T0292434

From Semantics to Computer Science

Gilles Kahn was one of the most influential figures in the development of computer science and information technology, not only in Europe but throughout the world. This volume of articles by several leading computer scientists serves as a fitting memorial to Kahn's achievements and represents the broad range of subjects to which he contributed, whether through his scientific research or his work at INRIA, the French National Institute for Research in Computer Science and Control.

The authors reflect upon the future of computing, discussing how it will develop as a subject in itself and how it will affect other disciplines, from biology and medical informatics, to the web and networks in general. Its breadth of coverage, topicality, originality and depth of contribution, make this book a stimulating read for all those interested in the future development of information technology.

From Semantics to Computer Science

Essays in Honour of Gilles Kahn

Edited by
Yves Bertot
INRIA Sophia-Antipolis Méditerranée

Gérard Huet and Jean-Jacques Lévy
INRIA Rocquencourt

Gordon Plotkin
University of Edinburgh

Shaftesbury Road, Cambridge CB2 8EA, United Kingdom

One Liberty Plaza, 20th Floor, New York, NY 10006, USA

477 Williamstown Road, Port Melbourne, VIC 3207, Australia

314–321, 3rd Floor, Plot 3, Splendor Forum, Jasola District Centre, New Delhi – 110025, India

103 Penang Road, #05–06/07, Visioncrest Commercial, Singapore 238467

Cambridge University Press is part of Cambridge University Press & Assessment,
a department of the University of Cambridge.

We share the University's mission to contribute to society through the pursuit of
education, learning and research at the highest international levels of excellence.

www.cambridge.org
Information on this title: www.cambridge.org/9780521518253

© Cambridge University Press & Assessment 2009

This publication is in copyright. Subject to statutory exception and to the provisions
of relevant collective licensing agreements, no reproduction of any part may take
place without the written permission of Cambridge University Press & Assessment.

First published 2009

A catalogue record for this publication is available from the British Library

ISBN   978-0-521-51825-3   Hardback

Cambridge University Press & Assessment has no responsibility for the persistence
or accuracy of URLs for external or third-party internet websites referred to in this
publication and does not guarantee that any content on such websites is, or will
remain, accurate or appropriate.

Contents

v

List of contributors

Roberto Amadio
PPS, Université Paris Diderot

Nicholas Ayache
INRIA Sophia Antipolis Méditerranée

François Baccelli
Ecole Normale Supérieure

Jean-Pierre Banâtre
INRIA/IRISA Université de Rennes

Alain Bensoussan
University of Texas at Dallas

Pierre Bernhard
I3S, Université de Nice Sophia Antipolis and CNRS

Yves Bertot
INRIA Sophia Antipolis Méditerranée

Luca Cardelli
Microsoft Research, Cambridge

Giovanna Carofiglio
Ecole Normale Supérieure and Politecnico di Torino

Olivier Clatz
INRIA Sophia Antipolis Méditerranée

Thierry Coquand
Chalmers University of Technology and Göteborg University

Bruno Courcelle
Institut Universitaire de France and LABRI, Université de Bordeaux 1

Pierre-Louis Curien
PPS, CNRS and Université de Paris 7

Hervé Delingette
INRIA Sophia Antipolis Méditerranée

Mehdi Dogguy
PPS, Université Paris Diderot

Serguei Foss
Heriot-Watt University, Edinburgh

Pascal Fradet
INRIA Rhône-Alpes

Frédéric Hamelin
I3S, Université de Nice Sophia Antipolis and CNRS

Laurent Hascoët
INRIA Sophia Antipolis Méditerranée

Andrew Herbert
Microsoft Research, Cambridge

Gilles Kahn

Yoshiki Kinoshita
National Institute of Advanced Industrial Science and Technology (AIST), Japan

Paul Klint
Centrum voor Wiskunde en Informatica and University of Amsterdam

Emmanuel Ledinot
Dassault Aviation

Edward A. Lee
University of California, Berkeley

Jean-Jacques Lévy
INRIA and Microsoft Research-INRIA Joint Centre

David B. MacQueen
University of Chicago

Grégoire Malandain
INRIA Sophia Antipolis Méditerranée

Eleftherios Matsikoudis
University of California, Berkeley

Robin Milner
University of Cambridge

Tobias Nipkow
TU München

Bengt Nordström
Chalmers University of Technology and Göteborg University

Christine Paulin-Mohring
INRIA Saclay - Île-de-France and Université Paris-Sud

Xavier Pennec
INRIA Sophia Antipolis Méditerranée

Yann Radenac
INRIA/IRISA Université de Rennes

G. Ramalingam
Microsoft Research India, Bangalore

Aarne Ranta
Chalmers University of Technology and Göteborg University

Thomas Reps
University of Wisconsin, Madison

Erik Sandewall
Linköping University and Royal Institute of Technology, Stockholm

Maxime Sermesant
INRIA Sophia Antipolis Méditerranée

Makoto Takeyama
National Institute of Advanced Industrial Science and Technology (AIST), Japan

Christian Urban
TU München

Jean Vuillemin
Ecole Normale Supérieure

Preface

Gilles Kahn was born in Paris on April 17th, 1946 and died in Garches, near Paris, on February 9th, 2006. He received an engineering diploma from Ecole Polytechnique (class of 1964), studied for a few years in Stanford and then joined the computer science branch of the French Atomic Energy Commission (CEA), which was to become the CISI company. He joined the French research institute in computer science and control theory (IRIA, later renamed INRIA) in 1976. He stayed with this institute until his death, at which time he was the chief executive officer of the institute. He was a member of Academia Europaea from 1995 and a member of the French Academy of Science from 1997.

Gilles Kahn's scientific achievements

Gilles Kahn's scientific interests evolved from the study of programming language semantics to the design and implementation of programming tools and the study of the interaction between programming activities and proof verification activities. In plain words, these themes addressed three questions. How do programmers tell a computer to perform a specific task? What tools can we provide to programmers to help them in their job? In particular, how can programmers provide guarantees that computers will perform the task that was requested?

Programming language semantics

In the early 1970s, Gilles Kahn proposed that programs should be described as collections of processes communicating through a network of channels, a description style that is now known as *Kahn networks*. He quickly proposed a format for the description of these networks and addressed the question of giving a precise meaning to this format. This is how Gilles Kahn came to be interested in programming language semantics. Part of the work to define this language of communicating processes was done in collaboration with David MacQueen, then at the University of Edinburgh.

In particular, Kahn networks could contain loops, which invite infinite behavior. The data on the communication channels could then appear as infinite streams of data and Gilles needed to refine the existing theory of domains to provide an adequate treatment of potentially infinite data structures. This led to the description of *concrete domains*, in collaboration with Gordon Plotkin, also at the University of Edinburgh.

The work on concrete domains followed the style of denotational semantics, where the meaning of each program is described as a function from some domain of input data to some domain of output data. Denotational semantics requires that a meaning should be ascribed to each construct of the programming language: this meaning should then be a function mapping the semantics of the sub-components to the meaning of whole expression. In any meaningful language, this implies that one should be able to find solutions to recursive equations, in other words, equations in which the defined object appears on both sides.

With this work, Gilles Kahn became recognized as an expert in the domain of programming language semantics. For instance, Gilles Kahn and his student Véronique Donzeau-Gouge were invited to work on the formal semantics of Ichbiah's LIS language, which was to become the Ada language after winning a competition from the American Department of Defense. Moreover, the theory of concrete domains was to have a wide impact, through the contributions of Gérard Berry and Pierre-Louis Curien on the definition of *sequential algorithms* and then on game semantics and the study of fully abstract models for sequential programming.

Gilles Kahn then set out to change the general point of view for describing programming language semantics: instead of looking for a meaning for programs, he proposed the provision of a clear description of how programs operate. He started from an earlier proposal of Gordon Plotkin, known as *structural operational semantics* and suggested considering complete executions of programs. In parallel with denotational semantics, it is then necessary to associate with each programming language construct and each possible behavior of this construct a description of an execution of this construct as a composition of the execution of its sub-components. Gilles Kahn noted the similarity of this approach with the concept of natural deduction used in proof theory and proposed that this description style should be called *natural semantics*.

Programming environments

From the middle of the 1970s, Gilles Kahn was also interested in developing practical tools to enable programmers to perform their job more efficiently and more reliably. The first aspect, studied from 1975, was the structured manipulation of programs, in which the elementary constructs of programming languages were directly understood by the program development tools. With the advent of graphical workstations, structured programming environments became very powerful: the mouse could be used to select whole expressions in one gesture and the display of programs could benefit from varied colors and fonts and from the enhanced readability of bi-dimensional layout. Several versions of interactive programming environments were developed, the first one was called Mentor and was developed in Pascal.

An offspring of the work on Mentor was the development of Mentor-Rapport by another of Gilles' students, Bertrand Mélèse. This tool was specialized for the production of structured documents. Mentor-Rapport was later to become Grif and have an important influence on the development of SGML and XML.

The next generation of programming environments was developed in Le_Lisp, another output of INRIA's research. This version was called Centaur. The development of Centaur started in the middle of the 1980s. Again, the tool was based on the structured manipulation of programs, but the project had the ambitious goal that a programming language should be entirely described with formal specifications of its syntax and its semantics; from which all programming tools could be derived. In particular, the language of inference rules that was already advocated by Gilles Kahn and Gordon Plotkin to describe operational semantics had also been in use for some time to describe type systems: this language could be used as a universal tool to describe many aspects of programming languages; it could also be given a computational behavior, through a translation into Prolog. This language was integrated in Centaur under the name of Typol, thanks to the work of Thierry Despeyroux. Typol was used to describe a wide variety of programming languages and tools for these languages: interpreters, compilers, partial evaluators, etc.

Generic programming environments are now part of the programmer's palette of tools. The Eclipse environment, produced by IBM is a well-known example. More characteristically, the advent of XML as a widespread communication standard also shows that the industry and the academic world are now convinced of the importance of structured data, as opposed to plain text. This predominance of structured data was already asserted in the Mentor tool, developed around 1975 by Gilles Kahn and his team.

Proving environments

Structured manipulation as found in Centaur could be used in other domains than just programming environments. Gilles Kahn was soon interested in applying it to tools that support mathematics on the computer. In particular, Gilles Kahn thought that *real theorem provers deserve real user-interfaces* and the Centaur technology was a good instrument to implement powerful man–machine interfaces for these tools. The readability of mathematical formula could benefit from the strong layout capabilities, a structure-based translation could be used to transform formal proofs into natural language mathematical text, and moreover the selection of positions in logical formula could be used to guide the proof process. The latter capability was called *proof-by-pointing* and attracted some notoriety to Gilles Kahn's team.

From proof environments, it was a natural step to get involved in the theme of computer-aided proof, in particular with the Coq system that was developed at INRIA, initially under the supervision of Gérard Huet. Gilles Kahn contributed in many ways to the growth of this system, studying formal descriptions of his own theory of concrete domains or some aspects of constructive geometry. Gilles also contributed to a tutorial to the Coq system.

In 1996, Gilles Kahn was appointed to the inquiry board that studied the failure of the inaugural flight of the Ariane 5 launcher. He played a crucial role in identifying the cause of the failure as a software bug. He saw this as an opportunity to promote the systematic analysis of software by automatic tools and made sure the best researchers of INRIA had an opportunity to apply their skills on this example of a complex system involving mission-critical software components.

The scientific themes that Gilles Kahn studied during his career exhibit both a wide variety of styles, from the most practical concerns of developing program editors to the most theoretical ones of devising a theory of domains for infinite data-structures; from programming language semantics to proof theory. However, all these themes contribute to the same focal motivation: making programmers more efficient and reliable in their work. The question of proving that programs satisfied some specification was already present in the early work on Kahn Networks; networks of communicating processes and co-routines were also used in the architecture of the Centaur system; questions of semantics are still among the most active application areas of theorem proving tools.

Gilles Kahn's influence on computer science in France

Beyond his own scientific achievements, Gilles Kahn helped in shaping modern computer science, mostly through his influence on INRIA's evolution. He was widely recognized for his scientific culture, thanks to which he was able to understand the key aspects of many scientific fields. He was good at sensing important new trends and at supporting the colleagues who explored them.

J.-L. Lions, the director of IRIA in the early 1970s, was quick to recognize Gilles' ability to understand the challenges of new research domains and gave Gilles the responsibility to preside over IRIA's project evaluation committee. Thus, Gilles was a researcher at INRIA, but with this specific task, he was already in a position to follow and appreciate the activity of colleagues in a much wider area than his own domain of expertise.

When INRIA decided to create a center in Sophia Antipolis, Gilles Kahn was again appointed as the head of the project committee, in effect being recognized by P. Bernhard as his main scientific adviser. At INRIA Sophia Antipolis, Gilles was a key actor in supporting the evolution of computer science in several domains. Gilles had a clear vision of the growth of personal computers linked together by a wide-area network and he insisted that INRIA should attract a high-level research team on networking. Later on, he supported the collaboration of INRIA in the World-Wide-Web consortium, an effort that helped shape the Internet as we know it today. In a similar vein, Gilles Kahn was an early supporter of interactions between computer science, biology, and medicine and he made sure that INRIA Sophia Antipolis would provide the right conditions for the growth of teams interested in artificial vision, computer-based analysis of medical imagery, or neuroscience.

Gilles Kahn also had an acute understanding of computer science's industrial impact. He was an early advocate of INRIA's approach to spawning start-up companies. For instance, he took in the early 1980s the initiative of meeting the top management of the Bull company to incite them to enter the market for personal workstations; he had noticed the SM-90 experimental architecture, then developed in the French telecommunication company's research laboratory (CNET). He convinced J.-F. Abramatic to start the Gipsy company on this market. Later, Gilles also convinced Pierre Haren to start the Ilog adventure with a team of bright young researchers. Ilog is now a much-cited success. Of course, the start-up movement around INRIA also had a few failures, some of them on topics that were directly derived from Gilles and his team's research, but Gilles made sure the dynamics would be maintained.

Gilles Kahn's vision on the future of computer science and control theory was more and more appreciated, this led to A. Bensoussan, the head of INRIA in 1994, appointing him as scientific director. When B. Larrouturou took over as Chief Executive Officer, he confirmed Gilles Kahn in this position. At the time, Gilles supervised the evolution of around 80 research teams and promoted new domains, in particular, the theme of bio-informatics was brought to the forefront.

In 2004, Gilles Kahn was appointed as INRIA's Chief Executive Officer. His influence at this position continued his work as scientific director. However, new aspects appeared, especially in his will to establish collaborations with the best research centers in the world, including research centers affiliated with major software companies.

The selection of articles in this book

In this book, we collected articles to contribute to Gilles Kahn's memory. Some of the contributions are directly related to one of Gilles' scientific interests. The articles by R. Amadio and M. Dogguy, J.-P. Banâtre, P. Fradet, and Y. Radenac, P.-L. Curien, E. Lee and E. Matsikoudis, and D. MacQueen show the continued influence of Kahn Networks in computer science. In particular, D. MacQueen's article gives a comprehensive historical perspective of the influence of this work. The articles of T. Coquand, Y. Kinoshita, B. Nordström, and M. Takeyama, B. Courcelle, G. Kahn, and J. Vuillemin, J.-J. Lévy, and G. Ramalingam and T. Reps are related to the larger field of programming language semantics. In particular, the article by Courcelle, Kahn, and Vuillemin is an English translation of an article on recursive equations that was published in French and is reproduced here with the kind permission of Springer Science and Business Media. The articles by P. Klint, B. Nordström, A. Ranta, and E. Sandewall are more closely related to Gilles' interest in developing programming tools and environments. The articles of Y. Bertot, C. Urban and T. Nipkow, and C. Paulin-Mohring are more closely related to computer-based proofs of programming language properties. In particular, C. Paulin-Mohring's contribution demonstrates how computer-based proof can be applied to Kahn Networks.

Other contributions attempt to give a wider view of Gilles Kahn's influence on computer science. Because of his positions as scientific director, Gilles Kahn had supported many domains of computer science and control theory. We thus have a wide variety of themes being considered: N. Ayache and his team describe the interaction of computer science and medical imaging; F. Baccelli, G. Carofiglio, and S. Foss provide an article on the efficiency analysis of some networking techniques; P. Bernhard and F. Hamelin contribute a study of game theory applied to biological systems; and L. Hascoët describes advanced techniques in automatic differentiation.

In a third group of contributions, authors have attempted the difficult exercise of paying tribute to the visionary qualities of Gilles Kahn. A. Bensoussan's article evokes Gilles' influence on the evolution of INRIA; L. Cardelli studies the ways in which computer science can help biologists address the daunting task of understanding living objects; A. Herbert investigates the impact of computers on science at large; E. Ledinot evokes the influence of Gilles' work on programming environments; and R. Milner questions the links and difference between software science and software engineering.

Acknowledgments

We wish to thank D. Tranah, C. Dennison, and C. Appleton from Cambridge University Press for their help in elaborating this book. Other people who helped in preparing the articles are A. Appel, K. Avratchenko, G. Berry, J. Bertot, J.-D. Boissonnat, G. Boudol, F. Boussinot, M. Brady, R. Bryant, D. Caucal, O. Corby, Y. Coscoy, S. Coupet-Grimal, T. Despeyroux, D. Doligez, C. Dubois, F. Fages, S. Gaubert, T. Jensen, J.-M. Jezequel, C. Kirchner, J.-W. Klop, V. Komendantsky, B. Larrouturou, J. Laird, X. Leroy, Z. Luo, R. Marlet, C. Munoz, F. Pottier, L. Pottier, M. Pouzet, L. Rideau, M. Sorine, T. Streicher, L. Théry, B. Werner.

Determinacy in a synchronous π-calculus

Roberto M. Amadio
Université Paris Diderot, PPS, UMR-7126

Mehdi Dogguy
Université Paris Diderot, PPS, UMR-7126

Abstract

The $S\pi$-calculus is a *synchronous* π-calculus which is based on the SL model. The latter is a relaxation of the ESTEREL model where the reaction to the *absence* of a signal within an instant can only happen at the next instant. In the present work, we present and characterize a compositional semantics of the $S\pi$-calculus based on suitable notions of labelled transition system and bisimulation. Based on this semantic framework, we explore the notion of determinacy and the related one of (local) confluence.[1]

1.1 Introduction

Let P be a program that can repeatedly interact with its environment. A *derivative* of P is a program to which P reduces after a finite number of interactions with the environment. A program *terminates* if all its internal computations terminate and it is *reactive* if all its derivatives are guaranteed to terminate. A program is *determinate* if after any finite number of interactions with the environment the resulting derivative is unique up to *semantic equivalence*.

Most conditions found in the literature that entail determinacy are rather intuitive, however the formal statement of these conditions and the proof that they indeed guarantee determinacy can be rather intricate in particular in the presence of name mobility, as available in a paradigmatic form in the π-calculus.

Our purpose here is to provide a streamlined theory of determinacy for the *synchronous* π-calculus introduced in [2]. It seems appropriate

---

[1] Work partially supported by ANR-06-SETI-010-02.

From Semantics to Computer Science Essays in Honour of Gilles Kahn, eds Yves Bertot, Gérard Huet, Jean-Jacques Lévy and Gordon Plotkin. Published by Cambridge University Press. © Cambridge University Press 2009.

to address these issues in a volume dedicated to the memory of Gilles
Kahn. First, Kahn networks [14] are a classic example of concurrent *and*
deterministic systems. Second, Kahn networks have largely inspired the
research on *synchronous* languages such as LUSTRE [9] and, to a lesser
extent, ESTEREL [6]. An intended side-effect of this work is to illustrate
how ideas introduced in concurrency theory well after Kahn networks
can be exploited to enlighten the study of determinacy in concurrent
systems.

Our technical approach will follow a process calculus tradition, as
listed here.

(i) We describe the interactions of a program with its environment
through a *labelled transition system* to which we associate a compositional notion of *labelled bisimulation.*

(ii) We rely on this semantic framework, to introduce a notion of
determinacy and a related notion of *confluence.*

(iii) We provide *local* confluence conditions that are easier to check
and that combined with *reactivity* turn out to be equivalent to
determinacy.

We briefly trace the path that has led to this approach. A systematic study of determinacy and confluence for calculus of communicating
systems (CCS) is available in [17] where, roughly, the usual theory of
rewriting is generalized in two directions: first rewriting is labelled and
second diagrams commute up to semantic equivalence. In this context,
a suitable formulation of Newman's lemma [19], has been given in [11].
The theory has been gradually extended from CCS, to CCS with values,
and finally to the π-calculus [20].

Calculi such as CCS and the π-calculus are designed to represent
asynchronous systems. On the other hand, the $S\pi$-calculus is designed
to represent *synchronous* systems. In these systems, there is a notion of
instant (or phase, or pulse, or round) and at each instant each thread
performs some actions and synchronizes with all other threads. One may
say that all threads proceed at the same speed and it is in this specific
sense that we will refer to *synchrony* in this work.

In order to guarantee determinacy in the context of CCS *rendez-vous*
communication, it seems quite natural to restrict the calculus so that
interaction is *point-to-point*, *i.e.*, it involves exactly one sender and one
receiver.[2] In a synchronous framework, the introduction of *signal*-based

---

[2] Incidentally, this is also the approach taken in Kahn networks but with an interaction mechanism based on unbounded, ordered buffers. It is not difficult to represent

communication offers an opportunity to move from point-to-point to a more general multi-way interaction mechanism with multiple senders and/or receivers, while preserving determinacy. In particular, this is the approach taken in the ESTEREL and SL [8] models. The SL model can be regarded as a relaxation of the ESTEREL model where the reaction to the *absence* of a signal within an instant can only happen at the next instant. This design choice avoids some paradoxical situations and simplifies the implementation of the model. The SL model has gradually evolved into a general purpose programming language for concurrent applications and has been embedded in various programming environments such as C, JAVA, SCHEME, and CAML (see [7, 22, 16]). For instance, the Reactive ML language [16] includes a large fragment of the CAML language plus primitives to generate signals and synchronize on them. We should also mention that related ideas have been developed by Saraswat *et al.* [21] in the area of constraint programming.

The $S\pi$-calculus can be regarded as an extension of the SL model where signals can carry values. In this extended framework, it is more problematic to have both concurrency *and* determinacy. Nowadays, this question is frequently considered when designing various kind of synchronous programming languages (see, e.g. [16, 10]). As we have already mentioned, our purpose here is to address the question with the tool-box of process calculi following the work for CCS and the π-calculus quoted above. In this respect, it is worth stressing a few interesting variations that arise when moving from the 'asynchronous' π-calculus to the 'synchronous' $S\pi$-calculus. First, we have already pointed-out that there is an opportunity to move from a point-to-point to a multi-way interaction mechanism while preserving determinacy. Second, the notion of confluence and determinacy happen to coincide while in the asynchronous context confluence is a strengthening of determinacy which has better compositionality properties. Third, reactivity appears to be a reasonable property to require of a synchronous system, the goal being just to avoid instantaneous loops, i.e. loops that take no time.[3]

The rest of the paper is structured as follows. In Section 1.2, we introduce the $S\pi$-calculus, in Section 1.3, we define its semantics based on

---

unbounded, ordered buffers in a CCS with value passing and show that, modulo this encoding, the determinacy of Kahn networks can be obtained as a corollary of the theory of confluence developed in [17].

[3] The situation is different in asynchronous systems where reactivity is a more demanding property. For instance, [11] notes: "*As soon as a protocol internally consists in some kind of correction mechanism (e.g., retransmission in a data link protocol) the specification of that protocol will contain a τ-loop*".

a standard notion of labelled bisimulation on a (non-standard) labelled transition system and we show that the bisimulation is preserved by static contexts, in Section 1.4 we provide alternative characterisations of the notion of labelled bisimulation we have introduced, in Section 1.5, we develop the concepts of determinacy and (local) confluence. Familiarity with the π-calculus [18, 23], the notions of determinacy and confluence presented in [17], and synchronous languages of the ESTEREL family [6, 8] is assumed.

1.2 Introduction to the $S\pi$-calculus

We introduce the syntax of the $S\pi$-calculus along with an informal comparison with the π-calculus and a programming example.

1.2.1 Programs

Programs $P, Q, \ldots$ in the $S\pi$-calculus are defined as follows:

$$
\begin{aligned}
P &::= \quad 0 \mid A(\mathbf{e}) \mid \overline{s}e \mid s(x).P, K \mid [s_1 = s_2]P_1, P_2 \mid [u \trianglerighteq p]P_1, P_2 \\
&\quad \mid \nu s\, P \mid P_1 \mid P_2 \\
K &::= \quad A(\mathbf{r})
\end{aligned}
$$

We use the notation $\mathbf{m}$ for a vector $m_1, \ldots, m_n$, $n \geq 0$. The informal behaviour of programs follows. 0 is the terminated thread. $A(\mathbf{e})$ is a (tail) recursive call of a thread identifier A with a vector $\mathbf{e}$ of expressions as argument; as usual the thread identifier A is defined by a unique equation $A(\mathbf{x}) = P$ such that the free variables of P occur in $\mathbf{x}$. $\overline{s}e$ evaluates the expression e and emits its value on the signal s. $s(x).P, K$ is the *present* statement which is the fundamental operator of the SL model. If the values $v_1, \ldots, v_n$ have been emitted on the signal s then $s(x).P, K$ evolves non-deterministically into $[v_i/x]P$ for some v_i ($[\_/\_]$ is our notation for substitution). On the other hand, if no value is emitted then the continuation K is evaluated at the end of the instant. $[s_1 = s_2]P_1, P_2$ is the usual matching function of the π-calculus that runs P_1 if s_1 equals s_2 and P_2, otherwise. Here both s_1 and s_2 are free. $[u \trianglerighteq p]P_1, P_2$, matches u against the pattern p. We assume u is either a variable x or a value v and p has the shape $\mathsf{c}(\mathbf{x})$, where c is a constructor and $\mathbf{x}$ is a vector of distinct variables. We also assume that if u is a variable x then x does not occur free in P_1. At run time, u is always a *value* and we run θP_1 if $\theta = match(u, p)$ is the substitution matching u against p, and P_2 if such substitution does not exist (written $match(u, p) \uparrow$). Note that as usual the variables occurring in the pattern p (including signal names) are bound in P_1. $\nu s\ P$ creates a new signal name s and runs P. $(P_1 \mid P_2)$ runs in parallel P_1 and P_2. A continuation K is simply a recursive call whose arguments are either expressions or values associated with signals at the end of the instant in a sense that we explain below. We will also write pause.K for $\nu s\ s(x).0, K$ with s not free in K. This is the program that waits till the end of the instant and then evaluates K.

1.2.2 Expressions

The definition of programs relies on the following syntactic categories:

$$
\begin{array}{lll}
Sig & ::= & s \mid t \mid \cdots & \text{(signal names)} \\
Var & ::= & Sig \mid x \mid y \mid z \mid \cdots & \text{(variables)} \\
Cnst & ::= & * \mid \mathsf{nil} \mid \mathsf{cons} \mid \mathsf{c} \mid \mathsf{d} \mid \cdots & \text{(constructors)} \\
Val & ::= & Sig \mid Cnst(Val, \ldots, Val) & \text{(values } v, v', \ldots) \\
Pat & ::= & Cnst(Var, \ldots, Var) & \text{(patterns } p, p', \ldots) \\
Fun & ::= & f \mid g \mid \cdots & \text{(first-order function symbols)} \\
Exp & ::= & Var & \\
 & & \mid Cnst(Exp, \ldots, Exp) & \\
 & & \mid Fun(Exp, \ldots, Exp) & \text{(expressions } e, e', \ldots) \\
Rexp & ::= & !Sig & \\
 & & \mid Var & \\
 & & \mid Cnst(Rexp, \ldots, Rexp) & \\
 & & \mid Fun(Rexp, \ldots, Rexp) & \text{(exp. with deref. } r, r', \ldots).
\end{array}
$$

As in the π-calculus, signal names stand both for signal constants as generated by the ν operator and signal variables as in the formal parameter of the present operator. Variables Var include signal names as well as variables of other types. Constructors $Cnst$ include $*$, nil, and cons. Values Val are terms built out of constructors and signal names. Patterns Pat are terms built out of constructors and variables (including signal names). If P, p are a program and a pattern then we denote with $fn(P), fn(p)$ the set of free signal names occurring in them, respectively. We also use $FV(P), FV(p)$ to denote the set of free variables (including signal names). We assume first-order function symbols $f, g, \ldots$ and an evaluation relation $\Downarrow$ such that for every function symbol f and values $v_1, \ldots, v_n$ of suitable type there is a unique value v such that $f(v_1, \ldots, v_n) \Downarrow v$ and $fn(v) \subseteq \bigcup_{i=1,\ldots,n} fn(v_i)$. Expressions Exp are terms built out of variables, constructors, and function symbols. The evaluation relation $\Downarrow$ is extended in a standard way to expressions whose only free variables are signal names. Finally, *Rexp* are expressions that may include the value associated with a signal s at the end of the instant (which is written $!s$, following the ML notation for dereferenciation). Intuitively, this value is a *list of values* representing the *set of values* emitted on the signal during the instant.

1.2.3 Typing

Types include the basic type 1 inhabited by the constant $*$ and, assuming σ is a type, the type $Sig(\sigma)$ of signals carrying values of type σ, and the type $List(\sigma)$ of lists of values of type σ with constructors nil and cons. In the examples, it will be convenient to abbreviate $\mathsf{cons}(v_1, \ldots, \mathsf{cons}(v_n, \mathsf{nil}) \ldots)$ with $[v_1; \ldots; v_n]$. 1 and $List(\sigma)$ are examples of *inductive types*. More inductive types (booleans, numbers, trees,...) can be added along with more constructors. We assume that variables (including signals), constructor symbols, and thread identifiers come with their (first-order) types. For instance, a function symbols f may have a type $(\sigma_1, \sigma_2) \to \sigma$ meaning that it waits two arguments of type σ_1 and σ_2, respectively, and returns a value of type σ. It is straightforward to define when a program is well-typed. We just point out that if a signal name s has type $Sig(\sigma)$ then its dereferenced value $!s$ has type $List(\sigma)$. In the following, we will tacitly assume that we are handling well typed programs, expressions, substitutions, ...

1.2.4 Comparison with the π-calculus

The syntax of the $S\pi$-calculus is similar to the one of the π-calculus, however, there are some important *semantic* differences that we highlight in the following simple example. Assume $v_1 \neq v_2$ are two distinct values and consider the following program in $S\pi$:

$$P = \nu\, s_1, s_2 \left(\begin{array}{cc} \overline{s_1}v_1 \quad | & \overline{s_1}v_2 \quad | \\ s_1(x).\ (s_1(y).\ (s_2(z).\ A(x,y)\ ,B(!s_1))\ ,0) & ,0 \end{array} \right)$$

If we forget about the underlined parts and we regard s_1, s_2 as *channel names* then P could also be viewed as a π-calculus process. In this case, P would reduce to

$$P_1 = \nu s_1, s_2\ (s_2(z).A(\theta(x), \theta(y))$$

where θ is a substitution such that $\theta(x), \theta(y) \in \{v_1, v_2\}$ and $\theta(x) \neq \theta(y)$. In $S\pi$, *signals persist within the instant* and P reduces to

$$P_2 = \nu s_1, s_2 \ (\overline{s_1}v_1 \mid \overline{s_1}v_2 \mid (s_2(z).A(\theta(x), \theta(y)), \underline{B(!s_1)}))$$

where $\theta(x), \theta(y) \in \{v_1, v_2\}$. What happens next? In the π-calculus, P_1 is *deadlocked* and no further computation is possible. In the $S\pi$-calculus, the fact that no further computation is possible in P_2 is detected and marks the *end of the current instant*. Then an additional computation represented by the relation $\xrightarrow{N}$ moves P_2 to the following instant:

$$P_2 \xrightarrow{N} P_2' = \nu s_1, s_2 \ B(v)$$

where $v \in \{[v_1; v_2], [v_2; v_1]\}$. Thus at the end of the instant, a dereferenced signal such as $!s_1$ becomes a list of (distinct) values emitted on s_1 during the instant and then all signals are reset.

1.2.5 A programming example

We introduce a programming example to illustrate the kind of synchronous programming that can be represented in the $S\pi$-calculus. We describe first a 'server' handling a list of requests emitted in the previous instant on the signal s. For each request of the shape $\mathsf{req}(s', x)$, it provides an answer which is a function of x along the signal s'.

$$
\begin{aligned}
Server(s) \ \ &= \ \ \mathsf{pause}.Handle(s, !s) \\
Handle(s, \ell) \ \ &= \ \ [\ell \triangleright \mathsf{req}(s', x) {::} \ell'](\overline{s'}f(x) \mid Handle(s, \ell')), Server(s) \ .
\end{aligned}
$$

The programming of a client that issues a request x on signal s and returns the reply on signal t could be the following:

$$Client(x, s, t) \ \ = \ \ \nu s' \ (\overline{s}\mathsf{req}(s', x) \mid \mathsf{pause}.s'(x).\overline{t}x, 0) \ .$$

1.3 Semantics of the $S\pi$-calculus

In this section, we define the semantics of the $S\pi$-calculus by a 'standard' notion of labelled bisimulation on a 'non-standard' labelled transition system and we show that labelled bisimulation is preserved by 'static' contexts. A distinct notion of labelled bisimulation for the $S\pi$-calculus has already been studied in [2] and the following Section 1.4 will show that the two notions are (almost) the same. A significant advantage of the presentation of labelled bisimulation we discuss here is that in the 'bisimulation game' all actions are treated in the same way. This allows

for a considerable simplification of the diagram chasing arguments that
are needed in the study of determinacy and confluence in Section 1.5.

1.3.1 Actions

The actions of the forthcoming labelled transition system are classified
in the following categories:

$$
\begin{array}{lll}
act & ::= \alpha \mid aux & \text{(actions)} \\
\alpha & ::= \tau \mid \nu\mathbf{t}\,\overline{s}v \mid sv \mid N & \text{(relevant actions)} \\
aux & ::= s?v \mid (E, V) & \text{(auxiliary actions)} \\
\mu & ::= \tau \mid \nu\mathbf{t}\,\overline{s}v \mid s?v & \text{(nested actions)}
\end{array}
$$

The category *act* is partitioned into relevant actions and auxiliary
actions.

The *relevant actions* are those that are actually considered in the
bisimulation game. They consist of: (i) an internal action τ; (ii) an emis-
sion action $\nu\mathbf{t}\,\overline{s}v$ where it is assumed that the signal names $\mathbf{t}$ are distinct,
occur in v, and differ from s; (iii) an input action sv; and (iv) an action
N (for *Next*) that marks the move from the current to the next instant.

The *auxiliary actions* consist of an input action $s?v$ which is coupled
with an emission action in order to compute a τ action and an action
(E, V) which is just needed to compute an action N. The latter is
an action that can occur exactly when the program cannot perform τ
actions and it amounts (i) to collect in lists the set of values emitted on
every signal, (ii) to reset all signals, and (iii) to initialize the continuation
K for each present statement of the shape $s(x).P, K$.

In order to formalize these three steps we need to introduce some
notation. Let E vary over functions from signal names to finite sets of
values. Denote with $\emptyset$ the function that associates the empty set with
every signal name, with $[M/s]$ the function that associates the set M
with the signal name s and the empty set with all the other signal names,
and with $\cup$ the union of functions defined point-wise.

We represent a set of values as a list of the values contained in the
set. More precisely, we write $v \Vdash M$ and say that v *represents* M if
$M = \{v_1, \ldots, v_n\}$ and $v = [v_{\pi(1)}; \ldots; v_{\pi(n)}]$ for some permutation π over
$\{1, \ldots, n\}$. Suppose V is a function from signal names to lists of values.
We write $V \Vdash E$ if $V(s) \Vdash E(s)$ for every signal name s. We also write
$dom(V)$ for $\{s \mid V(s) \neq []\}$. If K is a continuation, i.e. a recursive call
$A(\mathbf{r})$, then $V(K)$ is obtained from K by replacing each occurrence $!s$ of

a dereferenced signal with the associated value $V(s)$. We denote with $V[\ell/s]$ the function that behaves as V except on s where $V[\ell/s](s) = \ell$.

With these conventions, a transition $P \xrightarrow{(E,V)} P'$ intuitively means that (1) P is suspended, (2) P emits exactly the values specified by E, and (3) the behaviour of P in the following instant is P' and depends on V. It is convenient to compute these transitions on programs where all name generations are lifted at top level. We write $P \succeq Q$ if we can obtain Q from P by repeatedly transforming, for instance, a subprogram $\nu s P' \mid P''$ into $\nu s(P' \mid P'')$ where $s \notin fn(P'')$.

Finally, the *nested actions* $\mu, \mu', \ldots$ are certain actions (either relevant or auxiliary) that can be produced by a sub-program and that we need to propagate to the top level.

1.3.2 Labelled transition system

The labelled transition system is defined in Table 1.1 where rules apply to programs whose only free variables are signal names and with standard conventions on the renaming of bound names. As usual, one can rename bound variables, and the symmetric rules for (*par*) and (*synch*) are omitted. The first 12 rules from (*out*) to (ν_{ex}) are quite close to those of a polyadic π-calculus with asynchronous communication (see [4, 12, 13]) with the following exception: rule (*out*) models the fact that the emission of a value on a signal *persists* within the instant. The last five rules from (0) to (*next*) are quite specific of the $S\pi$-calculus and determine how the computation is carried on at the end of the instant (cf. discussion in Section 1.3.1).

The relevant actions different from τ, model the possible interactions of a program with its environment. Then the notion of reactivity can be formalized as follows.

Definition 1.1 (derivative) *A derivative of a program P is a program Q such that*

$$P \xrightarrow{\alpha_1} \cdots \xrightarrow{\alpha_n} Q, \qquad \text{where: } n \geq 0 .$$

Definition 1.2 (reactivity) *We say that a program P is reactive, if for every derivative Q every τ-reduction sequence terminates.*

Table 1.1. *Labelled transition system.*

$$(out) \quad \frac{e \Downarrow v}{\overline{s}e \xrightarrow{\overline{s}v} \overline{s}e} \qquad\qquad (in_{aux}) \quad \frac{}{s(x).P, K \xrightarrow{s?v} [v/x]P}$$

$$(in) \quad \frac{}{P \xrightarrow{sv} (P \mid \overline{s}v)} \qquad\qquad (rec) \quad \frac{A(\mathbf{x}) = P, \quad \mathbf{e} \Downarrow \mathbf{v}}{A(\mathbf{e}) \xrightarrow{\tau} [\mathbf{v}/\mathbf{x}]P}$$

$$(=_1^{sig}) \quad \frac{}{[s=s]P_1, P_2 \xrightarrow{\tau} P_1} \qquad\qquad (=_2^{sig}) \quad \frac{s_1 \neq s_2}{[s_1=s_2]P_1, P_2 \xrightarrow{\tau} P_2}$$

$$(=_1^{ind}) \quad \frac{match(v,p) = \theta}{[v \trianglerighteq p]P_1, P_2 \xrightarrow{\tau} \theta P_1} \qquad\qquad (=_1^{ind}) \quad \frac{match(v,p) = \uparrow}{[v \trianglerighteq p]P_1, P_2 \xrightarrow{\tau} P_2}$$

$$(comp) \quad \frac{P_1 \xrightarrow{\mu} P_1' \quad bn(\mu) \cap fn(P_2) = \emptyset}{P_1 \mid P_2 \xrightarrow{\mu} P_1' \mid P_2} \qquad\qquad (synch) \quad \frac{\begin{array}{c} P_1 \xrightarrow{\nu \mathbf{t} \, \overline{s}v} P_1' \\ P_2 \xrightarrow{s?v} P_2' \\ \{\mathbf{t}\} \cap fn(P_2) = \emptyset \end{array}}{P_1 \mid P_2 \xrightarrow{\tau} \nu \mathbf{t} \, (P_1' \mid P_2')}$$

$$(\nu) \quad \frac{P \xrightarrow{\mu} P' \quad t \notin n(\mu)}{\nu t \, P \xrightarrow{\mu} \nu t \, P'} \qquad\qquad (\nu_{ex}) \quad \frac{\begin{array}{c} P \xrightarrow{\nu \mathbf{t} \, \overline{s}v} P' \quad t' \neq s \\ t' \in n(v) \backslash \{\mathbf{t}\} \end{array}}{\nu t' \, P \xrightarrow{(\nu t', \mathbf{t})\overline{s}v} P'}$$

$$(0) \quad \frac{}{0 \xrightarrow{\emptyset, V} 0} \qquad\qquad (reset) \quad \frac{e \Downarrow v \quad v \text{ occurs in } V(s)}{\overline{s}e \xrightarrow{[\{v\}/s], V} 0}$$

$$(cont) \quad \frac{s \notin dom(V)}{s(x).P, K \xrightarrow{\emptyset, V} V(K)} \qquad\qquad (par) \quad \frac{P_i \xrightarrow{E_i, V} P_i' \quad i = 1, 2}{(P_1 \mid P_2) \xrightarrow{E_1 \cup E_2, V} (P_1' \mid P_2')}$$

$$(next) \quad \frac{P \succeq \nu \mathbf{s} \, P' \quad P' \xrightarrow{E, V} P'' \quad V \Vdash E}{P \xrightarrow{N} \nu \mathbf{s} \, P''}$$

1.3.3 A compositional labelled bisimulation

We introduce first a rather standard notion of (weak) labelled bisimulation. We define $\xRightarrow{\alpha}$ as:

$$\xRightarrow{\alpha} = \begin{cases} (\xrightarrow{\tau})^* & \text{if } \alpha = \tau \\ (\xRightarrow{\tau}) \circ (\xrightarrow{N}) & \text{if } \alpha = N \\ (\xRightarrow{\tau}) \circ (\xrightarrow{\alpha}) \circ (\xRightarrow{\tau}) & \text{otherwise} \end{cases}$$

This is the standard definition except that we insist on *not* having internal reductions after an N action. Intuitively, we assume that an observer can control the execution of programs so as to be able to test them at the very beginning of each instant.[4] We write $P \xrightarrow{\alpha} \cdot$ for $\exists P' \ (P \xrightarrow{\alpha} P')$.

Definition 1.3 (labelled bisimulation) *A symmetric relation $\mathcal{R}$ on programs is a labelled bisimulation if*

$$\frac{P \, \mathcal{R} \, Q, \quad P \xrightarrow{\alpha} P', \quad bn(\alpha) \cap fn(Q) = \emptyset}{\exists Q' \ (\ Q \overset{\alpha}{\Rightarrow} Q', \qquad P' \, \mathcal{R} \, Q' \ )}$$

We denote with $\approx$ the largest labelled bisimulation.

The standard variation where one considers weak reduction in the hypothesis ($P \overset{\alpha}{\Rightarrow} P'$ rather than $P \xrightarrow{\alpha} P'$) leads to the same relation. Furthermore, relying on this variation, one can show that the concept of bisimulation up to bisimulation makes sense, i.e. a bisimulation up to bisimulation is indeed contained in the largest bisimulation. An important property of labelled bisimulation is that it is preserved by static contexts. The proof of this fact follows [2] and it is presented in Appendix A.2.

Definition 1.4 *A static context C is defined as follows:*

$$C ::= [\ ] \mid C \mid P \mid \nu s \ C \tag{1.1}$$

Theorem 1.5 (compositionality of labelled bisimulation) *If $P \approx Q$ and C is a static context then $C[P] \approx C[Q]$.*

1.4 Characterizations of labelled bisimulation

The labelled transition system presented in Table 1.1 embodies a number of technical choices which might not appear so natural at first sight. To justify these choices, it is therefore interesting to look for alternative characterizations of the induced bisimulation equivalence. To this end we recall the notion of *contextual* bisimulation introduced in [2].

---

[4] This decision entails that, *e.g.*, we distinguish the programs P and Q defined as follows: $P = \mathsf{pause}.(\bar{s}_1 \oplus \bar{s}_2)$, $Q = \nu s \ (\mathsf{pause}.A(!s) \mid \bar{s}0 \mid \bar{s}1)$, where $A(x) = [x \rhd [0;1]](\bar{s}_1 \oplus \bar{s}_2), \bar{s}_1$, and $\oplus$, 0, and 1 are abbreviations for an internal choice and for two distinct constants, respectively (these concepts can be easily coded in the $S\pi$-calculus). On the other hand, P and Q would be equivalent if we defined $\overset{N}{\Rightarrow}$ as $\overset{\tau}{\Rightarrow} \circ \xrightarrow{N} \circ \overset{\tau}{\Rightarrow}$.

Definition 1.6 *We write:*

$$P \downarrow \quad if \quad \neg(P \xrightarrow{\tau} \cdot) \qquad\qquad (suspension)$$
$$P \Downarrow \quad if \quad \exists P' \ (P \xRightarrow{\tau} P' \ and \ P' \downarrow) \quad (weak \ suspension)$$
$$P \Downarrow_L \quad if \quad \exists P' \ (P \mid P') \Downarrow \qquad\quad (L\text{-}suspension)$$

Obviously, $P \downarrow$ implies $P \Downarrow$ which in turn implies $P \Downarrow_L$ and none of these implications can be reversed (see [2]). Furthermore, note that all the derivatives of a reactive program enjoy the weak suspension property.

Definition 1.7 (commitment) *We write* $P \searrow \bar{s}$ *if* $P \xrightarrow{\nu \mathbf{t} \ \bar{s}v} \cdot$ *and say that P commits to emit on s.*

Definition 1.8 (barbed bisimulation) *A symmetric relation $\mathcal{R}$ on programs is a barbed bisimulation if whenever $P \mathcal{R} Q$ the following holds:*

(B1) *If $P \xrightarrow{\tau} P'$ then $\exists Q' \ (Q \xRightarrow{\tau} Q'$ and $P' \mathcal{R} Q')$.*

(B2) *If $P \searrow \bar{s}$ and $P \Downarrow_L$ then $\exists Q' \ (Q \xRightarrow{\tau} Q', Q' \searrow \bar{s}$, and $P \mathcal{R} Q')$.*

(B3) *If $P \downarrow$ and $P \xrightarrow{N} P''$ then $\exists Q', Q'' \ (Q \xRightarrow{\tau} Q', Q' \downarrow, P \mathcal{R} Q', Q' \xrightarrow{N} Q''$, and $P'' \mathcal{R} Q'')$.*

We denote with $\approx_B$ the largest barbed bisimulation.

Definition 1.9 (contextual bisimulation) *A symmetric relation $\mathcal{R}$ on programs is a contextual bisimulation if it is a barbed bisimulation (conditions $(B1-3)$) and moreover whenever $P \mathcal{R} Q$ then*

(C1) $C[P] \mathcal{R} C[Q]$, *for any static context C.*

We denote with $\approx_C$ the largest contextual barbed bisimulation.

We arrive at the announced characterization of the labelled bisimulation.

Theorem 1.10 (characterization of labelled bisimulation) *If P, Q are reactive programs then $P \approx Q$ if and only if $P \approx_C Q$.*

The proof of this result takes several steps summarized in Table 1.2 which provides three *equivalent* formulations of the labelled bisimulation $\approx$.

In [2], the contextual bisimulation in Definition 1.9 is characterized as a variant of the bisimulation $\approx_3$ where the condition for the output is formulated as follows:

$$\frac{P \mathcal{R} Q, \quad P \Downarrow_L, \quad P \xrightarrow{\nu \mathbf{t} \ \bar{s}v}_2 P', \quad \{\mathbf{t}\} \cap fn(Q) = \emptyset}{Q \xRightarrow{\nu \mathbf{t} \ \bar{s}v}_2 Q', \quad P' \mathcal{R} Q'}$$

Table 1.2. *Equivalent formulations of labelled bisimulation.*

Labelled transition systems

$(\xrightarrow{\alpha}_1)$	Rule (in_{aux}) replaced by $$(in^1_{aux}) \quad \frac{}{s(x).P, K \xrightarrow{s?v} [v/x]P \mid \overline{s}v}$$
$(\xrightarrow{\alpha}_2)$	Rule (in) removed and action $s?v$ replaced by sv
$(\xrightarrow{\alpha}_3)$	Coincides with $\xrightarrow{\alpha}_2$

Bisimulation games

$(\approx_1)$	As in Definition 1.3
$(\approx_2)$	As above if $\alpha \neq sv$. Require: $$(Inp) \quad \frac{P \; \mathcal{R} \; Q}{(P \mid \overline{s}v) \; \mathcal{R} \; (Q \mid \overline{s}v)}$$
$(\approx_3)$	As above if $\alpha \neq sv$. Replace (Inp) with : $$\frac{P \; \mathcal{R} \; Q, \qquad P \xrightarrow{sv}_2 P'}{\exists Q' \; (\; Q \stackrel{sv}{\Rightarrow}_2 Q' \wedge P' \; \mathcal{R} \; Q') \vee \\ (Q \stackrel{\tau}{\Rightarrow}_2 Q' \wedge P' \; \mathcal{R} \; (Q' \mid \overline{s}v) \;)}$$ and for $\alpha = N$ require: $$\frac{P \; \mathcal{R} \; Q, \; (P \mid S) \xrightarrow{N} P', \\ S = \overline{s}_1 v_1 \mid \cdots \mid \overline{s}_n v_n}{\exists Q', Q'' \; (\; (Q \mid S) \stackrel{\tau}{\Rightarrow}_2 Q'', \quad (P \mid S) \; \mathcal{R} \; Q'', \\ Q'' \xrightarrow{N}_2 Q', \quad P' \; \mathcal{R} \; Q' \;)}$$

Clearly, if P is a reactive program then $P \Downarrow_L$. Note also that the Definition 1.2 of a reactive program refers to the labelled transition system 1.1 for which it holds that $P \xrightarrow{sv} (P \mid \overline{s}v)$. Therefore, if P is reactive then $(P \mid \overline{s}v)$ is reactive too and if we start comparing two reactive programs then all programs that have to be considered in the bisimulation game will be reactive too. This means that on reactive programs the condition $P \Downarrow_L$ is always satisfied and therefore that the bisimulation $\approx_3$ coincides with the labelled bisimulation considered in [2].[5]

---

[5] On non-reactive programs, labelled bisimulation makes more distinctions than contextual bisimulation. For instance, the latter identifies all the programs that do not L-suspend.

Remark 1.11 (on determinacy and divergence) One may notice that the notions of labelled bisimulation and contextual bisimulation we have adopted are only *partially* sensitive to divergence. Let $\Omega = \tau.\Omega$ be a looping program. Then $\Omega \not\approx_C 0$ since 0 may suspend while Ω may not. On the other hand, consider a program such as $A = \tau.A \oplus \tau.0$. Then $A \approx 0$ and therefore $A \approx_C 0$ and we are led to conclude that A is a determinate program. However, one may also argue that A is *not* determinate since it may either suspend or loop. In other words, determinacy depends on the notion of semantic equivalence we adopt. If the latter is not sensitive enough to divergence then the resulting notion of determinacy should be regarded as a *partial* property of programs, *i.e.* it holds provided programs terminate. In practice, these distinctions do not seem very important because, as we have already argued, *reactivity* is a property one should always require of synchronous programs and once reactivity is in place the distinctions disappear.

1.5 Determinacy and (local) confluence

In this section, we develop the notions of determinacy and confluence for the $S\pi$-calculus which turn out to coincide. Moreover, we note that for reactive programs a simple property of local confluence suffices to ensure determinacy.

We denote with ϵ the empty sequence and with $s = \alpha_1 \cdots \alpha_n$ a finite sequence (possibly empty) of actions different from τ. We define:

$$\stackrel{s}{\Rightarrow} = \begin{cases} \stackrel{\tau}{\Rightarrow} & \text{if } s = \epsilon \\ \stackrel{\alpha_1}{\Rightarrow} \cdots \stackrel{\alpha_n}{\Rightarrow} & \text{if } s = \alpha_1 \cdots \alpha_n \end{cases}$$

Thus s denotes a finite (possibly empty) sequence of interactions with the environment. Following Milner [17], a program is considered determinate if performing twice the same sequence of interactions leads to the same program up to semantic equivalence.

Definition 1.12 (determinacy) *We say that a program P is determinate if for every sequence s, if $P \stackrel{s}{\Rightarrow} P_i$ for $i = 1, 2$ then $P_1 \approx P_2$.*

Determinacy implies τ-inertness which is defined as follows.

Definition 1.13 (τ-inertness) *A program is τ-inert if for all its derivatives Q, $Q \stackrel{\tau}{\rightarrow} Q'$ implies $Q \approx Q'$.*

Next, we turn to the notion of confluence. To this end, we introduce first the notions of action compatibility and action residual.

Definition 1.14 (action compatibility) *The* compatibility predicate $\downarrow$ *is defined as the least reflexive and symmetric binary relation on actions such that $\alpha \downarrow \beta$ implies that either $\alpha, \beta \neq N$ or $\alpha = \beta = N$.*

In other words, the action N is only compatible with itself while any action different from N is compatible with any other action different from N.[6] Intuitively, confluence is about the possibility of commuting actions that happen in the *same instant*. To make this precise we also need to introduce a notion of action residual $\alpha \backslash \beta$, which specifies what remains of the action α once the action β is performed.

Definition 1.15 (action residual) *The residual operation $\alpha \backslash \beta$ on actions is only defined if $\alpha \downarrow \beta$ and in this case it satisfies:*

$$\alpha \backslash \beta = \begin{cases} \tau & \text{if } \alpha = \beta \\ \nu \mathbf{t} \backslash \mathbf{t}' \overline{s} v & \text{if } \alpha = \nu \mathbf{t} \ \overline{s} v \text{ and } \beta = \nu \mathbf{t}' \overline{s'} v' \\ \alpha & \text{otherwise} \end{cases}$$

Confluence is then about closing diagrams of compatible actions up to residuals and semantic equivalence.

Definition 1.16 (confluence) *We say that a program P is confluent, if for all its derivatives Q:*

$$\frac{Q \overset{\alpha}{\Rightarrow} Q_1, \quad Q \overset{\beta}{\Rightarrow} Q_2, \quad \alpha \downarrow \beta}{\exists Q_3, Q_4 \ (\ Q_1 \overset{\beta \backslash \alpha}{\Rightarrow} Q_3, \quad Q_2 \overset{\alpha \backslash \beta}{\Rightarrow} Q_4, \quad Q_3 \approx Q_4 \ )}$$

It often turns out that the following weaker notion of *local* confluence is much easier to establish.

Definition 1.17 (local confluence) *We say that a program is locally confluent, if for all its derivatives Q:*

$$\frac{Q \overset{\alpha}{\rightarrow} Q_1 \quad Q \overset{\beta}{\rightarrow} Q_2 \quad \alpha \downarrow \beta}{\exists Q_3, Q_4 \ (\ Q_1 \overset{\beta \backslash \alpha}{\Rightarrow} Q_3, \quad Q_2 \overset{\alpha \backslash \beta}{\Rightarrow} Q_4, \quad Q_3 \approx Q_4 \ )}$$

---

[6] The reader familiar with [20] will notice that, unlike in the π-calculus with *rendezvous* communication, we do not restrict the compatibility relation on input actions. This is because of the particular form of the input action in the labelled transition system in Table 1.1 where the input action does not actually force a program to perform an input. We expect that a similar situation would arise in the π-calculus with asynchronous communication.

It is easy to produce programs which are locally confluent but not confluent. For instance, $A = \bar{s}_1 \oplus B$ where $B = \bar{s}_2 \oplus A$. However, one may notice that this program is *not* reactive. Indeed, for reactive programs local confluence is equivalent to confluence.

Theorem 1.18

(1) *A program is determinate if and only if it is confluent.*

(2) *A reactive program is determinate if and only if for all its derivatives Q:*

$$\frac{Q \xrightarrow{\alpha} Q_1, \quad Q \xrightarrow{\alpha} Q_2, \quad \alpha \in \{\tau, N\}}{\exists Q_3, Q_4 \; (Q_1 \xRightarrow{\tau} Q_3, \quad Q_2 \xRightarrow{\tau} Q_4, \quad Q_3 \approx Q_4)}$$

The fact that confluent programs are determinate is standard and it essentially follows from the observation that confluent programs are τ-inert. The observation that determinate programs are confluent is specific of the $S\pi$-calculus and it depends on the remark that input and output actions automatically commute with the other compatible actions.[7]

Part (2) of the theorem is proved as follows. First one notices that the stated conditions are equivalent to local confluence (again relying on the fact that commutation of input and output actions is automatic) and then following [11] one observes that local confluence plus reactivity entails confluence.

We conclude this section by noticing a strong commutation property of τ actions that suffices to entail τ-inertness and determinacy. Let $\xrightarrow{\alpha}$ be $\xrightarrow{\alpha} \cup Id$ where Id is the identity relation.

Proposition 1.19 *A program is determinate if for all its derivatives Q:*

$$\frac{Q \xrightarrow{\tau} Q_1, \quad Q \xrightarrow{\tau} Q_2}{\exists Q' \; (Q_1 \overset{\tau}{\leadsto} Q', \quad Q_2 \overset{\tau}{\leadsto} Q')} \qquad \frac{Q \xrightarrow{N} Q_1, \quad Q \xrightarrow{N} Q_2}{Q_1 \approx Q_2}$$

This is proven by showing that the strong commutation of the τ-actions entails τ-inertness.

---

[7] We note that the commutation of the inputs arises in the π-calculus with asynchronous communication too, while the commutation of the outputs is due to the fact that messages on signals unlike messages on channels persist within an instant (for instance, in CCS, if $P = \bar{a} \mid a.\bar{b}$ then $P \xrightarrow{\bar{a}} a.\bar{b}$, $P \xrightarrow{\tau} \bar{b}$, and there is no way to close the diagram).

1.6 Conclusion

We have developed a framework to analyse the determinacy of programs in a *synchronous* π-calculus. First, we have introduced a compositional notion of labelled bisimulation. Second, we have characterized a relevant contextual bisimulation as a standard bisimulation over a modified labelled transition system. Third, we have studied the notion of confluence which turns out to be equivalent to determinacy, and we have shown that under reactivity, confluence reduces to a simple form of local confluence.

According to Theorem 1.18(2), there are basically two situations that need to be analysed in order to guarantee the determinacy of (reactive) programs. (1) At least two distinct values compete to be received within an instant, for instance, consider: $\bar{s}v_1 \mid \bar{s}v_2 \mid s(x).P, K$. (2) At the end of the instant, at least two distinct values are available on a signal. For instance, consider: $\bar{s}v_1 \mid \bar{s}v_2 \mid \mathsf{pause}.A(!s)$. Based on this analysis, we are currently studying an *affine* type system in the style of [15] that avoids completely the first situation and allows the second provided the behaviour of the continuation A does not depend on the order in which the values are collected.

Bibliography

[1]   R. Amadio. The SL synchronous language, revisited. *Journal of Logic and Algebraic Programming*, 70:121–150, 2007.

[2]   R. Amadio. A synchronous π-calculus. *Information and Computation*, 205(9):1470–1490, 2007.

[3]   R. Amadio, G. Boudol, F. Boussinot and I. Castellani. Reactive programming, revisited. *In Proc. Workshop on Algebraic Process Calculi: the first 25 years and beyond, Electronic Notes in Theoretical Computer Science*, 162:49–60, 2006.

[4]   R. Amadio, I. Castellani and D. Sangiorgi. On bisimulations for the asynchronous π-calculus. *Theoretical Computer Science*, 195:291–324, 1998.

[5]   R. Amadio and F. Dabrowski. Feasible reactivity in a synchronous π-calculus. In *Proc. ACM SIGPLAN Symp. on Principles and Practice of Declarative Programming*, 2007.

[6]   G. Berry and G. Gonthier. The Esterel synchronous programming language. *Science of Computer Programming*, **19**(2):87–152, 1992.

[7]   F. Boussinot. Reactive C: An extension of C to program reactive systems. *Software Practice and Experience*, **21**(4):401–428, 1991.

[8]   F. Boussinot and R. De Simone. The SL synchronous language. *IEEE Trans. on Software Engineering*, **22**(4):256–266, 1996.

[9] P. Caspi, D. Pilaud, N. Halbwachs and J. Plaice. Lustre: A declarative language for programming synchronous systems. In *Proc. ACM-POPL*, pp. 178–188, 1987.

[10] S. Edwards and O. Tardieu. SHIM: A deterministic model for heterogeneous embedded systems. *IEEE Transactions on Very Large Scale Integration Systems*, **14**(8), 2006.

[11] J. Groote, M. Sellink. Confluence for process verification. *Theoretical Computer Science* **170**(1–2):47–81, 1996.

[12] K. Honda and M. Tokoro. On asynchronous communication semantics. In *Object-based concurrent computing*, SLNCS 612, 1992.

[13] K. Honda and N. Yoshida. On reduction-based process semantics. *Theoretical Computer Science*, **151**(2):437–486, 1995.

[14] G. Kahn. The semantics of simple language for parallel programming. IFIP Congress, 1974.

[15] N. Kobayashi, B. Pierce and D. Turner. Linearity and the π-calculus. *ACM Transactions on Programming Languages and Systems* (TOPLAS), **21**(5), 1999.

[16] L. Mandel and M. Pouzet. ReactiveML, a reactive extension to ML. In *Proc. ACM Principles and Practice of Declarative Programming*, pp. 82–93, 2005.

[17] R. Milner. *Communication and Concurrency*. Prentice-Hall, 1989.

[18] R. Milner, J. Parrow and D. Walker. A calculus of mobile processes, parts 1–2. *Information and Computation*, **100**(1):1–77, 1992.

[19] M. Newman. On theories with a combinatorial definition of equivalence. *Annals of Mathematics*, **43**(2):223–243, 1942.

[20] A. Philippou and D. Walker. On confluence in the π-calculus. In *Proc. ICALP*, pp. 314–324, SLNCS 1256, 1997.

[21] V. Saraswat, R. Jagadeesan and V. Gupta. Timed default concurrent constraint programming. *Journal of Symbolic Computation*, **22**(5,6) 475–520, 1996.

[22] M. Serrano, F. Boussinot and B. Serpette. Scheme fair threads. In *Proc. ACM Principles and Practice of Declarative Programming*, pp. 203–214, 2004.

[23] D. Sangiorgi and D. Walker. *The π-calculus*. Cambridge University Press, 2001.

A.1 Basic properties of labelled bisimulation

We collect some basic properties of the notion of labelled bisimulation. First, we consider a standard variation of Definition 1.3 of bisimulation where transitions are weak on both sides of the bisimulation game.

Definition 1.20 (w-bisimulation) *A symmetric relation $\mathcal{R}$ on programs is a w-bisimulation if*

$$\frac{P \mathcal{R} Q, \quad P \overset{\alpha}{\Rightarrow} P', \quad bn(\alpha) \cap fn(Q) = \emptyset}{\exists Q' \ (\ Q \overset{\alpha}{\Rightarrow} Q', \quad P' \mathcal{R} Q' \ )}$$

We denote with $\approx_w$ the largest w-bisimulation.

With respect to this modified definition we introduce the usual notion of bisimulation up to bisimulation.[8]

Definition 1.21 (w-bisimulation up to w-bisimulation) *A symmetric relation $\mathcal{R}$ on programs is a w-bisimulation up to w-bisimulation if*

$$\frac{P \mathcal{R} Q, \quad P \overset{\alpha}{\Rightarrow} P', \quad bn(\alpha) \cap fn(Q) = \emptyset}{\exists Q' \ (\ Q \overset{\alpha}{\Rightarrow} Q', \quad P' \approx_w \circ \mathcal{R} \circ \approx_w Q' \ )}$$

We denote with $\approx_w$ the largest w-bisimulation.

Proposition 1.22

(1) *The relation $\approx$ is an equivalence relation.*

(2) *The relations $\approx$ and $\approx_w$ coincide.*

(3) *If $\mathcal{R}$ is a w-bisimulation up to w-bisimulation then $\mathcal{R} \subseteq \approx_w$.*

Proof (1) The identity relation is a labelled bisimulation and the union of symmetric relations is symmetric. To check transitivity, we prove that $\approx \circ \approx$ is a labelled bisimulation by standard diagram chasing.

(2) By definition a w-bisimulation is a labelled bisimulation, therefore $\approx_w \subseteq \approx$. To show the other inclusion, prove that $\approx$ is a w-bisimulation again by a standard diagram chasing.

(3) First note that by (1) and (2), it follows that the relation $\approx_w$ is transitive. Then one shows that if $\mathcal{R}$ is a w-bisimulation up to w-bisimulation then the relation $\approx_w \circ \mathcal{R} \circ \approx_w$ is a w-bisimulation. $\qquad \square$

---

[8] We recall that it is important that this notion is defined with respect to w-bisimulation. Indeed, proposition 1.22(3) below fails if w-bisimulation is replaced by bisimulation.

A.1.1 Structural equivalence

In the diagram chasing arguments, it will be convenient to consider programs up to a notion of 'structural equivalence'. This is the least equivalence relation $\equiv$ such that (1) $\equiv$ is preserved by static contexts, (2) parallel composition is associative and commutative, (3) $\nu s \ (P \mid Q) \equiv \nu s \ P \mid Q$ if $s \notin fn(Q)$, (4) $\overline{s}v \mid \overline{s}v \equiv \overline{s}v$, and (5) $\overline{s}e \equiv \overline{s}v$ if $e \Downarrow v$. One can check for the different labelled transition systems we consider that equivalent programs generate exactly the same transitions and that the programs to which they reduce are again equivalent.

A.2 Proof of Theorem 1.5

The theorem follows directly from the following Lemma 1.23(4).

Lemma 1.23

(1) *If $P_1 \approx P_2$ and σ is an injective renaming then $\sigma P_1 \approx \sigma P_2$.*

(2) *The relation $\approx$ is reflexive and transitive.*

(3) *If $P_1 \approx P_2$ then $(P_1 \mid \overline{s}v) \approx (P_2 \mid \overline{s}v)$.*

(4) *If $P_1 \approx P_2$ then $\nu s \ P_1 \approx \nu s \ P_2$ and $(P_1 \mid Q) \approx (P_2 \mid Q)$.*

Proof (1), (2) Standard arguments.
(3) Let $\mathcal{R}' = \{((P \mid \overline{s}v), (Q \mid \overline{s}v)) \mid P \approx Q\}$ and $\mathcal{R} = \mathcal{R}' \cup \approx$. We show that $\mathcal{R}$ is a bisimulation. Suppose $(P \mid \overline{s}v) \xrightarrow{\alpha} \cdot$ and $P \approx Q$. There are two interesting cases to consider.

($\alpha = \tau$) Suppose $(P \mid \overline{s}v) \xrightarrow{\tau} (P' \mid \overline{s}v)$ because $P \xrightarrow{s?v} P'$. By definition of the lts, we have that $P \xrightarrow{sv} (P \mid \overline{s}v) \xrightarrow{\tau} (P' \mid \overline{s}v)$. By definition of bisimulation, $Q \xRightarrow{sv} (Q'' \mid \overline{s}v) \xRightarrow{\tau} (Q' \mid \overline{s}v)$ and $(P' \mid \overline{s}v) \approx (Q' \mid \overline{s}v)$. We conclude, by noticing that then $(Q \mid \overline{s}v) \xRightarrow{\tau} (Q' \mid \overline{s}v)$.

($\alpha = N$) Suppose $(P \mid \overline{s}v) \xrightarrow{N} P'$. Notice that $P \xrightarrow{sv} (P \mid \overline{s}v)$. Hence:

$$Q \xRightarrow{sv} (Q'' \mid \overline{s}v) \xRightarrow{\tau} (Q''' \mid \overline{s}v) \xrightarrow{N} Q', \quad (P \mid \overline{s}v) \approx (Q'' \mid \overline{s}v) \approx (Q''' \mid \overline{s}v),$$
$$\text{and} \quad P' \approx Q' \ .$$

Then $(Q \mid \overline{s}v) \xRightarrow{N} Q'$.
(4) We show that $\mathcal{R} = \{(\nu\mathbf{t} \ (P_1 \mid Q), \nu\mathbf{t} \ (P_2 \mid Q)) \mid P_1 \approx P_2\} \cup \approx$ is a labelled bisimulation up to the structural equivalence $\equiv$.

(τ) Suppose $\nu\mathbf{t} \ (P_1 \mid Q) \xrightarrow{\tau} \cdot$. This may happen because either P_1 or Q perform a τ action or because P_1 and Q synchronize. We analyse the various situations.

$(\tau)[1]$ Suppose $Q \xrightarrow{\tau} Q'$. Then $\nu\mathbf{t} \, (P_2 \mid Q) \xrightarrow{\tau} \nu\mathbf{t} \, (P_2 \mid Q')$ and we can conclude.

$(\tau)[2]$ Suppose $P_1 \xrightarrow{\tau} P_1'$. Then $P_2 \xRightarrow{\tau} P_2'$ and $P_1' \approx P_2'$. So $\nu\mathbf{t} \, (P_2 \mid Q) \xRightarrow{\tau} \nu\mathbf{t} \, (P_2' \mid Q)$ and we can conclude.

$(\tau)[3]$ Suppose $P_1 \xrightarrow{s?v} P_1'$ and $Q \xrightarrow{\nu\mathbf{t}' \, \bar{s}v} Q'$. This means $Q \equiv \nu\mathbf{t}' \, (\bar{s}v \mid Q'')$ and $Q' \equiv (\bar{s}v \mid Q'')$. By (3), $(P_1 \mid \bar{s}v) \approx (P_2 \mid \bar{s}v)$. Moreover, $(P_1 \mid \bar{s}v) \xrightarrow{\tau} (P_1' \mid \bar{s}v)$. Therefore, $(P_2 \mid \bar{s}v) \xRightarrow{\tau} (P_2' \mid \bar{s}v)$ and $(P_1' \mid \bar{s}v) \approx (P_2' \mid \bar{s}v)$. Then we notice that the transition $\nu\mathbf{t} \, (P_1 \mid Q) \xrightarrow{\tau} \cdot \equiv \nu\mathbf{t}, \mathbf{t}' \, ((P_1' \mid \bar{s}v) \mid Q'')$ is matched by the transition $\nu\mathbf{t} \, (P_2 \mid Q) \xrightarrow{\tau} \cdot \equiv \nu\mathbf{t}, \mathbf{t}' \, ((P_2' \mid \bar{s}v) \mid Q'')$.

$(\tau)[4]$ Suppose $P_1 \xrightarrow{\nu\mathbf{t}' \, \bar{s}v} P_1'$ and $Q \xrightarrow{s?v} Q'$. Then $P_2 \xRightarrow{\nu\mathbf{t}' \, \bar{s}v} P_2'$ and $P_1' \approx P_2'$. And we conclude noticing that $\nu\mathbf{t} \, (P_2 \mid Q) \xRightarrow{\tau} \nu\mathbf{t}, \mathbf{t}' \, (P_2' \mid Q')$.

(out) Suppose $\nu\mathbf{t} \, (P_1 \mid Q) \xrightarrow{\nu\mathbf{t}' \, \bar{s}v} \cdot$. Also assume $\mathbf{t} = \mathbf{t_1}, \mathbf{t_2}$ and $\mathbf{t}' = \mathbf{t_1}, \mathbf{t_3}$ up to reordering so that the emission extrudes exactly the names $\mathbf{t_1}$ among the names in $\mathbf{t}$. We have two subcases depending which component performs the action.

$(out)[1]$ Suppose $Q \xrightarrow{\nu\mathbf{t_3} \, \bar{s}v} Q'$. Then $\nu\mathbf{t} \, (P_2 \mid Q) \xrightarrow{\nu\mathbf{t}' \, \bar{s}v} \nu\mathbf{t_2} \, (P_2 \mid Q')$ and we can conclude.

$(out)[2]$ Suppose $P_1 \xrightarrow{\nu\mathbf{t_3} \, \bar{s}v} P_1'$. Then $P_2 \xRightarrow{\nu\mathbf{t_3} \, \bar{s}v} P_2'$ and $P_1' \approx P_2'$. Hence $\nu\mathbf{t} \, (P_2 \mid Q) \xRightarrow{\nu\mathbf{t}' \, \bar{s}v} \nu\mathbf{t_2} \, (P_2' \mid Q)$ and we can conclude.

(in) It is enough to notice that, modulo renaming, $\nu\mathbf{t} \, (P_i \mid Q) \mid \bar{s}v \equiv \nu\mathbf{t} \, ((P_i \mid \bar{s}v) \mid Q)$ and recall that by (3), $(P_1 \mid \bar{s}v) \approx (P_2 \mid \bar{s}v)$.

(N) Suppose $\nu\mathbf{t} \, (P_1 \mid Q) \downarrow$. Up to structural equivalence, we can express Q as $\nu\mathbf{t}_Q \, (S_Q \mid I_Q)$ where S_Q is the parallel composition of emissions and I_Q is the parallel composition of receptions. Thus we have: $\nu\mathbf{t} \, (P_1 \mid Q) \equiv \nu\mathbf{t}, \mathbf{t}_Q \, (P_1 \mid S_Q \mid I_Q)$, and $\nu\mathbf{t} \, (P_2 \mid Q) \equiv \nu\mathbf{t}, \mathbf{t}_Q \, (P_2 \mid S_Q \mid I_Q)$ assuming $\{\mathbf{t}_Q\} \cap fn(P_i) = \emptyset$ for $i = 1, 2$.

If $\nu\mathbf{t} \, (P_1 \mid Q) \xrightarrow{N} P$ then $P \equiv \nu\mathbf{t}, \mathbf{t}_Q \, (P_1'' \mid Q')$ where in particular, we have that $(P_1 \mid S_Q) \downarrow$ and $(P_1 \mid S_Q) \xrightarrow{N} (P_1' \mid 0)$.

By the hypothesis $P_1 \approx P_2$, and by definition of bisimulation we derive that: (i) $(P_2 \mid S_Q) \xRightarrow{\tau} (P_2'' \mid S_Q)$, (ii) $(P_2'' \mid S_Q) \downarrow$, (iii) $(P_2'' \mid S_Q) \xrightarrow{N} (P_2' \mid 0)$, (iv) $(P_1 \mid S_Q) \approx (P_2'' \mid S_Q)$, and (v) $(P_1' \mid 0) \approx (P_2' \mid 0)$.

Because $(P_1 \mid S_Q)$ and $(P_2'' \mid S_Q)$ are suspended and bisimilar, the two programs must commit (cf. Definition 1.7) on the same signal names and moreover on each signal name they must emit the same set of values up to renaming of bound names. It follows that the program $\nu\mathbf{t}, \mathbf{t}_Q \, (P_2'' \mid$

$S_Q \mid I_Q$) is suspended. The only possibility for an internal transition is that an emission in P_2'' enables a reception in I_Q but this contradicts the hypothesis that $\nu \mathbf{t}, \mathbf{t}_Q$ ($P_1 \mid S_Q \mid I_Q$) is suspended. Moreover, ($P_2'' \mid S_Q \mid I_Q$) $\xrightarrow{N}$ ($P_2' \mid 0 \mid Q'$).

Therefore, we have that

$$\nu \mathbf{t}\ (P_2 \mid Q) \equiv \nu \mathbf{t}, \mathbf{t}_Q\ (P_2 \mid S_Q \mid I_Q) \xRightarrow{\tau} \nu \mathbf{t}, \mathbf{t}_Q\ (P_2'' \mid S_Q \mid I_Q),$$

$\nu \mathbf{t}, \mathbf{t}_Q$ ($P_2'' \mid S_Q \mid I_Q$) $\downarrow$, and $\nu \mathbf{t}, \mathbf{t}_Q$ ($P_2'' \mid S_Q \mid I_Q$) $\xrightarrow{N} \nu \mathbf{t}, \mathbf{t}_Q$ ($P_2' \mid 0 \mid Q'$). Now $\nu \mathbf{t}, \mathbf{t}_Q$ ($P_1 \mid S_Q \mid I_Q$) $\mathcal{R}$ $\nu \mathbf{t}, \mathbf{t}_Q$ ($P_2'' \mid S_Q \mid I_Q$) because ($P_1 \mid S_Q$) $\approx$ ($P_2'' \mid S_Q$) and $\nu \mathbf{t}, \mathbf{t}_Q$ ($P_1' \mid Q'$) $\mathcal{R}$ $\nu \mathbf{t}, \mathbf{t}_Q$ ($P_2' \mid Q'$) because $P_1' \approx P_2'$.   □

A.3 Proof of Theorem 1.10

We start with the labelled transition system defined in Table 1.1 and the notion of bisimulation in Definition 1.3. In Table 1.2, we incrementally modify the labelled transition system and/or the conditions in the bisimulation game. This leads to three equivalent characterizations of the notion of bisimulation. We prove this fact step by step.

Lemma 1.24 *The bisimulation $\approx$ coincides with the bisimulation $\approx_1$.*

Proof The only difference here is in the rule (in_{aux}), the bisimulation conditions being the same. Now this rule produces an action $s?v$ and the latter is an auxiliary action that is used to produce the relevant action τ thanks to the rule ($synch$). A simple instance of the difference follows. Suppose $P = \overline{s}e \mid s(x).Q, K$ and $e \Downarrow v$. Then:

$$P \xrightarrow{\tau} \overline{s}e \mid [v/x]Q = P' \text{ and } P \xrightarrow{\tau}_1 \overline{s}e \mid ([v/x]Q \mid \overline{s}v) = P''\ .$$

In the $S\pi$-calculus, we do not distinguish the situations where the same value is emitted once or more times within the same instant. In particular, P' and P'' are structurally equivalent (cf. Section A.1.1).
     □

Next, we focus on the relationships between the labelled transitions systems $\xrightarrow{act}_1$ and $\xrightarrow{act}_2$. In $\xrightarrow{act}_2$, the rule (in) is removed and in the rule (in_{aux}), the label $s?v$ is replaced by the label sv (hence the auxiliary action $s?v$ is not used in this labelled transition system).

Lemma 1.25 (1) *If $P \xrightarrow{act}_1 P'$ and $act \neq sv$ then $P \xrightarrow{act'}_2 P'$ where $act' = sv$ if $act = s?v$, and $act' = act$ otherwise.*

(2) *If $P \xrightarrow{act}_2 P'$ then $P \xrightarrow{act'}_1 P'$ where $act' = s?v$ if $act = sv$, and $act' = act$ otherwise.*

We also notice that 1-bisimulation is preserved by parallel composition with an emission; the proof is similar to the one of Lemma 1.23(3).

Lemma 1.26 *If $P \approx_1 Q$ then $(P \mid \bar{s}v) \approx_1 (Q \mid \bar{s}v)$.*

Lemma 1.27 *The bisimulation $\approx_1$ coincides with the bisimulation $\approx_2$.*

Proof ($\approx_1 \subseteq \approx_2$) We check that $\approx_1$ is a 2-bisimulation. If $\alpha = sv$ then we apply Lemma 1.26. Otherwise, suppose $\alpha \neq sv$, $P \approx_1 Q$, and $P \xrightarrow{\alpha}_2 P'$. By Lemma 1.25(2), $P \xrightarrow{\alpha}_1 P'$. By definition of 1-bisimulation, $\exists Q' \; Q \stackrel{\alpha}{\Rightarrow}_1 Q'$, $P' \approx_1 Q'$. By Lemma 1.25(1), $Q \stackrel{\alpha}{\Rightarrow}_2 Q'$.

($\approx_2 \subseteq \approx_1$) We check that $\approx_2$ is a 1-bisimulation. If $\alpha = sv$ and $P \xrightarrow{sv}_1 (P \mid \bar{s}v)$ then by definition of the lts, $Q \xrightarrow{sv}_1 (Q \mid \bar{s}v)$. Moreover, by definition of 2-bisimulation, $(P \mid \bar{s}v) \approx_2 (Q \mid \bar{s}v)$. Otherwise, suppose $\alpha \neq sv$, $P \approx_2 Q$, and $P \xrightarrow{\alpha}_1 P'$. By Lemma 1.25(1), $P \xrightarrow{\alpha}_2 P'$. By definition of 2-bisimulation, $\exists Q' \; Q \stackrel{\alpha}{\Rightarrow}_2 Q'$, $P' \approx_2 Q'$. By Lemma 1.25(2), $Q \stackrel{\alpha}{\Rightarrow}_1 Q'$. $\qquad\square$

Next we move to a comparison of 2 and 3 bisimulations. Note that both definitions share the same lts denoted with $\xrightarrow{\alpha}_2$. First we remark the following.

Lemma 1.28 (1) *If $P \approx_2 Q$ and $P \xrightarrow{N} P'$ then $\exists Q', Q'' \; (Q \stackrel{\tau}{\Rightarrow}_2 Q'', Q'' \xrightarrow{N} Q', P \approx_2 Q'', P' \approx_2 Q')$.*

(2) *If $P \approx_3 Q$ then $(P \mid \bar{s}v) \approx_3 (Q \mid \bar{s}v)$.*

Proof (1) If $P \xrightarrow{N} P'$ then P cannot perform τ moves. Thus if $P \approx_2 Q$ and $Q \stackrel{\tau}{\Rightarrow}_2 Q''$ then necessarily $P \approx_2 Q''$.

(2) Again we follow the proof of Lemma 1.23(3). Let $\mathcal{R}' = \{((P \mid \bar{s}v), (Q \mid \bar{s}v)) \mid P \approx_3 Q\}$ and $\mathcal{R} = \mathcal{R}' \cup \approx_3$. We show that $\mathcal{R}$ is a 3-bisimulation. Suppose $(P \mid \bar{s}v) \xrightarrow{\alpha}_1 \cdot$ and $P \approx_3 Q$. There are two interesting cases to consider.

$(\alpha = \tau)$ Suppose $(P \mid \bar{s}v) \xrightarrow{\tau}_2 (P' \mid \bar{s}v)$ because $P \xrightarrow{sv}_2 P'$. By definition of 3-bisimulation, either (i) $Q \xRightarrow{sv}_2 Q'$ and $P' \approx_3 Q'$ or (ii) $Q \xRightarrow{\tau}_2 Q'$ and $P' \approx_3 (Q' \mid \bar{s}v)$. In case (i), $(Q \mid \bar{s}v) \xRightarrow{\tau} (Q' \mid \bar{s}v)$ and we notice that $((P' \mid \bar{s}v), (Q' \mid \bar{s}v)) \in \mathcal{R}$. In case (ii), $(Q \mid \bar{s}v) \xRightarrow{\tau} (Q' \mid \bar{s}v)$ and we notice that $(P' \mid \bar{s}v, (Q' \mid \bar{s}v) \mid \bar{s}v) \in \mathcal{R}$ and $(Q' \mid \bar{s}v) \mid \bar{s}v \equiv (Q' \mid \bar{s}v)$.

$(\alpha = N)$ Suppose $((P \mid \bar{s}v) \mid S) \xrightarrow{N} P'$. By definition of 3-bisimulation, taking $S' = (\bar{s}v \mid S)$ $(Q \mid S') \xRightarrow{\tau} Q'' \xrightarrow{N} Q'$, $(P \mid S') \approx_3 Q''$, and $P' \approx_3 Q'$. □

Lemma 1.29 *The bisimulation $\approx_2$ coincides with the bisimulation $\approx_3$.*

Proof $(\approx_2 \subseteq \approx_3)$ We show that $\approx_2$ is a 3-bisimulation. We look first at the condition for the input. Suppose $P \approx_2 Q$ and $P \xrightarrow{sv}_2 P'$. By definition of 2-bisimulation, $(P \mid \bar{s}v) \approx_2 (Q \mid \bar{s}v)$. Also $(P \mid \bar{s}v) \xrightarrow{\tau}_2 (P' \mid \bar{s}v) \equiv P'$. By definition of 2-bisimulation, $(Q \mid \bar{s}v) \xRightarrow{\tau} (Q' \mid \bar{s}v)$ and $P' \equiv (P' \mid \bar{s}v) \approx_2 (Q' \mid \bar{s}v)$. Two cases may arise.

(1) If $Q \xRightarrow{sv} Q'$ then $Q' \mid \bar{s}v \equiv Q'$ and we satisfy the first case of the input condition for 3-bisimulation.

(2) If $Q \xRightarrow{\tau} Q'$ then, up to structural equivalence, we satisfy the second case of the input condition for 3-bisimulation.

Next we consider the condition for the end of the instant. Suppose $P \approx_2 Q$, $S = \bar{s_1}v_1 \mid \cdots \mid \bar{s_n}v_n$, and $(P \mid S) \xrightarrow{N}_2 P'$. By condition (Inp), $(P \mid S) \approx_2 (Q \mid S)$. Then, by Lemma 1.28(1), the condition of 3-bisimulation is entailed by the corresponding condition for 2-bisimulation applied to $(P \mid S)$ and $(Q \mid S)$.

$(\approx_3 \subseteq \approx_2)$ We show that $\approx_3$ is a 2-bisimulation. The condition (Inp) holds because of Lemma 1.28(2). The condition of 2-bisimulation for the end of the instant is a special case of the condition for 3-bisimulation where we take S empty. □

A.4 Proof of Theorem 1.18 and Proposition 1.19

First, relying on proposition 1.22(3), one can repeat the proof in [17] that confluence implies τ-inertness and determinacy.

Proposition 1.30 *If a program is confluent then it is τ-inert and determinate.*

Proof Let $\mathcal{S} = \{(P, P') \mid P \text{ confluent and } P \stackrel{\tau}{\Rightarrow} P'\}$ and define $\mathcal{R} = \mathcal{S} \cup \mathcal{S}^{-1}$. We show that $\mathcal{R}$ is a w-bisimulation up to w-bisimulation (cf. Lemma 1.22(3)). Clearly $\mathcal{R}$ is symmetric. Then suppose P confluent and $P \stackrel{\tau}{\Rightarrow} Q$ (the case where Q reduces to P is symmetric). If $Q \stackrel{\alpha}{\Rightarrow} Q_1$ then $P \stackrel{\alpha}{\Rightarrow} Q_1$ and $Q_1 \mathcal{R} Q_1$. On the other hand, if $P \stackrel{\alpha}{\Rightarrow} P_1$ then by confluence there are P_2, Q_1 such that $P_1 \stackrel{\tau}{\Rightarrow} P_2$, $Q \stackrel{\alpha}{\Rightarrow} Q_1$, and $P_2 \approx Q_1$. Thus $P_1 \mathcal{R} \circ \approx Q_1$.

Therefore if P is confluent and $P \stackrel{\tau}{\Rightarrow} P'$ then $P \approx P'$. Also recall that if Q is a derivative of P then Q is confluent. Thus we can conclude that if P is confluent then it is τ-inert.

Next, we show that:

$$\frac{P_1 \approx P_2, \quad P_1 \stackrel{\alpha}{\Rightarrow} P_3, \quad P_2 \stackrel{\alpha}{\Rightarrow} P_4}{P_3 \approx P_4}.$$

By definition of bisimulation, $\exists P_5 \ (\ P_2 \stackrel{\alpha}{\Rightarrow} P_5, P_3 \approx P_5\ )$. By confluence, $\exists P_6, P_7 \ (\ P_5 \stackrel{\tau}{\Rightarrow} P_6, P_4 \stackrel{\tau}{\Rightarrow} P_7, P_6 \approx P_7\ )$. By τ-inertness and transitivity, $P_3 \approx P_4$.

Finally, we can iterate this observation to conclude that if $P \stackrel{\alpha_1}{\Rightarrow} \cdots \stackrel{\alpha_n}{\Rightarrow} P_1$ and $P \stackrel{\alpha_1}{\Rightarrow} \cdots \stackrel{\alpha_n}{\Rightarrow} P_2$ then $P_1 \approx P_2$. □

We pause to point-out the particular properties of the input and output actions in the labelled transition system in Table 1.1. It is easily verified that if $P \xrightarrow{\nu \mathbf{t} \bar{s} v} P'$ then $P \equiv \nu \mathbf{t}(\bar{s}v \mid P'')$ and $P' \equiv (\bar{s}v \mid P'')$. This entails that in the following Table A.4.1 the cases that involve an output action are actually general up to structural equivalence.

Note that, up to symmetry (and structural equivalence), the Table A.4.1 covers *all* possible commutations of two compatible actions α, β but the two remaining cases where $\alpha = \beta$ and $\alpha \in \{\tau, N\}$.

Proposition 1.31 *If a program is deterministic then it is confluent.*

Proof We recall that if P is deterministic then it is τ-inert. Suppose Q is a derivative of P, $\alpha \downarrow \beta$, $Q \stackrel{\alpha}{\Rightarrow} Q_1$ and $Q \stackrel{\beta}{\Rightarrow} Q_2$.

If $\alpha = \beta$ then the definition of determinacy implies that $Q_1 \approx Q_2$. Also note that $\alpha \backslash \beta = \beta \backslash \alpha = \tau$ and $Q_i \stackrel{\tau}{\Rightarrow} Q_i$ for $i = 1, 2$. So the conditions for confluence are fulfilled.

So we may assume $\alpha \neq \beta$ and, up to symmetry, we are left with five cases corresponding to the five situations considered in Table A.4.1.

Table A.4.1. *Input–output commutations.*

$(in - \tau)$

$$\frac{P \xrightarrow{sv} (P \mid \overline{s}v), \quad P \xrightarrow{\tau} P'}{(P \mid \overline{s}v) \xrightarrow{\tau} (P' \mid \overline{s}v), \quad P' \xrightarrow{sv} (P' \mid \overline{s}v)}$$

$(in - in)$

$$\frac{P \xrightarrow{sv} (P \mid \overline{s}v), \quad P \xrightarrow{s'v'} (P \mid \overline{s'}v')}{(P \mid \overline{s}v) \xrightarrow{s'v'} (P \mid \overline{s}v) \mid \overline{s'}v', \quad (P \mid \overline{s'}v') \xrightarrow{sv} (P \mid \overline{s'}v') \mid \overline{s}v, \\ (P \mid \overline{s}v) \mid \overline{s'}v' \equiv (P \mid \overline{s'}v') \mid \overline{s}v}$$

$(out - \tau)$

$$\frac{\nu \mathbf{t}(\overline{s}v \mid P) \xrightarrow{\nu \mathbf{t} \ \overline{s}v} (\overline{s}v \mid P), \quad \nu \mathbf{t}(\overline{s}v \mid P) \xrightarrow{\tau} \nu \mathbf{t}(\overline{s}v \mid P')}{(\overline{s}v \mid P) \xrightarrow{\tau} (\overline{s}v \mid P'), \quad \nu \mathbf{t}(\overline{s}v \mid P') \xrightarrow{\nu \mathbf{t} \ \overline{s}v} (\overline{s}v \mid P')}$$

$(out - in)$

$$\frac{\nu \mathbf{t}(\overline{s}v \mid P) \xrightarrow{\nu \mathbf{t} \ \overline{s}v} (\overline{s}v \mid P), \quad \nu \mathbf{t}(\overline{s}v \mid P) \xrightarrow{s'v'} \nu \mathbf{t}(\overline{s}v \mid P) \mid \overline{s'}v'}{(\overline{s}v \mid P) \xrightarrow{s'v'} (\overline{s}v \mid P) \mid \overline{s'}v', \quad \nu \mathbf{t}(\overline{s}v \mid P) \mid \overline{s'}v' \xrightarrow{\nu \mathbf{t} \ \overline{s}v} (\overline{s}v \mid P) \mid \overline{s'}v'}$$

$(out - out)$

$$\frac{\nu \mathbf{t}(\overline{s_1}v_1 \mid \overline{s_2}v_2 \mid P) \xrightarrow{\nu \mathbf{t_1} \ \overline{s_1}v_1} \nu \mathbf{t} \backslash \mathbf{t_1} \ (\overline{s_1}v_1 \mid \overline{s_2}v_2 \mid P), \\ \nu \mathbf{t}(\overline{s_1}v_1 \mid \overline{s_2}v_2 \mid P) \xrightarrow{\nu \mathbf{t_2} \ \overline{s_2}v_2} \nu \mathbf{t} \backslash \mathbf{t_2} \ (\overline{s_1}v_1 \mid \overline{s_2}v_2 \mid P)}{\nu \mathbf{t} \backslash \mathbf{t_1} \ (\overline{s_1}v_1 \mid \overline{s_2}v_2 \mid P) \xrightarrow{\nu \mathbf{t_2} \backslash \mathbf{t_1} \ \overline{s_2}v_2} (\overline{s_1}v_1 \mid \overline{s_2}v_2 \mid P), \\ \nu \mathbf{t} \backslash \mathbf{t_2} \ (\overline{s_1}v_1 \mid \overline{s_2}v_2 \mid P) \xrightarrow{\nu \mathbf{t_1} \backslash \mathbf{t_2} \ \overline{s_2}v_2} (\overline{s_1}v_1 \mid \overline{s_2}v_2 \mid P)}$$

In the two cases where $\beta = \tau$ we have that $Q \approx Q_2$ by τ-inertness. Thus, by bisimulation $Q_2 \xRightarrow{\alpha} Q_3$ and $Q_1 \approx Q_3$. Now $\alpha \backslash \tau = \alpha$, $\tau \backslash \alpha = \tau$, and $Q_1 \xRightarrow{\tau} Q_1$. Hence the conditions for confluence are fulfilled.

We are left with three cases where α and β are distinct input or output actions. By using τ-inertness, we can focus on the case where $Q \xRightarrow{\alpha} Q_1$ and $Q \xrightarrow{\beta} Q_2' \xRightarrow{\tau} Q_2$. Now, by iterating the commutations in Table A.4.1, we can prove that:

$$\frac{Q \ (\xrightarrow{\tau})^n \ Q_1', \quad n \geq 1, \quad Q \xrightarrow{\beta} Q_2'}{\exists Q_2'' \ (\ Q_1' \xrightarrow{\beta} Q_2'', \quad Q_2' \ (\xrightarrow{\tau})^n \ Q_2'' \ )} \ .$$

So we are actually reduced to consider the situation where $Q \xrightarrow{\alpha} Q_1' \xRightarrow{\tau} Q_1$ and $Q \xrightarrow{\beta} Q_2' \xRightarrow{\tau} Q_2$. But then by Table A.4.1, we have: $Q_1' \xrightarrow{\beta \backslash \alpha} Q_3$,

$Q'_2 \xrightarrow{\alpha \backslash \beta} Q_4$, and $Q_3 \equiv Q_4$. Then using τ-inertness and bisimulation, it is easy to close the diagram. $\qquad \square$

This concludes the proof of the first part of Theorem 1.18(1). To derive the second part, we rely on the following fact due to [11].

Fact 1.32 ([11]) If a program is reactive and locally confluent then it is confluent.

Thus to derive the second part of Theorem 1.18(2) is enough to prove this fact.

Proposition 1.33 *A program is locally confluent if (and only if) for all its derivatives Q:*

$$\frac{Q \xrightarrow{\alpha} Q_1, \quad Q \xrightarrow{\alpha} Q_2, \quad \alpha \in \{\tau, N\}}{Q_1 \xRightarrow{\tau} Q_3 \quad Q_2 \xRightarrow{\tau} Q_4 \quad Q_3 \approx Q_4}$$

Proof The stated condition is a special case of local confluence thus it is a necessary condition. To show that it is sufficient to entail local confluence, it is enough to appeal again to Table A.4.1 (same argument given at the end of the proof of Proposition 1.31). $\qquad \square$

Proof of Proposition 1.19

Proof Say that P is *strong confluent* if it satisfies the hypotheses of Proposition 1.19.
Let $\mathcal{S} = \{(P, Q) \mid P \text{ strong confluent and } (P \equiv Q \text{ or } P \xrightarrow{\tau} Q)\}$.
Let $\mathcal{R} = \mathcal{S} \cup \mathcal{S}^{-1}$. We show that $\mathcal{R}$ is a bisimulation. Hence strong confluence entails τ-inertness. Note that if $P \xrightarrow{\alpha} P_i$, for $i = 1, 2$, and α is either an input or an output action then $P_1 \equiv P_2$. By Table A.4.1 and diagram chasing, we show that if P is strong confluent and $P \xRightarrow{\alpha} P_i$, for $i = 1, 2$, then $P_1 \approx P_2$. This suffices to show that P is determinate (and confluent). $\qquad \square$

2

Classical coordination mechanisms in the chemical model

Jean-Pierre Banâtre

INRIA/IRISA, Université de Rennes 1

Pascal Fradet

INRIA Rhône-Alpes

Yann Radenac

INRIA/IRISA, Université de Rennes 1

In memory of Gilles Kahn

The essence of this paper stems from discussions that the first author (Jean-Pierre Banâtre) had with Gilles on topics related with programming in general and chemical programming in particular. Gilles liked the ideas behind the Gamma model [6] and the closely related Berry and Boudol's CHAM [7] as the basic principles are so simple and elegant. The last opportunity Jean-Pierre had to speak about these ideas to Gilles, was when he presented the LNCS volume devoted to the Unconventional Programming Paradigms workshop [1]. The 10 minutes appointment (at that time, he was CEO of INRIA) lasted a long time. Gilles was fine and in good humour, as often, and he was clearly happy to talk about a subject he loved. He spoke a lot about λ-calculus, the reduction principle, the β-reduction. . . a really great souvenir!

Abstract

Originally, the chemical model of computation has been proposed as a simple and elegant parallel programming paradigm. Data is seen as "molecules" and computation as "chemical reactions": if some molecules satisfy a predefined reaction condition, they are replaced by the "product" of the reaction. When no reaction is possible, a normal form is reached and the program terminates. In this paper, we describe classical coordination mechanisms and parallel programming models in the chemical setting. All these examples put forward the simplicity and expressivity of the chemical paradigm. We pay a particular attention

From Semantics to Computer Science Essays in Honour of Gilles Kahn, eds Yves Bertot, Gérard Huet, Jean-Jacques Lévy and Gordon Plotkin. Published by Cambridge University Press. © Cambridge University Press 2009.

to the chemical description of the simple and successful parallel computation model known as Kahn Process Networks.

2.1 Introduction

The Gamma formalism was proposed 20 years ago to capture the intuition of computation as the global evolution of a collection of atomic values interacting freely [6]. Gamma can be introduced intuitively through the chemical reaction metaphor. The unique data structure in Gamma is the multiset which can be seen as a chemical solution. A simple program is made of a *reaction condition* and an *action*. Execution proceeds by replacing elements satisfying the reaction condition by the elements specified by the action. The result of a Gamma program is obtained when a stable or *inert* state is reached, that is to say, when no more reactions can take place.

For example, the computation of the maximum element of a non-empty multiset of comparable elements can be described by the reaction rule

$$\textbf{replace}\, x, y \,\textbf{by}\, x \,\textbf{if}\, x \geq y$$

meaning that any couple of elements x and y of the multiset such that x is greater or equal to y is replaced by x. This process goes on till a stable state is reached, that is to say, when only the maximum element remains. Note that, in this definition, nothing is said about the order of evaluation of the comparisons. If several disjoint pairs of elements satisfy the condition, reactions can be performed in parallel.

Gamma can be formalized as a multiset AC-rewriting language. The Gamma formalism, and its derivative works as summarized in [2], is based on finite multisets of basic values. However, this basic concept can be extended by allowing elements of multisets to be reactions themselves (*higher-order multisets*), to have an infinite multiplicity (*infinite multisets*) and even to have a negative multiplicity (*hybrid multisets*). In [4], we have investigated these unconventional multiset structures (higher-order, infinite and hybrid multisets) and shown how they can be interpreted in a chemical programming framework. In particular, we have introduced the γ-calculus, a minimal higher-order calculus that summarizes the fundamental concepts of chemical programming. From this basic language, we have derived HOCL (the Higher Order Chemical Language), a programming language built by extending the γ-calculus with constants, operators, types and expressive patterns. The reflexive CHAM [10] is another approach to higher-order multiset programming.

The objective of this paper is to show how many well-known parallel mechanisms from basic mutual exclusion to Kahn Process Networks can be expressed in the same unified framework: the chemical model. This work illustrates one more time the expressivity of chemical languages. It also paves the way to formal comparisons of classical coordination structures and models.

2.2 The higher-order chemical language

The HOCL language [4] is a higher-order extension of Gamma based on the γ-calculus [3]. Here, we present briefly and informally the features of HOCL used in this article. The interested reader will find a more complete and formal presentation in [4].

In HOCL, programs, solutions, data and reaction rules are all molecules. A program is a solution of atoms

$$\langle A_1, \ldots, A_n \rangle$$

that is, a multiset of constants, reaction rules and (sub-)solutions. The associativity and commutativity of the operator "," formalize the Brownian motion within a chemical solution. These laws can always be used to reorganize molecules in solutions. Atoms are either basic constants (integers, booleans, etc.), pairs $(A_1:A_2)$, sub-solutions $(\langle M \rangle)$ or reaction rules. A reaction rule is written

$$\mathbf{one}\, P \,\mathbf{by}\, M \,\mathbf{if}\, C$$

where P is a pattern which selects some atoms, C is the reaction condition and M the result of the reaction. If P matches atoms which satisfy C, they are replaced by M. For example,

$$\langle (\mathbf{one}\, x{::}\mathrm{Int}\, \mathbf{by}\, x + 1 \,\mathbf{if}\, x \,\mathrm{div}\, 2), 4, 9, 15 \rangle \longrightarrow_\gamma \langle 5, 9, 15 \rangle.$$

The pattern $x{::}\mathrm{Int}$ matches any integer, the condition imposes the integer to be even and the action replaces it by the next odd integer. In the rest of this article, we omit types in patterns when there is no ambiguity.

Such reaction rules are said to be *one-shot* since they are consumed when they react. In Gamma, rewrite rules were outside the multiset and remained as long as they could be applied. In HOCL, such recursive rules are called *n-shot* and, like in Gamma, these are written as

$$\mathbf{replace}\, P \,\mathbf{by}\, M \,\mathbf{if}\, C.$$

The execution of a chemical program consists in performing reactions (non-deterministically and possibly in parallel) until the solution becomes inert i.e. no reaction can take place anymore. For example, the following HOCL program computes the prime numbers lower than 10 using a version of the Eratosthenes' sieve:

$$\langle(\textbf{replace}\, x, y \,\textbf{by}\, x \,\text{if}\, x \,\text{div}\, y), 2, 3, 4, 5, 6, 7, 8, 9, 10\rangle.$$

The reaction removes any element y which can be divided by another one x. Initially several reactions are possible. For example, the pair $(2, 10)$ can be replaced by 2, the pair $(3, 9)$ by 3 or $(4, 8)$ by 4, etc. The solution becomes inert when the rule cannot react with any pair of integers in the solution; that is to say, when the solution contains only prime numbers. Even if there are many possible executions, the result of the computation in our example is always $\langle(\textbf{replace}\, x, y \,\textbf{by}\, x \,\text{if}\, x \,\text{div}\, y), 2, 3, 5, 7\rangle$.

A molecule inside a solution cannot react with a molecule outside the solution (the construct $\langle.\rangle$ can be seen as a membrane). Reaction rules can access the content of a sub-solution only if it is inert. This important restriction allows the evaluation order to be controlled in an otherwise highly non-deterministic and parallel model. All reactions should be performed in a sub-solution before its content may be accessed or extracted. So, the pattern $\langle P\rangle$ matches only inert solutions whose content matches the pattern P.

Rules can be named (or tagged) using the syntax

$$\text{name} = \textbf{replace}\, P \,\textbf{by}\, M \,\textbf{if}\, C.$$

Names are used to match and extract specific rules using the same syntax (name $= x$). We often use the **let** operator to name rules and assume that

$$\textbf{let}\, \text{name} = M \,\textbf{in}\, N \overset{\text{def}}{=} N[(\text{name} = M)/\text{name}]$$

that is, the occurrences of name in N are replaced by name $= M$.

We also often make use of the pattern ω which can match any molecule or nothing. This pattern is very convenient to extract elements from a solution.

Using all these features, the Eratosthenes' sieve can be rewritten in order to remove the n-shot reaction rule sieve at the end of the computation:

$$\textbf{let } \text{sieve} = \textbf{replace } x, y \textbf{ by } x \textbf{ if } x \text{ div } y \textbf{ in}$$
$$\textbf{let } \text{clean} = \textbf{one}\langle \text{sieve} = x, \omega \rangle \textbf{ by } \omega \textbf{ in}$$
$$\langle \text{clean}, \langle \text{sieve}, 2, 3, 4, 5, 6, 7, 8, 9, 10 \rangle \rangle$$

The reduction proceeds as follows:

$$\langle \text{clean} = \dots, \langle \text{sieve} = \dots, 2, 3, 4, 5, 6, 7, 8, 9, 10 \rangle \rangle$$
$$\xrightarrow{\ *\ } \quad \langle \text{clean} = \dots, \langle \text{sieve} = \dots, 2, 3, 5, 7 \rangle \rangle$$
$$\longrightarrow \quad \langle 2, 3, 5, 7 \rangle$$

The reaction rule clean cannot be applied until the sub-solution is inert. The rule sieve reacts until all primes are computed. Then, the one-shot rule clean extracts the prime numbers and suppresses the reaction rule sieve.

2.3 The basic coordination structures of HOCL

HOCL is a programming language that, as explained below, provides some primitive coordination structures: namely, parallel execution, mutual exclusion, the atomic capture and the serialization and parallelization of computations.

2.3.1 Parallel execution

When two reactions involve distinct tuples of elements, both reactions can occur at the same time.

For example, when computing the sum of a multiset of integers:

$$\langle 42, 6, 14, 5, 2, 8, 5, 42, 89, \text{add} = \textbf{replace } x, y \textbf{ by } x + y \rangle$$

several reactions involving the rule add may occur at the same time provided that the couples of integers involved are distinct. Parallel execution relies on a fundamental property of HOCL : mutual exclusion.

2.3.2 Mutual exclusion

The mutual exclusion property states that a molecule cannot take part to several reactions at the same time. For example, several reactions can occur at the same time in the previous solution (e.g. (42,89) at the same time as (5,5), etc.). Without mutual exclusion, the same integer could occur in several reactions at the same time. In this case, our previous program would not represent the sum of a multiset since, for example, 89 would be allowed to react with 2 and 6 and be replaced by 91 and 95.

2.3.3 Atomic capture

Another fundamental property of HOCL is the atomic capture. A reaction rule takes all its arguments atomically. Either all the required arguments are present or no reaction occurs. If all the required arguments are present, none of them may take part in another reaction at the same time.

Atomic capture is useful to express non-blocking programs. For example, the famous dining philosophers problem can be expressed in HOCL as follows. Initially the multiset contains N forks (i.e. N pairs Fork:1, ..., Fork:N) and the two following n-shot reaction rules eat and think:

$$\text{eat} = \textbf{replace } \text{Fork:}f_1, \text{ Fork:}f_2$$
$$\textbf{by } \text{Phi:}f_1$$
$$\textbf{if } f_2 = f_1 + 1 \bmod N$$
$$\text{think} = \textbf{replace } \text{Phi:}f$$
$$\textbf{by } \text{Fork:}f, \text{ Fork:}(f + 1 \bmod N)$$
$$\textbf{if true}$$

The eat rule looks for two adjacent forks Fork:f_1 and Fork:f_2 with $f_2 = f_1 + 1 \bmod N$ and "produces" the eating philosopher Phi:f_1. This reaction relies on the atomic capture property: the two forks are taken simultaneously (atomicity) and this prevents deadlocks. The think rule "transforms" an eating philosopher into two available forks. This rule models the fact that any eating philosopher can be stopped non-deterministically at anytime.

2.3.4 Serialization

A key motivation of chemical models in general, and HOCL in particular, is to be able to express programs without any artificial sequentiality (i.e. sequentiality that is not imposed by the logic of the algorithm). However, even within this highly unconstrained and parallel setting, sequencing of actions can be expressed. Sequencing relies on the fact that a rule needing to access a sub-solution has to wait for its inertia. The reaction rule will react after (in sequence) all the reactions inside the sub-solution have completed.

The HOCL program that computes all the primes lower than a given integer N can be expressed by a sequence of actions that first computes the integers from 1 to N and then applies the rule sieve:

$$\langle\langle\text{iota}, \overline{N}\rangle, \text{thensieve}\rangle$$

where

$$\text{thensieve} = \mathbf{one}\langle\text{iota} = r, \overline{x}, \omega\rangle \, \mathbf{by} \, \text{sieve}, \omega$$
$$\text{iota} = \mathbf{replace} \, \overline{x} \, \mathbf{by} \, x, \overline{x-1} \, \mathbf{if} \, x > 1$$
$$\text{sieve} = \mathbf{replace} \, x, y \, \mathbf{by} \, x \, \mathbf{if} \, x \, \text{div} \, y$$

The rule iota generates the integers from N to 1 using the notation $\overline{x}$ to denote a distinguished (e.g. tagged) integer. The one-shot rule thensieve waits for the inertia of the sub-solution. When it is inert, the generated integers are extracted and put next to the rule sieve (iota and the tagged integer $\overline{1}$ are removed). The wait for the inertia has serialized the iota and sieve operations.

Most of the existing chemical languages share these basic features. They all have conditional reactions with atomic capture of elements. On the other hand, they usually do not address fairness issues.

2.4 Classical coordination in HOCL

In this section, we consider well known coordination mechanisms and express them in HOCL. Most of them are communication patterns between sequential processes. We first show how to model such sequential processes as chemical solutions. Then, we propose a chemical version of communications using rendezvous, shared variables, Linda primitives and Petri nets.

2.4.1 Sequential processes in HOCL

In order to represent sequential and deterministic processes in the chemical model, we encode them at a fairly low level. For instance, the program counter and addresses of instructions will be represented explicitly. It should be clear that syntactic sugar could be used to express sequential processes (and many subsequent communication schemes) more concisely. However, for simplicity and uniformity reasons, we will stick to pure and basic HOCL programs.

A process is a solution made of:

- a local store storing variables represented by pairs of the form *name:value*;

- a code represented by a sequence of instructions encoded by pairs of the form *address:instruction* where *address* is an integer and *instruction* is a reaction rule to modify local variables;
- a program counter PC:*address* recording the next instruction to be executed.

A process is an inert solution that contains both the program to execute and its local store. A reaction rule, named run, executes the current instruction (i.e. the instruction pointed to by PC) of processes.

For example, the process $P = \{\text{TEMP} := \text{X}; \ \text{X} := \text{Y}; \ \text{Y} := \text{TEMP}; \}$ that swaps the content of two variables X and Y is represented by the sequence of instructions:

$$code \equiv \left\{ \begin{array}{l} 1{:}\langle\text{assign}(\text{TEMP}, \text{X})\rangle, \\ 2{:}\langle\text{assign}(\text{X}, \text{Y})\rangle, \\ 3{:}\langle\text{assign}(\text{Y}, \text{TEMP})\rangle \end{array} \right.$$

where assign(A, B) is the rule

$$\text{assign}(A, B) \equiv \textbf{one } A{:}a, \ B{:}b \\ \textbf{by } A{:}b, \ B{:}b$$

which performs the assignment $A := B$.

Assuming an initial store where the local variables X, Y and TEMP have the values 10, 23 and 0, respectively, the process P in its initial state is represented by the solution

$$\langle\text{P}{:}\langle\text{PC}{:}1, \text{X}{:}10, \text{Y}{:}23, \text{TEMP}{:}0, code\rangle, \text{run}\rangle$$

with

$$\text{run} = \textbf{replace } p{:}\langle\text{PC}{:}a, \ a{:}\langle c\rangle, \ \omega\rangle \\ \textbf{by } p{:}\langle\text{PC}{:}(a+1), \ a{:}\langle c\rangle, \ c, \ \omega\rangle$$

The run rule extracts the instruction pointed to by PC from the list of instructions and increments the program counter. The rule representing the instruction (i.e. c) reacts and modifies the local store. When the solution representing the process is inert again, the run rule can be applied again. In our example, it is easy to convince oneself that the solution will be rewritten into the final inert solution

$$\langle\text{P}{:}\langle\text{PC}{:}4, \ \text{X}{:}23, \ \text{Y}{:}10, \ \text{TEMP}{:}10, \ code\rangle, \ \text{run}\rangle$$

Since there is no instruction at address 4, the run rule cannot react anymore. Other instructions are easily defined, for example:

- the neg rule

$$\text{neg}(A) \equiv \textbf{one } A{:}a$$
$$\textbf{by } A{:}(\text{not } a)$$

corresponds to the statement $A := \text{not } A$.

- the add rule

$$\text{add}(A, B, C) \equiv \textbf{one } A{:}a, \ B{:}b, \ C{:}c$$
$$\textbf{by } A{:}(b + c), \ B{:}b, \ C{:}c$$

corresponds to the statement $A := B + C$.

- the jmp instruction

$$\text{jmp}(b) \equiv \textbf{one } \text{PC}{:}a$$
$$\textbf{by } \text{PC}{:}b$$

sets PC to a new address.

- the ncondJmp instruction

$$\text{ncondJmp}(B, b) \equiv \textbf{one } \text{PC}{:}a, B{:}k$$
$$\textbf{by } B{:}k, \ \text{PC}{:}(\textbf{if } k \textbf{ then } a \textbf{ else } b)$$

sets PC to a new address or leaves it unchanged depending on the value of the boolean variable B.

The run rule can be placed into a solution with several processes like:

$$\langle \text{run}, \ P_1{:}\langle\ldots\rangle, \ldots, \ P_n{:}\langle\ldots\rangle \rangle$$

In the absence of the coordination rule, run will rewrite all processes step by step potentially in parallel or non-deterministically. We now describe coordination (communication, synchronization) instructions between two (or more) processes. Contrary to standard imperative instructions which are of the form $a{:}\langle i \rangle$ (i.e. within a solution), coordination instructions will be of the form $a{:}i{:}x{:}y$ (i.e. in tuples). They cannot be executed by the run rule. The coordination mechanism relies on specific reaction rules taking as parameters all actors (processes, shared variables, queues, etc.) involved in the interaction.

2.4.2 Rendezvous in HOCL

We consider concurrently executing processes communicating by atomic, instantaneous actions called "rendezvous" (or sometimes, "synchronous message passing"). If two processes are to communicate, and one reaches the point at which it is ready to communicate first, then it stalls until the other process is ready as well. The exchange (communication) is atomic in that it is initiated and completed in a single uninterruptable step. Examples of rendezvous models include Hoare's communicating sequential processes (CSP) [11] and Milner's calculus of communicating systems (CCS) [13].

Rendezvous models are particularly well suited to applications where resource sharing is a key element, such as client–server database models and multitasking or multiplexing of hardware resources. A key feature of rendezvous-based models is their ability to cleanly model non-determinate interactions.

In HOCL, the rendezvous is represented as an atomic capture of two processes in a particular state. The sender should be ready to send something and the receiver should be ready to receive. The rule runRdV, below, implements a rendezvous communication in one atomic step:

$$
\begin{aligned}
\text{runRdV} = \ &\textbf{replace } p_1{:}\langle \text{PC}{:}a,\ a{:}\text{send}{:}p_2{:}x,\ x{:}k,\ \omega_1\rangle, \\
&\qquad\quad p_2{:}\langle \text{PC}{:}b,\ b{:}\text{recv}{:}p_1{:}y,\ y{:}l,\ \omega_2\rangle \\
&\textbf{by } p_1{:}\langle \text{PC}{:}(a+1),\ a{:}\text{send}{:}p_2{:}x,\ x{:}k,\ \omega_1\rangle, \\
&\qquad\ \ p_2{:}\langle \text{PC}{:}(b+1),\ b{:}\text{recv}{:}p_1{:}y,\ y{:}k,\ \omega_2\rangle
\end{aligned}
$$

The communication between two processes p_1 and p_2 takes place when the active instruction of p_1 is of the form send:p_2:x ("send the value of variable x to p_2") and the active instruction of p_2 is of the form recv:p_1:y ("place the value received from p_1 in variable y"). The value of x is placed into y and both program counters are incremented.

Typically, a collection of sequential processes communicating by rendezvous will be represented by a solution of the form:

$$\langle \text{run},\ \text{runRdV},\ \text{P}_1{:}\langle\ldots\rangle,\ldots,\ \text{P}_n{:}\langle\ldots\rangle\rangle$$

The reaction run will execute (in parallel and non-deterministically) processes unwilling to communicate. At the same time, runRdV will execute (potentially several) pairs of processes waiting for a rendezvous.

2.4.3 Shared variables

Local variables are inside the solution representing the associated process. Shared variables are represented by data in the top-level solution containing the processes. For example, the shared variable X whose value is 3 is represented as:

$$\langle \ldots,\ \text{P}_i{:}\langle\ldots\rangle,\ \ldots, \text{X}{:}3\rangle$$

A shared variable is manipulated using two instructions:

- a:Wshare:X:Y which writes the value of the local variable Y in the shared variable X;
- a:Rshare:X:Y which reads the value of the shared variable Y and stores it in the local variable X.

The associated reaction rules are

$$\text{runWshare} = \textbf{replace } p\text{:}\langle \text{PC}\text{:}a,\ a\text{:Wshare:}x\text{:}y,\ y\text{:}k,\ \omega\rangle,$$
$$x\text{:}l$$
$$\textbf{by } p\text{:}\langle \text{PC}\text{:}(a+1),\ a\text{:Wshare:}x\text{:}y,\ y\text{:}k,\ \omega\rangle,$$
$$x\text{:}k$$
$$\text{runRshare} = \textbf{replace } p\text{:}\langle \text{PC}\text{:}a,\ a\text{:Rshare:}x\text{:}y,\ x\text{:}k,\ \omega\rangle,$$
$$y\text{:}l$$
$$\textbf{by } p\text{:}\langle \text{PC}\text{:}(a+1),\ a\text{:Wshare:}x\text{:}y,\ x\text{:}l,\ \omega\rangle,$$
$$y\text{:}l$$

To let processes communicate using shared variables A and B, the system is represented by a solution of the form:

$$\langle \text{run, runWshare, runRshare, } \text{P}_1\text{:}\langle\ldots\rangle,\ldots, \text{P}_n\text{:}\langle\ldots\rangle,\ \text{A:}0,\ \text{B:}841\rangle$$

Again, the atomic capture of reaction rules is key to ensure the atomicity of the operations on shared variables. If several processes want to write the same shared variable concurrently, an ordering will be non-deterministically chosen.

2.4.4 Linda primitives in HOCL

The Linda model of communication [8] has mainly two operations, *out* and *in*, that modify a unique data structure called a tuple space. The operation $out(X_1\text{:}\cdots\text{:}X_n)$ stores a tuple $l_1\text{:}\cdots\text{:}l_n$ (where l_i is the value of the variable X_i) in the tuple space. The operation $in(X_1\text{:}\cdots\text{:}X_n)$ removes a tuple that matches the given tuple pattern. The tuple pattern contains variable names or constants. A corresponding tuple must be the same size and the constants must concur. Then, the ith variable X_i

is assigned to the ith value. In HOCL these are implemented by the two following reaction rules:

$$\text{runLindaOut} = \textbf{replace } p\text{:}\langle \text{PC:}a,\ a\text{:out:}r,\ \omega_P\rangle$$
$$\textbf{by } p\text{:}\langle \text{PC:}a,\ a\text{:}\overline{\text{out}}\text{:}r,\ \omega_P\rangle,$$
$$r$$

$$\text{runLindaIn} = \textbf{replace } p\text{:}\langle \text{PC:}a,\ a\text{:in:}r,\ \omega_P\rangle$$
$$\textbf{by } p\text{:}\langle \text{PC:}a,\ a\text{:}\overline{\text{in}}\text{:}r,\ \omega_P\rangle,$$
$$r$$

In both rules, the variable r stands for a one-shot rule that is extracted to be executed. In a out-rule, r has the following form:

$$\textbf{one } p\text{:}\langle \text{PC:}a,\ a\text{:}\overline{\text{out}}\text{:}r,\ X_1\text{:}l_1,\ldots,\ X_n\text{:}l_n,\ \omega_p\rangle,$$
$$\text{TS:}\langle\omega\rangle$$
$$\textbf{by } p\text{:}\langle \text{PC:}(a+1),\ a\text{:out:}r,\ X_1\text{:}l_1,\ldots,\ X_n\text{:}l_n,\ \omega_p\rangle,$$
$$\text{TS:}\langle l_1\text{:}\ldots\text{:}l_n,\ \omega\rangle$$

Conversely, in a in-rule, r has the following form:

$$\textbf{one } p\text{:}\langle \text{PC:}a,\ a\text{:}\overline{\text{in}}\text{:}r,\ X_1\text{:}l'_1,\ldots,\ X_n\text{:}l'_n,\ \omega_p\rangle,$$
$$\text{TS:}\langle l_1\text{:}\ldots\text{:}l_n,\ \omega\rangle$$
$$\textbf{by } p\text{:}\langle \text{PC:}(a+1),\ a\text{:in:}r,\ X_1\text{:}l_1,\ldots,\ X_n\text{:}l_n,\ \omega_p\rangle,$$
$$\text{TS:}\langle\omega\rangle$$

The in and out operations are implemented in a two-step fashion. In the first step, the corresponding rule is extracted. The instruction name in or out is converted to $\overline{\text{in}}$ or $\overline{\text{out}}$ to prevent a second shot, and the PC is not incremented. In the second step, the extracted one-shot rule looks for all the data it needs inside the process p (read or write variables) and inside the tuple space TS (matched tuple). It increments the PC and resets the instruction name to in or out.

The extracted one-shot rule corresponding to a in-rule is blocked until a tuple matching $l_1\text{:}\ldots\text{:}l_n$ is found in the considered tuple space, and so the corresponding process is blocked too. The pattern $l_1\text{:}\ldots\text{:}l_n$ may contain variables and constants (e.g. $1\text{:}x$).

Consider the server process of the Server–Clients example from [8]. A server treats a stream of requests encoded as a triple ("request", $index$, $data$) in the tuple space. Starting from index 1, the server extracts such a triple from the tuple space, assigns $data$ to its local variable req, treats the request and produces the result as a triple ("response", $index$, $data$) in the tuple space. The index is then incremented to treat the next

```
            server()
            {
                int index = 1;
                ...
                while (1) {
                    in("request", index, ? req);
                    ...
                    out("response", index++, response);
                }
            }
```

Fig. 2.1. Server in C-Linda.

$$\langle run, runLindaIn, runLindaOut, TS:\langle\rangle,$$
$$Server:\langle\ index:1,$$
$$PC:0,$$
$$req:0,$$
$$0:in:request,$$
$$...$$
$$n:out:response,$$
$$(n+1):jmp(0)$$
$$\rangle,\ ...$$
$$\rangle$$

with $\quad request = \textbf{one}\ Server:\langle PC:a,\ a:\overline{in}:r,\ index:i,\ req:j,\ \omega_p\rangle,$
$\qquad\qquad\qquad\qquad TS:\langle(\text{``request''}:i:X),\ \omega\rangle$
$\qquad\qquad \textbf{by}\ Server:\langle PC:(a+1),\ a:in:r,\ index:i,\ req:X,\ \omega_p\rangle,$
$\qquad\qquad\qquad\quad TS:\langle\omega\rangle$

$\quad response = \textbf{one}\ Server:\langle PC:a,\ a:\overline{out}:r,\ index:i,\ req:j,\ \omega_p\rangle,$
$\qquad\qquad\qquad\qquad TS:\langle\omega\rangle$
$\qquad\qquad\quad \textbf{by}\ Server:\langle PC:(a+1),\ a:out:r,\ index:(i+1),\ req:X,\ \omega_p\rangle,$
$\qquad\qquad\qquad\qquad TS:\langle(\text{``response''}:i:X),\ \omega\rangle$

Fig. 2.2. Encoding of the C-Linda server into HOCL.

request. The C-Linda code implementing the server is shown in Figure 2.1.

Figure 2.2 shows the encoding of this program into HOCL. The sequential code of the process is similar. The in and out operations are encoded using the two one-shot rules *request* and *response*. The rule *request* extracts a tuple of the form ("request":i:X), where i is the current index and assigns the data X to the local variable req. The rule *response* stores a tuple of the form ("response":i:X) where X is the value of the local variable req and increments the current index i. In both cases, the program counter is incremented and the in and out instructions are reset to an executable form.

2.4.5 Petri nets in HOCL

A Petri net [14] consists in places and transitions. A place may contain any number of tokens. A transition takes some tokens from its input places and produces tokens in its output places.

The notions of places and transitions are very close to the chemical notions of solutions and reaction rules. We represent a place as a solution of tokens $\langle \mathrm{Tok}, \mathrm{Tok}, \ldots \rangle$ and transitions as reaction rules rewriting atomically input and output places. Places and transitions are named P_i and t_j, respectively. For example, a transition t_1 taking two tokens from P_1 and producing one token into P_2 is represented by the rule

$$t_1 = \mathbf{replace}\ P_1{:}\langle \mathrm{Tok}, \mathrm{Tok}, \omega_1 \rangle,\ P_2{:}\langle \omega_2 \rangle$$
$$\mathbf{by}\ P_1{:}\langle \omega_1 \rangle,\ P_2{:}\langle \mathrm{Tok}, \omega_2 \rangle$$

The main issue is that two transitions consuming tokens in the same place (that has enough tokens) cannot be fired simultaneously since a sub-solution can only take part in one reaction at a time.

An alternative encoding, that allows two transitions with common input places to be fired concurrently is to represent a token in place P_i as the constant P_i. All tokens are placed in the top-level solution and the previous transition t_1 would be expressed as:

$$t_1 = \mathbf{replace}\ P_1, P_1\ \mathbf{by}\ P_2$$

The drawback of this encoding is to prevent the expression of inhibitor arcs. An inhibitor arc from place P to t enables the transition t to fire only if no tokens are in the place P. Testing the absence of elements with the second encoding is a global operation which cannot be expressed as a single atomic rule. With the first encoding, inhibitor arcs can be encoded easily by testing whether a sub-solution is empty. For example:

$$t_2 = \mathbf{replace}\ P_1{:}\langle \mathrm{Tok}, \omega_1 \rangle,\ P_2{:}\langle \rangle,\ P_3{:}\langle \omega_3 \rangle$$
$$\mathbf{by}\ P_1{:}\langle \omega_1 \rangle,\ P_2{:}\langle \rangle,\ P_3{:}\langle \mathrm{Tok}, \omega_3 \rangle$$

The Petri net shown in Figure 2.3 (taken from [14]) represents a readers–writers synchronization, where the k tokens in place P_1 represent k processes which may read and write in a shared memory represented by place P_3. Up to k process may be reading concurrently, but when one process is writing, no other process can be reading or writing.

The encoding of that Petri net in HOCL is the solution given in Figure 2.4. Tokens are represented by constants, and the four transitions are represented by four n-shot rules. For instance, the rule t2 takes and removes one token P1 and k tokens P3, and generates one token P4.

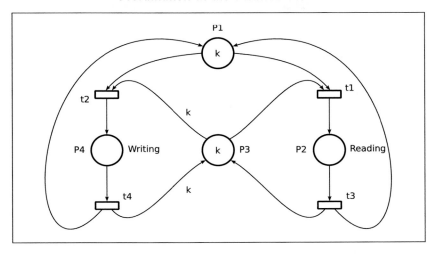

Fig. 2.3. Petri net of a readers–writers synchronization.

$$
\begin{aligned}
&\textbf{let } t1 = \textbf{replace } P1, P3 \textbf{ by } P2 \textbf{ in} \\
&\textbf{let } t2 = \textbf{replace } P1, \underbrace{P3, \ldots, \ P3}_{k} \textbf{ by } P4 \textbf{ in} \\[2pt]
&\textbf{let } t3 = \textbf{replace } P2 \textbf{ by } P1, P3 \textbf{ in} \\
&\textbf{let } t4 = \textbf{replace } P4 \textbf{ by } P1, \underbrace{P3, \ldots, \ P3}_{k} \textbf{ in} \\[2pt]
&\langle t1, \ t2, \ t3, \ t4, \ P1, \ \underbrace{P3, \ldots, \ P3}_{k} \rangle
\end{aligned}
$$

Fig. 2.4. Encoding of the Petri net in HOCL.

2.5 Kahn Process Networks in a chemical setting

The Kahn Process Network (KPN) model of computation [12] assumes a network of concurrent autonomous and deterministic processes that communicate over unbounded FIFO channels. Communication is asynchronous and point to point; it is based on a blocking read primitive and a non-blocking send primitive. Each process in the network is specified as a sequential program that executes concurrently with other processes. A KPN is deterministic, meaning that the result of the computation is independent of its schedule.

2.5.1 A simple example

Gilles Kahn gave in [12] an example made out of the three following sequential processes:

```
Process f(integer in U,V; integer out W) ;
  Begin integer I ; logical B ;
    B := true ;
    Repeat Begin
      I := if B then wait(U) else wait(V) ;
      print (I) ;
      send I on W ;
      B := not B ;
    End ;
  End ;

Process g(integer in U ; integer out V, W ) ;
  Begin integer I ; logical B ;
    B := true ;
    Repeat Begin
      I := wait(U) ;
      if B then send I on V else send I on W ;
      B := not B ;
    End ;
  End ;

Process h(integer in U ; integer out V; integer INIT ) ;
  Begin integer I ;
    Repeat Begin
      I := wait(U) ;
      send I on V ;
    End ;
  End ;
```

A process writes the value of a local variable X on a channel C using the command send X on C. It reads the channel C and stores the value in the local variable X using the command X := wait(C).

The network is built using one instance of each process f and g and two instances of process h (with its third parameter set to 0 and 1) and connecting them using the FIFO channels X, Y, Z, T1 and T2. Using par for the parallel composition, the network is specified as

```
f(Y,Z,X) par g(X,T1,T2) par h(T1,Y,0) par h(T2,Z,1) ;
```

A graphical representation of the complete network is given by Figure 2.5 where nodes represent processes and arcs communication channels between processes.

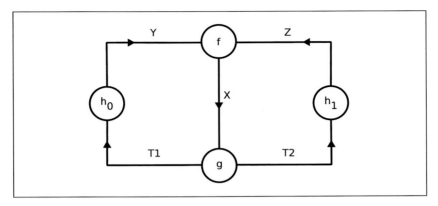

Fig. 2.5. Graphical representation of the KPN example.

2.5.2 Chemical queues

In KPNs, communication between processes uses queues to implement asynchronous communication. In HOCL, a queue can be represented by a solution of pairs *rank:value*. That solution includes also two counters CW (resp. CR) storing the rank to write (resp. to read) a value. Using the operation **send**, a producer adds a value at the rank CW and increments the counter CW. Using the operation **wait**, a consumer takes the value at rank CR and increments the counter CR. The counters CW and CR are always present in the solution representing the queue. Initially, the queue is empty and both counters are equal.

The **send X on C** operation is represented in HOCL by the instruction a:send:C:X and **X := wait(C)** by a:wait:C:X. The corresponding rules are:

$$\text{runSend} = \textbf{replace } p{:}\langle \text{PC}{:}a,\ a{:}\text{send}{:}q{:}u,\ u{:}k,\ \omega\rangle,$$
$$q{:}\langle \text{CW}{:}cw,\ \omega_Q\rangle$$
$$\textbf{by } p{:}\langle \text{PC}{:}(a+1),\ a{:}\text{send}{:}q{:}u,\ u{:}k,\ \omega\rangle,$$
$$q{:}\langle \text{CW}{:}(cw+1),\ cw{:}k,\ \omega_Q\rangle$$

$$\text{runWait} = \textbf{replace } p{:}\langle \text{PC}{:}a,\ a{:}\text{wait}{:}q{:}u,\ u{:}k,\ \omega\rangle,$$
$$q{:}\langle \text{CR}{:}cr,\ cr{:}l,\ \omega_Q\rangle$$
$$\textbf{by } p{:}\langle \text{PC}{:}(a+1),\ a{:}\text{wait}{:}q{:}u,\ u{:}l,\ \omega\rangle,$$
$$q{:}\langle \text{CR}{:}(cr+1),\ \omega_Q\rangle$$

The instructions send and wait can be seen as a rendezvous between a process p and a queue q. That implementation supports unbounded queues but does not allow a producer and a consumer to access the same queue at the same time. We present other possible encoding at the end of the section.

2.5.3 Chemical KPNs

Typically, a KPN is represented by several sequential processes and queues in the main solution. The solution contains also the three reaction rules run, runSend and runWait which can be performed at the same time (as long as they do not involve the same queues or processes). Chemical reactions make the network evolve according a unspecified, non-deterministic and parallel schedule. The only synchronization constraints are enforced by queues. Of course, even if there is much potential interleaving, the functional semantics of chemical KPNs is deterministic.

The example of Section 2.5.1 can be written in HOCL using the previous encoding for sequential commands (see Section 2.4.1) and queues as follows:

$$
\begin{array}{lll}
processF(u,v,w) \equiv & processG(u,v,w) \equiv & processH(u,v,init) \equiv \\
\quad \langle \text{PC:0,} & \quad \langle \text{PC:0,} & \quad \langle \text{PC:0,} \\
\quad \text{I:0, B:true,} & \quad \text{I:0, B:true,} & \quad \text{I:0,} \\
\quad 0{:}\langle \text{ncondJmp}(\text{B},3)\rangle, & \quad 0{:}\text{wait}{:}u{:}\text{I,} & \quad 0{:}\text{send}{:}v{:}init, \\
\quad 1{:}\text{wait}{:}u{:}\text{I,} & \quad 1{:}\langle \text{ncondJmp}(\text{B},4)\rangle, & \quad 1{:}\text{wait}{:}u{:}\text{I,} \\
\quad 2{:}\langle \text{jmp}(4)\rangle, & \quad 2{:}\text{send}{:}v{:}\text{I,} & \quad 2{:}\text{send}{:}v{:}\text{I,} \\
\quad 3{:}\text{wait}{:}v{:}\text{I,} & \quad 3{:}\langle \text{jmp}(5)\rangle, & \quad 3{:}\langle \text{jmp}(1)\rangle\rangle \\
\quad 4{:}\langle \text{print}, \text{I}\rangle, & \quad 4{:}\text{send}{:}w{:}\text{I,} & \\
\quad 5{:}\text{send}{:}w{:}\text{I,} & \quad 5{:}\langle \text{neg}(\text{B})\rangle, & \\
\quad 6{:}\langle \text{neg}(\text{B})\rangle, & \quad 6{:}\langle \text{jmp}(0)\rangle\rangle & \\
\quad 7{:}\langle \text{jmp}(0)\rangle\rangle & &
\end{array}
$$

The processes have local variables (I and B, or just I) and their program counter set to 0. The network of Figure 2.5 is represented by the following solution:

$$
\begin{array}{l}
\langle processF(\text{Y},\text{Z},\text{X}),\ processG(\text{X},\text{T1},\text{T2}), \\
\quad processH(\text{T1},\text{Y},0),\ processH(\text{T2},\text{Z},1), \\
\quad \text{Y}{:}\langle \text{CW:0, CR:0}\rangle,\ \text{Z}{:}\langle \text{CW:0, CR:0}\rangle,\ \text{X}{:}\langle \text{CW:0, CR:0}\rangle, \\
\quad \text{T1}{:}\langle \text{CW:0, CR:0}\rangle,\ \text{T2}{:}\langle \text{CW:0, CR:0}\rangle, \\
\quad \text{run, runWait, runSend}\rangle
\end{array}
$$

The solution is made of four instances of processes, five queues (initially empty), and the reaction rules implementing sequential execution (run) and communication (runWait, runSend). Our implementation remains close to the original example, the key difference being that sequential execution and communications are made explicit by reaction rules.

2.5.4 Other implementations of queues

We conclude our study of KPNs by presenting some other possible implementations of queues in the same chemical framework.

Bounded queues A bounded queue is a solution $q{:}n{:}\langle\ldots\rangle$ tagged by its name q and maximum size n. If a queue is bounded, the corresponding counters are incremented modulo its maximum size n. The rule runSendB is now a blocking primitive since it may only react when the queue is not full:

$$
\begin{aligned}
\text{runSendB} = \ &\textbf{replace } p{:}\langle\text{PC}{:}a,\ a{:}\text{send}{:}q{:}u,\ u{:}k,\ \omega\rangle, \\
&\qquad\quad q{:}n{:}\langle\text{CW}{:}cw,\ \text{CR}{:}cr,\ \omega_Q\rangle \\
&\textbf{by } p{:}\langle\text{PC}{:}(a+1),\ a{:}\text{send}{:}q{:}u,\ u{:}k,\ \omega\rangle, \\
&\qquad\quad q{:}n{:}\langle\text{CW}{:}(cw+1) \bmod n,\ \text{CR}{:}cr,\ cw{:}k,\ \omega_Q\rangle \\
&\textbf{if } (cw+1) \bmod n \neq cr
\end{aligned}
$$

$$
\begin{aligned}
\text{runWaitB} = \ &\textbf{replace } p{:}\langle\text{PC}{:}a,\ a{:}\text{wait}{:}q{:}u,\ u{:}k,\ \omega\rangle, \\
&\qquad\quad q{:}n{:}\langle\text{CR}{:}cr,\ cr{:}l,\ \omega_Q\rangle \\
&\textbf{by } p{:}\langle\text{PC}{:}(a+1),\ a{:}\text{wait}{:}q{:}u,\ u{:}l,\ \omega\rangle, \\
&\qquad\quad q{:}n{:}\langle\text{CR}{:}(cr+1) \bmod n,\ \omega_Q\rangle
\end{aligned}
$$

The queue is full when the next free rank $(\text{CW}+1)$ is equal modulo n to CR. In this case, the send operation blocks.

Non-exclusive queues When a queue is represented by a sub-solution, it cannot react simultaneously with several processes, especially between one producer and one consumer. In this case, using independent atoms to represent a queue solves this problem and the representations of all queues are mixed together. The two counters of a queue are tagged by the name of the queue ($\text{CW}{:}q{:}cw$, $\text{CR}{:}q{:}cr$). The values are also tagged and are represented as triples $q{:}r{:}v$ (name of queue, rank, value). The reaction rules implementing writing and reading become:

$$\text{runSendNEx} = \textbf{replace } p{:}\langle\text{PC}{:}a, \ a{:}\text{send}{:}q{:}u, \ u{:}k, \ \omega\rangle,$$
$$\text{CW}{:}q{:}cw$$
$$\textbf{by } p{:}\langle\text{PC}{:}(a+1), \ a{:}\text{send}{:}q{:}u, \ u{:}k, \ \omega\rangle,$$
$$\text{CW}{:}q{:}(cw+1), \ q{:}cw{:}k$$

$$\text{runWaitNEx} = \textbf{replace } p{:}\langle\text{PC}{:}a, \ a{:}\text{wait}{:}q{:}u, \ u{:}k, \ \omega\rangle,$$
$$\text{CR}{:}q{:}cr, \ q{:}cr{:}l$$
$$\textbf{by } p{:}\langle\text{PC}{:}(a+1), \ a{:}\text{wait}{:}q{:}u, \ u{:}l, \ \omega\rangle,$$
$$\text{CR}{:}q{:}(cr+1)$$

These operations are no longer rendezvous with the queue but instead with the counter CW for runSendNEx and the counter CR and an individual value for runWaitNEx. The same queue can be written and read at the same time as long as it has at least one value.

2.6 Conclusion

Originally, the Gamma formalism was invented as a basic paradigm for parallel programming [6]. It was proposed to capture the intuition of a computation as the global evolution of a collection of atomic values evolving freely. Gamma appears as a very high level language which allows programmers to describe programs in a very abstract way, with minimal constraints and no artificial sequentiality. In fact, from experience, it is often much harder to write a sequential program in Gamma than a parallel one. Later, it became clear that a necessary extension to this simple formalism was to allow elements of a multiset to be Gamma programs themselves, thus introducing higher order. This led to the HOCL language used in this paper.

The idea behind the present paper was to show how traditional coordination mechanisms can be readily described in a chemical setting. Basically, the chemical paradigm (as introduced in HOCL) offers four basic properties: mutual exclusion, atomic capture, parallelization and serialization. We have exploited these properties in order to give a chemical expression of well known coordination schemes. After presenting how to encode sequential processes as chemical solutions, we have expressed the CSP rendezvous, shared variables, Linda's primitives, Petri nets and Kahn Process Networks in HOCL. All these examples put forward the simplicity and expressivity of the chemical paradigm. A natural research direction would be to complete and use these descriptions in the same chemical framework to compare and classify the different coordination schemes.

The chemical paradigm has been used in several other areas. For example, an operating system kernel [15] has been specified in Gamma and proved correct in a framework inspired by the Unity logic [9]. The system is represented as a collection of quadruples (P_i, S_i, M_i, C_i) where S_i, M_i, and C_i represent, respectively, the state, the mailbox and the channel associated with process P_i. The P_i's are functions called by the system itself. The system includes rules such as

$$\textbf{replace}(P_i, S_i, M_i, C_i) \textbf{ by}(P_i', S_i', M_i', C_i') \textbf{ if } Ready(P_i, S_i)$$

An important aspect of this work is the derivation of a file system (written in Gamma) by successive refinements from a temporal logic specification.

More recently, we have used HOCL to specify autonomic systems [5]. Such self-organizing systems behave autonomously in order to maintain a predetermined quality of service which may be violated in certain circumstances. Very often, such violations may be dealt with by applying local corrections. These corrections are easily expressed as independent HOCL reaction rules. Comparisons with models related to HOCL and the underlying γ-calculus may be found in [4]. We do not come back on these comparisons here.

As a final comment, let us point out that, unlike Gamma, HOCL allows reaction rules (programs) to be elements of multisets, to be composed by taking (resp. returning) reactions as parameters (resp. result) and to be recursive (as expressed by the **replace** rule). In that sense, it complies with the principle stated in the conclusion of Gilles's paper [12]:

"A *good* concept is one that is closed under arbitrary composition and under recursion."

Acknowledgements

Thanks are due to the anonymous reviewers for their comments and suggestions.

Bibliography

[1]   J.-P. Banâtre, P. Fradet, J.-L. Giavitto and O. Michel (eds). *Unconventional Programming Paradigms (UPP'04)*, volume 3566 of Lecture Notes in Computer Science, Revised Selected and Invited Papers of the International Workshop, 2005. Springer-Verlag.

[2]   J.-P. Banâtre, P. Fradet and D. Le Métayer. Gamma and the chemical reaction model: Fifteen years after. In *Multiset Processing*, volume 2235 of Lecture Notes in Computer Science, pp. 17–44. Springer-Verlag, 2001.

[3]   J.-P. Banâtre, P. Fradet and Y. Radenac. Principles of chemical programming. In S. Abdennadher and C. Ringeissen (eds), *Proceedings of the 5th International Workshop on Rule-Based Programming (RULE 2004)*, volume 124 of *ENTCS*, pp. 133–147. Elsevier, June 2005.

[4]   J.-P. Banâtre, P. Fradet and Y. Radenac. Generalised multisets for chemical programming. *Mathematical Structures in Computer Science*, 16(4):557–580, 2006.

[5]   J.-P. Banâtre, P. Fradet and Y. Radenac. Programming self-organizing systems with the higher-order chemical language. *International Journal of Unconventional Computing*, 2007.

[6]   J.-P. Banâtre and D. Le Métayer. Programming by multiset transformation. *Communications of the ACM (CACM)*, 36(1):98–111, 1993.

[7]   G. Berry and G. Boudol. The chemical abstract machine. *Theoretical Computer Science*, 96:217–248, 1992.

[8]   N. Carriero and D. Gelernter. Linda in Context. *Communications of the ACM*, 32(4):444–458, 1989.

[9]   K. Mani Chandy and J. Misra. *Parallel Program Design : A Foundation*. Addison-Wesley, 1988.

[10]   C. Fournet and G. Gonthier. The reflexive CHAM and the join-calculus. In *Proceedings of the 23rd ACM Symposium on Principles of Programming Languages*, pp. 372–385. ACM Press, 1996.

[11]   C. A. R. Hoare. Communicating sequential processes. *Communications of the ACM*, 21(8):666–677, 1978.

[12]   G. Kahn. The semantics of a simple language for parallel programming. *Information Processing*, 74:471–475, 1974.

[13]   R. Milner. *A Calculus of Communicating Systems*, volume 92 of Lecture Notes in Computer Science. Springer-Verlag, 1980.

[14]   T. Murata. Petri nets: Properties, analysis and applications. *Proceedings of the IEEE*, 77(4):541–580, 1989.

[15]   H. R. Barradas. *Une approche à la dérivation formelle de systèmes en Gamma*. PhD thesis, Université de Rennes 1, France, 1993.

3

Sequential algorithms as bistable maps

Pierre-Louis Curien

CNRS – Université Paris 7

En guise de prologue

Gilles Kahn, pour moi, ce fut d'abord un article, en français s'il vous plait, texte qui fut le point de départ de ma recherche:

G. Kahn et G. Plotkin, Domaines concrets, TR IRIA-Laboria 336 (1978), paru en version anglaise en 1993 – signe de son influence dans le temps – dans le volume d'hommage à Corrado Böhm [14].

On ne pouvait imaginer un meilleur appât pour le jeune homme que j'étais, arrivé à l'informatique par le fruit d'une hésitation entre mathématiques (intimidantes) et langues (les vraies). Un autre collègue trop tôt disparu, Maurice Gross, m'avait aidé à choisir une tierce voie et m'avait guidé vers le DEA d'Informatique Théorique de Paris 7. Les cours de Luc Boasson et de Dominique Perrin m'avaient déjà bien ferré, mais la rencontre des domaines concrets m'a définitivement "attrapé", et parce qu'il s'agissait de structures ressemblant aux treillis – rencontrés assez tôt dans ma scolarité grâce aux Leçons d'Algèbre Moderne de Paul Dubreil et Marie-Louise Dubreil Jacotin que m'avait conseillées mon professeur de mathématiques –, et parce que Gérard Berry qui m'avait mis ce travail entre les mains avait une riche idée pour bâtir sur cette pierre.

L'idée directrice de cet article était de donner une définiton générale de structure de données, comprenant les listes, les arbres, les enregistrements, les enregistrements avec variantes, etc..., et, comme l'on fait dans toute bonne mathématique, une bonne notion de morphisme entre ces structures: Cette définition était donnée sous deux facettes équivalentes et reliées par un *théorème de représentation*: l'une concrète, en termes de cellules (nœuds d'arbres, champs d'enrigistrements, ...) et de valeurs, l'autre abstraite, en termes d'ordres partiels. Ce théorème,

From Semantics to Computer Science Essays in Honour of Gilles Kahn, eds Yves Bertot, Gérard Huet, Jean-Jacques Lévy and Gordon Plotkin. Published by Cambridge University Press. © Cambridge University Press 2009.

le premier du genre, a servi de modèle à des travaux ultérieurs (ceux de Winskel sur les structures d'événements en particulier).

S'agissant des morphismes, la contribution n'était pas moins importante. Après celles de Vuillemin et de Milner qui ne s'apppliquaient bien qu'au premier ordre, la définition de fonction séquentielle de Kahn–Ploktin était "la bonne". Cette notion, couplée au théorème de séquentialité de Berry obtenu à la même époque, ouvrait la voie à la construction d'un modèle séquentiel du λ-calcul, et c'est ici qu'intervint l'idée de Berry: passer des fonctions (séquentielles) à une notion plus concrète de morphisme.

Les algorithmes séquentiels [3], nés de cette intuition initiale, et que nous revisitons ici, sont, je l'espère, restés fidèles à l'esprit des domaines concrets, qui se voulaient formaliser des structures données *observables*. Dans un langage comme CAML, les types fonctionnels ne sont pas observables, mais dans le langage CDS (concrete data structure) que Berry a proposé et qui a été développé sur les fondements théoriques établis dans ma thèse, ils le sont [4]. Last but not least, la première sémantique opérationnelle du langage (décrite dans ma thèse d'Etat [9]) bien que séquentielle, s'inspire beaucoup du modèle des coroutines, présenté dans autre article fondateur de Gilles Kahn [13].

Sur un plan plus pratique, c'est sur la table traçante du (mythique) bâtiment 8 de l'INRIA Rocquencourt que j'ai pu sortir les beaux transparents (je ne crois pas en avoir réalisé, sans effort particulier, de plus esthétiques depuis) de ma soutenance de Thèse d'Etat, écrits en FLIP.

Elégance, profondeur, et sens pratique, cela ne résume pas Gilles Kahn, mais c'est ce dont je puis témoigner ici. De sa voix aussi, joviale et impérieuse, voire impériale, qui m'a sauvé la mise lors d'une présentation de mes travaux dans un colloque franco-américain à Fontainebleau. Je m'apprêtais à écrire au feutre, non sur le transparent, mais sur la table du projecteur...

Abstract

We describe the Cartwright–Curien–Felleisen model of observably sequential algorithms as a full subcategory of Laird's bistable biorders, thereby reconciling two views of functions: functions-as-algorithms (or programs), and functions-as-relations. We then characterize affine sequential algorithms as affine bistable functions in the full subcategory of locally boolean orders.

3.1 Introduction

This paper reconciles two views of functions: functions-as-algorithms (or programs), and functions-as-relations. Our functions-as-algorithms are the observably sequential algorithms on sequential data structures of Cartwright, Curien and Felleisen [5–7], and our functions-as-relations are Laird's bistable and pointwise monotonic functions on bistable biorders [15]. We exhibit a full embedding from the former to the latter.

Since the moment when the first version of these notes was circulated privately (2002), Laird has further improved the understanding of the connection by defining a full sub-category of bistable biorders, the category of locally boolean domains, whose intensional behaviour may be "synthesized" through decomposition theorems. A consequence of these theorems is that every locally boolean domain is isomorphic to a sequential data structure. Hence the results presented here actually yield an equivalence of categories (and another one between the respective subcategories of affine morphisms).

In order to make the paper relatively self-contained, we provide the necessary definitions in Sections 3.2 and 3.3. The main full embedding result is proved in Section 3.4, and the affine case is addressed in Section 3.5.

3.2 Sequential data structures

We define sequential data structures, which are concrete descriptions of partial orders whose elements are called strategies (there is indeed a game semantical reading of these structures, see e.g. [7]).

Definition 3.1 *A sequential data structure (sds) [1] is a triple* $\mathbf{S} = (C, V, P)$, *where*

- C *is a set of* cells,
- V *is a set of* values (C *and* V *disjoint*),
- P *is a prefix-closed set of non-empty alternating sequences* $c_1 v_1 c_2 \ldots$ (*with the* c_i's *in* C *and the* v_i's *in* V), *which are called* positions.

We denote by Q (resp. R) the subset of sequences of odd (resp. even) length of P, which are called *queries* (resp. *responses*).

One moreover assumes two special values $\perp$ and $\top$, not in V (nor in C) (in earlier work [6], $\top$ was called error, and in ludics [12] it is called demon). We let w range over $V \cup \{\perp, \top\}$.

Here are a few examples of sds's (described by their forest of positions):

$$bool \qquad\qquad bool \times bool$$

$$?\left\{\begin{array}{l} tt \\ ff \end{array}\right. \qquad\qquad \left\{\begin{array}{l} ?_1\left\{\begin{array}{l} tt \\ ff \end{array}\right. \\ ?_2\left\{\begin{array}{l} tt \\ ff \end{array}\right. \end{array}\right.$$

Thus, *bool* has one cell ? and two values *tt* and *ff*, while *bool* $\times$ *bool* is made of two copies of *bool*, tagged by 1 and 2, respectively.

Our last example is the sds of terms over a signature, say, $\Sigma = \{f^2, g^1, a^0\}$:

$$\epsilon\left\{\begin{array}{l} f\left\{\begin{array}{l} 1\left\{\begin{array}{l} f\left\{\begin{array}{l} 11\cdots \\ 12\left\{\begin{array}{l} f\cdots \\ g\{~121\cdots \\ a \end{array}\right. \end{array}\right. \\ g\{~11\cdots \\ a \end{array}\right. \\ 2\cdots \end{array}\right. \\ g\{~1\cdots \\ a \end{array}\right.$$

Here, the cells are words over the alphabet $\{1, 2\}$ (occurrences!) and the values are the function symbols.

Definition 3.2 *An* observable strategy *(or* strategy *for short) is a set* $x \subseteq R \cup \{q\top \mid q \in Q\} \cup \{q\bot \mid q \in Q\}$ *which satisfies the following properties:*

- *x is closed under (even length) prefixes,*
- *whenever* $qw_1, qw_2 \in x$, *then* $w_1 = w_2$,
- *whenever* $r \in x$, *then for all c such that* $rc \in Q$, *there exists w such that* $rcw \in x$.

The second condition is the crucial one: it tells us that queries are answered uniquely in a strategy. The other conditions are there for technical convenience.

A typical strategy, represented as a forest, i.e. as a set of branches, looks like this:

$$
\left\{
\begin{array}{l}
\vdots \\
c_0\ v_0 \left\{
\begin{array}{l}
c_1\ v_1 \left\{
\begin{array}{l}
c_3\ \bot \\
\vdots \\
c_4\ \top \\
\vdots \\
c_5\ \{ \\
\end{array}
\right. \\
c_2\ v_2 \left\{ \ \vdots \right. \\
\end{array}
\right. \\
\vdots
\end{array}
\right.
$$

Here are some concrete strategies (below each strategy, we give the corresponding boolean, pair of booleans, or term):

bool	$?\bot$	$?tt$	$?\!f\!f$	$?\top$
	$\bot$	tt	$f\!f$	$\top$

$$
bool \times bool \qquad
\left\{
\begin{array}{l}
?_1\bot \\
?_2\bot
\end{array}
\right.
\quad
\left\{
\begin{array}{l}
?_1\bot \\
?_2 tt
\end{array}
\right.
\quad
\left\{
\begin{array}{l}
?_1 f\!f \\
?_2\bot
\end{array}
\right.
\quad \cdots
$$

$$
(\bot, \bot) \qquad (\bot, tt) \qquad (f\!f, \bot) \qquad \cdots
$$

$$
\epsilon\ f \left\{
\begin{array}{l}
1\ f \left\{
\begin{array}{l}
11\ a \\
12\ g\ \{\ 121\ a
\end{array}
\right. \\
2\ a
\end{array}
\right.
$$

$$
f(f(a, g(a)), a)
$$

The above definition of strategy does not do justice to the arborescent structure of strategies, as in the examples just given. We now give a syntax of strategies-as-terms.

$$
\frac{rc \in Q}{c\bot : \mathrm{strat}(rc)} \qquad\qquad \frac{rc \in Q}{c\top : \mathrm{strat}(rc)}
$$

$$\frac{rc_0v_0 \in R \qquad x_c\text{:strat}(rc_0v_0c) \quad (rc_0v_0c \in Q)}{c_0v_0\{x_c \mid rc_0v_0c \in Q\}\text{:strat}(rc_0)}$$

$$\frac{x_c\text{:strat}(c) \quad (c \in Q)}{\{x_c \mid c \in Q\}\text{:strat}}$$

A strategy is a set $x = \{x_c \mid c \in Q\}$: strat. The strategy-as-set-of-responses associated to a strategy-as-term is defined as $\{r \mid r \in x\}$, where $r \in x$ is defined by the following rules:

$$\frac{}{c\bot \in c\bot} \qquad \frac{}{c\top \in c\top}$$

$$\frac{r_1 \in x_{c_1}}{c_0v_0r_1 \in c_0v_0\{x_c \mid rc_0v_0c \in Q\}} \qquad \frac{}{c_0v_0 \in c_0v_0\{x_c \mid rc_0v_0c \in Q\}}$$

$$\frac{r \in x_c}{r \in \{x_c \mid c \in Q\}}$$

This defines an injection, whose image is easily seen to be the set of strategies x that do not have any infinite branch, in the sense that there is no sequence

$$c_1\, v_1\, c_2\, v_2\, \ldots\, c_n\, v_n\, \ldots$$

whose even prefixes all belong to x. We shall call such strategies *finitary*. Hence we have two alternative definitions of finitary strategies: one by extension, and a "procedural" one.

We denote the set of strategies by $D^\top(\mathbf{S})$, and we use $D(\mathbf{S})$ for the set of strategies obtained by removing the rule introducing $c\top$. We write:

- $q \in A(x)$ if $q\bot \in x$,
- $q \in F(x)$ if $qv \in x$ for some $v \in V$ or if $q\top \in x$, and
- $x <_q y$ when $q \in A(x)$ and $q \in F(y)$.

If $q_1 = r_1c_1, \ldots, q_n = r_nc_n \in A(x)$, we denote by $x[q_1 \leftarrow x_1, \ldots, q_n \leftarrow x_n]$ the strategy obtained by replacing $c_i\bot$ by x_i:strat(q_i), for all i, in x.

We shall abbreviate $q = rc \leftarrow c\perp$ as $q \leftarrow \perp$, and similarly with $\top$. We shall use the convention that writing

$$x = x[q_0 \leftarrow \perp, \ldots, q_n \leftarrow \perp]$$

means that $A(x) = \{q_0, \ldots, q_n\}$.

Definition 3.3 *We define four orders $\leq^s$ (stable), $\leq^c$ (costable), $\leq$ (bistable), and $\sqsubseteq$ (pointwise) as the congruence closures of, respectively:*

for $\leq^s$:

$$\frac{rc \in Q \quad x \in \mathrm{strat}(rc)}{c\perp \leq^s x}$$

for $\leq^c$:

$$\frac{x \in \mathrm{strat}(rc)}{x \leq^c c\top}$$

for $\leq$:

$$\frac{rc \in Q}{c\perp \leq c\top}$$

for $\sqsubseteq$:

$$\frac{rc \in Q \quad x \in \mathrm{strat}(rc)}{c\perp \sqsubseteq x} \qquad \frac{rc \in Q \quad x \in \mathrm{strat}(rc)}{x \sqsubseteq c\top}$$

By congruence closure, we mean, say for $\sqsubseteq$, the following rules:

$$\frac{rc_0v_0 \in R \qquad x_c \sqsubseteq y_c \quad (rc_0v_0c \in Q)}{c_0v_0\{x_c \mid rc_0v_0c \in Q\} \sqsubseteq c_0v_0\{y_c \mid rc_0v_0c \in Q\}}$$

$$\frac{x_c \sqsubseteq y_c \quad (c \in Q)}{\{x_c \mid c \in Q\} \sqsubseteq \{y_c \mid c \in Q\}}$$

In words, replacing a $\perp$ by a (correctly typed) tree results in a stable increase, while removing a subtree and replacing it by $\top$ results in a costable increase. The bistable order is the intersection of the stable and the costable order: an increase in this order consists only in changing $\perp$'s to $\top$'s. The bistable order turns out to play a crucial role in the axiomatization (see Section 3.3). The pointwise order is the order generated by the union of the stable and the costable orders.

Streicher has remarked that $\sqsubseteq$ and $\leq$ make an sds a bistable biorder. This is an easy check left to the reader (after reading Section 3.3). Here, we extend this to a full and faithful embedding of the category of sds's and sequential algorithms into the category of bistable and $\sqsubseteq$-monotonic maps. Therefore, we now move on to define the relevant *categories* [1, 15].

Definition 3.4 *Given sets $A, B \subseteq A$, for any word $w \in A^*$, we define $w\lceil_B$ as follows*:

$$\epsilon\lceil_B = \epsilon \qquad (wm)\lceil_B = \begin{cases} w\lceil_B & \text{if } m \in A \backslash B \\ (w\lceil_B)m & \text{if } m \in B . \end{cases}$$

Definition 3.5 *Given two sds's $\mathbf{S} = (C, V, P)$ and $\mathbf{S}' = (C', V', P')$, we define $\mathbf{S} \multimap \mathbf{S}' = (C'', V'', P'')$ as follows. The sets C'' and V'' are disjoint unions*:

$$\begin{aligned} C'' &= C' \cup V \\ V'' &= V' \cup C . \end{aligned}$$

P'' *consists of the alternating positions s starting with a c', and which are such that*:

$$s\lceil_{\mathbf{S}'} \in P', (s\lceil_{\mathbf{S}} = \epsilon \text{ or } s\lceil_{\mathbf{S}} \in P), \text{ and}$$
$$s \text{has no prefix of the form } scc'.$$

The strategies of $\mathbf{S} \multimap \mathbf{S}'$ are called observably affine sequential algorithms from $\mathbf{S}$ to $\mathbf{S}'$.

A typical affine sequential algorithm looks like this:

$$
\left\{
\begin{array}{l}
\vdots \\
c_1'\, c_1 \left\{
\begin{array}{l}
\vdots \\
v_1\, c_2 \left\{
\begin{array}{l}
\vdots \\
v_2\, v_1' \left\{
\begin{array}{l}
\vdots \\
c_2' \cdots \\
\vdots
\end{array}
\right. \\
\vdots
\end{array}
\right. \\
\vdots
\end{array}
\right. \\
\vdots
\end{array}
\right.
$$

The initial query c_1' of the output prompts a query c_1 to the input. If the answer to this query is v_1, then the strategy wants to further explore the input and asks the query $c_1 v_1 c_2$, and so on, until enough of the input is known to answer the query c_1' with v_1', and then the output may launch a new query c_2', etc...

We next move on to define observably sequential algorithms (not necessarily affine). Our model follows linear logic's decomposition $\mathbf{S} \to \mathbf{S}' = (!\mathbf{S}) \multimap \mathbf{S}'$ [11]. The decomposition for sequential algorithms on sequential data structures was discovered by Lamarche [17, 7].

Definition 3.6 (exponential – sds) *Let $\mathbf{S} = (C, V, P)$ be a sds. The following recursive clauses define a set $P_!$ of alternating words over $Q \cup R = P$:*

$$
\frac{(\mathbf{r} = \epsilon \text{ or } \mathbf{r} \in P_!) \quad q \in A(state(\mathbf{r}))}{\mathbf{r}q \in P_!}
\qquad
\frac{\mathbf{q} \in P_! \text{ and } state(\mathbf{q}r) \in D(\mathbf{S})}{\mathbf{q}r \in P_!}
$$

where state *is the following function mapping responses (or ϵ) of $P_!$ to strategies of $\mathbf{M}$:*

$$
\frac{}{state(\epsilon) = \{c\perp \mid c \text{ initial}\}}
\qquad
\frac{q = r_1 c_1 \quad r = q v_1}{state(\mathbf{r}qr) = state(\mathbf{r})[q \leftarrow c_1 v_1 \{c\perp \mid rc \in Q\}]}
$$

The sds $(Q, R, P_!)$ is called $!\mathbf{S}$.

The above definition looks technical, but it just amounts to saying that the cells and values of $!\mathbf{S}$ are the queries and the responses of $\mathbf{S}$, and that the queries and responses of $!\mathbf{S}$ are sequences obtained from some tree traversal of the strategies of $\mathbf{S}$. This is in spirit similar to the coherence space semantics of linear logic [11].

Definition 3.7 *Given two sds's $\mathbf{S}$ and $\mathbf{S}'$, the strategies of $!\mathbf{S} \multimap \mathbf{S}'$ are called* observably sequential algorithms *from $\mathbf{S}$ to $\mathbf{S}'$.*

Despite their appearance, observably sequential algorithms are (in bijection with) functions: this key insight did not wait for Laird's work, and was indeed one of the contributions of Cartwright and Felleisen [5, 6, 1] to the older work of Berry and Curien on sequential algorithms on concrete data structures [3].

Definition 3.8 *Let f be an observably sequential algorithm from $\mathbf{S}$ to $\mathbf{S}'$ and x a strategy of $\mathbf{S}$. We define $f \cdot x$ (also written $f(x)$) as the normal form of $\langle f \mid x \rangle$ for the following rewriting system, which is easily seen to be confluent (no critical pairs) and terminating on finitary strategies.*

$$
\begin{array}{llll}
\langle c'v'\{x_i'' \mid i \in I\} \mid x \rangle & \rightarrow & c'v'\{\langle x_i'' \mid x \rangle \mid i \in I\} & \\
\langle c'\bot \mid x \rangle & \rightarrow & c'\bot & \\
\langle c'\top \mid x \rangle & \rightarrow & c'\top & \\
\langle c'q\{x_r'' \mid r''c'qr \in Q''\} \mid x \rangle & \rightarrow & c'?(\langle x_{r_0}'' \mid x \rangle) \ \ (r_0 \in x) & (\text{in } \mathrm{strat}(r''c')) \\
\langle c'q \mid x \rangle & \rightarrow & c'\bot & (q\bot \in x) \ \ (\text{in } \mathrm{strat}(r''c')) \\
\langle c'q \mid x \rangle & \rightarrow & c'\top & (q\top \in x) \ \ \text{in } \mathrm{strat}(r''c')) \\
\langle r_0q\{x_r'' \mid r''r_0qr \in Q''\} \mid x \rangle & \rightarrow & \langle x_{r_1}'' \mid x \rangle & (r_1 \in x) \ \ (\text{in } \mathrm{strat}(r''r_0)) \\
?(\langle r_0q\{x_r'' \mid r''r_0qr \in Q''\} \mid x \rangle) & \rightarrow & \bot & (q\bot \in x) \ \ (\text{in } \mathrm{strat}(r''r_0)) \\
?(\langle r_0q\{x_r'' \mid r''r_0qr \in Q''\} \mid x \rangle) & \rightarrow & \top & (q\top \in x) \ \ (\text{in } \mathrm{strat}(r''r_0)) \\
?(\langle rv'\{x_i'' \mid i \in I\} \mid x \rangle) & \rightarrow & v'\{\langle x_i'' \mid x \rangle \mid i \in I\} & \\
?(\langle r\bot \mid x \rangle) & \rightarrow & \bot & \\
?(\langle r\top \mid x \rangle) & \rightarrow & \top &
\end{array}
$$

For example, if $c'\,c_1\,v_1\,\ldots\,c_n\,v_n\,v'\,c_1'\,c\,v\,v_1' \in f$ and $c_1\,v_1\,\ldots\,c_n\,v_n\,c\,v \in x$, then $c'\,v'\,c_1'\,v_1' \in f \cdot x$. (The reader should have in mind here that potentially f (resp. x) branches after $c_1, \ldots, c_n, c$ (resp. after $v_1, \ldots, v_n$), and that the choice of strategies determine alternately which branch to choose.)

Definition 3.9 *Let $\mathbf{S}$ and $\mathbf{S}'$ be two sds's. A $\leq^s$-monotonic function $f : D^\top(\mathbf{S}) \to D^\top(\mathbf{S}')$ is called* sequential *at x if for any $q' \in A(f(x))$ one of the following properties hold:*

(i) $\forall y \geq^s x \ \ q' \notin F(f(y))$.

(ii) $\exists q \in A(x) \ \ \forall y > x \ (f(x) <_{q'} f(y)) \ \Rightarrow \ x <_q y)$.

A query q satisfying condition (2) is called a *sequentiality index* of f at (x, q'). The index is called strict if (1) does not hold. If (1) holds, then any q in $A(x)$ is a (vacuous) sequentiality index.

If q is a sequentiality index at (x, q') and if moreover $q'\top \in f(x[q \leftarrow \top])$, then we say that f is *observably sequential* at x, q', with index q (note then that the index is strict and that there can be no other sequentiality index).

The function f is called *sequential (resp. observably sequential) from* **S** *to* **S**$'$ if it is sequential (resp. *observably sequential*) at all points.

With the notation introduced above and using the $\leq^s$ monotonicity, we can rephrase the definition of observably sequential function more symmetrically as follows, at $x = x[q_1 \leftarrow \bot, \ldots, q_n \leftarrow \bot]$:

$$\forall x_1, \ldots, x_{i-1}, x_{i+1}, \ldots, x_n$$
$$q'\bot \in x[q_1 \leftarrow x_1, \ldots q_{i-1} \leftarrow x_{i-1}, q_i \leftarrow \bot, q_{i+1} \leftarrow x_{i+1}, \ldots, q_n \leftarrow x_n]$$

$$\forall x_1, \ldots, x_{i-1}, x_{i+1}, \ldots, x_n$$
$$q'\top \in x[q_1 \leftarrow x_1, \ldots q_{i-1} \leftarrow x_{i-1}, q_i \leftarrow \top, q_{i+1} \leftarrow x_{i+1}, \ldots, q_n \leftarrow x_n]$$

Or, alternatively, using instead the $\sqsubseteq$-monotonicity (which is established below), we get the following quantifier-free definition:

$$q'\bot \in x[q_1 \leftarrow \top, \ldots q_{i-1} \leftarrow \top, q_i \leftarrow \bot, q_{i+1} \leftarrow \top, \ldots, q_n \leftarrow \top]$$

$$q'\top \in x[q_1 \leftarrow \bot, \ldots q_{i-1} \leftarrow \bot, q_i \leftarrow \top, q_{i+1} \leftarrow \bot, \ldots, q_n \leftarrow \bot]$$

Theorem 3.10 *Observably sequential algorithms and observably sequential functions are in one-to-one correspondence, and under the bijection, the pointwise (resp. the stable) (resp. the bistable) ordering defined above indeed becomes the pointwise ordering (resp. Berry's stable ordering [2]) (resp. Laird's bistable ordering [15]):*

$$f \sqsubseteq g \ \ \Leftrightarrow \ \ (\forall x \ f(x) \sqsubseteq g(x))$$
$$f \leq^s g \ \ \Leftrightarrow \ \ (f \sqsubseteq g \text{ and } (\forall x, y \ (x \leq^s y \Rightarrow f(x) = f(y) \wedge^s g(x))))$$
$$f \leq g \ \ \Leftrightarrow \ \ (f \sqsubseteq g \text{ and } (\forall x, y \ (x \leq y \Rightarrow f(x) = f(y) \wedge g(x)) \text{ and}$$
$$g(y) = f(y) \vee g(x)))$$

The notation $\wedge^s$ *denotes the greatest lower bound with respect to the stable ordering, while* $\wedge$ *and* $\vee$ *refer to the bistable ordering (all these bounds exist, because* $f(y), g(x) \sqsubseteq g(y)$).

Proof Except for the last equivalence, the theorem is proved in [6]. We check here only that if f, g are observably sequential, $f \leq g$, and $x \leq y$, then $g(y) = g(x) \vee f(y)$. Suppose that $g(y) > g(x) \vee f(y)$. Let q' be filled in $g(y)$ and accessible from $g(x) \vee f(y)$. It follows that q' is accessible from $g(x)$ and from $f(y)$. The only way for g to make the difference w.r.t. f on input y is to use one of its additional $\top$'s, say, $q' \top$, in the interaction with y. More precisely, one of the $\top$'s of g is responsible for the filling of q'. But the interaction of g with y is the same as with x. Hence q' must be filled in $g(x)$, contrary to our assumption. $\square$

As an illustration of what is going on, suppose that $f_1, f_2 : \mathbf{S} \to \mathbf{S}'$ are $\leq^s$-minimal observably sequential algorithms such that

$$c' \, c_1 \, (c_1 v_1) \, c_2 \, (c_2 v_2) \, c \in f_1$$
$$c' \, c_2 \, (c_2 v_2) \, c_1 \, (c_1 v_1) \, c \in f_2$$

It looks like f_1 and f_2 define the same function (and indeed they do define the same function from $D(\mathbf{S})$ to $D(\mathbf{S}')$), but on $x = \{c_1 \bot, c_2 \top\}$ we have:

$$f_1 \cdot x = \{c' \bot\}$$
$$f_2 \cdot x = \{c' \top\}$$

Here, both $\bot$ and $\top$ act very much like colours used in chemical experiments: they track the presence of a proper value in c_1 and c_2, respectively. The special values $\bot$ and $\top$ play entirely symmetric roles as long as no infinite computations take place.

If we allow general, non-finitary strategies, the abstract machine of Definition 3.8 may well diverge (i.e. not terminate). Following Scott-Ershov's tradition, a non-terminating computation receives $\bot$ as value, and then $\bot$ and $\top$ cease to be symmetrical, since $\bot$ has become overloaded: it is both a symbol for non-termination, and an explicit symbol for a special error value that could be called "stop by lack of information". The other error value $\top$ could be called "deliberate stop" (see [10, 12, 8]).

3.3 Bistable biorders

So far, so good: we have a characterization of our notion of functions-as-algorithms as functions-as-relations. But still, the definition of sequential function (originally due to Kahn and Plotkin [14]) requires a rather concrete, "algorithmic" definition of domain (here, sequential data structures). We can get rid of this too, using Laird's notion of bistability, which can be defined more abstractly. In this section, we recall Laird's definitions [15].

Definition 3.11 *A bistable biorder is a set* $(D, \leq, \sqsubseteq)$ *equipped with two partial orders, such that whenever* x, y *have a lower or an upper bound for* $\leq$ *then* $x \vee y$ *and* $x \wedge y$ *exist (for* $\leq$*), and then* $x \vee y = x \sqcup y$ *and* $x \wedge y = x \sqcap y$*, hence the two orders coincide for* $\leq$*-connected components. Moreover* $\wedge$ *and* $\vee$ *distribute over each other in each component. One writes* $x \updownarrow y$ *when* x, y *have a* $\leq$*-upper bound (or equivalently a* $\leq$*-lower bound). A bistable function is a* $\leq$*-monotonic function such that for any* $x \updownarrow y$*:*

$$f(x \wedge y) = f(x) \wedge f(y)$$
$$f(x \vee y) = f(x) \vee f(y)$$

(we refer to the two halves of this property as $\wedge$*-bistability and* $\vee$*-bistability, respectively).*

We observe (for the reader with some linear logic culture) that the preservation of $\vee$ in the above definition is not a requirement of linearity, as it is taken with respect to $\leq$, not $\leq^s$.

In [15], the following theorem is proved:

Proposition 3.12 *The category of bistable biorders and bistable and* $\sqsubseteq$*-monotonic functions is cartesian closed.*

3.4 Full embedding

In this section, we show that the category of observably sequential algorithms embeds fully in Laird's category of bistable biorders and bistable and $\sqsubseteq$-monotonic functions. This amounts to the following proposition:

Theorem 3.13 *Given two sds's* **S** *and* **S**$'$*, a function* $f \colon D^\top(\mathbf{S})$ *to* $D^\top(\mathbf{S}')$ *is observably sequential if and only if it is bistable and* $\sqsubseteq$*-monotonic.*

Proof The proof of ($f \sqsubseteq$-monotonic and bistable $\Rightarrow f$ sequential) follows the steps of (and generalizes) Laird's proof of this property at $x = \bot$ [15]. Suppose that q' is accessible from $f(x)$ (with $x = x[q_0 \leftarrow \bot, \ldots, q_n \leftarrow \bot]$), and suppose moreover that none of the q_i's is a sequentiality index. Then by $\sqsubseteq$ monotonicity we have that q' is filled in all of the $f(x[q_0 \leftarrow$

$\top, \ldots, q_{i-1} \leftarrow \top, q_i \leftarrow \bot, q_{i+1} \leftarrow \top, \ldots, q_n \leftarrow \top])$. By $\leq$-monotonicity it is also filled in $f(x[q_0 \leftarrow \top, \ldots, q_n \leftarrow \top])$, and hence it is filled with the same value in all of the $f(x[q_0 \leftarrow \top, \ldots, q_{i-1} \leftarrow \top, q_i \leftarrow \bot, q_{i+1} \leftarrow \top, \ldots, q_n \leftarrow \top])$. Now, by $\wedge$-bistability, it should also be filled in $f(x)$ since

$$x = \bigwedge_{i=1\ldots n} x[q_0 \leftarrow \top, , \ldots, q_{i-1} \leftarrow \top, q_i \leftarrow \bot, q_{i+1} \leftarrow \top, \ldots, q_n \leftarrow \top] \, .$$

We show that if f is $\sqsubseteq$-monotonic and bistable, then it is observably sequential. That is, we have to show that if f has, say, q_0 as sequentiality index at (x, q'), then $q'\top \in f(x[q_0 \leftarrow \top])$. Suppose not. Then, if y is such that $x \leq^s y$ and q' is filled in $f(y)$, we have $y \sqsubseteq y[q_0 \leftarrow \top]$ and $x[q_0 \leftarrow \top] \leq y[q_0 \leftarrow \top]$. Since by pointwise monotonicity q' is filled in $f(y[q_0 \leftarrow \top])$, there exists a sequentiality index q_1 for f at $(x[q_0 \leftarrow \top], q')$. Continuing in this way, we would exhaust all the $\bot$'s of x. So we get that q' is filled in, say, $f(x[q_0 \leftarrow \top, q_1 \leftarrow \top, \ldots, q_n \leftarrow \top])$, and hence by $\vee$-bistability in one of the $f(x[q_i \leftarrow \top])$. But it cannot be an $i > 0$ since q_0 is a sequentiality index at x, hence it is $i = 0$, which contradicts the assumption.[1]

Conversely, if f observably sequential, we first show that f is $\sqsubseteq$-monotonic. It is enough to check that if $x \leq^c y$ then $f(x) \leq^c f(y)$. To show this – actually, the natural thing to show is that more generally if $f \leq^c g$ and $x \leq^c y$ then $f(x) \leq^c f(y)$ –, we extend the definition of $\leq^c$ by congruence to all the terms involved in the rewriting system of Definition 3.8. It is straightforward to show, for each of the rules of the rewriting system, that if $t \leq^c t'$ and $t' \rightarrow t'_1$ then there exists t_1 such that $t \rightarrow t_1$. Informally, the only difference of behaviour is that $\langle\, g \mid y\,\rangle$ might terminate before $\langle\, f \mid x\,\rangle$, because of a new $\top$ in g or y. Notice that

---

[1] Here, and also in the next section, we make the simplifying assumption that the strategies are finite. We sketch here what adjustments have to be made to remove the finiteness restriction. This is rather standard domain theory: bistable biorders have to be directed complete, and bistable functions have to be Scott-continuous. We refer to [15] for the relevant definitions. With a little care, all our arguments go through, making use of the continuity assumption. For example, to prove observable sequentiality, we used the finiteness assumption when writing $x = x[q_0 \leftarrow \bot, \ldots, q_n \leftarrow \bot]$, with n finite. If instead we have

$$x = x[q_0 \leftarrow \bot, \ldots, q_n \leftarrow \bot, \ldots,] \, ,$$

then the proof of sequentiality goes through because by continuity the $\wedge$-bistability extends to preservation of greatest lower bounds of arbitrary subsets of a $\uparrow$-component. For the proof of observable sequentiality, the finiteness of n was essential. But continuity saves us again: by continuity, we can take x, y finite, and we need only care about the q_j's that are filled in y, which are finitely many.

this argument is the same as the one used in the separation theorem of ludics (and, by the way, Girard's designs also form a bistable biorder) [12, 8].

Finally, we show that if f is observably sequential then it is bistable. One proves that f is $\leq$-monotonic much in the same way as for $\sqsubseteq$-monotonicity. The argument for $\wedge$-bistability is standard. One proves actually the preservation of all $\leq^s$ compatible binary $\leq^s$ greatest lower bounds (glb). Suppose that $x, y \leq^s z$ and $f(x \wedge^s y) <^s f(x) \wedge^s f(y)$. Let q' be accessible from $f(x \wedge^s y)$ and filled in $f(x)$ and $f(y)$. Let q be a sequentiality index at $x \wedge^s y, c'$. Then by sequentiality q is filled in both x and y, and with the same value since x, y have a $\leq^s$ upper bound. But then q is also filled in $x \wedge^s y$, contrary to the assumption. This shows a fortiori $\wedge$-bistability since $x \updownarrow y$ implies a fortiori that x, y have a $\leq^s$-upper bound, and that $x \wedge y = x \wedge^s y$.

As for $\vee$-bistability, suppose that $f(x) \vee f(y) < f(x \vee y)$. Let q' be accessible from $f(x) \vee f(y)$ and filled in $f(x \vee y)$. Then q' must be already accessible from $f(x \wedge y)$, as the order $\leq$ does not add new queries. Let q be the sequentiality index for q' at $x \wedge y$. Then we have that q is filled in $x \vee y$ by sequentiality, i.e. it is filled in either x or y, say, in x. By definition of $\leq$, since q is accessible from $x \wedge y$, q must be filled with $\top$ in x. But then q' is filled with $\top$ in $f(x)$ (and a fortiori in $f(x \vee y)$), by observable sequentiality: contradiction. $\qquad\square$

Proposition 3.14 *The category of sds's and observably sequential algorithms is cartesian closed.*

Proof This is an easy corollary of Theorem 3.13, Proposition 3.12, and Theorem 3.10. Indeed, all we have to check for a full subcategory of a cartesian closed category to be itself cartesian-closed is that the (product and) function space construction of the larger category, when applied to objects of the smaller, yields an object of the smaller. Laird's function space $D^\top(\mathbf{S}) \to D^\top(\mathbf{S}')$ is the set of bistable and $\sqsubseteq$-monotonic functions, equipped with the pointwise and bistable orderings, which is isomorphic to $D^\top(\mathbf{S} \to \mathbf{S}')$. $\qquad\square$

A direct proof of Proposition 3.14 is given in [6], but it is more complicated than the proof of Proposition 3.12.

3.5 Affine decomposition

In this section, we prove that affine sequential algorithms can also be defined as observably sequential functions that are affine with respect to the stable order, and hence as affine bistable and $\sqsubseteq$-monotonic functions (provided this makes sense, see below).

Definition 3.15 *An* affine function *is a function that preserves stable upper bounds of stably compatible elements.*

(The difference with linear functions, which may be more familiar to the linear logic oriented reader, is that preservation of $\perp$ is not required.)

Proposition 3.16 *Affine sequential algorithms are in order-isomorphic correspondence with affine observably sequential functions.*

Proof Let f be a sequential algorithm which is not affine. It contains at least a query of the form $r\,c'q_1\,r_1\,q_2$, where r_1 is not a prefix of q_2. Let x be the input strategy read off along the path from the root up to q_2. Formally, $x = state(\mathbf{r})$, where $\mathbf{r}$ is the projection of $r\,c'\,q_1\,r_1$ on the input sds. Let $y = (x \setminus \{r_1\}) \cup \{q_2\top\}$. Let q' be the projection of rc' on the output sds. Then q' is filled neither in $f(x)$ nor in $f(y)$, but is filled (with $\top$) in $f(x \vee^s y)$. Conversely, suppose that f is an affine sequential algorithm, and let $q'w' \in f(x \vee^s y)$. Let s be the position of f visited along the normalization against $x \vee^s y$ towards $q'w'$ (it is obtained by travelling in f from the root starting with the initial move of q', and solving ambiguities using $x \vee^s y$ and $q'w'$ when going up after a player's move, cf. Definition 3.8). Consider the last input response r on this position of f. Then r belongs to either x or y, say x. But all other responses along the path are prefixes of r, by the constraint of affinity, hence all belong to x. Therefore $q'w' \in f(x)$ (or $q'w' \in f(y)$). $\qquad\square$

However, bistable biorders are too poor to express the stable ordering. In further work, Laird [16] has defined the full subcategory of locally boolean domains in which not only the pointwise and bistable orders can be defined, but also the stable one [16] (we refer to this paper for the definition, which takes as primitive an operation $\neg$ of involution which in terms of sds's consists in exchanging $\perp$'s with $\top$'s). In fact, Laird shows a *representation theorem*, by means of elegant abstract decompositions: every locally boolean domain is isomorphic to the set of strategies of some sds (and every such set is a locally boolean domain). Summing up, we end up with an equivalence (actually two equivalences) of categories.

Proposition 3.17 *The categories of sds's and (observably) sequential algorithms and of locally boolean domains and $\sqsubseteq$-monotonic and bistable functions are equivalent. This equivalence cuts down to an equivalence between the respective subcategories of affine morphisms (Definitions 3.5 and 3.15).*

Proof Propositions 3.13 and 3.16 have established full embeddings. The equivalence of categories follows from the fullness on objects of the functors co-restricted to locally boolean domains. □

Since both in [17, 7] and [16] the comonads leading to models of (affine, intuitionistic) linear logic are defined as adjoint to an inclusion functor from the affine subcategory, the two decompositions are the same up to isomorphism. In other words, Laird's work provides a completely traditional domain-theoretic account of Berry–Cartwright–Curien–Felleisen–Lamarche's sequential algorithms model.

Finally, we mention two properties which add to the ambient symmetry:

Proposition 3.18

(i) *Observably sequential functions are* costable, *i.e.:*

$$\forall x, y \quad (\exists z \; z \leq^c z \text{ and } z \leq^c y) \;\Rightarrow\; f(x \vee^c y) = f(x) \vee^c f(y)$$

(ii) *Affine observably sequential functions are* coaffine, *i.e.:*

$$\forall x, y \quad (\exists z \; z \leq^c z \text{ and } z \leq^c y) \;\Rightarrow\; f(x \wedge^c y) = f(x) \wedge^c f(y)$$

The proofs are not difficult and are in the same vein as the ones given above.

However, observably sequential functions fail to be cocontinuous, i.e. they fail to preserve costable glbs of costable filters (see [18], Example 3.5.8, for a counter-example): this demonstrates the operational dissymmetry between $\top$ and $\bot$, since the latter is also used to denote non-termination.

We end the section with a brief sketch of how the concrete structure of sds's can be "abstracted" to that of a locally boolean domain. More precisely, we exhibit Laird's decomposition first in concrete terms, and then more abstractly, thus suggesting some of the ideas underlying Laird's representation theorem mentioned above.

First, we observe that the compact primes (i.e. the elements x such that, for any Y, $x \leq^s \bigvee Y$ implies $x \leq^s y$ for some $y \in Y$) of $D^\top(\mathbf{S})$

are in one-to-one correspondence with the queries and the responses of **S**:

$$
r \left\{ \begin{array}{c} c_1 \perp \\ \vdots \\ c_n \perp \end{array} \right.
\qquad\qquad
r \left\{ \begin{array}{c} c_1 \perp \\ \vdots \\ c \top \\ \vdots \\ c_n \perp \end{array} \right.
$$

$$\text{response} \quad (x = x \cap \neg x) \qquad \text{query} \quad (x \neq x \cap \neg x)$$

Next, any sds **S** can be written as

$$D^\top(\mathbf{S}) \approx \prod_i D_i$$

where

$$D_i \;=\; \{x \mid x \;\leq^c\; \{c_i \top\} \cup \{c \perp \mid c \in Q \text{ and } c \neq c_i\}$$

Abstractly:

$$D^\top(\mathbf{S}) \approx \prod_{\{p \mid p \,\leq^c - \text{maximal compact prime}\}} \{x \mid x \;\leq^c\; p\}$$

Each D_i is represented by an sds $\mathbf{S}_i$ (i.e., $D_i \approx D^\top(\mathbf{S}_i)$) that has a unique initial cell c_i. This property can be captured abstractly as:

$$\top \text{ is prime (and } \neq \perp)$$

The next step in the decomposition is to write

$$D_i = D_i' \cup \{\perp, \top\} \stackrel{\text{def}}{=} (D_i')^\uparrow$$

with $D_i' = D^\top(\mathbf{S}'_i)$, where $\mathbf{S}'_i$ is obtained from $\mathbf{S}_i$ by stripping off the unique initial cell c_i.

Finally, we decompose D_i' as follows:

$$D_i' \approx \Sigma_j D_{ij}$$

where

$$D_{ij} = \{x \in D_i \mid x \text{ starts with } v_j\} = \{x \mid x \;\geq^s\; \{v_j \perp\}\}$$

or, abstractly:

$$D_i' \approx \sum_{\{m \mid m \,\leq^s - \text{minimal}\}} \{x \mid x \;\geq^s\; m\}$$

Summing up, we have:

$$D^\top(\mathbf{S}) \quad \approx \quad \textstyle\prod_i D_i \qquad \text{(product of domains indexed}$$
$$\text{over } \leq^c -\text{maximal prime elements)}$$

$$D_i \quad = \quad (D_i')^\uparrow \qquad \text{(lifting of predomain)}$$

$$D_i' \quad \approx \quad \textstyle\sum_j D_{ij} \qquad \text{(sum of domains indexed}$$
$$\text{over } \leq^s -\text{minimal elements)}$$

3.6 Conclusion

We should note that a (weaker) version of the full embedding was proved indirectly in Laird's paper [15]: he proves that the bistable model is fully abstract for the language $\Lambda_\perp^\top$ (the simply typed λ-calculus with a single base type, and two constants $\perp$ and $\top$ of base type). This calculus is essentially the same as Cartwright–Curien–Felleisen's language SPCF with respect to which the model of sequential algorithms is fully abstract [6]. Hence, by uniqueness up to isomorphism of fully abstract models, the two models are isomorphic *on the simply typed hierarchy*. Our result is more general and does not refer to (the interpretation of) types.

As for every correspondence result, there are mutual benefits in the equivalence that we have proved. The algorithmic side provides an operational explanation of the various orders. The abstract domain-theoretic side provides simpler proofs sometimes (for example, of cartesian closedness,[2] and opens the way to extend the coverage of standard domain-theoretic tools for reasoning about sequential languages. Laird's current work goes in that direction.

Bibliography

[1]   R. Amadio and P.-L. Curien, *Domains and Lambda-calculi*, Cambridge University Press (1998).
[2]   G. Berry, Stable models of typed lambda-calculi. In *Proc. ICALP 1978*, Lecture Notes in Computer Science 62 Springer-Verlag (1978).
[3]   G. Berry and P.-L. Curien, Sequential algorithms on concrete data structures, *Theoretical Computer Science* **20**:265–321 (1982).

---

[2] Note however that it is not known whether the subcategory of locally boolean domains is cartesian closed. We have used here the cartesian closedness of the larger category of bistable biorders.

[4]   G. Berry and P.-L. Curien, Theory and practice of sequential algorithms: the kernel of the applicative language CDS. In *Algebraic Methods in Semantics*, M. Nivat, J. Reynolds (eds), Cambridge University Press, pp. 35–87 (1985).

[5]   R. Cartwright and M. Felleisen, Observable sequentiality and full abstraction. In *Proc. POPL 1992* (1992).

[6]   R. Cartwright, P.-L. Curien and M. Felleisen, Fully abstract semantics for observably sequential languages, *Information and Computation* **111**(2):297–401 (1994).

[7]   P.-L. Curien, On the symmetry of sequentiality. In *Proceedings of Mathematical Foundations of Programming Semantics 1993*, Lecture Notes in Computer Science 802, Springer-Verlag, pp. 29–71 (1994).

[8]   P.-L. Curien, Introduction to Linerar logic and ludics, parts I and II, *Advances of Mathematics (China)* **34**(5):513–544 (2005) and **35**(1):1–44 (2006).

[9]   P.-L. Curien, *Combinateurs Catégoriques, Algorithmes Séquentiels et Programmation Fonctionnelle*, Thèse d'Etat, Université Paris 7 (1983); English version: *Categorical Combinators, Sequential Algorithms and Functional Programming*, Research Notes in Theoretical Computer Science, Pitman (1986); second, revised edition, Birkhaüser (1993).

[10]   P.-L. Curien, Symmetry and interactivity in programming, *Bulletin of Symbolic Logic* **9**(2):169–180 (2003).

[11]   J.-Y. Girard, Linear logic, *Theoretical Computer Sciences* **50**:1–102 (1987).

[12]   J.-Y. Girard, Locus Solum, *Mathematical Structures in Computer Science* (2001).

[13]   G. Kahn and D. MacQueen, Coroutines and networks of parallel processes. In *Proc. IFIP 1977*, B. Gilchrist (ed.), North-Holland, pp. 993–998 (1977).

[14]   G. Kahn and G. Plotkin, Concrete domains, *Theoretical Computer Science* **12**:187–277 (1993).

[15]   J. Laird, Bistability: an extensional characterization of sequentiality. In *Proc. Computer Science and Logic 2003*, Lecture Notes in Computer Science 2803, Springer-Verlag (2003).

[16]   J. Laird, Locally boolean domains, *Theoretical Computer Science* **342**:132–248 (2005).

[17]   F. Lamarche, Sequentiality, games and linear logic. In *Proc. CLICS Workshop*, Aarhus University, DAIMI-397-II (1992).

[18]   T. Loew, *Locally Boolean Domains and Universal Models for Infinitary Sequential Languages*, PhD Thesis, Technische Universität Darmstadt (2006).

[19]   T. Streicher, Laird domains, draft (2002).

4

The semantics of dataflow with firing

Edward A. Lee

University of California, Berkeley

Eleftherios Matsikoudis

University of California, Berkeley

Abstract

Dataflow models of computation have intrigued computer scientists since the 1970s. They were first introduced by Jack Dennis as a basis for parallel programming languages and architectures, and by Gilles Kahn as a model of concurrency. Interest in these models of computation has been recently rekindled by the resurrection of parallel computing, due to the emergence of multicore architectures. However, Dennis and Kahn approached dataflow very differently. Dennis' approach was based on an operational notion of atomic firings driven by certain firing rules. Kahn's approach was based on a denotational notion of processes as continuous functions on infinite streams. This paper bridges the gap between these two points of view, showing that sequences of firings define a continuous Kahn process as the least fixed point of an appropriately constructed functional. The Dennis firing rules are sets of finite prefixes satisfying certain conditions that ensure determinacy. These conditions result in firing rules that are strictly more general than the blocking reads of the Kahn–MacQueen implementation of Kahn process networks, and solve some compositionality problems in the dataflow model. This work was supported in part by the Center for Hybrid and Embedded Software Systems (CHESS) at UC Berkeley, which receives support from the National Science Foundation (NSF awards #0720882 (CSR-EHS: PRET), #0647591 (CSR-SGER), and #0720841 (CSR-CPS)), the US Army Research Office (ARO #W911NF-07-2-0019), the US Air Force Office of Scientific Research (MURI #FA9550-06-0312 and AF-TRUST #FA9550-06-1-0244), the Air Force Research Lab (AFRL), the State of California Micro Program, and the following companies: Agilent, Bosch, DGIST, National Instruments, and Toyota.

From Semantics to Computer Science Essays in Honour of Gilles Kahn, eds Yves Bertot, Gérard Huet, Jean-Jacques Lévy and Gordon Plotkin. Published by Cambridge University Press. © Cambridge University Press 2009.

4.1 Introduction

Three major variants of the dataflow model of computation have emerged in the literature: Kahn process networks [15], Dennis dataflow [10], and dataflow synchronous languages [2]. The first two are closely related, while the third is quite different. This paper deals only with the first two, which have a key difference. In Dennis dataflow, a process is implemented as an execution of atomic firings of actors. Although Dennis dataflow can be viewed as a special case of Kahn process networks [18], the notion of firing has been absent from semantic models, which are most developed for Kahn process networks and dataflow synchronous languages.

Dennis and Kahn approach dataflow very differently. Dennis' approach is based on an operational notion of atomic firings driven by the satisfaction of firing rules. Kahn's approach is based on a denotational notion of processes as continuous functions on infinite streams. Dennis' approach influenced computer architecture [1, 26], compiler design, and concurrent programming languages [14]. Kahn's approach has influenced process algebras (see for example [6]) and semantics of concurrent systems (see for example [4, 20]). It has had practical realizations in stream languages [28] and operating systems (such as Unix pipes). Recently, interest in these models of computation has been rekindled by the resurrection of parallel computing, motivated by multicore architectures [8]. Dataflow models of computation are being explored for programming parallel machines [30], distributed systems [17, 21, 24], and embedded systems [19, 13]. Considerable effort is going into improved execution policies [31, 11, 32, 18] and standardization [22, 12].

This paper bridges the gap between Dennis and Kahn, showing that the methods pioneered by Kahn extend naturally to Dennis dataflow, embracing the notion of firing. This is done by establishing the relationship between a firing function and the Kahn process implemented as a sequence of firings of that function. A consequence of this analysis is a formal characterization of firing rules and firing functions that preserve determinacy.

4.2 Review of Kahn process networks

4.2.1 Ordered sets

We begin with a brief review of ordered sets [9].

An *order relation* $\leqslant$ on a set A is a binary relation on A that is *reflexive* ($a \leqslant a'$), *transitive* (if $a \leqslant a'$ and $a' \leqslant a''$, then $a \leqslant a''$), and *antisymmetric* (if $a \leqslant a'$ and $a' \leqslant a$, then $a = a'$). Of course, we can define a corresponding *irreflexive* relation, denoted by $<$, with $a < a'$ if and only if $a \leqslant a'$ and $a \neq a'$. The structure $\langle A, \leqslant \rangle$ is an *ordered set*. If the order relation is *partial*, in the sense that there exist $a, a' \in A$ such that $a \not\leqslant a'$ and $a' \not\leqslant a$, then we will often refer to $\langle A, \leqslant \rangle$ as a *partially ordered set*, or simply a *poset*. If, on the other hand, the order relation is *total*, in the sense that for all $a, a' \in A$, $a \leqslant a'$ or $a' \leqslant a$, then we will refer to $\langle A, \leqslant \rangle$ as a *totally ordered set*, or a *chain*.

For any ordered set $\langle A, \leqslant \rangle$ and any $B \subseteq A$, an element a is an *upper bound* of B in $\langle A, \leqslant \rangle$, iff for any $b \in B$, $b \leqslant a$. a is the *least upper bound* of B in $\langle A, \leqslant \rangle$ iff it is an upper bound of B, and for any other upper bound a' of B, $a \leqslant a'$. We write $\bigvee B$ to denote the least upper bound of B. The notion of *lower bound* and that of *greatest lower bound* are defined dually. In the case of two elements a_1 and a_2, we typically write $a_1 \vee a_2$ and $a_1 \wedge a_2$, instead of $\bigvee \{a_1, a_2\}$ and $\bigwedge \{a_1, a_2\}$. These are called the *join* and *meet* of a_1 and a_2.

A set $D \subseteq A$ is *directed* in $\langle A, \leqslant \rangle$ iff it is non-empty and every finite subset of D has an upper bound in $\langle A, \leqslant \rangle$. If every directed subset of A has a least upper bound in $\langle A, \leqslant \rangle$, then $\langle A, \leqslant \rangle$ is a *directed-complete ordered set*. If $\langle A, \leqslant \rangle$ is directed-complete and has a least element, then $\langle A, \leqslant \rangle$ is a *complete partial order*, or *cpo*. If $\langle A, \leqslant \rangle$ is directed-complete, and every non-empty subset of A has a greatest lower bound in $\langle A, \leqslant \rangle$, then $\langle A, \leqslant \rangle$ is a complete semilattice.

4.2.2 Sequences

We henceforth assume a non-empty set $\mathcal{V}$ of *values*. Each value represents a token, an atomic unit of data exchanged between the autonomous computing stations. We consider the set of all finite and infinite sequences over $\mathcal{V}$.

A *finite sequence of values*, or simply a *finite sequence*, is a function from the set $\{0, \ldots, n-1\}$ for some natural number n into the set $\mathcal{V}$. Notice that in the case of $n = 0$, $\{0, \ldots, n-1\} \rightarrow \mathcal{V} = \emptyset \rightarrow \mathcal{V} = \{\emptyset\}$. The empty set is therefore a finite sequence, which we call the *empty sequence* and denote by ε. We denote the set of all finite sequences of values by $\mathcal{V}^*$. This is of course the well known Kleene closure of the set $\mathcal{V}$.

An *infinite sequence of values*, or simply an *infinite sequence*, is a function from the set of all natural numbers ω into the set $\mathcal{V}$. We denote the set of all infinite sequences of values by $\mathcal{V}^\omega$. This is just another notation for the set $\omega \to \mathcal{V}$. We denote the set of all such sequences of values, finite or infinite, by $\mathcal{S}$; that is, $\mathcal{S} = \mathcal{V}^* \cup \mathcal{V}^\omega$.

For any finite sequence s, the *length* of s is the cardinal number of $\text{dom}\, s$, which we denote by $|s|$. This is just the number of elements in s.

Informally, a sequence is just an ordered list of values. For any particular sequence s, we often list its values explicitly, writing $\langle v_0, v_1, \ldots, v_{|s|-1} \rangle$ if s is finite, and $\langle v_0, v_1, \ldots \rangle$ if s is infinite. If s is the empty sequence ε, then we simply write $\langle\ \rangle$.

A sequence s_1 is a *prefix* of a sequence s_2, and we write $s_1 \sqsubseteq s_2$, if and only if $s_1 \subseteq s_2$. We make use of the set-theoretic definition of function here, according to which the graph of a function is the function itself. We caution the reader not to misread our statement: not every subset of a sequence is a prefix. If that subset is a sequence, however, then it must be a prefix of the original sequence.

Informally, s_1 is a prefix of s_2 if and only if the first $|s_1|$ values of s_2 are the values of s_1 in the same order as in s_1; that is, for any natural number $i \in \text{dom}\, s_1$, $s_2(i) = s_1(i)$.

The prefix relation $\sqsubseteq \subset \mathcal{S} \times \mathcal{S}$ is of course an order relation, and for any sequence s, $\varepsilon \sqsubseteq s$. The ordered set $\langle \mathcal{S}, \sqsubseteq \rangle$ is actually a complete semilattice. For any subset X of $\mathcal{S}$, we write $\bigsqcap X$ to denote the greatest lower bound of X in $\langle \mathcal{S}, \sqsubseteq \rangle$, namely the greatest common prefix of the sequences in X, and $\bigsqcup X$ to denote the least upper bound of X in $\langle \mathcal{S}, \sqsubseteq \rangle$, provided of course that this exists. In the case of two sequences s_1 and s_2, we typically write $s_1 \sqcap s_2$ and $s_1 \sqcup s_2$ for the meet and join of s_1 and s_2.

If s_1 is a finite sequence and s_2 an arbitrary sequence, then we write $s_1.s_2$ to denote the *concatenation* of s_1 and s_2. It is the unique sequence s with $\text{dom}\, s = \{0, \ldots, |s_1| + |s_2| - 1\}$ if s_2 is finite, and $\text{dom}\, s = \omega$ otherwise, such that for any $i \in \text{dom}\, s$, $s(i) = s_1(i)$ if $i < |s_1|$, and $s(i) = s_2(i - |s_1|)$ otherwise.

Informally, $s_1.s_2$ is the result of appending the ordered list of values of s_2 right after the end of s_1. Note that any finite s_1 is a prefix of a sequence s iff there is a sequence s_2 such that $s_1.s_2 = s$. It should be clear that s_2 is unique.

4.2.3 Tuples of sequences

A sequence of values models the traffic of tokens over a single communication line. A typical process network will have several communication lines, and a typical process will communicate over several of those. Thus, it will be useful to group together several different sequences and manipulate them as a single object. We do this using the notion of tuple.

A tuple is just a finite enumeration of objects. Here we are interested in tuples of sequences. For any natural number n, an *n-tuple of sequences*, or simply a *tuple*, is a function from $\{0, \ldots, n-1\}$ into $\mathcal{S}$. We let $\mathcal{S}^n$ denote the set of all n-tuples of sequences. For convenience, we identify $\mathcal{S}^1$ with $\mathcal{S}$. Note that when $n = 0$, $\mathcal{S}^n = \emptyset \to \mathcal{S} = \{\emptyset\}$. The empty set is thus a tuple, which we call the *empty tuple*.

We use boldface letters to denote tuples. If $\boldsymbol{s}$ is an n-tuple, then for any $i \in \{0, \ldots, n-1\}$, we often write $\boldsymbol{s}_i$ instead of $\boldsymbol{s}(i)$. Also, we often list the sequences within a tuple explicitly, writing $\langle s_0, \ldots, s_{n-1} \rangle$.

We say that an n-tuple is *finite* if and only if for any $i \in \{0, \ldots, n-1\}$, s_i is a finite sequence. This is of course vacuously true for the empty tuple.

The prefix order on sequences induces an order on n-tuples for any fixed n. The order we have in mind is the pointwise order. We say that an n-tuple $\boldsymbol{s}_1$ is a *prefix* of an n-tuple $\boldsymbol{s}_2$, and we write $\boldsymbol{s}_1 \sqsubseteq \boldsymbol{s}_2$, if and only if for any $i \in \{0, \ldots, n-1\}$, $\boldsymbol{s}_1(i) \sqsubseteq \boldsymbol{s}_2(i)$. Notice that the n-tuple of empty sequences, denoted by $\boldsymbol{\varepsilon}_n$, is a prefix of every other n-tuple. The ordered set $\langle \mathcal{S}^n, \sqsubseteq \rangle$ is a complete semilattice, where infima and suprema are calculated pointwise, simply because $\langle \mathcal{S}, \sqsubseteq \rangle$ is a complete semilattice itself.

If $\boldsymbol{s}_1$ is a finite n-tuple and $\boldsymbol{s}_2$ an arbitrary n-tuple, then we write $\boldsymbol{s}_1.\boldsymbol{s}_2$ to denote the pointwise concatenation of $\boldsymbol{s}_1$ and $\boldsymbol{s}_2$. It is the unique n-tuple $\boldsymbol{s}$ such that for any $i \in \{0, \ldots, n-1\}$, $\boldsymbol{s}(i) = \boldsymbol{s}_1(i).\boldsymbol{s}_2(i)$.

When $n = 0$, $\mathcal{S}^n$ has only one element, the empty tuple $\emptyset$. Hence, it must be the case that $\emptyset.\emptyset = \emptyset$. This is precisely what the pointwise concatenation evaluates to. Note again that for any finite $\boldsymbol{s}_1$, $\boldsymbol{s}_1 \sqsubseteq \boldsymbol{s}$ if and only if there is some tuple $\boldsymbol{s}_2$ such that $\boldsymbol{s}_1.\boldsymbol{s}_2 = \boldsymbol{s}$, in which case, this tuple $\boldsymbol{s}_2$ is unique.

4.2.4 Kahn processes

Before we can formalize the notion of a process, we must review a technical condition that we will need to impose.

A function $F : \mathcal{S}^m \to \mathcal{S}^n$ is *monotone* if and only if for all $\boldsymbol{s}_1, \boldsymbol{s}_2 \in \mathcal{S}^m$,

$$\boldsymbol{s}_1 \sqsubseteq \boldsymbol{s}_2 \implies F(\boldsymbol{s}_1) \sqsubseteq F(\boldsymbol{s}_2).$$

Informally, feeding a computing station that realizes a monotone function with additional input can only cause it to produce additional output. This is really a notion of causality, in that "future input concerns only future output" (see [15]).

A function $F:\mathcal{S}^m \to \mathcal{S}^n$ is *Scott-continuous*, or simply *continuous*, if and only if F is monotone, and for any subset D of $\mathcal{S}^m$ that is directed in $\langle \mathcal{S}^m, \sqsubseteq \rangle$,

$$F(\bigsqcup D) = \bigsqcup \{F(\boldsymbol{s}) \mid \boldsymbol{s} \in D\}.$$

Notice here that since F is monotone, the set $\{F(\boldsymbol{s}) \mid \boldsymbol{s} \in D\}$ is itself directed in $\langle \mathcal{S}^n, \sqsubseteq \rangle$, and hence has a least upper bound therein.

In order to better understand the importance of this notion, we must take notice of the additional structure that our ordered sets have. For any natural number m, the complete semilattice $\langle \mathcal{S}^m, \sqsubseteq \rangle$ is *algebraic*: for every $\boldsymbol{s} \in \mathcal{S}^m$,

$$\boldsymbol{s} = \bigsqcup \{\boldsymbol{s}' \sqsubseteq \boldsymbol{s} \mid \boldsymbol{s}' \text{ is finite}\}.$$

The set $\{\boldsymbol{s}' \sqsubseteq \boldsymbol{s} \mid \boldsymbol{s}' \text{ is finite}\}$ is of course directed in $\langle \mathcal{S}^m, \sqsubseteq \rangle$. Hence, we can obtain every m-tuple as the least upper bound of a set of finite tuples that is directed in $\langle \mathcal{S}^m, \sqsubseteq \rangle$. The response of a continuous function to an input tuple is therefore completely defined by its responses to the finite prefixes of that tuple. This is really a computability notion, in that a computing station cannot churn out some output only after it has received an infinite amount of input.

We remark here that continuity in this context is exactly the topological notion of continuity in a particular topology, which is called the *Scott topology*. In this topology, the set of all tuples with a particular finite prefix is an open set, and the collection of all these sets is a base for the topology.

A *Kahn process*, or just a *process*, is a continuous function $F:\mathcal{S}^m \to \mathcal{S}^n$ for some m and n. If $m = 0$, then we say that F is a *source*; $\mathcal{S}^m = \mathcal{S}^0 = \{\emptyset\}$ has a single member, the empty tuple, and hence F is trivially constant. If $n = 0$, then we say that F is a *sink*. In either case, F is trivially continuous.

Not every monotone function is continuous, and thus a Kahn process. For instance, consider a function $F:\mathcal{S} \to \mathcal{S}$ such that for any sequence s,

$$F(s) = \begin{cases} \langle\ \rangle & \text{if } \boldsymbol{s} \text{ is finite;} \\ \langle v \rangle & \text{otherwise.} \end{cases}$$

Here v is some arbitrary value. It is easy to verify that F is monotone but not continuous.

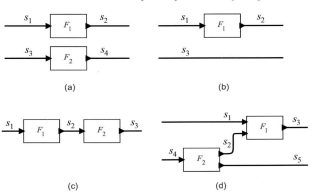

Fig. 4.1. Examples of compositions of processes.

For an example of a continuous function, consider the *unit delay* process $D_v{:}\mathcal{S} \to \mathcal{S}$, such that for any sequence s,

$$D_v(s) = \langle v \rangle . s, \tag{4.1}$$

where v is an arbitrary but fixed value. The effect of this process is to output an initial token of value v before starting to churn out the tokens arriving at its input, in the same order in which they arrive. We will have more to say about the unit delay below.

4.2.5 Compositions of Kahn processes and determinacy

A finite composition of Kahn processes is a collection $\{s_1, \ldots, s_p\}$ of sequences and a collection $\{F_1, \ldots, F_q\}$ of processes relating them, such that no sequence is the output of more than one process. Any sequence that is not the output of any of the functions is an input to the composition.

A composition is determinate if and only if given the input sequences, all other sequences are uniquely determined. Obviously, a Kahn process by itself is determinate, since it is a functional mapping from input sequences to output sequences.

Examples of finite compositions of Kahn processes are shown in Figure 4.1. In each of these examples, given the component processes, it is obvious how to construct a process that maps the input sequences (those that are not outputs of any process) to the other sequences. Each of these compositions is thus determinate. Following Broy [5], we can iteratively compose processes using patterns like those in Figure 4.1 to

Fig. 4.2. Feedback (a directed self-loop).

argue that arbitrary compositions are determinate. The most challenging part of this strategy is to handle feedback. (An alternative approach to this composition problem is given by Stark [27]).

Feedback compositions of Kahn processes may or may not be determinate. Consider for example the identity function I, such that for any sequence s, $I(s) = s$. I is trivially continuous, and thus a Kahn process. Suppose that we form a very simple composition of the identity process by feeding back the output to the input, letting $F = I$ in Figure 4.2. There are no inputs to the composition, which is therefore determinate if and only if the sequence s is uniquely determined. However, any sequence s satisfies the constraint of the composition, so it is not uniquely determined.

4.2.6 Least-fixed-point semantics

There is an alternative interpretation due to Kahn [15] that makes the example in Figure 4.2 determinate. Under this interpretation, any process composition is determinate. Moreover, this interpretation is consistent with the execution policies often used for such systems (their operational semantics), and hence it is an entirely reasonable denotational semantics for the composition. This interpretation is known as the least-fixed-point semantics, and in particular as the Kahn principle.

The Kahn principle is based on a well-known fixed-point theorem stating that a continuous function $F{:}X \to X$ on a cpo $\langle X, \leqslant \rangle$ has a least fixed point x in $\langle X, \leqslant \rangle$; that is, there is an $x \in X$ such that $F(x) = x$, and for any other $y \in X$ for which $F(y) = y$, $x \leqslant y$. Furthermore, the theorem is constructive, providing an algorithmic procedure for finding the least fixed point: the least fixed point of F is the least upper bound of all finite iterations of F starting from the least element in $\langle X, \leqslant \rangle$.

To put it into our context, suppose that $F{:}\mathcal{S}^n \to \mathcal{S}^n$ is a process, and consider the following sequence of n-tuples:

$$\boldsymbol{s}_0 = \boldsymbol{\varepsilon}_n, \ \boldsymbol{s}_1 = F(\boldsymbol{s}_0), \ \boldsymbol{s}_2 = F(\boldsymbol{s}_1), \ \dots. \tag{4.2}$$

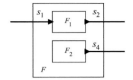

Fig. 4.3. Composition with a source of an infinite sequence.

Since F is monotone, and the tuple of empty sequences ε_n is a prefix of any other n-tuple, $s_i \sqsubseteq s_j$ if and only if $i \leq j$. Hence, $\{s_0, s_1, \ldots\}$ is a chain, and thus directed in $\langle \mathcal{S}^n, \sqsubseteq \rangle$, and since the latter is directed-complete, $\{s_0, s_1, \ldots\}$ has a least upper bound in $\langle \mathcal{S}^n, \sqsubseteq \rangle$. The fixed-point theorem states that this least upper bound is the least fixed point of F.

This theorem is quite similar to the well-known Knaster–Tarski fixed-point theorem, which applies to complete lattices rather than complete partial orders. For this reason, this approach to semantics is sometimes called Tarskian. The application of the theorem to programming language semantics was pioneered by Scott [25]. However, Kahn [15] was the first to recognize its potential in modelling and design of complex distributed systems.

Under this least-fixed-point principle, the value of s in Figure 4.2 is uniquely determined as the empty sequence ε when F is the identity process I. This is consistent with our intuition; the identity process will not produce an output token, unless there is some input token to cause it to.

Notice that (4.2) might suggest a reasonable execution policy for a network: start with every sequence empty, and begin iterating the evaluation of every process. In the limit, every sequence will converge to the least fixed point of the composite process, in accordance with the interpretation suggested by the Kahn principle.

4.2.7 Practical issues

There are serious practical problems with using (4.2) as an execution policy. If any process in the composition evaluates to an infinite tuple at some stage of the iteration, then the execution of that process will never terminate, and thus preclude the progress of the iteration. This will happen immediately in a composition like the one in Figure 4.3, where the process F_2 is a source of an infinite sequence.

In practice, we need to partially evaluate processes, carefully controlling the length of each sequence. The problem is addressed by Parks [23], who devises a general strategy to avoid accumulating unbounded numbers of unconsumed tokens, whenever it is possible to do so. All partially evaluated sequences are guaranteed to be prefixes of the sequences corresponding to the denotational semantics of the process composition (although, as pointed out in [11], there is no assurance of convergence to those sequences, which may not be desirable anyway).

4.3 Dataflow with firing

4.3.1 Dataflow actors

We begin with a simple definition and generalize later. Our first attempt will serve as a gentle introduction, and help motivate the need for the more general case.

A *dataflow actor*, or simply an *actor*, with m *inputs* and n *outputs* is a pair $\langle R, f \rangle$, where

(i) R is a set of finite m-tuples;
(ii) $f : \mathcal{S}^m \to \mathcal{S}^n$ is a (possibly partial) function defined at least on R;
(iii) $f(\boldsymbol{r})$ is finite for every $\boldsymbol{r} \in R$;
(iv) for all $\boldsymbol{r}, \boldsymbol{r}' \in R$, if $\boldsymbol{r} \neq \boldsymbol{r}'$, then $\{\boldsymbol{r}, \boldsymbol{r}'\}$ does not have an upper bound in $\langle \mathcal{S}^m, \sqsubseteq \rangle$.

We call each $\boldsymbol{r} \in R$ a *firing rule*, and f the *firing function* of the actor. The last condition is equivalent to the following statement: for any given m-tuple $\boldsymbol{s}$, there is at most one firing rule $\boldsymbol{r}$ in R such that $\boldsymbol{r} \sqsubseteq \boldsymbol{s}$. We remark here that because $\langle \mathcal{S}^m, \sqsubseteq \rangle$ is a complete semilattice, $\boldsymbol{r}$ and $\boldsymbol{r}'$ have an upper bound in $\langle \mathcal{S}^m, \sqsubseteq \rangle$ if and only they have a least upper bound in $\langle \mathcal{S}^m, \sqsubseteq \rangle$, or alternatively, if their join $\boldsymbol{r} \sqcap \boldsymbol{r}'$ is defined.

If $m = 0$, then R is a subset of the singleton set $\{\emptyset\}$, and condition (iv) is trivially satisfied. If $n = 0$, then condition (iii) is trivially satisfied.

4.3.2 Dataflow processes

Let $\langle R, f \rangle$ be a dataflow actor with m inputs and n outputs. We want to define a Kahn process $F : \mathcal{S}^m \to \mathcal{S}^n$ based on this actor, and a reasonable condition to impose is that for any m-tuple $\boldsymbol{s}$,

$$F(\boldsymbol{s}) = \begin{cases} f(\boldsymbol{r}).F(\boldsymbol{s}') & \text{if there exists } \boldsymbol{r} \in R \text{ such that } \boldsymbol{s} = \boldsymbol{r}.\boldsymbol{s}'; \\ \varepsilon_n & \text{otherwise.} \end{cases} \quad (4.3)$$

Of course, this is not a definition. It is by no means obvious that such an F exists, nor that this F is unique, or even a process. Nonetheless, it is possible to use the least-fixed-point principle to resolve these issues, and turn (4.3) into a proper definition. Before we can do this, however, we will need to review some order-theoretic facts about functions over tuples of sequences.

For fixed m and n, we write $\mathcal{S}^m \to \mathcal{S}^n$ to denote the set of all functions from $\mathcal{S}^m$ into $\mathcal{S}^n$. The prefix order on n-tuples induces a pointwise order on this set. We shall say that the function $F:\mathcal{S}^m \to \mathcal{S}^n$ is a *prefix* of the function $G:\mathcal{S}^m \to \mathcal{S}^n$, and write $F \sqsubseteq G$, if and only if $F(\boldsymbol{s}) \sqsubseteq G(\boldsymbol{s})$ for any m-tuple $\boldsymbol{s}$. Notice that the function $\boldsymbol{s} \mapsto \varepsilon_n$ mapping every m-tuple $\boldsymbol{s}$ to the n-tuple of empty sequences is a prefix of any other function in the set. The ordered set $\langle \mathcal{S}^m \to \mathcal{S}^n, \sqsubseteq \rangle$ is a complete semilattice, simply because $\langle \mathcal{S}^n, \sqsubseteq \rangle$ is a complete semilattice. For our purposes here, however, it suffices to know that $\langle \mathcal{S}^m \to \mathcal{S}^n, \sqsubseteq \rangle$ is a cpo.

Now consider the functional $\phi:(\mathcal{S}^m \to \mathcal{S}^n) \to (\mathcal{S}^m \to \mathcal{S}^n)$ associated with the actor $\langle R, f \rangle$, defined such that for any $F \in \mathcal{S}^m \to \mathcal{S}^n$ and any m-tuple $\boldsymbol{s}$,

$$\phi(F)(\boldsymbol{s}) = \begin{cases} f(\boldsymbol{r}).F(\boldsymbol{s}') & \text{if there exists } \boldsymbol{r} \in R \text{ such that } \boldsymbol{s} = \boldsymbol{r}.\boldsymbol{s}'; \\ \varepsilon_n & \text{otherwise.} \end{cases}$$

$$(4.4)$$

Theorem 4.1 ϕ *is monotone.*

Proof Let F_1 and F_2 be arbitrary functions of type $\mathcal{S}^m \to \mathcal{S}^n$, and suppose that $F_1 \sqsubseteq F_2$.

If there is a firing rule $\boldsymbol{r} \in R$ such that $\boldsymbol{r} \sqsubseteq \boldsymbol{s}$, then by condition (iv), $\boldsymbol{r}$ is unique, and hence $\phi(F_1)(\boldsymbol{s}) = f(\boldsymbol{r}).F_1(\boldsymbol{s}')$ and $\phi(F_2)(\boldsymbol{s}) = f(\boldsymbol{r}).F_2(\boldsymbol{s}')$, where $\boldsymbol{s} = \boldsymbol{r}.\boldsymbol{s}'$. However, by assumption, $F_1(\boldsymbol{s}') \sqsubseteq F_2(\boldsymbol{s}')$ for any m-tuple $\boldsymbol{s}'$, and hence $\phi(F_1)(\boldsymbol{s}) \sqsubseteq \phi(F_2)(\boldsymbol{s})$.

Otherwise, $\phi(F_1)(\boldsymbol{s}) = \varepsilon_n = \phi(F_2)(\boldsymbol{s})$.

In either case, $\phi(F_1)(\boldsymbol{s}) \sqsubseteq \phi(F_2)(\boldsymbol{s})$, and hence ϕ is monotone. $\quad\square$

Since ϕ is a monotone function over the cpo $\langle \mathcal{S}^m \to \mathcal{S}^n, \sqsubseteq \rangle$, it has a least fixed point F in $\langle \mathcal{S}^m \to \mathcal{S}^n, \sqsubseteq \rangle$ [9], which must satisfy (4.3). This is reassuring, but we can actually go a step further, and give a constructive procedure for finding that least fixed point.

Theorem 4.2 ϕ *is continuous.*

Proof Let $D \subseteq \mathcal{S}^m \to \mathcal{S}^n$ be directed in $\langle \mathcal{S}^m \to \mathcal{S}^n, \sqsubseteq \rangle$, and s an arbitrary m-tuple.

If there is a firing rule $r \in R$ such that $r \sqsubseteq s$, then by condition (iv), r is unique, and hence for every $F \in \mathcal{S}^m \to \mathcal{S}^n$, $\phi(F)(s) = f(r).F(s')$, where $s = r.s'$. Thus,

$$
\begin{aligned}
\bigsqcup \{ \phi(F)(s) \mid F \in D \} &= \bigsqcup \{ f(r).F(s') \mid F \in D \} \\
&= f(r).\bigsqcup \{ F(s') \mid F \in D \} \\
&= f(r).(\bigsqcup D)(s') \\
&= \phi(\bigsqcup D)(s).
\end{aligned}
$$

Notice that since D is directed in $\langle \mathcal{S}^m \to \mathcal{S}^n, \sqsubseteq \rangle$, it has a least upper bound therein, $\langle \mathcal{S}^m \to \mathcal{S}^n, \sqsubseteq \rangle$ being a cpo.

Otherwise, for every $F \in \mathcal{S}^m \to \mathcal{S}^n$, $\phi(F)(s) = \varepsilon_n$, and hence

$$
\bigsqcup \{ \phi(F)(s) \mid F \in D \} = \varepsilon_n = \phi(\bigsqcup D)(s).
$$

In either case,

$$
\bigsqcup \{ \phi(F)(s) \mid F \in D \} = \phi(\bigsqcup D)(s),
$$

and hence ϕ is continuous. $\qquad\qquad\square$

Since ϕ is continuous, not only does it have a least fixed point, but there is a constructive procedure for finding that least fixed point [9]. We can start with the least element in $\langle \mathcal{S}^m \to \mathcal{S}^n, \sqsubseteq \rangle$, the function $s \mapsto \varepsilon_n$ mapping every m-tuple s to the empty sequence, and iterate ϕ to obtain the following sequence of functions:

$$
F_0 = s \mapsto \varepsilon_n, \ F_1 = \phi(F_1), \ F_2 = \phi(F_1), \ \ldots . \tag{4.5}
$$

Since ϕ is monotone, and $s \mapsto \varepsilon_n$ is a sequence of every other function, the set $\{F_0, F_1, \ldots\}$ is a chain, and hence directed in $\langle \mathcal{S}^m \to \mathcal{S}^n, \sqsubseteq \rangle$. Thus, it has a least upper bound therein, which is the least fixed point of ϕ.

Let us examine this chain more closely for some fixed m-tuple s. Suppose that there is some sequence of firing rules $\langle r_1, r_2, \ldots \rangle$ such that $s = r_1.r_2.\ldots.$ Then, for this particular m-tuple, we can rewrite (4.5) in the following form:

$$
\begin{aligned}
F_0(s) &= \varepsilon_n \\
F_1(s) &= f(r_1) \\
F_2(s) &= f(r_1).f(r_2) \\
&\cdots
\end{aligned}
\tag{4.6}
$$

This is an exact description of the operational semantics in Dennis dataflow, with respect to a single actor. Start with the actor producing only the empty sequence. Then find the prefix of the input that matches a firing rule, and invoke the firing function on that prefix, producing a partial output. Notice here that because of condition (iv), no more than one firing rule can match a prefix of the input at any time. Then find the prefix of the remaining input that matches another firing rule, invoke the firing function on that prefix, and concatenate the result with the output.

In general, even when s is infinite, it is possible that there is only a finite sequence of firing rules $\langle r_0, \ldots, r_p \rangle$ such that $s = r_0. \ldots .r_p.s'$, with s' having no prefix in R. In both the operational semantics of Dennis dataflow and the denotational interpretation of (4.6), the firings simply stop, and the output is finite.

When $m = 0$, the least fixed point of ϕ is a source process, and if $\emptyset \in R$, then it produces the sequence $f(\emptyset).f(\emptyset). \cdots$. If $f(\emptyset)$ is non-empty, then this is infinite and periodic. This might seem limiting for dataflow processes that act as sources, but in fact it is not; a source with a more complicated output sequence can be constructed using a feedback composition, as in Figure 4.2.

When $n = 0$, the least fixed point of ϕ is a sink process, producing the sequence $\emptyset.\emptyset. \cdots = \emptyset$.

In view of this perfect coincidence with the operational semantics, we are tempted to define a Kahn process based on the actor $\langle R, f \rangle$ as this least fixed point of ϕ. In order to do this, however, we still need to prove that in the general case, this least fixed point of ϕ is actually a continuous function, and thus a Kahn process. It suffices to prove the following theorem.

Theorem 4.3 *For any $F: \mathcal{S}^m \to \mathcal{S}^n$, if F is continuous, then $\phi(F)$ is also continuous.*

Proof Let $F: \mathcal{S}^m \to \mathcal{S}^n$ be a continuous function, and $D \subseteq \mathcal{S}^m$ directed in $\langle \mathcal{S}^m, \sqsubseteq \rangle$.

Suppose, toward contradiction, that there are $r_1, r_2 \in R$ and $s_1, s_2 \in D$ such that $r_1 \neq r_2$, but $r_1 \sqsubseteq s_1$ and $r_2 \sqsubseteq s_2$. Then since D is directed in $\langle \mathcal{S}^m, \sqsubseteq \rangle$, $\{s_1, s_2\}$ has an upper bound in D, which is also an upper bound of $\{r_1, r_2\}$, in contradiction to (iv).

Therefore, there is at most one $r \in R$ that is a prefix of some tuple in D.

If there is such an $\boldsymbol{r} \in R$, then

$$\bigsqcup\{\phi(F)(\boldsymbol{s}) \mid \boldsymbol{s} \in D\} = \bigsqcup\{f(\boldsymbol{r}).F(\boldsymbol{s}') \mid \boldsymbol{r}.\boldsymbol{s}' \in D\}$$
$$= f(\boldsymbol{r}).\bigsqcup\{F(\boldsymbol{s}') \mid \boldsymbol{r}.\boldsymbol{s}' \in D\}$$
$$= f(\boldsymbol{r}).F(\bigsqcup\{\boldsymbol{s}' \mid \boldsymbol{r}.\boldsymbol{s}' \in D\})$$
$$= \phi(F)(\bigsqcup D).$$

Notice that since D is directed in $\langle \mathcal{S}^m, \sqsubseteq \rangle$, $\{\boldsymbol{s}' \mid \boldsymbol{r}.\boldsymbol{s}' \in D\}$ is also directed in $\langle \mathcal{S}^m, \sqsubseteq \rangle$, and in particular, $\boldsymbol{r}.\bigsqcup\{\boldsymbol{s}' \mid \boldsymbol{r}.\boldsymbol{s}' \in D\} = \bigsqcup D$.

Otherwise, there is no firing rule in R that is a prefix of some tuple in D, and hence

$$\bigsqcup\{\phi(F)(\boldsymbol{s}) \mid \boldsymbol{s} \in D\} = \varepsilon_n = \phi(F)(\bigsqcup D).$$

In either case,

$$\bigsqcup\{\phi(F)(\boldsymbol{s}) \mid \boldsymbol{s} \in D\} = \phi(F)(\bigsqcup D),$$

and hence $\phi(F)$ is continuous. $\qquad\square$

Since $\boldsymbol{s} \mapsto \varepsilon_n$ is trivially continuous, and continuous functions are closed under pointwise suprema [9], an easy induction suffices to see that the least fixed point of ϕ is a continuous function. Note here that the firing function f need not be continuous. In fact, it does not even need to be monotone. The continuity of the least fixed point of ϕ is guaranteed if $\langle R, f \rangle$ is a valid actor description according to conditions (i) through (iv).

4.3.3 Examples of firing rules

Consider a system where the set of token values is $\mathcal{V} = \{0, 1\}$. Let us examine some possible sets $R \subset \mathcal{S}$ of firing rules for unary firing functions $f : \mathcal{S} \to \mathcal{S}$.

The following sets of firing rules all satisfy condition (iv) above:

$$\begin{aligned} &\{\langle \ \rangle\}; \\ &\{\langle 0 \rangle\}; \\ &\{\langle 0 \rangle, \langle 1 \rangle\}; \\ &\{\langle 0, 0 \rangle, \langle 0, 1 \rangle, \langle 1, 0 \rangle, \langle 1, 1 \rangle\}. \end{aligned} \qquad (4.7)$$

The first of these corresponds to a function that consumes no tokens from its input sequence, and can fire infinitely regardless of the length of the input sequence. The second consumes only the leading zeros from the input sequence, and then stops firing. The third consumes one token from the input on every firing, regardless of its value. The fourth consumes two tokens on the input on every firing, again regardless of the values.

An example of a set of firing rules that does not satisfy condition (iv) is:

$$\{\langle\ \rangle, \langle 0\rangle, \langle 1\rangle\}. \tag{4.8}$$

Such firing rules would correspond to an actor that could non-deterministically consume or not consume an input token upon firing.

The firing rules in (4.8) would also correspond to the firing rules of the unit delay defined in (4.1), so such a process cannot be a dataflow actor under this definition. In fact, delays in dataflow actor networks are usually implemented directly as initial tokens on an arc. Thus, if we admit such an implementation, then there is no loss of generality here. The implementation cost is lower, and this strategy avoids having to have special firing rules for delays that, if allowed in general, could introduce non-determinism. Furthermore, once we admit this sort of implementation for the unit delay, it is easy to model arbitrary actors with state using a single self-loop initialized to their initial state.

Let us examine now some possible sets $R \subset \mathcal{S}^2$ of firing rules for binary firing functions $f:\mathcal{S}^2 \to \mathcal{S}$.

The following sets of firing rules all satisfy condition (iv):

$$\{\langle\langle 0\rangle, \langle 0\rangle\rangle, \langle\langle 0\rangle, \langle 1\rangle\rangle, \langle\langle 1\rangle, \langle 0\rangle\rangle, \langle\langle 1\rangle, \langle 1\rangle\rangle\};$$
$$\{\langle\langle 0\rangle, \langle\ \rangle\rangle, \langle\langle 1\rangle, \langle 0\rangle\rangle, \langle\langle 1\rangle, \langle 1\rangle\rangle\}; \tag{4.9}$$
$$\{\langle\langle 0\rangle, \langle\ \rangle\rangle, \langle\langle 1\rangle, \langle\ \rangle\rangle\}.$$

The first of these corresponds to an actor that consumes one input token from each of its inputs. For example, this could implement a logic function such as AND or OR. The second corresponds to a conditional actor, where the first input provides a control token on every firing. If the control token has value '1', then a token is consumed from the second input. Otherwise, no token is consumed from the second input. The third corresponds to an actor that has effectively one input, never consuming a token from the second input.

The following set of firing rules does not satisfy condition (iv):

$$\{\langle\langle 0\rangle, \langle\ \rangle\rangle, \langle\langle 1\rangle, \langle\ \rangle\rangle, \langle\langle\ \rangle, \langle 0\rangle\rangle, \langle\langle\ \rangle, \langle 1\rangle\rangle\}. \tag{4.10}$$

These would be the firing rules of a non-determinate merge, a process that can consume a token on either input and copy it to its output. The non-determinate merge is not a monotone process, and so use of it in a Kahn process network could result in non-determinism.

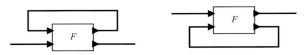

Fig. 4.4. If F is an identity process, the appropriate firing rules are (4.10).

It is interesting to notice that the sets of firing rules of (4.7) and (4.9) can all be implemented in a blocking-read fashion, according to the Kahn–MacQueen implementation of Kahn process networks [16]. An example of a process that cannot be implemented using blocking reads has the firing rules:

$$\{\langle\langle 1\rangle,\langle 0\rangle,\langle\ \rangle\rangle,\langle\langle 0\rangle,\langle\ \rangle,\langle 1\rangle\rangle,\langle\langle\ \rangle,\langle 0\rangle,\langle 1\rangle\rangle\}. \qquad (4.11)$$

These firing rules satisfy (iv) and correspond to the Gustave function [3], a function defining a process which is stable, but not sequential as the other examples.

While actors that satisfy conditions (i) through (iv) above yield continuous Kahn processes, these conditions are somewhat more restrictive than what is really necessary. The firing rules in (4.10), for example, are not only the firing rules for the dangerous non-determinate merge, but also the firing rules for a perfectly harmless two-input, two-output identity process. At first glance, it might seem that this sort of identity process could be implemented using the first set of firing rules of (4.9), though this will not work. The two examples in Figure 4.4 show why not. In the first example, the first (top) input and output should be the empty sequence under the least-fixed-point semantics, so there will never be a token to trigger any firing rule of (4.9). In the second of these examples, the second (bottom) input and output present the same problem. The firing rules of (4.10), however, have no difficulty with these cases. We next replace condition (iv) with a more general rule that solves such problems.

4.3.4 Commutative firings

Many dataflow models having a notion of firing are not compositional. These compositionality issues are discussed in a very general framework by Talcott [29]. In our context, the problem is simply that an aggregation of actors that can be individually described using firing rules and firing functions cannot be collectively described in this way. This problem was alluded to in the final example of the last sub-section, which is the

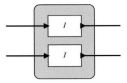

Fig. 4.5. A two-input, two-output identity process described as an aggregation of two one-input one-output identity processes.

simplest example illustrating the problem. It is possible to think of a two-input, two-output identity process as an aggregation of two one-input, one-output identity processes, as in Figure 4.5. One-input, one-output identity processes are trivially described as actors that satisfy conditions (i) through (iv), but a two-input, two-output identity process cannot be so described.

In order to solve this problem, we replace condition (iv) with the following more elaborate condition:

(iv′) for all $r, r' \in R$, if $r \neq r'$ and $\{r, r'\}$ has an upper bound in $\langle S^m, \sqsubseteq \rangle$, then $f(r).f(r') = f(r').f(r)$ and $r \sqcap r' = \varepsilon_m$.

This condition states that if any two firing rules are consistent, namely they have a common upper bound, and therefore can possibly be enabled at the same time, then it makes no difference in what order we use these firing rules; the values of the firing function at these consistent rules commute with respect to the concatenation operator. Furthermore, any two consistent firing rules have no common prefix other than the m-tuple of empty sequences.

It is easy to see that when condition (iv′) is satisfied,

$$r \sqcup r' = r.r' = r'.r; \tag{4.12}$$

that is, the least common extension (least upper bound) of any two consistent firing rules is their concatenation, in either order.

We also need to reconstruct the functional that we used to define the Kahn process. For convenience, let $P_R(s)$ denote the set $\{r \in R \mid r \sqsubseteq s\}$. This is a possibly empty finite set. The functional ϕ' is defined such that for any function $F:S^m \to S^n$ and any m-tuple s,

$$\phi'(F)(s) = \begin{cases} f(r_1).\cdots.f(r_p).F(s') & \text{if } P_R(s) \neq \emptyset \text{ and } \{r_1, \ldots, r_p\} = P_R(s); \\ \varepsilon_n & \text{otherwise.} \end{cases}$$

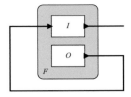

Fig. 4.6. A composition that is invalid under condition (iv), but not under condition (iv′).

Here, we assume, as before, that $s = r_1.\ldots.r_p.s'$. Notice that because of (4.12), for any permutation π on $\{1, \ldots, p\}$,

$$r_1.\ldots.r_p = r_{\pi(1)}.\ldots.r_{\pi(p)},$$

and similarly, because of condition (iv′),

$$f(r_1).\cdots.f(r_p) = f(r_{\pi(1)}).\cdots.f(r_{\pi(p)}).$$

Therefore, it makes no difference in what order we invoke the enabled firing rules. As before, we define the Kahn process F corresponding to the dataflow actor $\langle R, f \rangle$ to be the least fixed point of the functional ϕ'.

Although notationally tedious, it is straightforward to extend the results on ϕ to conclude that both the functional ϕ' and its least fixed point F are continuous; the proofs are practically identical.

Going back to the example of Figure 4.5, we see that we can use the firing rules of (4.10), and a firing function $f:\mathcal{S}^2 \to \mathcal{S}^2$ such that for any firing rule r, $f(r) = r$, to obtain a dataflow actor for the two-input, two-output identity process that is valid under condition (iv′). More interestingly, we can use the same firing rules to implement a process with firing function $f:\mathcal{S}^2 \to \mathcal{S}$ such that for each firing rule r,

$$f(r) = \begin{cases} \langle 1 \rangle & \text{if } r = \langle \langle 1 \rangle, \langle \ \rangle \rangle \text{ or } r = \langle \langle \ \rangle, \langle 1 \rangle \rangle; \\ \langle \ \rangle & \text{otherwise.} \end{cases}$$

This process is interesting because it is neither sequential nor stable, and thus cannot be implemented under condition (iv).

As a final example, consider the composition of Figure 4.6. The top process is an identity process, and the bottom one a source of the infinite sequence $\langle 0, 0, \ldots \rangle$. A reasonable firing function for the source process would be the function $\emptyset \mapsto \langle 0 \rangle$. The question now is how to define the firing rules R and firing function f of the composition.

A first, naive attempt would be to let $R = \{\langle 0\rangle, \langle 1\rangle\}$. However, with the feedback arc in Figure 4.6, this results in no firing rule ever becoming enabled. Instead, we need $R = \{\langle 0\rangle, \langle 1\rangle, \langle \ \rangle\}$, which violates condition (iv). However, if we define the firing function such that

$$f(\langle 0\rangle) = \langle\langle 0\rangle, \langle \ \rangle\rangle,$$
$$f(\langle 1\rangle) = \langle\langle 1\rangle, \langle \ \rangle\rangle, \text{ and}$$
$$f(\langle \ \rangle) = \langle\langle \ \rangle, \langle 0\rangle\rangle,$$

then condition (iv') is satisfied and the composition behaves as an aggregate of its parts.

4.3.5 Compositionality

The examples of Figure 4.5 and 4.6 indicate certain compositionality issues that can be successfully resolved using the notion of commutative firings. We can generalize this to every composition of the same type.

Consider a slight generalization of Figure 4.1(a), where s_1 is an m-tuple, s_2 is an n-tuple, s_3 is a p-tuple, and s_4 is a q-tuple. It is possible to prove that the aggregation of F_1 and F_2 is compositional, in the sense that it can always be described as a set of firing rules and a firing function.

Assume for simplicity that $m > 0$ and $p > 0$ (generalizing to allow zero values is easy), and suppose that F_1 is defined by $\langle R_1, f_1\rangle$ and F_2 by $\langle R_2, f_2\rangle$. Let

$$R_1' = \{r_1 \times \varepsilon_p \mid r_1 \in R_1\}$$

and

$$R_2' = \{\varepsilon_m \times r_2 \mid r_2 \in R_2\},$$

where we loosely write $r_1 \times \varepsilon_p$ to denote the unique $(m+p)$-tuple s that has $s(i) = r_1(i)$ if $i < m$, and $s(i) = \varepsilon_p(i-m)$ otherwise, etc. The set R of firing rules for the composite process $F : \mathcal{S}^{m+p} \to \mathcal{S}^{n+q}$ is defined by

$$R = R_1' \cup R_2'.$$

The firing function $f : \mathcal{S}^{m+p} \to \mathcal{S}^{n+q}$ of the composite process is defined such that for any finite $(m+p)$-tuple r,

$$f(r) = \begin{cases} f_1(r_1) \times \varepsilon_q & \text{if } r \in R_1' \text{ and } r = r_1 \times \varepsilon_p; \\ \varepsilon_n \times f_2(r_2) & \text{if } r \in R_2' \text{ and } r = \varepsilon_m \times r_2; \\ \varepsilon_{n+q} & \text{otherwise.} \end{cases}$$

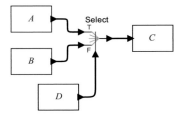

Fig. 4.7. An example of a process network where it might be undesirable from a practical perspective to insist that the operational semantics coincide with the denotational semantics.

It is now straightforward to verify that if $\langle R_1, f_2 \rangle$ and $\langle R_2, f_2 \rangle$ both satisfy condition (iv′), then so does $\langle R, f \rangle$.

4.3.6 Practical issues

The constructive procedure given by (4.6) ensures that repeated firings converge to the appropriate Kahn process defined by the actor. If any such sequence of firings is finite, then it is only necessary to invoke a finite number of firings. In practice, it is common for such firing sequences to be infinite, in which case a practical issue of fairness arises. In particular, since there are usually many actors in a system, in order to have the operational semantics coincide with the denotational semantics, it is necessary to fire each actor infinitely often, if possible.

It turns out that such a fairness condition is not always desirable. It may result in unbounded memory requirements for execution of a dataflow process network. In some such cases, there is an alternative firing schedule that is also infinite, but requires only bounded memory. That schedule may not conform to the denotational semantics, and nonetheless be preferable to one that does.

A simple example is shown in Figure 4.7. The actor labeled 'SELECT' has the following set of firing rules:

$$\{\langle\langle 1 \rangle, \langle \ \rangle, \langle 1 \rangle\rangle, \langle\langle 0 \rangle, \langle \ \rangle, \langle 1 \rangle\rangle, \langle\langle \ \rangle, \langle 1 \rangle, \langle 0 \rangle\rangle, \langle\langle \ \rangle, \langle 0 \rangle, \langle 0 \rangle\rangle\},$$

where the order of inputs is top-to-bottom. If the bottom input (the control input) has value '1' (for TRUE), then a token of any value is consumed from the top input, and no token is consumed from the middle input. If the control input has value '0' (for FALSE), then a token of any value is consumed from the middle input, and no token is consumed from the top input.

Suppose that the actors A, B, and D, all of which are sources, are defined to each produce an infinite sequence, and that C, which is a sink, is defined to consume an infinite sequence. Suppose further that the output from D is the constant sequence $\langle 0, 0, \ldots \rangle$. Then tokens produced by actor A will never be consumed. In most practical scenarios, it is preferable to avoid producing them if they will never be consumed, despite the fact that this violates the denotational semantics, which state that the output of actor A is an infinite sequence. This problem is solved by Parks [23], who also shows that the obvious solution for the example in Figure 4.7, the demand-driven execution, does not solve the problem in general. Another, more specialized solution, achieved by restricting the semantics, is presented by Caspi in [7].

4.4 Conclusion

We have shown how the formal semantic methods of Kahn dataflow can be adapted to Dennis dataflow, which is based on the notion of an actor firing. Kahn dataflow is defined in terms of continuous processes, which map input sequences to output sequences, while Dennis dataflow is defined in terms of firing functions, which map input tokens to output tokens, and are evaluated only when input tokens satisfy certain firing rules. We have formally defined firing rules and firing functions, and have shown how a Kahn process can be defined as the least fixed point of a continuous functional that is constructed using the firing rules and firing function of an actor. Furthermore, we have specified conditions on the firing rules and firing functions that solve certain compositionality problems in dataflow, in the sense that certain compositions of actors are actors themselves.

Bibliography

[1] Arvind, L. Bic and T. Ungerer. Evolution of data-flow computers. In J.-L. Gaudiot and L. Bic (eds), *Advanced Topics in Data-Flow Computing*. Prentice-Hall, 1991.

[2] A. Benveniste, P. Caspi, P. L. Guernic and N. Halbwachs. Data-flow synchronous languages. In J. W. d. Bakker, W.-P. d. Roever and G. Rozenberg, (eds), *A Decade of Concurrency – Reflections and Perspectives*, Volume 803 Lecture Notes in Computer Science, pp. 1–45. Springer-Verlag, 1994.

[3] G. Berry. Bottom-up computation of recursive programs. *Revue Française d'Automatique, Informatique et Recherche Opérationnelle*, **10**(3):47–82, 1976.

[4]   J. D. Brock and W. B. Ackerman. Scenarios, a model of non-determinate computation. In *Conference on Formal Definition of Programming Concepts*, volume 107, Lecture Notes in Computer Science, pp. 252–259. Springer-Verlag, 1981.

[5]   M. Broy. Functional specification of time-sensitive communicating systems. *ACM Transactions on Software Engineering and Methodology*, **2**(1):1–46, 1993.

[6]   M. Broy and G. Stefanescu. The algebra of stream processing functions. *Theoretical Computer Science*, **258**:99–129, 2001.

[7]   P. Caspi. Clocks in dataflow languages. *Theoretical Computer Science*, **94**(1), 1992.

[8]   M. Creeger. Multicore CPUs for the masses. *ACM Queue*, **3**(7):63–64, 2005.

[9]   B. A. Davey and H. A. Priestley. *Introduction to Lattices and Order*. Cambridge University Press, 1990.

[10]   J. B. Dennis. *First Version Data Flow Procedure Language*. Technical Report MAC TM61, MIT Laboratory for Computer Science, 1974.

[11]   M. Geilen and T. Basten. Requirements on the execution of Kahn process networks. In *European Symposium on Programming Languages and Systems*, Lecture Notes in Computer Science, pp. 319–334, Springer, 2003.

[12]   C.-J. Hsu, F. Keceli, M.-Y. Ko, S. Shahparnia and S. S. Bhattacharyya. DIF: An interchange format for dataflow-based design tools. In *International Workshop on Systems, Architectures, Modeling, and Simulation*, Samos, Greece, July 2004.

[13]   A. Jantsch and I. Sander. Models of computation and languages for embedded system design. *IEE Proceedings on Computers and Digital Techniques*, **152**(2):114–129, 2005.

[14]   W. M. Johnston, J. R. P. Hanna and R. J. Millar. Advances in dataflow programming languages. *ACM Computing Surveys*, **36**(1):1–34, 2004.

[15]   G. Kahn. The semantics of a simple language for parallel programming. In *Proc. of the IFIP Congress 74*. North-Holland Publishing Co., 1974.

[16]   G. Kahn and D. B. MacQueen. Coroutines and networks of parallel processes. In B. Gilchrist (ed.), *Information Processing*, pages 993–998. North-Holland Publishing Co., 1977.

[17]   D. Lazaro Cuadrado, A. P. Ravn and P. Koch. Automated distributed simulation in Ptolemy II. In *Parallel and Distributed Computing and Networks (PDCN)*. Acta Press, 2007.

[18]   E. A. Lee and T. M. Parks. Dataflow process networks. *Proceedings of the IEEE*, **83**(5):773–801, 1995.

[19]   Y. Lin, R. Mullenix, M. Woh, S. Mahlke, T. Mudge, A. Reid and K. Flautner. SPEX: A programming language for software defined radio. In *Software Defined Radio Technical Conference and Product Exposition*, Orlando, 2006.

[20]   S. G. Matthews. An extensional treatment of lazy data flow deadlock. *Theoretical Computer Science*, **151**(1):195–205, 1995.

[21]   A. G. Olson and B. L. Evans. Deadlock detection for distributed process networks. In *ICASSP*, 2005.

[22]   O. M. G. (OMG). A UML profile for MARTE, beta 1. OMG Adopted Specification ptc/07–08–04, August 2007.

[23]   T. M. Parks. *Bounded Scheduling of Process Networks*. PhD, UC Berkeley, 1995.

[24]   T. M. Parks and D. Roberts. Distributed process networks in Java. In *International Parallel and Distributed Processing Symposium*, Nice, France, April 2003.

[25]   D. Scott. Outline of a mathematical theory of computation. In *4th Annual Princeton Conference on Information Sciences and Systems*, pp. 169–176, 1970.

[26]   V. Srini. An architectural comparison of dataflow systems. *Computer*, **19**(3), 1986.

[27]   E. W. Stark. An algebra of dataflow networks. *Fundamenta Informaticae*, **22**(1-2):167–185, 1995.

[28]   R. Stephens. A survey of stream processing. *Acta Informatica*, 34(7), 1997.

[29]   C. L. Talcott. Interaction semantics for components of distributed systems. In *Formal Methods for Open Object-Based Distributed Systems (FMOODS)*, 1996.

[30]   W. Thies, M. Karczmarek and S. Amarasinghe. StreamIt: A language for streaming applications. In *11th International Conference on Compiler Construction*, volume 2304, Lecture Notes in Computer Science, Grenoble, France, 2002, Springer-Verlag.

[31]   W. Thies, M. Karczmarek, J. Sermulins, R. Rabbah and S. Amarasinghe. Teleport messaging for distributed stream programs. In *PPoPP*, Chicago, Illinois, USA, 2005. ACM.

[32]   A. Turjan, B. Kienhuis and E. Deprettere. Solving out-of-order communication in Kahn process networks. *Journal on VLSI Signal Processing-Systems for Signal, Image, and Video Technology*, 2003.

Kahn networks at the dawn of functional programming

David B. MacQueen
University of Chicago

5.1 Introduction

The evolution of programming languages involves isolating and describing abstractions that allow us to solve problems more elegantly, efficiently, and reliably, and then providing appropriate linguistic support for these abstractions. Ideally, a new abstraction can be described precisely with a mathematical semantics, and the semantics leads to logical techniques for reasoning about programs that use the abstraction. Gilles Kahn's early work on stream processing networks is a beautiful example of this process at work.

Gilles began thinking about parallel graph programs at Stanford, and he developed his ideas in a series of papers starting in 1971: [44], [45], and [46]. Gilles' original motivation was to provide a formal model for reasoning about aspects of operating systems programming, based on early data flow models of computation. But the model he developed turned out to be of much more general interest, both in terms of program architecture and in terms of semantics. During his Edinburgh visit in 1975–76, Gilles and I collaborated on a prototype implementation of the model that allowed further development and experimentation, reported in [47]. By 1976 it was clear that his model, while inspired by early data flow research, was also closely connected to several other developments, including coroutines, Landin's notion of streams, and the then emerging lazy functional languages.

While staying in Edinburgh, Gilles was also working with Gordon Plotkin on a general theory of "concrete" domains that could make a precise distinction between functions and data [48, 43]. This theory provided a semantic explanation of streams and other incrementally computed, potentially infinite data structures. This work not only

From Semantics to Computer Science Essays in Honour of Gilles Kahn, eds Yves Bertot, Gérard Huet, Jean-Jacques Lévy and Gordon Plotkin. Published by Cambridge University Press. © Cambridge University Press 2009.

strengthened the theoretical foundations of stream processing networks, but also contributed to deeper understanding of fundamental concepts such as sequentiality.

Gilles' key insight was that the behavior of a program organized as a graph of communicating sequential processes could be adequately represented by the sequences of data passing over the communication channels (the *channel histories*), and that these histories could be modeled as members of a complete lattice (or complete partial order) ordered by the prefix relation, following Scott's pioneering work on domain theory [72, 73]. Because of their sequential nature, communicating processes expressed continuous functions mapping histories of their input channels to histories of their output channels. The semantics of a parallel graph program could then be expressed as the least fixpoint of a set of recursive equations defining the channel histories in terms of the continuous functions representing processes. The uniqueness of the least fixpoint guaranteed determinacy of the program viewed as a function on histories.

The translation of a parallel graph program into a set of continuous stream functions and recursive stream equations was originally intended to provide a semantics for an imperative language of communicating processes. But this equational form of expression could also be considered as a language in its own right, and if we assume a coroutine-like, demand-driven execution strategy for this language it could be considered the earliest description of a pure, lazy functional language capable of computing with infinite data structures. The naturalness of this formulation is confirmed by the fact that Gilles' stream processing networks are easily expressed in modern lazy languages like Haskell [66].

The elegant and powerful abstraction of functional stream processing that Gilles developed has become a common idiom of programming in lazy and strict functional languages and has inspired many developments in areas such as reactive languages (e.g. LUSTRE [22]), digital signal processing, and semantics of concurrency.

In this paper, we will start by providing some historical context, discussing earlier data flow models, coroutines, and Landin's streams. We then summarize the development of Kahn networks through the series of papers Gilles published in the early to mid 1970s [14, 44, 45, 47]. We will briefly review the related Kahn–Plotkin development of concrete data types [43]. Next we will consider the roughly contemporary development of lazy functional languages, and finally we will discuss a few samples of the vast quantity of later work that built on or exploited these ideas.

Our goal is to illuminate this particular aspect of Gilles Kahn's scientific contributions by exploring its development in some detail and relating it to both earlier and contemporary developments.

5.2 Some precursors of Kahn networks

Three lines of conceptual development arising in the 1960s played a part in the origins of Kahn networks. One was the modeling of concurrent programs as data flow graphs, the second was Landin's introduction of the notion of functional streams, and the third was the investigation of coroutines. In this section we briefly review these precursors.

5.2.1 Graph models and data flow

In the late 1960s researchers began investigating new graph-based models of computation which later came to be known as data flow models.[1] The basic idea underlying programs as graphs is that edges represent channels carrying data values between nodes that represent operations or computational processes. These models typically involve concurrency, since it is usually assumed that multiple nodes can be active simultaneously. A large number of variations on graph models were proposed over the following years, including Kahn networks. A 1973 survey by Baer [11] covers several of the early graph models.

The earliest data flow language was probably the "block diagram" language, BLODI, developed at Bell Laboratories around 1960 [50]. BLODI enabled engineers to solve problems in digital acoustic signal processing by connecting elements from a library of predefined processing programs. A BLODI program specified a *circuit*, which was a graph consisting of *blocks*, or function nodes, connected by channels called *signals*. A block could have multiple input signals but only a single output signal, which could be shared as input by several other blocks. Some blocks performed pure arithmetic operations like addition to compute the next output in terms of the current inputs, while other blocks had internal state (e.g. delay blocks and accumulator blocks). Signals, which represent communication channels, carried a single value at a time, and the operation of the circuit was synchronous: the output of a block at one clock tick becomes the input for its consumers on the next clock tick. BLODI was the first of a line of block-diagram languages designed for digital signal processing [52].

---

[1] The term "data flow" may have originated in the title of Duane Adam's thesis [3].

The first theoretical model for a form of data flow computation was described by Karp and Miller in 1966 [49]. In this model, programs are fixed graphs whose nodes represent atomic operations, and whose edges transmit data between nodes, but in this case the edges can store a queue of values in transit. A node is enabled if it has sufficiently many input values on each input edge (an example of *data-driven* control flow), and an enabled node may execute, consuming a predetermined number of values from each input and producing a predetermined number of values on each output. The model is not very flexible or realistic, since the graph is fixed and the rates of consumption or production of each node on each connected edge are fixed independent of the values consumed. An execution of a graph program is modeled as a sequence of sets of simultaneously firing nodes, and the main theoretical result is that the behavior of a program is determinate when viewed in terms of the history of values on edges.

The Karp–Miller model introduced several important ideas: (1) modeling channels as unbounded queues of values, (2) characterizing a computation in terms of complete channel histories, and (3) data-driven execution. Furthermore, it provided an example of a parallel, nondeterministic operational model that produces deterministic global behavior.

The next major development in data flow models was the 1967 MIT thesis of Jorge Rodriguez [71], a student of Jack Dennis. This work was the beginning of a long line of data flow models intended to explore new ways to organize computations to achieve high levels of concurrency. The Rodriguez model was intended to be more realistic than the Karp–Miller model. The model is quite complex, with two types of edges and seven types of nodes. The two varieties of edges are data edges that carry a single unstructured value and have one of four statuses, or control edges, which have only a status. One type of node performs basic operations on data, while six other types of node perform various control functions. The model is basically data-driven, but the edge status values also play a part in enabling execution of a node. The program graphs are fixed, as in the Karp–Miller model, and edges can carry at most one value at a time. The thesis defined an operational semantics for the model and proved that it was determinate.

This data flow model was followed by a similar one presented by Duane Adams in his 1968 Stanford PhD thesis [3]. In this model, edges have only two status values (locked or unlocked), and as in Karp–Miller they can carry an unbounded queue of values of a specified type. Execution is data-driven, conditioned on input edge status values. Only one value is consumed from each unlocked input edge at each node execution, but multiple values (or none) can be output on each output edge. Nodes come in two flavors: r-nodes that perform unconditional operations on input values to compute output values, and s-nodes that implement status-dependent conditional operations, yielding both outputs and modified input statuses. An r-node may be a *procedure node*, whose function is itself defined in terms of a program graph. Procedure node graphs may be recursive, and may fail to terminate.

The operational model for Adams' graph programs is quite complex compared to Karp and Miller's and Rodriguez's models, because executions of r-nodes, though they must terminate before producing output, have duration and are allowed to overlap in a pipelined fashion. Thus Adams's model supports both spacial concurrency where multiple nodes are firing at the same time, and overlapped concurrent executions of a single node. Despite this complication, the operational semantics is shown to be determinate like the earlier models.

Adams presented several examples of data flow graph programs, including the factorial function (in iterative and recursive versions), Gaussian elimination, a merge sort, and a program for simplifying arithmetic terms.

Meanwhile, Jack Dennis, following up on Rodriguez's work, published another model in 1968 [29] that included a notion of graph procedures similar to that of Adams, except that a more general *procedure apply* node takes the name of a procedure to be applied as one of its inputs, making the model "higher-order" in a sense. Because data values could be modified, a read/write capability and signaling system had to be added to ensure mutual exclusion and determinacy of the model. The paper also sketches a machine architecture designed to directly execute the graph model. Like the Rodriguez model, this model has at most one value per edge and is supply-driven.

In a series of papers during the early to mid-1970s [31, 30, 32], Dennis continued to develop and refine his determinate, data-driven data flow models and corresponding computer architectures that could execute them [34], with the goal of achieving greater concurrency while maintaining a relatively simple, deterministic semantics. These models all involved single value edges and a distinction between operation nodes and control nodes. These ideas led to experimental data flow computer designs at MIT (Monsoon), the University of Manchester [37], and Imperial College (the Alice machine [27]).

5.2.2 Landin's streams

In Landin's paper "A correspondence between ALGOL 60 and Church's lambda-notation: Part I" [53], he introduces the concept of a *stream* as an open-ended and potentially infinite sequence of values, and uses them to translate the Algol 60 `for` statement.[2]

Landin's representation of a stream is simply a nullary function that, when called, produces an element and another stream function. Thus to "cons" an element x onto a stream s, we form the lambda abstraction $\lambda().(x, s)$, for which Landin introduced the special syntax "$x : * s$". This is a fully lazy cons operator, since it suspends the evaluation of both the head and tail of the stream. The basic list operators are then easily defined; for instance:

$$\texttt{nulls}(S) \;=\; \texttt{null}(S())$$
$$\texttt{hds}(S) \;=\; \texttt{fst}(S())$$

Landin's streams are a precursor to lists in lazy functional languages, but they differ from lazy lists in the absence of memoization in a data structure, and stream cons is strict in its first argument, so initial segments of streams must consist of fully defined elements.

Programming with these functional streams is straightforward, as shown by Burge in [17, 16]. For instance, it is easy to define functionals like map, fold, and filter over streams. Since streams are functions, it is also possible to define a recursive stream, as in "`let rec s` $= \lambda().(1, s)$ `in s`." Because the values of a stream are not consolidated into a data structure and are therefore ephemeral, using Landin's streams in situations where the streams are shared usually requires recomputation of their elements. Burge also notes that one can construct a cascade of stream processing functions that work like the coroutine pipelines described by Conway [25].

In the early 1970s, Landin's streams inspired the feature called dynamic lists in POP-2 [19]. A dynamic list is created by applying a primitive function `fntolist` to a *generator function*, which produces a new value each time it is called (normally depending on modified state). Dynamic lists were typically used to model input sources, but it was possible to use them for rudimentary stream processing applications. Landin's streams were also one inspiration of the notion of process that Milner began to explore in [64].

---

[2] Burge comments that he learned about the stream concept from Landin as early as 1962.

5.2.3 Coroutines

The concept of a coroutine is usually attributed to Melvin Conway, who coined the term in 1958 and originally used coroutines in the implementation of an assembler. He described the notion in his paper [25], which is concerned with the design of a compact, single-pass Cobol compiler.[3] In Conway's scheme, two communicating coroutines interact by transferring control back and forth at read and write operations (one is the producer, performing writes, and one is the consumer, performing reads). Each read/write interaction passes a single value directly between the coroutines. It is not indicated which coroutine is the driver, so the interaction could be either data-driven or demand driven. Such coroutines could be decoupled into separate passes, where the producer writes all its output values to a tape, and then the consumer runs in a separate pass and reads the values from the tape. This multi-pass variant is a form of data-driven execution, with buffered communication. The reason this decoupling is possible is that transfer of control is performed indirectly and implicitly by the input/output operations on a connecting channel.

Conway's version of coroutines allows them to have multiple outputs and multiple inputs, but he doesn't admit cycles. He goes on to describe the architecture of his Cobol compiler as a graph of communicating coroutines passing values along the links.

In 1968, Doug McIlroy gave a talk on coroutines at the Cambridge University Computer Laboratory, the contents of which later appeared as an unpublished note [59]. McIlroy cites Conway and mentions stream processes as one of the main applications for coroutines. McIlroy sketches a coroutine facility as an extension to a PL/I-like language, generalizing the mechanisms associated with PL/I procedures. He uses the term *connection* for ports through which coroutines communicate and by which control is transferred via either a *resume* operation or a function call notation using the port name as the function. The passing of parameters and results via connected ports is symmetrical, meaning connected ports can pass values (and control) both ways.

Connections are externally accessible attributes of coroutine instances, and a *connect* operation can create new linkages between connections. This makes it possible for a coroutine program to reconfigure itself,

---

[3] In a footnote, Conway notes that the coroutine concept was independently invented by Joel Erdwinn, then at the Computer Sciences Corporation. An article on coroutines in [67] attributes the independent invention to Erdwinn and Jack Merner.

anticipating the process reconfigurations of [47] that we will discuss in Section 4. McIlroy used a coroutine implementation of the Sieve of Eratosthenes to demonstrate how one can exploit the ability to dynamically generate new coroutine instances and reconfigure connections. This was the direct inspiration of the sieve example in [47].[4] He also mentions an idea suggested by David Park called "functional assignment", which corresponds to function closures, and he notes that some, but not all, coroutine programs can be expressed using function closures.[5]

5.3 The origin of Kahn networks

5.3.1 Early data flow research

Three years before the milestone publication of [46], while Gilles was a student at Stanford, he was already working on the idea of processes communicating via queue-like channels, and he published his first paper, "An approach to systems correctness," [44], in the 1971 Symposium on Operating Systems Principles (SOSP 71). This paper describes a graph model of computation as a formalism for specifying the functional behavior of systems programs (e.g. components of an operating system). It cites Duane Adams' thesis [3] and was probably also influenced by earlier data flow work, but it introduces a much simpler model.

A program is organized as a graph. Vertexes in the graph represent operations or processes, chosen from a predefined library, and they may execute independently and in parallel. Edges of the graph represent communication lines that convey values of various types between the processes, and processes communicate exclusively via these channels. A communication line behaves as a FIFO queue of values, with a capacity that may be either unbounded or bounded.

The vertexes of the graph are of two kinds. Multiplexer vertices take the values arriving on either of two input lines and send them as they arrive on a single output line, resulting in a fair but nondeterministic merge of the input sequences. The second kind of vertex is a computational node, which can have multiple inputs and multiple outputs. Some of these nodes perform discrete or atomic operations to transform inputs

---

[4] A functional version of the sieve also appears in [40], attributed there to P. Quarendon.

[5] A few years later, McIlroy's familiarity with stream processing coroutines and their pipeline composition influenced the design of the Unix shell [70] and led to Ken Thompson's adding the pipe combinator to an early version of the shell.

into outputs, while others represent a continuing sequential process (e.g. a number-generating process that emits an infinite increasing sequence of integers on its output line). Some sorts of computational nodes have local memory. The internal details of how computational nodes are defined are not discussed, but a basic set of sample nodes are described and used in examples.

Some node operations perform actions conditioned on the input values available (they perform *lookahead* on their input lines), and they can selectively input values from a subset of their input lines. An example would be the ordered merge operation, called M, that waits for integer values on its two input lines, compares those two values, then consumes only the larger value and sends it on its output line.

There is no explicit discussion of the execution model for graph programs, other than the statement that "nodes will represent processes that may operate independently" implying parallel execution. There is also a fairness assumption that any node that has inputs on all of its incoming edges will eventually become "active", i.e. will execute. This suggests a data-driven mode of execution similar to previous data flow models.

Gilles discusses the functional description of graph programs, including how to characterize the correctness of a program. A functional description involves an *input condition* that restricts the sequences of values supplied on the input lines (those lines that do not have a source within the program), and an *output condition* in the form of a relation between input sequences and output sequences (the sequences appearing on output lines, which are lines having no target within the program). The paper presents no formal semantics for graph programs, nor does it develop a theory for formally proving programs to be correct with respect to a functional description, but several example proofs are sketched using informal reasoning about the sequences representing communication histories. These example proofs involve a simple pipeline computation operating on two inputs and producing two outputs, a binary merge tree, a simple filtering program involving a cycle, and a couple variations on mutual exclusion mechanisms for managing resources. This approach to the description and analysis of program behavior through communication histories goes beyond anything appearing in the earlier data flow work of Karp and Miller, Rodriguez, and Adams [49, 71, 3], and anticipates the formal semantic model and reasoning techniques Gilles described in [45] and [46].

As mentioned, the graph model of [44] was probably most directly influenced by that of Adams. It is considerably simpler than Adams' model in that it eliminates the idea of channel status and procedure nodes. It also differs from Adams' model in that it is nondeterministic, because of the multiplex nodes, and it allows for channels of bounded capacity.

The data flow model of [44] is a transitional step between the data flow models of Karp and Miller, Rodriguez, and Adams and the more streamlined, elegant model described in [45] and [46]. In the later papers, Gilles returns to a deterministic model with sequential processing nodes, and develops the informal techniques for reasoning about communication histories into a functional semantics for graph programs.

5.3.2 Process networks

In an early IRIA report entitled "A Preliminary Theory for Parallel Programs" [45], followed by the 1974 IFIP Congress paper "The semantics of a simple language for parallel programming" [46], Gilles presented a new model for parallel programs consisting of communicating sequential processes. As in earlier models, programs consist of graphs where edges are communication channels and vertices are computational processes performing input and output on the connecting channels. Like the earlier data flow models of Karp–Miller and Adams, but unlike the model in [44] with its multiplexer nodes, this model is determinate when program behaviors are abstracted in terms of channel histories. Both [45] and [46] follow [44] in motivating the design of the model by its potential to clarify aspects of programming operating systems ([45] cites [75] in support of this objective).

This model is distinguished from earlier data flow models by the fact that the computations performed at nodes are modeled as continuously running sequential programs, or *processes*, performing data processing interspersed with occasional input and output operations. In most data flow models, nodes are associated with discrete operations that are initiated when inputs are available, perform some operation on the available input values, and terminate after producing some output values. In Gilles' model, availability of input does not activate a node, but nonavailability of input values on a channel may cause an active process to block (usually temporarily) waiting on an input operation. Even assuming parallel execution, it is fundamentally a demand-driven model, with the node processes driving the computation, rather than a data-driven model of processing where data flowing through the graph activates the operations at the nodes.

The key innovation in these two papers, however, is the development of a denotational semantics for these graph programs that abstracts away from the details of processing within the nodes and the timing of input/output interactions. The behavior of programs is represented abstractly through the histories of the channels, with the processes implementing continuous functions over these histories. The meaning of the program is then defined as a fixpoint of a set of stream equations. Beyond explaining the sequential process language, this formalized semantics actually provides an alternate purely functional language for implementing stream processing programs.

5.3.3 Basic assumptions

The key assumption underlying the functional semantics is that the communicating processes are executing *sequential* programs. Reference [45] is not specific about how these processes are expressed, suggesting as possibilities Turing machines communicating via one-way tapes, or, more concretely, assembly language programs. Reference [46] was more specific about the nature of the process language, sketching a simple ALGOL-like imperative language enriched with *wait* and *send* operations for communications via channels (see Figure 5.1). Regardless of the exact nature of the language used to express processes, it was assumed to be "sequential" in an intuitive sense, meaning that the primitive operations and control structures of the language dictated a single, completely determined sequence of computational steps, with no ambiguity about the order in which events occur. This intuition about sequentiality of processes implies certain principles of operation.

(i) Processes communicate only via input/output operations on channels (i.e. no shared variables or other implicit means of communication).

(ii) Values sent on communication channels will be received within a finite though indefinite amount of time (i.e. values communicated on a channel will not be lost or delayed forever in transit).

(iii) At most one process will output on a given channel, and at most one process will input from a given channel (i.e. two processes cannot share the same end of a channel).

(iv) Channels act like FIFO queues, so values will be received in the same order that they were sent.

(v) The only operations on channels are outputting a value, which cannot block, and inputting a value, which, if the channel is empty, will block until a value appears on the channel.

The last condition implies that there is no *polling* operation to query whether input is available on a channel without blocking, nor is there a *select* operation that can wait for input on any of several channels. Such operations would introduce behavior that depends on timing of events, introducing nondeterminacy. The third restriction is based on the assumption that `wait` and `send` are destructive operations on channels. Not being able to share channels for input is not much of a limitation, since it is easy to define a duplicator process that duplicates each input value on two output channels.

With respect to processes, we have the following assumptions.

- Processes have finite but unbounded internal memory.
- Processes run independently (except as constrained by communication), and multiple processes can run simultaneously, in parallel.

Since the output operation is nonblocking and processes can run in parallel it follows that channels have unbounded capacity. It is also assumed that channels are typed, i.e. each channel carries only values from a specified value domain D. In [45] these values could be either basic or structured, while in [46] it is assumed that only values of *simple* types are communicated, but the exact nature of the values communicated is not important as long as the primitive operations on those values are determinate and the values are not mutable.

Two other crucial intuitive properties of this model are: (1) as a process consumes more input values, it can only produce more output values, and additional inputs cannot affect earlier outputs, and (2) when a process produces an output, it can have performed only finitely many input operations, and hence any output value can only depend on finitely many input values. Viewing processes as functions over channel histories (ordered by the prefix relation), these two properties imply that they are *monotonic* and *continuous*.

5.3.4 An imperative stream processing language

Reference [46] begins with a sketch of a simple language for parallel programming based on processes communicating via channels. The language is anonymous, but we might retroactively name it ISPL, for "imperative stream processing language". The details of the base language are taken for granted, as the language is mainly meant as a concrete illustration of how sequential processes might be programmed, and the main focus was the study of the semantics of the parallel programs. The salient features of ISPL are listed here.

(i) Declarations introducing and naming typed *channels*, which are used to transmit values of specified base types like integer, real, logical (or boolean).

(ii) Operations of `wait` (blocking) and `send` (nonblocking) for performing input and output, respectively, on channels.

(iii) Declarations of *processes*, which are like procedures that when called, execute autonomous imperative programs that perform `wait` and `send` operations on input and output channels passed as arguments to the process.

(iv) A *par* operator for parallel execution of a set of process activations, linked by globally declared channels passed as parameters to the process procedures.

The principles discussed above are assumed to be satisfied by programs in this language, in particular that the processes will perform sequential computations. The body of a process is expressed in an Algol-like simple imperative language with assignment, conditionals, and loops. Process declarations are neither nested nor recursive, so a program will consist of a fixed, finite number of processes instances invoked at top level and connected in a fixed geometry determined by the channel arguments. Ordinary assignable variables can only be declared locally within process bodies.

To illustrate these concepts, we use the same program that served as the main example in [47], shown in Figure 5.1. This program gives rise to a fixed network pictured in Figure 5.2.

In the example of Figures 5.1 and 5.2, the network is closed, in the sense that all channels originate and terminate within the network. It is not obvious which channel should be regarded as representing the "result" of the computation, but we assume that it is possible to observe all of the channel histories generated during computation. In an *open* network with "dangling" channels that either have no source or no sink in the network, the dangling channel ends serve as top-level I/O ports that the network uses to communicate with the external environment.

```
Begin
   Integer channel X, Y, Z, T1, T2;
   Process f(integer in U,V; integer out W);
     Begin integer I; logical B;
        B := true;
        Repeat Begin
          I := if B then wait(U) else wait(V);
          print (I);
          send I on W;
          B := ¬ B;
          End;
     End;
   Process g(integer in U; integer out V, W);
     Begin integer I; logical B;
        B := true;
        Repeat Begin
          I := wait(U);
          if B then send I on V else send I on W;
          B := ¬ B;
          End;
     End;
   Process h(integer in U; integer out V; Integer INIT);
     Begin integer I;
        Repeat Begin
          I := wait(U);
          print (I);
          send I on V;
          End;
     End;

   f(Y,Z,X) par G(X,T1,T2) par h(T1,Y,0) par h(T2,Z,1);
End;
```

Fig. 5.1. Simple parallel program S.

Control flow is not explicitly addressed in the informal description of ISPL. The assumption is that all the processes activated in a *par* statement will run concurrently, so there is no control hierarchy among the processes (i.e. no main driver process), and all processes will run unless they are blocked waiting for input on an input channel. However, if one wanted to have a sequential control model for the process networks, the natural choice would be a demand-driven model, with demand initiated by a driver process. In this example, we might decided to view X as the principle output of the program, making the f process the obvious choice for the driver.

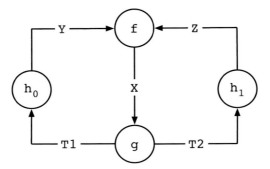

Fig. 5.2. The network for program S.

5.3.5 Semantics

As discussed above, the point of the imperative stream processing language is essentially to give concrete expression to the idea of *sequential processes*. The sequential nature of the basic process language, together with the characteristics of the wait and send operations, the restrictions placed on the way processes and channels are connected, and the assumptions about the behavior of channels mentioned above allow us to abstract from the details of what goes on within a process, and the timing of communication events. The behavior of a process can be characterized as a computable, and hence continuous, function from its input channel histories to its output channel histories. Thus by focusing on complete channel histories, we can translate any process network into a simple functional program over these histories, which we will call streams.

The stream of values transmitted over a channel carrying values from a domain D is a finite or infinite sequence of elements of D, and this domain of streams is denoted D^ω. D^ω is a complete partial order under the prefix ordering, which we can denote as $\sqsubseteq$, with the least element being Λ, the empty sequence (Reference [45] views it as a complete lattice by adding a top element).

Three basic operations are defined [45] over D^ω:

$$
\begin{aligned}
\text{HD} \quad &: \quad D^\omega \to D^\omega \\
\text{TL} \quad &: \quad D^\omega \to D^\omega \\
\text{CONS} \quad &: \quad D^\omega \times D^\omega \to D^\omega
\end{aligned}
$$

Mnemonically, HD stands for *head* (the first element of a sequence), TL stands for *tail*, and CONS stands for *construct*.[6] These are roughly the same as the conventional list operators *head*, *tail*, *cons*, except that HD returns a singleton sequence instead of an element of D and the first argument of CONS is a sequence rather than an element. They also differ from the conventional operators in terms of their behavior on Λ, where we have

$$\text{HD}(\Lambda) = \Lambda \qquad \text{TL}(\Lambda) = \Lambda \qquad \text{CONS}(\Lambda, X) = \Lambda$$

The point of these somewhat unconventional definitions is that they simplify some equations by avoiding having to move between sequence and element types and by avoiding some tests for the null sequence.

An important attribute of a sequence in D^ω is its length. The *length* of a sequence is the obvious function from D^ω to $\bar{\mathbf{N}}$, where $\bar{\mathbf{N}} = \mathbf{N} \cup \{\infty\}$ is $\mathbf{N}$ (the natural numbers) ordered numerically and topped with a maximal element ∞.

Now a network such as the one shown in Figure 5.2 can be viewed as a program schema (a graph with nodes labeled by function names and edges labeled by channel names) together with an interpretation of each node in the form of a tuple of history functions, one for each outgoing edge, taking the input streams as arguments. Thus for our example, we have functions

$$
\begin{aligned}
f \quad &: \quad \mathbf{N}^\omega \times \mathbf{N}^\omega \to \mathbf{N}^\omega \\
h \quad &: \quad \mathbf{N}^\omega \times \mathbf{N} \to \mathbf{N}^\omega \\
g_1 \quad &: \quad \mathbf{N}^\omega \to \mathbf{N}^\omega \\
g_2 \quad &: \quad \mathbf{N}^\omega \to \mathbf{N}^\omega
\end{aligned}
$$

where the node labeled **g** has two associated functions, $\mathbf{g}_1$ and $\mathbf{g}_2$, each defining the history of one of the two output channels for that node.

The recursive definitions of these history functions can be derived from the bodies of the process procedures by a variation on classical methods going back to McCarthy [57] for translating simple imperative code into recursive functions, and using the operators HD, TL, and CONS to express the effects of *waits* and *sends*. The details of this process are taken for granted in [45] and [46], and the results are illustrated by example. For

---

[6] In [46], Gilles used different names for these operators: HD becomes F (short for *first*), TL becomes R (*rest*), and CONS becomes A (*append*).

instance, the process applied to our example program yields the following set of function definitions:

$$
\begin{aligned}
f(U, V) &= \text{CONS}(\text{HD}(U), \text{CONS}(\text{HD}(V), f(\text{TL}(U), \text{TL}(V)))) \\
g_1(U) &= \text{CONS}(\text{HD}(U), g_1(\text{TL}(\text{TL}(U)))) \\
g_2(U) &= \text{CONS}(\text{HD}(\text{TL}(U)), g_2(\text{TL}(\text{TL}(U)))) \\
h(U, x) &= \text{CONS}(\langle x \rangle, U)
\end{aligned}
$$

This translation also makes manifest the determinacy of the process behaviors with respect to I/O histories, since these equations do indeed define functions. The resulting functions are also continuous, since they are defined by composition and recursion starting with continuous primitives.

Finally, the graph schema can be re-expressed as a set of equations on the sequence names representing streams. In our example, this yields the following system of equations:

$$
\begin{aligned}
X &= f(Y, Z) \\
Y &= h(T_1, 0) \\
Z &= h(T_2, 1) \\
T_1 &= g_1(X) \\
T_2 &= g_2(X)
\end{aligned}
$$

As the basis for interpreting such equations over streams, Gilles uses a generalization of the construction of fixpoints of equations over continuous operators originally due to Kleene [51], as generalized by Scott. The initial approximation to the streams is given by a tuple of empty sequences, and an ascending chain of successive approximations is built by iterating the stream functions defined by the equations to get the next approximation. The limit of this sequence is the least fixpoint solving the equations. The global determinacy of the parallel program is then a consequence of the uniqueness of the least fixpoint of such equations. [45] looks at several examples of networks and their fixed points, including the one above. As a very simple example, he shows that for the equation

$$
S = \text{CONS}(a, S)
$$

the successive approximations of the solution for X are $a, aa, \ldots a^n, \ldots$ and the value of S is the limit of this sequence of approximations, which is a^ω.

Gilles continued by showing that one could prove properties of such definitions using recently developed techniques for proving properties of recursively defined functions, including Scott and deBakker's computation induction ([74], [76]) and structural induction. As an illustration of such proof techniques, Gilles shows that the history X in the example above is equal to the sequence $0, 1, 0, 1, \ldots$.

Another technique first used in [45] is to use a simple abstract interpretation mapping sequences to their lengths to prove that a history is infinite. For instance, for the simple loop above this yields

$$length(X) \;=\; 1 \;+\; length(X)$$

and the only solution of this in the domain $\bar{\mathbf{N}}$ is ∞, thus showing that X is an infinite sequence.

5.3.6 Recursive schema – evolving process networks

Initially, Gilles' functional model deals with process programs with a fixed set of processes and fixed network geometries. The style of recursion used in defining process functions like f, g_1, g_2, and h has a particular form resulting from the translation of the iterative loops in the sequential process programs. The definitions are *quasi-tail-recursive*, i.e tail-recursive except for a leading CONS operation representing a send operation. This limited form of recursion is appropriate for stream functions representing stable, continuing elements of a network.

But Gilles next goes beyond the limitations of fixed networks by realizing that once one has functional representations of the network programs, one can use more general, non-tail-recursive definitions to express networks that evolve during computation, with processes and channels being created and destroyed dynamically. In terms of program graphs, he introduces recursive graph schemas, where a named program graph (or graphs) contain nodes labeled by that same name, and as the graph program is executed, the named node can be unfolded into another copy of the graph schema. The named schema and the corresponding named nodes have to have consistent "types", in the sense that the numbers and types of their input and output channels have to agree. The example used in [46] is illustrated in Figure 5.3, where the types of channels I, I′, and I″ have to agree, and similarly for O, O′, and O″.

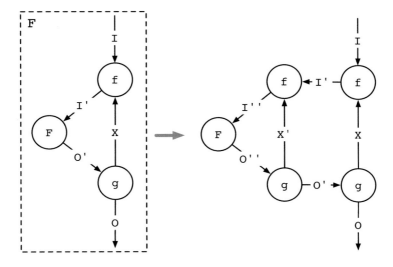

Fig. 5.3. A recursive schema.

The functional representation for this particular recursive network is defined by the (non-tail-recursive!) equations:

$$O \;=\; F(I)$$
$$F(I) \;=\; g_2(F(f(I,X)))$$
$$X \;=\; g_1(F(f(I,X)))$$

The concept of dynamic networks is just sketched in [45] and [46], and illustrated using abstract examples involving uninterpreted schemas. No operational model for executing such programs is suggested, and in particular there is no discussion of how the imperative process language (ISPL) might be extended to support dynamic networks. There are also no realistic applications presented in these papers. However, dynamic networks became a major topic in the next paper in the series, [47], which we will consider in the next section.

5.3.7 Schematology

Schematology (roughly, the study of properties of generic programs involving uninterpreted function symbols) was a fairly active area in the early 1970s [54], and Gilles was able to apply or generalize some known results to his process networks via their functional interpretation. Between [45] and [46], Gilles collaborated with Bruno Courcelle and Jean Vuillemin [26], to prove several general results that apply in particular to the basic graph program schemas representing static process networks with uninterpreted process nodes. These results show that the equivalence of such schemas is decidable and there exists a unique minimal schema equivalent to any given schema. Another observation is that general equations for fixpoints such as the following (from [81])

$$\mu x.g(f(x, i)) \quad = \quad g(\mu x.f(g(x, i)))$$

can be translated into equivalences between corresponding graph schema programs.

5.3.8 Observations and summary

Gilles argues that despite the limitations imposed to maintain determinacy, this language is still expressive enough to be useful. And determinism simplifies reasoning, because we are able to reason about complex systems without having to deal with the complications of state and nondeterministic changes in state in a parallel program, or the details of timing and synchronization of events. The sequentiality property guarantees that the behavior of processes can be modeled by continuous *functions* mapping their input streams to their output streams, and the communication discipline based on queue-like, non-shared channels ensures that the behavior of whole programs can be expressed as a unique fixpoint of equations derived from the connection topology of the program. Another desirable property of the model that follows from this semantics is that the concepts are closed under composition and recursion.

Gilles also notes that in principle, proofs can be mechanically checked in a theorem proving system like Milner's prover for LCF, the earliest version of which had recently been developed by Milner and Weyrauch at Stanford [63, 65].

Another major contribution of these papers that emerges in retrospect is that they include what can be viewed as the earliest description of a lazy functional language. The functional translation of network programs introduces non-strict functions over the data structure of lazy lists or streams, and cycles in the network introduce recursive definitions of stream data structures. The model also shows that such functional programs support parallel execution without losing determinacy.

5.4 Implementation, evolution, experimentation

Now we turn to the part of the history of Kahn networks in which I personally was involved, and which was reported in [47]. Gilles and I were both in Edinburgh for the 1975–76 academic year: I had arrived in May to join Rod Burstall's research group in the School of Artificial Intelligence and Gilles arrived in the late summer for a year's visit.

I had become interested in coroutines and related "nonstandard" control structures, and by the winter of 1976 I was experimenting with implementing coroutines in the POP-10 language[7] [19], which was the main language used in the School of Artificial Intelligence at Edinburgh at that time. POP-10 had provided a kind of delimited first-class continuation, with operations `barrierapply` (a control delimiter), `appstate` (call/cc), and `reinstate` (throw).[8] I told Gilles about my experiments and he suggested that we try implementing the language from his 1974 paper. We soon had a prototype running complete with new concrete syntax using POP-10's syntax macros.

The resulting language was described in [47], but it was not given a name, so let us retroactively call it ISPL-POP since it is embedded in POP-10. The basic expression and statement syntax of ISPL-POP was inherited from POP-10, so it differed superficially from the Algol-based syntax of ISPL in [46]. The primitive I/O operations on channels were also renamed, with *wait* replaced by GET and *send* e *on* C being written as PUT(e,C). The *par* operation was replaced by a statement of the form

    doco <channel decls>; <process calls> closeco

in which a declaration of fresh local channels is followed by a sequence of process calls applying process functions to channels. A *doco* statement could appear at top level as the argument of a *start* command, or embedded as the last statement in the body of a process function. In the later case, the process instance would use the *doco* statement to permanently *reconfigure* itself into the specified subnetwork, and the channels passed to process invocations could be either freshly created or

---

[7] POP-10 was a port of POP-2 to the DEC 10 computer recently acquired by Edinburgh [28].

[8] My coroutine experiments revealed some performance and semantic bugs in this feature that were corrected by Robert Rae later in 1976.

```
Process INTEGERS out QO;
  Vars N; 1 -> N; repeat INCREMENT N; PUT(N,QO) forever
Endprocess;

Process FILTER PRIME in QI out QO;
  Vars N;
  repeat GET(QI) -> N;
          if (N MOD PRIME) \= 0 then PUT(N,QO) close
  forever
Endprocess;

Process SIFT in QI out QO;
  Vars PRIME; GET(QI) -> PRIME;
  PUT(PRIME,QO);
  doco channels Q;
        FILTER(PRIME,QI,Q); SIFT(Q,QO)
  closeco
Endprocess;

Process OUTPUT in QI;
  repeat PRINT(GET(QI)) forever
Endprocess;

Start doco channels Q1 Q2;
          INTEGERS(Q1); SIFT(Q1,Q2); OUTPUT(Q2)
      closeco;
```

Fig. 5.4. Sieve of Eratosthenes.

inherited from the parent process. This gives rise to dynamic changes in the geometry of networks, as anticipated by the recursive network schemes described in [45] and [46].

As an example, Figure 5.4 reproduces the ISPL-POP version of the Sieve of Eratosthenes program inspired by McIlroy's coroutine version in [59]. Note that the body of the process SIFT ends in a *doco* statement that effectively replaces the SIFT process with a network of two new processes that inherit the current instance's input and output channels and communicate between themselves on a fresh internal channel, Q. This is a concrete example of the recursive schema from [45, 46].

The I/O operations GET and PUT have essentially the same semantics as the *wait* and *send* operations of the earlier ISPL, and there is the same restriction that a channel can only have one source, i.e. only one process (at a time) performs output on it. But ISPL-POP treats reading from a channel as nondestructive, so that two or more processes can consume input from a channel without interfering with one another. This is because channels are implemented as dynamically generated linked lists,[9] and when a channel is bound to an input port variable Q, Q is just a pointer into the list representing the channel, and `GET(Q)` returns the next element of the list designated by Q while setting `Q := tail(Q)`.

5.4.1 Toward a functional notation

As in References [45] and [46], the critical observation is that processes express *functions* from their input channel histories to their output channel histories, or in other words, stream functions. In order to more directly reflect the functional semantics of [45, 46], we wanted to evolve the ISPL-POP language into a more functional form, principally by treating the input and output channels of processes as stream *values* constituting arguments and results of a process call.

The first step toward a more functional notation was, for the common case of processes with a single output channel, to treat the output channel not as a parameter but as a result of process invocation. Following the POP-10 notation for functions with named return values, we use the alternate declaration notation:

```
Process SIFT in QI => QO;
```

This allows us to create a pipeline of process activations (with anonymous connecting streams) using an applicative expression:

```
doco SIFT(FILTER(PRIME,QI)) => QO closeco
```

This also expresses, with the notation "`=> QO`" the *splicing* of the result stream of the expression `SIFT(FILTER(PRIME,QI))` as the *stream continuation* of the output stream `QO` of the parent process.

```
Process SIFT in QI => QO;
  Vars PRIME; GET(QI) -> PRIME;
  PUT(PRIME,QO);
  doco SIFT(FILTER(PRIME,QI)) => QO closeco
Endprocess;
```

This *doco* statement can occur only at the end of the SIFT process (a *tail doco*?), as shown above, and the effect is that the parent SIFT process terminates and continuation of its output stream becomes the

---

[9] This was a natural choice for a POP-10 based implementation, because of its dynamic lists.

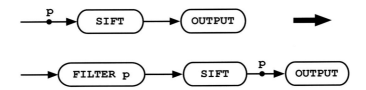

Fig. 5.5. The evolving Sieve network.

responsibility of the new SIFT process created by the nested *doco*. The result is that we have an *evolving* network, as illustrated in Figure 5.5.

As another step toward a functional stream language, we use splicing to define a *cons* process for consing a value onto an input stream, corresponding to the semantic CONS primitive in [45] (or the A operator of [46]):

```
Process CONS in QI => QO;
  PUT(A,QO)
  doco QI => QO closeco
Endprocess;
```

Then we can use this stream function to make SIFT even more functional by replacing the imperative PUT command with a call of CONS in the continuation expression.

```
Process SIFT in QI => QO;
  Vars PRIME; GET(QI) -> PRIME;
  doco CONS(PRIME,SIFT(FILTER(PRIME,QI))) => QO closeco
Endprocess;
```

One more language construct, a version of Landin's *whererec*, is added to allow *doco* reconfiguration statements to create cyclic subnetworks, thus eliminating the need for explicit channel declarations and the passing of output channels to processes in order to create cyclic networks. As a simple example, the following program generates the sequence of all natural numbers, assuming PLUS(n,Q) adds n to each element of the stream Q.

```
Start doco OUTPUTF(X)
         where channels X is CONS(0,PLUS(1,X))
       closeco
```

Or for a more complicated example here is our often cited solution of a problem posed by Dijkstra (to generate the sequence of all positive integers of the form $2^a 3^b 5^c$ where $a, b, c \geq 0$, in order):

```
Start doco OUTPUTF(X)
       where channels X,Y,Z are
    CONS(1,MERGE(TIMES(2,X),Y)),
    CONS(3,MERGE(TIMES(3,Y),Z)),
    CONS(5,TIMES(5,Z))
    closeco
```

where `TIMES` is scalar multiplication of an integer stream by an integer, and `MERGE` merges two ordered streams into one (suppressing duplicates, though in this version there will be none).

Having replaced the imperative `PUT` with `CONS`, we can also express input in a functional style by introducing `HEAD` and `TAIL` operations on streams. However, the emerging functional language for stream processing is still embedded in the imperative language, and at the top level a program must consist of one or more process calls, linked by channels either explicitly in the procedural style, or by applicative expressions with *where*-definitions for cycles. Thus streams were still not quite first-class values and the simple functional language for streams is approximated but not quite achieved.

Another obvious limitation is that our functional form of process can only have a single output channel (i.e. only return a single output stream). Thus we have to fall back to the imperative style to express some natural stream operations like splitting a stream into two streams by taking alternate elements, which is naturally performed by the process g in Figure 5.1. In the functional semantics of Kahn73/74, this problem is handled by splitting the process into multiple processes, (in this case $g1$ and $g2$) each responsible for just one of the output streams, but typically duplicating work. A more efficient functional programming solution would be to express the g process as a mutually recursive definition of two stream functions, each mapping a stream to a pair of output streams, but there is still some extra overhead in constructing and destructing the stream pairs at each level of recursion.

5.4.2 Operational semantics

Now let us consider execution strategies for ISPL-POP programs. The the initial implementation used a sequential, demand-driven, coroutine mode of execution. In this mode, when a network is created there is a designated driver process (by convention the last process created). Control passes from a consumer of a stream to the producer of the stream when input from the stream is attempted and there are no elements available (the channel is designated *hungry*), and control returns to the consumer when the producer outputs on a hungry channel. Later we added a fair process scheduler to simulate parallel execution as envisioned in [46].

The coroutine mode performs the minimum computation, while the concurrent mode can take advantage of multiple processors but may perform nonessential computation, including the creation of unnecessary processes and channels. Both modes are capable of encountering deadlocks, where a process is waiting for input on a stream whose producer is also blocked on input that in turn ultimately depends on the first process making progress.

For the concurrent mode of execution, where there is a danger of runaway computation, we experimented with a throttling method involving an integer *anticipation coefficient* $A(C)$ for each channel C. A single producer process will run until the number of unconsumed items in its output channel reaches $A(C)$. This is easily implemented for the imperative process language by having the state of a channel include the number of unconsumed items in the channel, and having this number be updated by the GET and PUT operations. This scheme is limited by the restriction to single-output processes, and it also doesn't transfer naturally to the functional interpretation of channels where channels are just pointers to a position in a pure stream value.

In terms of program proofs, [47] reiterated the techniques described in [46], providing additional proof sketches for the Dijkstra program and the Sieve of Eratosthenes. As before, the proofs depended on a variant of recursion induction [58] and a form of structural induction (co-induction) for proving that properties hold on an infinite stream by showing that they hold for a set of finite initial segments of unbounded lengths, and that the property is *admissible* (the analog of continuity for predicates).

We also applied a technique from [45] to prove freedom from deadlock by showing that an output stream was infinite in length, using a simple form of abstract interpretation where we map a stream to its length and interpret a stream function abstractly as a mapping from lengths (of input streams) to lengths (of output streams).

5.4.3 Stream programming experiments

Once ISPL-POP was implemented, we had motivation and opportunity to explore a wide range of stream processing applications beyond the small examples found in the previous papers. We implemented a variety of standard algorithms and data structures.

- Sorting algorithms (bubble sort, insertion sort, merge sort, topological sort).
- Several additional variants on the prime sieve program, including one that used priority queues.
- Generating the stream of Fibonacci numbers.
- A coroutine version of the equalfringe function using streams [41].
- A generator of the Pascal triangle.
- A generator of lucky numbers.
- A program that searches for solutions of $x_1^n + y_1^n = x_2^n + y_2^n$.
- A pipeline version of Yates' method for the discrete Fourier transform.

A more extensive example involved representing formal power series as streams of coefficients and writing stream programs to implement a variety of operations on power series, such as arithmetic operations, differentiation and integration, logarithms and exponentials, and trigonometric functions (sine, cosine, etc.). An interesting discovery about the series operations was that many of the operations could be expressed in terms of cyclic process networks. For instance, the inverse function on power series was defined as follows:

```
Process INVERSE in V => W;
  Vars V0; GET(V) -> V0;
  if V0 = 0 then COMPLAIN('Div by zero') close;
  doco T ==> W
      where T is CONS(1/V0,(-1/V0) */ T /*/ V) closeco
Endprocess;
```

where `*/` is scalar multiplication by a number, and `/*/` gives the product of two power series. Some years later, Doug McIllroy continued to develop the power series example and implemented it in a variety of stream-supporting languages [60, 61, 62].

The final relatively large-scale example that we developed involved infinite precision real arithmetic using algorithms developed by Wiedmer in [84]. Real numbers were represented as streams of variable radix coefficients. This application proved more challenging and the expression of the operations less elegant, mainly because the streams had to be renormalized frequently to prevent the radixes from growing excessively.

Through these experimental applications, we verified that the ISPL-POP language was adequate for expressing the stream-based algorithms that we had in mind, and that in certain applications, like power series, there were interesting ways of exploiting recursive stream definitions (i.e. cyclic networks). In the course of debugging and informal performance analysis of the programs, we discovered a couple of pitfalls. One of these was that it was quite possible to have bugs that would lead to deadlock, but when this occurred it was usually fairly easy, for the relatively small programs we were writing, to analyze the source of the deadlock. Deadlocks were typically caused by mismatched production rates or lack of adequate "priming" of channels.

The other pitfall was that some programs had serious space leaks due to a phenomenon that might be called "demand mismatch." This occurred in two related situations: (1) if a stream was being shared by two (or more) consumers, with one consumer reading the stream at a much faster rate than the other, then a longer and longer segment of live stream elements would build up in the interval between the positions of the two consumers in the stream, and (2) a process with two outputs might have a fast consumer on one output and a much slower consumer on the other output (this is really a generalization of the first situation to processes generating pairs of streams). With pseudo-concurrent execution, there was also the problem of runaway execution and creation of redundant processes whose outputs would never be used, or would be used only long after they were generated.

The source code for many of these examples is still available from the current author, though unfortunately the POP-10 source code for the implementation of ISPL-POP itself has been lost.

5.4.4 Summary

The main contribution of [47] was to report on an actual implementation, ISPL-POP, of the imperative stream processing language ISPL sketched in [46], and to show how that imperative language could evolve by the addition of a few features (functional processes, `CONS`, `HEAD`, and `TAIL` operations, and recursive stream definitions using *where*) most of the way toward the functional language for streams given as a semantics for the imperative language in the earlier papers [45, 46]. The other main enhancement of ISPL-POP relative to the earlier ISPL was the ability to implement the dynamically evolving networks that were suggested by the recursive network schemas of [45, 46].

The implementation was fairly straightforward: it was embedded in POP-2 which supplied the basic data structures and basic imperative/ functional control constructs. Additional special syntax was provided through macros, while processes were implemented using POP-2's delimited continuation feature, and streams were represented using POP-2's dynamic lists. Performance was not a primary concern, but it was good enough that all our experimental programs ran acceptably fast on the hardware of the day (DEC PDP10).

In terms of semantics, [47] described two modes of execution – the concurrent or parallel mode assumed in the earlier papers, and also a sequential, demand-driven coroutine mode. A key observation was that the choice between these execution modes had no effect on the denotational semantics of programs as stream functions. The semantics remains exactly the same as in the earlier papers, but the language evolved so that it could come fairly close to directly expressing that semantics.

Meanwhile, more or less contemporarily with the research reported in [47], lazy functional languages were being described and implemented that could even more directly capture the functional semantic definitions from [45, 46]. These included Ashcroft and Wadge's Lucid [5, 6], which in its early form could express a subset of the functional stream programs, Turner's SASL [78], which could handle all of them, and probably also the lazy LISP variants described in [40] and [35]. These parallel developments in lazy functional languages are explored further below in Section 5.6.

5.5 Theoretical foundations: concrete domains

Although [46] presented a semi-formal denotational semantics for his process networks, based on an informal notion of sequentiality of the processes, Gilles wanted to develop a more rigorous semantic foundation for stream processing networks and similar modes of incremental computation on data structures. When he arrived in Edinburgh at the end of the summer of 1975, he began collaborating with Gordon Plotkin on this problem.

The result, first written up as a manuscript draft dated December 1975 [48], was a theory of *concrete domains*, which were designed to model forms of data, in contrast with domains modeling functions or procedures. Concrete domains were meant not only to encompass familiar finite data values like integers and finite structures built from them, such as tuples, sums, and lists, but also potentially infinite structures like streams that could be computed incrementally, as, for example, in Kahn networks.

The definition of concrete domains started with a standard notion of domain (ω-algebraic, coherent, complete partial orders) and added additional order-theoretic properties that distinguish "data" domains from more general domains. They also developed a representation theory for this class of concrete domains in terms of concrete structures they called *information matrices*, and which Gérard Berry later called *concrete data structures*. In further unpublished work Gilles and Gordon Plotkin showed that concrete domains could be used as the basis for defining a precise notion of sequential function.

The Kahn–Plotkin theory of concrete domains and sequential functions provided a rigorous basis for specifying the semantics of Kahn networks with the coroutine mode of execution discussed in [47]. The manuscript of 1975 lead to an INRIA technical report [42], and then eventual publication in *Theoretical Computer Science* [43]. That publication was accompanied by an excellent historical introduction by Stephen Brookes [15] that explains both the origins of the work in developing a semantics for Kahn networks, and the substantial further development (up to 1993) by many researchers, notably Gerard Berry and Pierre-Louis Curien (sequential algorithms, CDS [12, 13]), Glynn Winskel (event structures [85]), and Brookes himself [14]. The concrete domains that arose out of the theoretical investigation of Kahn networks are highly relevant to several foundational problems, including the notion of a sequential function, fully abstract models, the semantics of parallel computation, and the semantics of lazy functional languages.

5.6 Lazy functional languages

Functional programming is a particularly natural context for the stream-processing paradigm, and particularly lazy functional programming. We have seen that Gilles' work was preceded by Landin's design ISWIM (the first true functional language) in the mid-1960s and his invention of a functional representation of streams. But when *lazy* functional languages began to emerge in the mid-1970s it quickly became apparent that the functional semantics of Gilles' graph programs could be directly expressed in such languages. The development of *lazy* functional languages began with the theoretical insights of Wadsworth and Vuillemin.

Wadsworth and Vuillemin in their PhD theses [82], [80] independently developed theoretical models for pure functional programming that included a technique for eliminating wasted computation. Wadsworth called this "call-by-need" while Vuillemin called his version the "delay rule". These techniques were similar in that they modified the classic call-by-name discipline to avoid duplicating computational tasks by sharing them and memoizing their results. Wadsworth achieved sharing by maintaining the terms being reduced as directed acyclic graphs.

The lazy functional languages followed LISP in making lists the central data structure, but they incorporated suspended computation and memoization into these data structures so that they could also represent potentially infinite streams. Although Gilles presented the functional form of stream processing as a semantics for an imperative process language, and did not describe an operational semantics for the functional form, this language did anticipate the kinds of programs one could write with (potentially infinite) lists in later lazy functional languages. A demand driven, i.e. lazy, mode of execution for these functional stream programs was a natural operational semantics, corresponding to the coroutine mode of execution.

Several other investigations of lazy evaluation were going on in parallel during the mid 1970s. These included Ashcroft and Wadge's Lucid language, the 1976 papers by Henderson and Morris, and Friedman and Wise, and the SASL language of David Turner. At the same time, Milner and his colleagues[10] at Edinburgh were resurrecting and enhancing Landin's ISWIM as ML, the metalanguage of the LCF theorem prover.

5.6.1 Lucid

Work on Lucid began at Waterloo University in 1974, and several papers emerged in 1975 through 1977 [5, 6, 8]. The central idea of Lucid was to abstract from the semantics of a simple imperative language with variables and assignment, conditional expressions and loops by focusing on the history of values assigned to a variable through the iterations of a loop. These iteration variable histories are sequences of values, which may be infinite in the case of a nonterminating loop, and even in the case of a terminating loop they can be extended to an infinite sequence by repeating the last value.

Lucid treated its variables as representing these complete histories, instead of the value at any particular instant. To simulate the effect of imperative loops, Lucid used limited forms of declarative equations

---

[10] Lockwood Morris, Malcolm Newey, Mike Gordon, and Chris Wadsworth

on variables, in conjunction with certain operators on histories such as
`first`, `next`, and `as soon as`. Thus, an imperative program like

```
I := 0;
while true do
  I := I + 1
end
```

would be represented in Lucid by the equations

```
first I = 0;
next I = I + 1;
```

Constant integer values are represented by constant histories, and
arithmetic operators like $+$ are extended pointwise to apply to two
histories or a history and a number. Loop termination is modeled by
the "`as soon as`" operator: if T is a history of a boolean variable, then
J `as soon as` T yields a constant (history) equal to the element of J
corresponding to the first true element of T.

Many simple imperative programs can be translated into this
equational language, and it then becomes possible to reason about the
histories using a set of axioms reflecting the semantics of the basic
operators (plus some additional modal operators such as `eventually`
and `hitherto`), and standard logical and algebraic reasoning methods.
So Lucid is presented as both a declarative programming language and
a logic for proving properties of programs.

If we view Lucid's histories as streams, it is obvious that Lucid can be
used as a stream processing language, expressing streams as solutions
of recursive equations. For instance, the equations for I above are equivalent to:

```
I = 0 :: (I + 1);
```

More complicated programs can be modeled using nested loops that
allow subsidiary equations to be expressed relative to each iteration of
an outer loop. The operations on histories were enriched with a cons
operator, `followed by`, and a filter operator `whenever` [6].

Initially, Lucid lacked the ability to define functions on histories, so it
was not possible, for instance, to express an ordered merge operation on
two ordered histories. But soon user-defined pointwise operations, called
mappings, and then general recursive definitions of history functions,
called *transformations* were added [7] to the language. This made it
possible to define recursive functions over histories and thus perform
general stream-processing.

The semantics of Lucid's core equational language subsumed that of a typical lazy functional language, but it was more general because histories were treated as a "random access" rather than a sequential access data structure. This meant that it was possible to have rather unusual recursive definitions, where, for instance, a value in a history could be defined recursively in terms of the *future* of the history. These kinds of definitions, however, did not seem to usefully increase the power of the language, and Lucid programs would normally fall within the range of those expressible in conventional functional languages.

Later on [9, 10], the syntax of Lucid evolved to be more like other functional languages, and a combination of Lucid and Landin's ISWIM emerged, called *Luswim*.

5.6.2 Lazy pure LISP

Morris and Henderson proposed a lazy evaluator for a dialect of pure LISP [56]. The syntax is slightly simplified, static binding is assumed instead of dynamic binding, and a FUNARG expression form is added to represent suspended evaluations (i.e. a pair consisting of an expression and an environment). The lazy evaluator is defined by giving an interpreter that operates on expressions stored in labeled cells in a memory. Evaluation proceeds by overwriting cells with the value of their stored expressions, sometimes allocating new cells in the process (e.g. for function application). A denotational semantics is given for the lazy language, and a soundness argument is sketched, showing that the evaluator is consistent with the semantics.

The evaluator defines a fully lazy LISP variant that suspends evaluation of all function arguments until they are acted upon by strict primitive operations. CONS is treated as a nonstrict primitive that does not evaluate its arguments, so lists can represent infinite streams. Examples showing the capabilities of lazy evaluation include a recursive definition of an infinite list, the prime sieve example, and the same fringe example from [41] (a coroutine solution for the problem of testing whether two binary trees have the same list of leaf nodes).

Friedman and Wise [35] took a somewhat more implementation-oriented approach to defining a lazy variant of LISP. They start by simply suggesting that the primitive `cons` operation should separately suspend evaluation of its two arguments, storing those suspensions in the car and cdr fields of the newly allocated cons cell. The primitives `car` and `cdr` are correspondingly modified to coerce the suspensions of

the respective components when they are applied. They then modify
McCarthy's metacircular interpreter for LISP 1.0 [57] by simply substituting these new versions of `cons`, `car`, and `cdr` for the original strict
versions, and they observe that the result is a fully lazy LISP interpreter
where every function is lazy by default, except for the strict primitives
like `atom` and `eq`.

They note that any stream processing function written for Landin's
streams will also work with their lazy list data type, but that it is more
general since it supports traversal of lists where some of the list elements
may be undefined, as long as the traversal does not need their values.

The Henderson–Morris and Friedman–Wise versions of lazy LISP are
essentially equivalent in their behavior. The LABEL form traditionally
used for expressing a recursive function is generalized (at least
in Henderson and Morris's evaluator), to allow recursive stream
expressions.

5.6.3 SASL, KRC, and Miranda

David Turner began working on a simple functional language around
1972–73, and this evolved into SASL (Saint Andrews Static Language)
[78] in 1976, when lazy evaluation was added. SASL can be considered
the beginning of the evolution that lead to Haskell, and SASL programs
would look very familiar to anyone who knows Haskell.

SASL was dynamically typed, with a spare, calculator-like syntax.
Its fixed repertoire of data types included integers, booleans, strings,
and lists. It inherited a number of features from ISWIM, such as simple
structure definitions (bindings with list patterns), *where*-clauses, and the
use of the colon for list cons.

SASL had recursive function definitions with multiple equations or
clauses, and multi-argument functions were typically curried. There were
no lambda expressions or anonymous function expressions – all functions
were defined either at top-level or in a where clause. Lists as well as
functions could be defined recursively.

Since SASL is a lazy functional language with lists and recursive
definitions of both functions and lists, it is easy to express examples like
the prime sieve and the Hamming problem in SASL.

Turner followed SASL with a second-generation language called
KRC (Kent Recursive Calculator) [79]. KRC was a relatively minor
update from SASL, with almost identical syntax except for the use of
square brackets for lists. The major language innovation introduced by

KRC was the addition of list comprehensions (*ZF expressions*).[11] KRC
retained the features of SASL supporting stream processing programs,
but list comprehensions could sometimes produce even more concise
expressions of these algorithms, as illustrated by this KRC version of
the prime sieve program (where "%" is the integer mod function):

```
primes = sieve [2..]
sieve (p:x) = p : sieve n; n <- x; n%p > 0
```

Miranda [77] followed SASL and KRC in the mid-1980s and added a
statically checked type system with polymorphic types based on the type
systems of ML and Hope. It also retained SASL and KRC's support
for stream processing. Miranda was a direct ancestor of Haskell [66],
which also inherited these earlier languages' stream processing features,
as shown by the following Haskell version of the Hamming Problem
program:

```
merge xs [] = xs
merge [] ys = ys
merge (x:xs) (y:ys) =
  if (x == y) then x : merge xs ys
  else if (x < y) then x : merge xs (y:ys)
  else y : merge (x:xs) ys
times n (x:xs) = (n * x) : times n xs
h = 1 : merge (times 2 h) (merge (times 3 h) (times 5 h))
```

5.6.4 Streams in strict functional languages

Although lazy functional languages have an obvious advantage in being
able to represent streams directly in terms of their built-in list types,
streams have become a very commonly used structure in strict functional
languages as well. It is, of course, possible to use Landin-style streams
in strict functional languages, but it is more common to use a stream
implementation supporting memoization.

Scheme, for instance, being a lexically scoped dialect of LISP, is
a strict functional language. As explained in Chapter 3 of [1] one
can define stream operations in terms of more basic delay and force
operations that respectively create a suspension and force evaluation
of it. A semi-lazy stream cons operation (`cons-stream`) can be defined
as a macro such that the expression (`cons-stream e1 e2`) expands to
(`cons e1 (delay e2)`). Then stream `head` is defined to the same as
`car` while the stream `tail` operation is given by:

---

[11] List comprehensions were also added to a later edition of SASL in 1979.

```
(define (tail stream) (force (cdr stream)))
```

The delay operator in turn is defined as a macro that suspends its argument expression by wrapping it with a lambda abstraction and passes it to a memoizing functional that produces a function equivalent to the suspension (assuming no side effects) but evaluating the suspended expression only the first time it is used. Since scheme supports data-level recursion, it is possible to define recursive streams:

```
(define ones (cons-stream 1 ones))
```

Another strict functional language, Hope, was developed in Edinburgh in the late 1970s [21], inspired by the functional equational language used by Burstall and Darlington in their research on program derivation [20, 18], and incorporating the polymorphic type system of LCF/ML [36] enhanced by algebraic data types and pattern matching. Although this was a strict language, a special lazy cons operation was added specifically to support lazy lists or streams, and a **whererec** declaration form supported direct recursive definitions of streams. Thus Hope had built-in facilities and syntax support for stream programming.

ML is a strict functional language directly inspired by ISWIM. Stream libraries are widely and routinely used in ML programming, though without macros, ML provides less syntactic sugar than Scheme and the suspension lambda abstractions are explicit. A typical definition of a semi-lazy stream type in Standard ML would be

```
datatype 'a susp = EVAL of 'a | UNEVAL of unit -> 'a
datatype 'a stream = Nils | Conss of 'a * 'a stream susp ref
fun cons (x, f) = Conss(x, ref(UNEVAL f))
fun head (Conss(x,_)) = x
fun force (ref(EVAL x)) = x
  | force (s as ref(UNEVAL f)) =
    let val x = f() in s := EVAL x; x end
fun tail (Conss(_,y) = force y
```

Use of the **cons** operator as in the function definition

```
fun ints n = cons(n, (fn () => ints(n+1)))
```

requires an explicit function abstraction to create the suspension. Also, because ML does not support data-level recursion, it is not possible to have direct recursive definitions of streams.

To overcome the problem of explicit suspensions, Phil Wadler, Walid Taha, and I developed an extension of Standard ML supporting the definition of lazy datatypes and lazy functions over such datatypes [55], and this design was implemented as an experimental feature of the SML/NJ compiler [4]. It is also possible in principle to add data-level recursive definitions to Standard ML.

The fundamental insight of [46] was that the computation performed by Kahn networks could be expressed as recursive operations on streams and recursive definitions of streams. This insight led us to evolve from an imperative process language toward a functional language for streams in [47]. But at the same time, lazy functional languages were emerging that proved to have the necessary features to express the functional semantics of Kahn networks, and the creators of these languages saw Kahn networks as a natural area of application demonstrating the expressive power of lazy functional programming. Some of the stream programs we developed have become standard examples in the literature of functional programming, and stream processing techniques have become part of the standard tool set in functional programming.

On the other hand, it has to be admitted that gems like the Hamming Problem and the recursive definition of the Fibonacci stream do not seem to be representative of applications of stream processing at a larger scale. Experience has shown that most realistic applications turn out to involve linear, or at least acyclic, networks.

5.7 Lasting impact of kahn networks

In the 30 years since Gilles' invention of Kahn networks and development of the related theory, the influence of this work has spread widely and touched many parts of computer science. In functional languages, both lazy and strict, the stream processing paradigm has become a routine aspect of programming. Even in conventional systems programming streams are a common abstraction, playing an important role in shell languages, I/O libraries (from Standard ML [68] to Java [39]), networking [69], signal processing [33], computer graphics and data management (e.g. streaming query languages). The notion has even leaked into the quotidian world of consumer technology and entertainment in the form of "streaming media."

Some of these manifestations of the stream concept, like filters and pipes in the Unix shell, or early data flow models, arose before or independently of Gilles' work on streams, but his work provided for the first time a clear, elegant, and principled understanding of these phenomena, and tools for reasoning about the behavior of stream processing. The theoretical legacy of Kahn networks is also connected to the development of Kahn–Plotkin concrete domains and the impact of that work on the development of the concept of sequentiality.

Several variations on Kahn networks and stream processing have been defined and studied in the succeeding years, including synchronous Kahn networks [23], N-synchronous Kahn networks [2], abstract synchronous networks [2], among many others, and Gilles' basic insight that networks can be modeled by recursive functions over streams has been elevated to the status of a general Principle (the Kahn Principle).

Finally, Kahn networks have a strong legacy for language design, with a number of important languages owing part of their inspiration to Gilles' work on streams. These would include the synchronous data flow language LUSTRE [22, 38], SISAL, and Functional Reactive Programming [83].

5.8 Conclusions

The development of Kahn networks as a programming technique, a semantic model, and a basis for tractable reasoning about concurrent programs is a model of clear development. The guiding principle behind Gilles' work in general, and Kahn networks in particular, is that mathematical abstractions and formal semantics are valuable tools in the design of computing artifacts.

My aim in this work has been to show how this work is connected to ideas from several important lines of development, including data flow, coroutines, Landin's streams, and the early development of lazy functional programming.

I also claim that the functional semantics of Kahn networks should be considered an early functional language supporting either a lazy, demand-driven or a concurrent operational model. The architectural ideas, semantics, and reasoning techniques associated with this model became a part of the core culture of functional programming.

However, the influence of these ideas was not restricted to functional programming. It had a continuing influence on modeling and analyzing concurrent programs, on specification languages, on software architecture, and on systems programming.

5.9 Acknowledgements

I wish to thank Doug McIlroy for useful background information on the history of coroutines and the development of the Unix shell, Jack Dennis for material on the early development of data flow models, and David Turner for information on the early history of SASL. I also thank the editors of this volume for their patience and forbearance during the long gestation of this paper, and the anonymous reviewers for their comments.

Bibliography

[1]   H. Abelson, G. J. Sussman, and J. Sussman. *Structure and Interpretation of Computer Programs*. McGraw-Hill, New York, 1985.

[2]   S. Abramsky. A generalized Kahn principle for abstract asynchronous networks. In *Mathematical Foundations of Programming Semantics, 5th International Conference*, pp. 1–21. Springer-Verlag, 1989.

[3]   D. A. Adams. *A Computation Model with Data Flow Sequencing*. PhD thesis, Computer Science Dept, Stanford University, December 1968. Technical Report CS-117.

[4]   A. Appel and D. B. MacQueen. Standard ml of new jersey. In J. Maluszynski and M. Wirsing (eds) *Programming Language Implementation and Logic Programming, Proceedings of the 3rd International Symposium*, volume 528 Lecture Notes in Computer Science, pp. 1–13. Springer Verlag, 1991.

[5]   A. E. Ashcroft. Program proving without tears. In G. Huet and G. Kahn (eds) *Symposium on Proving and Improving Programs*, pp. 99–111. INRIA Rocquencourt, July 1975.

[6]   A. E. Ashcroft and W. W. Wadge. Lucid – a formal system for writing and proving programs. *SIAM J. Comput.*, **5**:519–526, 1976.

[7]   A. E. Ashcroft and W. W. Wadge. *Lucid: Scope Structures and Defined Functions*. Technical Report Rep. CS-76-22, Computer Science Dept., University of Waterloo, 1976.

[8]   A. E. Ashcroft and W. W. Wadge. Lucid, a nonprocedural language with iteration. *Commun. ACM*, **20**(7):519–526, 1977.

[9]   A. E. Ashcroft and W. W. Wadge. *Structured Lucid*. Technical Report CS-79-21, Computer Science Department, University of Waterloo, 1979.

[10]   A. E. Ashcroft and W. W. Wadge. *Lucid, the Dataflow Programming Language*. Number 22 in APIC Studies in Data Processing. Academic Press, 1985.

[11]   J. L. Baer. A survey of some theoretical aspects of multiprocessing. *ACM Comput. Surv.*, **5**(1):31–80, 1973.

[12]   G. Berry and P.-L. Currien. Sequential algorithms on concrete data structures. *Theoret. Comput. Sci.*, **20**:265–322, 1982.

[13]   G. Berry and P.-L. Currien. The kernel of the applicative language cds: theory and practice. In *Proc. French-US Seminar on the Applications of Algebra to Language Definition and Compilation*, pp. 35–87. Cambridge University Press, 1985.

[14]   S. Brookes and S. Geva. Continuous functions and parallel algorithms on concrete data structures. In *Proc. 7th International Conf. on Mathematical*

Foundations of Programming Semantics, volume 598 in Lecture Notes in Computer Science, 1991.

[15] S. Brookes. Historical introduction to "concrete domains" by G. Kahn and G. D. Plotkin. *Theoret. Comput. Sci.*, **121**(1-2):179–186, 1993.

[16] W. H. Burge. *Recursive Programming Techniques*. Addison Wesley, 1975.

[17] W. H. Burge. Stream processing functions. *IBM J. Res. Develop.*, pp. 12–25, 1975.

[18] R. M. Burstall. Design considerations for a functional programming language. In *Infotech State of the Art Conference: The Software Revolution*, Copenhagen, October 1977.

[19] R. M. Burstall, J. S. Collins, and R. J. Popplestone. *Programming in POP-2*. Edinburgh University Press, 1977.

[20] R. M. Burstall and J. Darlington. A tranformation system for developing recursive programs. *J. ACM*, **24**(1), 1977.

[21] R. M. Burstall, D. B. MacQueen, and D. Sannella. Hope: An experimental applicative language. In *Conference Record of the 1980 Lisp Conference*, pp. 136–143, August 1980. Stanford.

[22] P. Caspi, D. Pilaud, N. Halbwachs and J. A. Plaice. LUSTRE: a declarative language for real-time programming. In *POPL '87: Proceedings of the 14th ACM SIGACT-SIGPLAN Symposium on Principles of Programming Languages*, pp. 178–188, New York, NY, USA, 1987. ACM Press.

[23] P. Caspi and M. Pouzet. Synchronous Kahn networks. In *ICFP '96: Proceedings of the first ACM SIGPLAN International Conference on Functional Programming*, pp. 226–238, New York, NY, USA, 1996. ACM Press.

[24] A. Cohen, M. Duranton, C. Eisenbeis, C. Pagetti, F. Plateau and M. Pouzet. N-synchronous Kahn networks: a relaxed model of synchrony for real-time systems. In *POPL '06: Conference Record of the 33rd ACM SIGPLAN-SIGACT Symposium on Principles of Programming Languages*, pp. 180–193, New York, NY, USA, 2006. ACM Press.

[25] M. E. Conway. Design of a separable transition-diagram compiler. *Commun. ACM*, **6**(7):396–408, 1963.

[26] B. Courcelle, G. Kahn and J. Vuillemin. Algorithmes d'equivalence et de reduction a des expressions minimales dans une classe d'equations recursives simples. In *Proceedings of the 2nd Colloquium on Automata, Languages and Programming*, pp. 200–213, London, UK. Springer-Verlag, 1974.

[27] J. Darlington and M. Reeve. Alice a multi-processor reduction machine for the parallel evaluation cf applicative languages. In *FPCA '81: Proceedings of the 1981 Conference on Functional Programming Languages and Computer Architecture*, pp. 65–76, New York, NY, USA, 1981. ACM Press.

[28] J. Davies. *POP-10 User's Manual*. Technical Report CS R25, University of Western Ontario Computer Science Dept., 1976.

[29] J. B. Dennis. Programming generality, parallelism, and computer architecture. In *Information Processing 68*, pp. 484–492. North Holland, 1969.

[30] J. B. Dennis. First version of a data flow procedure language. In *Programming Symposium, Proceedings Colloque sur la Programmation*, volume 19 of Lecture Notes in Computer Science, pp. 362–376, Springer-Verlag, 1974.

[31] J. B. Dennis, J. B. Fosseen and J. P. Linderman. Data flow schemas. In G. Goos and J. Hartmanis (eds), *International Symposium on Theoretical Programming*, volume 5, Lecture Notes in Computer Science, pp. 187–216, Springer-Verlag, 1974.

[32] J. B. Dennis. A language design for structured concurrency. In J. H. Williams and D. A. Fisher (eds), *Proceedings of the DoD Sponsored Workshop on Design and Implementation of Programming Languages*, volume 54, Lecture Notes in Computer Science, pp. 231–242. Springer-Verlag, 1977.

[33] J. B. Dennis. *Stream Data Types for Signal Processing*. Computation Structures Group Memo 36, MIT LCS, October 1994.

[34] J. B. Dennis and D. P. Misunas. A preliminary architecture for a basic data-flow processor. In *ISCA '75: Proceedings of the 2nd Annual Symposium on Computer Architecture*, pp. 126–132, New York, NY, USA, 1975. ACM Press.

[35] D. P. Friedman and D. S. Wise. Cons should not evaluate its arguments. In S. Michaelson and R. Milner (eds), *Automata, Languages and Programming*, pp. 257–284. Edinburgh University Press, 1976.

[36] M. J. C. Gordon, A. J. R. G. Milner, L. Morris, M. C. Newey and C. P. Wadsworth. A metalanguage for interactive proof in LCF. In *Fifth ACM Symposium on Principles of Programming Languages*, New York, 1978. ACM Press.

[37] J. R Gurd, C. C Kirkham and I. Watson. The Manchester prototype dataflow computer. *Commun. ACM*, **28**(1):34–52, 1985.

[38] N. Halbwachs, P. Caspi, P. Raymond and D. Pilaud. The synchronous dataflow programming language LUSTRE. *Proceedings of the IEEE*, **79**(9):1305–1320, Sept. 1991.

[39] E. Harold. *Java I/O, 2nd Edition*. O'Reilly Media, 2006.

[40] P. Henderson and J. H. Morris. A lazy evaluator. In *Third ACM Symposium on Principles of Programming Languages*, pp. 123–42, New York, 1976. ACM Press.

[41] C. Hewitt, P. Bishop, R. Steiger, I. Greif, B. Smith, T. Matson and R. Hale. Behavioral semantics of nonrecursive control structures. In *Programming Symposium, Proceedings Colloque sur la Programmation*, volume 19, Lecture Notes in Computer Science, pp. 385–407. Springer-Verlag, 1974.

[42] G. Kahn and G. D. Plotkin. *Domaines concrets*. INRIA Rapport 336, INRIA, 1978.

[43] G. Kahn and G. D. Plotkin. Concrete domains. *Theoret. Comput. Sci.*, **121**(1–2):187–277, 1993.

[44] G. Kahn. An approach to systems correctness. In *SOSP '71: Proceedings of the Third ACM Symposium on Operating Systems Principles*, pp. 86–94, New York, NY, USA, 1971. ACM Press.

[45]   G. Kahn. *A Preliminary Theory for Parallel Programs.* Technical Report Rapport Laboria no. 6, IRIA Rocquencourt, January 1973.

[46]   G. Kahn. The semantics of a simple language for parallel programming. In *Information Processing 74, Proceedings of the IFIP Congress 74*, pp. 471–475. Elsevier North Holland, 1974.

[47]   G. Kahn and D. B. MacQueen. Coroutines and networks of parallel processes. In B. Gilchrist (ed.), *Information Processing 77*, pp. 993–998. North Holland, 1977.

[48]   G. Kahn and G. Plotkin. *Concrete Data-types.* first draft manuscript, December 1975.

[49]   R. M. Karp and R. E. Miller. Properties of a model for parallel computations: Determinacy, termination, queueing. *SIAM J. Appl. Maths*, **14**(6):1390–1411, 1966.

[50]   J. Kelly, C. Lochbaum and V. Vyssotsky. A block diagram compiler. *Bell System Tech. J.*, **40**(3):669–676, May 1961.

[51]   S. Kleene. *Introduction to Metamathematics.* Van Nostrand, 1952.

[52]   G. Kopec. A high-level block-diagram signal processing language. In *IEEE International Conference on Acoustics, Speech, and Signal Processing*, pp. 684–687, 1979.

[53]   P. J. Landin. A correspondence between ALGOL 60 and Church's lambda-notation: Part I. *Commun. ACM*, **8**(2):89–101, 1965.

[54]   D. C. Luckham, D. M. R. Park and M. S. Paterson. On formalized computer programs. *J. System Sci.*, **4**(3):220–249, 1970.

[55]   D. B. MacQueen, P. Wadler and W. Taha. How to add laziness to a strict language without even being odd. In *Proceedings of the 1998 ACM Workshop on ML*, pp. 24–30, September 1998. Baltimore, MD.

[56]   J. McCarthy, P. W. Abrahams, D. J. Edwards, T. P. Hart and M. E. Levin. *LISP 1.5 Programmer's Manual.* MIT Press, 1962.

[57]   J. McCarthy. Towards a mathematical science of computation. In *Proceedings of the IFIP Congress 1962*, pp. 21–28. North-Holland, 1962.

[58]   J. McCarthy. A basis of a mathematical theory of computation. In P. Braffort and D. Hirshberg (eds), *Computer Programming and Formal Systems*, pp. 33–70. North-Holland, 1963.

[59]   M. D. McIlroy. Coroutines. unpublished note, May 1968.

[60]   M. D. McIlroy. Squinting at power series. *Software Pract. Exper.*, **20**:661–683, 1990.

[61]   M. D. McIlroy. *Power Series as Lazy Streams.* Technical Report BL011276-970313-02TMS, Bell Laboratories, Lucent Technologies, 1997.

[62]   M. D. McIlroy. Power series, power serious. *J. Funct. Program.*, **9**(3):325–337, May 1999.

[63]   R. Milner. Implementation and applications of Scott's logic for computable functions. In *Proceedings of ACM Conference on Proving Assertions About Programs*, pp. 1–6, New York, NY, USA, 1972. ACM.

[64]   R. Milner. Processes: A mathematical model of computing agents. In *Proceedings of the Colloquium in Mathematical Logic*, pp. 157–173. North-Holland, 1973.

[65] R. Milner and R. Weyrauch. Proving compiler correctness in a mechanized logic. In *Machine Intelligence 7*. Edinburgh University Press, 1972.

[66] S. Peyton-Jones (ed.) *Haskell98, Languages and Libraries, The Revised Report*. Cambridge University Press, 2003.

[67] E. D. Reilly. *Milestones in Computer Science and Information Technology*. Greenwood Press, 2003.

[68] J. Reppy and E. Gansner. *The Standard ML Basis Library*. Cambridge University Press, 2006.

[69] D. M. Ritchie. A stream input-output system. *AT&T Bell Laboratories Tech. J.*, **63**(8):1897–1910, 1984.

[70] D. M. Ritchie and K. Thompson. The UNIX time-sharing system. *Commun. ACM*, **17**(7):365–375, 1974.

[71] J. E. Rodriguez. *A Graph Model for Parallel Computations*. Technical Report TR-64, MIT Project MAC, September 1969.

[72] D. Scott. *Outline of a Mathematical Theory of Computation*. Technical Report Technical Monograph PRG-2, Programming Research Group, Oxford University, November 1970.

[73] D. Scott. *Continuous Lattices*. Technical Report Technical Monograph PRG-7, Programming Research Group, Oxford University, August 1971.

[74] D. Scott. Data types as lattices. *SIAM J. Comput.*, **5**:522–587, 1976.

[75] D. Seror. *D.C.P.L: A Distributed Control Programming Language*. PhD thesis, University of Utah, 1970.

[76] S. F. Smith. A computational induction principle. unpublished note, July 1991.

[77] D. A. Turner. An overview of Miranda. *SIGPLAN Notices*, 21, 1986.

[78] D. A. Turner. *SASL Language Manual*. Technical report, St. Andrews University, Department of Computational Science, December 1976.

[79] D. A. Turner. The semantic elegance of applicative languages. In *Proceedings of the 1981 Conf. on Functional Programming and Computer Architecture*, 1981.

[80] J. Vuillemin. Correct and optimal implementations of recursion in a simple programming language. In *STOC '73: Proceedings of the Fifth Annual ACM Symposium on Theory of Computing*, pp. 224–239, New York, NY, USA, 1973. ACM Press.

[81] J. Vuillemin. Correct and optimal implementations of recursion in a simple programming language. *J. Comput. System Sci.*, **9**(3):332–354, December 1974.

[82] C. P. Wadsworth. *Semantics and Pragmatics of the Lambda-calculus*. PhD thesis, Oxford University, 1971.

[83] Z. Wan and P. Hudak. Functional Reactive Programming from first principles. In *Proceedings of the ACM SIGPLAN'00 Conference on Programming Language Design and Implementation (PLDI'00)*, 2000.

[84] E. Wiedmer. *Exaktes rechnen mit reellen zahlen*. Technical Report Bericht no. 20, Eidgenössische Technische Hocchschule, Zurich, July 1976.

[85] G. Winskel. *Events in Computation*. PhD thesis, Edinburgh University, 1981.

6

A simple type-theoretic language: Mini-TT

Thierry Coquand
Chalmers University of Technology and Göteborg University

Yoshiki Kinoshita
*National Institute of Advanced Industrial Science
and Technology (AIST), Japan*

Bengt Nordström
Chalmers University of Technology and Göteborg University

Makoto Takeyama
*National Institute of Advanced Industrial Science and
Technology (AIST), Japan*

Abstract

This paper presents a formal description of a small functional language with dependent types. The language contains data types, mutual recursive/inductive definitions and a universe of small types. The syntax, semantics and type system is specified in such a way that the implementation of a parser, interpreter and type checker is straightforward. The main difficulty is to design the conversion algorithm in such a way that it works for open expressions. The paper ends with a complete implementation in Haskell (around 400 lines of code).

6.1 Introduction

We are going to describe a small language with dependent types, its syntax, operational semantics and type system. This is in the spirit of the paper "A simple applicative language: Mini-ML" by Clément, Despeyroux, and Kahn [5], where they explain a small functional language. From them we have borrowed the idea of using patterns instead of variables in abstractions and let-bindings. It gives an elegant way to express mutually recursive definitions. We also share with them the view that a programming language should not only be formally specified, but it should also be possible to reason about the correctness of its implementation. There should be a small step from the formal

From Semantics to Computer Science Essays in Honour of Gilles Kahn, eds Yves Bertot, Gérard Huet, Jean-Jacques Lévy and Gordon Plotkin. Published by Cambridge University Press. © Cambridge University Press 2009.

operational semantics to an interpreter and also between the specification of the type system to a type checker.

Our type checking algorithm reduces the problem to checking convertibility of terms.[1] A central feature of our Mini-TT presentation is that we compute normal forms of open terms for convertibility checking.

A major problem has been to define the computation of normal forms in such a way that checking convertibility can be reduced to checking syntactic identity of the normal forms. This is done in two steps: first evaluating an expression to its value and then applying a readback function taking the value to a normal expression. Values are representations of expressions in weak head normal form. There are connections between our work and the work of B. Gregoire and X. Leroy on compilation of strong reductions [10, 9]. As in their work, our approach for conversion is based on weak reductions on open terms, complemented by a recursive "read back" procedure.

Two main differences with this work are the following. First, there is the use of patterns mentioned above to encode mutual recursive definitions and our representation of data types as labelled sums. These two features allow us to represent some inductive recursive definitions in a natural way. Second, our way of comparing functions defined by case is less refined than the one in [10]. Although less refined, we think that our approach is simpler to implement at a machine level. The programming language associated to type theory is usually presented as λ-calculus extended with some primitive constants (constructors) and constants implicitly defined by pattern-matching equations [13]. Our simple treatment is actually more faithful to this usual presentation than structural equality. It also has the advantage that our syntax is very close to the one of an ordinary functional programming language, with arbitrary mutual recursive definitions.

Our approach should also allow us to apply the results of [4, 7]. This should provide a modular and semantical sufficient condition ensuring strong normalization and hence decidability of our type-checking algorithm.

This paper is organized as follows. In Section 6.2, the syntax of Mini-TT is given, as well as some syntactic sugar. Some programming examples, such as booleans and natural numbers, are given in Section 6.3. Section 6.4 introduces values and the evaluation function that sends

---

[1] Conversely, the convertibility of two terms t, u of type A can be reduced to the problem of whether the term $\lambda T.\lambda x.x$ has type $\Pi T{:}A \to \mathsf{U}.\ T\ t \to T\ u$.

$$
\begin{array}{rcl}
\text{expressions} \quad M, N, A, B & ::= & \lambda\, p\,.\, M \mid x \mid M\,N \mid \Pi\, p{:}A\,.\,B \mid \mathsf{U} \mid \\
& & M, N \mid M.1 \mid M.2 \mid \Sigma\, p{:}A\,.\,B \mid \\
& & 0 \mid \mathsf{T} \mid \\
& & c\,M \mid \mathsf{fun}\, S \mid \mathsf{Sum}\, S \mid \\
& & D;\, M \\
\text{patterns} \quad p & ::= & x \mid p, p \mid \_ \\
\text{choices} \quad S & ::= & (\,) \mid (c\,M, S) \\
\text{declarations} \quad D & ::= & p{:}A = M \mid \mathsf{rec}\, p{:}A = M \\
\text{syntactic sugar} \quad A \to B & = & \Pi\,\_{:}A\,.\,B \\
A \times B & = & \Sigma\,\_{:}A\,.\,B \\
c\,A \mid S & = & (c, A), S \\
c \to M \mid S & = & (c, M), S
\end{array}
$$

Fig. 6.1. Syntax of Mini-TT.

expressions to values. Our semantics is not based on a reduction relation between expressions. Intuitively, a value represents an expression in weak head normal form and the evaluation function implements the weak head reduction. Section 6.5 defines normal expressions and the readback function that sends a value to a normal expression. We check the convertibility of expressions by first evaluating them to values, then applying the readback function, and finally checking for syntactic identity. Typing rules are presented in Section 6.6, metamathematical remarks in Section 6.7 and Section 6.8 discusses variations possibly applied to mini-TT as given here. Finally Section 6.9 concludes the paper. In the Appendix, we attach a Haskell code which checks the typing relation, i.e. given two expressions, it checks whether the latter is a type expression and the former has the latter as its type.

6.2 Syntax

A brief summary of the syntax can be found in Figure 6.1.

In this presentation of the language, we are using patterns to introduce variables. An abstraction of the form $\lambda\,(x, y)\,.\, e$ is an abstraction of two variables x and y, so $(\lambda\,(x, y)\,.\, e)\, u$ reduces to $e[x := u.1, y := u.2]$ while an abstraction of the form $\lambda\,\_\,.\, e$ is an abstraction of no variables, so $(\lambda\,\_\,.\, e)\, u$ reduces to e.

A program is an expression of type T, usually just a list of declarations. A declaration is a definition of a constant with its type. We will first explain the syntax of the declarations, then continue to describe the various ways of forming expressions associated with each type-forming operation (unit type, dependent product, labelled sum and universe).

Declarations: recursive and explicit definitions There are two kinds of definitions, let expression $p{:}A = M;\ N$, and letrec expression $\mathsf{rec}\,p{:}A = M;\ N$. Use of patterns is not strictly necessary but simplifies the definition of mutually recursive definitions.

We allow definitions of non-terminating functions. This is essential if Mini-TT is going to be a core language for programming. Non-terminating functions are essential for interactive programs. Of course, it causes problems for type checking to be terminating, so we assume that termination is checked in a separate phase.

Unit type The unit type T has the unit element 0.

Dependent product, lambda abstraction, application The dependent product type $\Pi\,p{:}A\,.\,B$ is the type of functions taking an object M in the type A to an object in the type B (where B may depend on M). Lambda abstractions are written $\lambda\,p\,.\,M$ and application $M\,N$. It is possible to use the notation $A \to B$ as syntactic sugar for $\Pi\,\_{:}A\,.\,B$.

Dependent sum, pairs and projections The dependent sum $\Sigma\,p{:}A\,.\,B$ is the type of pairs M, N, where $M \in A$, $N \in B[M/p]$. The projections are written $M.1$ and $M.2$. It is possible to use the notaton $A \times B$ as syntactic sugar for $\Sigma\,\_{:}A\,.\,B$.

Labelled sum, constructor application and case An inductive set is regarded as a labelled sum $\mathsf{Sum}(c_1\ A_1, \ldots, c_n\ A_n)$, which contains objects of the form $c_i\,E$, where E is an object in A_i. We will also write this as $\mathsf{Sum}(c_1\ A_1 \mid \cdots \mid c_n\ A_n)$. It is possible to skip the type A_i in the case that it is the unit type T. For instance, the type of Boolean values can be written as $\mathsf{Sum}\ (\mathsf{true} \mid \mathsf{false})$ instead of $\mathsf{Sum}\ (\mathsf{true}\ \mathsf{T} \mid \mathsf{false}\ \mathsf{T})$.

The case-analysis function has the shape $\mathsf{fun}(c_1\ M_1, \ldots, c_n\ M_n)$. It is a function which when applied to an object of the form $c_i\,N$ is equal to $M_i\,N$. The choice $c_i\ (\lambda\,p\,.\,M_i)$ is written $c_i\ p \to M_i$ and the choice $c_i\ (\lambda\,\_\,.\,M_i)$ is written $c_i \to M_i$.

Universe The type of small types is written U. The objects in this are types not built up using U.

6.3 Examples of programs

Here are some examples of programs (a list of declarations $D_1; \cdots ; D_n$) that we can write in Mini-TT. The generic identity function will be represented by the program

$$\text{id:}\Pi \, A\text{:U} \,.\, A \to A = \lambda \, A \,.\, \lambda \, x \,.\, x$$

A simple example is the data type of Booleans and the corresponding elimination function

$$
\begin{aligned}
\text{Bool} \quad &: \; \text{U} = \text{Sum (true | false)} \\
\text{elimBool} \quad &: \; \Pi \, C\text{:Bool} \to \text{U} \,.\, C \, \text{false} \to C \, \text{true} \to \Pi \, b\text{:Bool} \,.\, C \, b \\
&= \lambda \, C \,.\, \lambda \, h_0 \,.\, \lambda \, h_1 \,.\, \text{fun (true} \to h_1 \mid \text{false} \to h_0)
\end{aligned}
$$

The type of natural numbers is represented as a recursively defined labelled sum

$$\text{rec Nat:U} = \text{Sum (zero | succ Nat)}$$

Similarly, the type of lists is described by

$$\text{rec List :U} \to \text{U} = \lambda \, A \,.\, \text{Sum (nil} \mid \text{cons} \, A \times \text{List} \, A)$$

The elimination function of the type of natural numbers is the recursively defined function

$$
\begin{aligned}
\text{rec natrec} \quad : \; &\Pi \, C\text{:Nat} \to \text{U} \,.\, C \, \text{zero} \to (\Pi \, n\text{:Nat} \,.\, C \, n \to C(\text{succ} \, n)) \to \\
&\Pi \, n\text{:Nat} \,.\, C \, n \\
= \; &\lambda \, C \,.\, \lambda \, a \,.\, \lambda \, g \,.\, \text{fun (zero} \to a \mid \text{succ} \, n_1 \to g \, n_1 \, (\text{natrec} \, C \, a \, g \, n_1))
\end{aligned}
$$

If we work in this fragment, and we do not introduce new definitions using rec, Sum and fun, we obtain a faithful representation of the corresponding fragment of type theory described in Chapter 20 of [12].

In Mini-TT, we can directly introduce other recursive functions on natural numbers, even if they can be defined without recursion using natrec. A simple example is the addition function

$$
\begin{aligned}
\text{rec add} \quad : \; &\text{Nat} \to \text{Nat} \to \text{Nat} \\
= \; &\lambda \, x \,.\, \text{fun (zero} \to x \mid \text{succ} \, y_1 \to \text{succ} \, (\text{add} \, x \, y_1))
\end{aligned}
$$

A more complex example is provided by the decidable equality function

$$
\begin{aligned}
\text{rec eqNat} \quad : \; &\text{Nat} \to \text{Nat} \to \text{Bool} \\
= \; &\text{fun (zero} \quad \to \text{fun (zero} \to \text{true} \mid \text{succ} \, y \to \text{false)} \\
&\mid \text{succ} \, x \to \text{fun (zero} \to \text{false} \mid \text{succ} \, y \to \text{eqNat} \, x \, y))
\end{aligned}
$$

$$\begin{aligned}
\text{values} \quad u, v, t \quad ::= \quad & [k] \mid \lambda f \mid \Pi\, t\, g \mid \mathsf{U} \mid \\
& u, v \mid 0 \mid \Sigma\, t\, g \mid \mathbf{1} \mid \\
& c\, v \mid \mathsf{fun}\, s \mid \mathsf{Sum}\, s
\end{aligned}$$

$$\begin{aligned}
\text{neutral values (accumulators)} \quad k \quad &::= \quad \mathsf{x}_n \mid k\, v \mid k.1 \mid k.2 \mid s\, k \\
\text{function closures} \quad f, g \quad &::= \quad \langle \lambda p.M, \rho \rangle \mid f \circ c \\
\text{choice closures} \quad s \quad &::= \quad \langle S, \rho \rangle \\
\text{environments} \quad \rho \quad &::= \quad () \mid \rho, p = v \mid \rho, D
\end{aligned}$$

Fig. 6.2. Values.

Our representation of this function corresponds to the system of pattern-matching equations

eqNat zero   zero = true,   eqNat zero   (succ y) = false,
eqNat (succ x) zero = false,   eqNat (succ x) (succ y) = eqNat $x\ y$,

compiled using two auxiliary functions

eqNat zero   = f, f zero = true, f (succ y) = false,
eqNat (succ x) = $g\, x$, $g\, x$ zero = false, $g\, x$ (succ y) = eqNat $x\ y$

The last example is the inductive-recursive definition [8] of a universe containing a code of the type of natural numbers and the dependent product formation, defined in a mutual recursive way with its corresponding decoding function:

$$\begin{aligned}
\mathsf{rec}\,(\mathsf{V}, \mathsf{T}) \ : \ & \Sigma\, X{:}\mathsf{U}\,.\, X \to \mathsf{U} \\
= \ (\ & \mathsf{Sum}\,(\mathsf{nat} \mid \mathsf{pi}\,(\Sigma\, x{:}\mathsf{V}\,.\, \mathsf{T}\, x \to \mathsf{V})), \\
& \mathsf{fun}\,(\mathsf{nat} \to \mathsf{Nat} \mid \mathsf{pi}\,(x, f) \to \Pi\, y{:}\mathsf{T}\, x\,.\, \mathsf{T}\,(f\, y))) \ ;
\end{aligned}$$

6.4 Operational semantics

In order to define the semantics of the language, it is necessary to first define the set of values (Fig. 6.2).

6.4.1 Values

A *value* represents an open expression in weak head normal form. It is either a *neutral value* [k] which represents an expression whose computation stopped because of an attempt to compute a variable, or a *canonical value*, the form of which makes clear the head construction of an expression: λ-abstraction λf, Π-abstraction $\Pi\, t\, g$, etc.

The neutral value x_n is a primitive (not defined) constant which is used to represent the value of a free variable. It is a constant about which we know nothing. It is called a *generic value* in [6].

Other neutral values are built up from evaluation contexts in which attempts are made to compute neutral values. For instance, we obtain the neutral value $k\,v$ when trying to evaluate an application and the value of the function is the neutral value k and the argument is v. Similarly, the neutral values $k.1$ and $k.2$ are the results of trying to project from a neutral value k. The neutral value $\langle S, \rho \rangle\,k$ is the result of trying to apply a choice function $\mathsf{fun}\,S$ to a neutral value k in an environment ρ. Neutral values are called *accumulators* by Grégoire and Leroy [10].

6.4.2 Value operations

There is a small set of functions defined on values. They are in general not defined for all arguments, e.g. the projections are not defined for functions. This does not lead to problems since the operations are only applied when evaluating well typed expressions.

There is a function which instantiates a function closure to a value. It is defined by:

$$
\begin{aligned}
\mathsf{inst}\langle \lambda p.M, \rho \rangle\,v &= \;\Downarrow M(\rho, p = v) \\
\mathsf{inst}(f \circ c)\,v &= \;\mathsf{inst}\,f(c\,v)
\end{aligned}
$$

Application $\mathsf{app}\,u\,v$ of values is defined using instantiation. Notice how a neutral value is built up in the case that the function is a neutral value:

$$
\begin{aligned}
\mathsf{app}(\lambda f)\,v &= \mathsf{inst}\,f\,v \\
\mathsf{app}(\mathsf{fun}\langle S, \rho \rangle)(c_i\,v) &= \mathsf{app}(\mathrm{J}M_i\mathrm{K}\rho)\,v \\
&\quad \text{where } S = (c_1 \rightarrow M_1 \mid \cdots \mid c_n \rightarrow M_n) \\
\mathsf{app}(\mathsf{fun}\,s)[k] &= [s\,k] \\
\mathsf{app}[k]\,v &= [k\,v]
\end{aligned}
$$

The projection function for pairs of values follows the same pattern:

$$
\begin{aligned}
(u, v).1 &= u \\
[k].1 &= [k.1] \\
(u, v).2 &= v \\
[k].2 &= [k.2]
\end{aligned}
$$

The function to look up the value $\rho(x)$ of a variable x in an environment ρ is only defined for ρ in which x is defined. Type checking guarantees that this is the case.

$$
\begin{array}{rcl}
\Downarrow \lambda p . M \rho & = & \langle \lambda p.M, \rho \rangle \\
\Downarrow x \rho & = & \rho(x) \\
\Downarrow M\, N \rho & = & \mathsf{app}(\Downarrow M\rho)(\Downarrow N\rho) \\
\Downarrow \Pi\, p{:}A . B \rho & = & \Pi\,(\Downarrow A\rho)\,\langle \lambda p.B, \rho \rangle \\
\Downarrow \mathsf{U} \rho & = & \mathsf{U} \\
\Downarrow D; M \rho & = & \Downarrow M(\rho, D)
\end{array}
$$

$$
\begin{array}{rcl}
\Downarrow M, N \rho & = & (\Downarrow M\rho, \Downarrow N\rho) \\
\Downarrow 0 \rho & = & 0 \\
\Downarrow M.1 \rho & = & (\Downarrow M\rho).1 \\
\Downarrow M.2 \rho & = & (\Downarrow M\rho).2 \\
\Downarrow \Sigma\, p{:}A . B \rho & = & \Sigma\,(\Downarrow A\rho)\,\langle \lambda p.B, \rho \rangle \\
\Downarrow \mathsf{T} \rho & = & 1
\end{array}
$$

$$
\begin{array}{rcl}
\Downarrow c\, M \rho & = & c\,(\Downarrow M\rho) \\
\Downarrow \mathsf{fun}\, S \rho & = & \mathsf{fun}\langle S, \rho \rangle \\
\Downarrow \mathsf{Sum}\, S \rho & = & \mathsf{Sum}\langle S, \rho \rangle
\end{array}
$$

Fig. 6.3. Semantics of Mini-TT.

If x is in p,

$$
\begin{array}{rcl}
(\rho, p = v)(x) & = & \mathsf{proj}_x^p(v) \\
(\rho, p{:}A = M)(x) & = & \mathsf{proj}_x^p(\Downarrow M\rho) \\
(\rho, \mathsf{rec}\, p{:}A = M)(x) & = & \mathsf{proj}_x^p(\Downarrow M(\rho, \mathsf{rec}\, p{:}A = M))
\end{array}
$$

If x is not in p,

$$
\begin{array}{rcl}
(\rho, p = v)(x) & = & \rho(x) \\
(\rho, D)(x) & = & \rho(x)
\end{array}
$$

The notation $\mathsf{proj}_x^p(v)$ is well-defined under the precondition that x is in p.

$$
\begin{array}{rcll}
\mathsf{proj}_x^x(v) & = & v & \\
\mathsf{proj}_x^{(p_1, p_2)}(v) & = & \mathsf{proj}_x^{p_1}(v.1) & \text{if } x \text{ is in } p_1, \\
\mathsf{proj}_x^{(p_1, p_2)}(v) & = & \mathsf{proj}_x^{p_2}(v.2) & \text{if } x \text{ is in } p_2
\end{array}
$$

6.4.3 Semantics

In Figure 6.3 we give the semantics of Mini-TT by equations of the form $\Downarrow M\rho = v$, meaning that the expression M evaluates to the value v in the environment ρ.

$$
\begin{array}{ll}
E & ::= \quad \lambda \mathsf{x}_i \,.\, E \mid \Pi \mathsf{x}_i{:}E_1 \,.\, E_2 \mid \mathsf{U} \mid [K] \\
& \quad\quad E_1, E_2 \mid 0 \mid \Sigma \mathsf{x}_i{:}E_1 \,.\, E_2 \mid \mathsf{T} \\
& \quad\quad c\,E \mid \mathsf{fun}\langle S, \alpha \rangle \mid \mathsf{Sum}\langle S, \alpha \rangle \\
K & ::= \quad \mathsf{x}_i \mid KE \mid K.1 \mid K.2 \mid \langle S, \alpha \rangle\, K \\
\alpha & ::= \quad () \mid (\alpha, p = E) \mid (\alpha, D)
\end{array}
$$

Fig. 6.4. Normal expressions.

$$
\begin{array}{lcl}
\mathsf{R}_i(\lambda f) & = & \lambda \mathsf{x}_i \,.\, \mathsf{R}_{i+1}(\mathsf{inst}\, f[\mathsf{x}_i]) \\
\mathsf{R}_i(u, v) & = & (\mathsf{R}_i\, u, \mathsf{R}_i\, v) \\
\mathsf{R}_i\, 0 & = & 0 \\
\mathsf{R}_i(c\, v) & = & c\,(\mathsf{R}_i\, v) \\
\mathsf{R}_i(\mathsf{fun}\langle S, \rho \rangle) & = & \mathsf{fun}\langle S, \mathsf{R}_i\, \rho \rangle \\
\mathsf{R}_i(\mathsf{Sum}\langle S, \rho \rangle) & = & \mathsf{Sum}\langle S, \mathsf{R}_i\, \rho \rangle \\
\mathsf{R}_i\, \mathsf{U} & = & \mathsf{U} \\
\mathsf{R}_i\, \mathbf{1} & = & \mathsf{T} \\
\mathsf{R}_i(\Pi\, t\, g) & = & \Pi \mathsf{x}_i{:}\mathsf{R}_i\, t \,.\, \mathsf{R}_{i+1}(\mathsf{inst}\, g[\mathsf{x}_i]) \\
\mathsf{R}_i(\Sigma\, t\, g) & = & \Sigma \mathsf{x}_i{:}\mathsf{R}_i\, t \,.\, \mathsf{R}_{i+1}(\mathsf{inst}\, g[\mathsf{x}_i]) \\
\mathsf{R}_i[k] & = & [\mathsf{R}_i\, k] \\
& & \\
\mathsf{R}_i\, \mathsf{x}_j & = & \mathsf{x}_j \\
\mathsf{R}_i(k\, v) & = & (\mathsf{R}_i\, k)(\mathsf{R}_i\, v) \\
\mathsf{R}_i(k.1) & = & (\mathsf{R}_i\, k).1 \\
\mathsf{R}_i(k.2) & = & (\mathsf{R}_i\, k).2 \\
\mathsf{R}_i(\langle S, \rho \rangle\, k) & = & \langle S, \mathsf{R}_i\, \rho \rangle\, (\mathsf{R}_i\, k) \\
& & \\
\mathsf{R}_i(\rho, p = v) & = & \mathsf{R}_i\, \rho,\; p = \mathsf{R}_i\, v \\
\mathsf{R}_i(\rho, D) & = & \mathsf{R}_i\, \rho, D \\
\mathsf{R}_i() & = & ()
\end{array}
$$

Fig. 6.5. The readback notation.

6.5 Normal expressions and readback

The readback function R_i takes a value to a normal expression (Fig. 6.4). The purpose of R_i is to facilitate convertibility checking. Notice that normal expressions are first-order objects, and have a decidable (syntactic) equality. Two convertible values are mapped to the same normal expression (i.e. identical, including choice of bound variables). This is similar to [10].

We overload the notation $\mathsf{R}_i(-)$ ($i \in \mathbb{N}$) for three cases (Fig. 6.5): the readback of a value $\mathsf{R}_i\, v$ is a normal expression E, that of a neutral value $\mathsf{R}_i\, k$ is a neutral expression K, and that of an environment $\mathsf{R}_i\, \rho$ is a normal environment α.

6.6 Typing rules

Typing context A typing context consists of an environment ρ and a *type environment* Γ:

$$\Gamma :: = ()\ |\ \Gamma,\ x{:}t$$

The lookup operation $\Gamma(x)$ is expressed not as a function but as an inductive predicate since it may fail and signals incorrectness of expression being type checked.

$$\frac{}{(\Gamma, x{:}t)(x) \to t} \qquad \frac{\Gamma(x) \to t}{(\Gamma, y{:}t')(x) \to t}\ y \neq x$$

That Γ is updated by binding $p{:}t = v$ to Γ' is written $\Gamma \vdash p{:}t = v \Rightarrow \Gamma'$. It decomposes the pattern binding to bindings of simple variables while checking that the shape of p fits the type t. The bound value v is needed to compute the type of subpatterns of p.

$$\frac{}{\Gamma \vdash x{:}t = v \Rightarrow \Gamma, x{:}t} \qquad \frac{}{\Gamma \vdash \_{:}t = v \Rightarrow \Gamma}$$

$$\frac{\Gamma \vdash p_1{:}t_1 = v.1 \Rightarrow \Gamma_1 \quad \Gamma_1 \vdash p_2{:}\, \mathsf{inst}\, g(v.1) = v.2 \Rightarrow \Gamma_2}{\Gamma \vdash (p_1, p_2){:}\Sigma\, t_1\, g = v \Rightarrow \Gamma_2}$$

6.6.1 Overview

There are four forms of judgements.

checkD	$\rho, \Gamma \vdash_l D \Rightarrow \Gamma'$	D is a correct declaration and extends Γ to Γ'.
checkT	$\rho, \Gamma \vdash_l A$	A is a correct type expression.
check	$\rho, \Gamma \vdash_l M \Leftarrow t$	M is a correct expression of the given type t.
checkI	$\rho, \Gamma \vdash_l M \Rightarrow t$	M is a correct expression and its type is inferred to be t.

The inference rules are syntax directed and constitute a standard bidirectional type-checking (semi-)algorithm. It is an important property of the checking algorithm that $\Downarrow M\rho$ is never computed without first checking that M is well-formed.

checkD: check that a declaration is correct

$$\frac{\rho,\Gamma \vdash_l A \quad \rho,\Gamma \vdash_l M \Leftarrow t \quad \Gamma \vdash p{:}t =\Downarrow M\rho \Rightarrow \Gamma_1}{\rho,\Gamma \vdash_l p{:}A = M \Rightarrow \Gamma_1} \; (t =\Downarrow A\rho)$$

$$\frac{\begin{array}{c} \rho,\Gamma \vdash_l A \\ \Gamma \vdash p{:}t = [\mathsf{x}_l] \Rightarrow \Gamma_1 \\ (\rho, p = [\mathsf{x}_l]),\Gamma_1 \vdash_{l+1} M \Leftarrow t \\ \Gamma \vdash p{:}t = v \Rightarrow \Gamma_2 \end{array}}{\rho,\Gamma \vdash_l \mathsf{rec}\, p{:}A = M \Rightarrow \Gamma_2} \left(\begin{array}{l} t = \Downarrow A\rho, \\ v = \Downarrow M(\rho, \mathsf{rec}\, p{:}A = M) \end{array} \right)$$

The rule for a let binding is as expected. We check that A is a type, M is an expression of that type, and extend Γ while checking that p fits the type. In the rule for a letrec binding, the body M is checked in a temporarily extended context, in which p is bound to a generic value. This means that while checking M, recursively defined identifiers are treated as fresh constants about which we assume nothing but their typing. Once M is checked, Γ is extended using the 'real' value $\Downarrow M(\rho, \mathsf{rec}\, p{:}A = M)$ for p.

checkT: check that something is a type

$$\frac{}{\rho,\Gamma \vdash_l \mathsf{U}} \qquad \frac{\rho,\Gamma \vdash_l A \quad \Gamma \vdash p{:} \Downarrow A\rho = [\mathsf{x}_l] \Rightarrow \Gamma_1 \quad (\rho, p = [\mathsf{x}_l]),\Gamma_1 \vdash_{l+1} B}{\rho,\Gamma \vdash_l \Pi\, p{:}A . B}$$

$$\frac{\rho,\Gamma \vdash_l A \quad \Gamma \vdash p{:} \Downarrow A\rho = [\mathsf{x}_l] \Rightarrow \Gamma_1 \quad (\rho, p = [\mathsf{x}_l]),\Gamma_1 \vdash_{l+1} B}{\rho,\Gamma \vdash_l \Sigma\, p{:}A . B}$$

$$\frac{\rho,\Gamma \vdash_l A \Leftarrow \mathsf{U}}{\rho,\Gamma \vdash_l A} \; \text{(if other rules are not applicable)}$$

If A is expected to be a type but not any of U, Π, or Σ, then it must be a small type of type U (the last rule).

check: check that an expression has a given type

$$\frac{\Gamma \vdash p{:}t = [\mathsf{x}_l] \Rightarrow \Gamma_1 \quad (\rho, p = [\mathsf{x}_l]), \Gamma_1 \vdash_{l+1} M \Leftarrow \mathsf{inst}\, g\, [\mathsf{x}_l]}{\rho, \Gamma \vdash_l \lambda p \,.\, M \Leftarrow \Pi\, t\, g}$$

$$\frac{\rho, \Gamma \vdash_l M \Leftarrow t \quad \rho, \Gamma \vdash_l N \Leftarrow \mathsf{inst}\, g(\Downarrow M\rho)}{\rho, \Gamma \vdash_l (M, N) \Leftarrow \Sigma\, t\, g}$$

$$\frac{\rho, \Gamma \vdash_l M \Leftarrow \mathsf{J}A_i\mathsf{K}\nu}{\rho, \Gamma \vdash_l c_i\, M \Leftarrow \mathsf{Sum}\langle c_1\, A_1 \mid \cdots \mid c_n\, A_n,\ \nu \rangle}$$

$$\frac{\begin{array}{c}\rho, \Gamma \vdash_l M_1 \Leftarrow \Pi\, (\mathsf{J}A_1\mathsf{K}\nu)\, (g \circ c_1)\\ \cdots \\ \rho, \Gamma \vdash_l M_n \Leftarrow \Pi\, (\mathsf{J}A_n\mathsf{K}\nu)\, (g \circ c_n)\end{array}}{\begin{array}{c}\rho, \Gamma \vdash_l \mathsf{fun}(c_1 \to M_1 \mid \cdots \mid c_n \to M_n) \Leftarrow\\ \Pi\, (\mathsf{Sum}\langle c_1{:}A_1 \mid \cdots \mid c_n{:}A_n, \nu \rangle)\, g\end{array}}$$

$$\frac{\rho, \Gamma \vdash_l D \Rightarrow \Gamma_1 \quad (\rho, D), \Gamma_1 \vdash_l M \Leftarrow t}{\rho, \Gamma \vdash_l D; M \Leftarrow t}$$

$$\frac{}{\rho, \Gamma \vdash_l 0 \Leftarrow \mathbf{1}} \qquad \frac{}{\rho, \Gamma \vdash_l \mathsf{T} \Leftarrow \mathsf{U}}$$

$$\frac{\rho, \Gamma \vdash_l A \Leftarrow \mathsf{U} \quad \Gamma \vdash p{:} \Downarrow A\rho = [\mathsf{x}_l] \Rightarrow \Gamma_1 \quad (\rho, p = [\mathsf{x}_l]), \Gamma_1 \vdash_{l+1} B \Leftarrow \mathsf{U}}{\rho, \Gamma \vdash_l \Pi\, p{:}A \,.\, B \Leftarrow \mathsf{U}}$$

$$\frac{\rho, \Gamma \vdash_l A \Leftarrow \mathsf{U} \quad \Gamma \vdash p{:} \Downarrow A\rho = [\mathsf{x}_l] \Rightarrow \Gamma_1 \quad (\rho, p = [\mathsf{x}_l]), \Gamma_1 \vdash_{l+1} B \Leftarrow \mathsf{U}}{\rho, \Gamma \vdash_l \Sigma\, p{:}A \,.\, B \Leftarrow \mathsf{U}}$$

$$\frac{\rho, \Gamma \vdash_l A_1 \Leftarrow \mathsf{U} \quad \cdots \quad \rho, \Gamma \vdash_l A_n \Leftarrow \mathsf{U}}{\rho, \Gamma \vdash_l \mathsf{Sum}(c_1\, A_1 \mid \cdots \mid c_n\, A_n) \Leftarrow \mathsf{U}}$$

$$\frac{\rho, \Gamma \vdash_l M \Rightarrow t' \quad \mathsf{R}_l\, t = \mathsf{R}_l\, t'}{\rho, \Gamma \vdash_l M \Leftarrow t} \text{ (if other rules are not applicable)}$$

This deals with expressions in canonical forms (weak head normal forms). For an expression in a non-canonical form, the last rule infers its type and checks that the inferred type is equal to the expected one. This is the single place where type checking uses conversion checking.

In the rule for a case-analysis function, it must be checked against a Π type whose domain is a Sum type. For simplicity, we require the constructors in case branches to match exactly the constructors listed in the Sum type, including the order. From the right-hand side of the equation

$$\mathsf{app}(\mathsf{Jfun}(c_1 \rightarrow M_1 \mid \cdots \mid c_n \rightarrow M_n)\mathsf{K}\rho)(c_i\,v) = \mathsf{app}(\mathsf{J}M_i\mathsf{K}\rho)\,v$$

we expect the branch expression M_i to have a Π type with the domain $\mathsf{J}A_i\mathsf{K}\nu$. The closure $g \circ c_i$ in the codomain part is what is needed to make both sides of the equation to have the same type, namely $\mathsf{inst}\,g(c_i\,v)$.

The rules for Π, Σ, T, and Sum here make the universe U to be directly closed under those operations, unlike the type **Set** of Logical Framework.

checkI: infer the type of an expression

$$\frac{\Gamma(x) \rightarrow t}{\rho, \Gamma \vdash_l x \Rightarrow t} \qquad \frac{\rho, \Gamma \vdash_l M \Rightarrow \Pi\,t\,g \quad \rho, \Gamma \vdash_l N \Leftarrow t}{\rho, \Gamma \vdash_l M\,N \Rightarrow \mathsf{inst}\,g(\Downarrow N\rho)}$$

$$\frac{\rho, \Gamma \vdash_l M \Rightarrow \Sigma\,t\,g}{\rho, \Gamma \vdash_l M.1 \Rightarrow t} \qquad \frac{\rho, \Gamma \vdash_l M \Rightarrow \Sigma\,t\,g}{\rho, \Gamma \vdash_l M.2 \Rightarrow \mathsf{inst}\,g((\Downarrow M\rho).1)}$$

We check and infer types of expressions in non-canonical forms here.

6.7 Metamathematical remarks

As we explained in the introduction, the work [4, 7] should provide a general *semantical* condition ensuring termination of type-checking: it is enough that the *strict* denotational semantics of the program is $\neq \bot$. As in [4, 7], one can ensure this by proving *totality* of the program. In turn, there are sufficient purely syntactical criteria ensuring totality. One such criteria is, for instance, *size-change termination* [11, 15].

6.8 Variations

NBE and η-conversion We can adopt the typed NBE algorithm by Abel, Dybjer, and Coquand [2] for our evaluation to obtain the version of Mini-TT with η-conversion. There are two points to modify our presentation of Mini-TT. First, when type checking under a binder, we extend a context not by a generic value $[\mathsf{x}_l]$ ($l = |\rho|$) but by its reflected form $\uparrow^t [\mathsf{x}_l]$, where t is the type of the generic value. Second, when we compare the expected type t and the inferred type t' in the last of **check**, we compare the readbacks of their redefined form $\mathsf{R}_i \Downarrow t$ and $\mathsf{R}_i \Downarrow t'$. These modifications make the comparison to be between η-long normal forms, thus making Mini-TT a language type checked with η-conversion.

Higher order values A function closures f is a first-order representation of a semantic function from values to values. We do not need to "look inside" it (cf. [10]). This can be made clear by replacing closures with these semantic functions themselves, thus making values higher order. Then, closure instantiation and constructions are replaced by the following.

$$
\begin{aligned}
\mathsf{inst}\, f\, v &= f\, v \\
\langle \lambda p.M, \rho \rangle &= (v \mapsto \Downarrow M(\rho, p = v)) \\
f \circ c &= (v \mapsto f(c\, v))
\end{aligned}
$$

6.9 Conclusion

We have presented a dependently typed language Mini-TT with its semantics and type checking rules. Mini-TT has dependent products, dependent sums and unit type, labelled sums, recursive definitions, and pattern abstractions and bindings.

Mini-TT is a step towards a simple and definitive core language for the proof-assistant Agda [3] based on versions of Martin-Löf Type Theory. To make development of large proofs and programs feasible, the full language must support various advanced features such as incomplete terms with meta-variables and synthesis of implicit arguments. Directly giving semantics to them and justifying its complex implementation is difficult. Our approach is to translate the full language to a well-understood simple core language. We would have a simple theory and implementation of the core language, with respect to which a full-fledged proof assistant is specified, implemented, and tested.

Our future work is towards that goal. This includes a strong normalization theorem for Mini-TT using the denotational semantics of [4, 7], non-uniform inductive families of types, universe hierarchy, proven correct compilation to abstract machine code as in [10], etc.

Bibliography

[1]   M. Abadi, L. Cardelli, P.-L. Curien and J.-J. Lévy. Explicit substitutions. In *Conference Record of the Seventeenth Annual ACM Symposium on Principles of Programming Languages, San Francisco, California*, pp. 31–46. ACM, 1990.

[2]   A. Abel, K. Aehlig and P. Dybjer. Normalization by evaluation for Martin-Löf type theory with one universe. *Electronic Notes in Theoretical Computer Science*, **173**:17–39, 2007.

[3]   Agda homepage. http://unit.aist.go.jp/cvs/Agda/.

[4]   U. Berger. Strong normalization for applied lambda calculi. *Logical Methods in Computer Science*, **1**(2), 2005.

[5]   D. Clément, J. Despeyroux, T. Despeyroux and G. Kahn. A simple applicative language: Mini-ML. In *LISP and Functional Programming*, pp. 13–27, 1986.

[6]   T. Coquand. An algorithm for type-checking dependent types. *Science of Computer Programming*, **26**(1–3):167–177, 1996.

[7]   T. Coquand and A. Spiwack. A proof of strong normalisation using domain theory. In *LICS*, pp. 307–316. IEEE Computer Society, 2006.

[8]   P. Dybjer. A general formulation of simultaneous inductive-recursive definitions in type theory. *Journal of Symbolic Logic*, **65**(2):525–549, 2000.

[9]   B. Grégoire. *Compilation des termes de preuves: un (nouveau) mariage entre Coq et Ocaml.* Thèse de doctorat, spécialité informatique, Université Paris 7, École Polytechnique, France, December 2003.

[10]   B. Grégoire and X. Leroy. A compiled implementation of strong reduction. In *International Conference on Functional Programming 2002*, pp. 235–246. ACM Press, 2002.

[11]   C. S. Lee, N. D. Jones and A. M. Ben-Amram. The size-change principle for program termination. In *Conference Record of the Twenty-eighth Annual ACM Symposium on Principles of Programming Languages*, volume 28 of *ACM SIGPLAN Notices*, pp. 81–92. ACM Press, January 2001.

[12]   B. Nordström, K. Petersson and J. M. Smith. *Programming in Martin-Löf's Type Theory*, volume 7, Monographs on Computer Science. Oxford University Press, 1990.

[13]   B. Nordström, K. Petersson, and J. M. Smith. Martin-Löf's type theory. In S. Abramsky, D. M. Gabbay and T. S. E. Maibaum, (eds), *Handbook of Logic in Computer Science*, volume 5. Oxford Science Publications, 2000.

[14]   M. Pellauer, M. Forsberg and A. Ranta. *BNF Converter Multilingual Front-end Generation from Labelled BNF Grammars.* Technical Report 2004-09, Department of Computing Science, Chalmers University of Technology and Göteborg University, 2004. available from http://www.cs.chalmers.se/~markus/BNFC/.

[15]   D. Wahlstedt. *Dependent Type Theory with Parameterized First-Order Data Types and Well-Founded Recursion.* PhD thesis, Chalmers University of Technology, 2007.

Appendix: Implementation

The inference rules are directly translated to Haskell using a simple error monad G a. The Haskell typing of the routines that corresponds to the four forms of judgements are:

```
data G a = Success a | Fail Name
```

```
instance  Monad G  where
    (Success x) >>= k     = k x
    Fail s   >>= k        = Fail s
    return                = Success
    fail                  = Fail
```

```
checkD :: Int -> Rho -> Gamma -> Decl -> G Gamma
checkT :: Int -> Rho -> Gamma -> Exp -> G ()
check  :: Int -> Rho -> Gamma -> Exp -> TVal -> G ()
checkI :: Int -> Rho -> Gamma -> Exp -> G TVal
```

If these routines return without producing error messages, then there are derivations that conclude corresponding judgements. The clause for the application rule of checkI judgement is

$$\frac{\rho, \Gamma \vdash_l M \Rightarrow \Pi t\, g \quad \rho, \Gamma \vdash_l N \Leftarrow t}{\rho, \Gamma \vdash_l M\, N \Rightarrow \mathsf{inst}\, g(\Downarrow N \rho)}$$

```
checkI k rho gma (EApp e1 e2) =
  do t1 <- checkI k rho gma e1
     (t, g) <- extPiG t1
     check k rho gma e2 t
     return (g * eval e2 rho)
  where
  extPiG (Pi t g) = return (t, g)
  extPiG u        = fail ("extPiG " ++ showVal u)
```

The implementation supposes a parser function. One can either write a parser directly in Haskell, or use the *BNF Converter* compiler construction tool [14]. From a description of concrete syntax in a labelled BNF grammar, BNFC generates modules for the data type for abstract syntax trees, a parser, and a pretty printer.

The implementation can be obtained from `http://www.cs.chalmers.se/Cs/Research/Logic/Mini-TT/`

```
------------------------------------------
-- Main module
------------------------------------------

module Main where

import Prelude hiding ((*))

----------------------------------------------------------------
-- Expressions
----------------------------------------------------------------

type Name = String

data Exp =
   ELam Patt Exp
 | ESet
 | EPi Patt Exp Exp
 | ESig Patt Exp Exp
 | EOne
 | Eunit
 | EPair Exp Exp
 | ECon Name Exp
 | ESum Branch
 | EFun Branch
 | EFst Exp
 | ESnd Exp
 | EApp Exp Exp
 | EVar Name
 | EVoid
 | EDec Decl Exp
   deriving (Eq,Ord,Show)

data Decl =
   Def Patt Exp Exp
 | Drec Patt Exp Exp
   deriving (Eq,Ord,Show)

data Patt =
   PPair Patt Patt
```

```
 | Punit
 | PVar Name
   deriving (Eq,Ord,Show)

type Branch = [(Name,Exp)]


-----------------------------------------------------------
-- Values
-----------------------------------------------------------

data Val =
     Lam Clos
   | Pair Val Val
   | Con Name Val
   | Unit
   | Set
   | Pi  Val Clos
   | Sig Val Clos
   | One
   | Fun SClos
   | Sum SClos
   | Nt Neut
   deriving Show

data Neut = Gen  Int
          | App  Neut Val
          | Fst  Neut
          | Snd  Neut
          | NtFun SClos Neut
   deriving Show

type SClos = (Branch, Rho)

-- Function closures
data Clos = Cl Patt Exp Rho | ClCmp Clos Name
   deriving Show

-- instantiation of a closure by a value
(*) :: Clos -> Val -> Val
(Cl p e rho) * v = eval e (UpVar rho p v)
```

```
(ClCmp f c ) * v = f * Con c v


mkCl :: Patt -> Exp -> Rho -> Clos
mkCl p e rho = Cl p e rho


clCmp :: Clos -> Name -> Clos
clCmp g c  = ClCmp g c


get s [] = error ("get " ++ show s)
get s ((s1,u):us) | s == s1 = u
get s ((s1,u):us)          = get s us


app :: Val -> Val -> Val
app (Lam f)              v       = f * v
app (Fun (ces, rho)) (Con c v)   =
  app (eval (get c es) rho) v
app (Fun s)          (Nt k)      = Nt(NtFun s k)
app (Nt k)           m           = Nt(App k m)
app w u = error "app "


vfst :: Val -> Val
vfst (Pair u1 _) = u1
vfst (Nt k)      = Nt(Fst k)
vfst w = error "vfst "


vsnd :: Val -> Val
vsnd (Pair _ u2) = u2
vsnd (Nt k)      = Nt(Snd k)
vsnd w =  error "vsnd "


---------------------------------------------
-- Environment
---------------------------------------------


data Rho = RNil | UpVar Rho Patt Val | UpDec Rho Decl
  deriving Show


getRho :: Rho -> Name -> Val
getRho (UpVar rho p v) x | x 'inPat' p = patProj p x v
                         | otherwise   = getRho rho x
```

```
getRho (UpDec rho (Def  p _ e)) x
  | x 'inPat' p = patProj p x (eval e rho)
  | otherwise   = getRho rho x
getRho rho0@(UpDec rho (Drec p _ e)) x
  | x 'inPat' p = patProj p x (eval e rho0)
  | otherwise   = getRho rho x
getRho RNil _ = error "getRho"


inPat :: Name -> Patt -> Bool
inPat x (PVar y)       = x == y
inPat x (PPair p1 p2) = inPat x p1 || inPat x p2
inPat _ Punit         = False


patProj :: Patt -> Name -> Val -> Val
patProj (PVar y)      x v | x == y        = v
patProj (PPair p1 p2) x v | x 'inPat' p1 = patProj p1 x (vfst v)
                          | x 'inPat' p2 = patProj p2 x (vsnd v)
patProj _ _ _ = error "patProj"


lRho :: Rho -> Int
lRho RNil             = 0
lRho (UpVar rho _ _) = lRho rho + 1
lRho (UpDec rho _  ) = lRho rho


eval :: Exp -> Rho -> Val
eval e0 rho = case e0 of
    ESet          -> Set
    EDec d e      -> eval e (UpDec rho d)
    ELam p e      -> Lam $ mkCl p e rho
    EPi  p a b    -> Pi  (eval a rho) $ mkCl p b rho
    ESig p a b    -> Sig (eval a rho) $ mkCl p b rho
    EOne          -> One
    Eunit         -> Unit
    EFst e        -> vfst (eval e rho)
    ESnd e        -> vsnd (eval e rho)
    EApp e1 e2    -> app (eval e1 rho) (eval e2 rho)
    EVar x        -> getRho rho x
    EPair e1 e2   -> Pair  (eval e1 rho) (eval e2 rho)
    ECon c e1     -> Con c (eval e1 rho)
    ESum cas      -> Sum (cas, rho)
```

```
    EFun ces      -> Fun (ces, rho)
    e -> error $ "eval: " ++ show e


------------------------------------------------------------
-- Normal forms
------------------------------------------------------------


data NExp =
      NLam Int NExp
    | NPair NExp NExp
    | NCon Name NExp
    | NUnit
    | NSet
    | NPi NExp Int NExp
    | NSig NExp Int NExp
    | NOne
    | NFun NSClos
    | NSum NSClos
    | NNt NNeut
    deriving (Eq,Show)

data NNeut = NGen Int
           | NApp NNeut NExp
           | NFst NNeut
           | NSnd  NNeut
           | NNtFun NSClos NNeut
    deriving (Eq,Show)

type NSClos = (Branch, NRho)

data NRho = NRNil | NUpVar NRho Patt NExp | NUpDec NRho Decl
    deriving (Eq,Show)


--------------------------------------------
-- Readback functions
--------------------------------------------


rbV :: Int -> Val  -> NExp

rbV k v0 = case v0 of
```

```
        Lam f          -> NLam k (rbV (k+1) (f * genV k))
        Pair u v       -> NPair (rbV k u) (rbV k v)
        Con  c v       -> NCon  c (rbV k v)
        Unit           -> NUnit
        Set            -> NSet
        Pi   t g       -> NPi (rbV k t) k (rbV (k+1) (g * genV k))
        Sig  t g       -> NSig (rbV k t) k (rbV (k+1) (g * genV k))
        One            -> NOne
        Fun (s,rho)    -> NFun (s,rbRho k rho)
        Sum (s,rho)    -> NSum (s,rbRho k rho)
        Nt l           -> NNt (rbN k l)

rbN :: Int -> Neut -> NNeut
rbN i k0 = case k0 of
        Gen j      -> NGen j
        App k m -> NApp (rbN i k) (rbV i m)
        Fst k      -> NFst (rbN i k)
        Snd k      -> NSnd (rbN i k)
        NtFun (s,rho) k -> NNtFun (s,rbRho i rho) (rbN i k)

rbRho :: Int -> Rho -> NRho
rbRho _ RNil = NRNil
rbRho i (UpVar rho p v) = NUpVar (rbRho i rho) p (rbV i v)
rbRho i (UpDec rho d  ) = NUpDec (rbRho i rho) d


------------------------------------------------
-- Error monad and type environment
------------------------------------------------


data G a = Success a | Fail Name

instance  Monad G  where
    (Success x) >>= k    = k x
    Fail s   >>= k       = Fail s
    return               = Success
    fail                 = Fail


type Gamma = [(Name, Val)]

lookupG :: (Show a, Eq a) => a -> [(a,b)] -> G b
```

```
lookupG s [] = fail ("lookupG " ++ show s)-- should never occur
lookupG s ((s1,u):us) | s == s1 = return u
lookupG s ((s1,u):us)           = lookupG s us

-- Updating type environment    Gamma |- p : t = u => Gamma'
upG :: Gamma -> Patt -> Val -> Val -> G Gamma
upG gma Punit          _         _ = return gma
upG gma (PVar x)       t         _ = return $ (x,t):gma
upG gma (PPair p1 p2) (Sig t g) v =
  do gma1 <- upG gma p1 t (vfst v)
     upG gma1 p2 (g * vfst v) (vsnd v)
upG _   p              _         _ =
  fail $ "upG: p = " ++  show p


-------------------------------------------------
-- Type checking rules
-------------------------------------------------


genV :: Int -> Val
genV k = Nt (Gen k)

checkT :: Int -> Rho -> Gamma -> Exp  -> G ()
check  :: Int -> Rho -> Gamma -> Exp  -> Val -> G ()
checkI :: Int -> Rho -> Gamma -> Exp  -> G Val
checkD :: Int -> Rho -> Gamma -> Decl -> G Gamma

checkT k rho gma e0 =
  case e0 of
    EPi  p a b -> do checkT k rho gma a
                     gma1 <- upG gma p (eval a rho) (genV k)
                     checkT (k+1) (UpVar rho p (genV k)) gma1 b
    ESig p a b -> checkT k rho gma (EPi p a b)
    ESet       -> return ()
    a          -> check k rho gma a Set

check k rho gma e0 t0 =
  case (e0, t0) of
    (ELam p e   , Pi  t g )->
        do let gen = genV k
           gma1 <- upG gma p t gen
```

```
                    check (k+1) (UpVar rho p gen) gma1 e (g * gen)
      (EPair e1 e2, Sig t g )->
        do check k rho gma e1 t
           check k rho gma e2 (g * eval e1 rho)
      (ECon c e   , Sum (cas,rho1))->
        do a <- lookupG c cas
           check k rho gma e (eval a rho1)
      (EFun ces, Pi (Sum (cas, rho1)) g) ->
        if map fst ces == map fst cas
          then sequence_ [check k rho gma e (Pi (eval a rho1)
                     (clCmp g c)) | ((c,e), (_,a)) <- zip ces cas]
          else fail "case branches does not match the data type"
      (Eunit      , One)-> return ()
      (EOne       , Set)-> return ()
      (EPi  p a b , Set)->
          do check k rho gma a Set
             let gen = genV k
             gma1 <- upG gma p (eval a rho) gen
             check (k+1) (UpVar rho p gen) gma1 b Set
      (ESig p a b , Set)-> check k rho gma (EPi p a b) Set
      (ESum cas, Set)  ->
          sequence_ [check k rho gma a Set | (_,a) <- cas]
      (EDec d e   , t  )-> do gma1 <- checkD k rho gma d
                             check k (UpDec rho d) gma1 e t
      (e          , t  )-> do t1 <- checkI k rho gma e
                             eqNf k t t1
    where
    eqNf :: Int -> Val -> Val -> G ()
    eqNf i m1 m2
      | e1 == e2  = return ()
      | otherwise = fail $ "eqNf: " ++ show e1 ++ "=/=" ++ show e2
      where e1 = rbV i m1
            e2 = rbV i m2


checkI k rho gma e0 =
  case e0 of
    EVar x      -> lookupG x gma
    EApp e1 e2 -> do t1 <- checkI k rho gma e1
                     (t, g) <- extPiG t1
                     check k rho gma e2 t
```

```
                             return (g * eval e2 rho)
      EFst e      -> do t <- checkI k rho gma e
                        (a,_) <- extSigG t
                        return a
      ESnd e      -> do t <- checkI k rho gma e
                        (_, g) <- extSigG t
                        return (g * vfst (eval e rho))

      e           -> fail ("checkI: " ++ show e)
    where
    extPiG :: Val -> G (Val, Clos)
    extPiG (Pi t g) = return (t, g)
    extPiG u        = fail ("extPiG " ++ showVal u)

    extSigG :: Val -> G (Val, Clos)
    extSigG (Sig t g) = return (t, g)
    extSigG u         = fail ("extSigG " ++ showVal u)

showVal u = show (rbV 0 u)

checkD k rho gma d@(Def  p a e) = do
  checkT k rho gma a
  let t = eval a rho
  check k rho gma e t
  upG gma p t (eval e rho)

checkD k rho gma d@(Drec p a e) = do
  checkT k rho gma a
  let t   = eval a rho
      gen = genV k
  gma1 <- upG gma p t gen
  check (k+1) (UpVar rho p gen) gma1 e t
  let v = eval e (UpDec rho d)
  upG gma p t v


--------------------------------------------------------
-- Main checking routines
--------------------------------------------------------
```

```
-- The input is checked as an expression of type One.
checkMain :: Exp -> G ()
checkMain e = check 0 RNil [] e One

-- checking a string input
checkStr :: String -> IO()
checkStr s =
  case parseExp $ myLex s of -- parsing using routines
    Fail msg -> putStrLn $ "Parse error: " ++ msg
    Success (e,_) ->
      case checkMain e of
        Fail  msg' ->
         putStrLn ("type-checking failed:\n" ++ msg')
        Success _  ->
         putStrLn ("type-checking succeded.")

-- checking the content of a file.
checkFile :: String -> IO()
checkFile file = checkStr =<< readFile file
```

7

Program semantics and infinite regular terms

Bruno Courcelle

Institut Universitaire de France
Université Bordeaux 1,
Laboratoire Bordelais de Recherche en Informatique

Abstract

The communication by Gilles Kahn, Jean Vuillemin and myself at the second International Colloquium on Automata, Languages and Programming, held in Saarbrücken in 1974 is in French in the proceedings, and has not been published as a journal article. However, Todd Veldhuizen wrote in 2002 an English translation that is reproduced in the next chapter.

À propos Chapter 8

It was quite a surprise for me to receive a message from Todd Veldhuizen saying that he had translated from French a 30-year-old conference paper presented at the second International Colloquium on Automata, Languages and Programming, held in Saarbrücken in 1974, of which I am coauthor with G. Kahn and J. Vuillemin. He did that work because he felt the paper was "seminal". First of all I would like to thank him for this work. The publication of his translation in a volume dedicated to the memory of Gilles Kahn is a testimony of the gratitude of Jean Vuillemin and myself to him, and the recognition of an important scientific contribution of Gilles among many others.

In this overview, I indicate a few research directions that can be traced back to that communication. I give only a few related references, this overview is not a thorough bibliographical review of related articles.

In the late 1960s, D. Scott constructed the first model of lambda-calculus, and his construction has been a corner stone for the theory of semantic domains and for denotational semantics [10,12]. Formal semantics of programming languages was beginning during these years.

From Semantics to Computer Science Essays in Honour of Gilles Kahn, eds Yves Bertot, Gérard Huet, Jean-Jacques Lévy and Gordon Plotkin. Published by Cambridge University Press. © Cambridge University Press 2009.

In the early 1970s, this formalization was also considered in a different, more syntactic perspective in the research group lead by Maurice Nivat at INRIA (INRIA, Institut National de Recherche en Informatique et Automatique, was called Laboria in 1974) and at Paris 7 University. This group has developed a theory of program schemes with uninterpreted conditional operators, handling them as basic functions rather than as control structures, which was the usual approach at that time. One obtains in this way a smoother algebraic treatment and more decidability results (although most problems are undecidable, and the decidable ones are actually intractable). This theory is exposed in the book by I. Guessarian [9], and in a chapter of the *Handbook of Theoretical Computer Science* [6].

This approach uses in a fundamental way *infinite terms* (comparable to formal power series) as syntactic objects representing the behaviours of program schemes under all interpretations. (Such terms are traditionally called "trees", in particular in my works, but this terminology is actually inadequate, because trees are different objects in graph theory.) The ICALP communication deals with *regular terms*, i.e. with infinite terms described as unique solutions of certain finite equation systems. Other, less abstract, recursive program schemes correspond to more complex infinite terms (called *algebraic trees*). These terms are related to deterministic context-free languages like regular terms are to regular languages. Regular and algebraic "trees" are surveyed in [4].

Another feature of the ICALP communication, which was developed later, is the focus on systems of equations and their least fixed points. In this way, program schemes get closer to denotational semantics than to operational semantics. This is coherent with the use of uninterpreted conditional operators. However, term rewriting systems are still useful for proving properties of program schemes depending on equational axioms satisfied by the base functions. The term "algebraic semantics" referring to this approach was in current use in the late 1970s. See [6,9].

Program transformations by "folding and unfolding" recursive definitions have raised a lot of interest. The characterization of equivalences of programs in terms of formal proof systems has certainly benefited from these developments. Recursive program schemes and grammars of various types are treated in a uniform way in my survey [5]. The existence of a formal system able to express the equivalence of recursive program schemes is the central fact proved by G. Sénizergues from which follows the decidability of the equivalence problem for deterministic pushdown automata [14,15]. (Deciding equality of infinite terms is also relevant in the study of recursive data types [1]). A system for proving the equivalence of *monadic recursion schemes* linked with simple deterministic languages was proposed shortly after ICALP'74 by J. Vuillemin and myself [8]. On the other hand, I. Walukiewicz has proved in [16] the completeness of a formal proof system for the μ-calculus, a language based on least and greatest fixed-points of systems of equations.

Regular infinite terms arise in a natural way as most general first-order unifiers of regular infinite terms, but also of finite ones. This extension of the results of the ICALP'74 communication has been studied by G. Huet and G. Kahn (but their projected article has never been completed[1]) and included in G. Huet's doctoral dissertation [11]. A detailed account is given in my survey [4], and the idea of using regular infinite terms as most general unifiers has been used by A. Colmerauer in some version of PROLOG [3]. Regular infinite terms also arise in the decidability proof of monadic second-order logic on the infinite complete binary tree given by M. Rabin [13], also in the late 1960s. They form the ground level of a hierarchy of infinite graphs having a decidable monadic second-order theory defined by D. Caucal [2], and the base of a definition of certain higher-order recursion schemes by T. Knapik and myself [7].

References

[1] F. Cardone and M. Coppo, Decidability properties of recursive types. *ICTCS 2003*, Bertinoro, Italy, Lecture Notes in Computer Science 2841, pp. 242–255, Springer-Verlag, 2003.

[2] D. Caucal, On infinite terms having a decidable monadic theory. *MFCS 2002*, Lecture Notes in Computer Science 2420, pp. 165-176, Springer-Verlag, 2002.

[3] A. Colmerauer, Prolog and infinite trees, logic programming, In: W. Clark and S.Tarnlund (eds.), pp. 153–172. Academic Press, 1982.

[4] B. Courcelle, Fundamental properties of infinite trees, *Theoretical Computer Science*, **25**:95–169, 1983.

[5] B. Courcelle, Equivalences and transformations of regular systems. Applications to recursive program schemes and grammars. *Theoretical Computer Science*, **42**:1–122, 1986.

[6] B. Courcelle, Recursive applicative program schemes. In: J. Van Leeuwen (ed.), *Handbook of Theoretical Computer Science, Volume B*, pp. 459–492. Elsevier, 1990.

[7] B. Courcelle and T. Knapik, The evaluation of first-order substitution is monadic second-order compatible. *Theoretical Computer Science*, **281**:177–206, 2002.

[8] B. Courcelle and J. Vuillemin, Completeness results for the equivalence of recursive schemas. *Journal of Computing Systems Science*, **12**:179–197, 1976.

[9] I. Guessarian, *Algebraic Semantics*, Lecture Notes in Computer Science 99, Springer Verlag, 1981.

---

[1] G. Huet, private communication.

[10] C. Gunter and D. Scott, Semantic domains. In: J. Van Leeuwen (ed.), *Handbook of Theoretical Computer Science, Volume B*, pp. 633–674. Elsevier, 1990.

[11] G. Huet, *Résolution d'équations dans des langages d'ordre* $1, 2, \ldots, \omega$. Doctoral dissertation, Université Paris 7, 1976.

[12] P. Mosses, Denotational semantics. In: J. Van Leeuwen (ed.), *Handbook of Theoretical Computer Science, Volume B*, pp. 575–632. Elsevier, 1990.

[13] M. Rabin, Decidability of second-order theories and automata on infinite trees, *Transactions of the American Mathematical Society*, **141**:1–35, 1969.

[14] G. Sénizergues, Complete formal systems for equivalence problems, *Theoretical Computer Science*, **231**:309–334, 1999.

[15] G. Sénizergues, L(A) = L(B) ?, *Theoretical Computer Science*, **251**:1–166, 2001.

[16] I. Walukiewicz, Completeness of Kozen's axiomatization of propositional μ-calculus, *Information and Computation*, **157**:142–182, 2000.

8

Algorithms for equivalence and reduction to minimal form for a class of simple recursive equations

Bruno Courcelle, Gilles Kahn, Jean Vuillemin

IRIA Laboria, Rocquencourt, France

Foreword

This document presents a translation for historical perspective of the paper: "B. Courcelle, G. Kahn, and J. Vuillemin. Algorithmes d'équivalence et de réduction à des expressions minimales dans une classe d'équations récursives simples, in, Jacques Loeckx, editor, *Automata, Languages and Programming*, volume 14 of *Lecture Notes in Computer Science*, pages 200–213. Springer Verlag, 1974". This text is published with kind permission of Springer Science and Business Media. This text was translated from French to English by T. Veldhuizen of Waterloo University, Canada.

Abstract

In this paper, we describe an algorithm for deciding equivalence in a domain whose objects are defined by uninterpreted fixpoint equations. The algorithm is then applied to finding minimal representations of those objects.

8.1 Introduction

Many recent works, for example [4, 8, 9, 11] use the notion of fixpoint equation to express semantics of programming languages. We study here a "pure language of fixpoints" with uninterpreted function symbols, which omits in particular the conditional operator *if-then-else*.

In the study of fixpoint equations, of which a typical example is the equation $X = f(X, g(X))$, we ask certain questions, for example:

From Semantics to Computer Science Essays in Honour of Gilles Kahn, eds Yves Bertot, Gérard Huet, Jean-Jacques Lévy and Gordon Plotkin. Published by Cambridge University Press. © Cambridge University Press 2009.

- is the equation $X = f(X, g(X))$ equivalent to the equation $Y = f(f(Y, g(Y)), g(Y))$?
- does there exist a simpler equation equivalent to

$$Z = g(g(Z))$$

or to the system

$$\begin{cases} X &=& f(Y, g(X), Y) \\ Y &=& g(X) \end{cases}$$

- can the variable X defined by the system

$$\begin{cases} X &=& f(X, Y) \\ Y &=& g(X, Y) \end{cases}$$

be defined by a single equation?

In the second section, we study *simple recursive equations*. We show the existence of *canonical forms* characterizing a class of equivalent equations. The canonical form minimizes the size of the equation in its equivalence class.

The third section, independent of the first (except where definitions of syntax and semantics are concerned), studies the same problems for *systems of recursive equations*, deriving a *notion of canonical form* that minimizes the *number of equations in the system*. This last problem is then addressed and resolved.

This work is motivated by a variety of questions such as the study of recursive datatype definitions in Algol 68 (C. Lewis and B. Rosen [6]), the formalization of equivalence proofs of parallel programs (G. Kahn [4]) and the study of decidable sub-theories of the theory of program schemas.

Other authors (J. Engelfriet [3], C. Pair [10], J. Kral [5]) have independently obtained related results in syntactically and semantically different frameworks.

8.2 Simple recursive equations

For clarity of exposition, we start by defining fixpoint equations in a single unknown.

8.2.1 Syntax

Terms are constructed from function symbols $\{F, G, H, \ldots\}$ each having some arity, and from the variable symbol X by the rules.

(i) Function symbols of arity 0 (or *constants*) and the symbol X are terms.
(ii) If $T_1, T_2, \ldots, T_n$ are terms and F is a function symbol of arity n, then $F(T_1, T_2, \ldots, T_n)$ is a term.

If T is a term, $X = T$ is a fixpoint equation.

In what follows, it is useful to define a partial order $\leq$ on the set of terms by the following rules:

(i) For all terms T, we have $X \leq T$.
(ii) If $T_1 \leq T_1', \ldots, T_n \leq T_n'$ then $F(T_1, \ldots, T_n) \leq F(T_1', \ldots, T_n')$.

For other terms, $T_1 \leq T_2$ if and only if T_2 is the result of substituting in T_1 some terms for some occurrences of X.

Example 8.1

$$F(X, G(X, X)) \leq F(H(X), G(X, H(X)))$$

but $F(X, G(X, X)) \not\leq F(X, H(X))$.

When given two terms T and T', we can define a lower bound $\Sigma(T, T')$ such that $\Sigma(T, T') \leq T$ and $\Sigma(T, T') \leq T'$ in the following manner:

$$\Sigma(T, X) = \Sigma(X, T) = X$$
$$\Sigma(F(T_1, T_2, \ldots, T_n), G(T_1', T_2', \ldots, T_m')) = X \quad \text{if } F \neq G$$
$$\Sigma(F(T_1, T_2, \ldots, T_n), F(T_1', T_2', \ldots, T_n')) = F(\Sigma(T_1, T_1'), \ldots, \Sigma(T_n, T_n'))$$

Example 8.2 $\Sigma(F(X, G(X)), F(G(X), H(X))) = F(X, X)$

Notation For a term T in which the letter X occurs m times, we denote by $T\{T_1, \ldots, T_m\}$ the result of substituting the term T_i for the ith occurrence of X in T, for each i in $[1, m]$.

Lemma 8.3 *For all terms T and T' there exist terms $T_1, \ldots, T_m$ and $T_1', \ldots, T_m'$ such that:*

$$T = \Sigma(T, T')\{T_1, \ldots, T_m\}$$
$$T' = \Sigma(T, T')\{T_1', \ldots, T_m'\}$$

8.2.2 Semantics

(a) We interpret fixpoint equations in a *domain* $\mathcal{D}$ which must satisfy the following requirements:

   (i) The set $\mathcal{D}$ is provided with a partial order relation $\subseteq$. We write $\equiv$ for the induced equivalence relation.
   (ii) There exists in $\mathcal{D}$ a least element $\bot$.
   (iii) Every denumerable ascending chain has a least upper bound.

   This structure, which is slightly less restrictive than that of complete lattice, used by D. Scott [11], and was also used in [7], [8] and [12].

(b)

   (i) With each constant symbol C is associated an element c in $\mathcal{D}$.
   (ii) With each function symbol F of arity n is associated a map f from $\mathcal{D}^n$ to $\mathcal{D}$ which is *monotone* and *continuous* in each of its arguments. (See R. Milner [7] for a definition of these notions).
   (iii) With each term T is associated in a natural way a map t from $\mathcal{D}$ to $\mathcal{D}$, and with the fixpoint equation $X = T$ we associate the least fixpoint of $t{:}\mathcal{D} \to \mathcal{D}$ which we again call the least fixpoint of the equation. It is defined as the upper bound in $\mathcal{D}$ of the set $\{t^n(\bot) \mid n \geq 0\}$. (See again [7]).

Convention We systematically use upper-case letters to designate syntactic objects, and lower-case letters to designate the associated semantic objects.

(c) We are now going to construct a *canonical interpretation* of our language, which plays the role of the Herbrand universe for first-order theories. The domain $\mathcal{D}$ of the canonical interpretation consists of the set of infinite sequences of terms $\{T_i \mid i \in \mathbb{N}\}$ constructed with the variable X such that $T_i \leq T_{i+1}$ for all $i \geq 0$.

   We now define an order relation $\subseteq$ on $\mathcal{D}$: if $\tau = \{T_i \mid i \in \mathbb{N}\}$ and $\tau' = \{T_i' \mid i \in \mathbb{N}\}$ are two elements of $\mathcal{D}$, then $\tau \subseteq \tau'$ if and only if $\forall i \, \exists j \; T_i \leq T_j'$.

   The minimal element of $\mathcal{D}$ is $\bot = \{T_i \mid \forall i \in \mathbb{N}, T_i = X\}$. Every chain $\tau_1 \subseteq \tau_2 \subseteq \cdots \subseteq \tau_i \subseteq \cdots$ in which $\tau_i = \{T_i^i \mid j \in \mathbb{N}\}$ admits an upper bound $\tau = \bigcup_{i \in \mathbb{N}} \tau_i = \{T_i' \mid i \in \mathbb{N}\}$ where for all i, $T_i' = T_{n_i}^i$, and the sequence n_i chosen so that $\forall i (n_i \geq i$ and $T_{n_i}^i \leq T_{n_{i+1}}^{i+1})$. (There exists such a sequence since the τ_i's form an ascending chain.)

A constant C is therefore interpreted as the sequence:

$$c = \{T_i \mid T_i = C, i \in \mathbb{N}\}$$

The interpretation f of an n-ary symbol F maps n sequences $\{T_k^i \mid k \in \mathbb{N}\}$ for i in $[1, n]$ to the sequence $\{F(T_k^1, T_k^2, \ldots, T_k^n) \mid k \in \mathbb{N}\}$. It is easy to verify that we have a legitimate interpretation. (More rigorously, the interpretation domain that we have considered is $\mathcal{D}/\equiv$).

We write $P\{A/X\}$ for the result of substituting A for all occurrences of X in a term P. We can verify that in our canonical interpretation $Y(t) = \{T^i \mid i \in \mathbb{N}\}$ with

$$T^1 = T \text{ and } T^{i+1} = T\{T^i/X\}$$

The interest in the canonical interpretation arises from the following lemma:

Lemma 8.4 *Two fixpoint equations are equivalent if and only if they are equivalent in the canonical interpretation.*

Proof It suffices to demonstrate that if $X = T$ and $X = T'$ are equivalent in the canonical interpretation c, they must be equivalent in all other interpretations I.

Let the fixpoints of these equations be $Y(t) = \{T^i \mid i \in \mathbb{N}\}$ and $Y(t') = \{T'^j \mid j \in \mathbb{N}\}$ in the canonical interpretation. It is easy to verify that $T_1 \leq T_2$ implies $t_1(\bot) \subseteq_I t_2(\bot)$ for all interpretations I. From $\forall i \, \exists j \, T^i \leq T'^j$ we deduce

$$\forall i \, \exists j \, t^i(\bot) \subseteq_I t'^j(\bot)$$

and by symmetry

$$\forall k \, \exists l \, t'^k(\bot) \subseteq_I t^l(\bot).$$

Consequently, in I, $\bigcup_{i \in \mathbb{N}} t^i(\bot) \equiv_I \bigcup_{i \in \mathbb{N}} t'^j(\bot)$. $\quad\square$

We can now state two technical lemmas that will be useful later.

Lemma 8.5 *If two terms $F(T_1, \ldots, T_n)$ and $G(T_1', \ldots, T_m')$ are equal in the canonical interpretation, then $F = G$, $n = m$, and for all i, $T_i = T_i'$ in the canonical interpretation.*

Proof Let $\{T_k^i \mid i \in \mathbb{N}\}$ and $\{T_k'^i \mid i \in \mathbb{N}\}$ be the interpretations of T_k and T_k'. Since:

$$\forall i \, \exists j \, F(T_1^i, \ldots, T_n^i) \leq G(T_1'^j, \ldots, T_m'^j)$$

from which we deduce $F = G$, $n = m$ and

$$\forall i \; \exists j \; T_k^i \leq T_k'^j \; (k \in [1, n])$$

and the opposite inequality also holds.   □

Lemma 8.6 *For all terms T and T', if $Y(t) \subseteq Y(t')$ in the canonical interpretation, then either $T = X$ or $Y(t) \equiv Y(t')$.*

Proof (a) First we define two notions of "depth" of a term T, $\mathrm{pmax}(T)$ and $\mathrm{pmin}(T)$:

$$\begin{cases} \mathrm{pmax}(X) = \mathrm{pmax}(C) = 1 \\ \quad \text{(if } C \text{ is a constant)} \\ \mathrm{pmax}(F(T_1, \ldots, T_n)) = 1 + \max_{1 \leq i \leq n} \{\mathrm{pmax}(T_i)\} \end{cases}$$

$$\begin{cases} \mathrm{pmin}(X) = 1 \; ; \; \mathrm{pmin}(C) = +\infty \\ \quad \text{(if } C \text{ is a constant)} \\ \mathrm{pmin}(F(T_1, \ldots, T_n)) = 1 + \min_{1 \leq i \leq n} \{\mathrm{pmin}(T_i)\} \end{cases}$$

These notions allow us to state the following "alignment" property: if T_1, T_2, T_3 satisfy $T_1 \leq T_3$ and $T_2 \leq T_3$ and $\mathrm{pmax}(T_1) \leq \mathrm{pmin}(T_2)$ then $T_1 \leq T_2$. The proof is done easily by structural induction. We can represent this situation by the following figure:

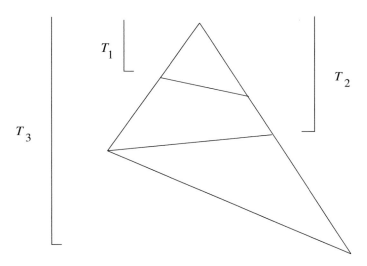

(b) Now, given two fixpoints $Y(t) = \{T^i \mid i \in \mathbb{N}\}$ and $Y(t') = \{T'^i \mid i \in \mathbb{N}\}$, if they satisfy $Y(t) \subseteq Y(t')$ then $\forall i\ \exists j\ T^i \leq T'^j$.

Let us also show that if we have $\forall j\ \exists i\ T'^j \leq T^i$, if $T \neq X$. Given T'^j, we can always find an i such that

$$\mathrm{pmin}(T^i) \geq \mathrm{pmax}(T'^j)$$

It is therefore possible to choose k such that $k \geq j$ and $T^i \leq T'^k$. Then $T'^j \leq T'^k$ and by the alignment property $T'^j \leq T^i$. Then $Y(t') \subseteq Y(t)$.

□

8.2.3 Normal form and equivalence algorithm

We are going to show that the set of terms leading to equivalent fixpoint equations is closed under the operation Σ.

Notation If two terms T and T' have interpretations t and t' in the canonical interpretation, we write $\sigma(t, t')$ for the interpretation of $\Sigma(T, T')$.

Lemma 8.7 *If $t(a) \equiv t'(a)$ for some a, then $\sigma(t, t')(a) \equiv t(a) \equiv t'(a)$.*

Proof By structural induction on T:

(1) If $T = X$ or $T = C$ the property is obvious.
(2) If $T = F(T_1, \ldots, T_n)$ two cases arise:

- $T' = X$, then $\Sigma(T, T') = X$ and the property holds;
- $T' = G(T'_1, \ldots, T'_m)$ and so necessarily $F = G$, $m = n$ and $t'_i(a) = t_i(a)$ for all i in $[1, n]$. By the induction hypothesis, $\sigma(t_i, t'_i)(a) = t_i(a)$ and therefore

$$t(a) = f(\sigma(t_1, t'_1)(a), \ldots, \sigma(t_n, t'_n)(a)) = \sigma(t, t')(a).$$

□

Lemma 8.8 *If two terms T and T' have the same fixpoint, then $\Sigma(T, T')$ also has the same fixpoint. In other words $Y(t) \equiv Y(t')$ implies $Y(t) = Y(\sigma(t, t'))$.*

Proof We have $Y(t) \equiv t(Y(t)) \equiv Y(t') \equiv t'(Y(t')) \equiv t'(Y(t))$. By Lemma 8.7 we obtain $\sigma(t, t')(Y(t)) = Y(t)$ and by minimality $Y(\sigma(t, t')) \subseteq Y(t)$. Lemma 8.6 therefore implies:

- either $Y(\sigma(t, t')) \equiv Y(t)$ and the proof is finished;
- or $\Sigma(T, T') \equiv X$, but this is compatible with $Y(t) = Y(t')$ only if $T = T' = X$ in which case we again have $Y(\sigma(t, t')) = Y(t)$.

$\square$

We are now ready to show (non-constructively) the existence of a minimal form for the set of terms leading to equivalent fixpoint equations.

We write $\|T\|$ for the size of a term T, defined recursively by:

(1) $\|X\| = 0$

(2) $\|F(T_1, \dots T_n)\| = 1 + \sum_{i=1}^{n} \|T_i\|$.

Lemma 8.9 *In the set $E(T) = \{T' \mid Y(t') \equiv Y(t)\}$ of terms having the same least fixpoint as T, there exists an element T^* of minimal size.*

Proof Let T_1 and T_2 be two different terms of $E(T)$ of minimal size. Then T_1 and T_2 are inevitably incomparable, otherwise, from Lemma 8.3, one of the two would be of size strictly less than the other. But then, again $\|\Sigma(T_1, T_2)\| < \|T_1\|$ from the lemma. Since $E(T)$ is closed under Σ by Lemma 8.8, T_1 and T_2 cannot be minimal. $\square$

For the moment, Lemma 8.9 does not allow the construction of T^*, but we will present a syntactic relation between all the terms having the same fixpoint as T^*. We write $T' \to T''$ for the relation defined by these axioms:

(i) $\vdash T \to T$

(ii) $T \to U \vdash T \to U\{\{X/T\}\}$

where the notation $U\{\{X/T\}\}$ indicates that some occurrences of X in U have been replaced by T. We write $D(T) = \{U \mid \vdash T \to U\}$.

Theorem 8.10 *The set $E(T)$ of terms having the same least fixpoint as T is identical to the set $D(T^*) = \{U \mid \vdash T^* \to U\}$ of terms deriving from the minimal element T^* of $E(T)$.*

Proof Of course $E(T) = E(T^*)$. The fact that $D(T^*) \subseteq E(T^*)$ is already known (for example cf. [10]). We now show that $E(T^*) \subseteq D(T^*)$: let T' be a term of minimal size belonging to $E(T^*)$ and not to $D(T^*)$. We necessarily have $T^* \leq T'$ because T^* is a normal form. So, $T' = T^*\{T_1, \dots T_k\}$. Since T' is in $E(T^*)$, we have

$$Y(t^*) \equiv Y(t') \equiv t'(Y(t')) \equiv t'(Y(t^*)).$$

Therefore $t^*(Y(t^*)) = t'(Y(t^*))$.

From Lemma 8.5, we deduce $Y(t^*) \equiv t_i(Y(t^*))$ for $i \in [1, k]$. By minimality and with Lemma 8.6, we obtain $Y(t_i) = Y(t^*)$. But since the T_i's are smaller than T' they are by hypothesis in $D(T^*)$. Consequently T' is in $D(T^*)$. $\qquad\square$

Theorem 8.10 implies that the normal form T^* of T is a subterm of T, namely the smallest subterm T^* such that $T^* \to T$. This gives us an algorithm for computing this normal form and a decision procedure for the equivalence of two fixpoint equations. Rather than presenting these two algorithms in greater detail here, we now proceed to the general case, that of systems of fixpoint equations.

8.3 Systems of recursive equations

The results obtained in the second section extend to the case of systems of fixpoint equations: with each system, one can associate a canonical system of minimal size (the "size" of a system is the sum of the sizes of its constituting equations). Thus, one obtains an algorithm for deciding the equivalence of two systems and one can also compute an equivalent system with a minimal number of equations. However, this last system is not necessarily unique.

8.3.1 Syntax

We use a set $\Xi = \{X_1, \dots, X_n\}$ of variables.

A *system* is:

(i) a family of fixpoint equations $X_i = T_i$, for $i = 1, 2, \dots n$. The terms T_i are constructed over the variables X_i, $i \in [1, n]$.

(ii) A *main variable* X_1.

A system is said to be *connected* if all its equations are needed to compute X_1, with the following definition: the equation $X_i = T_i$ and all the equations necessary for variables of T_i are needed to compute X_i. The *size* of a system $S = \{X_i = T_i \mid i \in [1, n]\}$ is defined by $\|S\| = \sum_1^n \|T_i\|$ and a system is said to be *uniform* if for all i, $\|T_i\| = 1$ i.e., if T_i contains a single function symbol.

8.3.2 Semantics

If we interpret terms as in Section 8.2.2 in a domain $\mathcal{D}$, then for the set $\{T_i \mid i \in [1, n]\}$ one gets an obvious map from $\mathcal{D}^n$ to $\mathcal{D}^n$ and thus a fixpoint in $\mathcal{D}^n$. We write $Y(x_i)$ for the component of this vector corresponding to the variable X_i.

Two systems S and S' are *equivalent* if, for all interpretations we have $Y(x_1) \equiv Y(x_1')$. The notion of canonical interpretation extends trivially and the reader may verify that Lemma 8.4 remains valid.

A system $\{X_i = T_i \mid i \in [1, n]\}$ is said to be *normal* if it is not equivalent to a system $\{X_j = T_j \mid j \in [1, n]\}$ in which the T_j's are subterms of the T_i and at least one of them is a proper subterm or a variable.

A proper subterm of T is a subterm of T different from T.

The case of a system containing a single equation, the system is normal if the equation is in normal form.

8.3.3 Canonical systems

Given a system $S = \{X_i = T_i \mid i \in [1, n]\}$ we start by constructing a uniform system $\overline{S}$ equivalent to it. For example:

$$S = \left\{ \begin{array}{lcl} X_1 & = & F(X_1, G(X_1, X_2)) \\ X_2 & = & H(F(X_1, X_2)) \end{array} \right.$$

(main variable X_1)

$$\overline{S} = \left\{ \begin{array}{lcl} Y_1 & = & F(Y_1, Y_3) \\ Y_2 & = & H(Y_4) \\ Y_3 & = & G(Y_1, Y_2) \\ Y_4 & = & F(Y_1, Y_2) \end{array} \right.$$

(main variable Y_1)

Formally, $\overline{S}$ is constructed as follows: let us call $\mathcal{J} = \{\tau_i \mid i \in [1, m]\}$ the set of proper subterms of S (in the case of our example: $\mathcal{J} = \{X_1, X_2, F(X_1, X_2), G(X_1, X_2)\}$.) The system $\overline{S}$ is constructed over new variables $Y_i, i \in [1, m]$ associated as follows with elements of $\mathcal{J}$:

(1) If $\tau_i = X_i$ and if $X_i = F(\tau_{i_1}, \ldots, \tau_{i_k})$ is an equation of S, then $Y_i = F(Y_{i_1}, \ldots, Y_{i_k})$ is an equation of $\overline{S}$.
(2) If $\tau_i = F(\tau_{i_1}, \ldots, \tau_{i_k})$ then $Y_i = F(Y_{i_1}, \ldots, Y_{i_k})$ is an equation of $\overline{S}$.
(3) The main variable of $\overline{S}$ is the new variable Y_1 associated with X_1.

Lemma 8.11 $S \equiv \overline{S}$

Lemma 8.12 *If S is connected, then $\overline{S}$ is connected. If S is normal, then $\overline{S}$ is normal.*

For a uniform system $S = \{X_i = F_i(X_{i_1}, \ldots, X_{i_{k(i)}}) \mid i \in I\}$ we compute the equivalence relation over variables defined by $Y(x_i) \equiv Y(x_j)$ for all interpretations, which we write $X_i \equiv X_j$. We inductively define an increasing sequence of subsets of $\Xi \times \Xi$, if $\Xi = \{X_i \mid i \in I\}$:

(1) $D_0 = \{(X_i, X_j) \in \Xi \times \Xi \mid F_i \neq F_j\}$
(2) $D_{n+1} = D_n \cup \{(X_i, X_j) \in \Xi \times \Xi \mid F_i = F_j \wedge$
$\quad \exists m \in [1, k(i)]$ such that $(X_{i_m}, X_{j_m}) \in D_n\}$

Lemma 8.13

(i) *There exists an integer l such that $D_l = \bigcup_{n=0}^{\infty} D_n$.*
(ii) *$X_i \equiv X_j$ if and only if the pair (X_i, X_j) does not appear in D_l.*

Proof (i) The existence of l comes simply from the fact that Ξ is finite. Let us prove (ii) by Scott induction (cf. [5]) on the formula Φ:

$$\bigwedge \{X_i \equiv X_j | (X_i, X_j) \notin D_l\}$$

First of all, $\bigwedge \Omega \equiv \Omega$. In addition, Φ implies:

$$\Phi\{T_1/X_1, \ldots, T_i/X_i, \ldots, T_n/X_n\}$$

since $(X_i, X_j) \notin D_l$ leads to $T_i \equiv T_j$. □

Theorem 8.14 *The equivalence of two systems of fixpoint equations is decidable.*

Proof Lemma 8.11 makes it possible to reduce to the case of uniform systems. If $S = \{X_i = T_i \mid i \in I\}$ and $S' = \{X_i' = T_i' \mid i \in I'\}$, it is always possible to ensure that $\Xi = \{X_i \mid i \in I\}$ and $\Xi' = \{X_i' \mid i \in I'\}$ are *disjoint* and to consider the system

$$S'' = \{X_i = T_i, \; X_j' = T_j' \mid i \in I, j \in I'\}.$$

The algorithm of Lemma 8.11 tells us whether $X_1 \equiv X_1'$. □

Corollary 8.15 *The equivalence $T \equiv T'$, where T and T' are any terms on the variables of the two systems S and S' is decidable.*

Proof One adds the equations $Z = T$ and $Z' = T'$ and verifies whether $Z \equiv Z'$. □

Theorem 8.16 *For any system S one can construct a corresponding equivalent system S' which is normal, whose size is at most the size of S and which has no more variables.*

Proof Let T be a proper subterm of S, $T \neq X_i$, such that $X_i \equiv T$. This equality permits to "reduce" the system S as follows:

- If T is a variable X_j, one replaces everywhere X_j by X_i and one removes from S the equation defining X_j, $X_j = T_j$. This transformation eliminates one variable from the system without increasing its size. One could also have eliminated X_i instead of X_j; this degree of freedom will be exploited later.
- If T is a subterm of size greater or equal to 1, we replace all its occurrences in S with X_i. The size of the system can only decrease and the system obtained is equivalent to the initial system.

This construction can only be iterated a finite number of times because there may be only a finite number of equivalences $X_i \equiv T$. By definition, the system which one then reaches is normal. □

Example 8.17
$$S_0 \begin{cases} X = F(F(X,Y), Z) \\ Y = G(X, Z) \\ Z = G(X, G(X, Y)). \end{cases}$$

One finds that $Y \equiv Z$. But S_0 is equivalent to S_1:
$$S_1 \begin{cases} X = F(F(X,Y), Y) \\ Y = G(X, Y). \end{cases}$$

But $X \equiv F(X, Y)$. Hence S_1 is therefore equivalent to S_2:
$$S_2 \begin{cases} X = F(X, Y) \\ Y = G(X, Y). \end{cases}$$

So S_2 is normal.

The construction of Theorem 8.16 can be more easily carried out on uniform systems where the only proper subterms are variables.

Lemma 8.13 defines an equivalence relation between these variables and the normal system associated with a uniform system connects to the equivalence classes.

Notation If S is uniform, we write $n(S)$ for the normal system to which it corresponds. With each system S, one associates an equivalent uniform system $\overline{S}$, and $\hat{S} = n(\overline{S})$ that is normal and uniform.

Lemma 8.18 *If R and S are two equivalent, connected systems, then $\hat{R} = \hat{S}$.*

Proof Of course, the equality between $\hat{R}$ and $\hat{S}$ is understood to be up to variable renaming. We first show that for each variable X_i of $\overline{R}$ there exists a variable X'_j of $\overline{S}$ such that $X_i \equiv X'_j$, by recurrence. Since $R \equiv S$ and $\overline{R} \equiv \overline{S}$, we have $X_1 \equiv X'_1$.

If $X_i \equiv X'_j$ and $X_i = F(X_{i_1}, \ldots, X_{i_n})$, $X'_j = F(X'_{j_1}, \ldots, X'_{j_n})$, then $X_{i_1} \equiv X'_{j_1}, \ldots, X_{i_n} \equiv X'_{j_n}$. Consequently, all the variables necessary to X_1 have a corresponding variable in $\overline{S}$. Since $\overline{R}$ is connected, these are all the variables of $\overline{R}$. Of course, the symmetric property is true:

$$\forall j \; \exists i \; X'_j \equiv X_i$$

Therefore there exists a bijection between the equivalence classes of $\overline{R}$ and $\overline{S}$. Since by construction the variables of (respectively) $\hat{R}$ and $\hat{S}$ are independent, we have $\hat{R} = \hat{S}$ modulo a renaming. □

Lemma 8.18 justifies calling the system $\hat{S}$ a canonical system.

Theorem 8.19 *In the set of systems equivalent to a given system S, the canonical system $\hat{S}$ is of minimal size.*

Proof From the construction of $\overline{S}$, it is clear that $\|S\| \geq \|\overline{S}\|$. Since $\|\overline{S}\| \geq \|n(\overline{S})\| = \|\hat{S}\|$ and $\hat{R} = \hat{S}$ for all R equivalent to S, $\hat{S}$ is of minimal size. □

Remark There may exist multiple equivalent systems of minimal size, but only one may be canonical, as the following example illustrates:

$$S_1 = \begin{cases} X = F(X, Y) \\ Y = G(Z) \\ Z = H(X, Y) \end{cases} \quad ; \quad S_2 = \begin{cases} X = F(X, Y) \\ Y = G(H(X, Y)) \end{cases} .$$

Here, $\|S_1\| = \|S_2\|$, $S_1 \equiv S_2$ and S_1 is canonical.

8.3.4 Minimizing the number of equations

One might be interested in a representation of a system that minimizes not the size but the number of equations. The following example illustrates that there is not always a unique system that is normal and minimal (in this sense):

$$S_1 = \left\{ \begin{array}{lll} X & = & F(X,Y) \\ Y & = & G(H(X,Y)) \end{array} \right. ; \qquad S_2 = \left\{ \begin{array}{lll} X' & = & F(X',G(Y')) \\ Y' & = & H(X',G(Y')) \end{array} \right. .$$

Thus S_1 and S_2 are equivalent ($X \equiv X'$), normal and each has a minimum number of equations. But S_1 and S_2 are not identical up to renaming of variables.

We now show how to construct all normal systems and all minimal normal systems.

Definition 8.20 *Let* $S = \{X_i = T_i \mid i \in I\}$ *and* C *be a set of variables of* S, $C = \{X_k \mid k \in K\}$, *containing* X_1 *and having the following property:*

$$\forall l \in I \setminus K, \exists T(l,C),$$

a term using only variables of C *such that* $X_l \equiv T(l,C)$.[1]

We call an S-*cut, denoted by* $C(S)$, *the system associated with such a set* C:

$$C(S) = \{X_i = T_i' \mid X_i \in C\}$$

in which T_i' *is obtained from* T_i *by replacing for all* l *in* $I \setminus K$ *the variable* X_l *by* $T(l,C)$. *To a set* C *containing a minimal number of variables corresponds a* minimal cut.

Theorem 8.21 *The normal systems equivalent to* S *are the cuts of* $\hat{S}$.

Proof If R is a cut of $\hat{S}$, then $R \equiv S$ and R is normal otherwise $\hat{S}$ would not be.

If R is normal and $R \equiv S$, then $\overline{R}$ is normal since $\overline{R} = \hat{R} = \hat{S}$.

But R is a cut of $\hat{S}$ if and only if $\overline{R} = \hat{S}$ and R is normal.   □

Corollary 8.22 *The minimal normal systems equivalent to* S *are the minimal cuts of* $\hat{S}$. *Since there are only a finite number of cuts of* $\hat{S}$, *one can effectively construct these minimal systems.*

---

[1] And by $T(l,C)$ we designate in what follows the least term allowing the definition of X_l.

Example 8.23

$$S = \begin{cases} X &=& F(F(X,Y),Y) \\ Y &=& G(H(X,G(Z))) \\ Z &=& H(X,G(Z)) \end{cases} \qquad \hat{S} = \begin{cases} X &=& F(X,Y) \\ Y &=& G(Z) \\ Z &=& H(X,Y) \end{cases}$$

$$C_1 = \{X,Y,Z\}, \quad C_1(\hat{S}) = \hat{S}$$

$$C_2 = \{X,Y\}, \qquad C_2(\hat{S}) = \begin{cases} X &=& F(X,Y) \\ Y &=& G(H(X,Y)) \end{cases}$$

$$C_3 = \{X,Z\}, \qquad C_3(\hat{S}) = \begin{cases} X &=& F(X,G(Z)) \\ Z &=& H(X,G(Z)) \end{cases}$$

So, we find the two minimal normal forms of S.

Remark If one starts from *a single* recursive equation as in the second section, one always finds a single minimal normal form, the normal form of this equation.

Example 8.24

$$S = \{X = F(X,G(F(X,G(X,X)),X))\}$$
$$\hat{S} = \begin{cases} X &=& F(X,X') \\ X' &=& G(X,X) \end{cases}$$
$$C = \{X\}, \quad C(\hat{S}) = \{X = F(X,G(X,X))\}.$$

8.4 Conclusion

In the opinion of the authors, the interest of this work lies not in the decidability results obtained (which can be with less effort) but in the methods used, in particular the construction of a canonical domain.

This method was used by B. Courcelle and J. Vuillemin [1] for functional systems.

Finally, it is possible to consider the results obtained as completeness results of subtheories of the logic LCF (Logic for Computable Functions) studied by R. Milner [7].

Acknowledgement

Some of the results obtained here were already known by R. Milner, who collaborated in the early phase of this work. B. Courcelle and J. Vuillemin thank T. Veldhuizen for the translation.

Bibliography

[1] B. Courcelle and J. Vuillemin, Completeness results for the equivalence of recursive schemes, *Journal of Computer System Science* **12**:179–197, 1976.

[2] W. P. De Roever, Operational and mathematical semantics for first-order recursive program schemas, (private communication).

[3] J. Engelfriet, A note on infinite trees, *Information Processing Letters* **1**:229–232, 1972.

[4] G. Kahn, A preliminary theory for parallel programs. (Rapport Laboria no. 6, January 1973).

[5] J. Kral, Equivalence of modes and the equivalence of finite automata, *Algol Bulletin* **35**:34–35, 1973.

[6] C. H Lewis and B. K. Rosen, Recursively defined data types: part 1. *Proceedings of the 1st annual ACM SIGACT-SIGPLAN Symposium on Principles of Programming Languages*, pp. 125–138. ACM, New York, 1973.

[7] R. Milner, Models of LCF. Stanford Computer Science Department Report. CS-332, 1973.

[8] R. Milner and R. Weyrauch, Proving compiler correctness in a mechanized logic. In B. Meltzer and D. Michie (eds), *Machine Intelligence* **7**, pp. 51–72. Edinburgh University Press, 1972.

[9] M. Nivat, Sur l'interprétation des schémas de programmes monadiques. Rapport Laboria No. 1, 1972.

[10] C. Pair, Concerning the syntax of Algol 68, *Algol Bulletin* **31**:16–27, 1970.

[11] D. Scott, *Outline of a Mathematical Theory of Computation*. Oxford Monograph PRG-2. Oxford University, 1970.

[12] J. Vuillemin, *Proof Techniques for Recursive Programs*. PhD thesis, Stanford Computer Science Department. 1973.

9

Generalized finite developments

Jean-Jacques Lévy

INRIA and Microsoft Research–INRIA Joint Centre

Abstract

The Finite Development theorem (FD) is a fundamental theorem in the theory of the syntax of the lambda-calculus. It gives sense to parallel reductions by stating that one can contract any given set of (possibly nested) redexes in any lambda term without looping and caring about the order in which these redexes are contracted. This theorem can be used to prove the Church–Rosser property, thus insuring determinism of reductions and uniqueness of normal forms. This paper explains how to extend the FD theorem to a finite number of creations of new redexes, i.e. redexes which do not exist in the initial term. This generalized theorem (gFD) also provides a proof technique to show the completeness of various reduction strategies. Finally it gives a natural intuition to the strong normalization property of the standard first-order typed lambda-calculus. The results in this article are not new, but were often mixed with other arguments; the aim of this paper is to stress on this sole gFD theorem.

9.1 Introduction

The basic operation of the lambda-calculus [6] is beta-reduction

$$(\lambda x.A)B \to A\{x := B\}$$

contracting any redex of the form $(\lambda x.A)B$ into its contractum $A\{x := B\}$ where every occurrence of the free variable x in A is replaced by B. Intuitively $\lambda x.A$ is a function of x producing the term A and beta-reduction describes the passing of the argument B to the function $\lambda x.A$ as in programming languages [4, 13, 22]. The lambda-calculus

From Semantics to Computer Science Essays in Honour of Gilles Kahn, eds Yves Bertot, Gérard Huet, Jean-Jacques Lévy and Gordon Plotkin. Published by Cambridge University Press. © Cambridge University Press 2009.

enjoys the Church–Rosser property, also named full confluence or simply confluence, which ensures the determinacy of results for beta-reductions. For instance if we write $\Delta = \lambda x.xx$ and $I = \lambda x.x$, then we have

$$M = (Ia)(Ia) \leftarrow \Delta(Ia) \rightarrow \Delta a = N$$

and $M \rightarrow a(Ia) \rightarrow aa \leftarrow N$. The common reduct aa of M and N can only be reached by performing two steps from M since the Ia redex is duplicated in M. The proof of the Church–Rosser theorem relies on an inductive argument on the length of *parallel reductions* starting from a given initial term, namely reductions whose parallel steps are of the form

$$M \xrightarrow{\mathcal{F}} M'$$

simultaneously contracting a set $\mathcal{F}$ of redexes in M. For instance, in the previous example, we have

$$M \xrightarrow{\mathcal{F}} aa \leftarrow N$$

where $\mathcal{F}$ is the set of the two Ia redexes in M and the usual reduction step $\rightarrow$ is identified to the contraction of a singleton set of redexes.

The exact definition of these parallel steps is not straightforward. Tait and Martin-Lof [3] axiomatize an anonymous parallel step as the contraction of a given set of redexes in an inside-out way. Curry and Feys [7] use the finite development (FD) theorem. This latter method is more ambitious since it shows that the notion of parallel step is consistent whatever the order in which redexes are contracted. An easy corollary of the FD theorem is the so-called lemma of parallel moves stating that if $\mathcal{F}_1$ and $\mathcal{F}_2$ are two sets of redexes in the lambda-term A and if

$$M \xleftarrow{\mathcal{F}_1} A \xrightarrow{\mathcal{F}_2} N$$

there exists a lambda-term B such that

$$M \xrightarrow{\mathcal{F}_2'} B \xleftarrow{\mathcal{F}_1'} N$$

The proof of the lemma just considers developments of $\mathcal{F}_1 \cup \mathcal{F}_2$. Then full confluence of the lambda-calculus follows easily.

In this article, we look more closely to the FD theorem and want to exhibit the property which makes it hold. Traditionally, the FD theorem is divided into two parts. Let $\mathcal{F}$ be a set of redexes in a given term M. Firstly any reduction relative to $\mathcal{F}$ terminates; secondly all maximal reductions relative to $\mathcal{F}$ end with the same term. In the previous statement, we say that a reduction is relative to $\mathcal{F}$ iff it only contracts residuals of redexes of $\mathcal{F}$. The FD theorem means that the set of reductions relative to $\mathcal{F}$ forms a *canonical system*, i.e. a set of confluent finite reductions. This situation is analogous to the one of the (first-order or higher-order) typed lambda-calculus where the set of all reductions from any given term also forms a canonical system. The difference between the typed lambda-calculus and relative reductions comes from the fact that in the latter case no redex is created. In the untyped lambda-calculus, strong normalization is not valid since reductions may be infinite as with $\Delta\Delta$ where a new redex is always created. But in the typed case, redexes may only be created in a limited form.

The main objective of this paper is to demonstrate that if there is no infinite chain of creations of redexes, the FD theorem may be extended. Therefore we will be able to characterize arbitrarily large canonical subsets of the reduction graph of any lambda-term in the untyped lambda-calculus. It will therefore enlighten strong normalization as the impossibility of producing infinite chains of redex creations.

The generalized FD theorem has been initially studied in [16]; it has been shown for term rewriting systems using recursive path orderings in [18]; it also holds in higher-order term rewriting, including Klop's CRSs, under the name Finite Family Developments in [24].

Some technique will be necessary in stating this generalized FD theorem. The notion of residual of redexes is subtle in the lambda-calculus since disjoint redexes may have nested residuals (this is not happening in term rewriting systems). We will also need the notion of permutation equivalence for reductions in order to define redex families. In Section 9.2, we introduce Hyland–Wadsworth lambda-calculus. In Section 9.3, we review definitions of residuals and finite developments. In Section 9.4, we define historical redexes and redex families. In Section 9.5, we show the generalized FD theorem and apply it to several lambda-calculi. Section 9.6 is the conclusion.

9.2 Hyland–Wadsworth lambda-calculus

Hyland–Wadsworth's lambda-calculus has been used for characterizing Scott's D_∞ model with Böhm trees. Here we use this calculus as a tool for proving termination of the generalized FD theorem.

In this calculus, the set Λ_e of terms is the usual set of lambda-terms but with every subterm equipped with an integer exponent.

Beta-conversion increments the exponents on borders of contracta. The rest of the calculus follows the traditional rules of the untyped lambda-calculus. We also assume that there is a global integer constant L which defines a lambda-calculus up-to-L, that we call in short the $hw(L)$-calculus, as follows:

$$m, n \ ::= \ \text{integer number} \qquad\qquad \text{exponents } (m, n \geq 0)$$

$$U, V \ ::= \ x^n \mid (UV)^n \mid (\lambda x.U)^n \qquad\qquad \text{terms}$$

$$((\lambda x.U)^n V)^m \rightarrow U\{x := V_{[n+1]}\}_{[n+1][m]} \qquad \text{beta-conversion}$$
$$\text{when } n \leq L$$

$$x^n_{[m]} = x^p \qquad\qquad\qquad\qquad\qquad\qquad\qquad \text{projection}$$
$$(UV)^n_{[m]} = (UV)^p \qquad\qquad\qquad\qquad\qquad \text{where } p = \lceil m, n \rceil$$
$$(\lambda x.U)^n_{[m]} = (\lambda x.U)^p$$

$$x^n\{x := W\} = W_{[n]} \qquad\qquad\qquad\qquad\qquad \text{substitution}$$
$$(UV)^n\{x := W\} = (U\{x := W\} \ V\{x := W\})^n$$
$$(\lambda y.U)^n\{x := W\} = (\lambda y.U\{x := W\})^n$$

where $p = \lceil m, n \rceil$ is the maximum of m and n.

The calculus presented here is a slight variant of the exact rules defined by Hyland and Wadsworth which followed rules of application in Scott's D_∞ model where application decrements exponents and a special rule exists for application of a function with a null exponent. Here, we notice that any term is in normal form in the $hw(-1)$ calculus. If $\Delta_n = (\lambda x.(x^0 x^0)^0)^n$ and $\Omega_n = (\Delta_n \Delta_n)^n$, we have Ω_n in normal form when $n > L$ and $\Omega_n \rightarrow \Omega_{n+1}$ when $n \leq L$.

We define the *degree* of a redex $R = ((\lambda x.U)^n V)^m$ to be the exponent n of its function part. We write $degree(R) = n$. In the up-to-L lambda-calculus, a redex is reducible if and only if its degree is not greater than L. Therefore by increasing the global constant L one gives more power to the calculus and reductions may go further. The reduction graph $\mathcal{R}_L(U)$ starting from a given term U get larger when L increases. We have

$$\mathcal{R}_0(U) \subset \mathcal{R}_1(U) \cdots \subset \mathcal{R}_L(U) \subset \mathcal{R}_{L+1}(U) \cdots$$

Theorem 9.1 $hw(L)$ *is a confluent and strongly normalizable calculus.*

Proof The proof is rather easy and follows the Tait–Martin Lof technique (for confluence) [3] and van Daalen [23, 20] (for strong normalization). Types are just replaced by integers. $\qquad\qquad\qquad\qquad\qquad \square$

We also call *canonical system* a calculus which enjoys both confluence and strong normalization. Therefore $hw(L)$ is a canonical system for any L. It can also be proved that $hw(\infty)$ is also confluent, but it may not terminate as in the usual lambda-calculus.

Let the forgetful function $U \mapsto ||U||$ be function which associate to every U the term $||U||$ obtained by erasing all exponents in U. For a given M, we can consider the term U_0 with all exponents equal to zero such that $||U_0|| = M$ and we may wonder what these increasing chains of sets $\mathcal{R}_L(U_0)$ represent. They approximate the reduction graph $\mathcal{R}(M)$ of M with an increasing set of canonical calculi.

9.3 Residuals and finite developments

Beta-reduction is written $\rightarrow$. Several steps (maybe none) of beta-reduction are written $\twoheadrightarrow$. We give names ρ, σ, ... to reductions and we write $\rho{:}M \twoheadrightarrow N$ to specify the initial and final terms of reduction ρ. The reduction graph of any lambda term M is written $\mathcal{R}(M)$. If two reductions ρ and σ start from M, we call them coinitial. Similarly, they are cofinal if they end on the same term N. Redexes may be tracked over reductions. Let $\rho \in \mathcal{R}(M)$ be the following reduction from M to N

$$\rho{:}M = M_0 \xrightarrow{R_1} M_1 \xrightarrow{R_2} M_2 \cdots \xrightarrow{R_n} M_n = N$$

contracting redex R_i in M_{i-1} at each step ($1 \leq i \leq n$). Let R be a redex in M. There could be several (may be none) residuals of R in N. We write $R\backslash\rho$ for the set of residuals of R in M by reduction $\rho \in \mathcal{R}(M)$. For instance, if we underline R and its residuals, we have

$$\rho{:}\Delta(\underline{Ix}) \rightarrow (\underline{Ix})\,(\underline{Ix})$$
$$\sigma{:}\underline{\Delta(Ix)} \rightarrow \underline{\Delta x}$$
$$\tau{:}\underline{\Delta(Ix)} \rightarrow (Ix)(Ix)$$

In the first case, Ix is copied by reduction ρ and has two residuals; in the second case, $\Delta(Ix)$ is modified by σ but is not copied by the contraction of an internal redex, and there is a single residual; in the third case, there is no residual of the contracted redex, since it disappeared. To define residuals precisely needs some work. We can either speak of occurrences of subterms and consider occurrences of both R and the redex contracted R_1 as in Curry and Feys [7]. An alternative method is Barendregt's underlining method [3]. We will refer to both methods here, and will not define precisely residuals. Just notice that residuals depend upon the reduction and that residuals of a redex may differ if we consider distinct reductions between two same terms. For instance, take $I(Ix) \to Ix$; then residuals are not the same if one contracts the external or internal redex.

Residuals are defined in a similar way in the $hw(L)$-calculus, since exponents do not modify the structure of terms. We first notice that residuals of a redex keep the degrees in $hw(L)$.

Lemma 9.2 *If $\rho{:}U \twoheadrightarrow V$ and $R = ((\lambda x.A)^n B)^m$ is a redex in U. Let R' be a redex in V such that $R' \in R \backslash \rho$, then $degree(R') = degree(R)$.*

We consider now the $hw(0)$-calculus in which we can only contract redexes of null degree. We also observe that there are only two cases for the creation of new redexes in the lambda-calculus. We can either pass an abstraction to the left of an application as in $(\lambda x. \cdots xB \cdots)(\lambda y.A)$ or we can create a redex upward as in $(\lambda x.A)BD$ when we have $(\lambda x.A)B \to \lambda y.C$. In both cases, in the $hw(L)$-calculus, we notice that the degree of the created redex is strictly greater than the degree of the contracted redex. This is due to the increment used in the projection rules around the contractum in the beta-rule.

Therefore in $hw(L)$-calculus, when $\rho{:}U \twoheadrightarrow V$, a redex in V with null degree is a residual of a redex in the initial term U.

We can now state the finite development theorem with the proof used in [16].

Theorem 9.3 (Finite developments+) *Let $\mathcal{F}$ be a set of redexes in M, consider relative reductions which contract only residuals of redexes in $\mathcal{F}$. Then:*

   (i) *there is no infinite reduction relative to $\mathcal{F}$;*
   (ii) *the developments of $\mathcal{F}$ (maximal relative reductions) end all at the same term;*
   (iii) *let R be a redex in M (maybe not in $\mathcal{F}$), then the residuals of R are the same by all developments of $\mathcal{F}$.*

Proof The proof is quite simple when using the Hyland–Wadsworth calculus. Consider the term M_0 where all subterms are equipped with a null exponent except degrees of redexes not in $\mathcal{F}$ which are equipped with degrees 2, 3, 4, etc. Then reductions relative to $\mathcal{F}$ are exactly the one of M_0 in $hw(0)$, since redexes of null degree can only be residuals of redexes in $\mathcal{F}$. Now as $hw(0)$ is a canonical system, one concludes on items 1 and 2. Furthermore, new redexes in $hw(0)$ can only have degree

1, and therefore redexes of degrees 2, 3, 4, etc can only be residuals of redexes in M_0 (not in $\mathcal{F}$). As the normal form is unique in $hw(0)$, the residuals of redexes not in $\mathcal{F}$ are the same by any development of $\mathcal{F}$.

□

One may notice the elegance of the previous proof since we escape the inspection of multiple cases by working with $hw(0)$ in which this inspection has been done in a systematic way within the confluence proof.

The third item of the FD theorem is often skipped. In fact, it is an important clause since it shows that the notion of residual is consistent with parallel steps. If we simultaneously contract a set $\mathcal{F}$ of redexes, we can speak of residuals of redexes without specifying the order in which redexes of $\mathcal{F}$ are contracted. We therefore write $R\backslash\mathcal{F}$ for the set of residuals of R by any (finite) development of $\mathcal{F}$ and we are also free of writing

$$M \xrightarrow{\mathcal{F}} N$$

for the relation linking M to N by a development of $\mathcal{F}$.

Going on with notations, when $\rho{:}M \twoheadrightarrow N$ and $\sigma{:}N \twoheadrightarrow P$, we write $\rho\sigma$ for the concatenation of these two reductions. Furthermore, we write o for the empty reduction of length 0. Therefore we have $\rho o = \rho = o\rho$. We also write $\mathcal{F}$ for the reduction consisting in a finite development of $\mathcal{F}$, and we define $\mathcal{F}_1 \sqcup \mathcal{F}_2$ as the two-step reduction $\mathcal{F}_1 \sqcup \mathcal{F}_2 = \mathcal{F}_1(\mathcal{F}_2\backslash\mathcal{F}_1)$. We finally forget braces when $\mathcal{F}$ is a singleton $\{R\}$. We can write $R\rho$ or ρR or $R\backslash S$ or $R \sqcup S$ etc.

There are two well-known corollaries of the FD theorem which will be useful for introducing the notion of redex history.

Lemma 9.4 (Parallel moves) *Let $\mathcal{F}_1$ and $\mathcal{F}_2$ be two sets of redexes in M. If $M_1 \xleftarrow{\mathcal{F}_1} M \xrightarrow{\mathcal{F}_2} M_2$, then there is a term N such that $M_1 \xrightarrow{\mathcal{G}_2} N \xleftarrow{\mathcal{G}_1} M_2$ with $\mathcal{G}_1 = \mathcal{F}_1\backslash\mathcal{F}_2$ and $\mathcal{G}_2 = \mathcal{F}_2\backslash\mathcal{F}_1$.*

With our new notations, an alternative statement of this lemma would be that $\mathcal{F}_1 \sqcup \mathcal{F}_2$ and $\mathcal{F}_2 \sqcup \mathcal{F}_1$ are cofinal. The proof is obvious by considering two developments of $\mathcal{F}_1 \cup \mathcal{F}_2$, one starting by contracting $\mathcal{F}_1$ and then $\mathcal{F}_2\backslash\mathcal{F}_1$, the second contracting $\mathcal{F}_2$ and then $\mathcal{F}_1\backslash\mathcal{F}_2$ (Fig. 9.1).

The lemma of parallel moves can also be named the square lemma, since a second corollary is the cube lemma which looks closer to properties of residuals.

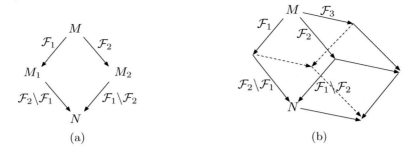

Fig. 9.1. (a) Parallel moves; (b) Cube lemma.

Lemma 9.5 (Cube lemma) *Let $\mathcal{F}_1$, $\mathcal{F}_2$ and $\mathcal{F}_3$ be three sets of redexes in M. Then $\mathcal{F}_3 \backslash (\mathcal{F}_1 \sqcup \mathcal{F}_2) = \mathcal{F}_3 \backslash (\mathcal{F}_2 \sqcup \mathcal{F}_1)$.*

This lemma is straightforward when we notice that $\mathcal{F}_1 \sqcup \mathcal{F}_2$ and $\mathcal{F}_2 \sqcup \mathcal{F}_1$ are two developments of $\mathcal{F}_1 \cup \mathcal{F}_2$. This argument may be extended by permutation on $\mathcal{F}_2$ and $\mathcal{F}_3$, or $\mathcal{F}_3$ and $\mathcal{F}_1$. We therefore get a nice cube whose each face is an application of the parallel moves lemma (Fig. 9.1).

9.4 Redex families

Redexes may be created by reductions when they are not residuals of redexes in the initial term. The notion of redex family aims to relate created redexes. As the reduction creating a redex interferes with its history, we define an *historical redex* (*hredex* in short) to be a pair $\langle \rho, R \rangle$ when $\rho : M \twoheadrightarrow N$ and R is a redex in N. Redexes in M with no history are of the form $\langle o, R \rangle$ where o is the empty reduction from M. But history of redexes has to be consistent with permutations of reduction steps, since the contraction of two independent redexes must be insensitive in the creation history of a redex.

Definition 9.6 *The* permutation equivalence $\sim$ *on reductions in $\mathcal{R}(M)$ starting from a given term M is defined inductively as follows:*
   (i) $\mathcal{F}_1 \sqcup \mathcal{F}_2 \sim \mathcal{F}_2 \sqcup \mathcal{F}_1$
   (ii) $\emptyset \sim o$ *and* $o \sim \emptyset$
   (iii) $\rho \sim \sigma$ *implies* $\tau\rho \sim \tau\sigma$
   (iv) $\rho \sim \sigma$ *implies* $\rho\tau \sim \sigma\tau$
   (v) $\rho \sim \sigma \sim \tau$ *implies* $\rho \sim \tau$.

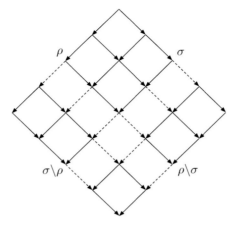

Fig. 9.2. $\rho\backslash\sigma$ is residual of reduction ρ by reduction σ.

Two reductions are equivalent if they differ by applying the lemma of parallel moves. A reduction step contracting an empty set of redexes can be erased, i.e. it is equivalent to the empty reduction. Permutation equivalence is also extended by concatenation and by transitivity. Alternative definitions of this equivalence can be found in [25, 21].

This relation is defined on parallel reductions, but it also relates regular reductions since their elementary steps can be considered as contracting singletons sets of redexes. In fact, the same relation can be generated by restricting the first case of the definition to be singleton sets.

Residuals of reductions can also be defined inductively as follows (see Fig. 9.2).

Definition 9.7 *Let ρ and σ be two reduction starting at M. The residual $\rho\backslash\sigma$ of reduction ρ by reduction σ is inductively defined by:*

  (i) *if $\rho = \mathcal{F}$ and $\sigma = \mathcal{G}$, then $\rho\backslash\sigma = \mathcal{F}\backslash\mathcal{G}$*
 (ii) $\rho\backslash(\sigma_1\sigma_2) = (\rho\backslash\sigma_1)\backslash\sigma_2$
(iii) $(\rho_1\rho_2)\backslash\sigma = (\rho_1\backslash\sigma)(\rho_2(\sigma\backslash\rho_1)$

When ρ and σ are two coinitial reductions, we define $\rho \sqcup \sigma$ as for single-step reductions by $\rho \sqcup \sigma = \rho(\sigma\backslash\rho)$. We also write $\emptyset^k$ for k steps of empty-set contractions. The following properties hold for the permutation equivalence.

Lemma 9.8 *Let ρ and σ be two coinitial reductions $(\rho, \sigma \in \mathcal{R}(M))$:*

    (i) $\rho \sqcup \sigma \sim \sigma \sqcup \rho$
    (ii) $\rho \sim \sigma$ *iff* $\forall \tau \in \mathcal{R}(M)$ $\tau \backslash \rho = \tau \backslash \sigma$
    (iii) $\rho \sim \sigma$ *iff* $\rho \backslash \sigma = \emptyset^k$ *and* $\sigma \backslash \rho = \emptyset^\ell$
    (iv) $\rho \sigma \sim \rho \tau$ *iff* $\sigma \sim \tau$

Proof The proofs use simple algebraic arguments. Clearly (i) is true by definition. The cube lemma gives (iia) which is that $\rho \sim \sigma$ implies $\tau \backslash \rho = \tau \backslash \sigma$. Then (iia) implies $(iiia)$ since $\emptyset^k = \rho \backslash \rho = \rho \backslash \sigma$ and $\sigma \backslash \rho = \sigma \backslash \sigma = \emptyset^\ell$. Conversely, when $\sigma \backslash \rho = \emptyset^\ell$, one gets $\rho \sim \rho(\sigma \backslash \rho) = \rho \sqcup \sigma$ since $\emptyset^\ell \sim o$. Similarly $\sigma \sim \sigma \sqcup \rho$ as $\rho \backslash \sigma = \emptyset^k$. We get $\rho \sim \sigma$ by transitivity and applying (i). Now to prove iib, if we have $\tau \backslash \rho = \tau \backslash \sigma$ for all τ, we get $\emptyset^k = \rho \backslash \rho = \rho \backslash \sigma$. Similarly for $\sigma \backslash \rho = \emptyset^\ell$. Therefore $\rho \sim \sigma$ by (iii). To prove (iv), the right-to-left direction is implied by the definition of $\sim$. Now let $\rho \sigma \sim \rho \tau$, we have $\rho \sigma \backslash \rho \tau = (\rho \sigma \backslash \rho) \backslash \tau$. But $\rho \sigma \backslash \rho = (\rho \backslash \rho)(\sigma \backslash (\rho \backslash \rho)) = \emptyset^k(\sigma \backslash (\emptyset^k)) = \emptyset^k \sigma$. Therefore $\rho \sigma \backslash \rho \tau = (\emptyset^k \sigma) \backslash \tau = \emptyset^k(\sigma \backslash \tau)$. Hence $\rho \sigma \backslash \rho \tau \sim \sigma \backslash \tau$. Therefore by (iii), if $\rho \sigma \sim \rho \tau$, we also have $\sigma \sim \tau$.   □

The permutation equivalence has many properties, most of them are due to the nice symmetry of the cube lemma. An interesting fact is that an upper semi-lattice can be constructed (or a push-out in categorical terminology). This lattice of reductions is derived by the following pre-ordering on coinitial reductions $\rho \leq \sigma$ iff $\rho \tau \sim \sigma$ for some τ. The interested reader is refer to [16, 3, 4, 11]. A permutation class of reductions is also characterized by its *unique* standard reduction. The permutation equivalence can also be viewed as the analogous of parse trees in context-free languages where several derivations equivalent by permutations correspond to the same parse tree. In formal grammars, the notion of ambiguity reveals two different parse trees corresponding to a same terminal sentence. In the lambda-calculus, this ambiguity often arises.

Take for instance $\rho : \Delta\Delta \to \Delta\Delta$ and $\sigma : \Delta\Delta \to \Delta\Delta \to \Delta\Delta$. Then ρ and σ are coinitial and cofinal, but $\rho \not\sim \sigma$. Similarly $o \not\sim \rho$. A more complex example is when the initial term M is $I((\lambda y.Ix)z)$. Then the reduction graph of M has no lattice structure, but the corresponding ordered structure induced by the permutation equivalence is indeed a lattice. Furthermore, the term M contains three redexes $R = I((\lambda y.Ix)z)$, $S = Ix$ and $K = (\lambda y.Ix)z$. When ρ and σ are two reductions defined by $\rho : I((\lambda y.Ix)z) \to (\lambda y.Ix)z \to Ix$ and $\sigma : I((\lambda y.Ix)z) \to I((\lambda y.x)z) \to Ix$, the hredex $\langle \rho, Ix \rangle$ is a residual of $\langle o, S \rangle$, but $\langle \sigma, Ix \rangle$ is a residual of $\langle o, R \rangle$. This kind of ambiguity cannot happen in the lattice of reductions where residuals are consistent with history, thanks to the cube lemma.

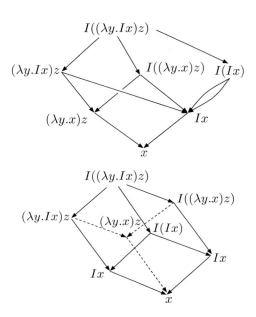

The interconnection between two created hredexes $\langle \rho, R \rangle$ and $\langle \sigma, S \rangle$ is not obvious as demonstrated by the following example. Take $M = \Delta(IIx)$ which contains two redexes $\Delta(IIx)$ and II. When the latter is contracted, it creates the new redex Ix which may appear in many reducts of M. One of them seems more representative, namely the one in $\Delta(Ix)$ where his history $\rho_0 : M \to \Delta(Ix)$ is entirely devoted to create the Ix redex. But to connect other instances of Ix in the reduction graph of M, it is necessary to close downward with residuals. For instance if $\rho_1 : M \to (IIx)(IIx) \to (Ix)(IIx)$ and $\rho_1 : M \to (IIx)(IIx) \to (IIx)(Ix)$, in order to connect $\langle \rho_1, Ix \rangle$ and $\langle \rho_2, Ix \rangle$, one has to link them to $\langle \rho_0, Ix \rangle$ through $\langle \rho_3, R_1 \rangle$ and $\langle \rho_3, R_2 \rangle$ where $\rho_3 : M \to (IIx)(IIx) \to (Ix)(IIx) \to (Ix)(Ix)$ (R_1 is left redex in $(Ix)(Ix)$ and R_2 is right redex in $(Ix)(Ix)$). More precisely $\langle \rho_1, Ix \rangle$ has residual $\langle \rho_3, R_1 \rangle$ which is residual of $\langle \rho_0, Ix \rangle$ which has $\langle \rho_3, R_2 \rangle$ as residual and this last one is residual of $\langle \rho_2, Ix \rangle$. Therefore created redexes can be connected by a zigzag of residuals related by consistent histories (i.e. using the permutation equivalence).

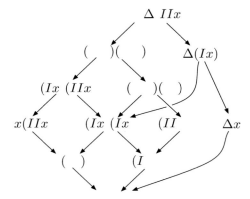

We can now define formally the residual and family relations between hredexes.

Definition 9.9 *Let two reductions ρ and σ be coinitial. The hredex $\langle \sigma, S \rangle$ is a residual of the hredex $\langle \rho, R \rangle$ iff there is a reduction τ such that $\rho\tau \sim \sigma$ and $S \in R\backslash\tau$. We write then $\langle \rho, R \rangle \leqslant \langle \sigma, S \rangle$.*

We say that the hredexes $\langle \rho, R \rangle$ and $\langle \sigma, S \rangle$ are in the same family if they are connected by the reflexive, symmetric and transitive closure of the previous residual relation on hredexes. We then write $\langle \rho, R \rangle \approx \langle \sigma, S \rangle$. Formally:

(i) $\langle \rho, R \rangle \approx \langle \rho, R \rangle$

(ii) $\langle \rho, R \rangle \approx \langle \sigma, S \rangle$ implies $\langle \sigma, S \rangle \approx \langle \rho, R \rangle$

(iii) $\langle \rho, R \rangle \approx \langle \sigma, S \rangle \approx \langle \tau, T \rangle$ implies $\langle \rho, R \rangle \approx \langle \tau, T \rangle$

(iv) $\langle \rho, R \rangle \leqslant \langle \sigma, S \rangle$ implies $\langle \rho, R \rangle \approx \langle \sigma, S \rangle$

We notice that the residual and family relations form, respectively, an ordering and an equivalence. Furthermore, one can easily show that, when $\langle \rho, R \rangle \leqslant \langle \rho, S \rangle$, there is a unique reduction τ up to the permutation equivalence such that $\rho\tau \sim \sigma$ and $S \in R\backslash\tau$ (Fig. 9.3). Therefore we may omit the specific reduction τ in the definition of residuals of hredexes. The residual and family relations on hredexes is also compatible with the permutation equivalence: when $\rho \sim \sigma$, one indeed has $\langle \rho, R \rangle \leqslant \langle \sigma, R \rangle$ since $\rho o = \rho \sim \sigma$ and $R \in R\backslash o$. Many other properties can be shown on redex families, one of the most striking is the connection with the labeled lambda-calculus, see [16]. We just mention here that when $\langle \rho, R \rangle$ and $\langle \sigma, S \rangle$ have a common residual $\langle \tau, T \rangle$, then there is a unique redex T_0 such that the hredex $\langle \rho \sqcup \sigma, T_0 \rangle$ is a residual of $\langle \rho, R \rangle$ and $\langle \sigma, S \rangle$. An

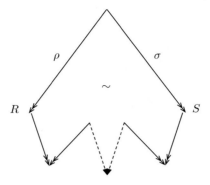

Fig. 9.3. $\langle \rho, R \rangle \approx \langle \sigma, S \rangle$: the hredexes $\langle \rho, R \rangle$ and $\langle \sigma, S \rangle$ belong to the same family.

alternative way is to state that $\langle \rho, R \rangle \leqslant \langle \tau, T \rangle$ and $\langle \sigma, S \rangle \leqslant \langle \tau, T \rangle$ implies there exists a (unique) $\langle \rho \sqcup \sigma, T_0 \rangle$ such that $\langle \rho, R \rangle \leqslant \langle \rho \sqcup \sigma, T_0 \rangle \leqslant \langle \tau, T \rangle$ and $\langle \sigma, S \rangle \leqslant \langle \rho \sqcup \sigma, T_0 \rangle \leqslant \langle \tau, T \rangle$.

The permutation equivalence and the family relation can also be defined in the $hw(\mathrm{L})$-lambda-calculus thanks to the two following lemmas. We write $||\rho||$ for ρ where the forgetful function is applied to every term in reduction ρ.

Lemma 9.10 *Let ρ and σ be two reductions starting from U. If $||\rho|| \sim ||\sigma||$, we have $\rho \sim \sigma$.*

Lemma 9.11 *Let ρ be any reduction starting from $||U||$. Then there is L sufficiently large and a reduction ρ' in $hw(L)$ such that $\rho = ||\rho'||$.*

Proof The proof is easy since the parallel-moves lemma can be applied in the $hw(L)$-lambda-calculus, since residuals keep redex degrees. Therefore, since $\rho \sim \sigma$, we have $\sigma \backslash \rho = \emptyset^n$ and $\rho \backslash \sigma = \emptyset^m$, which means ρ and σ are also cofinal in the $hw(L)$-lambda-calculus. $\square$

For the interested reader, the labeled lambda-calculus designed in [16] is sufficiently precise to characterize exactly the permutation equivalence, i.e. two reductions are equivalent iff they are coinitial and cofinal in the labeled lambda-calculus.

An easy corollary of this lemma is that residuals of hredexes are the same notion in the standard lambda-calculus and in the $hw(\infty)$-calculus.

Therefore the notion of redex families also coincide. A last remark is
that if two redexes R and S are in the same family, their degree are the
same (since residuals keep degrees).

9.5 Generalized finite developments

The usual finite development theorem deals with redexes who are in the
initial term. Now created redexes can be taken into account with redex
families.

Theorem 9.12 (GFD) *Let $\mathcal{F}$ be a finite set of redex families in $\mathcal{R}(M)$,
consider relative reductions which contract only redexes belonging to a
family in $\mathcal{F}$. Then:*

  (i) *there is no infinite reduction relative to $\mathcal{F}$;*

  (ii) *the developments of $\mathcal{F}$ (maximal relative reductions) end all at
       the same term;*

  (iii) *if ρ and σ are two developments of $\mathcal{F}$, then $\rho \sim \sigma$.*

Proof The proof is rather straightforward since the family relation
is identical in the usual lambda-calculus and in the $hw(\infty)$-lambda-
calculus. Let U_0 be the term corresponding to M with all subterms with
null exponents ($\|U_0\| = M$). Redexes in each family have same degree.
Let L be the largest degree for redexes in the finite family set $\mathcal{F}$. Then a
reduction relative to $\mathcal{F}$ is inside the $hw(L)$-lambda-calculus. As $hw(L)$
is a canonical system, we know that these relative reductions cannot be
infinite. Therefore all reductions relative to $\mathcal{F}$ are finite.

Now, if two reductions $\rho{:}M \twoheadrightarrow N$ and $\sigma{:}M \twoheadrightarrow P$ starting at M are
complete developments of $\mathcal{F}$ (i.e. maximum relative reductions to $\mathcal{F}$), we
notice that $\rho \sqcup \sigma$ and $\sigma \sqcup \rho$ are also reductions relative to $\mathcal{F}$ by definition
of the family relation. As ρ and σ are maximal, we have $\sigma \backslash \rho = \emptyset^n$ and
$\rho \backslash \sigma = \emptyset^m$. Therefore $\rho \sim \tau$. Hence we get $N = P$. But $\rho \sim \tau$ also means
that if τ is another reduction starting at M, we have $\tau \backslash \rho = \tau \backslash \sigma$. $\square$

Thus, the FD theorem has been extended to finite sets of families.
All developments of such a given finite set of redex families are
equivalent by permutations, and therefore the consistency of residuals
w.r.t. developments holds for the usual notion of redex residual and
for residuals of reductions. It means that if a term M can start an
infinite reduction, this infinite reduction contracts an infinite set of
redex families. Hence a term can have an infinite reduction iff it can

generate infinitely new redex families. This can be formalized in the following way.

Definition 9.13 *We say that the hredex $\langle \rho, R \rangle$ directly creates the hredex $\langle \sigma, S \rangle$ iff $\sigma \sim \rho R$ and the contraction of R creates S. We write $\langle \rho, R \rangle$ ◄ $\langle \sigma, S \rangle$.*

The hredex $\langle \rho, R \rangle$ creates $\langle \sigma, S \rangle$ if they are connected by transitive closure of direct creation and residual. We then write $\langle \rho, R \rangle \lhd \langle \sigma, S \rangle$. Formally:

- *(i) $\langle \rho, R \rangle$ ◄ $\langle \sigma, S \rangle$ implies $\langle \rho, R \rangle \lhd \langle \sigma, S \rangle$*
- *(ii) $\langle \rho, R \rangle \leqslant \langle \rho', R' \rangle \lhd \langle \sigma, S \rangle$ implies $\langle \rho, R \rangle \lhd \langle \sigma, S \rangle$*
- *(iii) $\langle \rho, R \rangle \lhd \langle \sigma', S' \rangle \leqslant \langle \sigma, S \rangle$ implies $\langle \rho, R \rangle \lhd \langle \sigma, S \rangle$*
- *(iv) $\langle \rho, R \rangle \lhd \langle \sigma, S \rangle \lhd \langle \tau, T \rangle$ implies $\langle \rho, R \rangle \lhd \langle \tau, T \rangle$*

So $\langle \rho, R \rangle$ directly creates $\langle \sigma, S \rangle$ if the reduction σ is equivalent by permutations to a reduction $M \twoheadrightarrow N \overset{R}{\to} P$ where the first part $M \twoheadrightarrow N$ is the reduction ρ and the contraction of R creates the new redex S in P, i.e. $S \notin S' \backslash R$ for any S' in N. By construction the notion of creation is consistent with the equivalence $\sim$. One also easily checks that the creation relation is antisymmetric, since with the $hw(\infty)$-lambda-calculus we know that degrees of redexes are kept invariant by residuals and increase in case of a direct creation. So the creation relation $\lhd$ is a strict ordering. We would like to prove that a term which does not contain an infinite chain of creations is strongly normalizable. Unfortunately this property seems to need more advanced technical arguments. We will show a broader property relying on the creation of families.

Definition 9.14 *The family of the hredex $\langle \rho, R \rangle$ creates the family of the hredex $\langle \sigma, S \rangle$ if a hredex in the family of $\langle \rho, R \rangle$ creates a hredex in the family of $\langle \sigma, S \rangle$. We write $\langle \rho, R \rangle \ll \langle \sigma, S \rangle$. Formally:*

- *(i) $\langle \rho, R \rangle$ ◄ $\langle \sigma, S \rangle$ implies $\langle \rho, R \rangle \ll \langle \sigma, S \rangle$*
- *(ii) $\langle \rho, R \rangle \approx \langle \rho', R' \rangle \ll \langle \sigma, S \rangle$ implies $\langle \rho, R \rangle \ll \langle \sigma, S \rangle$*
- *(iii) $\langle \rho, R \rangle \ll \langle \sigma', S' \rangle \approx \langle \sigma, S \rangle$ implies $\langle \rho, R \rangle \ll \langle \sigma, S \rangle$*
- *(iv) $\langle \rho, R \rangle \ll \langle \sigma, S \rangle \ll \langle \tau, T \rangle$ implies $\langle \rho, R \rangle \ll \langle \tau, T \rangle$*

Clearly this relation with creation of families is broader than the previous relation on creation of hredexes, since $\langle \rho, R \rangle \approx \langle \sigma, S \rangle$ when $\langle \rho, R \rangle \leqslant \langle \sigma, S \rangle$. It also defines a strict ordering on families with the same argument as the one used for hredex creation. With this new ordering, one can easily show that strong normalization is induced by the absence of infinite chains of family creations.

Lemma 9.15 *A term without infinite chains of family creations is strongly normalizable.*

Proof We consider the covering relation of the $\ll$ ordering (i.e. $\langle \rho, R \rangle \ll \langle \sigma, S \rangle$ when there is no intermediate $\langle \tau, T \rangle$ between $\langle \rho, R \rangle$ and $\langle \sigma, S \rangle$). This relation induces a directed acyclic graph with finite number of successors for each node. To see that the out-degree of each node is finite, one can work by induction on the length from the roots of this graph since for a given length n we know by the gFD theorem that we have the strong normalization property and therefore a finite number of redex families. Now if the total number of families (i.e. number of nodes in the dag) is infinite, we get by Koenig lemma that there is an infinite path from the roots. It means that there is an infinite chain of family creations, which is impossible by hypothesis of the lemma. So the total number of families for the given term is finite. By the gFD theorem, we get that this term strongly normalizes.   □

As corollary, we get strong normalization for the first-order typed lambda-calculus. In this calculus, we call degree of a redex the type of its function part. We notice that a redex of degree $\alpha \to \beta$ can only create redexes of type α or β (this can be proved by case inspection as in the paragraph following Lemma 9.2). Furthermore, when two redexes are in the same family, their degrees are equal. Thus, there are no infinite chains of family creations for any term of the first-order typed lambda-calculus. By the previous lemma, the calculus enjoys strong normalization.

9.6 Conclusion

The generalized Finite Development (gFD) theorem shows that relative reductions w.r.t. a finite set of redex families cannot be infinite and that all developments end with the same term.

The gFD theorem is an important tool in the understanding of strong normalisation. It defines arbitrary large canonical systems as subgraphs of the reduction graph of any term. In this sense, it expresses the *compactness* of the lambda-calculus. It was used in [15] for proving the completeness of inside-out reductions, i.e. for any ρ there is an inside-out reduction σ and a (inside-out) reduction τ such that $\rho\tau \sim \sigma$. But we can get completeness of many more reduction strategies with the gFD theorem as long as the strategy consists in reordering of contractions of redexes in the same family set.

Furthermore, it is an argument for proving strong normalization as soon as one can prove that there is no infinite chain of family creations. With the gFD theorem, the proof of strong normalization is reduced to the proof of the non existence of such infinite chains of creations. We took the example of the standard first-order typed lambda-calculus, but some effort remains to be done in the understanding of higher-order typed systems where we conjecture that such an argument must exist. If correct, we could get illuminating proofs of strong normalization.

The gFD theorem also holds in other calculi. In fact, this theorem is true in any calculus with some compactness property, i.e. nearly all calculi. In the lambda-calculus, it is simple to express, but it can also be easily stated in orthogonal term rewriting systems [11] or in combinatory reduction systems [12]. This theorem seems also correct in calculi with critical pairs, where permutation equivalence is more complex to define (see [5]) since the equivalence classes may be incompatibles due to different choices around critical pairs. Then the permutation equivalence is very close to event structures [14, 26].

Acknowledgements

Gilles Kahn has been a mentor in my research. He initiated me to denotational semantics and Scott's logic. Moreover he pointed out to me the first (interesting) papers I ever read about lambda-calculus. His constant help and support made the results of this paper and others possible.

This article has benefited from numerous comments by Jan-Willem Klop and Paul-André Melliès.

Bibliography

[1]   R. Amadio and P.-L. Curien. *Domains and Lambda-calculi*. Cambridge University Press, 1998.

[2]   H. Barendregt. *Handbook of Mathematical Logic*, chapter the type free lambda calculus. In North-Holland, 1977.

[3]   H. Barendregt. *The Lambda Calculus, Its Syntax and Semantics*. North-Holland, 1984.

[4]   G. Berry and J.-J. Lévy. Minimal and optimal computations of recursive programs. *JACM*, 26(1):148–175, January 1979.

[5]   G. Boudol. Computational semantics of term rewriting systems. In *Algebraic methods in Semantics*. Cambridge University Press, 1985.

[6]   A. Church. *The Calculi of Lambda-Conversion*. Princeton University Press – Oxford University Press, 1941.

[7]   H. Curry and R. Feys. *Combinatory Logic*, volume 1. North-Holland, 1958.

[8]   H. Curry, R. Feys and J. Seldin. *Combinatory Logic*, volume 2. North-Holland, 1972.

[9]   L. Damas and R. Milner. Principal type-schemes for functional programs. In *POPL*, pp. 207–212, 1982.

[10]   R. Hindley. *Basic Simple Type Theory*. Cambridge University Press, 1997.

[11]   G. Huet and J.-J. Lévy. Computations in orthogonal rewriting systems I and II, In *Computational Logic; Essays in Honor of Alan Robinson*. pp. 395–443. The MIT Press, 1991.

[12]   J.-W. Klop. *Combinatory Reduction Systems*. PhD thesis. Mathematical Centre Tracts 127, CWI, Amsterdam, 1980.

[13]   P. Landin. A correspondence between Algol 60 and Church's lambda-notation. *CACM*, **8**(2):89–101, 1965.

[14]   C. Laneve. Distributive evaluations of lambda-calculus. *Fundamenta Informaticae*, **20**(4):333–352, 1994.

[15]   J.-J. Lévy. An algebraic interpretation of the $\lambda\beta$-calculus and a labeled λ-calculus. In C. Böhm (ed.), *Lambda-Calculus and Computer Science Theory*, volume 37 of Lecture Notes in Computer Science, pp. 147–165. Springer, March 1975.

[16]   J.-J. Lévy. *Réductions correctes et optimales dans le lambda calcul*. PhD thesis, University of Paris 7, 1978. (in French).

[17]   J.-J. Lévy. Optimal reductions in the lambda-calculus. In *To H. B. Curry: Essays on Combinatory Logic, Lambda Calculus and Formalism*, pp. 159–191. Academic Press, 1980.

[18]   L. Maranget. *La stratégie paresseuse*. PhD thesis, University of Paris 7, July 1992.

[19]   P.-A. Melliès. A factorisation theorem in rewriting theory. In *Proceedings of the 7th Conference on Category Theory and Computer Science*, volume 1290, Lecture Notes in Computer Science, pp. 49–68, Santa Margherita Ligure. Springer, 1997.

[20]   R. Nederpelt, J. Geuvers and R. d. Vrijer. *Selected Papers on Automath*, volume 133, Studies in Logic and the Foundations of Mathematics. North-Holland, 1994.

[21]   V. V. Oostrom and R. D. Vrijer. Equivalence of reductions. In *Terese, Term Rewriting Systems*. Cambridge University Press, March 2003.

[22]   G. Plotkin. Call-by-name, call-by-value, and the lambda-calculus. *Theoretical Computer Science*, 1, 1975.

[23]   D. van Daalen. *The Language Theory of Automath*. PhD thesis, TUE, 1980.

[24]   V. van Oostrom. Finite family developments. In *Proceedings of the 8th International Conference on Rewriting Techniques and Applications (RTA*

'97), volume 1232, in Lecture Notes in Computer Science, pp. 308–322, Sitges, June 1997.

[25] V. van Oostrom and R. de Vrijer. Four equivalent equivalences of reductions. In *WRS'02*, volume 70(6), *ENTCS*, December 2002.

[26] G. Winskel. Event structure semantics for ccs and related languages. Technical report, DAIMI – AARhus University, April 1983.

10

Semantics of program representation graphs

G. Ramalingam

Microsoft Research India; Bangalore, India

Thomas Reps

University of Wisconsin; Madison, WI; USA

Dedicated to the memory of Gilles Kahn, 1946-2006.

Abstract

Program representation graphs (PRGs) are an intermediate representation for programs. (They are closely related to program dependence graphs.) In this paper, we develop a mathematical semantics for PRGs that, inspired by Kahn's semantics for a parallel programming language, interprets PRGs as dataflow graphs. We also study the relationship between this semantics and the standard operational semantics of programs. We show that (i) the semantics of PRGs is more defined than the standard operational semantics, and (ii) for states on which a program terminates normally, the PRG semantics is identical to the standard operational semantics.

10.1 Introduction

In this paper, we develop a mathematical semantics for program representation graphs (PRGs) and study its relationship to a standard (operational) semantics of programs. Program representation graphs are an intermediate representation of programs, introduced by Yang *et al.* [27] in an algorithm for detecting program components that exhibit identical execution behaviors. They combine features of static-single-assignment forms (SSA forms) [23, 2, 5, 21] and program dependence graphs (PDGs) [13, 6, 11]. (See Fig. 10.1 for an example program and its PRG.) PRGs have also been used in an algorithm for merging program variants [28].

From Semantics to Computer Science Essays in Honour of Gilles Kahn, eds Yves Bertot, Gérard Huet, Jean-Jacques Lévy and Gordon Plotkin. Published by Cambridge University Press. © Cambridge University Press 2009.

Program dependence graphs have been used as an intermediate program representation in various applications such as vectorization, parallelization [13], and merging program variants [11]. A number of variants of the PDG have been used as the basis for efficient program analysis by optimizing compilers as well as other tools (e.g., see [15, 17, 24]). All these uses of dependence graph representations vitally depend on a usually unstated or unproven assumption that the representation adequately captures the program semantics. Horwitz *et al.* [10] were the first to address the question of whether PDGs were "adequate" as program representations. They showed (for a simplified programming language) that if the program dependence graphs of two programs are isomorphic, the programs are equivalent in the following sense: for any initial state σ, either both programs diverge or both halt with the same final state.

Such an equivalence theorem makes it reasonable to try to develop a semantics for program dependence graphs that is consistent with the program semantics. In contrast to the indirect proof of the equivalence theorem given in [10], such a semantics would provide a direct proof of the theorem.

Two different semantics have so far been developed for PDGs (and thus each provides a direct proof of the equivalence theorem). Selke [22] provides a graph-rewriting semantics for PDGs. This semantics represents computation steps as graph transformations. The dependence edges are used to make sure that statements are executed in the right order. The store is embedded in the graph. When assignment statements are executed, the relevant portions of the graph are updated to reflect the new value of the corresponding variable. Evaluation of *if* predicates results in deletion of the part of the graph representing the *true* or *false* branch, as appropriate. Evaluation of *while* predicates results in the deletion of the body of the loop or creating a copy of it, as necessary.

Cartwright and Felleisen [4] start with a non-strict generalization of the denotational semantics of the programming language and use a staging analysis to decompose the meaning function into two functions: a *compiler* function that transforms programs into *code trees*, which resemble PDGs, and an *interpreter* function for *code trees*. The interpreter function provides an operational semantics for code trees.

A different (and perhaps more natural) way to develop a semantics for program dependence graphs would be to treat them as graphs of some dataflow programming language and use the conventional operational semantics of such programming languages. Although analogies between

PDGs and dataflow graphs have been made previously, this idea has not actually been formalized (i.e., to date no semantics has been developed that interprets PDGs as dataflow graphs). In fact, there are some problems in doing so, as will be explained in Section 10.4.

In [12], Kahn introduced a model for parallel or distributed computation consisting of a group of processing units connected by unidirectional communication channels to form a network of processes. In this setting, the output of each process (i.e. the possibly infinite sequence of values on the output channel of the process) is defined as a function of the sequence of values on the input channels of the process. In this paper, we show that, with minor modifications, PRGs—as opposed to PDGs—can be interpreted in a very similar fashion, with each vertex being interpreted as a process and each dependence edge as a communication channel. That is, we show how to develop a mathematical semantics for PRGs by formalizing the analogy between PRGs and the dataflow graphs used by Kahn in developing a semantics for a parallel programming language. We create a set of possibly mutually recursive equations that, as a function of the initial store, associate a sequence of values with each vertex in the PRG. The semantics of the PRG is defined to be the least-fixed-point solution of these equations.

The dataflow semantics for PRGs can be restricted so as to give a semantics for PRGs as store-to-store transformers. However, for some applications of PRGs, such as merging program variants, the more general semantic definition is preferable. The more general semantic definition also leads to a stronger form of the equivalence theorem for PRGs that relates the sequences of values computed at corresponding vertices of programs that have isomorphic PRGs.

In particular, we show that: (1) the sequence of values computed at any program point (according to the operational semantics) is, in general, a prefix of the sequence associated with that program point by the PRG semantics and (2) for normally terminating program executions the two sequences are identical. This yields the following equivalence theorem: If the PRGs of two programs are isomorphic, then for any initial state σ, either (1) both programs terminate normally, and the sequence of values computed at corresponding vertices are equal, or (2) neither program terminates normally and for any pair of corresponding vertices, the sequence of values computed at one of them will be a prefix of the sequence of values computed at the other. A similar equivalence theorem for program slices also follows as a consequence: If the PRG of one program is isomorphic to a subgraph of the PRG of another program, then whenever the second program terminates normally, the first program will also terminate normally, and produce the same sequence of values at every program point as the sequence produced by the second program at the corresponding program point. Indirect proofs of such equivalence theorems have been previously derived for PDGs [20] and PRGs [26]; this paper provides the first direct proof of the result.

The remainder of the paper is organized as follows: Section 10.2 describes the programming language under consideration. Section 10.3 defines program representation graphs, and Section 10.4 extends this definition. Section 10.5 presents the semantics of PRGs. Section 10.6 deals with various properties of the standard operational semantics. Section 10.7 considers the relationship between a program's standard operational semantics and the semantics of its PRG. Section 10.9 discusses related work. (In the interests of brevity, two of the proofs have been omitted; they may be found in reference [18].)

10.2 The programming language under consideration

We are concerned with a programming language with the following characteristics: expressions contain only scalar variables and constants; statements are either assignment statements, conditional statements, while-loops, or *end* statements. An *end* statement, which can only appear at the end of a program, names zero or more of the variables used in the program. The variables named in the *end* statement are those whose final values are of interest to the programmer. An example program is shown in the upper-left-hand corner of Figure 10.1 below.

Our discussion of the language's semantics is in terms of the following informal model of execution. We assume a standard operational semantics for sequential execution; the statements and predicates of a program are executed in the order specified by the program's control-flow graph; at any moment there is a single locus of control; the execution of each assignment statement or predicate passes control to a single successor; the execution of each assignment statement changes a global execution state. An execution of the program on an initial state yields a (possibly infinite) sequence of values for each predicate and assignment statement in the program; the ith element in the sequence for program component c consists of the value computed when c is executed for the ith time.

10.3 Program representation graphs

As mentioned previously, PRGs combine features of SSA forms and PDGs. In the SSA form of a program, special assignment statements (ϕ

assignments) are inserted so that exactly one assignment to a variable x, either an assignment from the original program or a ϕ assignment, can reach a use of x from the original program. The ϕ statements assign the value of a variable to itself; at most two assignments to a variable x can reach the use of x in a ϕ statement. For instance, consider the following example program fragments:

L_1:	$x := 1$		L_1:	$x := 1$
	if p **then**			**if** p **then**
L_2:	$\quad x := 2$		L_2:	$\quad x := 2$
	fi			**fi**
L_4:	$y := x + 3$		L_3:	$x := \phi_{if}(x)$
			L_4:	$y := x + 3$

In the source program (on the left), both assignments to x at L_1 and L_2 can reach the use of x at L_4; after the insertion of "$x := \phi_{if}(x)$" at L_3 (on the right), only the ϕ assignment to x can reach the use of x at L_4. Both assignments to x at L_1 and L_2 can reach the use of x at L_3.

Different definitions of program dependence graphs have been given, depending on the intended application; nevertheless, they are all variations on a theme introduced in [14], and share the common feature of having an explicit representation of data dependences. The program dependence graph defined in [6] introduced the additional feature of an explicit representation for control dependences. The program representation graph, defined below, has edges that represent control dependences and one kind of data dependence, called flow dependence.

The program representation graph of a program P, denoted by R_P, is constructed in two steps. First an augmented control-flow graph is built and then the program representation graph is constructed from the augmented control-flow graph. An example program, its augmented control-flow graph, and its program representation graph are shown in Fig. 10.1.

Step 1. The control-flow graph[1] [1] of program P is augmented by adding *Initialize*, *FinalUse*, ϕ_{if}, ϕ_{Enter}, and ϕ_{Exit} vertices, as follows:

(i) A vertex labeled "$x := \quad Initialize_x$" is added at the beginning of the control-flow graph for each variable x that may be used before

---

[1] In control-flow graphs, vertices represent the program's assignment statements and predicates; in addition, there are two additional vertices, *Start* and *Exit*, which represent the beginning and the end of the program. The *Start* vertex is interpreted as an *if* predicate that evaluates to *true*, and the whole program is interpreted as the *true* branch of the *if* statement (see [6]).

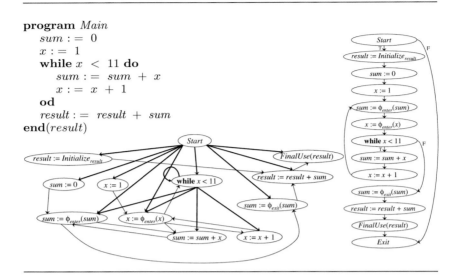

Fig. 10.1. An example program is shown on the top left. This example sums the integers 1 to 10 and adds the sum to the variable *result*. On the right is the augmented control-flow graph for the program. Note the absence of *Initialize* and *FinalUse* vertices for *sum* and *x* and of a ϕ_{Exit} vertex for *x*. On the bottom left is the program representation graph for the program. Note that there is a control-dependence edge from the *while* predicate $x < 11$ to itself. The boldface arrows represent control-dependence edges; thin arrows represent flow-dependence edges. The label on each control-dependence edge—*true* or *false*—has been omitted.

being defined in the program. (We say that a variable x *may be used before being defined* if there exists some path in the control-flow graph from the *Start* vertex to a vertex v that uses x such that none of the vertices in the path, excluding v, contains an assignment to variable x.) If there are many *Initialize* vertices for a program, their relative order is not important as long as they come immediately after the *Start* vertex.

(ii) A vertex labeled "*FinalUse(x)*" is added at the end of the control-flow graph for each variable x that appears in the *end* statement of the program. If there are many *FinalUse* vertices for a program, their relative order is not important as long as they come immediately before the *Exit* vertex.

(iii) For every variable x that is defined within an *if* statement, and that may be used before being redefined after the *if* statement, a vertex labeled "$x := \phi_{if}(x)$" is added immediately after the *if* statement. If there are many ϕ_{if} vertices for an *if* statement, their relative order is not important as long as they come immediately after the *if* statement.

(iv) For every variable x that is defined inside a loop, and that may be used before being redefined inside the loop or may be used before being redefined after the loop, a vertex labeled "$x := \phi_{Enter}(x)$" is added immediately before the predicate of the loop. If there are many ϕ_{Enter} vertices for a loop, their relative order is not important as long as they come immediately before the loop predicate. After the insertion of ϕ_{Enter} vertices, the first ϕ_{Enter} vertex of a loop becomes the entry point of the loop.

(v) For every variable x that is defined inside a loop, and that may be used before being redefined after the loop, a vertex labeled "$x := \phi_{Exit}(x)$" is added immediately after the loop. If there are many ϕ_{Exit} vertices for a loop, their relative order is not important as long as they come immediately after the loop.

Note that ϕ_{Enter} vertices are placed inside of loops, but ϕ_{Exit} vertices are placed outside of loops.

Step 2. Next, the program representation graph is constructed from the augmented control-flow graph. The vertices of the program representation graph are those in the augmented control-flow graph (except the *Exit* vertex). Edges are of two kinds: control-dependence edges and flow-dependence edges.

A control-dependence edge from a vertex u, representing an *if* or *while* predicate, to a vertex v, denoted by $u \rightarrow_c v$, means that, during execution, whenever the predicate represented by u is evaluated and its value matches the label—*true* or *false*—on the edge to v, then the program component represented by v will eventually be executed if the program terminates normally. Recall that we model the *Start* statement as an *if* predicate. Thus, the source of any control-dependence edge is either the *Start* vertex or some other predicate vertex.

There is a control-dependence edge from a predicate vertex u to a vertex v if, in the augmented control-flow graph, v occurs on every path from u to *Exit* along one branch out of u but not the other. This control-dependence edge is labeled by the truth value of the branch in which v always occurs.

Note that there is a control-dependence edge from a *while* predicate to itself. Methods for determining control-dependence edges for programs with unrestricted flow of control are given in [6, 5]; however, for our restricted language, control-dependence edges can be determined in a simpler fashion: Except for the extra control-dependence edge incident on a ϕ_{Enter} vertex, the control-dependence edges merely reflect the nesting structure of the program.

A flow-dependence edge from a vertex u to a vertex v, denoted by $u \rightarrow_f v$, means that the value produced at u may be used at v. There is a flow-dependence edge $u \rightarrow_f v$ if there is a variable x that is assigned a value at u and used at v, and there is an x-definition-free path from u to v in the augmented control-flow graph. The flow-dependence edges of a program representation graph can be computed using dataflow analysis.

The *imported variables* of a program P, denoted by Imp_P, are the variables that might be used before being defined in P, i.e. the variables for which there are *Initialize* vertices in the PRG of P.

Textually different programs may have isomorphic program representation graphs. However, it has been shown that if two programs have isomorphic program representation graphs, then the programs are semantically equivalent:

Theorem 10.1 (equivalence theorem for PRGs [26].) *Suppose that P and Q are programs for which R_P is isomorphic to R_Q. If σ is a state on which P halts, then for any state σ' that agrees with σ on the imported variables of P,*

   (i) *Q halts on σ',*

   (ii) *P and Q compute the same sequence of values at each corresponding program component, and*

   (iii) *the final states of P and Q agree on all variables for which there are final-use vertices in R_P and R_Q.*

10.4 Extensions to program representation graphs

Our aim is to treat PRGs as pure dataflow graphs. Dataflow graphs are a model of parallel computation, where vertices represent computing agents and edges represent unidirectional communication channels. Values computed at one vertex are transmitted to other vertices along the edges. In this model, the sequence of values "flowing" along an edge out of vertex u is a function of the sequences of values "flowing" along edges incident on vertex u.

The trouble with treating PDGs (as opposed to PRGs) as dataflow graphs is that multiple definitions of a variable may reach a vertex. In contrast, vertices in dataflow graphs tend to have only one incident edge per variable, the only exception being certain control vertices that choose the value from one of two incident edges based on a Boolean input. In contrast with PDGs, PRGs resemble dataflow graphs in this respect—normally only one definition of any variable reaches any vertex. The exceptions are the ϕ_{if} and ϕ_{Enter} vertices, which are reached by two definitions of a variable. Both ϕ_{if} and ϕ_{Enter} vertices are associated with predicate nodes, and are similar to the control vertices in dataflow graphs.

There is a small problem in treating PRGs as dataflow graphs. If $u \to_f v$ is a data dependence, then a particular value computed at u may be used zero or more times at v! However, in dataflow graphs a value flowing along an edge is consumed exactly once. To get around this problem, we introduce several new kinds of ϕ nodes that can consume unused data or duplicate them a certain number of times. These extra nodes make it possible to view PRGs as dataflow graphs and simplify the definition of PRG semantics.

The essential idea is to replace all data dependences $u \to_f v$ that can cause the above-mentioned problem by two data dependences $u \to_f w$ and $w \to_f v$, where w is an appropriate ϕ node, as described below.

(i) We first consider any data dependence $u \to_f v$ such that the value computed at u gets used at v only if an *if* predicate t evaluates to *true* at the appropriate instance. We introduce a ϕ_T vertex that, in the dataflow semantics, acts as a filter that transmits only those values that correspond to the *if* predicate evaluating to *true*. Let t be an *if* statement predicate and u a vertex outside the *if* statement. If there exists at least one vertex v such that (1) $u \to_f v$ is an edge in the PRG and (2) v is either in the *true* branch of the *if* statement or is a ϕ_{if} vertex associated with the *if* statement such that the definition u reaches v along the *true* branch of the control-flow graph, then introduce a ϕ_T vertex for the variable defined in u. Let w denote the new vertex. Add the control-dependence edge $t \to_c w$ labeled *true* and the data dependence edge $u \to_f w$. For each vertex v satisfying the above condition, replace $u \to_f v$ by the edge $w \to_f v$. See Figure 10.2 for an illustration of this definition.

Similarly, ϕ_F vertices are introduced in the *false* branches of *if* statements.

(ii) We now consider any data dependence $u \to_f v$ such that the value computed at u may be used several times at v due to multiple iterations of a *while* loop. We introduce a ϕ_{copy} vertex that, in the dataflow semantics, creates multiple copies of the value computed at u, one for each evaluation of the *while* predicate during the

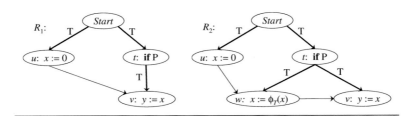

Fig. 10.2. The above example shows how ϕ_T vertices are introduced into PRGs.

execution of the loop. Let t be a *while* statement predicate and u a vertex outside the *while* statement. If there exists at least one non-ϕ_{Enter} vertex v inside the *while* statement such that $u \rightarrow_f v$ is an edge in the PRG, then introduce a ϕ_{copy} vertex for the variable defined in u. Let w denote the new vertex. Add control dependences $t \rightarrow_c w$ and $s \rightarrow_c w$, where s is t's parent, just as for a ϕ_{Enter} vertex. Add data dependence $u \rightarrow_f w$. For each vertex v satisfying the above condition, replace $u \rightarrow_f v$ by $w \rightarrow_f v$. See Figure 10.3 for an illustration of this definition.

(iii) We now consider any data dependence $u \rightarrow_f v$ such that the value computed at u gets used at v only if a *while* predicate t evaluates to *true* at the appropriate instance. We introduce a ϕ_{while} vertex that, in the dataflow semantics, filters out the values corresponding to an evaluation of the *while* predicate to *false*. Let t be a *while* statement predicate and u a ϕ_{Enter} or ϕ_{copy} vertex associated with the *while* statement. If there exists at least one vertex $v \neq t$ inside the *while* statement such that $u \rightarrow_f v$ is an edge in the PRG, then introduce a ϕ_{while} vertex w corresponding to the relevant variable. Add the control dependence $t \rightarrow_c w$ labeled *true* and the data dependence $u \rightarrow_f w$. For each vertex v satisfying the above condition, replace $u \rightarrow_f v$ by $w \rightarrow_f v$. See Figure 10.4 for an illustration of this definition.

Note: As may be seen from the informal explanations above, and the formal semantics presented later, ϕ_{while} and ϕ_T vertices have the same semantics and, hence, could be represented using the same type of ϕ vertex. Similarly, ϕ_{Exit} and ϕ_F vertices have the same semantics. However, we retain these distinct names for their mnemonic value.

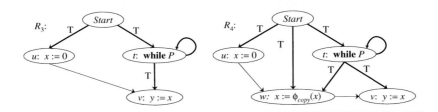

Fig. 10.3. The above example shows how ϕ_{copy} vertices are introduced into PRGs. Note that a ϕ_{while} vertex will subsequently be introduced between w and v.

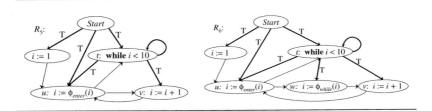

Fig. 10.4. The above example shows how ϕ_{while} vertices are introduced into PRGs.

The above transformations are performed in the following order: Traverse the control-dependence subtree of the PRG in a top-down fashion. For each predicate vertex t, for each suitable vertex u, perform either (1) or (2) and (3) (in that order) as appropriate.

Let us call the resulting structure an extended PRG. Note that the process guarantees that if there is any data dependence $u \rightarrow_f v$ and v is a non-ϕ vertex, then u and v have the same set of control-dependence predecessors, i.e., u and v execute under the same conditions. Thus, barring nontermination or abnormal termination, each value computed at u gets used exactly once at v. (Normally, a control-dependence predecessor of a vertex u is just a vertex v such that there exists a control-dependence edge $v \rightarrow_c u$. But occasionally, as above, we use the phrase to refer to a pair $\langle v, b \rangle$ such that there exists a control-dependence edge $v \rightarrow_c u$ labeled b).

The above extensions may be viewed as describing a graph transformation function $\mathbf{E}$—thus, if G is a PRG, then $\mathbf{E}(G)$ is the extended PRG. In the following section, we present a semantics for extended

PRGs, represented by the semantic function $\mathbf{M}$. The semantics of the (unextended) PRG G is then defined to be $\mathbf{M}(\mathbf{E}(G))$.

Let G be the PRG of a program P. We would like to relate the PRG semantics of G to the standard operational semantics of program P. To do this, we augment program P with ϕ-statements so that there is a one-to-one correspondence between the statements and predicates of the program so obtained (denoted by P') and the vertices of $\mathbf{E}(G)$. This is done just as in Section 10.3, with appropriate ϕ-statements being added to correspond to the ϕ vertices introduced in this section. (Thus, what we get is really an augmented control-flow graph, which has a standard operational semantics.) This simplifies various proofs relating the PRG semantics to the program semantics. Since each ϕ statement is an assignment of some variable to itself, the introduction of such statements hardly changes the standard semantics of the program. Consequently, the results we derive relating the semantics of $\mathbf{E}(G)$ to the semantics of extended program do relate the PRG semantics to the standard program semantics.

Here, it should be noted that $\mathbf{E}(G)$ may not be the PRG of the program P'. More precisely, the data dependence edges in $\mathbf{E}(G)$ may not correspond to the true data dependences in P'. For instance, consider the PRG G shown in Figure 10.5. G is the PRG of both programs P_1 and P_2, shown in augmented form below. The extended PRG $\mathbf{E}(G)$ turns out to be the PRG of extended program P_2', but not of P_1'.

L_1:	$x := 0$	L_1:	$x := 0$
	if p **then**	L_4:	$z := x$
L_2:	$x := \phi_T(x)$		**if** p **then**
L_3:	$y := x$	L_2:	$x := \phi_T(x)$
	fi	L_3:	$y := x$
L_4:	$z := x$		**fi**

$$\text{Program } P_1' \qquad\qquad\qquad \text{Program } P_2'$$

However, this difference between the actual dependences and the edges in the extended PRG causes no problem, as shown later.

Henceforth, the terms PRGs and programs will refer to extended PRGs (like $\mathbf{E}(G)$) and extended programs (like P'), respectively.

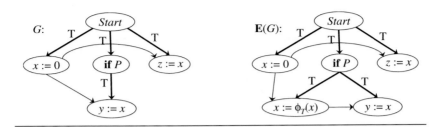

Fig. 10.5. An example of how extended PRGs may not represent the true data dependences of the extended program.

10.5 PRG semantics

10.5.1 Notation

Let u be a vertex in an extended PRG G. The vertex type of u must be one of {*assignment, if, while,* ϕ_T, ϕ_F, ϕ_{if}, ϕ_{while}, ϕ_{Enter}, ϕ_{Exit}, ϕ_{copy}, *Start, Initialize, FinalUse*}, and will be denoted by *typeOf(u)*. If u is an *assignment, if,* or *while* vertex, then *functionOf(u)*, a function of n variables, will represent the n-variable expression in vertex u. When the variables in the expression are abstracted to create a function, they have to be done so in some particular order. The variables, in the same order, are denoted by $var_1(u), \ldots, var_n(u)$. The data-dependence predecessor corresponding to $var_i(u)$ at u (where u is an *assignment, if,* or *while* vertex) is denoted by $dataPred_i(u)$. If u has a unique data dependence predecessor, $dataPred(u)$ will denote the predecessor vertex. Let *parent(u)* denote the unique control-dependence predecessor of vertex u, ignoring self-loops; in the case that u is a ϕ_{Enter} or a ϕ_{copy} vertex, *parent(u)* denotes the corresponding *while* predicate vertex. If $u \rightarrow_c v$ is a control-dependence edge, *label(u, v)* will denote the label (*true* or *false*) on that control-dependence edge. Let *controlLabel(u)* denote *label(parent(u), u)*. If u is an *Initialize, FinalUse,* or ϕ vertex, then *varOf(u)* denotes the corresponding variable.

If u is a ϕ_{if}, ϕ_T, or ϕ_F vertex, then *ifNode(u)* will denote the corresponding *if* predicate vertex. Similarly, if u is some ϕ node associated with a *while* loop, *whileNode(u)* will denote the corresponding *while* predicate vertex. If u is a ϕ_{Enter} vertex, then *innerDef(u)* and *outerDef(u)* denote the definitions that reach u from inside and outside the loop, respectively. If u is a ϕ_{if} vertex, then *trueDef(u)* and *falseDef(u)* are defined similarly. Let $CDP(u)$ denote the set of control-dependence predecessors of u, along with their associated labels.

Let Var denote the domain of variable names. Let Val denote the basic domain of first-order values manipulated by the programs—it includes the domain of *Booleans* and any other domains of interest: $Val = Boolean + integer + \ldots$

The domain *Sequence*, consisting of finite and infinite sequences of values belonging to Val, is defined by the following recursive domain equation, where NIL denotes the domain consisting of the single value *nil*.

$$Sequence = (NIL + (Val \times Sequence))_\perp$$

The *cons* operator is denoted by $\cdot$, as in $head \cdot tail$. Elements of the *Sequence* domain may be classified into three kinds: Finite sequences (such as $a_1 \cdot a_2 \cdot \ldots \cdot a_n \cdot nil$), infinite sequences ($a_1 \cdot a_2 \cdot \ldots$) and sequences whose suffix is unknown or undefined (such as $a_1 \cdot a_2 \cdot \ldots \cdot a_n \cdot \perp$). If a sequence X has at least i elements, then $X(i)$ is defined to be the ith element of X; otherwise, it is undefined. Similarly, $X(i \ldots j)$ denotes the corresponding subsequence of X, if all those elements are defined; otherwise, it is undefined. If X contains at least j occurrences of the value x, then $index(X, j, x)$ is defined and denotes the position in sequence X of the jth occurrence of x. $\#(X, j, x)$ denotes the number of occurrences of x in $X(1 \ldots j)$. A sequence X is said to be a prefix of sequence Y iff for every $X(i)$ that is defined, $Y(i)$ is defined and equal to $X(i)$.

The meaning function **M** that we want to define belongs to the domain

$$PRG \rightarrow Store \rightarrow Vertex \rightarrow Sequence,$$

where $Store = Var \rightarrow Val$.

10.5.2 The semantics

Let G be the PRG under consideration and σ the initial store. For each vertex u in G, we define a sequence $S(u)$ by an equation, which depends on the type of the vertex u. This set of equations can be combined into one recursive equation of the form

$$s = Fs,$$

where s combines all the sequences and hence effectively belongs to the domain *Vertex* → *Sequence*. The least fixed point S of this equation is given by

$$S = \bigsqcup_{i=0}^{\infty} F^i(\bot),$$

(where $\bot$ maps each vertex to the bottom value of *Sequence*). This least fixed point is taken to be the semantics of the given PRG with respect to the given store, i.e., $\mathbf{M}[G]\sigma = S$.

The equations are described below. (Note that the treatment of the bottom value in the following equations follows from the treatment of bottom by the primitive operations. Most importantly, the cons operator is non-strict in its second parameter. Similarly, "*if b then e_1 else e_2*" evaluates to e_1 if b evaluates to true, even if e_2 evaluates to bottom.)

- If u is the *Start* vertex, $S(u) = true \cdot nil$.
- If u is an *Initialize* vertex, $S(u) = \sigma(varOf(u)) \cdot nil$.
- If u is a *FinalUse* vertex, $S(u) = S(dataPred(u))$.
- If u is a ϕ_T vertex, $S(u) = select(true, S(parent(u)), S(dataPred(u)))$, where

$$select(x, y \cdot tail_1, z \cdot tail_2) = \begin{cases} z \cdot select(x, tail_1, tail_2) & \text{if } x = y \\ select(x, tail_1, tail_2) & \text{otherwise} \end{cases}$$

$$select(x, nil, z) = nil$$
$$select(x, y, nil) = nil$$

Note: The value of $select(x, s_1, s_2)$ is the sequence consisting of the values $s_2(i)$ such that $s_1(i)$ is the value x. More formally, let $s_3 = select(x, s_1, s_2)$. If $s_1(1 \ldots j)$ and $s_2(1 \ldots j)$ are defined and $j = index(s_1, i, x)$, then $s_3(i)$ is defined and equal to $s_2(j)$.

Conversely, if $s_3(i)$ is defined, then there must be a j such that $s_1(1 \ldots j)$ and $s_2(1 \ldots j)$ are defined and $j = index(s_1, i, x)$.

- If u is a ϕ_F vertex, $S(u) = select(false, S(parent(u)), S(dataPred(u)))$.
- If u is a ϕ_{if} vertex, $S(u) = merge(S(ifNode(u)), S(trueDef(u)), S(falseDef(u)))$, where

$$merge(true \cdot tail_1, x \cdot tail_2, s) = x \cdot merge(tail_1, tail_2, s)$$
$$merge(true \cdot tail_1, nil, s) = nil$$
$$merge(false \cdot tail_1, s, x \cdot tail_2) = x \cdot merge(tail_1, s, tail_2)$$
$$merge(false \cdot tail_1, s, nil) = nil$$
$$merge(nil, y, z) = nil$$

Note: Let $s_4 = merge(s_1, s_2, s_3)$. s_4 is the sequence obtained by merging the two sequences s_2 and s_3 according to s_1, a sequence of Boolean values. More formally, $s_4(i)$ is defined iff $s_1(1 \ldots i)$ is defined and $s_2(1 \ldots j)$ and $s_3(1 \ldots i - j)$ are defined, where $j = \#(s_1, i, true)$ and $i - j = \#(s_1, i, false)$. Furthermore, if the latter conditions are true, $s_4(i)$ will equal $s_2(j)$ if $s_1(i)$ equals *true* and $s_3(i - j)$ if $s_1(i)$ equals *false*.

- If u is a ϕ_{Exit} vertex, $S(u) = select(false, S(whileNode(u)), S(dataPred(u)))$.
- If u is a ϕ_{while} vertex, $S(u) = select(true, S(whileNode(u)), S(dataPred(u)))$.
- If u is a ϕ_{Enter} vertex,

$$S(u) = whileMerge(S(whileNode(u)), S(innerDef(u)), S(outerDef(u))),$$

where

$$whileMerge(s_1, s_2, x \cdot tail) = x \cdot merge(s_1, s_2, tail)$$
$$whileMerge(s_1, s_2, nil) = nil$$

Note: From the definition, it can be seen that the function *whileMerge* is quite related to *merge*. Let $s = whileMerge(s_1, s_2, s_3)$. $s(1)$ is defined and equal to $s_3(1)$ iff $s_3(1)$ is defined. For $i \geq 1$, $s(i+1)$ is defined iff $s_1(1 \ldots i)$ is defined and $s_2(1 \ldots j)$ and $s_3(1 \ldots i + 1 - j)$ are defined, where $j = \#(s_1, i, true)$ and $i - j = \#(s_1, i, false)$. If the latter conditions are true, then $s(i+1)$ will equal $s_2(j)$ if $s_1(i)$ equals *true* and $s_3(i+1-j)$ if $s_1(i)$ equals *false*.

- If u is a ϕ_{copy} vertex, $S(u) = whileCopy(S(whileNode(u)), S(dataPred(u)))$, where

$$whileCopy(s, x \cdot tail) = x \cdot copy(s, x \cdot tail)$$
$$whileCopy(s, nil) = nil$$
$$copy(true \cdot tail_1, x \cdot tail_2) = x \cdot copy(tail_1, x \cdot tail_2)$$
$$copy(false \cdot tail_1, x \cdot tail_2) = whileCopy(tail_1, tail_2)$$

Note: $whileCopy(s_1, s_2)$ is the sequence obtained by duplicating each element $s_2(i)$ (of the sequence s_2) $n + 1$ times, where n is the number of occurrences of 'true' between the $i - 1^{th}$ and i^{th} occurrence of 'false' in the sequence s_1. More formally, if $s = whileCopy(s_1, s_2)$, then (1) $s(1)$ is defined and equal to $s_2(1)$ iff $s_2(1)$ is defined and (2) $s(i + 1)$ is defined iff $s_1(1 \ldots i)$ is defined and $s_2(1 \ldots j)$ is defined, where $j = \#(s_1, i, false) + 1$. If the latter conditions hold, then $s(i+1)$ equals $s_2(j)$.

- The remaining possibilities are that u is an *assignment* vertex, an *if* predicate vertex, or a *while* predicate vertex. In these cases, if u has n data dependence predecessors, where $n > 0$, then

$$S(u) = map(functionOf(u))(S(dataPred_1(u)), \ldots S(dataPred_n(u))),$$

where

$$map(f)(x_1 \cdot tail_1, x_2 \cdot tail_2, \ldots, x_n \cdot tail_n)$$
$$= \quad f(x_1, x_2, \ldots, x_n) \cdot map(f)(tail_1, tail_2, \ldots, tail_n)$$
$$map(f)(nil, nil, \ldots, nil)$$
$$= \quad nil$$

Note: Let f be an n-variable function. Let $s = map(f)(s_1, \ldots, s_n)$. Then, $s(i)$ is defined and equal to $f(s_1(i), \ldots, s_n(i))$ if and only if $s_1(1 \ldots i), \ldots, s_n(1 \ldots i)$ are all defined.

If n is 0, then the expression in vertex u is a constant-valued expression. This case divides into two subcases. If u is anything other than a true-valued *while* predicate vertex, then

$$S(u) = replace(controlLabel(u), functionOf(u), S(parent(u))),$$

where

$$replace(x, y, z \cdot tail) = \begin{cases} y \cdot replace(x, y, tail) & \text{if } x = z \\ replace(x, y, tail) & \text{otherwise} \end{cases}$$

$$replace(x, y, nil) = nil$$

Note: Let $s_2 = replace(x, y, s_1)$. s_2 is essentially a sequence consisting of as many 'y's as s_1 has 'x's. Thus, all elements in s_1 that do not equal x are ignored, and the remaining elements are each replaced by y. More formally, $s_2(i)$ is defined and equal to y if and only if $index(s_1, i, x)$ is defined.

- If u is a true-valued *while* predicate vertex, then

$$S(u) = whileReplace(controlLabel(u), S(parent(u)),$$

where

$$whileReplace(x, nil) = nil$$
$$whileReplace(x, z \cdot tail) = \begin{cases} infinite\,Trues & \text{if } x = z \\ whileReplace(x, tail) & \text{otherwise} \end{cases}$$

and $infinite\,Trues = true \cdot infinite\,Trues$.

Note: whileReplace(x, s) is an infinite sequence of '*true*'s if the value x occurs in the sequence s, and the empty sequence otherwise.

10.6 Standard semantics

Consider the sequential execution of a program P on initial store σ, under the standard operational semantics. Let I denote the sequence of program points executed—i.e., $I(i)$ is the program point executed in the ith step. Let V denote the corresponding sequence of values computed. Thus, $V(i)$ denotes the value computed during the ith execution step. If a program point u executes at least i times, then $step(u, i)$ denotes the step number at which u executes for an ith time—i.e., $step(u, i) = index(I, i, u)$.

Let $A(u)$ denote the (possibly infinite) sequence of values computed at program point u. Thus, $A(u)(i)$ is defined iff $step(u, i)$ is defined, in which case it equals $V(step(u, i))$. Let $value(x, u, i)$ denote the value of the variable x at the begining of the $step(u, i)^{th}$ execution step. We will be interested in $value(x, u, i)$ only if x is used at program point u. We now observe some of the properties that hold among the various sequences. Our aim is to express $A(u)(i)$ in terms of values computed before $step(u, i)$.

All ϕ statements, *Initialize* statements, and *FinalUse* statements represent an assignment of a variable to itself. Other statements u compute the value

$$functionOf(u)(var_1(u), \ldots, var_n(u)).$$

This gives us the following property:

Property 1. If u is a ϕ, *Initialize*, or *FinalUse* statement, then the value of $A(u)(i)$ equals $value(varOf(u), u, i)$. Otherwise, $A(u)(i)$ equals $functionOf(u)(value(var_1(u), u, i), \ldots, value(var_n(u), u, i))$.

In the standard semantics, the store is used to communicate values between statements in the program. The following property follows directly from the way a store is used.

Property 2. Let $A = \{j \mid 1 \leq j < step(u, i)$ and $I(j)$ assigns to $x\}$ and let $\max(A)$ denote the maximum element in the set A. Then,

$$value(x, u, i) = \begin{cases} V(\max(A)) & \text{if } A \text{ is non-empty} \\ \sigma(x) & \text{otherwise} \end{cases}$$

The introduction of *Initialize* statements guarantees the following property.

Property 3. If x is some variable used at u and $step(u, i)$ is defined, then the set $\{j \mid 1 \leq j < step(u, i)$ and $I(j)$ assigns to variable $x\}$ is empty iff u is an *Initialize* statement.

Note that because the programming language has no aliasing mechanism, we can talk about assignments to variables rather than locations. It also makes it possible to compute statically the variable to which a statement dynamically assigns a value. Let $RD(u, x)$ denote the set of reaching definitions of variable x at statement u. (A statement v that assigns a value to variable x is said to be a reaching definition (of variable x) for statement u if there exists a path in the control-flow graph from v to u such that none of the vertices in the path, excluding v and u, is an assignment to variable x.) The following is a property of reaching definitions.

Property 4. If u is not an *Initialize* statement and x is some variable used at u, then $\max(\{j \mid 1 \leq j < step(u, i)$ and $I(j)$ assigns to variable $x\})$ is equal to $\max(\{j \mid 1 \leq j < step(u, i)$ and $I(j) \in RD(u, x)\})$.

The preceding three properties imply the following.

Property 5. If x is some variable used at u and A denotes the set $\{j \mid 1 \leq j < step(u, i)$ and $I(j) \in RD(u, x)\}$, then

$$value(x, u, i) = \begin{cases} \sigma(x) & \text{if } u \text{ is an } Initialize \text{ statement} \\ V(\max(A)) & \text{otherwise} \end{cases}$$

Let $DDP_G(u, x)$ denote the set of data-dependence predecessors that correspond to variable x of vertex u in graph G. We drop the subscript G if G is the extended PRG. If G is the PDG or PRG of the extended program, then $DDP_G(u, x) = RD(u, x)$, by definition (assuming that x is used at program point u). However, this need not be true if G is the extended PRG, as observed earlier. Yet, the data-dependence edges in the extended PRG are a sufficient-enough approximation to the reaching definitions for the following property to hold.

Property 6. If u is not an *Initialize* statement and x is some variable used at u, then

$$value(x, u, i) = V(\max(\{j \mid 1 \leq j < step(u, i) \text{ and } I(j) \in DDP(u, x)\}))$$

The justification for the above claim follows. Let $k = \max(\{j \mid 1 \leq j < step(u,i)$ and $I(j) \in DDP(u,x)\})$. Since $I(k) \in DDP(u,x)$, $I(k)$ must assign to x. Now, for any j such that $k < j < step(u,i)$, if $I(j)$ is an assignment to x, then $I(j)$ must be one of the new ϕ-statements introduced in the extension of PRGs (Section 10.4). (If not, consider the maximum j such that $k < j < step(u,i)$, $I(j)$ is an assignment to x and $I(j)$ is not one of the new ϕ-statements. Then, the data dependence $I(j) \rightarrow_f u$ must have been in the original PRG. Consequently, either $I(j) \rightarrow_f u$ must be present in the extended PRG, or there must be an m such that $j < m < step(u,i)$ and $I(m) \rightarrow_f u$ is present in the extended PRG. Either way, we have a contradiction with the maximality of k in its definition.) Since all the new ϕ-statements are assignments of a variable to itself, the above result follows.

Observe that all statements other than ϕ_{Enter} and ϕ_{if} statements have only one data dependence predecessor per variable. In such cases the above equation may be simplified to yield the following property.

Property 7. If $DDP(u,x) = \{v\}$, then

$$
\begin{aligned}
value(x,u,i) &= V(\max(\{j \mid 1 \leq j < step(u,i) \text{ and } I(j) = v\})) \\
&= V(\max(\{step(v,k) \mid step(v,k) < step(u,i)\})) \\
&= A(v)(k), \quad \text{where } k \text{ is such that} \\
&\qquad step(v,k) < step(u,i) < step(v,k+1)
\end{aligned}
$$

The notation $step(x,i) < step(y,j)$ essentially means that program point y executes for the jth time only after program point x executes for the ith time. However, we will also say that $step(x,i) < step(y,j)$ even if y does not execute j times.

The following properties concern control dependence and help identify the value of k in property 7. Observe that if v is a data-dependence predecessor of u, and u and v are non-ϕ statements, then u and v have the same control-dependence predecessor and v occurs to the left of u in the program's abstract syntax tree. More generally, if v is any kind of data-dependence predecessor of u and u is a non-ϕ vertex, then u and v have the same control-dependence predecessors and v dominates u in the extended control-flow graph.

Property 8. If $CDP(u) = CDP(v)$ and v dominates u, then $step(v,i) < step(u,i) < step(v,i+1)$, for all i. Furthermore, if the program execution terminates normally, u and v execute the same number of times.

The previous two properties combined with Property 1 gives us the following result.

Property 9. If u is an *assignment* statement, *if* predicate, or *while* predicate, and executes i times, then

$$A(u)(i) = functionOf(u)(A(dataPred_1(u))(i), \ldots, A(dataPred_n(u))(i)).$$

Let u have only one control-dependence predecessor, say v. Let this control-dependence edge be labeled *true*. Then, barring nontermination or abnormal termination, u is executed exactly once each time v is evaluated to *true*. More formally, we can state the following property:

Property 10. Let $v \rightarrow_c u$, labeled *true*, be the sole control-dependence edge that is incident on u. Then, if $A(u)(i)$ is defined, $j = index(A(v), i, true)$ must be defined and $step(v, j) < step(u, i)$. Conversely, if $index(A(v), i, true)$ is defined, then $A(u)(i)$ must be defined, barring nontermination or abnormal termination.

The above property can be extended to state that $step(u, i)$ occurs "soon after" $step(v, j)$—i.e., before any other statement at the same nesting level as v can be executed. Let w denote some vertex with the same control-dependence predecessors as v and occuring to the left of v. (As a specific example, let u be a ϕ_T vertex. Let v be $parent(u)$ and w be $dataPred(u)$.) It is easy to see that $step(w, j) < step(u, i) < step(w, j+1)$. This gives us the following property.

Property 11. Let u be a ϕ_T vertex. Let v denote $parent(u)$ and w denote $dataPred(u)$. If $A(u)(i)$ is defined, then $j = index(A(v), i, true)$ must be defined and

$$step(w, j) < step(v, j) < step(u, i) < step(w, j + 1)$$

and consequently, from Properties 1 and 7,

$$A(u)(i) = A(w)(j)$$

A similar extension of Property 10 to consider a vertex w with the same control-dependence predecessors as v and occurring to the right of v yields the following property.

Property 12. Let v be an *if* predicate and let $v \to_c u$, labeled *true*, be the only control-dependence edge incident on u. Let w be a ϕ_{if} vertex associated with v. Let $j = \#(A(v), i, \text{true})$. Then $step(u, j) < step(w, i) < step(u, j + 1)$.

Related versions of the above two properties may be obtained by replacing *true* by *false* and T by F. The following property of ϕ_{if} vertices is obtained from Properties 1, 6, and 12.

Property 13. Let u be a ϕ_{if} vertex. Let v be *ifNode(u)*, x be *trueDef(u)* and y be *falseDef(u)*. If $A(u)(i)$ is defined, then

$$A(u)(i) = \begin{cases} A(x)(j) & \text{if } A(v)(i) \\ A(y)(i - j) & \text{otherwise} \end{cases}$$

where $j = \#(A(v), i, \text{true})$.

A formal derivation of the above property follows. Assume that $A(v)(i)$ is *true*. Let $\#(A(v), i, \text{true})$ be j. Obviously, $\#(A(v), i - 1, \text{true}) = j - 1$, while $\#(A(v), i, \text{false}) = \#(A(v), i - 1, \text{false}) = i - j$. Hence, from property 12,

$$step(y, i - j) < step(u, i - 1) < step(x, j) < step(u, i) < step(x, j + 1)$$

and

$$step(u, i) < step(y, i - j + 1)$$

Properties 1 and 6 imply that $A(u)(i)$ must be $A(x)(j)$. Similarly, if $A(v)(i)$ is *false*, then $A(u)(i)$ must be $A(y)(i - j)$.

The following property concerns the execution behavior of a ϕ_{Enter} vertex. Here, it is useful to consider the execution of the whole loop (rather than just the loop predicate). The loop completes an execution when the loop predicate evaluates to *false*. Suppose the loop predicate v has been executed i times. Then, the number of times the loop has completed an execution is given by $\#(A(v), i, \text{false})$.

Property 14. Let u be a ϕ_{Enter} vertex. Let v, x, and y be *whileNode(u)*, *outerDef(u)*, and *innerDef(u)*, respectively. Let w be the parent of x and v. Let the control dependences $w \to_c v$ and $w \to_c u$ be labeled *true*. If $i > 1$, then the following hold

$$step(x, 1) < step(u, 1) < step(y, 1)$$
$$step(u, i - 1) < step(v, i - 1) < step(u, i)$$
$$step(x, j) < step(u, i) < step(x, j + 1), \text{where } j = \#(A(v), i - 1, \text{false}) + 1$$
$$step(y, j) < step(u, i) < step(y, j + 1), \text{where } j = \#(A(v), i - 1, \text{true})$$

In particular, from Property 6, if $A(u)(1)$ is defined, then

$$A(u)(1) = A(x)(1)$$

and for $i > 1$, if $A(u)(i)$ is defined, then

$$A(u)(i) = \begin{cases} A(y)(i-j) & \text{if } A(v)(i-1) \\ A(x)(j) & \text{otherwise} \end{cases}$$

where $j = \#(A(v), i-1, false) + 1$.

The derivation of the above property is very similar to the derivation of Property 13.

The following property concerns ϕ_{copy} vertices. It is similar to, though simpler than, the previous property.

Property 15. Let u be a ϕ_{copy} vertex. Let v denote *whileNode(u)*, and w denote *dataPred(u)*. Let $j = \#(A(v), i-1, false) + 1$ Then,

$$step(u, i-1) < step(v, i-1) < step(u, i)$$

and

$$step(w, j) < step(u, i) < step(w, j+1)$$

and if $A(u)(i)$ is defined, it must be equal to $A(w)(j)$.

10.7 Relationship to the standard operational semantics

We now consider the relationship between the semantics of the PRG of a program, as defined earlier, and the standard operational semantics of the program. We show that in general the sequence $S(u)$ (which is defined by the PRG semantics) may be more defined than the sequence $A(u)$ (the sequence of values computed by program point u, as defined by the operational semantics of the program)—or more formally, that $A(u)$ will be a prefix of $S(u)$. However, for input stores on which the program terminates normally, the sequence $S(u)$ will be shown to be equal to the sequence $A(u)$.

This difference in the case of nonterminating (or abnormally terminating) program execution maybe explained as follows. Dataflow semantics exposes and exploits the parallelism in programs. The eager or data-driven evaluation semantics lets a program point execute as soon as the data it needs is available. In the standard sequential execution of a program, however, the execution of a program point u may have to be delayed until completion of execution of some other part of the program, even if the result of that computation is unnecessary for the computation to be done at u. Moreover, if that computation never terminates or terminates abnormally, execution of program point u does not occur.

Let $S(u)$ denote the least-fixed-point solution of the set of recursive equations for the PRG of program P and initial store σ as defined in Section 10.5. As observed earlier, the set of equations can be combined into one recursive equation of the form $s = Fs$. Let $S^k(u)$ denote $F^k(\bot)(u)$, the kth approximation to the solution at vertex u. Now we are ready to state a sequence of lemmas and theorems that relate the standard operational semantics and the PRG semantics.

Lemma 10.2 *Let G be the extended PRG of a program P and σ be an input store. Let $S(u)$ denote $\mathbf{M}[G](\sigma)(u)$, $S^k(u)$ denote the kth approximation to $S(u)$, and $A(u)$ denote the sequence of values computed at program point u for input σ under the standard operational semantics. If $A(u)(i)$ is defined, then there exists a k such that $S^k(u)(i)$ is defined and equal to $A(u)(i)$.*

Proof: See [18].

Theorem 10.3 *Let G be the extended PRG of a program P and σ an input store. Let $S(u)$ denote $\mathbf{M}[G](\sigma)(u)$ and $A(u)$ denote the sequence of values computed at program point u for input σ under the standard operational semantics. Then, $A(u)$ is a prefix of $S(u)$.*

Proof: The theorem follows immediately from the previous lemma. Let $S^k(u)$ denote the kth approximation to $S(u)$. Thus, $S(u) = \bigsqcup_{i=0}^{\infty} S^i(u)$. If $A(u)(i)$ is defined, then there exists a k such that $S^k(u)(i)$ is defined and equal to $A(u)(i)$, from the previous lemma. Consequently, $S(u)(i)$ is defined and equal to $A(u)(i)$.

The preceding theorem concerns possibly nonterminating (or abnormally terminating) executions of the program. We now consider executions that terminate normally and show the stronger result that for all program points u, $S(u) = A(u)$.

Lemma 10.4 *Let G be the extended PRG of a program P and σ an input store on which P terminates normally. Let $S(u)$ denote $\mathbf{M}[G][\sigma](u)$, $S^k(u)$ denote the kth approximation to $S(u)$, and $A(u)$ denote the sequence of values computed at program point u for input σ under the standard operational semantics. For any k, $S^k(u)$ is a prefix of $A(u)$.* $\square$

Proof: See [18].

Theorem 10.5 *Let G be the extended PRG of a program P and σ an input store on which P terminates normally. Let $S(u)$ denote $\boldsymbol{M}[G][\sigma](u)$ and $A(u)$ denote the sequence of values computed at program point u for input σ under the standard operational semantics. Then $S(u)$ is a prefix of $A(u)$.* □

Proof: Let $S^k(u)$ denote the kth approximation to $S(u)$. If $S(u)(i)$ is defined, then there must be a k such that $S^k(u)(i)$ is defined (and, obviously, equal to $S(u)(i)$). It follows from the previous lemma that $A(u)(i)$ is defined and equal to $S(u)(i)$.

Theorem 10.6 *Let G be the extended PRG of a program P and σ an input store on which P terminates normally. $\boldsymbol{M}[G][\sigma](u)$ is equal to $A(u)$, the sequence of values computed at program point u for input σ under the standard operational semantics.* □

Proof: It follows from the last two theorems that $A(u)$ is a prefix of $\mathbf{M}[G][\sigma](u)$ and $\mathbf{M}[G][\sigma](u)$ is a prefix of $A(u)$. Hence, $A(u)$ and $\mathbf{M}[G][\sigma](u)$ must be equal.

A stronger form of the equivalence theorem for PRGs [26] (see Section 10.3) follows directly from the previous theorems.

Theorem 10.7 *Let P and Q be programs with isomorphic PRGs, R_P and R_Q, respectively. Let σ_1 and σ_2 be two states that agree on the imported variables of P and Q. Let x_1 and x_2 be two corresponding vertices of P and Q. Let $A_P(x_1)$ and $A_Q(x_2)$ denote the sequence of values computed at x_1 and x_2, on states σ_1 and σ_2, respectively. Then, either (1) P and Q terminate normally on σ_1 and σ_2, respectively, and $A_P(x_1)$ equals $A_Q(x_2)$, or (2) neither P nor Q terminates normally on σ_1 and σ_2, respectively, and $A_P(x_1)$ is a prefix of $A_Q(x_2)$ or vice versa.* □

Proof: Note that the dependence of the PRG semantics on the initial state is restricted to the values of the imported variables. Consequently, the semantics of the isomorphic PRGS R_P and R_Q for initial states σ_1 and σ_2, respectively, say S_P and S_Q, are identical. Thus $S_P(x_1) = S_Q(x_2)$. From the previous section, we also know that $A_P(x_1)$ is a prefix of $S_P(x_1)$ and that $A_Q(x_2)$ is a prefix of $S_Q(x_2)$. Consequently, $A_P(x_1)$ must be a prefix of $A_Q(x_2)$ or vice versa.

Note that $A_P(x)$ and $S_P(x)$ are finite for all vertices x in P iff the program P terminates normally. Hence, either P and Q both terminate normally (in which case $A_P(x_1) = S_P(x_1) = S_Q(x_2) = A_Q(x_2)$) or neither P nor Q terminates normally. The theorem follows immediately.

However, note that this stronger equivalence theorem can be derived from the Sequence–Congruence theorem [27], too.

10.8 Application to program slicing

We now show how the results established above can be used to reason about and establish the correctness of applications of a PRG. Specifically, we consider the application of PRGs to program slicing and derive an analogue of the Slicing theorem of [20] relating the semantics of a program's slice to the semantics of the program. A slice of a program with respect to a program point p and a variable v consists of all statements of the program that might affect the value of v at point p [25]. When the variable v is used or defined at program point p, the slice with respect to v at p can be obtained by identifying the subgraph of a PDG (or PRG) induced by all vertices that can reach p in the PDG (or PRG) and transforming the subgraph into a program [16].

Theorem 10.8 *Let P and Q be programs with PRGs R_P and R_Q, respectively; let q be a vertex of R_Q, and R_P be isomorphic to a subgraph of R_Q induced by all vertices that can reach q. Let σ_1 and σ_2 be two states that agree on the imported variables of P. Let x_1 and x_2 be two corresponding vertices of P and Q. Let $A_P(x_1)$ and $A_Q(x_2)$ denote the sequence of values computed at x_1 and x_2, on states σ_1 and σ_2, respectively. Then, (1) $A_P(x_1)$ is a prefix of $A_Q(x_2)$ or vice versa, and (2) if Q terminates normally on σ_2 then P terminates normally on σ_1 and $A_P(x_1)$ equals $A_Q(x_2)$.*   □

Proof: Note that the set of equations induced by R_P is isomorphic to the corresponding subset of the equations induced by R_Q. For $T \in \{P, Q\}$, let S_T denote the semantics of the PRG R_T, and let $S_T^k(u)$ denote the kth approximation to $S_T(u)$. One can establish by induction that $S_P^k(x_1) = S_Q^k(x_2)$ for any corresponding pair of vertices x_1 in P and x_2 in Q. It follows that $S_P(x_1) = S_Q(x_2)$.

Because $A_P(x_1)$ is a prefix of $S_P(x_1)$ and $A_Q(x_2)$ is a prefix of $S_Q(x_2)$, it follows that either $A_P(x_1)$ must be a prefix of $A_Q(x_2)$ or $A_Q(x_1)$ must be a prefix of $A_P(x_2)$.

Furthermore, if Q terminates normally on σ_2, then $S_Q(x_2)$ is finite and equal to $A_Q(x_2)$ for every vertex x_2 in Q. It follows that $S_P(x_1)$ is finite for every vertex x_1 in P and that P must terminate normally on σ_1. Hence, $A_P(x_1) = S_P(x_1) = S_Q(x_2) = A_Q(x_2)$, where x_1 and x_2 are corresponding vertices.

10.9 Related work

Selke's graph rewriting semantics for PDGs [22], and Cartwright and Felleisen's derivation of a semantics for PDGs [4] have already been discussed in Section 10.1.

The work described in this paper, which was originally described in a 1989 technical report [19], was motivated by the desire to apply Kahn's semantics for a parallel programming language [12] to the problem that Selke's and Cartwright and Felleisen's papers addressed. A somewhat similar approach was taken in two other papers from the same era.

- Ottenstein *et al.* [15] describe an augmented program-dependence representation, similar to the extended PRG, for programs with unstructured control flow, and indicate that it could be interpreted as a dataflow graph. Their work, however, focuses on constructing the representation, and they do not present a formal semantics for the representation.

- Pingali *et al.* [17] argue that intermediate representations of programs should themselves be programs, i.e., have a local execution semantics, to permit abstract interpretation over the intermediate representation. They describe yet another dependence-graph representation, for which they present a dataflow-like semantics; however, this semantics is based on a global store, rather than being a "pure dataflow" semantics. They show how the representation can be used for abstract interpretation to perform constant propagation.

Field [7] presents a rewriting semantics for programs, where programs are viewed as terms, and a set of equational axioms for such terms is used as the basis for rewriting terms. Rewriting applied to a term consisting of a program and its input corresponds to program execution. On the other hand, rewriting can also be applied to a program, without its input, to produce a "simplified" program equivalent to the original program. Field shows that this rewriting process can produce terms that are similar to program representations such as PRGs.

Weise *et al.* [24] present another dependence-graph representation, called the Value Dependence Graph; they argue that such representations are a better basis for compiler optimizations, and illustrate this via an algorithm for partial redundancy elimination. Weise *et al.* address a more complete language than we do.

Giacobazzi and Mastroeni [8] present a framework for defining programming language semantics for which the semantics of a program and a slice of the program are related, even when the slice changes the termination behavior. Their approach uses transfinite state traces, which allows the semantics to observe what happens "after" a divergent loop. This allows a program's behavior to be related to the behaviors of slices that change the termination status: the finite behavior of a slice that terminates on inputs that cause the original program to diverge can be related to the program's transfinite behavior.

Hatcliff et al. [9] relate the semantics of a concurrent program and the semantics of a slice of the program using the notion of weak simulation: a correspondence relation is defined between the execution states of the program and the execution states of the slice, and it is shown that for any observable transition that the program can make, the slice can make a corresponding transition. Amtoft [3] uses a similar approach for sequential programs.

Bibliography

[1]   A. Aho, R. Sethi and J. Ullman. *Compilers: Principles, Techniques and Tools*. Addison-Wesley, 1985.

[2]   B. Alpern, M. Wegman, and F. Zadeck. Detecting equality of variables in programs. In *POPL*, pp. 1–11, 1988.

[3]   T. Amtoft. Slicing for modern program structures: a theory for eliminating irrelevant loops. *Information Processing Letters*, **106**:45–51, 2008.

[4]   R. Cartwright and M. Felleisen. The semantics of program dependence. In *PLDI*, pp. 13–27, 1989.

[5]   R. Cytron, J. Ferrante, B. Rosen, M. Wegman and F. Zadeck. An efficient method of computing static single assignment form. In *POPL*, pp. 25–35, 1989.

[6]   J. Ferrante, K. Ottenstein and J. Warren. The program dependence graph and its use in optimization. *TOPLAS*, **3**(9):319–349, 1987.

[7]   J. Field. A simple rewriting semantics for realistic imperative programs and its application to program analysis. In *PEPM*, pp. 98–107, 1992.

[8]   R. Giacobazzi and I. Mastroeni. Non-standard semantics for program slicing. *HOSC*, **16**(4):297–339, 2003.

[9]   J. Hatcliff, J. Corbett, M. Dwyer, S. Sokolowski and H. Zheng. A formal study of slicing for multi-threaded programs with JVM concurrency primitives. In *SAS*, 1999.

[10] S. Horwitz, J. Prins and T. Reps. On the adequacy of program dependence graphs for representing programs. In *POPL*, pp. 146–157, 1988.

[11] S. Horwitz, J. Prins and T. Reps. Integrating non-interfering versions of programs. *TOPLAS*, **11**(3):345–387, 1989.

[12] G. Kahn. The semantics of simple language for parallel programming. In *IFIP Congress*, pp. 471–475, 1974.

[13] D. Kuck, R. Kuhn, B. Leasure, D. Padua and M. Wolfe. Dependence graphs and compiler optimizations. In *POPL*, pp. 207–218, 1981.

[14] D. Kuck, Y. Muraoka, and S. Chen. On the number of operations simultaneously executable in FORTRAN-like programs and their resulting speed-up. *IEEE Trans. on Computers*, **C-21**(12):1293–1310, 1972.

[15] K. Ottenstein, R. Ballance and A. MacCabe. The program dependence web: A representation supporting control-, data-, and demand-driven interpretation of imperative languages. In *PLDI*, pp. 257–271, 1990.

[16] K. Ottenstein and L. Ottenstein. The program dependence graph in a software development environment. In *Softw. Eng. Symp. on Practical Softw. Dev. Environments*, pp. 177–184, 1984.

[17] K. Pingali, M. Beck, R. Johnson, M. Moudgill, and P. Stodghill. Dependence flow graphs: An algebraic approach to program dependencies. In *Advances in Languages and Compilers for Parallel Processing*, pp. 445–467. M.I.T. Press, 1991.

[18] G. Ramalingam and T. Reps. Appendix A: Proofs. "www.cs.wisc. edu/wpis/papers/soprgs08-proofs.pdf".

[19] G. Ramalingam and T. Reps. Semantics of program representation graphs. TR-900, Computer Science Department, University of Wisconsin, Madison, WI, 1989.

[20] T. Reps and W. Yang. The semantics of program slicing and program integration. In *CCIPL*, pp. 360–374, 1989.

[21] B. Rosen, M. Wegman, and F. Zadeck. Global value numbers and redundant computations. In *POPL*, pp. 12–27, 1988.

[22] R. Selke. A rewriting semantics for program dependence graphs. In *POPL*, pp. 12–24, 1989.

[23] R. Shapiro and H. Saint. The representation of algorithms. Tech. Rep. CA-7002-1432, Massachusetts Computer Associates, 1970.

[24] D. Weise, R. Crew, M. Ernst and B. Steensgaard. Value dependence graphs: Representation without taxation. In *POPL*, pp. 297–310, 1994.

[25] M. Weiser. Program slicing. In *ICSE*, pp. 439–449, 1981.

[26] W. Yang. *A New Algorithm for Semantics-Based Program Integration*. PhD thesis, Computer Science Department, University of Wisconsin, Madison, WI, Aug. 1990.

[27] W. Yang, S. Horwitz and T. Reps. Detecting program components with equivalent behaviors. TR-840, Computer Science Department, University of Wisconsin, Madison, WI, Apr. 1989.

[28] W. Yang, S. Horwitz and T. Reps. A program integration algorithm that accommodates semantics-preserving transformations. *TOSEM*, **1**(3):310–354, July 1992.

11

From Centaur to the Meta-Environment: a tribute to a great meta-technologist

Paul Klint

Centrum voor Wiskunde en Informatica and University of Amsterdam

Abstract

Gilles Kahn was a great colleague and good friend who has left us much too early. In this paper I will sketch our joint research projects, the many discussions we had, some personal recollections, and the influence these have had on the current state-of-the-art in meta-level language technology.

11.1 Getting acquainted

> **Bâtiment 8.** *On a sunny day in the beginning of July 1983 I parked my beige Citroen Dyane on the parking lot in front of Bâtiment 8, INRIA Rocquencourt. At the time, the buildings made the impression that the US military who had constructed the premises in Rocquencourt were also the last that had ever used the paint brush. Inside, lived an energetic research family and I was hosted by project CROAP headed by Gilles Kahn. My roommates Veronique Donzeau-Gouge and Bertrand Mélèse helped me find a bureau in a corner in the cramped building and helped to set up a Multics account on the Honeywell-Bull mainframe.*

After some flirtations with computer graphics, software portability and the Unix operating system, I turned to the study of string processing languages on which I wrote a PhD in 1982 [55]. The main topic was the Summer programming language [52] that featured objects, success/failure driven control flow, string matching and composition,

From Semantics to Computer Science Essays in Honour of Gilles Kahn, eds Yves Bertot, Gérard Huet, Jean-Jacques Lévy and Gordon Plotkin. Published by Cambridge University Press. © Cambridge University Press 2009.

and a "try" mechanism that allowed the execution of an arbitrary sequence of statements and would undo all side effects in case this execution resulted in failure.

As part of this work, I got attracted to the question of how the semantics of such languages could be defined [53]. The approach I used was a meta-circular language definition that covered both syntax and semantics. However, this definition was written after the actual implementation had already been completed. Would it not be great if a language definition could be used to *generate* an efficient language implementation?

As described in more detail in [44], Jan Heering and I started the design of a dedicated programming environment for the Summer programming language. This led us to the notion of a *monolingual programming environment* [43] in which the various modes of the environment such as programming, command line execution and debugging were all done in the same language. We were aware of the formidable implementation effort of such a system for a specific language and, in addition to this, Summer had never been designed with that purpose in mind. As already described, we had some experience with language definitions and this naturally led to the idea of a programming environment based on language definitions.

This is how Jan and I became aware of the INRIA work on syntax-directed editing [36, 60], the formal definition of ADA [37], the language definition formalism Metal [50], and the abstract syntax tree manipulation system Mentor [39, 38, 40]. This work was motivated by Gilles's earlier work on semantic aspects of programming languages [47, 48, 51]. The best way to study this work was to pay a visit to the CROAP (Conception et Réalisation d'Outils d'Aide à la Programmation) team at INRIA, which was headed by Gilles. This is precisely what I did in July 1983. A lucky coincidence was that Tim Teitelbaum and his two PhD students Thomas Reps and Suzanne Horwitz were spending their sabbatical in Rocquencourt. This gave me the opportunity to compare three systems: the Mentor system (Gilles and coworkers), an early version of the synthesizer generator (Tim Teitelbaum and Thomas Reps), and Ceyx (a Mentor-like system built by Jean-Marie Hullot on top of Jerome Chailloux' LeLisp system). This comparison appeared as [54].

11.2 The GIPE projects

Take the money and run! *Phone call from Gilles early 1984: "Paul, did you hear about this new ESPRIT program? Shouldn't we submit a proposal and take the money and run?"*

11.2.1 GIPE proposal

And indeed, by the end of 1984 we submitted a proposal for the project *Generation of Interactive Programming Environments* or GIPE[1] for short. The prime contractor was SEMA METRA (France) and the partners were BSO (a Dutch software house that is currently part of ATOS ORIGIN), Centrum voor Wiskunde en Informatica (Netherlands) and INRIA (France). The objectives and envisaged approach were neatly summarized in the proposal.

The main objective of this project is to investigate the possibilities of automatically generating interactive programming environments from a language specification. An "interactive programming environment" is here understood as a set of integrated tools for the incremental creation, manipulation, transformation and compilation of structured formalized objects such as programs in a programming language, specifications in a specification language, or formalized technical documents. Such an interactive environment will be generated from a complete syntactic and semantic characterization of the formal language to be used. In the proposed project, a prototype system will be designed and implemented that can manipulate large formally described objects (these descriptions may even use combinations of different formalisms), incrementally maintain their consistency, and compile these descriptions into executable programs.

The following steps are required to achieve this goal.

- *Construction of a shared software environment as a point of departure for experimenting with and making comparisons between language specific techniques. The necessary elements of this – Unix-based – software environment are: efficient and mutually compatible implementations of Lisp and Prolog, a parser generator, general purpose algorithms for syntax-directed editing and prettyprinting, software packages for window management and graphics, etc. Most of these elements are already available or can be obtained; the main initial effort will be to integrate these components into one reliable, shared software environment.*

---

[1] We never settled on a proper pronunciation of this acronym.

- *A series of experiments that amount to developing sample specifications-based on different language specification formalisms, but initially based on inference rules and universal algebra–for a set of selected examples in the domain of programming languages, software engineering and man-machine interaction. The proposed formalisms have well-understood mathematical properties and can accommodate incremental and even reversible computing.*
- *Construction of a set of tools of the shared environment to carry out the above experiments. It will be necessary to create, manipulate and check (parts of) language specifications and to compile them into executable programs. The tools draw heavily upon techniques used in object-oriented programming (for manipulation of abstract syntax trees), automatic theorem proving (for inferring properties from given specifications to check their consistency and select potential compilation methods), expert systems (to organize the increasing number of facts that become known about a given specification) and Advanced Information Processing in general (man-machine interfaces, general inference techniques, maintenance and propagation of constraints, etc.)*
- *The above experiments will indicate which of the chosen formalisms is most appropriate for characterizing various aspects of programming languages and interactive programming environments. These insights will be used in constructing a prototype system for deriving programming environments from language specifications. The envisioned "programming environment generator" consists of an integrated set of tools and an adequate man-machine interface for the incremental creation, consistency checking, manipulation and compilation of language specifications.*

By performing some hype-aware substitutions (syntax $\mapsto$ model, generation $\mapsto$ model-driven, elements $\mapsto$ components) this vision is still relevant today. As in each proposal we had to oversell our ideas and we indeed needed GIPE (1985–1989), and its sequel project GIPE II (1989–1993) to create a proof-of-concept of this vision. In the GIPE II project, the companies GIPSI (France), Bull (France), Planet (Greece), PTT Research (the Netherlands), and the research partners TH Darmstadt (Germany), University of Amsterdam (the Netherlands) and PELAB (Linkoping Sweden) joined the team.

11.2.2 The importance of GUIs

Disoriented mice. *Demonstration sessions are a must for any subsidized research program and ESPRIT was no exception. As part of the yearly ESPRIT conference we gathered—with many colleagues from all over Europe who participated in other ESPRIT projects—in an underground parking lot of the Berlaymont building in Brussels. The parking garage had been turned into an exposition center but the smell of cars was still clearly present. Our two Sun workstations booted-up well but at the stage that the window system was up and running and interaction with the mouse was needed, everything messed up. Incompatible mouse drivers? A hardware error? After two hours of hectic discussions and experiments we discovered the cause of the problem. At that time of early optical mice, the specific grid on the mouse pad was used to determine the mouse's coordinates and simply switching the two mouse pads solved the problem. Or was this a case of overexposure to exhaust fumes after all?*

Gilles had from early on recognized the importance of a proper user-interface. His preoccupation with the user-interface was based on an earlier disappointing experience when the Mentor system was being demonstrated to a high-ranking official from a US government agency. The nifty thing to be demonstrated was that the knowledge of the abstract syntax of a program could be used to skip complete subtrees during a search operation. However, it turned out to be impossible to get this nice idea across because the official kept asking "where's the user-interface?".

In fact, during the GIPE project we had the same experience while demonstrating an early prototype of our syntax-directed editor to the board of directors of BSO, our Dutch commercial partner at the time. From our perspective everything was present in the demo: a parser generator, a parser, a syntax-tree manager, and a prettyprinter. All these tools were based on a well-understood theory and implemented with a lot of hard work. However, we learned the hard way that the most important part was still missing: a colorful user-interface that could attract the attention of the board.

It will come as no surprise, that user-interfaces have played an important role during and after the GIPE projects.

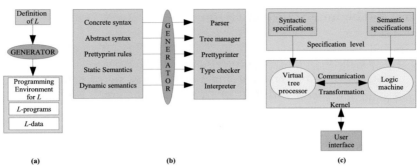

(a)   (b)   (c)

Fig. 11.1. Early architectural designs of the GIPE system: (a) End-user view of an L-environment for an arbitrary language L; (b) Relation between language definition and generated environment; (c) Global architecture.

11.2.3 GIPE results

The initial architecture of the environment generator was described in [28]. Figure 11.1 gives some snapshots of that design. Clearly visible are the generator-based approach and the internal representation of programs as trees.

It is amazing how much effort is often required to achieve goals described in innocently looking sentences in a project proposal, like "Most of these elements are already available or can be obtained; the main initial effort will be to integrate these components into one reliable, shared software environment". Recall, that the project started in the pre-X-windows era and we have experimented with a lot of now long forgotten systems: Brown Workstation Environment, LucasFilm, LeLisp Virtual Window System, and Graphical Objects.

Another fundamental choice that we made early on in the project was to use LeLisp [23] as the implementation language. LeLisp was a nice, flexible language that was ideal for prototyping and code generation. However, this decision turned out to be a major problem towards the end of GIPE II. LeLisp was transferred to the INRIA spinoff ILOG and we were stuck with a LeLisp version that was no longer maintained.

There have always been two different approaches in the GIPE projects: a "Dutch" approach and a "French" approach. As a Francophile, I liked Gilles' laissez-faire style that today would be called "just-in-time". Several of the younger members in the Dutch team preferred to have things organized weeks in advance. Not surprisingly this led to occasional excitement whether things would be ready for the review, the annual report, the demonstration or whatever. I can testify here, that things were always ready—just-in-time. The other differences in approach will be discussed below.

Initial results of the project were reported in [42] and several other ESPRIT-related conferences. The main outcome of the GIPE projects was the *Centaur system* that was the promised proof-of-concept environment generator [29, 14]. It consisted of the following items.

- The Virtual Tree Processor (VTP): a database for storing abstract syntax trees [61].
- Specification formalisms: Metal (syntax), PPML (prettyprinting) [65], TYPOL (static and dynamic semantics) [26, 33, 49], SDF (syntax) [41], ASF (static and dynamic semantics) [6], and ASF+SDF (the integrated version of the latter two) [6, 34].
- Various editors.
- A user-interface.

In addition to the design and implementation of the system itself various case studies such as for Mini-ML[24, 27], Pico [6], LOTOS [58], Eiffel [1], Esterel [9], Sisal [2], POOL [6] and others were carried out.

After so many years, I should confess that the system was a true Centaur: half human and half horse. On top of the common infrastructure (LeLisp, VTP, Graphical Objects) actually two subsystems were built: a French system using Metal, PPML and TYPOL versus a Dutch system consisting of ASF+SDF and the Generic Syntax-directed Editor (GSE). SDF was also used in the French subsystem for some experiments.

I always found that the French subsystem was ahead of us in terms of inspiring examples and user-interface integration, while we were struggling with issues like incremental parser generation, efficient execution of rewrite rules and understanding how modularization should work. In hindsight, the major results of the project as a whole were the following.

- The use of natural semantics to specify language semantics.
- The use of user-defined syntax and rewriting techniques to specify language semantics.
- A wide range of implementation techniques that showed the feasibility of these approaches.

At the end of GIPE II the interests of the partners started to diverge further and further. Gilles' team was moving in the direction of the interactive editing of proofs [69, 12] and converting proofs to text [31]. See [22] for an annotated bibliography. On the Dutch side, we were more interested in pursuing the original vision of a programming environment generator; this is documented in [42, 56, 34].

11.3 An ongoing scientific debate

> **A soldering job.** *In the same parking-lot-turned-into-exposition-centre as the year before we encountered communication problems. How to connect our two workstations in order to exchange relevant software needed for the demonstrations? Gilles and I ended up lying on the floor soldering a null-modem in order to make the connection. It did work, but we were without any doubt the most unqualified electricians in the exposition centre.*

One of the major benefits of the cooperation between the partners in the GIPE projects were the discussions on topics of common interest and the different views and arguments that were exchanged. Gilles was a passionate researcher and had outspoken opinions on all matters relevant to the project. I will briefly describe them below.[2] This scientific debate was the corner stone of the success of the projects. *European cooperative research would be better off if this kind of liberal, scientific debate would be more cherished by the European policy makers.*

11.3.1 Monolingual versus domain-specific languages

As mentioned earlier in Section 11.1, Jan Heering and I came from a "monolingual" background and we wanted to unify as much as possible. Looking at the Mentor approach, we observed that different languages were used for partially overlapping purposes.

- Metal defined concrete syntax, abstract syntax and a mapping from the former to the latter.
- PPML defined a mapping from abstract syntax to a language of boxes.
- Mentol, Mentor's command language, contained constructs for matching and control flow that were also present in Metal and PPML.

This approach has the advantage that each step is explicit and that there is more opportunity for manual tweaking in order to handle complex situations. The disadvantage is, however, that the specification writer has to be aware of several representations and mappings between

---

[2] Disclaimer: this paper focuses on work resulting from the GIPE projects and mostly ignores other related work.

them. We opted for a more integrated approach in SDF [41] and made the following assumptions.

- There exists a "natural" context-free grammar for the language we want to define. In this way the grammar does not contain idiosyncrasies caused by the use of specific parsing technologies.
- There is a fixed mapping between concrete and abstract syntax.
- Grammars are modules that can be composed.
- A default prettyprinter can be derived from the context-free grammar but can be overridden by user-defined preferences.

Of course, this approach places a tremendous load on the implementation but it leads—in my opinion—to a higher-level specification. So in the case of SDF, the monolingual approach worked well. However, the evolutionary pressures are such that opportunities, desires and needs to introduce specialized formalisms are abundant. Today, we have—in addition to ASF+SDF—dedicated formalisms for component interconnection, relational calculus, prettyprinting, and module configuration. From time to time I wonder if some of them can be eliminated .... Gilles' view that specialized formalisms are unavoidable was certainly the more realistic one.

11.3.2 Strings versus trees

With a background in string processing languages, it is not surprising that we had a certain bias in favor of a textual (re)presentation of programs, whereas Gilles always took the abstract syntax tree as central representation. This resulted in the following differences in point of view:

- In the parsing model, we opted to stay as close to the parse tree as possible, see Section 11.3.2.1.
- At the specification level, we wanted to have user-defined syntax and give the user complete textual freedom in the concrete textual notation of functions and datatypes. See Section 11.3.2.2.
- In the editing model, we took the user's text as the primary source of information. This is opposed to the view that the actual text entered is parsed, converted to an internal tree structure, and then presented to the user as the result of prettyprinting that tree. This is explained in more detail in Section 11.3.2.3.

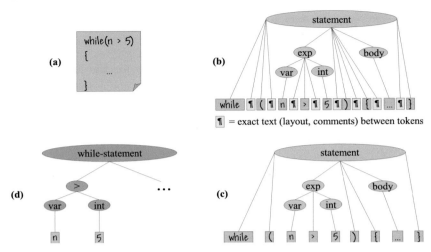

Fig. 11.2. Structured representation of source text: **(a)** Source text; **(b)** Full parse tree; **(c)** Conventional parse tree; **(d)** Abstract syntax tree.

11.3.2.1 Parse trees versus abstract syntax trees

What is the right abstraction for representing and manipulating programs? Syntax trees are the structures that are the result of syntax analysis (also known as parsing) of some program text. However, syntax trees exist in various flavors.

Parse trees are a faithful description of the manner in which a text has been been derived from its grammar. A *full* parse tree contains all the textual details of the text including whitespace, comments and the like. See Figure 11.2(b). Since there is no information loss, it is possible to literally reconstruct the original text from the parse tree. A *conventional* parse tree is a full parse tree with all the layout symbols removed, see Figure 11.2(c). In this case, the source text can be mostly reconstructed but all layout symbols have to be guessed by a prettyprinter.

Abstract syntax trees omit the textual representation but focus on structure. As shown in Figure 11.2(d), the abstract syntax tree for a while-statement is a tree node labeled "while-statement" with two children: an expression and the body of the while-statement. From such a *shallow* abstract syntax tree, the source text can only be recreated by means of prettyprinting (see Section 11.3.2.3). However the original layout (indentation, spacing, comments) is lost. The global advantage of abstract syntax trees is that they require less memory space.

The debate about the proper program representation was always centered around the question how "deep" the abstract syntax tree should be, in other words, how big could the distance between a parse tree and the corresponding "deep" abstract syntax tree be. Suppose that a language contains various iteration constructs, like a for-loop, a while-do-loop, do-until loop, etc. A "deep" abstract syntax tree could map all loop variants on a single, general, loop node. This has the advantage that a single semantic rule can handle all the different cases at once. The disadvantage is that it is no longer possible to know the construct in the original program or to reconstruct the original source text in any way.

Centaur mostly used shallow abstract syntax but had the functionality to build deep syntax trees when desired. In the developments after GIPE, we have focused our attention more and more on software renovation projects where it is mandatory to reconstruct the original source code even after source code transformations. So we moved closer to the source text and now use full parse trees as structured representation of programs.

11.3.2.2 User-defined syntax

Not surprisingly, our string bias led us to believe that the user should be free to write specifications in a domain-specific notation. In a way, this was our answer to the phenomenon of domain-specific languages. Why write `and(true, or(false, true))` while `true and (false or true)` looks more natural? Writing a compilation rule for an if-statement as

```
compile(if $Test then $Series1 else $Series2 endif) = ...
```

looks more appealing than using a strict prefix notation to represent program fragments. Note that $Test, $Series1 and $Series2 are meta-variables that represent program fragments. A real example—that has already transformed millions of lines of COBOL code—is the following [20]:

```
addEndIf(IF $Expr $OptThen $Stats) =
IF $Expr $OptThen $Stats END-IF
```

In COBOL, the THEN and END-IF keywords are optional in if-statements. The above rule inserts END-IF keywords in if-statements in order to increase readability and maintainability. Using abstract syntax, a dozen prefix functions would be needed to describe this rule while the version that uses concrete syntax is (almost) readable by the average COBOL programmer. This is another argument in favour of full parse trees.

We decided to aim for an approach where every function or datatype in a specification is in fact a mini-language which defines its own concrete syntax. Of course, these mini-languages should be composable into larger languages and so on. This is a very flexible approach that treats a simple datatype like the Booleans or a complete programming language like Java or COBOL in a uniform manner. The consequences of this decision, however, were staggering.

- Since language grammars had to be composed, we needed a parsing approach that permits grammar composition. Since none of the standard approaches supported this,[3] we started a journey, that has still not ended, in the area of Generalized LR parsing [59, 70, 13, 45].
- Since specification rules contain applications of user-defined grammar rules, it is impossible to define one, fixed, grammar for our specification formalism. As a consequence, we need a two-stage approach: first collect all user-defined grammar rules, generate a parser for them, and then parse the rules in the specification.

In addition to the conceptual challenges, it was also a major problem to implement this in a fashion that scales to really large cases. At several points in time I have thought that the decision to provide user-defined syntax in this way was fatal to our part of the project. Gilles was intrigued by this approach, started a brief study to add it to TYPOL but after a short while concluded that it was not practical and moved ahead to new interesting problems. Since he was not interested in syntax at all, this was probably a wise decision and avoided a lot of complications.

For us, the balance is different. Today we are one of the unique systems that provide fully general user-defined syntax and the major benefit is that program transformation rules can be written in a way that is as close as possible to ordinary source text. This helps in the acceptance of program transformations. However, we have still not solved all problems related to this approach. For instance, since we are working in the domain of full context-free grammars, it remains a challenge how to handle ambiguous grammars.

---

[3] General context-free grammars are compositional in the sense that they can be combined and form again a context-free grammar. Such a composition can be affected by interferences due to name clashes. Popular subclasses like LL(k) or LR(k) are not compositional at all: the combined grammar may require extensive restructuring in order to satisfy the requirements of the specific subclass.

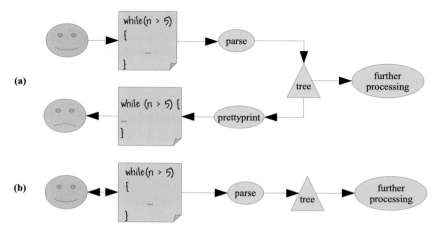

Fig. 11.3. Two editing models: **(a)** User types in source text and sees prettyprinted text; **(b)** User only sees source text as typed in.

11.3.2.3 From PPML to Pandora

Don't touch that link! *In the early days of the World Wide Web we were all excited about the new information infrastructure that was emerging. Gilles showed us the latest version of the Mosaic browser. "Don't touch that link since it connects all the way to Australia!" he said with concern in his voice when I tried it. At that time of expensive dial-in connections, today's cheap broadband connectivity was impossible to foresee. Later, Gilles played a key role in the transfer of the W3C consortium from CERN to INRIA.*

As mentioned above, during the editing of programs we took the text as entered by the user as the primary source of information. After a textual modification, the text was reparsed and the internal tree structure was updated. The textual image as presented to the user remained exactly as the user had typed it in. This is shown in Figure 11.3(b). In the standard editing model used by Centaur, the text was parsed, converted to a tree structure, and then presented to the user as the result of prettyprinting that tree. This is shown in Figure 11.3(a).

A *prettyprinter* takes an abstract syntax tree and transforms it into text according to user-defined rules; the subject had been pioneered by

Oppen [67]. At INRIA there was already extensive experience with the subject in the form of the Prettyprinting Meta-Language PPML [65]. PPML used a notion of "boxes" that originates from [32] and provides operators for the horizontal and vertical composition of text blocks. PPML provides matching constructs to identify language constructs in the abstract syntax tree, case distinctions, and construction recipes to build box expressions for specific language construction.

Due to our text-oriented view on editing we had no need for a prettyprinter and have lived without one for many years.

PPML was a typical case where our monolingual view clashed with Gilles' view on the use of specialized languages. The PPML constructs mentioned (matching, case distinction, term construction) were also present in the formalisms that performed semantic processing on the syntax tree (be it TYPOL or ASF+SDF) and this duplication of concepts was not appealing for us. Many years later, we gave up ignoring prettyprinting and built several prettyprinters based on the Box language [21, 19]. In our most recent prettyprinter, Pandora, all matching, case distinction and construction of boxes is done in ... ASF+SDF. So here is at least one exceptional case, where monolingualism prevailed.

11.3.3 From virtual tree processor to ATerms

The Virtual Tree Processor (VTP) [61] was a database system for abstract syntax trees. Given a signature describing the names of the constructor functions, as well as their number and type of arguments, the VTP allowed the construction of arbitrary, type-correct, trees over the defined signature.

In addition to functions for the creation, access and modification of trees, the VTP also provided functionality for creating, maintaining and merging *cursors* (or "paths" in VTP terminology) in each tree. Regarding internal data representation and functionality, the VTP was not unlike a present-day XML processor. The main difference was that the VTP only provided an API (Application Programmer's Interface) for manipulating trees. As a result, programs manipulating trees were restricted to LeLisp although later a C++ version was completed. A serialized form of the trees that could easily be shared by programs written in other languages was missing.

In today's Meta-Environment there is a similar need for manipulating and storing trees. We have taken a textual (and also a binary) representation for trees as starting point and they can be used and exchanged by programs written in arbitrary languages. The resulting format (ATerms and ATerm library [17, 18]) is, in many ways, simpler than the original VTP functionality. One distinctive feature is that it provides (and maintains) maximal subterm sharing, thus considerably reducing the size of large syntax trees.

11.3.4 Component architecture

Over the years Centaur had evolved into quite a large code base of 200 000–300 000 lines of (mostly LeLisp) code. There were three forces that made us aware of the fact that we needed to reflect on a more component-based approach.

- The French team was more and more interested in connecting external parsers (for instance, for parsing proof traces) and tools (for instance, provers and proof checkers).
- The Dutch team became more and more concerned about the modularity and maintainability of the code base.
- We were all aware of the need to write components in other programming languages than LeLisp; this was partly driven by the availability and support problems with LeLisp that we all were expecting (see Section 11.2.3).

And, as usual in this cooperation, both teams identified the same problem but ended-up with completely different solutions. Dominique Clément proposed a notion of "software IC", a software component that could be connected with other components via communication channels, not unlike hardware ICs. This approach evolved into Sophtalk [25, 30, 46], a basic, messaging-based, infrastructure for distributed programming. Quoting the Sophtalk website [68]:

Sophtalk is a set of tools that enable one to program the interaction between objects following an event model of communication. Sophtalk is an autonomous LeLisp system that provides facilities for programming communication between objects and processes. The system is composed of three packages: stnode, a multicast communication mechanism; stio an extension of the standard LeLisp asynchronous and synchronous i/o mechanisms; and stservice, a mechanism offering interprocess communication at the shell and LeLisp levels.

The Dutch team had, at the same time, been experimenting with the partitioning of the system in independently executing parts. The primary objective was to increase modularization and to start experiments with writing components in different languages. The initial project to build a new editor from existing components was a disaster [57]. All parts were implemented and tested individually and worked well in isolation. But, when put together, deadlock after deadlock manifested itself. This was a strong incentive to take concurrency seriously and has resulted in the ToolBus coordination architecture [7, 8] that is still in use today. The basic idea of the ToolBus is to have a central, programmable, "software bus" that is used to connect components that may be written in different programming languages, but adhere to a fixed protocol and exchange data in a fixed format (i.e., ATerms, see Section 11.3.3).

11.3.5 Other topics

In addition to the topics already discussed above, the cooperation in the GIPE projects has also been a catalyst for research in a wide range of other areas that were of common interest.

- Origin tracking [11, 35].
- Incremental evaluation [64, 3].
- Generic debugging [10, 66].

I refer the interested reader to the references for further discussion on each of these topics.

11.4 The post-GIPE era

11.4.1 The French side

The many roads to Route des Lucioles. *Living in a country where winters can be long and dark, I liked the occasional meetings in Sophia-Antipolis where Gilles was working since the mid-1980s. On one of the occasions that he picked me up from a hotel in Antibes he confessed that he was participating in a local competition to find as many new routes towards the INRIA premises as possible. I never recognized the route we took or how we managed to reach Route des Lucioles, on every successive visit.*

11.4.1.1 CROAP and OASIS

The CROAP project at INRIA was stopped in 1998 and research on generic programming environments was continued in the Oasis project under direction of Isabelle Attali who had, along with others, earlier worked on the incremental evaluation of TYPOL specifications. In this project, Didier Parigot developed the SmartTools system [4, 5] that can be seen as a second generation Centaur system with a strong emphasis on the use of XML as its tree representation mechanism. The user-interface is shown in Figure 11.4. It can provide several, simultaneous, views on the same document. The architecture is shown in Figure 11.5. Note that the user-interface itself is defined in a separate document (Document GI) and that the communication between components is achieved via an asynchronous message infrastructure.

Today, the SmartTools system focuses on domain-specific languages and software factories. Since the interests of the Oasis project gradually moved towards security analysis and smart cards, the SmartTools system has never become a primary focus of the project.

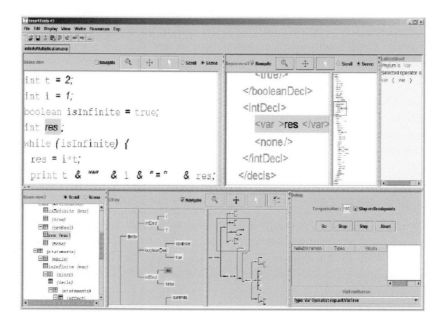

Fig. 11.4. User interface of SmartTools.

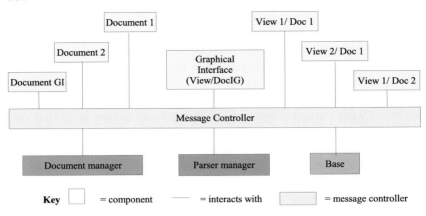

Fig. 11.5. Architecture of SmartTools.

Tragically, Isabelle and her two children died in the 2004 tsunami, while on holiday with her family in Sri Lanka.

11.4.2 Other impact of the Centaur legacy at INRIA

Many ideas from Centaur still survive in subsequent research activities at Inria. I will briefly mention some clear examples.

11.4.2.1 AXIS

The AXIS[4] is concerned with verification of information systems and web sites. They are applying Natural Semantics to help specify, check and maintain static semantics of Web sites and more generally of Web documents. Former GIPE team members Thierry Despeyroux (of TYPOL fame) and Anne-Marie Vercoustre are working in this project.

11.4.2.2 MARELLE

The MARELLE[5] is developing an environment for the computer-supported verification of mathematical proofs. The overall goal is to ensure the correctness of software. Examples are a graphical user-interface for the Coq prover (as already experimented with in GIPE) and the certified

---

[4] User-Centered Design, Analysis and Improvement of Information Systems, see http://www-sop.inria.fr/axis/.

[5] Computer aided verification of proofs and software, see http://www-sop.inria.fr/marelle/index_eng.html.

implementation of various algorithms. MARELLE is headed by Yves Bertot who was also on the GIPE team.

11.4.2.3 PARSIFAL

The PARSIFAL[6] project works on proofs of programs and protocols and emphasizes the underlying principles of proof search. Typical applications are in areas like proof-carrying code and model checkers. The vice-head of PARSIFAL Joëlle Despeyroux was on the GIPE team.

11.4.2.4 TROPICS

The TROPICS[7] team works on an environment for analysis and transformation of scientific programs, and aims at applying techniques from software engineering to numeric software for Computational Fluid Dynamics. Their Tapenade[8] system applies Automatic Differentiation to Fortran programs in order to derive optimized versions of the original program. TROPICS is headed by Laurent Hascoët, who was a member of the GIPE team.

11.4.3 Ariane V

On June 4, 1996 the first test flight of the Ariane 5 (flight 501) took place and was a dramatic failure. After 37 seconds the rocket exploded.

According to the report of the Inquiry Board [62] the Ariane 5 reused software from Ariane 4 beyond its specifications and this caused a floating point conversion to fail. For reasons of efficiency the Ada error handler had been disabled. This has become known as one of the more expensive software bugs.

Gilles, being an expert on programming language semantics in general and on Ada semantics in particular, was a member of the Inquiry Board. Is there a better example of theory meeting practice?

11.4.4 Evaluation committees and Scientific Council

In 1998 I participated in the evaluation committee for INRIA Programme 2A, in 1999 for the project OASIS and in the period

---

[6] Preuves Automatiques et Raisonnement sur des SpécIFicAtions Logiques, see `http://www.lix.polytechnique.fr/parsifal/`.

[7] Program transformations for scientific computing, see `http://www.inria.fr/recherche/equipes/tropics.en.html`.

[8] See ftp://ftp-sop.inria.fr/tropics/tapenade/README.html.

1998–2002 I served as member of INRIA's Scientific Council. All these occasions gave me ample opportunity to watch Gilles at work: friendly, hospitable and seemingly bored that yet another evaluation had to take place. At the same time he was very keen that the politically most desirable conclusions ended up in the final reports of these committees.

In the Scientific Council, Gilles acted as an excellent strategist with a keen eye for new scientific developments and for opportunities for INRIA to make a scientific or societal contribution. We shared an interest in the phenomenon of *spinoff companies*: attempts to bring scientific results to the market.

11.4.5 The Dutch side

On the Dutch side, we have seen slow progress in three generations of software.

1992 The initial LeLisp-based version of the ASF+SDF Meta-Environment.

2000 The first generation of a completely component-based Meta-Environment based on the ToolBus. The main implementation languages used were C, ASF+SDF and Tcl/TK (for the user-interface).

2007 The second generation, released in 2007, that contains a plugin architecture for the user-interface, visualization tools, and more, see Section 11.4.5.1 below and [15, 16, 63]. In this edition, Java has become one of the prominent implementation languages.

In the remainder of this section, I will give more details about this second generation system (The Meta-Environment version 2.0) as we present it today.

11.4.5.1 The Meta-Environment, Version 2.0

The Meta-Environment[9] is an open framework for language development, source code analysis and source code transformation. It consists of syntax analysis tools, semantic analysis and transformation tools, and an interactive development environment (see Fig. 11.6). It is supported by a growing open source community, and can easily be modified or extended with third party components.

---

[9] This section is based on a tool demonstration presented in [15]. See www. meta-environment.org for further details.

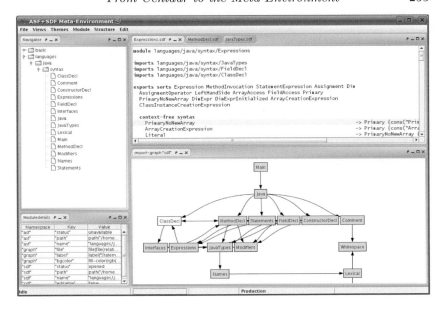

Fig. 11.6. User interface of the Meta-Environment.

The Meta-Environment is a generalization of the ASF+SDF Meta-Environment that has been successfully used in many analysis, transformation and renovation projects. The Meta-Environment has been used for applications such as the following.

- Parsing (new and old) programming languages, for further processing the parse trees.
- Analysis of source code (fact extraction, type analysis, and documentation generation).
- Transformation, refactoring, and source code generation.
- Design and implementation of Domain-specific languages.

11.4.5.2 Features of The Meta-Environment

From the background given in this paper, the features of The Meta-Environment can be easily recognized.

- Modular grammar definitions—a consequence of our generalized parsers.
- Declarative disambiguation filters used to resolve many common ambiguities in programming languages.

- Conditional term rewriting used to perform software transformations.
- Seamless integration of user-defined syntax in rewrite rules, enabling the definition of transformation rules in concrete syntax, as opposed to using abstract syntax and getting much more obscure rules. This also guarantees fully syntax-safe source code generation.
- A highly modular and extensible architecture based on the coordination of language processing tools.
- ATerms as a language-independent intermediate data exchange format between tools.
- An Integrated Development Environment (IDE) that provides interactive support and on-demand tool execution.

Version 2.0 of The Meta-Environment includes various new features.

- A grammar library containing grammars for C, Java, Cobol and other programming languages.
- Rewriting with layout. This enables fine-grained analysis and transformations such as high-fidelity source-to-source transformations that preserve comments and whitespace.
- Automatically generated syntax highlighting based on syntax definitions for arbitrary languages.
- Automatically generated prettyprinters that can be refined by the user.
- Rscript—a relational calculus engine that enables easy computing with facts extracted from source code.
- Advanced information visualization tools for the interactive display of relations, parse trees and dependencies.
- A fully customizable, plugin-based user-interface with dockable panes, and user-defined menus and buttons. Plugins can run user-defined scripts to interact with other tools.

A major architectural improvement in version 2.0 is the division of the system into several separate layers that enable the creation of a family of related applications that share common facilities such as user-interface, parsing infrastructure, and error reporting (the kernel layer). The facilities for syntax analysis (SDF layer) and transformation (ASF layer) are implemented on top of this kernel. See Figure 11.7 for an overview of this layered architecture. Observe that the system uses the ToolBus as coordination infrastructure and compare this with the Sophtalk approach (Section 11.3.4) and the architecture of SmartTools

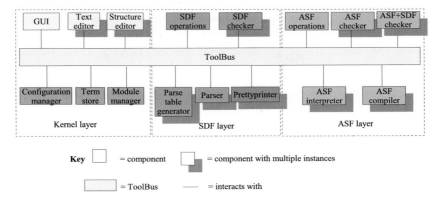

Fig. 11.7. Run-time architecture of the Meta-Environment.

(Fig. 11.5). All three systems achieve component decoupling by way of messaging middleware.

11.4.5.3 Applications of the Meta-Environment

In the area of software evolution, The Meta-Environment has been successfully applied to the transformation of database schemas, analysis of embedded SQL, Cobol prettyprinting and restructuring, PL/I parsing, analysis and restructuring of C++, dead-code detection in Java, and aspect mining in C.

Due to the many extension points (rules for defining syntax, prettyprinting, analysis and transformation; extensible user-interface; connection of third-party components; extensible architecture) the system can be easily adapted to the requirements of a specific software evolution or renovation problem.

In the area of domain-specific languages, the system has been applied to domains as disparate as financial systems and machine tooling.

11.4.6 Synthesis: the ATEAMS project

As in every classical story there are three parts: thesis, anti-thesis and synthesis. The GIPE story also seems to follow this structure: the GIPE projects (see Section 11.2) and the post-GIPE era (see Section 11.4) form thesis and anti-thesis. The synthesis suddenly enters the stage by way of a joint CWI/INRIA project team that is in preparation at the time of writing: ATEAMS[10] that will do research on *fact extraction, refactoring and transformation,* and *reliable middleware* with as overall aims to enable the evolution of large software systems to service-oriented systems and to use the service paradigm to scale up analysis and transformation tools.

11.5 Concluding remarks

> **Gilles the Meta-technologist.** *Gilles would often exclaim: "This is so meta" with a strong emphasis on the second syllable of the word "meta".*

Meta-approaches were, are and will remain crucial: meta-modeling, model-driven development, and domain-specific engineering are the current labels for the activities that played a prominent role in the objectives and results of the GIPE projects.

It comes as no surprise that generic language technology is in increasing demand for the design and implementation of domain-specific languages; for the analysis and transformation of software and software models; and for numerous forms of code generation. The increasing popularity of the Meta-Environment is one illustration of this.

As this brief historical overview shows, many of the ideas Gilles worked on are still in daily use today. This is mostly due to his conceptual approach to many problems. He liked to view things from a higher level of abstraction. First in studying meta-level descriptions of programming languages, later as scientific director of INRIA where he could supervise and steer technological developments and research directions. A true "meta-technologist" with a vision. As president of INRIA he could apply his meta-skills and vision to a large, bureaucratic but highly successful research organization. Gilles was the opposite of a bureaucrat, but he knew as no other that conquering the bureaucracy is the only way to realize one's vision.

---

[10] Analysis and transformation of EvolvAble Modules and Services.

Bibliography

[1] I. Attali. A natural semantics for Eiffel dynamic binding. *ACM Transactions on Programming Languages and Systems (TOPLAS)*, **18**(5), 1996.

[2] I. Attali, D. Caromel and A. L. Wendelborn. From a formal dynamic semantics of Sisal to a Sisal environment. In *HICSS (2)*, pp. 266–267, 1995.

[3] I. Attali, J. Chazarain and S. Gilette. Incremental evaluation of natural semantics specification. In M. Bruynooghe and M. Wirsing (eds), *PLILP*, volume 631, Lecture Notes in Computer Science, pp. 87–99. Springer, 1992.

[4] I. Attali, C. Courbis, P. Degenne, A. Fau, J. Fillon, Chr. Held, D. Parigot and C. Pasquie. Aspect and XML-oriented semantic framework generator: Smarttools. In *Second Workshop on Language Descriptions, Tools and Applications, LDTA'02*, volume 65 Electronic Notes in Theoretical Computer Science (ENTCS), pp. 1–20. Springer, 2002.

[5] I. Attali, C. Courbis, P. Degenne, A. Fau, D. Parigot and C. Pasquier. Smarttools: a generator of interactive environment tools. *Electr. Notes Theoritical Computer Science*, 44(2), 2001.

[6] J. A. Bergstra, J. Heering and P. Klint (eds), *Algebraic Specification*. ACM Press/Addison-Wesley, 1989.

[7] J. A. Bergstra and P. Klint. *The ToolBus: a Component Interconnection Architecture*. Technical Report P9408, University of Amsterdam, Programming Research Group, 1994.

[8] J. A. Bergstra and P. Klint. The discrete time ToolBus – a software coordination architecture. *Science of Computer Programming*, **31**(2-3):205–229, 1998.

[9] Y. Bertot. Implementation of an interpreter for a parallel language in Centaur. In *European Symposium on Programming*, pp. 57–69, 1990.

[10] Y. Bertot. Occurrences in debugger specifications. In *PLDI '91: Proceedings of the ACM SIGPLAN 1991 Conference on Programming Language Design and Implementation*, pp. 327–337, New York, NY, USA, 1991. ACM Press.

[11] Y. Bertot. Origin functions in lambda-calculus and term rewriting systems. In J.-C. Raoult (ed.), *CAAP*, volume 581, Lecture Notes in Computer Science, pp. 49–65. Springer, 1992.

[12] Y. Bertot, G. Kahn and L. Théry. Proof by pointing. In M. Hagiya and J. C. Mitchell (eds), *TACS*, volume 789 Lecture Notes in Computer Science, pp. 141–160. Springer, 1994.

[13] S. Billot and B. Lang. The structure of shared forests in ambiguous parsing. In *ACL*, pp. 143–151, 1989.

[14] P. Borras, D. Clément, Th. Despeyroux, J. Incerpi, G. Kahn, B. Lang and V. Pascual. CENTAUR: The system. In *Software Development Environments (SDE)*, pp. 14–24, 1988.

[15] M. G. J. van den Brand, M. Bruntink, G. R. Economopoulos, H. A. de Jong, P. Klint, T. Kooiker, T. van der Storm and J.J. Vinju. Using the meta-environment for maintenance and renovation. In *Proceedings of the 11th European Conference on Software Maintenance and Reengineering (CSMR'07)*, pp. 331–332. IEEE Computer Society, March 21–23 2007.

[16] M. G. J. van den Brand, A. van Deursen, J. Heering, H. A. de Jong, M. de Jonge, T. Kuipers, P. Klint, L. Moonen, P.A. Olivier, J. Scheerder, J. J. Vinju, E. Visser and J. Visser. The ASF+SDF Meta-Environment: a component-based language development environment. In R. Wilhelm (ed.), *Compiler Construction (CC '01)*, volume 2027, Lecture Notes in Computer Science, pp. 365–370. Springer-Verlag, 2001.

[17] M. G. J. van den Brand, H. A. de Jong, P. Klint and P. Olivier. Efficient Annotated Terms. *Software, Practice & Experience*, 30:259–291, 2000.

[18] M. G. J. van den Brand and P. Klint. ATerms for manipulation and exchange of structured data: It's all about sharing. *Information and Software Technology*, **49**(1):55–64, 2007.

[19] M. G. J. van den Brand, A. T. Kooiker, J. J. Vinju and N. P. Veerman. A Language Independent Framework for Context-sensitive Formatting. In *10th Conference on Software Maintenance and Reengineering (CSMR 2006)*, pp. 631–634. IEEE Computer Society Press, 2006.

[20] M. G. J. van den Brand, A. Sellink and C. Verhoef. Control flow normalization for COBOL/CICS legacy system. In *CSMR*, pp. 11–20. IEEE Computer Society, 1998.

[21] M. G. J. van den Brand and E. Visser. Generation of formatters for context-free languages. *ACM Transactions on Programming Languages and Systems*, **5**(1):1–41, 1996.

[22] Centaur web pp., Last visit December 2006. `http://www-sop.inria.fr/croap/centaur/centaur.html`.

[23] J. Chailloux, M. Devin, F. Dupont, J.-M. Hullot, B. Serpette and J. Vuillemin. *Le_Lisp version 15.2, le manuel de référence*. Technical report, INRIA, 1986.

[24] D. Clément. The natural dynamic semantics of Mini-Standard ML. In H. Ehrig, R. A. Kowalski, G. Levi and U. Montanari (eds), *TAPSOFT, Vol.2*, volume 250 Lecture Notes in Computer Science, pp. 67–81. Springer, 1987.

[25] D. Clément. A distributed architecture for programming environments. In R. N. Taylor (ed.), *Proceedings of the Fourth ACM SIGSOFT Symposium on Software Development Environments*, pp. 11–21, 1990.

[26] D. Clément, J. Despeyroux, Th. Despeyroux, L. Hascoet and G. Kahn. *Natural Semantics on the Computer*. Technical Report RR416, I.N.R.I.A., june 1985.

[27] D. Clément, J. Despeyroux, Th. Despeyroux and G. Kahn. A simple applicative language: Mini-ML. In *LISP and Functional Programming*, pp. 13–27, 1986.

[28] D. Clément, J. Heering, J. Incerpi, G. Kahn, P. Klint, B. Lang and V. Pascual. Preliminary design of an environment generator. Second annual review report: D9, GIPE, ESPRIT Project 348, January 1987.

[29] D. Clément, J. Incerpi and G. Kahn. CENTAUR: Towards a "software tool box" for programming environments. In F. Long (ed.), *SEE*, volume 467 Lecture Notes in Computer Science, pp. 287–304. Springer, 1989.

[30] D. Clément, V. Prunet and F. Montagnac. Integrated software components: A paradigm for control integration. In A. Endres and H. Weber

(eds), *Software Development Environments and CASE Technology*, volume 509, Lecture Notes in Computer Science, pp. 167–177. Springer, 1991.

[31] Y. Coscoy, G. Kahn and L. Théry. Extracting text from proofs. In M. Dezani-Ciancaglini and G. D. Plotkin (eds), *TLCA*, volume 902, Lecture Notes in Computer Science, pp. 109–123. Springer, 1995.

[32] J. Coutaz. *The Box, a Layout Abstraction for User Interface Toolkits*. Technical Report CMU-CS-84-167, Carnegie Mellon University, 1984.

[33] Th. Despeyroux. Executable specification of static semantics. In G. Kahn, D. B. MacQueen and G. D. Plotkin, editors, *Semantics of Data Types*, volume 173, Lecture Notes in Computer Science, pp. 215–233. Springer, 1984.

[34] A. van Deursen, J. Heering and P. Klint (eds). *Language Prototyping: An Algebraic Specification Approach*, volume 5, AMAST Series in Computing. World Scientific, 1996.

[35] A. van Deursen, P. Klint and F. Tip. Origin tracking. *Journal of Symbolic Computing* **15**(5-6):523–545, 1993.

[36] V. Donzeau-Gouge, G. Huet, G. Kahn, B. Lang and J.J. Lévy. A structure oriented program editor: a first step towards computer assisted programming. In *International Computing Symposium*. North Holland, 1975.

[37] V. Donzeau-Gouge, G. Kahn and B. Lang. On the formal definition of ADA. In N. D. Jones (ed.), *Semantics-Directed Compiler Generation*, volume 94 Lecture Notes in Computer Science, pp. 475–489. Springer, 1980.

[38] V. Donzeau-Gouge, G. Kahn, B. Lang and B. Mélèse. Documents structure and modularity in mentor. In *Software Development Environments (SDE)*, pp. 141–148, 1984.

[39] V. Donzeau-Gouge, G. Kahn, B. Lang, B. Mélèse and E. Morcos. Outline of a tool for document manipulation. In *IFIP Congress*, pp. 615–620, 1983.

[40] V. Donzeau-Gouge, B. Lang and B. Mélèse. Practical applications of a syntax directed program manipulation environment. In *ICSE*, pp. 346–357, 1984.

[41] J. Heering, P. R. H. Hendriks, P. Klint and J. Rekers. The syntax definition formalism SDF - reference manual. *SIGPLAN Notices*, **24**(11):43–75, 1989.

[42] J. Heering, G. Kahn, P. Klint and B. Lang. Generation of interactive programming environments. In *ESPRIT '85, Status Report of Continuing Work, Part I*, pp. 467–477. North-Holland, 1986.

[43] J. Heering and P. Klint. Towards monolingual programming environments. *ACM Transactions on Programming Languages and Systems*, **7**(2):183–213, April 1985.

[44] J. Heering and P. Klint. Prehistory of the ASF+SDF system (1980–1984). In M. G. J. van den Brand, A. van Deursen, T. B. Dinesh, J. Kamperman and E. Visser (eds), *Proceedings of ASF+SDF95 A workshop on Generating Tools from Algebraic Specifications*, number P9504 in

Technical Report. Programming Research Group, University of Amsterdam, 1995.

[45] J. Heering, P. Klint and J. Rekers. Incremental generation of parsers. *IEEE Transactions on Software Engineering*, **16**(12):1344–1350, 1990.

[46] I. Jacobs, F. Montignac, J. Bertot, D. Clément and V. Prunet. *The Sophtalk Reference Manual*. Technical Report 149, INRIA, February 1993.

[47] G. Kahn. An approach to system correctness. In *SOSP*, pp. 86–94, 1971.

[48] G. Kahn (ed.) *Semantics of Concurrent Computation, Proceedings of the International Sympoisum, Evian, France, July 2–4, 1979*, volume 70, Lecture Notes in Computer Science. Springer, 1979.

[49] G. Kahn. Natural semantics. In F.-J. Brandenburg, G. Vidal-Naquet and M. Wirsing (eds), *STACS*, volume 247, Lecture Notes in Computer Science, pp. 22–39. Springer, 1987.

[50] G. Kahn, B. Lang, B. Mélèse and E. Morcos. Metal: A formalism to specify formalisms. *Science of Computer Programming*, **3**(2):151–188, 1983.

[51] G. Kahn and D. B. MacQueen. Coroutines and networks of parallel processes. In *IFIP Congress*, pp. 993–998, 1977.

[52] P. Klint. An overview of the summer programming language. In *Conference Record of the 7th ACM Symposium on Principles of Programming Languages (POPL'80)*, pp. 47–55, 1980.

[53] P. Klint. Formal language definitions can be made practical. In *Algorithmic Languages*, pp. 115–132, 1981.

[54] P. Klint. *A Survey of Three Language-independent Programming Environments*. RR 257, INRIA, 1983.

[55] P. Klint. *A Study in String Processing Languages*, volume 205 of Lecture Notes in Computer Science. Springer-Verlag, 1985. Based on the dissertation *From Spring to Summer*, defended at the Technical University Eindhoven, 1982.

[56] P. Klint. A meta-environment for generating programming environments. *ACM Transactions on Software Engineering and Methodology*, **2**(2):176–201, April 1993.

[57] J. W. C. Koorn and H. C. N. Bakker. *Building an Editor from Existing Components: an Exercise in Software Re-use*. Technical Report P9312, Programming Research Group, University of Amsterdam, 1993.

[58] H. Korte, H. Joosten, V. Tijsse, A. Wammes, J. Wester, Th. Kuhne and Chr. Thies. *Design of a LOTOS Simulator: Centaur from a user's Perspective*. Fifth annual review report: D5, GIPE II, ESPRIT project 2177, 1993.

[59] B. Lang. Deterministic techniques for efficient non-deterministic parsers. In J. Loeckx (ed.) *ICALP*, volume 14, Lecture Notes in Computer Science, pp. 255–269. Springer, 1974.

[60] B. Lang. On the usefulness of syntax directed editors. In R. Conradi, T. Didriksen and D. H. Wanvik (eds) *Advanced Programming Environments*, volume 244, Lecture Notes in Computer Science, pp. 47–51. Springer, 1986.

[61] B. Lang. The virtual tree processor. In J. Heering J. Sidi and A. Verhoog (eds) *Generation of Interactive Programming Environments, Intermediate*

Report, number CS-R8620 in Technical Report. Centrum voor Wiskunde en Informatica, 1986.

[62]   J. L. Lions. ARIANE 5: Flight 501 Failure, Report by the Inquiry Board. `http://homepp..inf.ed.ac.uk/perdita/Book/ariane5rep.html`, 1996. Last visit January 2007.

[63]   Meta-Environment web pp., Last visit March 2008. `http://www.meta-environment.org`.

[64]   E. van der Meulen. Deriving incremental implementations from algebraic specifications. In M. Nivat, Ch. Rattray, T. Rus and G. Scollo (eds) *AMAST*, Workshops in Computing, pp. 277–286. Springer, 1991.

[65]   E. Morcos-Chounet and A. Conchon. PPML: a general purpose formalism to specify prettyprinting. In H.-J. Kugler (ed.) *Information Processing 86*, pp. 583–590. Elsevier, 1986.

[66]   P. A. Olivier. Debugging distributed applications using a coordination architecture. In D. Garlan and D. Le Métayer (eds) *COORDINATION*, volume 1282, Lecture Notes in Computer Science, pp. 98–114. Springer, 1997.

[67]   D. C. Oppen. Prettyprinting. *ACM Transactions on Programming Languages and Systems*, **2**(4):465–483, 1980.

[68]   Sophtalk web pp., Last visit December 2006. `http://www-sop.inria.fr/croap/sophtalk/sophtalk.html`.

[69]   L. Théry, Y. Bertot and G. Kahn. Real theorem provers deserve real user-interfaces. In *SDE 5: Proceedings of the Fifth ACM SIGSOFT Symposium on Software Development Environments*, pp. 120–129, New York, NY, USA, 1992. ACM Press.

[70]   M. Tomita. *Efficient Parsing for Natural Language: A Fast Algorithm for Practical Systems*. Kluwer Academic Publishers, Norwell, MA, USA, 1985.

12

Towards a theory of document structure

Bengt Nordström

Chalmers University of Technology and the University of Göteborg

Abstract

The structure of documents of various degree of formality, from scientific papers with layout information and programs with their documentation to completely formal proofs can be expressed by assigning a type to the abstract syntax tree of the document. By using dependent types – an idea from type theory – it is possible to express very strong syntactic criterion on wellformedness of documents. This structure can be used to automatically generate parsers, type checkers and structure-oriented editors.

12.1 Introduction

We are interested to find a general framework for describing the structure of many kinds of documents, such as

- books and articles
- "live" documents (like a web document with parts to be filled in)
- programs
- formal proofs.

Are there any good reasons why we use different programs to edit and print articles, programs and formal proofs? A unified view on these kinds of documents would make it possible to use only one structure-oriented editor to build all of them, and it would be easier to combine documents of different kinds, for instance scientific papers, programs with their documentation, informal and formal proofs and simple web forms.

Such a view requires that we have a good framework to express syntactic wellformedness (from things like the absence of a title in

From Semantics to Computer Science Essays in Honour of Gilles Kahn, eds Yves Bertot, Gérard Huet, Jean-Jacques Lévy and Gordon Plotkin. Published by Cambridge University Press. © Cambridge University Press 2009.

265

a footnote to correctness of a formal proof) and to express how the document should be edited and presented.

12.2 Examples

12.2.1 Proof editors and documented proofs

A proof editor is a program which helps a user to write a formal proof. In doing this, it can give suggestion of what proof rules to use and can check that the proof rules are correctly applied. There are also commands to delete part of the proof and to regret earlier steps.

Most proof editors are commmand-based; the user manipulates a proof state using a command language. But there are also WYSIWIG proof editors [15, 9, 3] where a proof is obtained by direct manipulation. The proof is presented on the screen to the user and edited by editing the presentation. The things which are edited are incomplete expressions, the missing parts are presented as placeholders. The basic editing step is to replace a placeholder with an (incomplete) expression or vice versa. In this article, we are mainly interested in these kind of editors.

Proof editors like Coq [5] and HOL Light [10] are becoming more and more mature. To become a tool which people can rely on, it it still necessary to develop a small and understood proof checker with a well-understood relationship between the proof checker and the logic. But this is not enough. The proofs must be readable by humans. The final product should be a document consisting of a mixture of formal proofs, programs whose values are formal proofs and informal mathematical text. The editor to produce this document is important.

12.2.2 Integrated development environments

An integrated development environment is a structure-oriented editor for a programming language together with other tools to develop programs (debugging etc). One of the first programming environments based on a structure-oriented editor was the MENTOR system [7] developed by Gilles Kahn et al in the 70's. In this system it was possible to mix different programming languages. The system was later generalized and simplified in the CENTAUR system [4]. An example of a more modern system is Eclipse [8] which is a framework for creating programming environments. New tools and languages can be added as plug-ins to the existing system.

A fundamental part of such a programming environment is a set of tools for documentation of programs. It is thus necessary to edit programs and documents with layout information.

12.2.3 Editable forms on the web

Documents on the web which contains forms to fill in are generally produced in an ad hoc manner. To create a form requires a lot of programming. For instance, a filled in date must be checked for correctness. These kind of interactive checks for syntactic wellformedness is something we recognize from proof editors. A proof editor (based on direct manipulation) is exactly doing this, it checks syntactic wellformedness and helps the user in other ways to build up a formal proof. Here we are looking at a document with slots to be filled in as an expression with holes in a WYSIWIG proof editor. If we have a type system which can express the syntactic restrictions of the placeholders, we could let the web browser use a built-in type checker to check that the forms are syntactically correct.

In this way, there would be no need to write ad hoc code checking the syntactic correctness, the expected types of the slots give enough information for a type checker to check this.

12.3 A first step

It is clear that documents (programs, proofs, etc.) have a common syntactical structure. They are built up from parts, where each part is either simple or compound.

The simple parts could be an individual character (for running text), an integer or an empty list (for programs), 0 or π (for mathematical expressions). A compound part in a document could be a section (with a section heading and a body), in a program it could be a while-statement (with a boolean expression and a statement) and in a mathematical expression it could be an addition (with two operands). We will look at a simple part as a functional constant without arguments, while a compound part is a functional constant applied to its arguments (parts). For instance, the expression $3 + 4 * 7$ is built up in the following way:

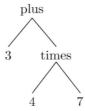

We need a notation for these kind of trees, we will write the tree above as

$$+\ 3\ (*\ 4\ 7).$$

The functional constants $+$ and $*$ are written before their arguments.

We will use ideas from type theory to express the structure of documents. The syntactic wellformedness of a document will be expressed by giving a type to its abstract syntax.

The advantages of being explicit about this structure becomes evident when writing programs that manipulate documents. This is one of the reasons that people are going over from the untyped HTML to the weakly-typed XML for describing documents on the web.

A type system has also advantages for a structure-oriented editor. The editor can be made more user-friendly since it will only suggest type-correct alternatives (completions become more meaningful if the number of suggestions is small).

It will be easier to write a program taking a typed document as input. There is no need to check syntactic wellformedness, since this will be done by the type-checker. If we have a programming language in which it is possible to use the type system to express the structure of a document, then we can discover erroneous document-processing programs already when they are type checked (i.e. at compile time). In this way, we are sure that the resulting document is structurally well formed.

12.4 Abstract and concrete syntax

A document is represented by an *abstract syntax tree* which gives all important syntactic structure to it. This is a mathematical object explaining how a document is built up from its parts. The document (program, proof, etc.) is presented by using a *linearization function*, which takes the abstract syntax to its *concrete syntax*. The concrete syntax is just a way to present the abstract object.

In general, it is possible to have many linearization functions, so that the same document can be presented in different ways. A proof, for instance, could (like in the Alfa proof editor [9]) be presented as a proof term, a natural deduction proof tree,

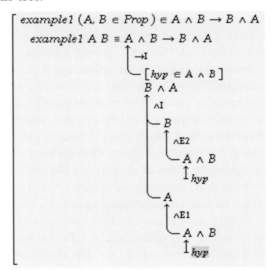

or a Fitch-like tree.

A web document would be presented in different ways on paper or screen (and different for screens of different sizes). A text in a natural language could be presented in English or Swedish by different linearization functions. This idea has been successfully used by Aarne Ranta in his GF project [20].

The inverse of the linearization function is *parsing*. There are two consequences of this view of parsing. First, parsing is in general ambiguous, since there is no requirement that the linearization function is injective. There are many abstract syntax trees with the same concrete syntax. The second consequence is that parsing is not computable in general (to compute the abstract syntax tree from the concrete syntax may require knowledge about the world, this is the case for expressions in an unrestricted natural language), or not feasible (for instance if we present a proof of a mathematical proposition with the word true, then it would be necessary to find the proof in order to build its abstract syntax tree).

If the document is built using a WYSIWYG structure editor, one is tempted to think that there is little need for abstract syntax. Only the concrete syntax of the document is presented and the editing is done by changing the concrete syntax. However, the editing commands (like navigation, insertions and deletions) should reflect the abstract syntax. In fact, these commands can uniformly be generated from the abstract syntax. A better understanding of its structure is essential to give better designs of these commands [18].

In such an editor, it is necessary to present the document being edited in a concrete syntax which has a computable unambigous parser. The list of input characters from the input should uniquely determine the corresponding abstract syntax. It is an advantage if the parser can be automatically generated from the linearization function, and this is often the case (but the resulting parser is often ambiguous) [21].

One important concrete syntax is the *text syntax*, which is a parsable, unambiguous concrete syntax constructed in such a way that it is easy to use when editing the document in an unstructured text editor. For a programming language, there is usually no difference between the text syntax and other concrete syntaxes. Knuth's WEB system [14] and some other systems for literate programming are exceptions, where the concrete syntax of programs is slightly improved over the text syntax. For a document which is a combination of informal text with layout information and formal mathematical text, the classic example of text syntax is LaTeX without macros. Programming languages are in general infeasible to use for this purpose, since they use a quoting mechanism for text strings. On the other hand, mathematical expressions containing infix, postfix and mixfix operators must also be easy to input. This rules out XML and prefix languages as good text syntax for mathematical documents. Only an experienced Lisp programmer prefers to read and write the expression $(+\ x\ (-\ (*\ y\ 3)\ 2))$ instead of the mathematical expression $x + y * 3 - 2$.

12.5 Expressing document structure

We will express the structure of a document by giving a type to the abstract syntax tree of the document. The abstract syntax tree is a mathematical object, and we will use ideas from Martin-Löf's type theory [16, 17, 1] to express the type. We assume that we have a syntactic category of identifiers, which either stand for variables or constants. We will use the notation i, x and c for identifiers, variables and constants.

The simple kind of abstract trees which was mentioned earlier were built up using application only. They had the shape $(c\ e_1\ \ldots\ e_n)$, where c is a constant and e_i are expressions. But in order to express variable binding, which is so common in mathematics and programming, we will also use expressions built up by abstracting n variables ($n \geq 1$) from an expression e. We will use the lambda notation $\lambda x_1 \ldots x_n.e$ for these kind of expressions.

So for instance, the mathematical expression $\int_0^1 e^x dx$ will be represented by

```
Int 0 1 \x.(power e x)
```

and $\sum_{i=1}^{100} 1/i$ will be represented by

```
sum 1 100 \i.(div 1 i).
```

We will start with a simple type system similar to a type system for functional programming languages. Then we will extend it to a system for dependent types. But before we do this, we have to explain how constants are declared.

12.5.1 Declaration of constants

There are two kinds of constants: primitive and defined. A defined constant gets its meaning by a definition, while a primitive constant gets its meaning outside the language. Our notion of computation is expansion of definitions and a computation terminates when there is no definition to expand. The type system must have the property that the type of an expression is preserved under computation.

Primitive constants. A constant is *primitive* when it has no definition, it can only be computed to itself. For instance, consider the following declarations:

$$\textbf{data} \quad \mathsf{N} \in \mathsf{Set} \quad \textbf{where}$$
$$\mathsf{nordzero} \in \mathsf{N};$$
$$\mathsf{s} \in \mathsf{N} \to \mathsf{N}$$
$$\textbf{data} \quad \mathsf{nordList} \ (A \in \mathsf{Set}) \in \ \mathsf{Set} \quad \textbf{where}$$
$$\mathsf{nordnil} \in \mathsf{nordList} \ A \ \mathsf{nordzero}$$
$$\mathsf{nordcons} \ \in (A \ (\mathsf{nordList} \ A)) \to \mathsf{nordList} \ A$$

This declares the primitive constants N, nordzero and s. It also expresses that N has the type Set (i.e. that it is a set), that the type of nordzero is N, and that s $x \in$ N whenever $x \in$ N. Furthermore, it expresses that this is an inductive definition of N, so there are no more primitive constants which produce objects in N. The only[1] way to introduce an object in Set is to use a declaration of this kind. The second declaration defines the set of lists in a similar way.

A set with no elements can be introduced by having an empty list of declaration after the keyword **where**.

Explicit definitions. A *defined* constant is a constant which has a definition, for instance

$$\mathsf{plus2} \in \mathsf{N} \to \mathsf{N}$$
$$\mathsf{plus2} = \lambda x. \ \mathsf{s} \ (\mathsf{s} \ x)$$

is an example of an *explicitly defined constant*. This gives the meaning of a new functional constant by a right hand side. In order for this kind of definition to be correct it is necessary that the type is correct and that the right hand side is an object in that type.

Implicit definitions. An implicitly defined constant is defined by pattern matching (over primitive constants) and recursion. The standard example is:

$$\mathsf{add} \ \in \mathsf{N} \to \mathsf{N} \to \mathsf{N}$$
$$\mathsf{add} \ \mathsf{nordzero} \ y = e$$
$$\mathsf{add} \ (\mathsf{s} \ x) \ y = \mathsf{s} \ (\mathsf{add} \ x \ y)$$

---

[1] It is however possible to give an object in Set a new name by using a definition.

This says that add is a constant which takes two objects in N as arguments and yields an object in N as result. It is defined by the defining equations in the declaration. In order for an implicit definition to be correct it is necessary that the patterns are defined for all arguments and that the definition is unambigous. We could for instance require that the patterns are disjoint and complete. It is also necessary that the expansion of definitional equality is terminating. Usually this is checked by finding some wellordering relation in the definition.

The distinction between implicit and explicit definitions is important because it separates the definitions according to how difficult it is to check them. There will always be a wish to extend the notion of a correct implicit definition, any fixed limitation of this concept will sometimes be a straitjacket.

12.6 A simple type system

In order to explain type theory, we will first describe a framework for a simple theory with nondependent types. This corresponds closely to the core of functional programming languages like ML and Haskell. The next step is to extend this to dependent types. The description will be very brief and no formal rules will be given.

Let us start with the system without dependent types. There is one basic type, the type Set whose objects are the sets. Then we have the following type-forming operations:

- El A, the type of elements in A (which must be an object in the type Set),
- $(A_1 \ldots A_n)$, the cartesian product,
- $A_1 \to A_2$, the function type,
- Record $(c_1 \in A_1) \ldots (c_n \in A_n)$, record type.

We will write El A as A, since it will always be clear from the context if A stands for an object in Set or the types of elements in A.

The type-forming operations are of course not minimal: records can be used to decode cartesian products, functions can be used to decode anything, natural numbers can decode anything. We want to present a system which can be used to express the abstract syntax of documents in a straightforward way, without any detours via complicated codings. For instance, we use cartesian products to express more than one argument of a function instead of currying since this is the most straightforward way of looking at a documents with several parts. Currying is some kind of coding. Another advantage of this approach is that we want it to be clear from the outer form of an expression whether it is computed or not. The alternative of using records would require an explanation of not only how to express a tuple, but also patterns in implicit definitions.

The type system is defined by induction over the type structure. Assume that $A_1, \ldots, A_n$ are given types. We will follow the tradition in type theory and explain a new type-forming operation by explaining what it means to be an object in it. This should be followed by an explanation what it means for two objects to be equal in the type (each type comes together with an equality defined on it). The definition of equality will only be given in cases where it is not obvious.

12.6.1 Cartesian product

An object may consist of a finite number of well-formed objects.

The *cartesian product* $(A_1 \; \ldots \; A_n)$ is a type for $n \geq 0$. The elements of this type are tuples of the form $(a_1 \; \ldots \; a_n)$, where $a_i \in A_i$. Notice that $() \in ()$.

12.6.2 Functions

The type of functions $A_1 \to A_2$ is explained by saying that $f \in A_1 \to A_2$ means that $f \; a_1 \in A_2$ whenever $a_1 \in A_1$.

12.6.3 Record types

A record is an object which like a tuple has a finite set of components, the difference is that the components in records have names. These names can be used to project the component from the record, the expression $e.c_i$ projects the component with the name c_i from the record e. We are also using the names as locally defined constants inside the record.

The *record type* (or labeled cartesian product) Record $(c_1 \in A_1) \ldots (c_n \in A_n)$ is a type, for $n \geq 0$. That we have an object e of this type means that $e.c_i \in A_i$, for $i \leq n$, and also that $e = $ record $(c_1 = e.c_1) \ldots (c_n = e.c_n) \in$ Record $(c_1 \in A_1) \ldots (c_n \in A_n)$

Two elements d and e in Record $(c_1 \in A_1) \ldots (c_n \in A_n)$ are equal if $d.c_i = e.c_i \in A_i$ for $i \leq n$.

So, each record type has its own equality relation defined, and if the expressions d and e are of a record type, then they are equal in the empty record type, i.e. $d = e \in$ Record . There is an inherent notion of sub-typing here, if $e \in$ Record $(c_1 \in A_1)(c_2 \in A_2)\ldots(c_n \in A_n)$ then $e \in$ Record $(c_1 \in A_1)(c_2 \in A_2)\ldots(c_j \in A_j)$ for all $j \leq n$.

We can use a record like a local definition in the sense of allowing the labels to occur in the definition of later fields. In an expression record $(c_1 = e_1)\ldots(c_n = e_n)$ the label c_i may occur in the expression e_j, for $j > i$, and the above expression is defined by the following equalities (we use $e[c: = a]$ for the expression obtained by substituting all free occurrences of the identifier c for the expression a in the expression e):

$$e.c_1 = e_1$$
$$e.c_2 = e_2[c_1: = e.c_1]$$
$$\ldots$$
$$e.c_n = e_n[c_1: = e.c_1, \ldots c_{n-1}: = e.c_{n-1}]$$

Records are used in documents when, for instance part of the document is a database (or is computed from a database). A typical example is a database of literature references (like BibTeX). A watered down version is also used in HTML and XML for expressing arguments to some primitive constants (attributes). In these languages, the type of elements are restricted to be strings.

12.7 Dependent types

If we have a type system where a type can depend on an object in another type, then we can generalize the type forming operations to dependent types.

This is the case in the type system just outlined. For instance, if $A \in$ Set, then A is a type. And the type A depends trivially on the object A in the type Set. This opens the possibility to consider tuples of the form $(a\ b)$, where $a \in A$ and $b \in B(a)$, where the type $B(a)$ depends on the object $a \in A$. We can also have functions f, where the type of $f\ a$ depends on the value of the argument a.

A simple example is the following declaration of the type of vectors (Vect $A\ n$) of length n:

data Vect $(A \in$ Set$)(n \in$ N$) \in$ Set **where**

vnil $\in$ Vect A nordzero

vcons $\in (a \in A)(as \in$ Vect $A\ n)$Vect A (s n)

The constructor vnil creates vectors of length 0, while the constructor vcons builds a vector of length $n + 1$ from a vector of length n.

We can use this type to express tables of fixed size: the type Vect (Vect A n) m can be used when we want to express a table of the dimensions $n * m$. On the other hand, the type nordList (Vect A n) expresses a table with arbitrary number of rows of length n.

12.7.1 Dependent functions

The expression $(x \in A)B$ is a type if A is a type and B x is a type for $x \in A$. This is the type of functions f, which when applied to an argument a in A yields an expression f a $\in B$ a. Notice here that the type of the application depends on the argument of the function.

12.7.2 Dependent records

The expression Record $(c_1 \in A_1)(c_2 \in A_2) \ldots (c_n \in A_n)$ is a type. Each type expression A_i may depend on previous labels c_j, $j < i$, so for instance A_4 may depend on c_1, c_2 and c_3.

Here the requirements on an object e of the type are that $e.c_i \in A_i$, and we know that $e =$ record $(c_1 = a_1)(c_2 = a_2) \ldots (c_n = a_n)$ where $a_i = e.c_i$.

Example from mathematics. The disjoint union of a family of sets $\sum_{n \in \mathsf{N}} A^n$ is the type of pairs, the first being a natural number n and the second a vector $(a_1, ..., a_n)$ of length n.

Example from logic Dependent types are used to represent the universal and existential quantifiers (using the Curry–Howard–Kolmogorof isomorphism).

Example from semiformal language. A form which contain a part whose structure is dependent on the value of a previous part. For instance, when you fill in a form for your address, the structure of the address depends on the country you live in. The syntax of a telephone number depends on the area code of the number (for instance in Gothenburg we can only have 6 or 7 digits after the area code).

12.8 An application: a web browser with a built in type checker

Using these ideas it would be possible to integrate an interactive type checker (a proof editor[2]) in a web browser. When we want to present a form with slots to fill in, we just produce a document with typed place holders. Using dependent types it is possible to express very strong requirements on syntactic wellformedness, requirements which are currently expressed in an ad hoc way. For instance, if we had a placeholder (year, month, day) for a date, we can express that the type for this would be

```
record (year: Year)(month: Fin 12)(day: Fin (f year month))
```

where `Year` is a type of integers in some range around 2000, `Fin x` is the interval `[1,x]` and `f` is a function computing the maximal number of days in a specific year and month.

12.9 Related work

The main source of inspiration of this work comes from proof editors like Agda, Coq, HOL, Isabelle, Lego [1, 5, 13, 19] in the Types consortium [11, 12, 22] during the last 15 years. Many of these systems use dependent types to express mathematical propositions. The objects in such a type are the formal proofs of the proposition. So, a false proposition is represented by an empty type.

The view of the abstract syntax as the fundamental syntactical structure is persistent in computer science. It is a standard way of modularizing compilers and other program-manipulation programs. It is also implicit in denotational semantics, where the semantics is expressed by induction over the abstract syntax. This is probably the reason why the abstract syntax trees are sometimes called semantical (for instance, in linguistics and in the semantical web)

The idea of distinguishing between abstract and concrete syntax was introduced in linguistics by Curry [6] who used the words tectogrammatical and phenogrammatical structure. In Aarne Ranta's

---

[2] The idea of identifying type checking with proof checking comes from the proposition-as-types principle in which you identify a proposition with the set of its proofs. To write a proof of a given proposition then becomes the same as writing a program with a given type. For instance, to write a proof of $A \wedge B \supset B \wedge A$ consists in writing a program which takes a proof of $A \wedge B$ to a proof of $B \wedge A$.

Grammatical Framework this is a major idea for obtaining multilinguality (the same abstract syntax tree is presented by many concrete syntaxes, one for each language involved) and translation between different fragments of natural languages. Linguists in general tend to refuse to distinguish between abstract and concrete syntax.

The idea of using abstract syntax trees for documents is also present in the XML community.

12.10 Acknowledgements

I would like to thank the reviewers for many helpful comments.

It was during my visit to INRIA at the end of the 1970s that I learned about the MENTOR project and learned about a more general view on programming environments. I will always be grateful to Gilles Kahn for his endless source of inspiration, his ability to ask good questions and suggest good solutions.

Bibliography

[1] Agda homepage. `unit.aist.go.jp/cvs/Agda/`.

[2] A. Asperti, G. Bancerek and A. Trybulec (eds). *Mathematical Knowledge Management, Third International Conference, MKM 2004, Bialowieza, Poland, September 19-21, 2004, Proceedings*, volume 3119, Lecture Notes in Computer Science. Springer, 2004.

[3] R. Bornat and B. Sufrin. Animating formal proof at the surface: The Jape proof calculator. *Computer Journal*, **42**(3):177–192, 1999.

[4] P. Borras, D. Clement, Th. Despeyrouz, J. Incerpi, G. Kahn, B. Lang, and V. Pascual. CENTAUR: The system. In *Proceedings of the ACM SIGSOFT/SIGPLAN Software Engineering Symposium on Practical Software Development Environments (PSDE)*, volume 24, pp. 14–24, New York, NY, 1989. ACM Press.

[5] Coq homepage. `pauillac.inria.fr/coq/`, 1999.

[6] H. B. Curry. Some logical aspects of grammatical structure. In R. O. Jakobson (ed.) *Structure of Language in its Mathematical Aspects. Proceedings of the 12th Symposium in Applied Mathematics*, pp. 56–68, 1961.

[7] V. Donzeau-Gouge, G. Huet, G. Kahn and B. Lang. Programming environments based on structured editors: The MENTOR experience, 1984.

[8] Eclipse homepage. `www.eclipse.org`.

[9] T. Hallgren. Alfa homepage. `www.cs.chalmers.se/~hallgren/Alfa/`, 1996-2000.

[10] J. Harrison. The HOL light theorem prover. `www.cl.cam.ac.uk/~jrh13/hol-light/`, 2006.

[11]   G. Huet and G. Plotkin (eds) *Logical Frameworks: First International Workshop on Logical Frameworks, Antibes, May, 1990*. Cambridge University Press, 1991.

[12]   G. Huet and G. Plotkin (eds) *Logical Environments: Second International Workshop on Logical Frameworks, Edinburgh, May, 1991*. Cambridge University Press, 1993.

[13]   Isabelle Homepage. `www.cl.cam.ac.uk/Research/HVG/Isabelle/`, 2003.

[14]   D. E. Knuth. *Literate Programming*. CSLI, 1992.

[15]   L. Magnusson and B. Nordström. The ALF proof editor and its proof engine. In *Types for Proofs and Programs*, volume 806, Lecture Notes in Computer Science, pp. 213–237, Nijmegen, 1994. Springer-Verlag.

[16]   P. Martin-Löf. *Intuitionistic Type Theory*. Bibliopolis, Napoli, 1984.

[17]   B. Nordström, K. Petersson and J. M. Smith. *Martin-Löf's Type Theory*, chapter 1, pp. 1–33. Oxford University Press, 2001.

[18]   L. Padovani and R. Solmi. An investigation on the dynamics of direct-manipulation editors for mathematics. In Asperti *et al.* [2], pp. 302–316.

[19]   R. Pollack. The LEGO proof assistant. `www.dcs.ed.ac.uk/home/lego/`, 1997.

[20]   A. Ranta. Grammatical Framework Homepage. `www.cs.chalmers.se/~aarne/GF/`, 1999–2005.

[21]   A. Ranta. Grammatical Framework: A Type-Theoretical Grammar Formalism. *Journal of Functional Programming*, **14**(2):145–189, 2004.

[22]   The Types Project Homepage. `www.cs.chalmers.se/Cs/Research/Logic/Types/`.

[23]   L. Théry, Y. Bertot and G. Kahn. Real theorem provers deserve real user-interfaces. In *Proceedings of the Fifth ACM SIGSOFT Symposium on Software Development Environments*, pp. 120–129, 1992.

13

Grammars as software libraries

Aarne Ranta

Chalmers University of Technology and University of Gothenburg

à la mémoire de Gilles Kahn

Abstract

Grammars of natural languages are needed in programs such as natural language interfaces and dialogue systems, but also more generally, in software localization. Writing grammar implementations is a highly specialized task. For various reasons, no libraries have been available to ease this task. This paper shows how grammar libraries can be written in GF (Grammatical Framework), focusing on the software engineering aspects rather than the linguistic aspects. As an implementation of the approach, the GF Resource Grammar Library currently comprises ten languages. As an application, a translation system from formalized mathematics to text in three languages is outlined.

13.1 Introduction

How can we generate natural language text from a formal specification of meaning, such as a formal proof? Coscoy, Kahn and Théry [10] studied the problem and built a program that worked for all proofs constructed in the Coq proof assistant [30]. Their program translates structural text components, such as *we conclude that*, but leaves propositions expressed in formal language:

```
We conclude that Even(n) -> Odd(Succ(n)).
```

A similar decision is made in Isar [32], whereas Mizar [31] permits English-like expressions for some predicates. One reason for stopping at this level is certainly that typical users of proof systems are comfortable

From Semantics to Computer Science Essays in Honour of Gilles Kahn, eds Yves Bertot, Gérard Huet, Jean-Jacques Lévy and Gordon Plotkin. Published by Cambridge University Press. © Cambridge University Press 2009.

with reading logical formulas, so that only the proof-level formalization needs translation.

Another good reason for not translating propositions in a system like [10] is the difficulty of the task. It is enough to look at any precise formalization of natural language syntax to conclude that a lot of work and linguistic knowledge is demanded to get it right. This knowledge is largely independent of the domain of translations: the very same grammatical problems appear in tasks as different from proofs as, for instance, systems for hands-free controling of an MP3 player in a car [23].

In this paper, we will introduce a (to our knowledge) novel approach to natural language programming tasks. We view grammar rules as specialist knowledge, which should be encapsulated in **libraries**. Using a grammar in an application program then becomes similar to, for instance, using a numerical analysis library in a graphics rendering programme. The user of the library just has to specify on a high abstraction level what she wants—for instance, that she wants to build a sentence from a certain noun phrase and a certain adjective. The library takes care of picking the proper forms of words (which e.g. in French must obey the rules of gender and number agreement) and putting the words in right order (which e.g. in German depends on whether the sentence is subordinate or a main clause).

To introduce the grammar-related problems in programming, we will start with a simple example from the area of **software localization** – a task of natural language rendering of messages produced by a program. We continue with an outline of GF (Grammatical Framework, [25]), which is a special-purpose programming language for writing grammars, in particular designed to permit modularity and information hiding [26]. One major asset of GF is a Resource Grammar Library, which formalizes the central grammatical structures of ten languages [27]. We give an outline of this library, with the main focus on the organization, presentation, and evaluation of the library from the software engineering point of view (rather than the linguistic point of view, which is treated in other publications). As an example of the use of the library, we show how to use the library for the translation of formalized mathematics to natural language, which can be seen as complementing the work of [10].

13.2 Grammars and software localization

13.2.1 A very simple example

Many programs produce natural-language output in the form of short messages. In software localization, these messages must be translated to new languages. One important property of translation is grammatical correctness. Even in English, this is often violated: an email program may tell you,

```
You have 1 messages
```

If a little more thought has been put into the program, it might say

```
You have 1 message(s)
```

The code that should be written to get the grammar right is of course

```
msgs n = "You have" ++ show n ++ messages
   where
      messages = if n==1 then "message" else "messages"
```

Now, what is it we need in order to generate this in a new language?

First of all, we have to know the words *you*, *have*, and *message* in the new language. This is not quite as simple as it may sound. For instance, looking up the word *message* in an English–Swedish dictionary on the web[1] gives the variants *bud* and *budskap*. Which one to choose? In fact, the correct answer is neither: the translation of *message* in the domain of emails is *meddelande*.

In addition to the dictionary forms of the words, we need to know how they are inflected. Only when we know that the plural of *meddelande* is *meddelanden*, can we write the Swedish rule

```
msgs n = "Du har" ++ show n ++ messages
   where
      if n == 1 then "meddelande" else "meddelanden"
```

However, it is not universal that only the one/many distinction affects inflection. In Arabic, there are five cases [13]:

```
if n ==  1 then "risAlatun" else
if n ==  2 then "risAlatAni" else
if n <  11 then "rasA'ila" else
if n % 100 == 0 then "risAlatin" else
                    "risAlatan"
```

---

[1] www.freedict.com/onldict/swe.html

From these strictly grammatical decisions we arrive to more pragmatic, or cultural, ones. In many languages, we have to know the proper way to politely address the user. In Swedish, one tends to use the familiar *du har 3 meddelanden* rather than the formal *ni har 3 meddelanden*. In French, the preference is the opposite: *vous avez 3 messages* rather than *tu as 3 messages*. The preferred choice depends not only on language but also on the intended audience of the program.

Localization clearly needs more knowledge than what can be found in a dictionary. Hiring native-speaker programmers is one solution, but only if these programmers have explicit grammatical knowledge of their native languages. In general, the expertise that is needed is the linguist's expertise. At the same time, localization may require expertise on the application domain rather than in linguistics, so that truly appropriate terminology is used. Can we find these two experts in one and the same person? Or do we have to hire two programmers per language?

13.2.2 A library-based solution

A common technique used in localization are databases that contain words and standard texts in different languages. Such a library may contain a key, `YouHaveMessages`, or simply, `sentence_2019`, which is rendered as a function of language. Companies may have databases of thousands of sentences used for localizing their products.

If a localization library is really sophisticated, the renderings are not just constant strings but can be templates, so that e.g. `YouHaveMessages` is a template in which a number is filled and the proper rendering is chosen by case analysis on the number.

Now, an unlimited number of sentences of the same form as *you have 3 messages* can be produced by changing the subject and the object:

```
You have 4 points.
We have 2 cases.
```

The first example could be from a game, whereas the second appears in the proof renderings of [10]. To cover all possible variations, a database is not enough: something like a **grammar** is needed. However, grammars as usually written by linguists do not have a format that is usable for this task. For instance, a context-free grammar or a unification grammar defines the set of strings of a language, but it does not provide explicit functions for rendering particular structures.

To see what format is required of a grammar, let us take a cue from databases with keys to ready-made sentences and templates. Keys to sentences can be seen as constants, and keys to templates as functions:

```
Hello : Sentence
YouHaveMessages : Number -> Sentence
```

A grammar arises from this picture in a natural way: we just add more types of expressions and more complex functions, including recursive ones:

```
Modify : Adjective -> Noun -> Noun
```

Following a tradition in grammar, we call these types the **categories** of the grammar. The "keys" could be called **grammatical functions**. The categories and the function type signatures together form the **API** (Application Programmer's Interface) of the grammar library: they are everything the user of the library needs in order to build grammatically correct expressions. In addition, the library has to provide a **rendering function**, such that for each category C,

```
render : Language -> C -> String
```

The linguistic knowledge contained in the library is hidden behind the API showing the categories, the grammatical functions, and the rendering functions; the user of the library does not need to care about how they are implemented. Notice, moreover, that the API is independent of rendering language: the same combinations of grammatical functions can be rendered to different languages by varying the Language parameter.

Returning to the *n messages* example, we would need a grammar library API containing the categories

```
Sentence, NounPhrase, Noun, Number
```

and the constructor functions

```
Have     : NounPhrase -> NounPhrase -> Sentence
NumberOf : Number -> Noun -> NounPhrase

PoliteYou, FamiliarYou, We : NounPhrase
Message, Point, Case : Noun
```

Then we can translate the examples above by using different values of lang in

```
render lang (Have PoliteYou   (NumberOf 1 Message))
render lang (Have FamiliarYou (NumberOf 4 Point))
render lang (Have We          (NumberOf 2 Case))
```

13.2.3 Searching translations by parsing

If localization is implemented with an ordinary database, we can use a string in one language to search translations in other languages. In a grammar, the corresponding technique is **parsing**, i.e. the inverse of the rendering function.

```
parse : Language -> String -> C
```

This would enable us to write

```
msgs lang n = render lang (parse english "you have n messages")
```

thus avoiding the manual construction of grammatical function applications. This can be a very efficient way to use a grammar library. However, since natural languages are ambiguous, `parse` may give many results:

```
"you have 3 messages"
```

```
Have PoliteYou   (NumberOf 3 Message)
Have FamiliarYou (NumberOf 3 Message)
Have PluralYou   (NumberOf 3 Message)
```

It then remains to the user of the library to select the correct alternative, and she must thus have at least some understanding of the grammatical functions.

13.3 Implementing a grammar library in GF

Those who know GF [25] must have recognized the introduction as a seduction argument eventually leading to GF. The main components of a grammar library correspond exactly to the main components of GF:

- categories and grammatical functions = **abstract syntax**
- rendering and parsing = **concrete syntax**
- abstract library objects = **abstract syntax trees.**

We refer to [25, 26, 27] for the details of GF. Let us just show a set of GF modules forming a very simple English–French language library.

First, there is an abstract syntax module listing categories (`cat`) and grammatical functions (`fun`):

```
abstract Lib = {
  cat
    Noun ;
    Adjective ;
  fun
    Modify : Adjective -> Noun -> Noun ;
}
```

This module has adjectives and nouns, and a function that modifies a noun by an adjective (e.g. *even number*, *nombre pair*).

Second, there is a concrete syntax module of this abstract syntax, assigning a **linearization type** (`lincat`) to each category, and a **linearization function** (`lin`) to each function. Linearization may involve **parameters** (`param`) that control the rendering of abstract syntax trees.

```
concrete LibEng of Lib = {
  lincat
    Noun = {s : Number => Str} ;
    Adjective = {s : Str} ;
  lin
    Modify adj noun = {
      s = table {n => adj.s ++ noun.s ! n}
    } ;
  param
    Number = Singular | Plural ;
}
```

Linearization is a homomorphism that obeys the linearization types. Linearization types, in general, are record types that contain all relevant linguistic information. Minimally, they contain just a string, as `Adjective` does in this English example. But `Noun` in this example has a **table** (a **finite function**), which produces a string as a function of `Number` (defined by the constructors `Singular` and `Plural`). The linearizarion of modification passes the number parameter (variable `n`) to the noun (where `!` marks selection from a table) and concatenates (`++`) the adjective with the resulting noun form. In this way, we get (*one*) *new message* and (*three*) *new messages*

In the French module, we have different linearization types and different word order.

```
concrete LibFre of Lib = {
  lincat
    Noun = {s : Number => Str ; g : Gender} ;
    Adjective = {s : Gender => Number => Str ; isPre : Bool} ;
  lin
    Modify adj noun = {
      s = table {n => case adj.isPre of {
              True  => adj.s ! noun.g ! n ++ noun.s ! n ;
              False => noun.s ! n ++ adj.s ! noun.g ! n
              }
          } ;
      g = noun.g
    } ;
  param
    Number = Singular | Plural ;
    Gender = Masculine | Feminine ;
    Bool = True | False ;
}
```

The modification rule shows **agreement** between the noun and the adjective: the adjective is inflected by selecting the gender of the noun. In this way, we get *nombre pair* but *somme paire*. Unlike in English, the adjective can be placed after the noun; a boolean parameter is used to take care of whether the adjective is placed before of after the noun (e.g. *nouveau message*, "new message" vs. *message privé*, "private message").

This simple example is enough to show that natural languages have complex grammars but also, more importantly, that the abstract syntax can abstract away from complexities like word order and agreement, which are different from one language to another. An application programmer using the library can thus be freed from thinking about these details. With the adjective `new` and the noun `message` added to the abstract and the concrete syntaxes, the abstract syntax tree `Modify new message` will produce all desired forms of this combination in both languages.

The example we just showed is a a **multilingual grammar**: an abstract syntax together with a set of concrete syntaxes. A multilingual grammar can be used as a translator, where translation is the composition of parsing from one language with linearization to another. But it is also a suitable format for a grammar library. As the API of the library, the abstract syntax can be used, together with the names of the concrete syntaxes, showing what languages are available.

The **render** method is a direct application of the linearization rules. Also a **parse** method is available, as a consequence of the **reversibility** property of GF grammars: a set of linearization rules automatically generates a parser.

13.3.1 Using GF grammars in other programming languages

A GF grammar library can obviously be used for writing GF grammars—but this is not yet very useful if the grammar is to be a part of an application written in another programming languages. The simplest way to make it usable is off-line: to construct texts that are cut and pasted to the application, or stored in databases of fixed phrases. But this is not always possible, since the proper natural-language output of a program may depend on the run-time input of the program, as was the case in the *n messages* example, and also in applications like natural-language interfaces to proof assistants.

A fully satisfactory method is to compile the multilingual grammar into code usable in other languages. These languages can then make the rendering functions available as ordinary functions. For instance, in Java 1.5, we have

```
String linearize(Language l, Tree t)
Collection<Tree> parse(Language l, Category c, String str)
```

(see [5]). In order to use these functions, the programmer also has to be able to construct and analyse objects of type **Tree**. This can be done in two ways. The first alternative is a universal type of trees. This type has a constructor that builds a tree from a label representing an abstract syntax function, and an array of subtrees:

```
Tree(String label, Tree[] children)
```

While this tree type is powerful enough to represent all trees, it also permits false ones: the types of the abstract syntax functions do not constrain the construction of trees. A better alternative is to encode the abstract syntax types by using Java's class system, in the same way as Appel [1] does for the abstract syntax of programming languages. In this method, an abstract base class is created for every category of abstract syntax. Every function is encoded as a class extending its value category:

```
public abstract class Noun { ... }
public abstract class Adjective  { ... }
public class Modify extends Noun {
  public final Adjective adjective_ ;
  public final Noun noun_ ;
  public Modify(Adjective p1, Noun p2){ ... }
}
```

The concrete syntax implementation is not presented to the application programmer, and is in that sense uninteresting. But how does it work? The method we have used is to compile GF grammars into a simpler low-level format called PGF, Portable Grammar Format. This format consists essentially of arrays of strings and pointers to other arrays, implementing the linearization records of all well-typed trees. While the compiler from GF to PGF is a highly complex program, a PGF interpreter is fairly easy to write in any programming language. Such interpreters have been written in Java, Haskell, C++, and Prolog [27]. Also tree building is supported, so that e.g. a Java class system in the format shown above can be generated from an abstract syntax.

An alternative to the PGF interpreter is compilation from PGF to host program code. This method is useful if high performance is needed. For instance, in order to use GF grammars in portable devices with severe constraints, we have developed a compiler from PGF to C. In order to run language processing in web browsers, we compile PGF to JavaScript.

13.3.2 The GF Resource Grammar Library

By building the high-level grammar formalism GF and its compiler to the low-level format PGF, we have created two components of the infrastructure for grammar engineering. The next component, which we now want to focus on, is the **GF Resource Grammar Library** [27, 19]. The library project started in 2001, with the purpose of creating a standard library for GF, and thereby to make GF more usable for non-linguist programmers. As of version 1.2 (December 2007), the library covers ten languages: Danish, English, Finnish, French, German, Italian, Norwegian, Russian, Spanish, and Swedish. For these languages, a full coverage of the API is provided. Partial but already useful implementations exist for Arabic [14], Bulgarian, Catalan, and Urdu [18].

The GF Resource Grammar Library has had three major applications outside the group developing the library: in the KeY project, for translating between formal and informal software specifications [2, 6]; in the WebALT project, for translating mathematical exercises from formal representations to seven languages [8]; and in the TALK project, for localizing spoken dialogue systems to different languages [23]. These projects together have forced the library to cover both written technical language and spoken casual language. They have also involved library users with varying backgrounds: linguists, computer scientists, mathematicians, engineers.

In the following sections, we will discuss some critical questions of grammar libraries, including design, presentation, and programming language aspects. We will do this in the light of the experience gained from the GF Resource Grammar Library project.

13.4 Design questions for a grammar library

When designing a library, the first question is of course *coverage*. A grammar library should cover the grammars of the involved languages – but what this means is not so clear-cut for natural languages as it is for programming languages. Natural languages are open-ended: they evolve all the time, and the boundary between what is grammatical and what is not is often vague.

The second question is *organization and presentation*: division into modules, level of granularity, orthogonality. In the domain of grammars, we have also the choice between traditional "school grammar" concepts (which however do not suffice for all purposes) and modern, sophisticated linguistic concepts. (which however vary from one linguistic theory to another).

While these design questions have analogues in other areas of software libraries, the use of grammars as libraries has not been studied before. The reason is that grammars have mainly been written to provide stand-alone parsers and generators, with, so to say, `render` and `parse` as the only points of access.

13.5 The coverage of the library

13.5.1 Morphology

If we want the library to cover a language, the first thing that we need is **inflectional morphology**. This component enables the analysis and synthesis of all word forms in the language. What the rules of the

morphology are is a well understood question for all the languages in GF
Resource Grammar Library, so that the implementation is a question of
engineering. GF is a typed functional programming language, and it is
therefore natural to use similar techniques as in the Zen toolkit [17] and
in Functional Morphology [15].

A functional-style morphology implementation consists of an
inflection engine and a **lexicon**. The inflection engine is a set of
paradigms, that is, functions that compute a full inflection table from
a single word form. The lexicon can then be presented as a list of
word-paradigm pairs.

It is the lexicon that makes the morphology usable as a tool for
tasks like analysing texts. In a library, however, a static lexicon is less
important than the inflection engine. Domain-specific applications of the
library often require new words not appearing in any standard lexicon.
Fortunately, such technical words tend to follow regular inflection
patterns, and it is easy to provide paradigms for defining their inflection
without very much knowledge of linguistics. The most useful part of
a lexicon provided by a library is one containing irregular words, e.g.
the French irregular verbs, as well as function words, such as pronouns,
which are both frequent, domain-independent, and very irregular. These
lexica together result in some hundreds of words in each language.

13.5.2 Syntax

The most challenging part of the library is **syntax**. In the GF Resource
Grammar Library, we started from an extension of the PTQ fragment of
Montague ("Proper Treatment of Quantification in Ordinary English",
[21]) and ended up with a coverage similar to the CLE (Core Language
Engine [28]). This language fragment has proven sufficient for the
aforementioned large-scale applications of GF Resource Grammar
Library, as well as for many small-scale test applications.

The syntax in the GF Resource Grammar Library covers the usual
syntactic structures within sentences: predication, coordination, relative
clauses, indirect questions, embedded sentences, pronouns, determiners,
adjectives, etc. It also covers structures above the sentence level: the
topmost category is `Text`. Texts are lists of `Phrase`s, which can be
declarative sentences, questions, imperatives, and exclamations; also
subsentential phrases are covered, as they are needed in dialogues:
(*What do you want to drink?*) *Red wine.*

13.6 The organization and presentation of the library

13.6.1 Morphology

The morphology API is a set of paradigms. A paradigm takes a string (usually, the dictionary form also known as the **lemma**) and produces a complete inflection table. For instance, French verb paradigms look as follows:

```
v_besch56 : Str -> V  -- mettre
```

The naming of verb paradigms in French and other Romance languages follows the authoritative *Bescherelle* series of books [4]. Each paradigm in the API is endowed with a comment containing some example words.

Traditionally, as in the *Bescherelle* books, an inflectional paradigm is a function that takes one form and produces all the others (51 forms in the case of French verbs). Paradigm are identified by the sets of endings that are used for each word form: if two words show any difference in their endings, they belong to different paradigms. Thus the French *Bescherelle* contains 88 verb paradigms. This is a prohibitive number for the user of the library, and it is easy to make mistakes in picking a paradigm.

Fortunately, most paradigms in most languages are unproductive, in the sense that they apply only to a limited number of words—all new words can be treated with a handful of paradigms, often known as "regular". In *Bescherelle*, for instance, less than 10 of the 88 paradigms are regular in this sense. They are, moreover, predictable: to choose what paradigm to use, it is enough to consider the ending of the verb infinitive form. This prediction can be encoded as a **smart paradigm**, which inspects its argument using regular expression patterns, and dispatches to the productive *Bescherelle* paradigms:

```
mkV : Str -> V = \ v ->
  case v of {
    _ + "ir"              => v_besch19 v ;   -- finir
    _ + "re"              => v_besch53 v ;   -- rendre
    _ + "éger"              => v_besch14 v ;   -- assiéger
    _ + ("eler" | "eter") => v_besch12 v ;   -- jeter
    _ + "éder"              => v_besch10 v ;   -- céder
    _ + "cer"             => v_besch7  v ;   -- placer
    _ + "ger"             => v_besch8  v ;   -- manger
    _ + "yer"             => v_besch16 v ;   -- payer
    _                     => v_besch6  v     -- aimer
  } ;
```

The morphology API for French verbs now consists of this smart paradigm, together with a lexicon of those 379 verbs that do not follow it.

The smart paradigm idea was the single most important reason to add regular pattern matching to GF. The GF Resource Grammar Library has shown that it scales up well. For instance, in Finnish, which (together with Arabic) is morphologically the most complex of the library languages, 90% of words are covered by one-argument smart paradigms.

13.6.2 Syntax

Maybe the most useful and at the same time the most surprising feature of the GF Resource Grammar Library is that its syntax API is language-independent. In other words, the library describes all languages as having the same structure. To make this possible, the power of separating concrete syntax from abstract syntax is sometimes stretched to the extreme. However, since linearization is a homomorphism, the relation between trees and their linearizations remains compositional.

In version 1.2, the syntax API consists of an abstract syntax with 44 categories and 190 functions. If each language had a separate API, the library would have something like 440 categories and 1900 functions. The common syntax API thus improves the manageability of the library by an order of magnitude. Another advantage is that, once a programmer learns to use the library for one language, she can use it for all the other languages as well.

The disadvantages are mostly on the implementor's side: the concrete syntax is often more complex and less natural than it would be if each language had its own abstract syntax. The user of the library will mainly notice this disadvantage as long and memory-demanding compilations from time to time.

The common API is complete and sound in the sense that it permits the programmer to express everything in all languages with grammatically correct sentences. The resulting language is highly normalized and can be unidiomatic. Therefore the library also provides language-dependent syntax extensions. For instance, the great number of tenses in Romance languages (e.g. simple vs. composite past) has no counterpart in other languages. Just some of the tenses are accessible via the common API, and the rest via language-dependent extensions.

13.6.3 The common syntax API

The concepts of syntax are more abstract and less commonly known than the concepts of morphology. For instance, how many non-linguist programmers would know that a sentence is built from a **noun phrase** and a **verb phrases**, and that a verb phrase is formed by combining a verb with a sequence of **complements** that depend on the **subcategorization frame** of the verb?

Let us see how the library deals with sentence construction. There are several categories of verbs, corresponding to the different subcategorization frames. The API shows the category declarations, each commented with a description and an example. Here are some of the frames we use:

```
V    -- one-place verb              e.g. "sleep"
V2   -- two-place verb              e.g. "love"
V3   -- three-place verb            e.g. "show"
VS   -- sentence-complement verb    e.g. "claim"
```

For each category, there is a function that forms verb phrases:

```
UseV    : V   -> VP                 -- sleep
ComplV2 : V2  -> NP -> VP           -- use it
ComplV3 : V3  -> NP -> NP -> VP     -- send it to her
ComplVS : VS  -> S  -> VP           -- know that she runs
```

Verb phrases can moreover be formed from the copula (*be* in English) with different kinds of complements,

```
UseComp : Comp -> VP                -- be warm
CompAP  : AP   -> Comp              -- (be) small
CompNP  : NP   -> Comp              -- (be) a soldier
CompAdv : Adv  -> Comp              -- (be) here
```

These complements can again be built in many ways; for instance, an adjectival phrase (**AP**) can be built as the positive form of an the adjective (**A**), using the function

```
PositA  : A -> AP                   -- warm
```

On the top level, a **clause** (**Cl**) can be built by putting together a noun phrase and a verb phase:

```
PredVP  : NP -> VP -> Cl            -- this is warm
```

A clause is like a **sentence** (S), but with unspecified tense, anteriority (to do vs. to have done), and polarity (positive or negative). A complete sentence is thus produced by fixing these features:

```
UseCl   : Cl -> Tense -> Ant -> Pol -> S
```

The structure of this abstract syntax is motivated by the demands of completeness, succinctness, and non-redundancy. Similar ways of forming trees are factored out. The categories VP and Comp are examples of this: in a sense, they are artifacts of the linguistic theory.

13.6.4 Ground API vs. end-user API

In the common syntax API, trees become deeply hierarchical. The very simple sentence *this is warm* becomes

```
UseCl TPres ASimul PPos
  (PredVP this_NP (UseComp (CompAP (PositA (regA "warm")))))
```

Factoring out similar structures, as succinctness and non-redundancy in general, is good for the implementors of the resource grammars, since it minimizes the duplication of work. For users, however, constructing deeply nested trees, and even reading them, is intimidating, especially because it is difficult to make the naming conventions completely logical and easy to remember.

After the completion of the first version of GF Resource Grammar Library, the main attention was devoted to making the library easier to understand. The succinct, non-redundant API as described above is now called the **ground API**. Its main purpose is to serve as a specification of the functionalities that a resource implementation must provide. The **end-user API** has different requirements. For instance, redundancy can be helpful to the user. The resulting presentation of the end-user API was inspired by one of the most influential software libraries, the Standard Template Library (STL) of C++ [29].

13.6.5 Overloading

An important instrument in STL is **overloading**: the use of a common name for different functions that in some sense perform similar tasks. Two different criteria of similarity used in STL have proven useful in our library:

- functions that construct objects of the same type: **constructors** in STL
- functions that operate in the same way on their arguments, irrespectively to type: **algorithms** in STL

Overloading in GF is implemented by a compile-time resolution algorithm. As in C++ (and ALGOL68), it performs bottom-up type inference from the arguments. Unlike C++, GF has partial applications, and must therefore use the value type in resolution, in addition to argument types.

The implementation of overloading was unexpectedly simple and efficient. In conclusion, overloading is a small language feature from the implementation point of view but has a deep effect on the way in which the language is used.

13.6.6 Constructors

What is a constructor? In the technical sense of type theory, *all* functions of an abstract syntax are constructors, since they define the data forms of an inductive system of data types [20]. Overloading of constructors in this sense poses technical problems, for instance, when constructors are used as patterns in case analysis.

However, what corresponds to type-theoretical constructors in C++ is not the C++ constructor functions, but the forms of records of class variables. These variables are usually *not* disclosed to the user of a class. The very purpose of the C++ constructors is to hide the real data constructors. This distinction gives one more reason for GF to have an end-user API separate from the ground API: to achieve full data abstraction, the ground API must not be disclosed to users at all!

We have built a set of overloaded constuctors that covers the resource grammar syntax with just 22 function names. All these names have the form mkC, where C is the value category of the constructor. For instance, we have a set of Cl forming functions,

```
mkCl : NP -> V    -> Cl             -- he sleeps
mkCl : NP -> V2   -> NP -> Cl       -- he uses it
mkCl : NP -> V3   -> NP -> NP -> Cl -- he sends it to her
mkCl : NP -> VS   -> S  -> Cl       -- he knows that she runs
mkCl : NP -> A    -> Cl             -- he is warm
mkCl : NP -> AP   -> Cl             -- he is warmer than you
mkCl : NP -> NP   -> Cl             -- he is a man
mkCl : NP -> Adv  -> Cl             -- he is here
```

Notice that the set of constructors also flattens the structure of the ground API: the theoretical categories `VP` and `Comp` have been eliminated in favor of functions using their constituents directly. Furthermore, we have added a flattening constructor taking an adjective (`A`), which is a special case of the adjectival phrase (`AP`).

The constructor forming sentences from clauses shows yet another typical use of overloading: **default arguments**. Any of the arguments for tense, anteriority, and polarity may be omitted, in which case the defaults present, simultaneous, and positive are used, respectively. The API shows optional argument types in parentheses (for the GF compiler, parentheses have only their usual grouping function; the following is really implemented as a group of overloaded functions):

```
mkS : Cl -> (Tense) -> (Ant) -> (Pol) -> S
```

With this set of constructors, the sentence *this is warm* can now be written

```
mkS (mkCl this_NP (regA "warm"))
```

13.6.7 Combinators

What about the "algorithms" of STL? In grammar, one analogue are grammatical functions that operate on different categories, such as **coordination** (forming conjunctions and disjunctions). These functions are of course redundant because constructors cover the same ground, but often combinators give a more direct and intuitive access to the resource grammar. Here is an example, a part of the coordination function:

```
coord : Conj  -> ListAdv     -> Adv  -- here, now and fast
coord : Conj  -> ListAP      -> AP   -- warm and very tasty
coord : Conj  -> ListNP      -> NP   -- John, Mary and I
coord : Conj  -> ListS       -> S    -- I sleep and you walk
coord : Conj  -> Adv -> Adv -> Adv   -- here and now
coord : DConj -> Adv -> Adv -> Adv   -- both here and now
```

Altogether, there are $4*2*2 = 16$ coordination functions, since there are four categories that can be coordinated, two kinds of coodinated collections (lists of arbitrary length and the special case of two elements), and two kinds of coordinating conjunctions (types *and* and *both-and*). Since all of them have different types, they can be represented by one overloaded constant.

13.7 Success criteria and evaluation

Natural-language grammars are usually evaluated by testing them against some text corpus, such as the Wall Street Journal corpus. The current GF Resource Grammar Library would not perform well in such a test. Even if it did, the test would miss the most important points about the use of the grammar as a library, rather than as a stand-alone parser. Thus we need some new criteria for grammar evaluation, to a large extent similar to software libraries in general.

13.7.1 The success criteria

Correctness. This is the most important property of any library. The user of the library must be able to rely on the expertise of its authors, and all library functions must thus do the right thing. In the case of a grammar library, this means **grammatical correctness** of everything that is type-correct in the grammar.

Coverage. In tasks such as localization or document generation, this means above all **semantic coverage**: although limited, the language fragment must be sufficient for expressing whatever programmers need to express.

Usability. In this case, usability by non-linguists is the interesting question. The success in this point depends on presentation and documentation, rather than on the implementation.

Efficiency. This is a property often mentioned in the C++ community: using the library should not create any run-time overhead compared with hand-written code [29]. Interestingly, a considerable amount of compile-time overhead is created in both C++ (because of template instantiation) and GF (because of partial evaluation; see [25]).

13.7.2 These are not our success criteria

Completeness, in the sense of the grammar's being able to parse all expressions. While this would be useful in applications that need to parse user input, it would clutter the grammar with questionable constructions and compromise its correctness.

Semantic correctness, in the sense of the grammar only producing meaningful expressions. Now we can produce grammatically well-formed nonsense:

```
colourless green ideas sleep furiously
```

```
draw an equilateral line through the rectangular circle
```

It is difficult to rule out such sentences by general principles. The philosophy of the resource grammar library is that semantics is given in applications, not in the library. What is meaningful, and what meaning is, varies from one domain to the other.

Translation equivalence. The common syntax API does not guarantee common meanings, let alone common pragmatic value. In applications, it is often necessary to use the API in different ways for different languages. For instance, a standard English mathematical exercise uses the imperative, whereas French uses the infinitive:

```
Compute the sum X.    -- *Calculez la somme X.
Calculer la somme X. -- *To compute the sum X.
```

It is the programmer of the mathematics application who selects the right constructions in both languages. The grammar library only takes care of the proper renderings of these constructions. Of course, a special-purpose mathematics library can introduce a function for constructing exercises, which uses the ground library in different ways for English and French.

Linguistic innovation. The idea of the resource grammar library is to formalize a body of "known facts" about languages and offer them to non-linguist users. While we do believe that some innovation was needed to make the library work, the purpose of the API is to hide this from the users, and make it look natural and easy.

13.7.3 Evaluation

To evaluate correctness, coverage, and usability, it is good to have applications from different areas and by different users. In this sense, testing a grammar library is much like testing any software. An extra method for testing grammatical correctness is the possibility of automatically generating trees and linearizing them, and inspecting the results. Version 1.0 of the GF Resource Grammar Library was released when a stable point was reached in this process.

Completeness in the usual mathematical sense is even possible to prove, by writing a translator from a system of logic to the library API. This has been done for several systems, thus proving instances of expressive completeness.

Compile-time efficiency is a serious problem with some resource grammars (in particular, the Romance languages and Finnish). This has led us to looking for improvements to the partial evaluation method used. But grammars written by using resource grammars as libraries, when compiled, are free from overhead, because the partial evaluation specializes them accurately to the type system of the application, as shown in [25].

13.8 Example: rendering mathematical concepts

Mathematical text is a mixture of natural language and symbolic notation. While the proportion of symbolic notation varies, the following rules are usually obeyed.

- Only logically atomic sentences are symbolic: quantifiers and connectives are verbal.
- Some conventional, mostly 2-place, predicates are symbolic, e.g. = and <, while most new predicates are verbal, e.g. *x is even*.
- Singular terms are often symbolic, e.g. x + y, but also often verbal, e.g. *the greatest prime factor of x*.
- A symbolic expression may not contain parts expressed in words.

The last rule has an important consequence for a symbolic predicate that is given a verbal argument: either the predicate is rendered verbally,

```
the greatest prime factor of x is equal to x/2
```

or a symbol is locally defined for the argument,

```
p = x/2, where p is the greatest prime factor of x.
```

If we want a proof assistant to generate text of publication quality, we have to obey these rules. They are also important in educational applications [8]. Correct verbalization is a part of standard mathematical language as much as correct symbolic notation is. The symbolic notation problem is to a large extent solved in computer algebras and many proof assistants, e.g. by using TeX. But verbalization is a more difficult problem, since it involves so much linguistics.

On the topmost level of definitions and proofs, the main problem is proper order and structure, and these questions are studied in e.g. [9] and [33]. What a grammar library can contribute is the replacement of concrete text by abstract syntax trees. For instance, the formula *we have n cases* can be expressed by

```
mkCl (mkNP we_Pron) have_V2 (mkNP n case_N)
```

which will produce the correct forms for any language as function of n.

Going down to the level of propositional structure, we need to express quantifiers and connectives by using natural language. It is easy use the GF Resource Grammar Library to write rules such as

```
Conj A B = coord and_Conj A B   -- A and B
Disj A B = coord or_Conj A B    -- A or B
```

But now we encounter the problem of ambiguity. We cannot just compositionally translate A & (B v C) with *A and B or C*. This problem is solved in [6] by the use of grouping (indentation, bullets) and subsentential coordination (*x is prime and y is even or odd*), also known as **aggregation** in natural language generation literature. The translation of logical structures, although tricky, can be solved generically in the implementation of a proof system and then reused in applications on any domain, largely independently of language.

The vast majority of textual rendering problems is encountered when new concepts are defined by users as a part of proof construction. In [16], we presented a plug-in to the Alfa proof editor, where definitions can be seen as GF abstract syntax rules and annotated by concrete syntax rules telling how the new concepts are expressed in natural language. This idea is applicable in any proof assistant that is able to express the types of new concepts; it is also used in the KeY program verification system [2, 6].

At the time of [16], the GF Resource Grammar Library was not available, and users had to think of both grammar rules and mathematical idioms when writing annotations. For the WebALT project [8], a combinator library was written to cover the most frequent needs. It has a set of predication rules (`pred`) building clauses (`Cl`) to express prepositions, and a set of application rules (`app`) building noun phrases (`NP`) to express individual objects:

```
pred : V  -> NP -> Cl          -- x converges
pred : V  -> ListNP -> Cl      -- x, y and z intersect
pred : V2 -> NP -> NP -> Cl    -- x intersects y
pred : A  -> NP -> Cl          -- x is even
pred : A  -> ListNP -> Cl      -- x, y and z are equal
pred : A2 -> NP -> NP -> Cl    -- x is divisible by y
pred : N  -> NP -> Cl          -- x is a prime
pred : N  -> ListNP -> Cl      -- x, y and z are relative primes
```

```
pred : N2 -> NP -> NP -> Cl   -- x is a divisor of y

app  : N2 -> NP -> NP          -- the successor of x
app  : N2 -> ListNP -> NP      -- the sum of x, y and z
app  : N3 -> NP -> NP -> NP  -- the interval from x to y
```

Together with morphological paradigms, these combinators can be used for defining renderings of mathematical concepts easily and compactly.

The **pred** functions are very much like the **mkCl** constructors in Section 6.6 above, with the difference that the predicate (verb or adjective) is given the first argument position. In typical linearization rules for mathematical predicates, this has the advantage of permitting the use of partial application. This is what we do in the following examples, which produce English, French, and Finnish.

```
Succ : Nat -> Nat
Succ = app (mkN2 "successor")
Succ = app (mkN2 "successeur")
Succ = app (mkN2 "seuraaja")

Div : Nat -> Nat -> Prop
Div = pred (mkA2 "divisible" "by")
Div = pred (mkA2 "divisible" "par")
Div = pred (mkA2 "jaollinen" adessive)

Prime : Nat -> Prop
Prime = pred (mkA "prime")
Prime = pred (mkA "premier")
Prime = pred (mkA "jaoton")
```

13.8.1 A functor implementation of the translator

In the previous example, the languages use the syntax API in exactly the same way, and differ only in the lexicon. This results in repetition of code, which can actually be avoided in GF by using a **functor**. A functor in GF is, like in ML, a module that depends on **interfaces** (called **signatures** in ML), that is, modules that only show the types of constants and omit definitions. The resource API itself is an interface. In a typical GF application, the programmer builds herself another one to define a **domain lexicon**. In the present example, the domain lexicon interface declares the constants

```
successor_N2 : N2
divisible_A2 : A2
prime_A : A
```

The functor can then be written

```
Succ = app successor_N2
Div = pred divisible_A2
Prime = pred prime_A
```

To add a new language to a multilingual grammar implemented with a functor like this, it is enough to write a new instance of the domain lexicon. This technique is explained in more detail in [26] and [23].

13.9 Related work

13.9.1 Grammar formalisms

The fundamental idea of GF is the division of a grammar into an abstract and concrete syntax. It is this division that at the same time supports the communication between grammatical structures and other data structures, and permits the construction of multilingual grammars. The idea is first found in Curry [11], and it was used by Montague [21] with the purpose of giving denotational semantics to a fragment of English.

In linguistics, Curry's idea was for a long time ignored, with Montague as one of the few exceptions. The situation has however changed in the past ten years, with GF and related formalisms: ACG (Abstract Categorial Grammars [12]), HOG (Higher-Order Grammar, [24]), and Lambda Grammars [22]. Only GF has so far produced a large-scale implementation and grammar libraries.

13.9.2 Grammar libraries

CLE (Core Language Engine [28]) has been the closest point of comparison as for both the coverage and purpose of the GF Resource Grammar Library. The languages included in CLE are English, Swedish, French, and Danish, with similar but structurally distinct fragments covered. The "glue" between the languages is called QLF (Quasi-Logical Form), which in fact gives a structure rather similar to the ground API of the GF Resource Grammar. Like GF, CLE adresses the idea of sharing code between grammar implementations. It uses macros and file includes instead of functions and modules for this purpose. Moreover, specializing a large grammar to a small application is adressed by a technique called explanation-based learning. The effect is often similar to GF's partial evaluation.

The LinGO Matrix project [3] defines a methodology for building grammars of different languages that cover the same phenomena. The language-independent syntax API of GF can be seen as an extreme version of the same idea, using a common formal representation for all languages. LinGO grammars are aimed to parse real texts.

Pargram [7] is a project with the goal of building a set of parallel grammars. Its original purpose was machine translation between English, French, and German. The grammars are connected with each other by transfer functions, rather than a common representation. Currently the project covers more than ten languages.

13.9.3 Compiling to natural language

When introducing a proof-to-text translator, the paper [10] opens a new perspective to the problem: natural language generation is seen as similar to compilation. Thus it uses code optimization techniques to improve the generated text, in a partly similar way to what in main-stream natural language generation is known as aggregation. These optimizations operate on what in a compiler would be called intermediate code—a level between source code (Coq proofs) and target code (natural language). Now, if we see natural language as target code, or machine code, we can understand the nature of some of the difficulties of generating it. Natural language, just like machine code, is difficult to deal with directly: it is better to hide it under a level of abstraction. Assembly code is one such level, but it is even better if the compiler can generate intermediate code retargetable to many machines. The intermediate code of [10] was indeed retargeted to English and French. The language-independent abstract syntax of GF Resource Grammar Library can be seen as a format implementing the same idea, now retargeted to more languages.

13.10 Conclusion

We have discussed the GF Resource Grammar Library from the point of view of library-based software engineering. This is a novel perspective on grammars, which are usually seen as programs performing parsing and generation, rather than as libraries. Libraries are useful for software localization and applications such as proof assistants. A main problem is to make the library API intelligible for non-linguist users. The use of a common API for different languages helps considerably; another useful instrument is overloading, which helps to keep the function names memorizable and to create different views of the library.

Acknowledgments

It was Gilles Kahn who turned my attention to compiler techniques in natural language generation. I am deeply grateful for the invitation to visit him in Sophia-Antipolis in 1995, and also for the contact we had afterwards. GF was born from a combination of these compiler techniques and the type-theoretical view of abstract and concrete syntax, for which I am grateful to Per Martin-Löf.

The GF Resource Grammar Library has been built with the cooperation of many people, and gained from comments and suggestions from even more—to mention just some: Krasimir Angelov, Jean-Philippe Bernardy, Lars Borin, Björn Bringert, Lauri Carlson, Robin Cooper, Ali El Dada, Hans-Joachim Daniels, Elisabet Engdahl, Markus Forsberg, Harald Hammarström, Kristofer Johannisson, Janna Khegai, Peter Ljunglöf, Wanjiku Ng'ang'a, Bengt Nordström, and Jordi Saludes. During the past year, collaboration with the Software Methodology and Systems group at Chalmers (Andreas Priesnitz, Sibylle Schupp, and Marcin Zalewski) has brought to my attention the important conceptual work on software libraries done in the C++ community.

The research has been supported by the grant *Library-Based Grammar Engineering* from Vetenskapsrådet.

Bibliography

[1]   A. Appel. *Modern Compiler Implementation in Java*. Cambridge University Press, 1998.

[2]   B. Beckert, R. Hähnle and P. Schmitt. *Verification of Object-Oriented Software: The KeY Approach*, volume 4334 Lecture Notes in Computer Science. Springer-Verlag, 2006.

[3]   E. M. Bender and D. Flickinger. Rapid prototyping of scalable grammars: Towards modularity in extensions to a language-independent core. In *Proceedings of the 2nd International Joint Conference on Natural Language Processing IJCNLP-05 (Posters/Demos)*, Jeju Island, Korea, 2005.

[4]   Bescherelle. *La conjugaison pour tous*. Hatier, 1997.

[5]   B. Bringert. *Embedded Grammars*. MSc Thesis, Department of Computing Science, Chalmers University of Technology, 2004.

[6] D. A. Burke and K. Johannisson. Translating Formal Software Specifi-cations to Natural Language / A Grammar-Based Approach. In P. Blache, E. Stabler, J. Busquets and R. Moot (eds) *Logical Aspects of Computational Linguistics (LACL 2005)*, volume 3402 LNCS/LNAI, pp. 51–66. Springer-Verlag, 2005.

[7] M. Butt, H. Dyvik, T. Holloway King, H. Masuichi and C. Rohrer. The Parallel Grammar Project. In *COLING 2002, Workshop on Grammar Engineering and Evaluation*, pp. 1–7, 2002.

[8] O. Caprotti. WebALT! Deliver Mathematics Everywhere. In *Proceedings of SITE 2006. Orlando March 20–24*, 2006.

[9] Y. Coscoy. *Explication textuelle de preuves pour le calcul des constructions inductives*. PhD thesis, Université de Nice-Sophia-Antipolis, 2000.

[10] Y. Coscoy, G. Kahn and L. Thery. Extracting text from proofs. In M. Dezani-Ciancaglini and G. Plotkin (eds) *Proc. Second International Conference on Typed Lambda Calculi and Applications*, volume 902 Lecture Notes in Computer Science, pp. 109–123, Springer-Verlag, 1995.

[11] H. B. Curry. Some logical aspects of grammatical structure. In Roman Jakobson, editor, *Structure of Language and its Mathematical Aspects: Proceedings of the Twelfth Symposium in Applied Mathematics*, pp. 56–68. American Mathematical Society, 1963.

[12] Ph. de Groote. Towards abstract categorial grammars. In *Association for Computational Linguistics, 39th Annual Meeting and 10th Conference of the European Chapter, Toulouse, France*, pp. 148–155, 2001.

[13] A. El Dada. Implementation of the Arabic numerals and their syntax in GF. In *Computational Approaches to Semitic Languages: Common Issues and Resources, ACL-2007 Workshop, June 28, 2007, Prague*, 2007.

[14] A. El Dada and A. Ranta. Implementing an open source arabic resource grammar in GF. In M. A. Mughazy (ed.) *Perspectives on Arabic Linguistics XX*, pp. 209–232. John Benjamins, Amsterdam and Philadelphia, 2007.

[15] M. Forsberg and A. Ranta. Functional Morphology. In *ICFP 2004, Showbird, Utah*, pp. 213–223, 2004.

[16] T. Hallgren and A. Ranta. An extensible proof text editor. In M. Parigot and A. Voronkov (eds) *LPAR-2000*, volume 1955 LNCS/LNAI, pp. 70–84. Springer, 2000.

[17] G. Huet. A functional toolkit for morphological and phonological processing, application to a Sanskrit tagger. *Journal of Functional Programming*, **15**(4):573–614, 2005.

[18] M. Humayoun. *Urdu Morphology, Orthography and Lexicon Extraction*. MSc Thesis, Department of Computing Science, Chalmers University of Technology, 2006.

[19] J. Khegai. GF parallel resource grammars and Russian. In *Coling/ACL 2006*, pp. 475–482, 2006.

[20] P. Martin-Löf. Constructive mathematics and computer programming. In Cohen, Los, Pfeiffer and Podewski (eds) *Logic, Methodology and Philosophy of Science VI*, pp. 153–175. North-Holland, Amsterdam, 1982.

[21] R. Montague. *Formal Philosophy*. Yale University Press, New Haven, 1974. Collected papers edited by R. Thomason.

[22]   R. Muskens. Lambda grammars and the syntax-semantics interface. In R. van Rooy and M. Stokhof (eds) *Proceedings of the Thirteenth Amsterdam Colloquium*, pp. 150–155, Amsterdam, 2001.

[23]   N. Perera and A. Ranta. Dialogue System Localization with the GF Resource Grammar Library. In *SPEECHGRAM 2007: ACL Workshop on Grammar-Based Approaches to Spoken Language Processing, June 29, 2007, Prague*, 2007.

[24]   C. Pollard. Higher-order categorial grammar. In M. Moortgat (ed.) *Proceedings of the Conference on Categorial Grammars (CG2004), Montpellier, France*, pp. 340–361, 2004.

[25]   A. Ranta. Grammatical framework: a type-theoretical grammar formalism. *Journal of Functional Programming*, **14**(2):145–189, 2004.

[26]   A. Ranta. Modular grammar engineering in GF. *Research on Language and Computation*, **5**:133–158, 2007.

[27]   A. Ranta. Grammatical Framework Homepage, 2008. `digitalgrammars.com/gf`.

[28]   M. Rayner, D. Carter, P. Bouillon, V. Digalakis and M. Wirén. *The Spoken Language Translator*. Cambridge University Press, Cambridge, 2000.

[29]   B. Stroustrup. *The C++ Programming Language, Third Edition*. Addison-Wesley, 1998.

[30]   The Coq Development Team. The Coq Proof Assistant Reference Manual. `pauillac.inria.fr/coq/`, 1999.

[31]   A. Trybulec. The Mizar Homepage. `http://mizar.org/`, 2006.

[32]   M. Wenzel. Isar - a generic interpretative approach to readable formal proof documents. In Y. Bertot, G. Dowek, A. Hirschowitz, C. Paulin and L. Théry (eds) *Theorem Proving in Higher Order Logics, TPHOLs'99*, volume 1690 Lecture Notes in Computer Science, 1999.

[33]   F. Wiedijk. Formal proof sketches. In *Types for Proofs and Programs*, volume 3085 Lecture Notes in Computer Science, pp. 378–393. Springer, 2004.

14

The Leordo computation system

Erik Sandewall

Linköping University and Royal Institute of Technology, Stockholm, Sweden

Abstract

The purpose of the research reported here was to explore an alternative way of organizing the general software structure in computers, eliminating the traditional distinctions between operating system, programming language, database system, and several other kinds of software. We observed that there is a lot of costly duplication of concepts and of facilities in the conventional architecture, and believe that most of that duplication can be eliminated if the software is organized differently. This article describes Leordo, an experimental software system that has been built in order to explore an alternative design and to try to verify the hypothesis that a much more compact design is possible and that concept duplication can be eliminated or at least greatly reduced. Definite conclusions in those respects can not yet be made, but the indications are positive and the design that has been

14.1 Introduction

14.1.1 Project goal and design goals

Leordo is a software project and an experimental software system that integrates capabilities that are usually found in several different software systems:

- in the operating system
- in the programming language and programming environment
- in an intelligent agent system
- in a text formatting system

From *Semantics to Computer Science Essays in Honour of Gilles Kahn*, eds Yves Bertot, Gérard Huet, Jean-Jacques Lévy and Gordon Plotkin. Published by Cambridge University Press. © Cambridge University Press 2009.

and others more. I believe that it should be possible to make a much more concise, efficient, and user-friendly design of the total software system in the conventional (PC-type) computer by integrating capabilities and organizing them in a new way.

The purpose of the Leordo project[1] was *to verify or falsify this hypothesis.* This was done by designing and implementing an experimental system, by iterating on its design until it satisfied a number of well defined criteria, and by implementing a number of characteritic applications using the Leordo system as a platform.

The implementation of the experimental system has passed several such iterations, and a reasonably well-working system has been in daily use for several years. The following are the requirements that were specified for that system and that are satisfied by the present implementation. We expect to retain them in future system generations.

The system is of course organized in a modular fashion, where the modules are called *knowledge blocks* and contain both algorithms, data, and intermediate information such as ontologies and rules. There shall be a designated *kernel* consisting of one or a few knowledge blocks that is used as a basis on which other blocks can be built, for the purpose of additional services and for applications. The following were and are *the requirements on the kernel.*

- It shall contain self-describing information and corresponding procedural capabilities whereby it is able to administrate itself, its own structure, and its own updates.

- It shall provide the extension capabilities that make it possible to attach additional knowledge blocks to it and to administer them in the same way as the kernel administers itself.

- It shall provide adequate representations for the persistent storage of all contents of the blocks in the kernel, as well as the representations and the computational services for performing computations on the same contents.

- It shall provide capabilities for adaptation, in particular to facilitate moving a system between hosts, and for defining alternative configurations based on different sets of knowledge blocks.

- Although the experimental system will be based on an existing, conventional operating system and ditto programming language, it

---

[1] The project and the system were previously called Leonardo, but the name was changed to Leordo in order to avoid a name conflict.

shall be designed in such a way that it can be ported to the weakest possible, underlying software base.

The last item in these requirements is included because in principle we believe that the services of the operating system and the programming language and system, should just be parts of one integrated computation system. The longer-term goal is therefore that the Leordo system itself should contain the programming-language and operating-system services.

Furthermore, the facilities in the kernel have been, and will continue to be designed in such a way that they do not merely serve the above-mentioned requirements on the kernel itself; they shall also be general enough to provide a range of applications with similar services.

Above the kernel and below the specific application areas and applications, there shall also be an extensible *platform* consisting of knowledge blocks that are of general use for a number of applications of widely different character.

Illustration materials and annexes of the present article can be found on the article's persistent webpage at
`http://www.ida.liu.se/ext/caisor/pm-archive/leonardo/002/`. It is useful to have access to that webpage while reading the present article.

14.1.2 Main hypothesis for the leordo project

The main hypothesis for this project, for which we hope to obtain either strong positive evidence or a clear refutation, is as follows: *It is demonstrably possible to design the kernel and a platform in such a way that (1) repeated implementation of similar tasks is virtually eliminated in the kernel and platform, and (2) the total software structure that is obtained when several applications are built on this platform can also be essentially free from repeated implementations of similar tasks.*

14.1.3 Approach to the design

The design of the system does not start by defining a programming language, nor by defining a process structure or a virtual instruction set. In Leordo, the first step in the design is to define an object-oriented information structure that has some points in common with RDF[2]

---

[2] `http://www.w3.org/RDF/`

and OWL,[3] although also with significant differences. The notation used for this purpose is called KRE, the Knowledge Representation Expression language. It is used for all information in the system, including application data, procedures, ontologies, parameter structures, and whatever corresponds to data declarations in our system. Full KRE is a knowledge representation language but the present article will only describe those parts of KRE that are used for the Leordo system design.

The element in the KRE structure is called an *entity*, and entities can have *attributes* and *properties*. Attribute values can have structure and are not merely links to other entities; they can be constructed by the formation of sets, sequences, and records, even recursively. Moreover, entities can be composite expressions; they are not merely atoms with mnemonic names. Property values are like long strings and can be used for expressing e.g. a function definition, or a descriptive comment. Because of this expressive power, KRE is best viewed as a knowledge representation language.

We use the term 'entity' rather than 'object' for the elements in KRE since the term 'object' has a connotation of message passing and a fairly restrictive view of class hierarchy, which are not applicable in KRE.

Each knowledge block consists of a set of *entity files*; each entity file consists of a sequence of entities; and each entity has its attributes and properties.

The experimental system, which is based on conventional operating systems, has in addition the following design. A *Leordo individual* is a section of the file system in a computer hosting the individual, namely one directory and all its sub-directories, with all the files contained in them (with the exception of auxiliary files such as .bak files). Each entityfile in the Leordo sense (i.e. a sequence of entities) is represented by one file in the sense of the file system; this file is a text ('ascii') file adhering to a particular syntax. An *activation* of the individual is obtained by starting a run with a host programming language, where the run is initialized using some of the files contained in the individual. The run usually includes interactions with a human user, but maybe also with robotic equipment, Internet information sources and resources, or other Leordo individuals. Entityfiles in the individual can be read and written during the activation, for example for storing information that has been acquired during the activation, or for updating the software.

---

[3] http://www.w3.org/TR/owl-features/

In accordance with the specified goals for Leordo, as described above, the individual shall be self-contained and be able to model its own structure, and to update it. In that sense the individual is able to *modify itself* during the activation. The individual shall also contain facilities for moving itself, or allowing itself to be moved from one host to another, in ways that are reminiscent of mobile agents.[4]

The use of directories and files for representing aggregates of Leordo entities is an intermediate solution. In the longer run we wish to port Leordo to a persistent software system that is able to represent entities directly, so that the structures and services that are traditionally offered by an operating system and in particular by its file system, can instead be implemented in the Leordo kernel or platform.

Both the experimental system and the forthcoming persistent system must use a *host programming language*. Functions, procedures, classes, or whatever other building-blocks are used in the host language will be represented by Leordo entities, and the definition of a function (etc) is expressed in a property of that entity. Our main experimental system has been implemented in CommonLisp; a part of the core has also been implemented in Python. We expect that the persistent system will be based on a language similar to Scheme. Interpretation-oriented languages such as these are the best suited for our approach.

14.1.4 Notation vs. system

The language design and the system design in our approach are strongly interdependent. The language design has come first in the present project, but the system design is by far the largest part of the work and it has arguably the largest novelty value. The main purpose of the present report is to describe the system design, but it is necessary to describe the language design first.

14.2 An example of KRE

By way of introduction we show two examples of how the Leordo Data Expression language, KRE, is used in Leordo. A more detailed specification of KRE can be found in the report "The Leonardo Representation Language.[5]

---

[4] http://en.wikipedia.org/wiki/Mobile-agent
[5] http://www.ida.liu.se/ext/caisor/pm-archive/leonardo/001/

14.2.1 KRE in the Common Knowledge Library

The Common Knowledge Library[6] (CKL) is an open-source repository for structured information ranging from 'facts' to 'knowledge'. It presently contains more than 60 000 entitites each having a number of attributes. The KRE notation is the 'first language' used by the Common Knowledge Library. The reader is encouraged to browse its website in order to obtain an impression of how information can be represented using KRE.

One thing that is not immediately seen on the CKL website is, however, the representation of meta-information. We use two kinds of meta-information: type information and catalog information. Each entity has an attribute called `type` where the attribute value is a new entity representing the type of the given entity. Furthermore, for each entityfile there is one entity that serves as the name of the entityfile; one of the attributes of the naming entity is a sequence consisting of the entityfile's members. The name of an entityfile is itself the first member of that list.

The type system is quite simple. For use in some applications there is also a notion of *classes* which are similar to the 'concepts' of description languages, but this is not used in the system kernel.

Notice that entityfiles are used for expressing both programs and data. Each named unit in a program, such as a function or a procedure, is represented as a KRE entity, with the program code in a property of that entity. The entityfiles that are used within the system differ in some minor ways from those shown on the CKL website. For example, the provenance and IPR information occurs only in the published files and not in system-internal files.

The operation of *loading* an entityfile is performed by activations, and consists of reading the text file for the entityfile, such as the ones used in the CKL, and constructing the corresponding data structures in the activation. The operation of *storing* an entityfile is the reverse operation of re-writing its text file by converting data structures to corresponding, textual expressions. Loading and immediately storing an entityfile has a null effect on its text file.

---

[6] `http://piex.publ.kth.se/ckl/`

14.2.2 Cooperating agents

The next example shows how a distributed computational process is organized in Leordo, and how the KRE language is used for representing the control information. Consider the following method description in Leordo:

```
-----------------------------------------------------------
-- method6

[: type method]
[: plan {[intend: t1 t2 (remex: lar-004 (query: makebid))]
         [intend: t1 t3 (query: makebid)]
         [intend: t4 t5 (query: propose-compromise)]}]
[: time-constraints {[afterall: {t2 t3} t4]}]
-----------------------------------------------------------
```

This is a plan, i.e. a kind of high-level procedure, for a situation where two separate users have to give their respective bids for some purpose, and when both bids have been received, one user has to propose a compromise. This requires performing the action **query:** three times with different arguments. The time when the first two occurrences are to start is called **t1**; the third occurrence starts at a time **t4** which is defined as being when the first two occurrences have ended. The time when the first mentioned occurrence ends is called **t2**, and similarly for **t3**. The method consists of a set of intended actions, and set of time constraints between them.

This plan is supposed to be executed in a particular individual (called **lar-003** in our specific run of the plan) but the first mentioned action is to be remote executed (therefore **remex:**) in another individual called **lar-004**.

The KRE language is used for representing this plan, or script. In this example there is an entity called **method4** with three attributes **type**, **plan**, and **time-constraints**. The value of the **type** attribute determines what other attributes may be present.

This examples uses more of the KRE expressivity than in the first example. It shows how expressions in KRE may be atomic ones (symbols, strings, or numbers), or may be formed recursively using the operators $<\ldots>$ for sequences, $\{\ldots\}$ for sets, $[\ldots]$ for records, and $(\ldots)$ for forming composite entities. In the example, (**query: makebid**) is a composite entity that has a type and attributes, just like the atomic entity `method4`.

The webpage of the present article contains details from an activation using the method shown above, and it illustrates how KRE is used for the control information as the plan or script is executed, and for retaining some of that control information afterwards.

14.3 Information structure

14.3.1 The structure of Knowledgeblocks

The total information in a Leordo system is organized as a set of knowledgeblocks, and each activation of Leordo is initialized by loading one specific knowledgeblock in that set. Some knowledgeblocks *require* others, however, so that to load a knowledgeblock one first loads those other knowledgeblocks that it requires, recursively, and then one loads the entityfiles that are specified for the given knowledgeblock itself.

Each knowledgeblock consists of a set of entityfiles. One of those entityfiles represents the knowledgeblock as a whole and contains overall information about it; it is called the *index* of the knowledgeblock. The first entity in the index has the type `kb-index` which is a subtype of `entityfile`, and this entity is used to designate the knowledgeblock as a whole. This means that it can have both attributes that pertain to its role as describing its own entityfile, and attributes that pertain to the knowledgeblock as a whole.

One important use of the knowledgeblock index is to specify where the textfiles for other entityfiles in the same knowledgeblock are stored. The kb index specifies the mapping from entities as understood by Leordo, to actual file paths in the computer or filestore at hand.[7] This makes it straightforward to move entityfiles and to redirect references to them, which has a number of uses including that it makes it easy for several individuals to share some of their files.

A few of the entityfiles in a knowledgeblock have special properties or play special roles, besides its index. This applies in particular for ontology files. To the largest extent possible, entities in the core Leordo system and in its applications are organized in terms of an ontology which is subject to modularization like all other aspects of the

---

[7] Some Leordo individuals are placed on detachable memory devices, such as USB sticks, which means that they can have activations on different hosts without their file structure having been 'moved' in a conventional sense.

system. The kernel contains a 'core ontology', and every knowledgeblock contributes additional entities and links to the ontology, thereby extending the core. Each activation of an individual contains a working ontology that has been formed by loading and integrating the ontology files of the knowledgeblocks that have been loaded.

Entities in a knowledgeblock can be of three kinds with respect to mobility: *software specific, individual specific,* or *host specific.* These are defined as follows. If an individual is moved to another host, then it shall encounter host-specific entities of the new host instead of those it had on the old host, whereas software-specific and individual-specific entities are retained. On the other hand, if a knowledgeblock is exported from one individual to another then only the software-specific entities are exported and they will be used with the individual-specific entities of the receiving individual. Individual-specific information includes the history and experience of the individual; host-specific information includes, for example, the locations and properties of databases, printout devices, and other resources that the host can offer to a visiting software individual.

In the present Leordo design, each entityfile is required to have all its members of the same kind in this respect, so that the distinction between software specific, individual specific, and host specific applies to entityfiles as well. The knowledgeblock index specifies only the locations of software-specific entityfiles that belong to it. There are separate catalogs for all host-specific and for all individual-specific entityfiles.

14.3.2 Considerations for the design of KRE

Knowledge Representation Expressions (KRE) is a textual representation for information structures, and the above examples have given the flavor of this notation. The details of the syntax are described in a separate memo that is available on the Leordo website.[8] The present subsection shall discuss the design considerations that guided the definition of KRE.

The idea of allowing data structures to be expressed as text, and to define input and output of data structures accordingly, was pioneered by John McCarthy with Lisp 1.5.[9] It has been adopted in several interpretive or 'scripting' programming languages that are used

---

[8] http://www.ida.liu.se/ext/leonardo/
[9] http://www.lisp.org/alu/home

extensively, such as Perl[10] and Python.[11] It is also characteristic of high level message formats, such as the KQML.[12] With partly different goals, this tradition has also been continued in the XML family of information representation languages, including e.g. RDF and OWL besides XML itself.

There are several possible motivations for representing information structures textually, in text files or otherwise, and in particular, for the following situations.

 (i) For persistent storage of the information, between runs of computer programs.

 (ii) For presentation of the information to the user, and for allowing her or him to edit the information.

(iii) As a message format, for transmitting chunks of information from one executing process to another one.

(iv) For representation of internal system information, such as parameter settings for particular programs or services.

These alternatives apply regardless of whether the text files are used for representing pieces of code, application data, or declarations, ontologies, or other metadata.

The choice of representation may depend on which of these are the intended uses. In particular, if the second purpose is intended then it becomes important to have a representation that is convenient to read for the human. The poor lisibility of XML was apparently accepted because it was thought that XML coded information should mostly be seen and edited through graphical interfaces, and not directly by users or developers.

In our case, we wish to use KRE for all four of the above-mentioned purposes. We also have some other design requirements.

• The notation should be suitable for use in textbooks, research articles, and manuals. This strongly suggests that it should stay as close to conventional set theory notation as possible.

• Since the notation is going to be the basis for an entire computation system, including its programming-language aspects, it must be expressive enough for the needs of a programming language.

---

[10] http://www.perl.org/

[11] http://www.python.org/

[12] http://www.cs.umbc.edu/kqml/

- The notation is used for the ontology structure that is a backbone for the Leordo system. It must therefore be expressive enough for what is needed in ontologies.

These requirements led to the decision of not using an existing language or notation, but to design our own. The following aspects of the KRE language should be emphasized in particular.

(1) *The use of multiple bracket types.* Most programming languages use several kinds of parentheses and brackets, such as (...), [...], { ... }, and possibly others. On the other hand, representations for information structures often use a single kind of brackets, such as (...) in Lisp and < ... > in XML and other languages in the SGML tradition. This is sufficient in principle, but it makes it necessary to rewrite sets, sequences, and other "naturally parenthesized" structures along the lines of

```
(set a b c)
(sequence a b c)
```

and so on. LRX uses the multiple brackets approach and allows expressions such as

```
{a b c}
<a b c>
```

for sets and sequences, and in addition a few other kinds of brackets. This difference is trivial from an abstract point of view, but it makes surprisingly much difference for the ease of reading complex expressions. Compare, for example, the KRE reprsentation of the plan entity in example 2, which was as follows:

```
-----------------------------------------------------------
[: type method]
[: plan {[intend: t1 t2 (remex: lar-004 (query: makebid))]
        [intend: t1 t3 (query: makebid)]
        [intend: t4 t5 (query: propose-compromise)]}]
[: time-constraints {[afterall: {t2 t3} t4]}]
-----------------------------------------------------------
```

with a representation of *just the second line* of that information in an XML-style[13] single-bracket notation:

---

[13] http://www.w3.org/XML/

```
----------------------------------------------------------
<plan>
   <planstep-set>
      <planstep>
         <intendstep>
            <fromtime>t1</fromtime>
            <totime>t2</totime>
            <remote-execute>
               <execute-at>
                  <indiv-name>lar-004</indiv-name>
               </execute-at>
               <execute-what>
                  <query-action>
                     <phrase>makebid</phrase>
                  </query-action>
               </execute-what>
            </remote-execute>
         <intendstep>
      <planstep>
----------------------------------------------------------
```

Even the Lisp-style single-bracket representation is much less convenient to read than the multi-bracket representation:

```
----------------------------------------------------------
(maplet type method)
(maplet plan
   (set (record intend: t1 t2
           (term remex: lar-004 (term query: makebid)))
        (record intend: t1 t3 (term query: makebid))
        (record intend: t4 t5 (term query: propose-compromise))
           ))
(maplet time-constraints
   (set (constraint afterall (set t2 t3) t4)) )
----------------------------------------------------------
```

In a historical perspective it is interesting to compare the great interest in legibility issues when programming languages are designed, with the virtually complete disregard for the same issue in the design of so-called markup languages for representing structured information in general.

(2) *The use of composite expressions for entities.* KRE is similar to OWL, for example, in that it is based on the use of entities to which attributes and properties are assigned. In the simplest cases, entities are written as identifiers and attributes are expressions that are formed using set, sequence, and record forming operators. However, entities can also be composite expressions that are formed using a *symbolic function* and one or more arguments which are again atomic or composite expressions, for example as in

```
(payment: (membership: (member-number: 1452)
                       (year: 2006) ))
```

for "the payment for the membership during year 2006, by member number 1452", or

```
(b: 356 (remex: lar-004 (query: makebid)))
```

for "the instance of the action (query: makebid) that was initiated at time 356 for execution in the individual lar-004". Entities formed by composite expressions share the same characteristics as atomic entities, for example that they have a type and can be assigned attributes and properties, and that they can be included in entityfiles with their assignments.

The YAML (Yet Another Markup Language)[14] allows assigning attributes to composite structures, but does not make it possible to include such a composite structure as a term in a larger expression.

The use of composite entities has turned out to be very useful in the design of ontologies and other knowledge representations. It is included in the kernel of the Leordo system and is used in various ways even for representing "system" information in the kernel, as the second introductory example has showed. Another example is for intermediate structures in the version management subsystem. On higher levels of the design, there is an extension of LRX for representing formulas in first-order predicate calculus, in which case composite entities are identified with terms in the sense of logic.

(3) *The use of event-state records.* Records are formed in LRX using the notation of the following examples:

```
[date: 2006 10 24]
[quantity: meter 42195]
[quantity: (per: meter second) 46]
```

---

[14] http://www.yaml.org/

for the date of October 24, 2006, for the quantity of 42195 meters, and for the quantity of 46 meters per second, respectively. Records differ from composite entities in that they are passive data objects that can not be assigned attributes or properties.

One kind of records, called event-state records, actually allow some of their components to change, but in restricted ways. They are used for representing the current state of an action instance that the system is performing during a period of time, or the current observation state of an event that the system observes. An event record such as (simple example)

```
[move-robot: r14 pos12 pos14 :start 16:22
              :velocity [quantity: mps 4]
              :current-pos [xy-coordinate: 47 12]]
```

where `mps` is an abbreviation for (`per: meter second`), may represent the current state of an event where the robot `r14` moves from position `pos12` to position `pos14`. The record contains the three *direct arguments* of the operator `move-robot:`, and after them the three *state variables* of the event with the respective labels `:start`, `:velocity`, and `:current-pos`. The values of the state variables, except `:start`, can be changed while the event executes in order to reflect the current state of the robot concerned. When the event ends then the ending time is added as an additional state variable, other state variables are added or removed so that the record becomes a representation of the event as a whole and its final effects, the record freezes, and no further changes are possible in it.

An event-state record such as this may be the value of an attribute of an action-instance entity as formed by, for example, the symbolic function `b:` that was introduced previously.

14.4 The Leordo Kernel and platform

14.4.1 The structure and constituents

The Leordo Kernel consists of four knowledgeblocks, beginning with the *core* which is called `core-kb`. By convention, the names of knowledge-blocks end with "-kb". The core satisfies all the requirements on the kernel except version management. In addition there is `chronos-kb` that implements a representation of calendar-level time and of events in the lifecycle of an individual, `config-kb` that is used for creating new copies ("individuals") of the system and for configuring old and new individuals, and finally `syshist-kb` that implements version management. Both reproduction and version management add entries to the system's history of its own activities which is maintained by `chronos-kb`. For example, a so-called synchronization in the sense of version management is treated as an event in the representation provided by `chronos-kb`.

The more basic aspects of self-modification in the system are implemented in `core-kb`, however. This includes, for example, facilities for allowing the user to edit attributes and properties of an entity, and to add entities and entityfiles.

The core part of the Leordo ontology, called `coreonto`, is an entityfile within the the initial knowledgeblock `core-kb`. Every other knowledgeblock, including the other three kernel blocks, can have their own ontology files that extend preceding knowledgeblocks.

14.4.2 The Core Knowledgeblock, `core-kb`

The following are the contents of the core block, as organized in a number of entityfiles.

- The initial loading or 'bootstrap' machinery. It consists of a few entityfiles that are the very first ones to be loaded when an activation is started, and it prepares the ground for subsequent loading.

- The index file of the core knowledgeblock. (`core-kb`).

- The ontology file of the core knowledgeblock, which is at the same time the core or "top-level" ontology of Leordo as a whole. (`coreonto`).

- Miscellaneous additions to the core ontology that are needed for historical or other reasons. (`toponto`).

- Definitions of procedures for loading entityfiles and parsing the textual representation of entities. (`leo-preload`, `leoparse`).

- Definitions of elementary operations on the structured objects in the Leordo data representation, such as sequences, sets, and records. (`leoper`).

- Miscellaneous auxiliary functions that are needed in the other entityfiles but which have a general-purpose character. (`misc`).

- Major timepoints in the history of the present instance of the system (`mp-catal`).

- Functions for administrating entities, entityfiles, and knowledge-blocks, for example, for creating them and for editing their attributes. (`leo-admin`).
- Functions for writing the textual representation of entityfiles, and for producing the textual representation of Leordo datastructures from their internal ones. (`leoprint`).
- Definitions for a simple executive for command-line operation of the system. (`lite-exec`).

The entityfile `mp-catal` mostly serves `chronos-kb`, but it is initialized in the core block which is why it is present in this list.

Many of these blocks are straightforward and do not require further comment here; their details are described in the systems documentation. I have already described and discussed the data format for the textual representation of entityfiles. The files for loading and storing that representation (`leo-preload, leoparse, leoprint`) are direct implementations of the data format. Furthermore I shall discuss the ontology, the bootstrap machinery, the machinery for cataloguing entityfiles using knowledgebase index files, and the facility for defining multiple configurations within an individual. Final sections will describe the other parts of the kernel, namely, the facility for administrating and 'remembering' information about calendar-time-level events in the history of a Leordo individual, and the facility for version management of entityfiles.

14.4.3 The Leordo startup machinery

One of the basic requirements on the Leordo Kernel is that it shall be able to administrate itself, and in addition it shall provide facilities for self-administration of other knowledgeblocks that are built on top of the four knowledgeblocks in the kernel. This self-administration requirement includes several aspects.

- All program code in an implementation shall be represented as entityfiles, without exceptions. This guarantees that general facilities for administration and analysis of Leordo software can apply even to the initial parts of the bootstrap process.
- Since interactive sessions with the Leordo system typically involve loading information from the textual representation of entityfiles, modifying their contents, and re-storing those entityfiles, it shall be possible to edit all entityfiles for software in that way as well.

- However, it shall also be possible to text-edit the file representation of an entityfile and load it into an activation of Leordo, in order for the edits to take effect there.
- In addition, there shall be a version management system that applies to software entityfiles like for all other entityfiles.

The first three of these aspects is implemented using the `core-kb` knowledgeblock; the fourth one using the separate `syshist-kb` knowledgeblock. Notice, however, that the first aspect is a step towards (i.e. facilitates greatly) the fourth one.

The startup process for Leordo activations is actually a good illustration of how a somewhat complex process can be organized around its symbolic data structures. Appendix 4 describes this in some detail.

14.4.4 Configuration management

One Leordo individual may contain the software for a number of applications, for example for simulation, for robotics, for document management, and so on. However, it may not be necessary, or even desirable to have all of that software and its associated application data present in a particular activation of the system. The individual should therefore have several *configurations* that specify alternative ways of starting an activation. The startup files that were described above serve to define such configurations. In particular, the `kb-included` attribute specifies which knowledgeblocks are to be loaded when the system starts. Knowledgeblock dependencies whereby one knowledgeblock may require some other knowledgeblocks to be loaded first are supported, and are represented by particular attributes on the knowledgeblocks themselves.

Each configuration may also make some other specifications, for example for extra information that is to be loaded in order to start it. Furthermore, each configuration shall specify its user interface, in the sense of a command-line interpreter, a GUI, and/or a web-accessible service. This is done with the `execdef` attribute on the startup-file that was described in Appendix 4.

14.4.5 The Knowledgebase index files

Each Leordo individual is represented as a directory structure, consisting of a top-level directory and its various subdirectories on several levels, with their contents. In a predecessor to Leordo, the Software Individuals Architecture, we used fixed conventions for where the entityfiles would be located within the directory structure, and relative addressing for accessing them. This turned out to be too inflexible, and for Leordo we have a convention where each entity representing an entityfile is associated with the path to where the textual entityfile is to be found.

At first it would seem that this should be one of the attributes of the entity that names and describes the entityfile, and that is the first element in the entityfile. However, it would be pointless to put that attribute within the file itself, since the system needs it in order to find the file so it can load it. One can think of two ways out of this dilemma: either to divide the attributes of an entity into several groups that can be located in different physical files, or to construct a composite entity with the entityfile entity as its argument.

Both approaches have their pros and cons. Leordo does provide a mechanism for *overlays* whereby one can introduce entities and assign some attributes to them in one entityfile, and then add some more attributes in an overlay, which is a separate file. However, that facility is not part of the kernel, and we are reticent of putting too much into the kernel. Also, overlays require the entity as such to have been introduced first, before the overlay is added. The attribute for the location of an entityfile is needed before the entity itself is available.

We have therefore chosen the other alternative. The following is a typical entity in an index file for a knowledgeblock, such as `core-kb`:

```
----------------------------------------------------------
-- (location: leoadmin)

[: type location]
[: filepath "../../../leo-1/Coreblock/leoadmin"]

@Comment
Loading entityfiles and knowledgeblocks, creating new ones,
etc.


----------------------------------------------------------
```

It defines the location of the entityfile `leoadmin` by introducing a composite entity (`location: leoadmin`) whose type is `location`, and assigning a `filepath` attribute to it.[15] Among the files that occur at the beginning of the startup phase, `self-kb`, `kb-catal` and `core-kb` consist mostly or entirely of such entities.

14.5 Other kernel knowledgeblocks

Until this point we have described the design of the core knowledgeblock, `core-kb`. The Leordo kernel also contains three other knowledgeblocks, beginning with `chronos-kb` that enables the Leordo activation to register events and to have an awareness of the passing of time and a notion of its own history. Based on it there is the reproduction facility, `config-kb`, and the versions management facility, `syshist-kb`.

Both reproduction and version management are essential for the evolution of the Leordo software through concurrent strands of incremental change in several instances of the system, i.e. several Leordo individuals. This is the decisive factor for considering these to be an integral part of the system kernel. In addition, by doing so we also provide a set of tools that can be used in applications of several kinds. – The importance of having software tools for version administration do not need to be explained; it has been proven through the very widespread use of tools such as CVS.[16]

The following are brief summaries of the services that are provided by these knowledgeblocks in the kernel:

14.5.1 Awareness of time in the Leordo individual

The basic contributions in `chronos-kb` are listed here.

- A facility for defining and registering significant *timepoints*. Such a timepoint is registered with its date, hour, minutes, and seconds, and it can be associated with the starting or ending of events.
- A facility for introducing *events* in a descriptive sense: the system is told that a particular event starts or ends, and registers that information.
- A facility for defining *sessions* which are composite events corresponding to the duration of one activation of the Leordo system, and for defining individual events within the session.

---

[15] Actually this attribute is called `filename` in the current system, for historical reasons. This is due to be changed.

[16] `http://www.nongnu.org/cvs/`

All of this information is built up within the Leordo system, and is maintained persistently by placing it in entityfiles.

14.5.2 System history and version management

The system history is a kind of skeleton on which several kinds of contributions can be attached. The first of these is the version management facility which consists of two parts, one that is local within an individual, and one that requires the use of two individuals.

Local version management works as follows. The individual maintains a sequence of *archive-points* which are effectively a subset of the timepoints that are registered by `chronos-kb`. Archive-points have names of the form `ap-1234`, allowing up to 9999 archivepoints in one individual. Each archive-point is associated with the archiving of a selection of files from one particular knowledgeblock. The archiving *action* takes a knowledgeblock as argument, obtains a new archivepoint, and for each entityfile in the knowledgeblock it compares the current contents of the file with those of the latest archived version of the same file. It then allocates a new directory, named after the new archive-point, and places copies there of all entityfiles where a nontrivial difference has been identified. The archive-point is an entity that is provided with attributes specifying its timepoint, its knowledgeblock, the set of names for all entityfiles in the knowledgeblock at the present time, and the set of names for those entityfiles that have been archived.

However, the comparison between current and archived version of the entityfile also has a side-effect on the current file, namely, that each entity in the file is provided with an attribute specifying the most recent archive-point where a change has been observed in that particular entity. This makes it possible to make version management on the level of entities, and not merely on entire files, which is important for resolving concurrent updates of the same entityfile in different individuals.

Local version management is useful for backup if mistaken edits have destroyed existing code, but it does not help if several users make concurrent changes in a set of entityfiles. This is what *two-party version management* is for. In this case, there is one 'server' individual that keeps track of updates by several users, and one 'client' that does its own updates and sometimes 'synchronizes'[17] with the server. Such

---

[17] This is the usual term, although it is of course a terrible misuse of the word 'synchronize'.

synchronization must always be preceded by a local archiving action in the client. Then, downward synchronization allows the client to update its entityfiles with those changes that have been incorporated into the server at a time that succeeds the latest synchronized update in the client. If the current entityfile version in the client is not a direct or indirect predecessor of the version that is presently in the server, then no change is made. After that, an upward synchronization identifies those entityfiles whose contents still differ between the server and the client. If the version in the server precedes, directly or indirectly, the current version in the client, then the current version in the client is imposed on the server.

In the remaining cases, the system attempts to resolve concurrent changes in a particular entityfile by going to the level of the individual entities. If that is not sufficient, the user is asked to resolve the inconsistency.

A particular technical problem arises because these synchronization actions require the Leordo activation to read and compare several versions of the same entityfile. The problem is that normally, reading such a file makes assignments to attributes and properties of the entities in the file, but for synchronization purposes one does not wish the definitions in one file to replace the definitions that were obtained from another file. This problem is solved using composite entities, as follows: The procedure for reading an entityfile in KRE format has an optional parameter whose value, if it is present, should be a symbolic function of one argument. If it is absent then the file is read as usual. If it is present, on the other hand, then that function is applied to each entity that is read from the file, obtaining a 'wrapped' entity, and the attributes and properties in the file are assigned to the wrapped entity. After this, the comparisons and updates can proceed in the obvious way.

We have now seen two examples of how symbolic functions and composite entities have been useful even for internal purposes within the kernel. This illustrates the potential value of reorganizing the overall software architecture so that certain, generally useful facilities are brought into, or closer to the system kernel, instead of treating them as specific to applications.

14.5.3 Configuration and reproduction of individuals

One of the important ideas in Leordo is that the system shall be self-aware, so that it is able to represent its own internal state, to analyze it and to modify it, and it shall be able to represent and "understand" its own history. Furthermore, all of this shall occur in persistent ways and over calendar time, and not only within one activation or "run" of the system.

We believe that these properties are important for a number of applications, but in particular for those that belong to, or border on artificial intelligence, for example for "intelligent agents". A system that acquires information during its interactions with users and with the physical world, and that is able to learn from experience for example using case-based techniques, will certainly need to have persistence. It does not make sense for the system to start learning again each time a new activation is started. It is then a natural step to also provide the system with a sense of its own history.

One must then define what is "the system" that has that persistence and sense of its own history. What if the software is stored in a server and is used on a number of thin clients that only contain the activations? What if several copies of it are taken and placed on different hosts? What if a copy of the system is placed on a USB stick so that it can be used on several different hosts?

In the case of Leordo, the answer is in principle that each individual is a self-contained structure that contains all of the software that it needs. Different individuals may contain equal copies of that software, but in addition each of them contains its own history and its own "experience". However, it is also perfectly possible for each individual to modify its software so that it comes to differ from the software of its peers.

What if additional copies (individuals) are needed, for example because additional persons wish to use the system? The simplest solution is to have an archive individual from which one takes copies for distribution, but in any case that archive individual will change over time, so a notion of version or generation of the entire individual will be needed. But more importantly, separate strands of the Leordo species may develop in different directions, and a particular new user may be more interested in obtaining a copy of his friend's Leordo rather than one from the archive.

In principle, a new individual that is obtained from a Leordo individual by copying its software but erasing its history and other local information, is to be considered as an "offspring" and not as a "copy". If the copy is perfect and all history is preserved in it, then it shall be called a "clone". The administration of clones offers additional problems that will not be addressed here.

For offspring, the following conventions are adopted. The making of an offspring from an individual is to be considered as an action of that individual, and is to be recorded in its history. Each individual has a *name*, and the offspring of a particular individual are numbered from 1 and up. No individual is allowed to have more than 999 offspring. The first individual under this scheme was called `lar`, and its direct offspring are called `lar-001`, `lar-002`, etc. The offspring of `lar-002` are called `lar-002-001`, `lar-002-002`, and so forth. The abbreviation `lar` stands for "Leordo Ancestry Root".

The overall convention for the population of Leordo individuals is now that new individuals can only be produced as offspring of existing ones, so that the parent is aware of the offspring being produced and so that no name clashes can occur in the population. Additional information about when and where offspring are produced is of course valuable, but can be considered as add-on information.

Notice in particular that version management information is not inherited by offspring, and they start with an empty backup directory as well as an empty memory of past events.

In principle, each new individual should obtain a copy of all the software of its parent. In practice this is quite inconvenient when several individuals are stored on the same host; one would like them to be able to share some of the software files. This has been implemented as follows: Each individual may identify another individual that is known as its "provider", and when its index files specify the locations of entityfiles, they may refer both to files in its own structure, and files in its provider. An individual is only allowed to update entityfiles of its own, and is not supposed to update entityfiles in its provider.[18] When a new individual is created, then it is first produced with a minimal number of files of its own, and it relies on its parent as its provider for most of the entityfiles. After that, it is up to the offspring to copy whatever software it needs from its provider to itself, until it can cut that umbillical cord. Only then is it in a position to migrate to other hosts. Besides, given adequate software, it may be able to import knowledgeblocks and entityfiles from other individuals and not only from its parent.

What has been said so far applies to Leordo-specific software. In addition, applications in Leordo will often need to access other software that is available in the individual's host for its current activation, for

---

[18] This restriction is not enforced at present, but users violate it at their own risk.

example text editors and formatters. The kernel contains a systematic framework for administrating this.

Facilities for reproduction of individuals were first developed in the earlier project towards the *Software Individuals Architecture.* In that project we considered reproduction and knowledge transfer between individuals to be very central in the architecture, besides the abilities for self-modelling. In our present approch reproduction has been relegated to a somewhat less central position, due to the experience of the previous project.

14.5.4 Other facilities in the kernel

The four knowledgeblocks in the kernel also contain a number of other facilities that have not been described here. In particular, there is a concept of a "process" in a particular sense of that word. Leordo processes are persistent things, so they exist on calendar time and not only within one activation of the system. Each process has its own subdirectories where it maintains its local state between activations, and each activation is an activation *of* one particular process. Each process can only have one activation at a time, but different processes can have activations concurrently.

14.6 Platform facilities

The next layer in the Leordo software architecture, after the kernel, is called the *platform.* This layer is under construction and is intended to be open-ended, so that new contributions can be added continuously as the need is identified and the implementation is completed. The following are some platform-level knowledgeblocks that exist and are in use at present.

14.6.1 Channels

Leordo channels are a mechanism for sending messages between individuals, for the purpose of requesting actions or transmitting information. Each channel connects two specific individuals for two-way, ansynchronous communication and is associated with a number of attributes, including one specifying the data format to be used for the messages. The KRE data format is the default choice.

14.6.2 Communicable executive

The initial example in this article describing the interactions between two Leordo individuals was executed using our *communicable executive* (CX). The basic command-line executive in the kernel is not sufficient for it. CX performs incessantly a cycle where it does three things:

- Check whether an input line has been received from the user. If so, act on it.
- Check what messages have arrived in the incoming branch of the currently connected channels for this individual. If so, pick up the messages and act on them.
- Visit all the currently executing actions in the present individual, and apply an update procedure that is attached to each of them. This procedure may perform input and output, update the local state of the action, and terminate the action with success or failure, if appropriate.

The communicable executive is a natural basis for several kinds of applications, including for some kinds of robotic systems, dialog systems, and simulation systems.

14.7 The implemented leordo system

14.7.1 History of the experimental implementation

The design for Leordo started in early 2005. It was based on the earlier experience with the Software Individuals Architecture (SIA), and with several earlier systems before that. The SIA was used as the platform the a major part of the Linköping-WITAS Robotic Dialog Environment, RDE,[19] which contributed valuable background for the present system.

During the almost three years of Leordo development we have tried to make 'laboratory notes' documenting what steps were taken, what design changes were made, and so on. We shall study the possibility of extracting a more concise account of essential design decisions and design changes from these laboratory notes.

14.7.2 Current usage

The goal of the Leordo project, as stated in the introduction to this article, is to validate or refute the project's hypothesis concerning the possibility of a fully integrated software system architecture. In order to

---

[19] http://www.ida.liu.se/ext/casl/

test this hypothesis it is necessary both to implement the system kernel, and to use it for a few different applications of widely different character.

Two such applications have been fully implemented and are in regular use. This is a way of checking that the system is always kept operational while it is being revised and extended continuously.

The present author uses a Leordo-based software application as his standard tool for the preparation of articles and other documents and for website pages, including the extensive CAISOR website.[20] This application has been in daily use since the year 2006.

Secondly, Leordo is used for the management and extension of the Common Knowledge Library and its website. This support system is a fairly large collection of routines for acquisition, revision, and presentation of structured information, including version management, IPR management, and type checking of large information structures.

Plans for the future include the porting to Leordo of the previously written applications for simulation of a robotic environment and for user dialog with such a robot.

14.8 Discussion: the need for software system consolidation

The main goal of the Leordo project, as we stated initially, is to explore the possibility of obtaining a much simpler design of the overall software system in a computer, in particular by reorganizing and realigning its major parts so as to eliminate duplication of concepts and of software facilities. It is not yet possible to evaluate the concrete, experimental Leordo system design against that goal, but it is possible to identify how the new design relates to some of the concrete redundancies in conventional systems. They are listed here.

Duplication of procedural language between operating system (shell scripts) and programming languages. In Leordo there is a host language which may vary between generations of the system, but which shall in any case be a language of the 'interpretive' or 'script' type, such as Scheme, Python, etc. The Leordo kernel provides the command-script situation, and the language can be extended with more facilities, and restricted by using, for example, type system, in order to satisfy the needs of other usage situations.

Duplication of notations and systems for type declarations of data structures, between programming languages, database systems,

---

[20] http://www.ida.liu.se/ext/caisor/

communication systems e.g. CORBA, etc. The two-layered approach to the type system in Leordo was explained in the beginning of Section 14.2. Exactly because the type system is not built into the system kernel, we foresee that it shall be possible to design it in such a flexible way that it can satisfy the varying needs of several kinds of contemporary type systems. This is of course one aspect of the main design hypothesis that was stated at the beginning of the present report.

Scripting languages in various software tools, for example spreadsheet systems, webpage languages such as Javascript, etc. The idea is that such tools ought to be implemented based on the Leordo kernel and inherit its facilities, including in particular the use of the host language.

Duplication between the file-directory system and database systems. Although the present, temporary implementation of Leordo is based on a conventional operating system and makes fairly extensive use of its file system, the long-term idea is to replace it with an implementation of entities and aggregates of entities that is done on directly on the base software. This new information structure shall then subsume what the file-directory system does today.

In the continued work on Leordo we are going to build a number of applications for the purpose of obtaining additional experience with these and other aspects of duplication. At the same time we shall be vigilant in monitoring what new duplications may arise as the system and the applications grow in size and complexity.

References

Due to the character of this material, most of the references are to websites that provide information about a particular language or system. These references have been placed in footnotes on the page where the reference occurs.

References to published articles and released reports from the Leordo project can be found on the project website.[21] References to published articles from the preceding Software Individuals Architecture project (SIA) can be found on its past project website.[22]

---

[21] http://www.ida.liu.se/ext/leonardo/
[22] http://www.ida.liu.se/ext/caisor/systems/sia/page.html

15

Theorem-proving support in programming language semantics

Yves Bertot

INRIA Sophia-Antipolis Méditerranée

This paper is dedicated to the memory of Gilles Kahn, my thesis advisor, my mentor, my friend.

Abstract

We describe how the formal description of a programming language can be encoded in the Coq theorem prover. Four aspects are covered: Natural semantics (as advocated by Gilles Kahn), axiomatic semantics, denotational semantics, and abstract interpretation. We show that most of these aspects have an executable counterpart and describe how this can be used to support proofs about programs.

15.1 Introduction

Nipkow demonstrated in [25] that theorem provers could be used to formalize many aspects of programming language semantics. In this paper, we want to push the experiment further to show that this formalization effort also has a practical outcome, in that it makes it possible to integrate programming tools inside theorem provers in an uniform way. We re-visit the study of operational, denotational semantics, axiomatic semantics, and weakest pre-condiction calculus as already studied by Nipkow and we add a small example of a static analysis tool based on abstract interpretation.

To integrate the programming tools inside the theorem prover we rely on the possibility to execute the algorithms after they have been formally described and proved correct, a technique known as *reflection* [3, 11]. We also implemented a parser, so that the theorem prover can be used as a playground to experiment on sample programs. We performed this

From *Semantics to Computer Science Essays in Honour of Gilles Kahn*, eds Yves Bertot, Gérard Huet, Jean-Jacques Lévy and Gordon Plotkin. Published by Cambridge University Press. © Cambridge University Press 2009.

experiment using the Coq system [17, 8]. The tools that are formally described can also be "extracted" outside the proof environment, so that they become stand alone programs [23].

The desire to use computers to verify proofs about programming language semantics was probably one of the main incentives for the design of modern interactive theorem provers. The LCF system was a pioneer in this direction. The theory of programming languages was so grounded in basic mathematics that a tool such as LCF was quickly recognized as a tool in which mathematical reasoning can also be simulated and proofs can be verified by decomposing them in sound basic logical steps. LCF started a large family of theorem-proving tools, among which HOL [19] and Isabelle [26] have achieved an outstanding international recognition. Nipkow's experiments were conducted using Isabelle.

In the family of theorem-proving tools, there are two large sub-families: there are the direct descendants of the LCF system [20], which rely on simply-typed λ-calculus and the axioms of higher-order logic to provide foundations for a large portion of mathematics; on the other hand, there are systems descending from de Bruijn's Automath system and Martin-Löf's theory of types, where propositions are directly represented as types, "non-simple" types, namely dependent types, can be used to represent quantified statements, and typed functions are directly used to represent proofs. In systems of the LCF family, typed λ-terms are used in the representation of logical statements and proofs are objects of another nature. In systems of the latter family, usually called type theory-based theorem-proving tools, typed λ-terms are used both in the representation of logical statements and in the representation of proofs. Well-known members of the type theory-based family of theorem-proving tools are Nuprl [13], Agda [14], and Coq.

The fact that typed λ-terms are used both to represent logical statements and proofs in type theory-based theorem-proving tools has the consequence that computation in the typed λ-calculus plays a central role, because verifying that a theorem is applied to an argument of the right form may require an arbitrary large computation in these systems. By contrast, computation plays only a secondary role in LCF-style theorem-proving tools and facilities to execute programs efficiently to support proofs was only added recently [4].

With structural operational semantics and natural semantics, Gordon Plotkin and Gilles Kahn provided systematic approaches to describing programming languages relying mostly on the basic concepts of inductive types and inductive propositions. Execution states are represented as environments, in other words lists of pairs binding a variable name and a value. Programs themselves can also be represented as an inductive data-type, following the tradition of *abstract syntax* trees, a streamlined form of parsing trees. Execution of instructions can then be described as inductive propositions, where executing an instruction is described as a ternary relation between an input environment, an instruction, and an output value. The execution of each program construct is described by composing "smaller" executions of this construct or its sub-components.

Another approach to semantics is to express that a program links properties of inputs with properties of outputs. In other words, one provides a logical system to describe under which condition on a program's input a given condition on the program's output can be guaranteed (as long as the program terminates). This style of description is known as *axiomatic semantics* and was proposed by Hoare [21]. We can again use an inductive type to represent properties of input and output of programs. We will show that axiomatic semantics can easily be described using inductive properties and recursive functions and we will prove the consistency with the initial operational semantics. Axiomatic semantics also supports an algorithmic presentation, known as a *verification condition generator* for the *weakest pre-condition calculus* as advocated by Dijkstra [16]. Again, we provide an implementation of this generator, a proof that it is correct, and examples of using this through reflection to establish properties of sample programs.

The next style of semantic description that we will study will be the style known as *denotational semantics* or *domain theory*, actually the style that motivated the first implementation of the LCF system. Here, the semantics of the instructions is described as a collection of partial functions from a type of inputs to a type of outputs. The kind of functions that are commonly used in type-theory-based theorem-proving tools are not directly suited for this approach, for fundamental reasons. We will show which axioms of classical logical can be used to provide a simple encoding of the partial functions we need. However, using these axioms precludes computing inside the theorem prover, so that the function we obtain is executable only after extraction outside the theorem prover. This approach can still be used to derive an interpreter, a tool to execute programs, with a guarantee that the interpreter respects the reference operational semantics.

The last aspect is an approach to the static analysis of programs known as *abstract interpretation*. While other approaches aim at giving a completely precise understanding of what happens in programs, abstract interpretation focuses on hiding enough details so that the information that is obtained from the analysis is easier to manage and more importantly the computations to perform the analysis can be performed automatically with guaranteed termination.

These experiments are available as a Coq contribution [7].

15.1.1 Related work

The main reference we used on programming language semantics is Winskel's text book [32].

Many publications have been provided to show that these various aspects of programming language could be handled in theorem provers. Our first example is [9] where we described the correctness of a program transformation tool with respect to the language's operational semantics. This work was performed in the context of the Centaur system [10] where semantic descriptions could be executed with the help of a prolog interpreter or reasoned about using a translation to the Coq theorem prover [29]. The most impressive experiment is described in [25], who approximately formalizes the first 100 pages of Winskel's book, thus including a few more proofs around the relations between operational semantics, axiomatic semantics, and denotational semantics than we describe here. The difference between our work and Nipkow's is that we rely more on reflection and make a few different choices, like the choice to provide a minimal syntax for assertions, while Nipkow directly uses meta-level logical formulas and thus avoid the need to describe substitution. On the other hand, our choice of an abstract syntax for assertions makes it possible to integrate our verification generator with a parser, thus providing a more user-friendly approach to annotated programs.

The work on denotational semantics is a transposition and a reduction of the work on domain theory that could already be described formally in the framework of *logic of computable functions*, in Isabelle [24].

The study of interactions between abstract interpretation and theorem provers is the object of more recent work. Intermediate approaches use abstract interpreters to generate proofs of correctness of programs in axiomatics semantics as in [12]. Pichardie [27] provides a more advanced formal study than ours, however our approach has the advantage of being based on natural semantics: thanks to this, recursion can be based on the structure of programs, while his approach imposes using the style of well-founded induction, which makes it ill-suited for reflection.

Application domains for theorem prover-aware formal semantics of programming languages abound. Nipkow and his team [31], Jacobs and his team [30], and Barthe and his team [2, 6] showed the benefits there could be in describing the Java programming language and the Java virtual machine, to verify soundness properties of the byte-code verifier and apply this to the guarantees of the security that the Java language and its Smartcard-aware offspring, JavaCard. More recent work by Leroy and his team show that this work can be extended to the formalization of efficient compilers. The interest is also spreading in the community of researchers working on the design of programming language, as witnessed by the success of the PoplMark challenge [1].

15.2 Concrete and abstract syntax

We consider a *while loop* programing language with simple arithmetic expressions: it is the Imp language of [25] without the conditional instruction. The language has been trimmed to a bare skeleton, but still retains the property of being Turing complete. We will use ρ as meta-variables for variable declarations (we will also often use the word *environment*), e for expressions, b for boolean expressions, and i for instructions. We use an infinite denumerable set of variable names whose elements are written $x, y, x_1, \ldots$ and we use n, n_1, n' to represent integers. The syntactic categories are defined as follows:

$$\rho ::= (x, n) \cdot \rho | \emptyset \qquad e ::= n \mid x \mid e{+}e \qquad b ::= e < e$$

$$i ::= \text{skip} \mid x{:}{=}e \mid i;i \mid \text{while } b \text{ do } i \text{ done}$$

The intended meaning of most of these constructs should be obvious.

In the theorem prover, we use inductive types to describe these syntactic categories. The convention that numbers are expressions needs to be modified: there is a constructor **anum** in the type of arithmetic expression **aexpr** that maps a number to the corresponding expression. Similarly, variable names are transformed into arithmetic expressions and assignments just use variable names as first components.

Inductive aexpr : Type :=
  avar (s : string) | anum (n : Z) | aplus (e$_1$ e$_2$:aexpr).

Inductive bexpr : Type := blt (e$_1$ e$_2$: aexpr).

Inductive instr : Type :=
  assign (s: string)(e:aexpr) | sequence (i$_1$ i$_2$:instr)
  | while (b:bexpr)(i:instr) | skip.

15.3 Operational semantics

15.3.1 Evaluation and environment update

15.3.1.1 Inference rules

We will describe the evaluation of expressions using judgments of the form $\rho \vdash e \rightarrow v$ or $\rho \vdash b \rightarrow v$ (with a straight arrow). These judgments should be read as *in environment ρ, the arithmetic expression e (resp. the expression b) has the value v*. The value v is an integer or a boolean value depending on the kind of expression being evaluated. The rules describing evaluation are as follows:

$$\frac{}{\rho \vdash n \rightarrow n} \qquad \frac{}{(x,n) \cdot \rho \vdash x \rightarrow n}$$

$$\frac{\rho \vdash x \rightarrow n \quad x \neq y}{(y,n') \cdot \rho \vdash x \rightarrow n} \qquad \frac{\rho \vdash e_1 \rightarrow n_1 \quad \rho \vdash e_2 \rightarrow n_2}{\rho \vdash e_1 + e_2 \rightarrow n_1 + n_2}$$

$$\frac{\rho \vdash e_1 \rightarrow n_1 \quad \rho \vdash e_2 \rightarrow n_2 \quad n_1 < n_2}{\rho \vdash e_1 < e_2 \rightarrow \mathsf{true}}$$

$$\frac{\rho \vdash e_1 \rightarrow n_1 \quad \rho \vdash e_2 \rightarrow n_2 \quad n_2 \leq n_1}{\rho \vdash e_1 < e_2 \rightarrow \mathsf{false}}$$

During the execution of instructions, we will regularly need describing the modification of an environment, so that the value associated to a variable is modified. We use judgments of the form $\rho \vdash x, n \mapsto \rho'$, which should be read as *x has a value in ρ and ρ' and the value for x in ρ' is n; every other variable that has a value in ρ has the same value in ρ'.* This is simply described using two inference rules, in the same spirit as rules to evaluate variables.

15.3.1.2 Theorem prover encoding

Judgments of the form $\cdot \vdash \cdot \rightarrow \cdot$ are represented by three-argument inductive predicates named aeval and beval. We need to have two predicates to account for the fact that the same judgment is actually used to describe the evaluations of expressions of two different types. The encoding of premises is quite straightforward using nested implications, and we add universal quantifications for every variable that occurs in the inference rules. All inference rules for a given judgment are grouped in a single inductive definition. This makes it possible to express that the meaning of the judgment $\cdot \vdash \cdot \rightarrow \cdot$ is expressed by these inferences *and only these inferences rules.*

Environments are encoded as lists of pairs, so that the empty environment is encoded as nil and the environment $(x,n) \cdot \rho$ is (x,n)::r when r is the encoding of ρ.

Definition env := list(string*Z).

Inductive aeval : env → aexpr → Z → Prop :=
  ae_int : ∀ r n, aeval r (anum n) n
| ae_var$_1$: ∀ r x n, aeval ((x,n)::r) (avar x) n
| ae_var$_2$: ∀ r x y v v' , x ≠ y → aeval r (avar x) v → aeval ((y,v')::r) (avar x) v
| ae_plus : ∀ r e$_1$ e$_2$ v$_1$ v$_2$, aeval r e$_1$ v$_1$ → aeval r e$_2$ v$_2$ →
          aeval r (aplus e$_1$ e$_2$) (v$_1$ + v$_2$).

Inductive beval : env → bexpr → bool → Prop :=
| be_lt$_1$: ∀ r e$_1$ e$_2$ v$_1$ v$_2$, aeval r e$_1$ v$_1$ → aeval r e$_2$ v$_2$ → v$_1$ < v$_2$ →
          beval r (blt e$_1$ e$_2$) true
| be_lt$_2$: ∀ r e$_1$ e$_2$ v$_1$ v$_2$, aeval r e$_1$ v$_1$ → aeval r e$_2$ v$_2$ → v$_2$ ≤ v$_1$ →
          beval r (blt e$_1$ e$_2$) false.

The four place judgment $\cdot \vdash \cdot, \cdot \mapsto \cdot$ is also encoded as an inductive definition for a predicate named update.

Induction principles are automatically generated for these declarations of inductive predicates. These induction principles are instrumental for the proofs presented later in the paper.

15.3.2 Functional encoding

The judgment $\rho \vdash e \to n$ actually describes a partial function. To describe a partial function, we use the type constructor option, which defines a new type with an extra element None.

Inductive option (A:Type) : Type := Some : A → option A | None : option A.

We describe the evaluation function in two steps with lookup and af, which return values in option Z. When computing additions, we need to compose partial functions. For this, we define a bind function that takes care of undefined values in intermediate results. The pre-defined function string_dec is used to compare two strings.

Fixpoint lookup (r:env)(s:string){struct r} : option Z :=
match r with
nil ⇒ None | (a,b)::tl ⇒ if (string_dec a s) then Some b else lookup tl s
end.

Definition bind (A B:Type)(v:option A)(f:A→option B) : option B :=
  match v with Some x ⇒ f x | None ⇒ None end.

```
Fixpoint af (r:env)(e:aexpr) {struct e} : option Z :=
match e with
  avar index ⇒ lookup r index
| anum n ⇒ Some n
| aplus e₁ e₂ ⇒ bind (af r e₁) (fun v₁ ⇒ bind (af r e₂) (fun v₂ ⇒ Some (v₁+v₂)))
end.
```

We can define functions bf to evaluate boolean expressions and uf to compute updated environments in a similar way.

We use two functions to describe the evaluation of arithmetic expressions, the Fixpoint construct imposes that one states which argument is decreasing at each call: for lookup it is the environment and for af it is the expression.

With aeval and af, we have two encodings of the same concept. We show that these encodings are equivalent with the following lemmas.

Lemma lookup_aeval : ∀ r s v, lookup r s = Some v → aeval r (avar s) v.

Lemma af_eval : ∀ r e v, af r e = Some v → aeval r e v.

Lemma aeval_f : ∀ r e n, aeval r e n → af r e = Some n.

The proof of the first lemma is done by induction on the structure of r, the proof of the second lemma is done by induction on e, while the proof of the third lemma is done by induction on the structure of the proof for aeval (using the induction principle, which is generated when the inductive predicate is declared). Using simple proof commands, each of these proofs is less than ten lines long.

15.3.3 Natural semantics

With *natural semantics* [22], Gilles Kahn proposed that one should rely on judgments expressing the execution of program fragments until they terminate. The same style was also called *big-step* semantics. The main advantage of this description style is that it supports very concise descriptions for sequential languages. For our little language with four instructions, we only need five inference rules.

We rely on judgments of the form $\rho \vdash i \rightsquigarrow \rho'$ (with a twisted arrow). These judgments should be read as *executing i from the initial environment ρ terminates and yields the new environment ρ'*.

$$\frac{}{\rho \vdash \mathsf{skip} \rightsquigarrow \rho} \qquad \frac{\rho \vdash e \rightarrow n \qquad \rho \vdash x, n \mapsto \rho'}{\rho \vdash x{:}{=}e \rightsquigarrow \rho'}$$

$$\frac{\rho \vdash i_1 \rightsquigarrow \rho' \qquad \rho' \vdash i_2 \rightsquigarrow \rho''}{\rho \vdash i_1;i_2 \rightsquigarrow \rho''} \qquad \frac{\rho \vdash b \rightarrow \mathsf{false}}{\rho \vdash \mathsf{while}\ b\ \mathsf{do}\ i\ \mathsf{done} \rightsquigarrow \rho}$$

$$\frac{\rho \vdash b \rightarrow \mathsf{true} \quad \rho \vdash i \rightsquigarrow \rho' \quad \rho' \vdash \mathsf{while}\ b\ \mathsf{do}\ i\ \mathsf{done} \rightsquigarrow \rho''}{\rho \vdash \mathsf{while}\ b\ \mathsf{do}\ i\ \mathsf{done} \rightsquigarrow \rho''}$$

Because it is described using collections of rules, the judgment $\cdot \vdash \cdot \rightsquigarrow \cdot$ can be described with an inductive predicate exactly like the judgments for evaluation and update. We use the name exec for this judgment.

It is also possible to describe the programming language as a transition semantics in which each transition maps the pair of an environment and an instruction to a new environment and instruction. The transition only describes an elementary step of execution and the new instruction describes what remains to be done. This style is called *structural operational semantics* or *small step semantics* and was advocated by Plotkin [28]. We also developed a small-step description of the language and proved its consistency with the natural semantics, but we will not describe it in this paper, for lack of space.

As with the judgment $\rho \vdash e \rightarrow v$, the judgment $\rho \vdash i \rightsquigarrow \rho'$ actually describes a partial function. However, this partial function cannot be described as a structural recursive function as we did when defining the functions lookup and af. For while loops, such a function would present a recursive call where neither the environment nor the instruction argument would be a sub-structure of the corresponding initial argument. This failure also relates to the fact that the termination of programs is undecidable for this kind of language, while structural recursion would provide a terminating tool to compute whether programs terminate. In the later section on denotational semantics, we will discuss ways to encode a form of recursion that is powerful enough to describe the semantics as a recursive function.

15.4 Axiomatic semantics

We study now the encoding of axiomatic semantics as proposed by Hoare [21] and the weakest pre-condition calculus as proposed by Dijkstra [16].

The principle of this semantic approach is to consider properties that are satisfied by the variables of the program before and after the execution.

15.4.1 The semantic rules

To describe this approach, we use judgments of the following form: $\{P\}i\{Q\}$. This should be read as *if P is satisfied before executing i and executing i terminates, then Q is guaranteed to be satisfied after executing i.* These judgments are also called *Hoare triples*.

There are two key aspects in axiomatic semantics: first the behavior of assignment is explained by substituting variables with arithmetic expressions; second the behavior of control operators is explained by isolating properties that are independent from the choice made in the control operator and properties that can be deduced from this choice.

$$\frac{}{\{P\}\mathsf{skip}\{P\}} \qquad \frac{\{P\}i_1\{Q\} \quad \{Q\}i_2\{R\}}{\{P\}i_1;i_2\{R\}}$$

$$\frac{}{\{P[x \leftarrow e]\}x{:}{=}e\{P\}} \qquad \frac{\{b \wedge P\}i\{P\}}{\{P\}\mathsf{while}\ b\ \mathsf{do}\ i\ \mathsf{done}\{\neg b \wedge P\}}$$

$$\frac{P \Rightarrow P_1 \quad \{P_1\}i\{Q_1\} \quad Q_1 \Rightarrow Q}{\{P\}i\{Q\}}$$

In the rule for while loops, the property P corresponds to something that should be verified whether the loop body is executed 0, 1, or many times: it is independent from the choice made in the control operator. However, when the loop terminates, one knows that the test must have failed, this is why the output property for the loop contains $\neg b$. Also, P should be preserved through execution of the loop body, but only when the test is satisfied, this is why the premise has b in the left-hand side assertion.

We call the first four rules *structural rules*. The last rule, known as the *consequence* rule, makes it possible to include logical reasoning about the properties. To prove the two premises that are implications, it is necessary to master the actual meaning of the properties, conjunction, and negation.

15.4.2 Theorem-prover encoding

The first step is to define a data-type for assertions. Again, we keep things minimal. Obviously, the inference rules require that the language of assertions contain at least conjunctions, negations, and tests from the language's boolean expressions. We also include the possibility to have abitrary predicates on arithmetic expressions, represented by a name given as a string.

Inductive assert : Type :=
  a_b (b: bexpr) | a_not (a: assert) | a_conj (a a': assert)
  | pred (s: string)(l: int aexpr).

Inductive condition : Type := c_imp (a a':assert).

The type condition contains the implications that used for the consequence rule.

For variables that occur inside arithmetic expressions, we use valuation functions of type string$\rightarrow$ Z instead of environments and we define a new function af' (respectively bf', lf') to compute the value of an arithmetic expression (respectively boolean expressions, lists of arithmetic expressions) for a given valuation. The function af' is more practical to use and define than af because it is total, while af was partial.

Fixpoint af' (g:string$\rightarrow$Z)(e:aexpr) {struct e}: Z :=
match e with avar s $\Rightarrow$ g s | anum n $\Rightarrow$ n | aplus e_1 e_2 $\Rightarrow$ af' g e_1 + af' g e_2 end.

To give a meaning to assertion predicates, we use lists of pairs associating names and Coq predicates on lists of integers as *predicate* environments and we have a function f_p to map an environment and a string to a predicate on integers.

With all these functions, we can interpret assertions as propositional values using a function i_a and conditions using a function i_c.

Definition p_env := list(string*(list Z$\rightarrow$Prop)).

Fixpoint i_a (m: p_env)(g:string$\rightarrow$Z)(a:assert) : Prop :=
  match a with
    a_b e $\Rightarrow$ bf' g e | a_not a $\Rightarrow$ ~ i_a m g a
  | pred p l $\Rightarrow$ f_p m p (lf' g l) | a_conj a_1 a_2 $\Rightarrow$ i_a m g a_1 $\wedge$ i_a m g a_2
  end.

Definition i_c (m:p_env)(g:string$\rightarrow$Z)(c:condition) :=
  match c with c_imp a_1 a_2 $\Rightarrow$ i_a m g a_1 $\rightarrow$ i_a m g a_2 end.

The validity of conditions can be expressed for a given predicate environment by saying that their interpretation should hold for any valuation.

Definition valid (m:p_env)(c:condition) := ∀ g, i_c m g c.

We also define substitution for arithmetic expressions, boolean expressions, and so on, each time traversing structures. The function at the level of assertions is called a_subst. We can then define the axiomatic semantics.

Inductive ax_sem (m :p_env): assert → instr → assert → Prop:=
  ax$_1$: ∀ P, ax_sem m P skip P
| ax$_2$: ∀ P x e, ax_sem m (a_subst P x e) (assign x e) P
| ax$_3$: ∀ P Q R i$_1$ i$_2$, ax_sem m P i$_1$ Q → ax_sem m Q i$_2$ R →
          ax_sem m P (sequence i$_1$ i$_2$) R
| ax$_4$: ∀ P b i, ax_sem m (a_conj (a_b b) P) i P →
          ax_sem m P (while b i) (a_conj (a_not (a_b b)) P)
| ax$_5$: ∀ P P' Q' Q i,
          valid m (c_imp P P') → ax_sem m P' i Q' → valid m (c_imp Q' Q) →
          ax_sem m P i Q.

15.4.3 Proving the correctness

We want to certify that the properties of programs that we can prove using axiomatic semantics hold for actual executions of programs, as described by the operational semantics. We first define a mapping from the environments used in operational semantics to the valuations used in the axiomatic semantics. This mapping is noted $r@g$; for a variable x it returns the value of x in environment r when it is defined and $g\ x$ otherwise. We express the correctness of axiomatic semantics by stating that if "exec r i r'" and "ax_sem P i Q" hold, if P holds in the initial environment, Q should hold in the final environment r.

Theorem ax_sem_sound : ∀ g m i P Q r r', ax_sem m P i Q → exec r i r' →
    i_a m (r@g) P → i_a m (r'@g) Q.

This statement is best proved with two nested inductions, starting with an induction on the ax_sem statement. A key lemma shows that updating an environment for a variable and a value, as performed in operational semantics, and substituting an arithmetic expression for a variable, as performed in axiomatic semantics, are consistent:

Lemma a_subst_correct : forall a r1 e v m g r2 x,
    aeval r1 e v → s_update r1 x v r2 →
    (i_a m (r1@g) (a_subst a x e) ↔ i_a m (r2@g) a).

15.4.4 The weakest pre-condition calculus

The structure of a proof for a Hoare triple $\{P\}i\{Q\}$ can mostly be deduced from the structure of the instruction i, but the assertions in loop invariants and in consequence rules cannot be found automatically. Dijkstra proposed to annotate programs with the missing formulas and to gather the implications used in consequence steps as a collection of conditions to be proved on the side. The result is a *verification condition generator* which takes an annotated program as input and returns a list of conditions. We will now describe such a generator, called vcg.

We need to define a new data-type for these annotated programs.

Inductive a_instr : Type :=
  prec (a:assert)(i:a_instr) | a_skip | a_assign (s:string)(e:aexpr)
| a_sequence (i₁ i₂:a_instr) | a_while (b:bexpr)(a:assert)(i:a_instr).

The prec constructor is used to assert properties at any point in the program. The while statement has an extra field a for the invariant. We also provide a projection that maps annotated instructions to bare instructions by forgetting the assumptions, so that we can use an annotated instruction like plain instructions.

There are two main steps. The first step is to understand what is the pre-condition for an annotated instruction and a given post-condition. For the a_while and prec constructs, the pre-condition is simply the one declared in the corresponding annotation, for the other constructs, the pre-condition has to be computed using substitution and composition.

Fixpoint pc (i:a_instr)(a:assert) {struct i} : assert :=
  match i with
    prec a' i ⇒ a' | a_while b a' i ⇒ a' | a_skip ⇒ a
  | a_assign x e ⇒ a_subst a x e | a_sequence i₁ i₂ ⇒ pc i₁ (pc i₂ a)
  end.

The second step is to gather all the conditions that would appear in a minimal axiomatic semantics proof for the given post-condition and the pre-condition computed in the first step using pc.

Fixpoint vcg (i:a_instr)(post : assert) {struct i} : list condition :=

match i with
 a_skip ⇒ nil | a_assign _ _ ⇒ nil | prec a i ⇒ c_imp a (pc i post)::vcg i post
 | a_sequence i_1 i_2 ⇒ vcg i_2 post ++ vcg i_1 (pc i_2 post)
 | a_while e a i ⇒
   c_imp (a_conj (a_not (a_b e)) a) post
   :: c_imp (a_conj (a_b e) a) (pc i a) :: vcg i a
end.

We proved a correctness statement, which expresses that the validity of all the generated conditions suffices for the Hoare triple to hold. This proof is done by induction on the instruction. We can then obtain a statement that relates the condition generator and the operational semantics.

Theorem vcg_sound :
 ∀ m i A, (valid_l m (vcg i A)) → ∀ g r_1 r_2, exec r_1 i r_2 →
 i_a m (r_1@g) (pc i A) → i_a m (r_2@g) A.

15.4.5 *Using the generator in a proof by reflection*
In this example, we consider the program that adds the n first positive integers and we prove the usual identity about the result. We use a predicate environment ex_m that maps the names le and pp to predicates on lists of two integers x and y, which hold when $x \le y$ and $2 \times y = x \times (x + 1)$, respectively. With the help of a parser, we can state our claim in a concise manner:

Example ex_1 : ∀ g r_2, 0 < n →
 exec (("x", 0)::("y", 0)::("n",n)::nil)
   (parse "while x < n do [le(x,n) ∧ pp(y,x)] x:=x+1;y:=x+y done") r_2 →
   2*(r_2@g)"y" = (r_2@g)"x"*((r_2@g)"x"+1).

The conclusion actually is an instance of the pp predicate, and we apply the vcg_sound theorem, which leads to two requirements. The first is that the verification conditions hold:

valid_l ex_m
 (vcg (parse_instr' "while x < n do [le(x,n) ∧ pp(y,x)] x:=x+1;y:=x+y done")
   (parse_assert' "pp(y,n)"))

After forcing the computation of the parser and the condition generator, this leads to the following logical statement:

$\forall x\ y\ n.$
$(x \nleq n \wedge x \leq n \wedge 2y = x(x+1) \Rightarrow 2*y = n(n+1)) \wedge$
$(x < n \wedge x \leq n \wedge 2y = x(x+1) \Rightarrow x+1 \leq n \wedge$
$2(x+1+y) = (x+1)(x+2)).$

This is easily proved using regular Coq tactics. The second requirement is that the pre-condition should hold for the initial environment.

$$0 \leq n \wedge 2 \times 0 = 0 \times (0+1).$$

This statement is also proved easily. This example shows that we have a simple model of tools like Why [18].

15.5 Denotational semantics

In denotational semantics, the aim is to describe the meaning of instructions as functions. The functions need to be partial, because some instructions never terminate on some inputs. We already used partial functions for the functional encoding of expression evaluation. However, the partial recursive function that we defined were structural, and therefore guaranteed to terminate. The execution function for instructions does not fit in this framework and we will first define a new tool to define recursive function. Most notably, we will need to use non-constructive logic for this purpose.

Again the partial functions will be implemented with the **option** inductive type, but the **None** constructor will be used to represent either that an error occurs or that computation does not terminate.

15.5.1 *The fixpoint theorem*

The approach described in [32] relies on Tarski's fixpoint theorem, which states that every continuous function in a complete partial order with a minimal element has a least fixpoint and that this fixpoint is obtained by iterating the function from the minimal element.

Our definition of complete partial order relies on the notion of chains, which are monotonic sequences. A partial order is a type with a relation $\subseteq$ that is reflexive, antisymmetric, and transitive; this partial order is complete if every chain has a least upper bound. A function f is continuous if for every chain c with a least upper bound l, the value $f(l)$ is the least upper bound of the sequence $f(c_n)$. Notice that when defining continuous function in this way, we do not require f to be monotonic; actually, we prove that every continuous function is monotonic.

The proof of Tarski's theorem is quite easy to formalize and it can be formalized using intuitionistic logic, so the plain calculus of constructions is a satisfactory framework for this.

15.5.2 *The complete partial order of partial functions*

The main work in applying Tarski's theorem revolves around proving that types of partial functions are complete partial orders. A type of the form option A has the structure of a complete partial order when choosing as order the relation such that $x \subseteq y$ exactly when $x = y$ or $x =$ None. The element None is the minimal element. Chains have a finite co-domain, with at most two elements, the least upper bound of chains can be proved to exist using the non-constructive excluded-middle axiom.

Given an arbitrary complete partial order $(B, \subseteq)$, the type of functions of type $A \rightarrow B$ is a complete partial order for the order defined as follows:

$$f \subseteq g \Leftrightarrow \forall x, f(x) \subseteq g(x).$$

The proof that this is a complete partial order requires other non-constructive axioms: extensionality is required to show that the order is antisymetric and a description operator is required to construct the least upper bound of a chain of functions. We actually rely on the non-constructive ϵ operator proposed by Hilbert and already used in HOL or Isabelle/HOL. This ϵ operator is a function that takes a type T, a proof that T is inhabited, a predicate on T, and returns a value in T that is guaranteed to satisfy the predicate when possible.

For a sequence of functions f_n (not necessarily a chain), we can define a new function f, which maps every x to the value given by the ϵ operator for the predicate "to be the least upper bound of the sequence $f_n(x)$". Now, if it happens that f_n is a chain, then each of the sequences $f_n(x)$ is a chain, $f(x)$ is guaranteed to be the least upper bound, and f is the least upper bound of f_n.

In practice, Tarski's least fixpoint theorem gives us a programming tool, which we call Tarski_fix and a theorem about this tool, which we call Tarski_fix_prop. If one wishes to define a function with a recursive definition of the form

$$f\ x = e$$

such that f appears in e, it suffices that we have a theorem th stating that $\lambda f.\lambda x.e$ is continuous. The function f can then be defined by the following equation:

$$f = \mathsf{Tarski\_fix}\ (\lambda f x.e)$$

The theorem $\mathsf{Tarski\_fix\_prop}$ states that f is the least fixed-point of $\lambda f x.e$.

15.5.3 Defining the semantics

For a while loop of the form while b do i done, such that the semantic function for i is f_i, we want the semantic function to be the function $\phi_{b,i}$ such that :

$$\phi_{b,i}(\rho) = \begin{cases} \rho & \text{if bf } b{=}\text{false} \\ \phi_{b,i}(\rho') & \text{if bf } b{=}\text{true and } f_i(\rho) = \mathsf{Some}\ \rho' \\ \mathsf{None} & \text{otherwise} \end{cases}$$

This function $\phi_{b,i}$ is the least fixpoint of the function $\mathsf{F\_phi}$ obtained by combining a conditional construct, a sequential composition function (already described using the bind function), and a few constant functions. We encode $\mathsf{F\_phi}$ and phi as follows:

Definition ifthenelse (A:Type)(t:option bool)(v w: option A) :=
  match t with Some true $\Rightarrow$ v | Some false $\Rightarrow$ w | None $\Rightarrow$ None end.

Notation " 'IF x 'THEN a 'ELSE b" := (ifthenelse _ x a b) (at level 200).

Definition F_phi (A:Set)(t:A$\rightarrow$option bool)(f g :A$\rightarrow$option A)
  : A $\rightarrow$ option A := fun r $\Rightarrow$ 'IF (t r) 'THEN (bind (f r) g) 'ELSE (Some r).

We proved that each of the constructs and $\mathsf{F\_phi}$ are continuous. The semantics for instructions can then be described by the following functions:

Definition phi := fun A t f $\Rightarrow$ Tarski_fix (F_phi A t f).

Fixpoint ds(i:instr) : (list(string*Z)) $\rightarrow$ option (list(string*Z)) :=
match i with
  assign x e $\Rightarrow$ fun l $\Rightarrow$ bind (af l e)(fun v $\Rightarrow$ update l x v)
| sequence i_1 i_2 $\Rightarrow$ fun r $\Rightarrow$ (ds i_1 r)(ds i_2)
| while e i $\Rightarrow$ fun l $\Rightarrow$ phi env (fun l' $\Rightarrow$ bf l' e)(ds i) l |
| skip $\Rightarrow$ fun l $\Rightarrow$ Some l
end.

We also proved the equivalence of this semantic definition and the natural semantics specification:

Theorem ds_eq_sn : $\forall$ i l l', ds i l = Some l' $\leftrightarrow$ exec l i l'.

We actually rely on a lemma which states that the least fixpoint of a continuous function is the least upper bound of the chain obtained by iterating the function on the least element. In our case, this gives the following corollary:

$$\forall x\ v, \text{phi } x = \text{Some } v \Rightarrow \exists n, \text{F\_phi}^n \text{ (fun } y \rightarrow \text{None) } x = \text{Some } x$$

We can then proceed with a proof by induction on the number n.

Unlike the functions af, af', or vcg, the function phi is not usable for computation inside the theorem prover, but F_phi^n can be used to compute using approximations. We can still extract this code and execute it in Ocaml, as long as we extract the Tarski fixpoint theorem to a simple fixpoint function:

let rec fix f = f (fun y $\rightarrow$ fix f y)

This interpreter loops when executing a looping program; this is predicted in the Coq formalization by a value of None.

15.6 Abstract interpretation

The goal of abstract interpretation [15] is to infer automatically properties about programs based on approximations described as abstract values. Approximations make it possible to consider several executions at a time, for example all the executions inside a loop. This way the execution of arbitrary programs can be approximated using an algorithm that has polynomial complexity.

Abstract values are supposed to represent subsets of the set of concrete values. Each abstract interpreter works with a fixed set of abstract values, which must have a certain structure. An operation on abstract values must be provided for each operation in the language (in our case we only have to provide an addition). The subset represented by the result of an abstract operation must contain all the concrete values of the corresponding operation when applied to values in the input subsets. The domain of abstract values is also ordered, in a way that respects inclusion for the subsets they represent. Also, the type of abstract values should also contain an element corresponding to the whole set of integers. We will call this element the top abstract value. The theoretical foundations provided by Cousot and Cousot [15] actually enumerate all the properties that are required from the abstract values.

Given an abstract valuation where variable names are mapped to abstract values, we program an abstract evaluation function ab_eval for arithmetic expressions that returns a new abstract value. This function is programmed exactly like the function af' we used for axiomatic semantics, simply replacing integer addition with an abstract notion of addition on abstract values.

As a running example, we will use an abstract domain of intervals, whose bounds can be regular integers or infinite bounds, and we use a natural extension of addition to infinite bounds (we agree that $-\infty + \infty = \infty$, but this never occurs in our computation). The addition of intervals can be defined as the result of adding the lower bounds together and adding the upper bounds together.

When we need to evaluate with respect to an abstract environment I, i.e. a finite list of pairs of variable names and abstract values, we use the function (ab_lookup I) that associates the top value to all variables that do not occur in the abstract environment.

Abstract execution of instructions takes as input an abstract environment and a bare instruction and returns the pair of an annotated instruction and an optional final abstract environment. When the optional final environment is None, this means that the analysis detected guaranteed non-termination. The annotations in the result instruction describe information that is guaranteed to be satisfied when execution reaches the corresponding point.

Abstract execution for assignments, sequences, and skip instructions naturally follows the concrete semantics. For while loops, we depart from the concrete semantics to ensure that our tool always terminates even on non-terminating programs. The approach is to make over approximations with abstract environments that get coarser and coarser, until we reach an approximation that is stable through abstract interpretation of the loop body. Thus, we want to find an invariant abstract environment for loops, as we did in axiomatic semantics. We chose a simple strategy.

(i) We use information from the loop test, when this is possible.

(ii) We check whether the abstract environment after testing and executing the loop body once is *stable*, i.e. if abstract values in the output of the executing the loop body environment are included in the corresponding input values.

(iii) If this fails, we use a widen heuristic function to compute an over-approximation and we try again.

(iv) If this fails again, we use a drastic over-approximation that is guaranteed to succeed: the environment that maps the top abstract value to every variable.

To use information from the loop test, when it has the form $v < e$, where v is a variable, we refine the abstract value for v inside the loop and after exiting the loop. We may detect that the refined value represents the empty set, when the test can never succeed or never fail, and in this case we have found dead-code. This is performed by a function intersect_env. This function takes a first boolean argument that is used to express that we check whether the test is satisfied or falsified. This function returns None when the test can never be satisfied or can never be falsified. When dead-code is detected, we annotate the instruction with false assertions, to mark that the location is never reached, (this is done in mark).

For example, when using intervals, executing with respect to the environment $l_1 = (x,[1,1]).\emptyset$, and analyzing the instruction

while x < 10 do x := x+1 end,

we use intersect_env to discover that the test does not restrict the possible values for x. After executing the loop body, we obtain an environment $l_2 = (x,[2,2]).\emptyset$. After combining with the initial environment, we obtain a third environment $l_3 = (x, [1,2]).\emptyset$. This environment is not stable. We use the widen heuristic to propose an over-approximating interval for x and we start again with the environment $l_4 = (x,[1,+\infty]).\emptyset$. we use intersect_env to compute the environment l_5 that includes information from the test. We obtain $l_5 = (x,[1,9]).\emptyset$. After executing the assignment we obtain a new $l_6 = (x,[2,10]).\emptyset$. We combine l_6 and l_5 to obtain a new environment $l_7 = (x,[1,10]).\emptyset$. Using intersect_env again, but with l_7 as input, we obtain again l_5, then l_6, then combining again with l_7 we find that l_7 is stable. In this example, we find a fixed-point at the second stage. We can then compute the abstract environment at the exit of the loop, this time intersecting the fixed-point abstract environment with the negated test. The output abstract environment is $l_8 = (x,[10,10]).\emptyset$.

The three stages are described in a function fp that computes an abstract fixed-point for this abstract interpretation. This function has the following type:

fp : ab_env → bexpr → instr → (ab_env → a_instr*option ab_env) →
        a_instr*option ab_env

The function argument (fourth argument) is the function that computes abstract interpretation on the loop body.

Our abstract interpreter is then described as a recursive function abstract_i (here we use to_a to transform an environment into an assertion, and to_a' for optional environments, mapping None to false_assert).

```
Fixpoint abstract_i (i : instr)(l : ab_env) : a_instr*option ab_env :=
match i with
  skip ⇒ (prec (to_a l) a_skip, Some l)
| sequence i₁ i₂ ⇒
  let (i'1, l') := abstract_i i₁ l in
  match l' with
    None ⇒ (a_sequence i'1 (prec false_assert (mark i₂)), None)
  | Some l' ⇒ let (i'2, l'') := abstract_i i₂ l' in (a_sequence i'1 i'2, l'')
  end
| assign x e ⇒
  (prec (to_a l) (a_assign x e), Some (ab_update l x (ab_eval (ab_lookup l) e)))
| while b i ⇒
  match intersect_env true l b with
    None ⇒
  (prec (to_a l)(a_while b (a_conj (a_not (a_b b)) (to_a l)) (mark i)), Some l)
  | Some l' ⇒
    let (i',l'') := fp l b i (abstract_i i) in
      match l'' with
        None ⇒ (prec (to_a l) (a_while b (to_a l) i'), intersect_env false l)
      | Some l'' ⇒ (prec (to_a l) (a_while b (to_a l'') i'), intersect_env false l'' b)
      end
  end
end.
```

This abstract interpreter is a programming tool: it can be run with an instruction and initial approximations for variables. It returns the same instruction, annotated with properties about the variables at each location, together with the final abstract environment. We proved a correctness statement for this abstract interpreter. This statement relies on the verification condition generator that we described earlier.

Theorem abstract_i_sound:
  ∀ i e i' e', abstract_i i e = (i', e') → valid_l m (vcg i' (to_a' e'))).

This theorem is proved by induction on i. We need to establish a few facts.

(i) The order of variables does not change in successive abstract environments.

(ii) Abstract execution is monotonic: given wider approximations, execution yields wider results (assuming reasonable assumptions for widen and intersect_env).

(iii) The fp function either yields a result that is wider than its input or detects non-termination of the loop body.

(iv) The verification condition generator is monotonic with respect to implication: if the conditions generated for i and a post-condition P hold and $P \rightarrow P$ is valid, then the conditions generated for i and Q also hold and pc i P → pc i Q is also valid. This property is needed because abstract interpreters and condition generators work in reverse directions.

This abstract interpreter was developed in a modular fashion, in which the domain of abstract values is described using a module interface. We implemented an instance of this domain for intervals. This interpreter can actually be run inside Coq on small examples.

15.7 Conclusion

This overview of formalized programming language semantics is elementary in its choice of a very limited programming language. Because of this, some important aspects of programming languages are overlooked: *binding*, which appears as soon as local variables or procedures and functions are allowed; *typing*, which is a useful programming concept for the early detection of programming errors; *concurrency*, which is useful to exploit modern computing architectures, etc. Even for this simplistic programming language, we could also have covered two more aspects: program transformations [9] and compilation [5].

Three aspects of this work are original: we obtain tools that can be executed inside the Coq prover for proof by reflection; our work on denotational semantics shows that the conventional extraction facility of the Coq system can also be used for potentially non terminating functions, thanks to well chosen extraction for Tarski's fixpoint theorem; last, our description of an abstract interpreter is the first to rely on axiomatic semantics to prove the correctness of an abstract interpreter.

Concerning reflection, we find it exciting that the theorem prover can be used to execute programs in the object language (in work not reported here we show how to construct an incomplete interpreter from a structural operational semantics), to generate condition verifications about programs (thanks to the verification condition generator), and to prove the conditions as usual logical statements. More interestingly, the abstract interpreter can be run on programs to generate simultaneously annotated programs and the proof that these annotated programs are consistent.

Formal verification techniques based on verification condition generators suffer from the burden of explicitly writing the loop invariants. Chaieb already suggested that the loop invariants could be obtained through abstract interpretation [12], generating proof traces that can be verified in theorem provers. Our partial correctness theorem for the abstract interpreter suggests a similar approach here, except that we also proved the abstract interpreter correct. An interesting improvement would be to make manually written assertions collaborate with automatically generated ones; considering manual annotation as part of the input for the widen heuristic is an easy approach to this improvement.

Bibliography

[1] B. E. Aydemir, A. Bohannon, M. Fairbairn, J. N. Foster, B. C. Pierce, P. Sewell, D. Vytiniotis, G. Washburn, S. Weirich and S. Zdancewic. Mechanized metatheory for the masses: The POPLmark challenge. In *Proceedings of the Eighteenth International Conference on Theorem Proving in Higher Order Logics (TPHOLs 2005)*, pp. 50–65. Springer-Verlag, 2005.

[2] G. Barthe, G. Dufay, L. Jakubiec, S. Melo de Sousa and B. Serpette. A formal executable semantics of the JavaCard platform. In D. Sands (ed.) *Proceedings of ESOP'01*, volume 2028 Lecture Notes in Computer Science, pp. 302–319. Springer-Verlag, 2001.

[3] G. Barthe, M. Ruys and H. Barendregt. A two-level approach towards lean proof-checking. In *TYPES '95: Selected papers from the International Workshop on Types for Proofs and Programs*, London, UK, pp. 16–35. Springer-Verlag, 1996.

[4] S. Berghofer and T. Nipkow. Executing higher order logic. In P. Callaghan, Z. Luo, J. McKinna and R. Pollack (eds) *TYPES*, volume 2277, Lecture Notes in Computer Science, pp. 24–40. Springer-Verlag, 2000.

[5] Y. Bertot. *A Certified Compiler for an Imperative Language.* Research Report RR-3488, INRIA, 1998.

[6] Y. Bertot. Formalizing a jvml verifier for initialization in a theorem prover. In *Computer Aided Verification (CAV'2001)*, volume 2102, Lecture Notes in Computer Science, pp. 14–24. Springer-Verlag, 2001.

[7] Y. Bertot. A survey of semantics styles, 2007. available on the Coq site at `coq.inria.fr/Semantics_survey.html`.

[8] Y. Bertot and P. Castéran. *Interactive Theorem Proving and Program Development, Coq'Art:the Calculus of Inductive Constructions.* Springer-Verlag, 2004.

[9] Y. Bertot and R. Fraer. Reasoning with executable specifications. In *TAPSOFT'95*, volume 915, Lecture Notes in Computer Science, pp. 531–545, 1995.

[10] P. Borras, D. Clément, T. Despeyroux, J. Incerpi, G. Kahn, B. Lang and V. Pascual. Centaur: the system. In *Third Symposium on Software Development Environments*, 1988.

[11] S. Boutin. Using reflection to build efficient and certified decision procedures. In *Theoretical Aspects of Computer Science*, volume 1281, Lecture Notes in Computer Science, pp. 515–529. Springer-Verlag, 1997.

[12] A. Chaieb. Proof-producing program analysis. In K. Barkaoui, A. Cavalcanti and A. Cerone (eds) *ICTAC*, volume 4281, Lecture Notes in Computer Science, pp. 287–301. Springer-Verlag, 2006.

[13] R. Constable, S. F. Allen, H. M. Bromley, W. R. Cleaveland, J. F. Cremer, R. W. Harber, D. J. Howe, T. B. Knoblock, N. P. Mendler, P. Panangaden, J. T. Sasaki and S. F. Smith. *Implementing Mathematics with the Nuprl Proof Development System.* Prentice-Hall, 1986.

[14] C. Coquand. Agda. `www.cs.chalmers.se/~catarina/agda`.

[15] P. Cousot and R. Cousot. Abstract interpretation: a unified lattice model for static analysis of programs by construction or approximation of fixpoints. In *Conference Record of the Fourth Annual ACM SIGPLAN-SIGACT Symposium on Principles of Programming Languages*, pp. 238–252, Los Angeles, California, 1977. ACM Press, New York, NY.

[16] E. W. Dijkstra. *A discipline of Programming.* Prentice Hall, 1976.

[17] G. Dowek, A. Felty, H. Herbelin, G. Huet, C. Murthy, C. Parent, C. Paulin-Mohring and B. Werner. *The Coq Proof Assistant User's Guide.* INRIA, May 1993. Version 5.8.

[18] J.-C. Filliâtre. Proof of imperative programs in type theory. In *International Workshop TYPES'98*, volume 1657, Lecture Notes in Computer Science, pp. 78–92. Springer-Verlag, March 1998.

[19] M. J. C. Gordon and T. F. Melham. *Introduction to HOL : a theorem-proving environment for higher-order logic.* Cambridge University Press, 1993.

[20] M. J. C. Gordon, R. Milner and C. P. Wadsworth. *Edinburgh LCF*, volume 78, Lecture Notes in Computer Science. Springer-Verlag, 1979.

[21] C. A. R. Hoare. An axiomatic basis for computer programming. *Communications of the ACM*, **12**:576–580, 1969.

[22]   G. Kahn. Natural semantics. In K. Fuchi and M. Nivat (eds) *Programming of Future Generation Computers*, pp. 237–258. North-Holland, 1988. (also appears as INRIA Report no. 601).

[23]   P. Letouzey. A new extraction for Coq. In H. Geuvers and F. Wiedijk (eds) *TYPES 2002*, volume 2646, Lecture Notes in Computer Science, pp. 200–219. Springer-Verlag, 2003.

[24]   O. Müller, T. Nipkow, D. von Oheimb and O. Slotosch. HOLCF = HOL + LCF. *Journal of Functional Programming*, **9**:191–223, 1999.

[25]   T. Nipkow. Winskel is (almost) right: Towards a mechanized semantics. *Formal Asp. Computing*, **10**(2):171–186, 1998.

[26]   L. C. Paulson and T. Nipkow. *Isabelle : a Generic Theorem Prover*, volume 828, Lecture Notes in Computer Science. Springer-Verlag, 1994.

[27]   D. Pichardie. *Interprétation abstraite en logique intuitionniste : extraction d'analyseurs Java certifiés*. PhD thesis, Université Rennes 1, 2005. (In French).

[28]   G. Plotkin. Structural operational semantics. Lecture notes DAIMI FN-19, Aarhus University, 1981. (reprinted 1991).

[29]   D. Terrasse. Encoding natural semantics in Coq. In *Proceedings of the Fourth International Conference on Algebraic Methodology and Software Technology, AMAST'95*, Lecture Notes in Computer Science, pp. 230–244. Springer-Verlag, 1995.

[30]   J. van den Berg and B. Jacobs. The loop compiler for Java and JML. In *TACAS 2001*, pp. 299–312. Springer-Verlag, 2001.

[31]   D. von Oheimb. *Analyzing Java in Isabelle/HOL, Formalization, Type Safety, and Hoare Logic*. PhD thesis, Technische Universität München, 2000.

[32]   G. Winskel. *The Formal Semantics of Programming Languages, an introduction*. Foundations of Computing. The MIT Press, 1993.

16

Nominal verification of algorithm W

Christian Urban and Tobias Nipkow

TU München

Abstract

The Milner-Damas typing algorithm W is one of the classic algorithms in computer science. In this paper we describe a formalized soundness and completeness proof for this algorithm. Our formalization is based on names for both term and type variables, and is carried out in Isabelle/HOL using the Nominal Datatype Package. It turns out that in our formalization we have to deal with a number of issues that are often overlooked in informal presentations of W.

"Alpha-conversion always bites you when you least expect it."

A remark made by Xavier Leroy when discussing with us the informal proof about W in his PhD thesis [7].

16.1 Introduction

Milner's polymorphic type system for ML [8] is probably the most influential programming language type system. The second author learned about it from a paper by Clément *et al.* [2]. He was immediately taken by their view that type inference can be viewed as Prolog execution, in particular because the Isabelle system, which he had started to work on, was based on a similar paradigm as the Typol language developed by Kahn and his coworkers [1]. Milner himself had provided the explicit type inference algorithm W and proved its soundness. Completeness was later shown by Damas and Milner [4]. Neither soundness nor completeness of W are trivial because of the presence of the Let-construct (which is not expanded during type

From Semantics to Computer Science Essays in Honour of Gilles Kahn, eds Yves Bertot, Gérard Huet, Jean-Jacques Lévy and Gordon Plotkin. Published by Cambridge University Press. © Cambridge University Press 2009.

inference). Two machine-checked proofs for soundness and completeness were implemented previously [5, 9]. Both of these proofs code type and term variables using de Bruijn indices. This leads to slick proofs which, however, require strange lemmas about arithmetic on de Bruijn terms, not present in typical proofs done with "pencil-and-paper" (for example [7, 13]).

Here we will describe a formalization for soundness and completeness of W using the Nominal Datatype Package developed by Berghofer and the first author [14, 16]. This package is based on ideas pioneered by Pitts *et al.* [11, 12] and aims to provide all necessary infrastructure for reasoning conveniently about languages with bound variables. For this it provides mechanisms to deal with named binders and allows one to define datatypes modulo α-equivalence. For example, when defining the lambda-calculus with the terms

$$ a \quad | \quad t_1 \ t_2 \quad | \quad \lambda a.t $$

one defines term-constructors for variables, applications and lambdas and indicates in case of lambdas that a is bound in t. The Nominal Datatype Package constructs then a (nominal) datatype representing α-equivalence classes of those terms. Unlike constructions involving de Bruijn indices, however, the α-equivalence classes in the Nominal Datatype Package involve names. This is similar to the convention in "pencil-and-paper" proofs where one states that one identifies terms that differ only in the names of bound variables, but works with terms in a "naïve" way. However, dealing with α-equivalence classes has some subtle consequences: some functions cannot be defined anymore and α-equivalence classes do not immediately come equipped with a structural induction principle. Therefore the Nominal Datatype Package provides a recursion combinator that ensures functions respect α-equivalence classes and also provides two principles for performing proofs by structural induction over them. The first induction principle looks as follows:

$$ \frac{\begin{array}{l} \forall a. \ P \ (a) \\ \forall t_1 \ t_2. \ P \ t_1 \wedge P \ t_2 \longrightarrow P \ (t_1 \ t_2) \\ \forall a \ t. \ P \ t \longrightarrow P \ (\lambda a.t) \end{array}}{P \ t} $$

where a property P holds for all (α-equated) lambda-terms t provided the property holds for variables, applications and lambdas. In the latter two cases one can as usual assume the property holds for the immediate subterms. However, this principle is quite inconvenient in practice, since it requires the lambda-case to be proved for all binders, which often means one has to rename binders and establish auxiliary lemmas concerning such renamings. In informal reasoning this renaming is nearly always avoided by employing the variable convention for bound variables. Therefore the Nominal Datatype Package generates automatically the following stronger induction principle for α-equated lambda-terms

$$\frac{\begin{array}{l} \forall\, a\ C.\ P\ C\ (a) \\ \forall\, t_1\ t_2\ C.\ (\forall\, C.\ P\ C\ t_1) \wedge (\forall\, C.\ P\ C\ t_2) \longrightarrow P\ C\ (t_1\ t_2) \\ \forall\, a\ t\ C.\ a\ \#\ C \wedge (\forall\, C.\ P\ C\ t) \longrightarrow P\ C\ (\lambda a.t) \end{array}}{P\ C\ t}$$

where one only needs to prove the lambda-case for all fresh binders (w.r.t. some suitably chosen context C). With the stronger induction principle we can relatively easily formalize informal proofs employing the variable convention (for more details see [15, 16]). The reason is that the variable convention usually states which free variables the binder has to avoid. We can achieve the same with the stronger induction principle by instantiation C with what is informally avoided.

16.2 Terms, types and substitutions

16.2.1 Terms and types

Our *terms* represent λ-terms enriched with Let-expressions:

$$trm\ =\ Var\ var\ |\ App\ trm\ trm\ |\ Lam\ var.\ trm\ |\ Let\ var\ be\ trm\ in\ trm$$

where *var* is some infinite type of *term variables*. This definition looks like an ordinary recursive datatype, but its definition in Isabelle includes the keyword **nominal_datatype**. This means that *trm* is really a type of equivalence classes of terms modulo α-conversion. The definition also includes the information that the term-variable *var* in *Lam var. trm* binds all free occurrences *var* in *trm*, and similarly for *Let var be trm in trm'* that all occurrences of *var* are bound in *trm'*. Thus we really work with α-equivalence classes, as we have for example the equation *Lam a. Var a = Lam b. Var b*, which does not hold had we defined terms as an ordinary datatype.

However, *types* do not contain any binders and therefore are defined as an ordinary datatype *ty*

$$ty = TVar \ tvar \ | \ ty{\rightarrow}ty$$

based on some infinite type *tvar* of *type variables*.

Type schemes are universally quantified types. This quantification is again modelled via a nominal datatype, namely

$$tyS = Ty \ ty \ | \ \forall \ tvar.tyS$$

where in the latter clause a type variable is bound in a type scheme. With this definition we fix the order of the binders, and also allow type schemes with multiple occurrences of the same bound type variable, for example, $\forall X. \forall X. Ty \ (TVar \ X)$. This will require some care in the proofs we shall give later on. Ideally one would like to quantify over a whole set of variables in one go, as in $\forall \{X_1 \ldots X_n\}. \ ty$; however, this is not yet supported in either the nominal or any other approach to datatypes with binders. We are not the first to choose the representation using a fixed order for binders: it has been used in the description of W given by Gunter [6] and also by Damas in parts of his thesis (see [3] page 66).

Our naming conventions for term variables, terms, type variables, types and types-schemes are

$$a : var, \quad t : trm, \quad X : tvar, \quad T : ty, \quad S : tyS.$$

We use the following list notation: $x{::}xs$ is the list with head x and tail xs, $xs \ @ \ ys$ is the concatenation of two lists, and $x \in xs$ means that x occurs in the list xs. List inclusion is defined by

$$xs \subseteq ys \ \overset{\text{def}}{=} \ \forall \, x. \ x \in xs \ \longrightarrow \ x \in ys$$

and two lists of type variables are considered *equivalent* provided

$$xs \approx ys \ \overset{\text{def}}{=} \ xs \subseteq ys \ \wedge \ ys \subseteq xs.$$

16.2.2 Substitutions

We model substitutions as lists, namely $Subst = (tvar \times ty) \ list$, and reserve variables θ, σ and δ for them. Because lists are finite, one can always find a new type variable that does not occur in a substitution. We will use for this concept the notion of freshness, written $X \ \# \ \_$, from the nominal logic work [11, 16]. When modelling substitutions as functions, one has to require finiteness of their domain (the type variables not mapped to themselves) explicitly, which complicates matters. Since there is no free lunch, we have to define a number of concepts that would come for free with substitutions as functions.

- Application to a type

  $\theta(TVar\ X) = lookup\ \theta\ X$

  $\theta(T_1 {\rightarrow} T_2) = \theta(T_1){\rightarrow}\theta(T_2)$

  is defined in terms of the auxiliary function *lookup*:

  $lookup\ []\ X = TVar\ X$

  $lookup\ ((Y,\ T){::}\theta)\ X = (if\ X = Y\ then\ T\ else\ lookup\ \theta\ X)$

- Application to a type scheme:

  $\theta(Ty\ T) = Ty\ \theta(T)$

  $\theta(\forall\,X.S) = \forall\,X.\theta(S)$ provided $X\ \#\ \theta$

- Substitution composition:

  $\theta_1 \circ [] = \theta_1$

  $\theta_1 \circ ((X,\ T){::}\theta_2) = (X,\ \theta_1(T)){::}\theta_1 \circ \theta_2$

- Extensional equivalence:

  $\theta_1 \approx \theta_2 \overset{\text{def}}{=} \forall\,X.\ \theta_1(TVar\ X) = \theta_2(TVar\ X)$

- Domain of a substitution:

  $dom\ [] = []$

  $dom\ ((X,\ T){::}\theta) = X{::}dom\ \theta$

The only technically interesting point here is the application of a substitution to a type scheme. For a start, this definition is not by ordinary structural recursion since it operates on equivalence classes. Luckily the nominal datatype infrastructure provides a mechanism whereby one can specify the recursion equations as above and Isabelle generates verification conditions that imply that the definition is independent of the choice of representatives of the equivalence class. This is the case if X does not occur freely in θ. Note, however, that substitution application over type schemes is *not* a partial function, since type schemes are α-equivalence classes and one can always rename the X away from θ. We can easily show that substitution composition is associative, that is $\theta_1 \circ (\theta_2 \circ \theta_3) = (\theta_1 \circ \theta_2) \circ \theta_3$, and that $\theta_1 \circ \theta_2(\_) = \theta_1(\theta_2(\_))$ holds for types and type schemes. The substitution of a single type variable is defined as a special case:

$$(\_)[X{:}=T] \overset{\text{def}}{=} [(X,T)](\_)$$

16.2.3 Free type variables

Free type variables, *ftv*, of types and type-schemes are defined as usual

$$
\begin{aligned}
&ftv\ (TVar\ X) = [X] && ftv\ (Ty\ T) = ftv\ T \\
&ftv\ (T_1 {\rightarrow} T_2) = ftv\ T_1\ @\ ftv\ T_2 && ftv\ (\forall X.S) = ftv\ S - [X]
\end{aligned}
$$

except that *ftv* returns a list, which may contain duplicates (in the last clause the difference stands for removing all elements of the second list from the first). The reason for lists rather than sets is the following: The typing of Let-expressions (see Section 16.3) requires a type to be turned into a type scheme by quantifying over some free variables (see Section 16.2.4). If the free variables are given as a list, this is just recursion over the list. If they are given as a finite set, one faces the problem that recursion over a set is only well-defined if the order of elements does not matter [10]. But the order of quantifiers does matter in our representation of type schemes! Hence one would need to order the set artificially, for example via HOL's choice operator, which we prefer to avoid.

We shall also make use of the notion of free type variables for pairs and lists, defined by the clauses

$$
ftv\ (x,\ y) = ftv\ x\ @\ ftv\ y \qquad ftv\ [] = [] \qquad ftv\ (x{::}xs) = ftv\ x\ @\ ftv\ xs.
$$

For term and type variables we define $ftv\ a \overset{\text{def}}{=} []$ and $ftv\ X \overset{\text{def}}{=} [X]$. The free type variables for substitutions are therefore the free type variables in their domain and co-domain.

16.2.4 Generalization of types and unbinding of type schemes

Types can be turned into type schemes by generalizing over a list of type variables. This is formalized by the function *gen* defined by

$$
\begin{aligned}
&gen\ T\ [] = Ty\ T \\
&gen\ T\ (X{::}Xs) = \forall X.gen\ T\ Xs
\end{aligned}
$$

In the definitions and proofs that follow, we will also need an unbinding operation that for a type scheme, say *S*, provides a type *T* and a list of type variables *Xs* such that *S = gen T Xs*. Since type schemes are α-equated, we cannot expect this operation being a function from type schemes to lists of type variables and types: the reason is that such a function calculates with binders in a way that does not preserve α-equivalence classes. Indeed, the Nominal Datatype Package does not allow us to define

$$unbind \ (Ty \ T) = [\,] \cdot T$$
$$unbind \ (\forall X.S) = X :: (unbind \ S)$$

as it would lead to an inconsistency (because $\forall X. Ty \ (TVar \ X)$ can unbind to both $[X] \cdot (TVar \ X)$ and $[Y] \cdot (TVar \ Y)$). However, we can define the unbinding operation of a type scheme as a three-place relation inductively defined by the rules

$$\frac{}{Ty \ T \hookrightarrow [\,] \cdot T} \qquad \frac{S \hookrightarrow Xs \cdot T}{\forall X.S \hookrightarrow (X :: Xs) \cdot T}$$

One can easily establish the following three properties for the unbinding relations.

Lemma 16.1

   (*i*) $\exists Xs \ T. \ S \hookrightarrow Xs \cdot T$

   (*ii*) $gen \ T \ Xs \hookrightarrow Xs \cdot T$

  (*iii*)   If $S \hookrightarrow Xs \cdot T$ then $S = gen \ T \ Xs$.

Proof The first is by induction on the type scheme S, the second is by induction on Xs and last is by induction over $S \hookrightarrow Xs \cdot T$.   □

The property from Lemma 16.1(*i*) demonstrates that the unbinding relation is "total" if the last two parameters are viewed as results.

16.2.5 Instances of a type scheme

Types can be obtained as instances of type schemes by instantiating the bound variables. This we define inductively as follows

$$\frac{}{T \prec Ty \ T} \qquad \frac{X \ \# \ T' \qquad T \prec S}{T[X := T'] \prec \forall X.S}$$

where $X \ \# \ T'$ stands for X not occurring in T'. The main reason for this slightly non-standard definition is that for $\prec$ we can easily show that it is preserved under substitutions, namely:

Lemma 16.2 *If* $T \prec S$ *then* $\theta(T) \prec \theta(S)$.

Proof By induction on $\prec$; the only interesting case is the second rule. Since we added the side-condition $X \ \# \ T'$ in this rule, the Nominal Datatype Package provides us with a strengthened induction principle for $\prec$ that has the variable convention already built in [15]. As a result we can assume in this case that not only $X \# T'$ (which comes from the rule) but also that $X \# \theta$ (which comes from the variable convention). We need to show that $\theta(T[X:=T']) \prec \theta(\forall X.S)$ holds. By the freshness assumptions we have that the left-hand side is equal to $\theta(T)[X:=\theta(T')]$ and the right-hand side is equal to $\forall X.\theta(S)$. Moreover we have that $X \# \theta(T')$. Consequently we can apply the rule and are done. $\square$

A more standard definition for a type T being an instance of a type scheme $\forall\{X_1..X_n\}.T'$ involves a substitution θ whose domain is $\{X_1..X_n\}$ and which makes $\theta(T')$ equal to T. This translates in our setting to the following definition:

$$T \prec' S \stackrel{\text{def}}{=} \exists Xs\ T'\ \theta.\ S \hookrightarrow Xs \cdot T' \wedge dom\ \theta \approx Xs \wedge \theta(T') = T.$$

However, it is much harder to show Lemma 16.2 for the $\prec'$-relation: for a start there is no convenient induction principle; also we have to analyse how $\theta(S)$ unbinds, which means we have to rename the binders appropriately. Nevertheless, it is relatively straightforward to show that both relations are equivalent.

Lemma 16.3 $T \prec S$ if and only if $T \prec' S$.

To prove this lemma, we shall first establish the two facts.

Lemma 16.4
  (i)   If $T \prec S$ then $T \prec \forall X.S$.
  (ii)   If $S \hookrightarrow Xs \cdot T$ then $T \prec S$.

Proof For the first part, we choose a fresh type variable Y such that $Y \# (S, T, X)$. From the assumption and Lemma 16.2 we obtain $T[X:=TVar\ Y] \prec S[X:=TVar\ Y]$. Using the fact $Y \# TVar\ X$, we can derive $T[X:=TVar\ Y][Y:=TVar\ X] \prec \forall Y.S[X:=TVar\ Y]$ using the rule. Because of the manner in which we have chosen Y, the left-hand side is equal to T and the right-hand side is (alpha-)equal to $\forall X.S$. Using (i) we can show by a routine induction over $S \hookrightarrow Xs \cdot T$ the second part of the lemma. $\square$

Proof For Lemma 16.3. The left-to-right direction is by induction on $\prec$ and quite routine. For the other direction we have to show that $\theta(T') \prec S$ holds. We first use Lemma 16.4(ii) to infer $T' \prec S$ from $S \hookrightarrow Xs \cdot T'$. Appealing to Lemma 16.2, we can thus infer that $\theta(T') \prec \theta(S)$ holds. By a routine induction over $S \hookrightarrow Xs \cdot T'$, we can show that $\forall\, X \in Xs.\ X\ \#\ S$, which in turn implies that $\theta(S) = S$ since $dom\ \theta \approx Xs$. Consequently we can conclude with $\theta(T') \prec S$. $\qquad\square$

16.2.6 Subsumption relation for type-schemes

A type scheme S_1 is subsumed by another type scheme S_2 provided that

$$S_1 \ll S_2 \stackrel{\mathrm{def}}{=} \forall\, T.\ T \prec S_1 \longrightarrow T \prec S_2.$$

Damas shows in [3] (slightly adapted to our setting) that:

Lemma 16.5 If $S_1 \hookrightarrow Xs_1 \cdot T_1$ and $S_2 \hookrightarrow Xs_2 \cdot T_2$ then

$S_1 \ll S_2$ if and only if
$$\exists\, \theta.\ dom\ \theta \approx Xs_2 \,\wedge\, T_1 = \theta(T_2) \,\wedge\, (\forall\, X \in Xs_1.\ X\ \#\ S_2).$$

Proof The left-to-right directions is as follows: from the first assumption we know $T_1 \prec S_1$ by Lemma 16.4(*ii*) and thus $T_1 \prec S_2$. From this we obtain a θ such that $dom\ \theta \approx Xs_2$ and $T_1 = \theta(T_2)$ holds. The property $\forall\, X \in Xs_1.\ X\ \#\ S_2$ follows from the observation that all free type variables of S_2 are also free in T_1. The other direction follows from the fact that if $S_2 \hookrightarrow Xs_2 \cdot T_2$ and $dom\ \theta \approx Xs_2$ then $\theta(T_2) \prec S_2$. $\quad\square$

From Lemma 16.5 we can derive the following two properties of subsumption which will be useful later on.

Lemma 16.6
(*i*)   If $S_1 \ll S_2$ *then* $ftv\ S_2 \subseteq ftv\ S_1$.
(*ii*)   If $Xs_1 \subseteq Xs_2$ *then* $gen\ T\ Xs_1 \ll gen\ T\ Xs_2$.

Proof For the first part we obtain by Lemma 16.1(*i*) Xs_1, T_1, Xs_2 and T_2 such that $S_1 \hookrightarrow Xs_1 \cdot T_1$ and $S_2 \hookrightarrow Xs_2 \cdot T_2$. We have further that (*) $ftv\ S_1 \approx ftv\ T_1 - Xs_1$ and $T_1 \prec S_1$. From Lemma 16.5 we can infer that $\forall\, X \in Xs_1.\ X\ \#\ S_2$, which in turn implies that (**) $Xs_1 \cap ftv\ S_2 = \emptyset$. Using the assumption and $T_1 \prec S_1$ we obtain $T_1 \prec S_2$. By induction on $\prec$ we can show that $ftv\ S_1 \subseteq ftv\ T_1$. Using (**) we can infer that $ftv\ S_2 \subseteq ftv\ T_1 - Xs_1$ and hence conclude appealing to (*).

For the second part we have that $gen\ T\ Xs_1 \hookrightarrow Xs_1 \cdot T$ and $gen\ T\ Xs_2 \hookrightarrow Xs_2 \cdot T$ using Lemma 16.1(*ii*). By assumption it holds that $\forall\, X \in Xs_1.\ X\ \#\ gen\ T\ Xs_2$. Taking the identity substitution, written ε, which maps every $X \in Xs_2$ to $TVar\ X$, then $dom\ \varepsilon \approx Xs_2$ and $T = \varepsilon(T)$. Consequently we can conclude using Lemma 16.5. $\square$

16.3 Typing

16.3.1 Typing contexts

Typing contexts are lists of (term variable, type scheme)-pairs, i.e. *Ctxt* = (*var* × *tyS*) *list*. A typing context Γ is *valid* when it includes only a single association for every term variable in Γ. We can define the notion of validity by the two rules:

$$\frac{}{valid\ []} \qquad \frac{valid\ \Gamma \qquad a\ \#\ \Gamma}{valid\ ((a,\ S)::\Gamma)}$$

where we attach in the second rule the side-condition that a must be fresh for Γ, which in case of our typing contexts is equivalent to x not occurring in Γ. The application of a substitution θ to a typing context is defined as usual by

$$\theta([]) = [] \qquad \theta((a,\ S)::\Gamma) = (a,\ \theta(S))::\theta(\Gamma).$$

The subsumption relation is extended to typing contexts as follows:

$$\frac{}{[]\ \ll\ []} \qquad \frac{S_1\ \ll\ S_2 \qquad \Gamma_1\ \ll\ \Gamma_2}{(a,\ S_1)::\Gamma_1\ \ll\ (a,\ S_2)::\Gamma_2}$$

16.3.2 Typing rules

Now we have all the notions in order to define the typing judgment $\Gamma \vdash t : T$:

$$\frac{valid\ \Gamma \qquad (a,\ S) \in \Gamma \qquad T \prec S}{\Gamma \vdash Var\ a : T}$$

$$\frac{\Gamma \vdash t_1 : T_1 {\rightarrow} T_2 \qquad \Gamma \vdash t_2 : T_1}{\Gamma \vdash App\ t_1\ t_2 : T_2}$$

$$\frac{a\ \#\ \Gamma \qquad (a,\ Ty\ T_1)::\Gamma \vdash t : T_2}{\Gamma \vdash Lam\ a.\ t : T_1 {\rightarrow} T_2}$$

$$\frac{a\ \#\ \Gamma \qquad \Gamma \vdash t_1 : T_1 \qquad (a,\ close\ \Gamma\ T_1)::\Gamma \vdash t_2 : T_2}{\Gamma \vdash Let\ a\ be\ t_1\ in\ t_2 : T_2}$$

The complexity of this system comes from *close* Γ T_1 in the Let-rule, which stands for the *closure* of T_1 w.r.t. Γ. This means that all free type variables in T_1 are universally quantified, except for those that are also free in Γ

$$close\ \Gamma\ T \stackrel{\text{def}}{=} gen\ T\ (ftv\ T - ftv\ \Gamma).$$

The first formulation of the above set of rules that we are familiar with appeared in the Mini-ML paper [2] where it was proved equivalent to the system by Damas and Milner. The Mini-ML rules are derived from the Damas–Milner rules by incorporating the quantifier rules into the other rules (via *close* and $\prec$), thus making the system syntax-directed.

The above system is much more faithful to standard presentations in the literature than the two previous formalizations based on de Bruijn indices [5, 9]. In fact, it is nearly identical to standard presentations. One exception is that we explicitly require that a pair $(a, \_)$ can only be added to the context Γ if a does not occur in it already. In the literature this corresponds roughly to those formalizations where the authors assume that the a is implicitly renamed beforehand.

We have that the typing relation is preserved under substitutions and that it is monotone under the subsumption relation:

Lemma 16.7 *If* $\Gamma \vdash t : T$ *then* $\theta(\Gamma) \vdash t : \theta(T)$.

Lemma 16.8 *If* $\Gamma_1 \vdash t : T$ *and* $\Gamma_1 \ll \Gamma_2$ *then* $\Gamma_2 \vdash t : T$.

Proof For Lemma 16.7. For this lemma we derive a strong induction principle [15] for the typing relation that allows us in the Let-case to assume the bound type variables, that is $ftv\ T_1 - ftv\ \Gamma$, avoid θ. Then the variable case is as follows: we know that validity is preserved under substitution, which implies that $valid\ (\theta(\Gamma))$ holds; $(x, S) \in \Gamma$ implies $(x, \theta(S)) \in \theta(\Gamma)$; and by Lemma 16.2 we can infer $\theta(T) \prec \theta(S)$. In the Let-case we have that $\forall X \in ftv\ T_1 - ftv\ \Gamma.\ X \mathrel{\#} \theta$, which implies that $\theta(close\ \Gamma\ T) = close\ (\theta(\Gamma))\ (\theta(T))$. Consequently all cases can be established by straightforward application of the inference rules. $\square$

Proof For Lemma 16.8. We show first that $\Gamma_1 \ll \Gamma_2$ implies *close* Γ_1 T $\ll$ *close* Γ_2 T: Using Lemma 16.6(i) we show by induction that $ftv\ \Gamma_1 \subseteq ftv\ \Gamma_2$ holds; thus $ftv\ T - ftv\ \Gamma_2 \subseteq ftv\ T - ftv\ \Gamma_1$. By Lemma 16.6($ii$) we obtain *close* Γ_1 $T \ll$ *close* Γ_2 T. Lemma 16.8 is now by a routine induction on $\Gamma_1 \vdash t : T$ using in the variable case the fact that if $(x,$

$S_1) \in \Gamma_1$ and $\Gamma_1 \lll \Gamma_2$ then there exists an S_2 such that $S_1 \lll S_2$ and $(x, S_2) \in \Gamma_2$. $\qquad\qquad\square$

The completeness proof in Section 16.5 needs the following lemma.

Lemma 16.9 $close\ (\theta(\Gamma))\ (\theta(T)) \lll \theta(close\ \Gamma\ T)$.

Proof The proof is by a fiddly alpha-renaming for the type scheme on the right-hand side to move the substitution θ under the binders. Then we appeal to Lemma 16.5. $\qquad\qquad\square$

16.4 Algorithm W

16.4.1 The rules

At this point we depart from the standard formalization: instead of defining W as a recursive function $W(\Gamma, t) = (\theta, T)$ which can possibly fail, we define W as an inductive relation $(V, \Gamma, t) \mapsto (V', \theta, T)$ where the lists V and V' contain the type variables that have been used so far by the algorithm. With this we rigorously treat the process of issuing new type variables and also avoid the vagueness present in some presentations of W, which state that a fresh variable is created, but omitting the information as to what it should be fresh for. Again, we are not the first to thread through the algorithm a list of type variables that need to be avoided: for example Gunter [6] gives such rules, but does not give a soundness nor completeness proof for these rules; Leroy [7] gives both proofs but includes in the algorithm an infinite set of available type variables.

Our rules for W are as follows:

$$\frac{(a,\ S) \in \Gamma \qquad freshen\ V\ S\ T}{(V, \Gamma, Var\ a) \mapsto (V\ @\ ftv\ T, [], T)}$$

$$\frac{(V, \Gamma, t_1) \mapsto (V_1, \theta_1, T_1) \qquad (V_1, \theta_1(\Gamma), t_2) \mapsto (V_2, \theta_2, T_2)}{mgu\ \theta_3\ (\theta_2(T_1))\ (T_2 \to TVar\ X) \qquad X\ \#\ V_2}{(V, \Gamma, App\ t_1\ t_2) \mapsto (X :: V_2, \theta_3 \circ \theta_2 \circ \theta_1, \theta_3(TVar\ X))}$$

$$\frac{(X :: V, (a,\ Ty\ (TVar\ X)) :: \Gamma, t) \mapsto (V', \theta_1, T_1)}{a\ \#\ \Gamma \qquad X\ \#\ (\Gamma,\ V)}{(V, \Gamma, Lam\ a.\ t) \mapsto (V', \theta_1, \theta_1(TVar\ X) \to T_1)}$$

$$\frac{(V,\Gamma,t_1) \mapsto (V_1,\theta_1,T_1) \qquad a \# \Gamma}{\frac{(V_1,(a, \; close \; (\theta_1(\Gamma)) \; T_1)::\theta_1(\Gamma),t_2) \mapsto (V_2,\theta_2,T_2)}{(V,\Gamma,Let \; a \; be \; t_1 \; in \; t_2) \mapsto (V_2,\theta_2 \circ \theta_1,T_2)}}$$

In the variable rule, in order to obtain the most general instance of a type schema, also known as its *generic instance*, all its bound variables are instantiated by *fresh* variables. This is formalized as a predicate *freshen* $V \; S \; T$, where V stands for the type variables to be avoided and T is the generic instance of S. Note that *ftv* T contains the newly introduced type variables. The definition of *freshen* is inductive: type schemes are simply unpacked:

$$\frac{}{freshen \; V \; (Ty \; T) \; T}$$

Quantifiers are instantiated by new variables:

$$\frac{freshen \; V \; S \; T \qquad Y \# (V, \; X, \; S, \; T) \qquad X \# V}{freshen \; V \; (\forall X.S) \; (T[X:=TVar \; Y])}$$

We show that *freshen* is "total" if V and S are viewed as input, and that it produces an instance for S.

Lemma 16.10

   (i) $\exists T. \; freshen \; V \; S \; T.$
   (ii)   If *freshen* $V \; S \; T$ then $T \prec S.$

Proof The first property is by induction on S and involving α-renamings; the second is by induction on *freshen* $V \; S \; T.$ $\square$

16.4.2 Unification

We treat unification as a black box and merely specify its behaviour via a predicate *mgu* $\theta \; T_1 \; T_2$ which expresses that θ is a *most general unifier* of T_1 and T_2. We shall rely on the following four properties of *mgu*:

Proposition 16.11

   (i)   If *mgu* $\theta \; T_1 \; T_2$ then $\theta(T_1) = \theta(T_2).$
   (ii)   If *mgu* $\theta \; T_1 \; T_2$ and $\theta'(T_1) = \theta'(T_2)$ then $\exists \delta. \; \theta' \approx \delta \circ \theta.$
   (iii)   If *mgu* $\theta \; T_1 \; T_2$ then *ftv* $\theta \subseteq ftv \; (T_1, \; T_2).$
   (iv)   If $\theta(T_1) = \theta(T_2)$ then $\exists \theta'. \; mgu \; \theta' \; T_1 \; T_2.$

16.5 Soundness and completeness proofs

The soundness and completeness statements for W are as follows:

Theorem 16.12 (soundness)
If $(V,\Gamma,t) \mapsto (V',\theta,T)$ and valid Γ then $\theta(\Gamma) \vdash t : T$.

Theorem 16.13 (completeness)
If $[] \vdash t : T$ then $\exists V \ \theta \ T'. \ ([],[],t) \mapsto (V,\theta,T') \wedge (\exists \delta. \ T = \delta(T'))$.

The proof of the first theorem is by a strong induction over $(V,\Gamma,t) \mapsto (V',\theta,T)$ using Lemma 16.7. This induction is relatively straightforward and therefore we omit the details.

The proof of the completeness theorem is more interesting: it is by induction on the structure of t. However, the statement needs to be strengthened in order to succeed with the induction. The strengthened statement is given by the following theorem.

Theorem 16.14 If $\sigma(\Gamma) \vdash t : T'$ and $ftv \ \Gamma \subseteq V$ then there exist θ, T, δ and V' such that

$$
\begin{aligned}
&(i) \quad (V,\Gamma,t) \mapsto (V',\theta,T) \\
&(ii) \quad T' = \delta(T) \\
&(iii) \quad \sigma' \approx \delta \circ \theta \ inside \ V.
\end{aligned}
$$

where we use the notion of two substitutions being *equal over a list of type variables*. This notion is defined as

$$
\theta_1 \approx \theta_2 \ inside \ Xs \ \stackrel{\text{def}}{=} \ \forall X \in Xs. \ \theta_1(TVar \ X) = \theta_2(TVar \ X)
$$

This relation is reflexive, symmetric and transitive in the arguments θ_1 and θ_2. We can also show that:

Lemma 16.15
(i)   If $\theta_1 \approx \theta_2 \ inside \ Xs$ and $ftv \ \_ \subseteq Xs$ then $\theta_1(\_) = \theta_2(\_)$ where $\_$ stands for types, type schemes, typing contexts and substitutions.
(ii)   If $X \ \# \ Xs$ then $\theta \approx (X, \ T)::\theta \ inside \ Xs$.
(iii) If $\theta_1 \approx \theta_2 \ inside \ Xs$ and $ftv \ \theta \subseteq Xs$ and $Xs' \subseteq Xs$ then $\theta_1 \circ \theta \approx \theta_2 \circ \theta \ inside \ Xs'$.

Proof The first property holds for types, type schemes, typing contexts and substitutions. In each case the property is shown by structural induction. The second property is by a simple calculation. The last is by induction on θ using (i). $\qquad\square$

Next we show that the list of used variables increases in every "recursive call" in the algorithm and that the list of used variables indeed contains all used variables.

Lemma 16.16

(i) If $(V,\Gamma,t) \mapsto (V',\theta,T)$ then $V \subseteq V'$.

(ii) If $(V,\Gamma,t) \mapsto (V',\theta,T)$ and ftv $\Gamma \subseteq V$ then ftv $(\Gamma, \theta, T) \subseteq V'$.

Proof Both are by induction on the rules of W. $\qquad\square$

Now we have everything in place to establish the completeness of W.

Proof For Theorem 16.14: The proof is by strong structural induction over t avoiding Γ and generalizing over V, σ and T.

Variable-case: By assumption we have $\sigma(\Gamma) \vdash Var\ x : T'$. From this we obtain an S such that $T' \prec S$ and (i) $(x, S) \in \sigma(\Gamma)$. From (i) we obtain an S' such that (ii) $(x, S') \in \Gamma$ and $S = \sigma(S')$. By Lemma 16.10(i) we have an T such that (iii) *freshen* $V\ S'\ T$. From this and (ii) we can derive $(V,\Gamma, Var\ x) \mapsto (V\ @\ ftv\ T,[],T)$. Using (iii) and $T' \prec \sigma(S')$ we obtain a δ such that $T' = \delta(T)$ and $\sigma \approx \delta \circ []$ *inside* V, which concludes this case.

Lambda-case: By the variable convention we have built into the induction principle for the typing relation, we know $x\ \#\ \Gamma$, from which we can infer that also $x\ \#\ \sigma(\Gamma)$ holds. By assumption we have $\sigma(\Gamma) \vdash Lam\ x.\ t : T'$. Taking the last two facts together we obtain a T_1 and T_2 such that

$$(i)\ (x,\ Ty\ T_1)::\sigma(\Gamma) \vdash t : T_2 \quad \text{and} \quad (ii)\ T' = T_1 {\rightarrow} T_2.$$

We now choose a new type-variable X such that $X\ \#\ (\sigma,\ \Gamma,\ \sigma(\Gamma),\ V)$ holds. By assumption we have $ftv\ \Gamma \subseteq V$, which implies $ftv\ ((x,\ Ty\ (TVar\ X))::\Gamma) \subseteq X::V$. We also have that

$$(iii)\ (x,\ Ty\ T_1)::\sigma(\Gamma) = ((X,\ T_1)::\sigma)((x,\ Ty\ (TVar\ X))::\Gamma)$$

because by condition $X\ \#\ \sigma$ it holds that $((X,\ T_1)::\sigma)(\Gamma) = \sigma(\Gamma)[X:=T_1]$ and by condition $X\ \#\ \sigma(\Gamma)$ that $\sigma(\Gamma)[X:=T_1] = \sigma(\Gamma)$.

Fact (iii) allows us to apply the induction hypothesis obtaining a θ, T_1, δ and V' such that

(iv) $(X::V,(x,\ Ty\ (TVar\ X))::\Gamma,t) \mapsto (V',\theta,T)$
(v) $T_2 = \delta(T)$
(vi) $(X,\ T_1)::\sigma \approx \delta \circ \theta\ inside\ X::V$.

We can conclude the Lambda-case with

$$(V,\Gamma,Lam\ x.\ t) \mapsto (V',\theta,\theta(TVar\ X)\rightarrow T).$$

which follows from $x\ \#\ \Gamma$ and $X\ \#\ (\Gamma,\ V)$. By the calculation

$$
\begin{aligned}
T' &= T_1 \rightarrow T_2 &&\text{by } (ii) \\
   &= T_1 \rightarrow \delta(T) &&\text{by } (v) \\
   &= \delta \circ \theta(TVar\ X) \rightarrow \delta(T) &&\text{by } (vi)
\end{aligned}
$$

we have that $T' = \delta(\theta(TVar\ X)\rightarrow T)$. Finally we have that $\sigma \approx \delta \circ \theta$ *inside* V because

$$
\begin{aligned}
\sigma &\approx (X,\ T_1)::\sigma &&inside\ V &&\text{by } X\ \#\ V \text{ and Lemma } 16.15(ii) \\
       &\approx \delta \circ \theta &&inside\ V &&\text{by } (vi)
\end{aligned}
$$

Application-case: By assumption we have $\sigma(\Gamma) \vdash App\ t_1\ t_2 : T'$, from which we obtain a T'' such that

(i) $\sigma(\Gamma) \vdash t_1 : T''\rightarrow T'$ and (ii) $\sigma(\Gamma) \vdash t_2 : T''$

holds. Using (i) and the assumption $ftv\ \Gamma \subseteq V$, the induction hypothesis gives us a θ, T, δ and V' such that

(iii) $(V,\Gamma,t_1) \mapsto (V',\theta,T)$
(iv) $T''\rightarrow T' = \delta(T)$
(v) $\sigma \approx \delta \circ \theta\ inside\ V$.

From $ftv\ \Gamma \subseteq V$ and (v) we know that $\sigma(\Gamma) = \delta(\theta(\Gamma))$ holds. Using Lemma $16.16(ii)$ and (iii) we can infer $ftv\ (\theta,\ \Gamma,\ T) \subseteq V'$ which means $ftv\ (\theta(\Gamma)) \subseteq V'$ holds. In the induction hypothesis for t_2 we can set Γ to $\theta(\Gamma)$ and σ to δ. By using (ii) this gives us a θ', T''', δ' and V'' such that

(vi) $(V',\theta(\Gamma),t2) \mapsto (V'',\theta',T''')$
(vii) $T'' = \delta'(T''')$
$(viii)$ $\delta \approx \delta' \circ \theta'\ inside\ V'$.

We now choose a new type-variable X such that $X \mathbin{\#} (V'', T''', \theta'(T))$ holds. By calculation we can show that the type $((X,\ T')::\delta')(\theta'(T))$ is equal to $((X,\ T')::\delta')(T''' \rightarrow TVar\ X)$.

Let-case: By the variable convention again, we know $x \mathbin{\#} \Gamma$, from which we can infer that also $x \mathbin{\#} \sigma(\Gamma)$ holds. By assumption we have $\sigma(\Gamma) \vdash$ *Let x be t_1 in t_2* $: T'$. Taking the last two facts together we obtain a T'' such that

$$(i)\ \ \sigma(\Gamma) \vdash t_1 : T'' \qquad (ii)\ \ (x,\ close\ (\sigma(\Gamma))\ T'')::\sigma(\Gamma) \vdash t_2 : T'$$

hold. By assumption $(*)$ *ftv* $\Gamma \subseteq V$ and induction hypothesis for t_1, we obtain a θ, T_1, δ and V' such that

$$
\begin{aligned}
(iii)\quad & (V,\Gamma,t_1) \mapsto (V',\theta,T_1)\\
(iv)\quad & \qquad\qquad T'' = \delta(T_1)\\
(v)\quad & \qquad \sigma \approx \delta \circ \theta\ inside\ V.
\end{aligned}
$$

By the assumption $(*)$ and (v) we have $\sigma(\Gamma) = \delta(\theta(\Gamma))$. Using Lemma 16.9 and (iv) we can hence infer that

$$(x,\ close\ (\sigma(\Gamma))\ T'')::\sigma(\Gamma) \ll \delta((x,\ close\ (\theta(\Gamma))\ T_1)::\theta(\Gamma)).$$

Consequently we can use Lemma 16.8 and (ii) to infer

$$(vi)\ \ \delta((x,\ close\ (\theta(\Gamma))\ T_1)::\theta(\Gamma)) \vdash t_2 : T'$$

We can now use the induction hypothesis for t_2 where we instantiate σ with δ, and Γ with $(x,\ close\ (\theta(\Gamma))\ T_1)::\theta(\Gamma)$. Since from (iii), $(*)$ and Lemma 16.16(ii) we have $(**)$ *ftv* $(\theta,\ \Gamma,\ T_1) \subseteq V'$ and hence *ftv* $(\theta(\Gamma)) \subseteq V'$, we can show that *ftv* $((x,\ close\ (\theta(\Gamma))\ T_1)::\theta(\Gamma)) \subseteq V'$. This allows us to use the induction hypothesis for t_2 to obtain a θ', T_2, δ' and V'' such that

$$
\begin{aligned}
(vii)\quad & (V',(x,\ close\ (\theta(\Gamma))\ T_1)::\theta(\Gamma),t_2) \mapsto (V'',\theta',T_2)\\
(viii)\quad & T' = \delta'(T_2)\\
(ix)\quad & \delta \approx \delta' \circ \theta'\ inside\ V'.
\end{aligned}
$$

Using $(viii)$ we can conclude provided we can further show that

$$(V,\Gamma,\textit{Let } x \textit{ be } t_1 \textit{ in } t_2) \mapsto (V'',\theta' \circ \theta,T_2) \quad \text{and} \quad \sigma \approx \delta' \circ \theta' \circ \theta\ inside\ V$$

hold. The first follows from (iii), (vii) and the variable convention $x \mathbin{\#} \Gamma$. The second follows using $V \subseteq V'$ (from (iii)) and the calculation:

$$
\begin{aligned}
\sigma \quad &\approx \quad \delta \circ \theta & \textit{inside } V \qquad & \text{by } (v) \\
&\approx \quad \delta' \circ \theta' \circ \theta & \textit{inside } V \qquad & \text{by } (ix),\, (**) \text{ and Lemma } 16.15(iii)
\end{aligned}
$$

This concludes the proof.   □

16.6 Conclusion

While the typing algorithm W is a classic algorithm implemented numerous times, there are surprisingly few careful descriptions of soundness and completeness proofs that can be readily used in a formalization. For example in [13] a version of W is presented that leaves the choice of fresh variables implicit and only states our Theorems 16.12 and 16.13; [6] gives a rigorous description for how to choose fresh variables, but only presents the details for soundness and completeness where this choice is left implicit. Two slick machine-checked proofs for soundness and completeness were implemented previously [5, 9], but both of these proofs code type and term variables using de Bruijn indices. As a result they were not easily adaptable to our setting, since they were streamlined for the representation of type schemes based on de Bruijn indices. For example, many proofs in [9] are by induction over the structure of type schemes, which we could not follow with our representation involving iterated binders. Most of the inspiration for our formalized proofs we have drawn from the treatment of soundness and completeness given by Leroy [7]. He encodes type schemes by quantifying over a whole set of variables in one go, and it took, surprisingly, a lot of work to adapt his proofs to our representation where we can only bind a single type variable in each quantification-step.

Although the Nominal Datatype Package provides a convenient reasoning infrastructure for α-equivalence classes, it did not provide as much help for this formalization as one might hope. One reason is that the package is not yet up to the task of representing general binding structures, and thus it is not yet possible to implement type schemes with a set of quantified type variables. Another reason is that the algorithm W contains many subtle "low level" operations involving type variables. This necessitates many α-renamings that had to be formalized explicitly without much help from the nominal infrastructure. However, we do not think that this can be avoided in any representation technique for binders (bar de Bruijn indices) that has been put forward in various theorem provers. Our formalization is part of the Nominal Datatype Package, which can be downloaded at:

http://isabelle.in.tum.de/nominal/

Bibliography

[1]   D. Clément, J. Despeyroux, T. Despeyroux, L. Hascoet and G. Kahn. Natural semantics on the computer. In K. Fuchi and M. Nivat (eds), Proceedings of the France-Japan AI and CS Symposium, ICOT, Japan, pp. 49–89, 1986. Also Technical Memorandum PL-86-6 Information Processing Society of Japan and Rapport de recherche #0416, INRIA.

[2]   D. Clément, J. Despeyroux, T. Despeyroux and G. Kahn. A simple applicative language: Mini-ML. In *Proc. ACM Conf. Lisp and Functional Programming*, pp. 13–27, 1986.

[3]   L. Damas. *Type Assignment in Programming Languages*. PhD thesis, University of Edinburgh, 1984.

[4]   L. Damas and R. Milner. Principal type schemes for functional programs. In *Proc. 9th ACM Symp. Principles of Programming Languages*, pp. 207–212, 1982.

[5]   C. Dubois and V. Ménissier-Morain. Certification of a type inference tool for ML: Damas-Milner within Coq. *Journal of Automated Reasoning*, **23**:319–346, 1999.

[6]   C. A. Gunter. *Semantics of Programming Languages*. MIT Press, 1992.

[7]   X. Leroy. *Polymorphic Typing of an Algorithmic Language*. PhD thesis, University Paris 7, 1992. INRIA Research Report, No 1778.

[8]   R. Milner. A theory of type polymorphism in programming. *Journal of Computer Systems Science*, **17**:348–375, 1978.

[9]   W. Naraschewski and T. Nipkow. Type inference verified: Algorithm W in Isabelle/HOL. *Journal of Automated Reasoning*, **23**:299–318, 1999.

[10]   T. Nipkow and L. C. Paulson. Proof pearl: Defining functions over finite sets. In J. Hurd (ed.) *Theorem Proving in Higher Order Logics (TPHOLs 2005)*, volume 3603, Lecture Notes in Computer Science, pp. 385–396. Springer-Verlag, 2005.

[11]   A. M. Pitts. Nominal logic, A first order theory of names and binding. *Information and Computation*, **186**:165–193, 2003.

[12]   A. M. Pitts and M. J. Gabbay. A metalanguage for programming with bound names modulo renaming. In *Proc. of the 5th International Conference on Mathematics of Program Construction (MPC)*, volume 1837, Lecture Notes in Computer Science, pp. 230–255. Springer-Verlag, 2000.

[13]   M. Tofte. *Operational Semantics and Polymorphic Type Inference*. PhD thesis. Edinburgh University, 1988.

[14]   C. Urban and S. Berghofer. A recursion combinator for nominal datatypes implemented in Isabelle/HOL. In *Proc. of the 3rd International Joint Conference on Automated Reasoning (IJCAR)*, volume 4130, Lecture Notes in Artificial Intelligence, pp. 498–512. Springer-Verlag, 2006.

[15] C. Urban, S. Berghofer and M. Norrish. Barendregt's variable convention in rule inductions. In *Proc. of the 21th International Conference on Automated Deduction (CADE)*, volume 4603, Lecture Notes in Artificial Intelligence, pp. 35–50. Springer-Verlag, 2007.

[16] C. Urban and C. Tasson. Nominal Techniques in Isabelle/HOL. In *Proc. of the 20th International Conference on Automated Deduction (CADE)*, volume 3632, Lecture Notes in Computer Science, pp. 38–53, Springer-Verlag, 2005.

17

A constructive denotational semantics for Kahn networks in Coq

Christine Paulin-Mohring

INRIA Saclay - Île-de-France and Université Paris-Sud

Abstract

Semantics of programming languages and interactive environments for the development of proofs and programs are two important aspects of Gilles Kahn's scientific contributions. In his paper "The semantics of a simple language for parallel programming" [11], he proposed an interpretation of (deterministic) parallel programs (now called Kahn networks) as stream transformers based on the theory of complete partial orders (cpos). A restriction of this language to synchronous programs is the basis of the data-flow Lustre language which is used for the development of critical embedded systems [14, 10].

We present a formalization of this seminal paper in the Coq proof assistant [4, 15]. For that purpose, we developed a general library for cpos. Our cpos are defined with an explicit function computing the least upper bound (lub) of an increasing sequence of elements. This is different from what Kahn developed for the standard Coq library where only the existence of lubs (for arbitrary directed sets) is required, giving no way to explicitly compute a fixpoint. We define a cpo structure for the type of possibly infinite streams. It is then possible to define formally what is a Kahn network and what is its semantics, achieving the goal of having the concept closed under composition and recursion. The library is illustrated with an example taken from the original paper as well as the Sieve of Eratosthenes, an example of a dynamic network.

17.1 Introduction

Semantics of programming languages and interactive environments for the development of proofs and programs are two important aspects of

From Semantics to Computer Science Essays in Honour of Gilles Kahn, eds Yves Bertot, Gérard Huet, Jean-Jacques Lévy and Gordon Plotkin. Published by Cambridge University Press. © Cambridge University Press 2009.

Gilles Kahn's scientific contributions. In his paper "The semantics of a simple language for parallel programming" [11], he proposed an interpretation of (deterministic) parallel programs (now called Kahn networks) as stream transformers based on the theory of complete partial orders (cpos). A restriction of this language to synchronous programs is the basis of the data-flow Lustre language [14, 10], which is used now for the development of critical embedded systems. Because of the elegance and generality of the model, Kahn networks are also a source of inspiration for extensions of the data-flow synchronous paradigm to higher-order constructions [7] or to more permissive models of synchrony [8].

We present a formalization of this seminal paper in the Coq proof assistant [4, 15]. For that purpose, we developed a general library for cpos. Our cpos are defined with an explicit function computing the least upper bound (lub) of a monotonic sequence of elements. This is different from what Kahn developed for the standard Coq libraries where only the existence of lubs is required, giving no way to explicitly compute a fixpoint. However, Kahn's library was intended as the background for a computer formalisation of the paper "Concrete Domains" by Kahn and Plotkin [13] and it covers general cpos with the existence of a lub for arbitrary directed sets whereas our work only considers ω-cpos with lubs on monotonic sequences, which is a sufficient framework for modeling Kahn networks.

We define a cpo structure for the type of possibly infinite streams. This is done using a coinductive type in Coq with two constructors, one for adding an element in front of a stream, the second constructor add a silent step Eps. From the structural point of view, our streams are infinite objects; this is consistent with the fact that these streams are models for communication links which are continuously open even if there is no traffic on the line. However, we identify the empty stream with an infinite stream of Eps constructors, so our data type models both finite and infinite streams. We define the prefix order on this data type and the corresponding equality. We also develop useful basic functions: the functions for head, tail and append used by Kahn [11], but also a filtering and a map function.

It is then possible to define formally what is a Kahn network and what is its semantics, achieving the goal of having the concept closed under composition and recursion. A Kahn network will be defined by a concrete set of edges corresponding to links in the network, each one associated with the type of the objects which are transmitted on that link. With each noninput edge is associated a node which is a continuous function producing a stream of outputs from streams given as inputs. This type of Kahn networks has a natural cpo structure. The semantics of a Kahn network is obtained in the following way: we provide streams for the input edges of the system, then the system is interpreted as an equation on the streams corresponding to the traffic on all the edges, seen as a continuous function. The semantics of the network is the fixpoint of this continuous function. We prove that this solution is a continuous function both of the network and of the input streams. By selecting the appropriate outputs, a system can be interpreted as a new node to be used in another system. Furthermore, the continuity with respect to the system itself gives the possibility of recursively defining a system.

Our library is illustrated with an example taken from the original paper as well as the Sieve of Eratosthenes, an example of a dynamic network, recursively defined.

Outline The remaining part of the introduction gives the main notations used in this paper. Section 17.2 recalls Kahn's approach in [11], which introduces cpos as a natural structure for the semantics of a simple parallel language. Section 17.3 introduces our definition of cpo structures in Coq. It is based on a structure of ordered types. We define the cpos of monotonic and continuous functions as well as several constructions for product of cpos. Section 17.4 introduces the type of possibly infinite streams and defines a cpo structure on it (in particular a lub function). We start with the simpler case of the flat cpo. We define a general function on the cpo of streams computing the value depending on the head and tail of the stream (and giving the empty stream in case the input is empty). We derive from this operator the constructions for head, tail and append as well as functionals for mapping a function on all elements of the stream or filtering the elements of a stream with respect to a boolean condition. We derive a cpo structure for natural numbers as a particular case of streams. Section 17.5 defines a type for Kahn networks and the associated semantics. Section 17.6 illustrates our library with two examples, one taken from the original paper [11], the other is the Sieve of Eratosthenes.

Notation In this paper, we use mathematical notations close to the Coq notations.

The expression $A \to B$ represents both the type of functions from type A to type B and the proposition: "A implies B". The arrow associates to the right: $A \to B \to C$ represents $A \to (B \to C)$.

The expression $\forall x, P$ represents the proposition "for all x, P" or the type of dependent functions which associate with each x an object of type P. We can annotate a variable with its type and put several binders as in $\forall (x\,y : A)(z : B), P$ which represents the property: "for all x and y of type A and z of type B, P holds".

The function which maps a variable x of type A to a term t is written fun $x \Rightarrow t$ or fun $x : A \Rightarrow t$. We can introduce several binders at the same time.

We write $c\,x_1 \ldots x_n \overset{\text{def}}{=} t$ to introduce c as an abbreviation for the term fun $x_1 \ldots x_n \Rightarrow t$. We write $x = y$ for (polymorphic) definitional equality in Coq (i.e. terms that are structurally equal). We use the notation $x == y$ for a specific equivalence relation associated with the type of x and y, defined as a setoid equality.[1]

We shall also use the Coq notation $\{x : A|P\}$ for the type of pairs (a, p) with a of type A and p a proof of $P[a/x]$ and $\{x : A\&\{y : B|P\}\}$ for the type of triples (a, b, p) with a of type A, b of type B and p a proof of $P[a/x, b/y]$.

17.2 From a simple parallel languages to cpos

In [11], Kahn proposes an algol-like language to describe parallel system. Each process is defined as a procedure with input and output parameters which are interpreted as channels. In the body of the procedure, there is a possibility to wait for a value on an input parameter or to send a value on an output parameter. Global channels can be declared, the processus can be instantiated and executed in parallel. The idea is that each channel correponds to a fifo in which values can be stored or read. There is no bound on the size of the fifo and a process can be blocked waiting a value on an empty channel.

More precisely a Kahn network is built from autonomous computing stations linked together. The stations exchange information through communication lines. The assumptions are that a computing station receives data from input lines, computes using its own memory and produces result on some of the output lines. The communication lines

---

[1] In Type theory, there is a natural polymorphic equality called the Leibniz equality which corresponds to convertibility and which allows rewriting in an arbitrary context. This equality is sometimes too strong. It is also possible to associate with a type a specific equivalence relation. The type together with the relation is called a setoid. The relation can be used pretty-much like an equality for rewriting, but only under a context built using operators which are proved to preserve the setoid relation. Coq offers facilities to manipulate the setoids.

are the only medium of communication between stations and the transmission of data on these lines is done in a finite amount of time. With each communication line, we associate the type of data which transit on that line. Each node can use the history of the inputs to produce an output, so it can be seen as a function from the streams of inputs to the streams of outputs. This function is continuous, which means that an output can be delivered without waiting for an infinite amount of information on the inputs lines.

A Kahn network is represented as an oriented graph. The nodes are the computing stations and the edges are the communication lines. We distinguish the input lines which have no source node. The graphical representation of the example in Kahn's paper is given in Figure 17.1.

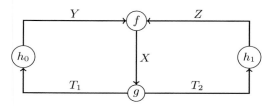

Fig. 17.1. A simple example of Kahn network.

In Kahn semantics, we look at the sequence of values that will be sent on each channel. This is a possibly infinite sequence (a stream). Locally each node is interpreted as a function taking as input a stream for each input edge and computing a stream for each output edge.

The system itself will behave as the solution of a set of equations defining the stream of values on the channels (one equation for each node). In our example, the system of equations will be:

$$X = f(Y, Z) \quad Y = h_0(T_1) \quad Z = h_1(T_2) \quad T_1 = g_1(X) \quad T_2 = g_2(X)$$

This is a recursive definition. In order to ensure the existence of a solution, we use a cpo structure on the set of streams (with the prefix order) and we prove that each node corresponds to a monotonic and continuous function.

Now if we have a system and we distinguish input and output edges, the solution is itself a continuous function from inputs to outputs so behaves like a node. This is an essential property for a modular design of systems. It gives also the possibility to recursively defined a system, like the Sieve of Eratosthenes which we describe in Section 17.6.2 and which corresponds to the network in Figure 17.2.

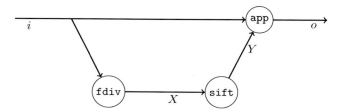

Fig. 17.2. A Kahn network for the Sieve of Eratosthenes.

The precise definition of nodes in the previous examples will be given in Section 17.6.

17.3 Formalizing cpos constructively

The basic structure used for the interpretation of Kahn networks is the ω-complete partial order. We developed a Coq library of general results on ω-cpos.

17.3.1 Definition

An ω-cpo is a type D with a partial order $\leq$, a least element (usually written $\bot$) and a least-upper bound (written $\mathtt{lub}\,h$) for any monotonic sequence h of elements in D ($h : nat \rightarrow D$ such that $\forall nm, n \leq m \rightarrow h\,n \rightarrow h\,m$).

An ω-cpo is actually a weaker structure than ordinary cpos where lubs exist for any directed set of elements. However, ω-cpos are sufficient for the construction of fixpoints. In the following we refer to ω-cpos simply as cpos.

17.3.1.1 Ordered structure

We define the type ord of ordered structures. An object in the type ord is a dependent record with a type A, a binary relation $\leq$ on A, and a proof that this relation is reflexive and transitive.

An example of an ordered structure is the type nat of natural numbers with the usual order. In the following, we shall abusively write nat for the object of type ord corresponding to this structure.

Notations When O is an ordered structure, we write $x : O$ to mean that x is an element of the carrier of O. The coercion mechanism in Coq allows us to support this abuse of notation: whenever a type is expected and an ordered structure O is provided, Coq automatically coerces the term O to its carrier.

When O is an ordered structure and $x, y : O$, the Coq notation mechanism allows us to write $x \leq y$ to express that x and y are in the relation associated with the ordered structure O. We shall write $x \leq_O y$ when we want to make the ordered structure explicit.

Equality We define an equality on an ordered structure by:
$x == y \stackrel{\text{def}}{=} x \leq y \wedge y \leq x$;
this is obviously an equivalence relation.

Order on functions Given an ordered structure O and a type A, there is a natural order on the type $A \to O$ of functions from A to O, called the pointwise order, which is defined by $f \leq_{A \to O} g \stackrel{\text{def}}{=} \forall x, f\, x \leq_O g\, x$. We write $A \stackrel{o}{\to} O$ for the corresponding ordered structure.

Monotonic functions Given two ordered structures O_1 and O_2, we introduce the type of monotonic functions from O_1 to O_2. Elements of this type are records with a function f of type $O_1 \to O_2$ (formally from the carrier of O_1 to the carrier of O_2) and a proof that this function is monotonic. With the pointwise order on functions, this type is an ordered structure written $O_1 \stackrel{m}{\to} O_2$.

If an object f has type $O_1 \stackrel{m}{\to} O_2$, it is formally a pair with a function and a proof of monotonicity. In Coq, we introduce a coercion from f to a function from O_1 to O_2, such that we can write $(f\, x)$ in a way consistent with mathematical practice. We consequently have the following property:
$\forall (f : O_1 \stackrel{m}{\to} O_2)(x\, y : O_1), x \leq y \to f\, x \leq f\, y$.
We also proved that any monotonic function preserves equality.

The composition of two monotonic functions is monotonic: when $f : O_1 \stackrel{m}{\to} O_2$ and $g : O_2 \stackrel{m}{\to} O_3$, we define $g@f$ of type $O_1 \stackrel{m}{\to} O_3$ the monotonic function such that $(g@f)\, x = g\, (f\, x)$

Notation fun $x \stackrel{m}{\Rightarrow} t$**.** If t is an expression of type O_2 depending on x of type O_1, we write fun $x \stackrel{m}{\Rightarrow} t$ for the object f in Coq of type $O_1 \stackrel{m}{\to} O_2$, which is a monotonic function such that $f\, x = t$. In Coq, the object f is formally a pair built from the function fun $x \Rightarrow t$ and a proof of monotonicity. The (informal) notation $\mathsf{fun}\, x \overset{m}{\Rightarrow} t$ hides the proof of monotonicity and helps us to insist on the functional behavior of f. In our Coq development we try to systematically define objects in $O_1 \overset{m}{\to} O_2$ using combinators like the composition of monotonic functions in order to get proof of monotonicity for free relying on the type system. After the definition of such an object f, we systematically prove a (trivial) lemma $f\, x = t$ which captures the functional behavior of the monotonic function. This lemma is useful for rewriting the expressions involving f.

17.3.1.2 Cpo structure

A cpo structure is defined as a record which contains:

- an ordered structure O;
- a least element $\bot$ of type O;
- a least upper-bound function $\mathtt{lub}$ for monotonic sequences; the constant $\mathtt{lub}$ has type: $(\mathtt{nat} \overset{m}{\to} O) \to O$;
- proofs of the following properties:
    - $\forall x : O, \bot \leq x$
    - $\forall (f : \mathtt{nat} \overset{m}{\to} O)(n : \mathtt{nat}), f\,n \leq \mathtt{lub}\, f$
    - $\forall (f : \mathtt{nat} \overset{m}{\to} O)(x : O), (\forall n, f\,n \leq x) \to \mathtt{lub}\, f \leq x.$

A cpo structure is implicitly identified with the underlying ordered structure. In particular, if D_1 and D_2 are two cpo structures, we can write $D_1 \overset{m}{\to} D_2$ for the ordered structure of monotonic functions from D_1 to D_2.

Continuity It is easy to show from the properties of $\mathtt{lub}$ that given D_1 and D_2 two cpo structures, $F : D_1 \overset{m}{\to} D_2$ a monotonic function from D_1 to D_2 and f a monotonic sequence on D_1, we have

$$\mathtt{lub}\,(F@f) \leq F\,(\mathtt{lub}\, f)$$

We say that F is *continuous* whenever the other direction is true, namely:

$$\forall f : \mathtt{nat} \overset{m}{\to} D_1, F\,(\mathtt{lub}\, f) \leq \mathtt{lub}\,(F@f).$$

We write $D_1 \overset{c}{\to} D_2$ for the ordered structure of continuous functions. When g has type $D_2 \overset{c}{\to} D_3$ and f has type $D_1 \overset{c}{\to} D_2$, we write $g@_f$ the element of $D_1 \overset{c}{\to} D_3$ which corresponds to the composition of f and g, ie such that $(g@_f)\, x = g\,(f\, x)$.

17.3.2 Cpo constructions

The structure of cpos is preserved by the usual constructions of functions and products. In this part we show constructions for the cpos of functions, monotonic functions and continuous functions as well as the product of two cpos, of an arbitrary family of cpos and the k-times product D^k of a cpo D.

17.3.2.1 Functional constructions

Given a cpo structure D and a type A, we can define a cpo structure on the set of functions from A to D using a pointwise construction for $\bot$ and `lub`:

$$\bot_{A \to D} \overset{\text{def}}{=} \mathsf{fun}\, x \to \bot_D \qquad \mathsf{lub}_{A \to D}\, h \overset{\text{def}}{=} \mathsf{fun}\, x \Rightarrow \mathsf{lub}_D(\mathsf{fun}\, n \overset{m}{\Rightarrow} h\, n\, x)$$

We write $A \overset{O}{\to} D$ for the cpo of simple functions from A to D.

Given an ordered type O, it is easy to show that $\bot_{O \to D}$ is a monotonic function and that `lub` preserves monotonicity. So we have a cpo structure written $O \overset{M}{\to} D$ on the type of monotonic functions.

If D_1 and D_2 are two cpo structures, then because $\bot_{D_1 \overset{m}{\to} D_2}$ is a continuous function and `lub` preserves continuity, we also have a cpo structure on continuous functions from D_1 to D_2. We write $D_1 \overset{C}{\to} D_2$ for this cpo structure.

17.3.2.2 Product constructions

We formalized other constructions on cpos corresponding to products.

Binary product The binary product $D_1 \times D_2$ of two cpo structures has a cpo structure written $D_1 \otimes D_2$.

$$\bot_{D_1 \otimes D_2} \overset{\text{def}}{=} (\bot_{D_1}, \bot_{D_2})$$

$$\mathsf{lub}_{D_1 \otimes D_2}\, h \overset{\text{def}}{=} (\mathsf{lub}_{D_1}(\mathsf{fun}\, n \overset{m}{\Rightarrow} \mathsf{fst}\,(h\, n)), \mathsf{lub}_{D_2}(\mathsf{fun}\, n \overset{m}{\Rightarrow} \mathsf{snd}\,(h\, n)))$$

The projection and pairing functions are continuous, we have defined

- `FST` : $\forall D_1 D_2, D_1 \otimes D_2 \overset{C}{\to} D_1$ `SND` : $\forall D_1 D_2, D_1 \otimes D_2 \overset{C}{\to} D_2$;
- `PAIR` : $\forall D_1 D_2, D_1 \overset{C}{\to} D_2 \overset{C}{\to} D_1 \otimes D_2$.

We also defined functions for currying and uncurrying

- `CURRY` : $\forall D_1 D_2 D_3, ((D_1 \otimes D_2) \overset{C}{\to} D_3) \overset{C}{\to} D_1 \overset{C}{\to} D_2 \overset{C}{\to} D_3$,
- `UNCURRY` : $\forall D_1 D_2 D_3, (D_1 \overset{C}{\to} D_2 \overset{C}{\to} D_3) \overset{C}{\to} (D_1 \otimes D_2) \overset{C}{\to} D_3$.

Indexed product $\prod D$ For modeling Kahn networks, it is useful to have a generalized product over an arbitrary number of cpos.

We take a set I of indexes and a family D of cpos indexed by I, that is, $D : I \to \mathsf{cpo}$. The cpo structure for the product written $\prod D$ is just a dependent generalization of the function type $I \overset{o}{\to} D$ in which the domain D may depend on the index. When D is a type expression depending on a free variable i, we write $\prod_i D$ for $\prod(\mathsf{fun}\, i \Rightarrow D)$

- Carrier: $\forall i : I, D\, i$
- Order: $x \leq_{\prod D} y \overset{\mathrm{def}}{=} \forall i, x\, i \leq_{D\, i} y\, i$
- Least element: $\bot_{\prod D} \overset{\mathrm{def}}{=} \mathsf{fun}\, i \Rightarrow \bot_{D\, i}$
- Least upper bound: $\mathsf{lub}_{\prod D}\, h \overset{\mathrm{def}}{=} \mathsf{fun}\, i \Rightarrow \mathsf{lub}_{D\, i}(\mathsf{fun}\, n \overset{m}{\Rightarrow} h\, n\, i)$.

The interesting constructions on that structure are listed here.

- A projection function $\mathtt{PROJ}$ of type: $\forall i : I, (\prod D) \overset{C}{\to} D\, i$.
- Given two indexed families D and D' over the set I, the mapping $\mathtt{MAPi}$ of a continuous function on the elements of an indexed product has type $(\forall i, D i \overset{C}{\to} D'i) \to \prod D \overset{C}{\to} \prod D'$ and is defined such that $\mathtt{MAPi}\, f\, p\, i = f\, i\, (p\, i)$.
- An operation to lift the indexes. Assume that we have two sets of indexes I and J, a family D of cpos indexed by I, and a function $f : J \to I$. We define a continuous function $\mathtt{LIFTi}$ of type $\prod D \overset{C}{\to} \prod_j D\,(f\, j)$ such that $\mathtt{LIFTi}\, p\, j = p\,(f\, j)$. It allows to select, reorganize or duplicate the elements in the product.

Finite product D^k It is also useful to have a finite product on the same cpo D. Given $k : \mathsf{nat}$, one possibility is to take the function space $\{i | i < k\} \overset{O}{\to} D$, but in that case we will have to deal with the subset type in Coq which is not always convenient. Instead we take the type $\mathsf{nat} \to D$ but instead of the pointwise order for functions, we introduce an order up-to k: $f \leq g \overset{\mathrm{def}}{=} \forall n, n < k \to f\, n \leq g\, n$. We write $k \to D$ for the cpo structure with this order. The least element is defined pointwise. For the lub, there is a small difficulty. The natural definition would be:

$$\mathsf{lub}_{k \to D}\, h\, n = \mathsf{lub}_D\, (\mathsf{fun}\, p \overset{m}{\Rightarrow} h\, p\, n)$$

But $(\mathsf{fun}\, p \Rightarrow h\, p\, n)$ is monotonic only when $n < k$. However, the value of $\mathsf{lub}_{k \to D}\, h\, n$ for $k \leq n$ is meaningless so we can choose an arbitrary one. Consequently we introduce h' such that $h'\,p\,n = h\,p\,n$ when $n < k$ and $\perp$ otherwise. Then taking:

$$\text{lub}_{k \to D}\,h\,n = \text{lub}_D\,(\text{fun}\,p \overset{m}{\Rightarrow} h'\,p\,n)$$

gives us the expected properties.

17.3.3 Fixpoints

Given a cpo structure D and a monotonic function F of type $D \overset{m}{\to} D$, we can define a monotonic function $(\text{iter}\,F)$ of type $\text{nat} \overset{m}{\to} D$ such that $\text{iter}\,F\,0 = \perp$ and $\text{iter}\,F\,(n+1) = F\,(\text{iter}\,F\,n)$.

We define the fixpoint of F as the least-upper bound of this sequence: $\text{fixp}\,F \overset{\text{def}}{=} \text{lub}\,(\text{iter}\,F)$.

The constant fixp has type $(D \overset{m}{\to} D) \to D$. It is itself a monotonic function.

It is easy to show that $\text{fixp}\,F \leq F\,(\text{fixp}\,F)$. The equality $\text{fixp}\,F == F\,(\text{fixp}\,F)$ is provable under the assumption that F is a continuous function.

We can also show that fixp is a continuous function from the cpo $(D \overset{C}{\to} D)$ of continuous functions on D to D. Consequently, we are able to define FIXP of type $(D \overset{C}{\to} D) \overset{C}{\to} D$, such that for all F of type $D \overset{C}{\to} D$:

$$\text{FIXP}\,F = \text{fixp}\,(\text{fun}\,x \overset{m}{\Rightarrow} F\,x) \qquad \text{FIXP}\,F == F\,(\text{FIXP}\,F).$$

Scott's induction principle We proved Scott's induction principle. A predicate is said to be *admissible* if it is true for the lub of a monotonic sequence when it is true for all the elements of the sequence: $\text{admissible}\,P \overset{\text{def}}{=} \forall f : \text{nat} \overset{m}{\to} D, (\forall n, P\,(f\,n)) \to P(\text{lub}\,f)$.

Scott's induction principle states that when a predicate is admissible, if it is true for $\perp$ and preserved by a monotonic function $F : D \overset{m}{\to} D$, then it is true for the fixpoint of F:

$$\forall P, \text{admissible}\,P \to P\,\perp \to (\forall x, P\,x \to P\,(F\,x)) \to P\,(\text{fixp}\,F)$$

Minimality It is easy to prove that the fixpoint of a monotonic function is the minimal solution for the equation. Namely:
$\forall (F : D \overset{m}{\to} D)(x : D), F\,x \leq x \to \text{fixp}\,F \leq x.$

17.4 The cpo of streams

We now want to define a cpo structure for concrete data types. Before developing the construction for streams, we show the simpler case of a flat cpo, which illustrates the main ideas.

17.4.1 The flat cpo

The simplest nontrivial (i.e. not reduced to $\bot$) cpo is the flat domain. Given a type A, we add an extra element $\bot$ and we have $x \leq b$ if and only if $x = \bot$ or $x = b$.

A natural solution could be to take as the carrier for this cpo the option type on A with values either None or Some a with $a : A$.

```
Inductive option (A:Type) : Type :=
   None :  option A | Some : A → option A
```

The constant None will be the least element. However we cannot define constructively a least upper bound. Indeed, given an increasing sequence of elements in our domain, we would have to decide whether all the elements are $\bot$ in which case the lub is $\bot$ or if there exists an element in the sequence which is of the form Some a in which case the lub is this element. Because we follow a constructive approach in Coq where functions correspond to algorithms, we cannot define a function which takes such a decision.

The computation of lubs is possibly an infinite process, a solution to represent infinite computations in Coq is to use coinductive types. This is the approach taken by Capretta [6] for dealing with general recursive functions in Coq. The solution is to introduce:

```
CoInductive flat (A:Type) : Type :=
   Eps : flat A → flat A | Val : A → flat A
```

A value in type flat is either finite of the form $\overbrace{\text{Eps}\,(\ldots(\text{Eps}\,(\text{Val}\,a))\ldots)}^{n}$ (written $\text{Eps}^{n}\,(\text{Val}\,a)$) in which case it represents the value a (with extra Eps steps corresponding to silent computations) or an infinite object Eps^{∞} coinductively defined by $\text{Eps}^{\infty} = \text{Eps}\,\text{Eps}^{\infty}$ corresponding to a diverging computation.

Eps^{∞} will be our least element and we need to identify all the representations of the value a ignoring the Eps constructors.

In order to achieve that, we define co-inductively the order on the flat domain with these three rules:

$$\frac{x \leq y}{\text{Eps}\, x \leq \text{Eps}\, y} \qquad \frac{x \leq \text{Val}\, a}{\text{Eps}\, x \leq \text{Val}\, a} \qquad \frac{y = \text{Eps}^n(\text{Val}\, a)}{\text{Val}\, a \leq y}$$

From this definition we proved reflexivity, transitivity and properties like $\text{Eps}^\infty \leq x$ or $\text{Val}\, a \leq x \to x == \text{Val}\, a$.

We can now look at the construction of lubs. We have a monotonic sequence h of elements in $\text{flat}\, A$ and we want (constructively) to build the least upper bound which can be either $\bot$ or a value.

If x is an element of $\text{flat}\, A$, we write $[x]_n$ for the same element but removing the n-th first Eps constructors (or less if we find a value before). We have $x == [x]_n$. Now in order to build the least upper bound, we look at $h\, 0$. If we find a value then we have our bound; if not, we produce an Eps and we continue by looking at $[h\, 0]_1$; $[h\, 1]_1$ if we find a value then we are done, if the elements start with an Eps then we produce an Eps in the least upper bound and we continue. At the n-th step we look at the sequence $[h\, 0]_n$; $[h\, 1]_n$; $\ldots$; $[h\, n]_n$, we try to find a direct value, otherwise we produce an Eps step and continue. This mechanism is illustrated in Figure 17.3; the Coq formalization will be given in the more involved case of streams. If one of the elements $(h\, k)$ in the sequence is a value,

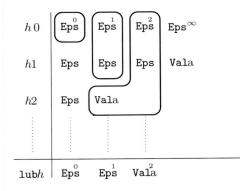

Fig. 17.3. Computation of lubs in a flat domain.

then there exists n such that $[h\, k]_n = \text{Val}\, a$ so we will eventually find this value before the p-th step with $k \leq p$ and $n \leq p$.

17.4.2 Streams

We now look at the case of streams which is developed following the same kind of reasoning.

17.4.2.1 Definition

The type of streams is co-inductively defined as:

CoInductive Str (A : Type) : Type :=
    Eps : Str A → Str A | cons : A → Str A → Str A

As before Eps^∞ can be coinductively defined by $\text{Eps}^\infty = \text{Eps Eps}^\infty$. It represents the empty stream and is also our $\perp$ element. We define a function $[\_]_n$ removing Eps in front of the stream by induction on n and case analysis on the stream.

$$[s]_0 = s \qquad [\text{Eps}\, x]_{n+1} = [x]_n \qquad [\text{cons}\, a\, x]_{n+1} = \text{cons}\, a\, x$$

17.4.2.2 Order

The order we consider on streams is the prefix order, we must also ignore the Eps steps which correspond to silent computations.

$$\frac{x \leq y}{\text{Eps}\, x \leq y} \qquad \frac{[y]_n = \text{cons}\, a\, z \qquad x \leq z}{\text{cons}\, a\, x \leq y}$$

The idea is that in order to show that $x \leq y$, there are two cases: if x is $\text{Eps}\, x'$ then we try to show $x' \leq y$, if x is $(\text{cons}\, a\, x')$ then after a finite number of Eps, y should be of the form $(\text{cons}\, a\, y')$ and we need to show that x' is less than y'. We do not know how many Eps steps we should remove so we cannot decide whether $x \leq y$ or not, and similarly we cannot decide whether a stream is finite or not. This corresponds well to the vision of the streams as a model of asynchronous communication links: it is not possible to know if more information will arrive and when. If we want to transmit a finite number of elements, we have to decide on a special character to indicate the end of the data.

Decidability of the empty stream is not required for the development we want to perform and it is the price to pay for having an explicit computation of lubs and fixpoints.

We can prove the expected properties of the order besides reflexivity and transitivity :

- $\text{Eps}^\infty \leq x$
- $\neg(\text{cons}\, a\, x \leq \text{Eps}^\infty)$
- $\text{cons}\, a\, x \leq \text{cons}\, b\, y \leftrightarrow a = b \wedge x \leq y$

Equality As in other ordered structures, equality on streams $x == y$ is defined as $x \leq y \wedge y \leq x$. It is important to distinguish this equality from intensional equality in Coq: $x = y$ means that x and y are structurally equal. For instance we have $x == \text{Eps}\,x$ for all x while $x = \text{Eps}\,x$ is only true for the Eps^∞ stream.

Simulation properties Coinductive definitions in Coq correspond to greatest fixpoints. The primitive way to build a proof of $x \leq y$ is to use fixpoint definitions in Coq, which should be guarded. This guarded condition is very syntactic and not always convenient to use in tactics. An alternative way is to define a co-induction principle which in this case corresponds to a simulation principle.

We introduce a principle which does not rely on the intensional representation of streams. We have to find a relation R on streams that is compatible with equality on streams and such that when $R\,x\,y$ holds and x is equal to a stream $\text{cons}\,a\,x'$ then y is also equal to $\text{cons}\,a\,y'$ and $R\,x'\,y'$ also holds. If such an R exists then it is included in the relation $\leq$ on streams. This principle can be written as follows:

$$\frac{\forall x\,y\,z\,t, x == z \to y == t \to R\,x\,y \to R\,z\,t \qquad \forall a\,x\,y, R\,(\text{cons}\,a\,x)\,y \to \exists z, y == \text{cons}\,a\,z \wedge R\,x\,z}{\forall x\,y, R\,x\,y \to x \leq y}$$

From this we can derive a principle which says that in order to prove $x \leq y$, it is enough to prove it in the particular case where $x == \text{cons}\,a\,x'$. This principle is in practice sufficient in order to avoid reasoning on whether x is the empty stream or not.

17.4.2.3 Least upper bounds

Destructuring streams We introduce a predicate is_cons on streams. It is defined as an inductive predicate with two constructors $\text{is\_cons}\,x \to \text{is\_cons}\,(\text{Eps}\,x)$ and $\text{is\_cons}\,(\text{cons}\,a\,x)$. We can prove that $\text{is\_cons}\,x$ is equivalent to $\exists a\,s, x == \text{cons}\,a\,s$.

In Coq is_cons is a *noninformative* proposition: we know the existence of a and s but we cannot use a and s to compute a value. However, if we know that a stream contains a cons constructor, the algorithm that removes Eps constructors will eventually stop on a cons constructor. In Coq, we defined a function uncons of type:

$$\forall x, \text{is\_cons}\,x \to \{a : A \& \{s : \text{Str}\,A \mid x == \text{cons}\,a\,s\}\}.$$

From the computational point of view, this function takes a (nonempty) stream as input and returns a pair (a, s) of its head and tail plus the proof that $x == \mathsf{cons}\, a\, s$. Technically, the function uncons is defined in Coq by a fixpoint doing a structural induction on the proof of $(\mathsf{is\_cons}\, x)$ and a case analysis on the structure of x.

Building lubs The construction of lubs for monotonic sequences of streams is a generalization of the idea used in the case of flat domains.

Consider a monotonic sequence h of streams, and a natural number n. We can look at the first constructor of $h\,0 \ldots h\,(n-1)$. Either we only have Eps steps or there exists $m < n$ such that $h\,m = \mathsf{cons}\, a\, s$. In this last case, the lub will start by $\mathsf{cons}\, a$ and we know that for all $p \geq m$, the stream $h\,p$ is equal to $\mathsf{cons}\, a\, s'$ (because $h\,m \leq h\,p$) such that we can extract a subsequence of h corresponding to the tails of $h\,p$ and recursively find the lub of this sequence. Following this idea, we built a function fCon which takes as argument a sequence of stream h and a natural number n and either answers that all $h\,m$ starts with Eps for all $m < n$ or find an element a and another sequence h' such that there exists $m < n$ such that each $h\,(k + m)$ is equal to $\mathsf{cons}\, a\,(h'\,k)$. Formally the Coq type of fCon is:

$$\forall (h : \mathsf{nat} \overset{m}{\to} \mathsf{Str}\,A)(n : \mathsf{nat}),$$
$$\{a : A\,\&\,\{h' : \mathsf{nat} \overset{m}{\to} \mathsf{Str}\,A|$$
$$\exists m, m < n \wedge \forall k, h\,(k + m) == \mathsf{cons}\, a\,(h'\,k)\}\}$$
$$+ \{\forall m, m < n \to h\,m = \mathsf{Eps}(\_)\}$$

This function is defined by structural recursion on n.

We write $[h] \overset{\mathsf{def}}{=} \mathsf{fun}\, n \overset{m}{\Rightarrow} [h\,n]_1$ for the sequence h where we have removed the first Eps step of each stream, our lub function is defined with a cofixpoint:

```
CoFixpoint lubn (h:nat→ StrA) (n:nat) : StrA :=
match fCon h n with
        (a,h',_) ⇒ cons a (lubn h' 1)
    |  _          ⇒ Eps (lubn [h] (n+1))
end
```

This recursive function is accepted by Coq because it is a *guarded fixpoint*: any recursive call in the body appears under a constructor of the type of streams.

The lub of a stream sequence h is just defined as $(\mathsf{lubn}\, h\, 1)$. We proved that this is the lub of the sequence of streams.

17.4.2.4 Useful functions on streams

In his paper, Gilles Kahn introduced several functions to manipulate streams: taking the first element, the stream without the first element or the concatenation of the first element of a stream to another.

All these functions are proved to be continuous. In our development, we derive them from the more general scheme of a function from streams to streams defined by case analysis on the structure of the input stream. If the input is equal to $\mathsf{cons}\,a\,x$ then the result is computed from a and x by a given function F, if it is Eps^∞ then the result is Eps^∞.

Let a parameter function F have type $A \to \mathsf{Str}A \overset{m}{\to} \mathsf{Str}B$. The function that we named case is coinductively defined by:

$$\mathsf{case}\,F\,(\mathsf{Eps}\,x) = \mathsf{Eps}\,(\mathsf{case}\,F\,x) \qquad \mathsf{case}\,F\,(\mathsf{cons}\,a\,x) = F\,a\,x$$

It is easy to check that $\mathsf{case}\,F\,\bot\,==\,\bot$ and that $x\,==\,\mathsf{cons}\,a\,y\,\to$ $\mathsf{case}\,F\,x\,==\,F\,a\,y$.

When F is a continuous function of type $A \to \mathsf{Str}A \overset{C}{\to} \mathsf{Str}B$, then $\mathsf{case}\,(\mathsf{fun}\,a\,s \overset{c}{\Rightarrow} F\,a\,s)$ is also a continuous function of type $\mathsf{Str}A \overset{C}{\to} \mathsf{Str}B$. The case construction is also continuous with respect to the argument F, such that we can build CASE of type $(A \overset{O}{\to} \mathsf{Str}A \overset{C}{\to} \mathsf{Str}B) \overset{C}{\to} \mathsf{Str}A \overset{C}{\to} \mathsf{Str}B$.

From this scheme, we derive the following functions:

- first has type $\mathsf{Str}\,A \to \mathsf{Str}\,A$ and is defined by:
  $\mathsf{first} \overset{\mathrm{def}}{=} \mathsf{case}\,(\mathsf{fun}\,a\,s \overset{m}{\Rightarrow} \mathsf{cons}\,a\,\bot)$
- rem has type $\mathsf{Str}\,A \to \mathsf{Str}\,A$ and is defined by:
  $\mathsf{rem} \overset{\mathrm{def}}{=} \mathsf{case}\,(\mathsf{fun}\,a\,s \overset{m}{\Rightarrow} s)$
- app has type $\mathsf{Str}\,A \to \mathsf{Str}\,A \to \mathsf{Str}\,A$ and is defined by:
  $\mathsf{app}\,x\,y \overset{\mathrm{def}}{=} \mathsf{case}(\mathsf{fun}\,a\,s \overset{m}{\Rightarrow} \mathsf{cons}\,a\,y)\,x$.
  We remark that $\mathsf{app}\,x\,y$ only takes the first element of x, and adds it in front of y. It corresponds to the "followed by" operation in synchronous data-flow languages and not to the usual append function on lists which cannot be defined in that framework.

We also build their continuous versions: FIRST and REM of type $\mathsf{Str}\,A \overset{C}{\to} \mathsf{Str}\,A$ and APP of type $\mathsf{Str}\,A \overset{C}{\to} \mathsf{Str}\,A \overset{C}{\to} \mathsf{Str}\,A$

We proved the properties which are given by Kahn [11]:

$$\mathsf{first}\,\bot\,==\,\mathsf{rem}\,\bot\,=\,\mathsf{app}\,\bot\,x\,==\,\bot$$

$$\mathsf{first}\,x\,==\,\mathsf{app}\,x\,\bot \qquad x\,==\,\mathsf{app}\,(\mathsf{first}\,x)\,(\mathsf{rem}\,x)$$

Instead of $x == \bot \vee \mathtt{rem}\,(\mathtt{app}\,x\,y) == y$ in Kahn [11], we proved that $\mathtt{is\_cons}\,x \rightarrow \mathtt{rem}\,(\mathtt{app}\,x\,y) == y$.

We also proved that $\mathtt{app}\,(\mathtt{first}\,x)\,y == \mathtt{app}\,x\,y$.

Bisimulation revisited Using the $\mathtt{rem}$ function, it is possible to express a bisimulation principle. In order to prove that two streams are equal, it is sufficient to find a relation R which is stable by equality, which implies equality on first elements and is preserved by remainders for nonempty streams. Such a relation R is included in equality:

$$\forall D\,(R : \mathtt{Str}\,A \rightarrow \mathtt{Str}\,A \rightarrow Prop),$$
$$(\forall x_1\,x_2\,y_1\,y_2, R\,x_1\,y_1 \rightarrow x_1 == x_2 \rightarrow y_1 == y_2 \rightarrow R\,x_2\,y_2)$$
$$\rightarrow (\forall x\,y, (\mathtt{is\_cons}\,x \vee \mathtt{is\_cons}\,y) \rightarrow R\,x\,y \rightarrow \mathtt{first}\,x == \mathtt{first}\,y)$$
$$\rightarrow (\forall x\,y, (\mathtt{is\_cons}\,x \vee \mathtt{is\_cons}\,y) \rightarrow R\,x\,y \rightarrow R\,(\mathtt{rem}\,x)\,(\mathtt{rem}\,y))$$
$$\rightarrow \forall x\,y, R\,x\,y \rightarrow x == y.$$

17.4.2.5 Mapping and filtering

Mapping A useful functional on streams is to apply a function $F : A \rightarrow B$ to any element of a stream of A in order to obtain a stream of B.

We easily build this function using our fixpoint construction and case analysis.

We first build a function $\mathtt{Mapf}$ of type $(\mathtt{Str}\,A \xrightarrow{C} \mathtt{Str}\,B) \xrightarrow{C} A \xrightarrow{O} \mathtt{Str}\,A \xrightarrow{C} \mathtt{Str}\,B$ such that $\mathtt{Mapf}\,f\,a\,s = \mathtt{cons}\,(F\,a)\,(f\,s)$.

Then we introduce $\mathtt{MAP} \stackrel{\mathrm{def}}{=} \mathtt{FIXP}\,(\mathtt{CASE}\,@\_\mathtt{Mapf})$ of type $\mathtt{Str}\,A \xrightarrow{C} \mathtt{Str}\,B$ and $\mathtt{map}$ the underlying function of type $\mathtt{Str}\,A \rightarrow \mathtt{Str}\,B$. From the properties of $\mathtt{FIXP}$, $\mathtt{CASE}$ and $\mathtt{Mapf}$, we obtain easily the expected equalities:

$$\mathtt{map}\,\bot == \bot \qquad \mathtt{map}\,(\mathtt{cons}\,a\,s) == \mathtt{cons}\,(F\,a)\,(\mathtt{map}\,s).$$

Of course, we could have defined $\mathtt{map}$ directly in Coq using a guarded fixpoint (a fixpoint where recursive calls are directly under a constructor) on the co-inductive type $\mathtt{Str}\,A$ which satisfies the following equations:

$$\mathtt{map}\,(\mathtt{Eps}\,x) = \mathtt{Eps}\,(\mathtt{map}\,x) \qquad \mathtt{map}\,(\mathtt{cons}\,a\,x) = \mathtt{cons}\,(F\,a)\,(\mathtt{map}\,x)$$

Proving monotonicity and continuity of this function requires specific co-recursive proofs. Our definition using $\mathtt{FIXP}$ and $\mathtt{CASE}$ gives us these results directly without extra work.

Our technique applies to recursive definitions of functions on streams which do not directly correspond to guarded fixpoints like the `filter` function.

Filtering Filtering is an operation that selects elements of a stream that satisfy a given (decidable) property P. This operator has been widely studied because it is the typical example of a nonguarded definition on co-inductively defined infinite streams.

Using p of type $A \rightarrow$ `bool` to decide the property P, a definition in an Haskell-like language would be:

$$\text{filter}\, p\,(\text{cons}\, a\, s) = \text{if}\ p\, a\ \text{then}\ \text{cons}\, a\,(\text{filter}\, p\, s)\ \text{else}\ \text{filter}\, p\ s$$

The problem is that if P only holds on a finite number of elements of the stream then the output is finite and there is no way to decide that.

Bertot [3] proposes a solution where there is an inductive proof that P holds infinitely many times in the input and this is used to produce an infinite stream as output. An alternative solution is to produce as output an infinite stream of values which are either a real value or a dummy constant.

With our representation of streams, we can simply define the stream in a similar way as for the map function using case analysis and fixpoint. We introduce $\text{Filterf}\, p$ of type $(\text{Str}\, A \xrightarrow{C} \text{Str}\, A) \xrightarrow{C} A \xrightarrow{O} \text{Str}\, A \xrightarrow{C} \text{Str}\, A$ such that $\text{Filterf}\, p\, f\, a\, s = \text{if}\ p\, a\ \text{then}\ \text{cons}\, a\,(f\, s)\ \text{else}\ f\, s$.

Then we introduce $\text{FILTER}\, p \stackrel{\text{def}}{=} \text{FIXP}\,(\text{CASE}\,@\_(\text{Filterf}\, p))$ of type $\text{Str}\, A \xrightarrow{C} \text{Str}\, A$ and $(\text{filter}\, p)$ the corresponding function of type $\text{Str}\, A \rightarrow \text{Str}\, A$. We easily check the expected property:

$$\text{filter}\, p\,(\text{cons}\, a\, s) == \text{if}\ p\, a\ \text{then}\ \text{cons}\, a\,(\text{filter}\, p\, s)\ \text{else}\ \text{filter}\, p\ s$$

17.4.2.6 *Finiteness*

We can define what it means for a stream to be finite or infinite. As usual, infinity is defined co-inductively and finiteness is an inductive predicate. We defined them the following way:

```
Inductive finite (s:Str A) : Prop :=
  fin_bot : s ≤ ⊥ → finite s
| fin_cons: finite (rem s) → finite s.

CoInductive infinite (s:Str A) : Prop :=
    inf_intro : is_cons s → infinite (rem s) → infinite s.
```

We were able to prove

- $s \leq t \to \mathtt{infinite}\, s \to \mathtt{infinite}\, t$
- $s \leq t \to \mathtt{finite}\, t \to \mathtt{finite}\, s$.
  This property is not provable if we take a different version of $\mathtt{finite}$ with an extra hypothesis $(\mathtt{is\_cons}\, s)$ in the constructor $\mathtt{fin\_cons}$. With such a definition of $\mathtt{finite}$, a proof of $\mathtt{finite}\, t$ is isomorphic to the number of $\mathtt{cons}$ in t. Assuming $s \leq t$, a proof of $\mathtt{finite}\, s$ should give us the exact number of elements in s, but there is no way to explicitly compute this number. With our definition of $\mathtt{finite}$, a proof of $\mathtt{finite}\, s$ just gives us an upper bound of the number of $\mathtt{cons}$ in the stream and is consequentely compatible with the order on the streams.
- $\mathtt{finite}\, s \to \neg\mathtt{infinite}\, s$

17.4.3 The particular case of natural numbers

We put an ordered structure on the type $\mathtt{nat}$ of natural numbers but this is not a cpo because there is no lub for the sequence $h\, n = n$. If we want a cpo structure, we need to add an infinite element. One way to define a cpo for natural numbers reusing our previous library is to take the type of streams on the trivial type $\mathtt{unit}$ with only one element $\mathtt{tt} : \mathtt{unit}$. The 0 element will be $\mathtt{Eps}^\infty$ as before, the successor function will be $\mathtt{S}\, x \stackrel{\text{def}}{=} \mathtt{cons}\, \mathtt{tt}\, x$. We can define the top element S^∞ with the cofixpoint $S^\infty = \mathtt{S}\, S^\infty$ and prove $\forall x, x \leq S^\infty$.

We write $\mathtt{Nat}$ for this cpo. There is an obvious monotonic function from $\mathtt{nat}$ to $\mathtt{Nat}$.

This domain is used in order to define the $\mathtt{length}$ function from $\mathtt{Str}\, A$ to $\mathtt{Nat}$. It is just an application of the $\mathtt{map}$ construction with the functional $\mathtt{fun}\, a \Rightarrow \mathtt{tt}$. We were able to show the following properties:

- $\forall s : \mathtt{Str}\, A, \mathtt{infinite}\, (\mathtt{length}\, s) \leftrightarrow \mathtt{infinite}\, s$
- $\forall n : \mathtt{Nat}, \mathtt{S}\, n \leq n \to \mathtt{infinite}\, n$

In the case of streams, we defined the append of streams x and y, just taking the first element of x (if it exists) and putting it in front of y. There is no way to define the usual append function on lists such that the concatenation of the empty stream and y is y, because we never know if x is empty by just looking at a finite prefix.

The situation is a bit different for the cpo of natural numbers where the concatenation corresponds to addition. When trying to add x with

y we might look alternatively at the head part of x and y. Whenever we find a successor, we can produce a successor on the output. If one of x or y is 0 then we will always find Eps step on this input and the output will be equal to the other argument with just extra Eps steps inserted.

Following this idea, we have been able to define the addition as a continuous function on Nat and prove that it is commutative and that $\mathsf{add}\,n\,0 == n$.

17.5 Kahn networks

We shall now explain our representation of Kahn networks in Coq.

17.5.1 Representing nodes

We define a shallow embedding of nodes. A *node* with inputs of type $A_1, \ldots, A_n$ and outputs in types $B_1, \ldots, B_p$ is a continuous function of type $\prod_i \mathsf{Str}\,A_i \xrightarrow{C} \prod_j \mathsf{Str}\,B_j$.

In general we allow arbitrary sets of indexes I for inputs and J for outputs. We associate with each index a type family $A : I \to \mathsf{Type}$ and $B : J \to \mathsf{Type}$, a *node of signature $A\ B$* is an element of $\prod_i \mathsf{Str}\,(A\,i) \xrightarrow{C} \prod_j \mathsf{Str}\,(B\,j)$.

We distinguish the particular case of a simple node with only one output. Given a set of indexes I for inputs, a type family $A : I \to \mathsf{Type}$ and a type B, we define a *simple node of signature $A\ B$* to be an element of $\prod_i \mathsf{Str}\,(A\,i) \xrightarrow{C} \mathsf{Str}\,B$.

A node with several outputs can just be seen as a set of simple nodes, each one corresponding to the projection on the corresponding output.

17.5.2 Representing systems

We start from a concrete set of edges and we distinguish input edges (given by a type I) from the other ones (given by a type J). We consider all the noninput edges to be output edges, it is not relevant for the system which outputs we want to observe.

We associate with each edge a type, so we have a type family $A : I + J \to \mathsf{Type}$. The type $I + J$ is the disjoint union of I and J. We write $(l\,i)$ (resp. $(r\,j)$) for the element of $I + J$ associated with $i : I$ (resp. $j : J$).

We define $SA \overset{\text{def}}{=} \text{fun}\, i \Rightarrow \text{Str}\,(A\,i)$ the type family indexed by $I + J$ of streams of elements of type $A\,i$ and $SA_I \overset{\text{def}}{=} \text{fun}\, i \Rightarrow SA\,(l\,i)$ the type family indexed by I associated with the inputs.

Now each edge which is not an input edge has a source which is a node. Actually each edge is associated with one particular output of the source node. We already mentioned that a general node with n outputs is equivalent to n simple nodes.

In our model, each noninput edge is associated to one simple node (its source).

A simple node in general is a function f of type $\prod_{k \in K} \text{Str}\, A'_k \overset{C}{\to} \text{Str}\, B$. We have to link the inputs of the node (indexed by K) with the edges of the system. This corresponds to producing a function $\sigma : K \to (I + J)$ which is compatible with the type system (i.e. A'_k is convertible with $A\,(\sigma\,k)$). Given f and σ, we could use the DLIFTi operation introduced in Section 17.3.2.2 in order to build a function f' of type $\prod SA \overset{C}{\to} \text{Str}\, B$, which can also be seen as a simple node but taking all the edges of the system as input.

Instead of introducing for each node the extra level of indirection with the set K and the map $\sigma : K \to (I + J)$, we directly consider that an output edge is associated with a (simple) node of the system which is a continuous map taking all streams associated with an edge as input, i.e. an element of $\prod SA \overset{C}{\to} \text{Str}\, B$. This gives us a very simple and uniform definition of the type of systems that we describe now.

A *system* with input edges I and output edges J of type $A : I + J \to \text{Type}$ is an object of type:

$$\text{system}\, A \overset{\text{def}}{=} \forall j : J, \left(\prod SA\right) \overset{C}{\to} \text{Str}\,(A\,(r\,j))$$

The set of systems has a cpo structure corresponding to an indexed product $\prod_j (\prod SA \overset{C}{\to} \text{Str}\,(A\,(r\,j)))$.

Equation associated with a system A system defines an equation on the streams associated with the edges, provided we give values for the input edges.

Formally if we have a system s on a type family $A : I + J \to \text{Type}$ as before and an input inp which is a product of streams on I such that inp has type $\prod SA_I$, then we can define the set of equations as a continuous function $(\text{EQN\_of\_system}\, s\, inp)$ of type $\prod SA \overset{C}{\to} \prod SA$ such that

$$\text{EQN\_of\_system}\, s\, inp\, X\,(l\,i) = inp\, i \qquad \text{EQN\_of\_system}\, s\, inp\, X\,(r\,j) = s\, j\, X$$

Taking the fixpoint of this function gives us the output observed on all the edges.

This function `EQN_of_system` is monotonic and continuous with respect to both the system and the input arguments. It has type:
$\texttt{system}\, A \xrightarrow{C} \prod SA_I \xrightarrow{C} (\prod SA \xrightarrow{C} \prod SA)$.

The solution of this equation for a system s and an input inp is obtained by taking the fixpoint of the functional $(\texttt{EQN\_of\_system}\, s\, inp)$. It is still a continuous function both of the system of the inputs, so we obtain for each system s, a new node `SOL_of_system` s of type $(\prod SA_I) \xrightarrow{C} (\prod SA)$ such that:

$$\texttt{SOL\_of\_system}\, s\, inp == \texttt{EQN\_of\_system}\, s\, inp\, (\texttt{SOL\_of\_system}\, s\, inp).$$

Now if we are only interested by a subset O of the output nodes, we use a mapping $\pi : O \to J$ and we use again the lift function in order to restrict our solution to a node indexed by I for inputs and O for outputs of type $(\prod SA) \xrightarrow{C} (\prod_{o:O} SA\, (r\, (\pi\, o)))$.

In the examples, we shall only be interested by one output $o : J$ which is simply obtained by applying `SOL_of_system` $s\, inp$ to $(r\, o)$.

17.5.3 Remarks

There are a few differences between our formalization and Kahn's original definition [11].

- Kahn defined a node as a continuous function, associated with edges for its inputs and outputs. In our formalism, we have the association between the edges and the output of a node but nothing on the link between the input of the node and the edges. The nodes are implicitly related to all edges. In practice, as we shall see in the examples, we shall start with a node defined as a continuous function with the appropriate number of arguments corresponding to the number of input edges in the node. Then, when defining the system, we simply project the relevant edges of the system on the corresponding inputs of the node.

- A noninput edge in our systems has one source node but may have several target nodes. This avoids the explicit use of duplication nodes which is discussed as a possible harmless extension in Kahn [11].

17.6 Examples

17.6.1 A simple example

We illustrate our approach with the same running example as in Kahn [11].

17.6.1.1 Definition

We first draw in Figure 17.4 the graphical scheme corresponding to the network.

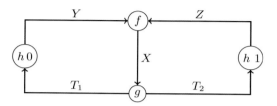

Fig. 17.4. A simple example of Kahn network.

The edges are X, Y, Z, T_1, and T_2. There is no input edge so the set I is defined as the empty type. The set J is an enumerated set with elements X, Y, Z, T_1, and T_2. All the links contain values in type $\mathtt{nat}$ such that the type family $A : I + J \to \mathsf{Type}$ is defined by $A\,k = \mathtt{nat}$ and we have $SA\,k = \mathtt{Str\,nat}$.

The functions corresponding to the nodes are f, g and h. The node g has two outputs corresponding to the functions g_1 and g_2. They satisfy the equations:

- $f\,U\,V = \mathtt{app}\,U\,(\mathtt{app}\,V\,(f\,(\mathtt{rem}\,U)\,(\mathtt{rem}\,V)))$
- $g_1\,U = \mathtt{app}\,U\,(g_1\,(\mathtt{rem}\,(\mathtt{rem}\,U)))$
- $g_2\,U = \mathtt{app}\,(\mathtt{rem}\,U)\,(g_2\,(\mathtt{rem}\,(\mathtt{rem}\,U)))$
- $h\,n\,U = \mathtt{cons}\,n\,U$

In Kahn [11], the equations involve an extra $\mathtt{first}$ application in the first argument of $\mathtt{app}$, but because we proved: $\mathtt{app}\,(\mathtt{first}\,x)\,y == \mathtt{app}\,x\,y$, we can eliminate it.

In order to define these nodes, we use the fixpoint construction and the composition of the (continuous) functions $\mathtt{app}$, $\mathtt{rem}$ and $\mathtt{cons}$ on streams.

The system itself (called $\mathtt{sys}$) is translated from the scheme in the Figure 17.4 which can also be seen as the set of equations:

$$X = f\,Y\,Z \quad Y = h\,0\,T_1 \quad Z = h\,1\,T_2 \quad T_1 = g_1\,X \quad T_2 = g_2\,X$$

In **Coq**, **sys** is a function from J to the continuous functions from $\prod SA \overset{C}{\to} \mathbf{Str}\,\mathtt{nat}$. Given p of type $\prod SA$, we have:

- $\mathtt{sys}\,X\,p = f\,(p\,(r\,Y))\,(p\,(r\,Z))$
- $\mathtt{sys}\,Y\,p = h\,0\,(p\,(r\,T_1))$
- $\mathtt{sys}\,Z\,p = h\,1\,(p\,(r\,T_2))$
- $\mathtt{sys}\,T_1\,p = g_1\,(p\,(r\,X))$
- $\mathtt{sys}\,T_2\,p = g_2\,(p\,(r\,X))$

Now the resulting stream (called **result**) of type ($\mathbf{Str}\,\mathtt{nat}$) is obtained the following way:

(i) The solution **sol** of the system **sys** has type $\prod SA_I \overset{C}{\to} \prod SA$.

(ii) Because I is empty, the type SA_I containts a trivial element **inp**, we apply **sol** to **inp** and get an object of type $\prod SA$.

(iii) The object **sol inp** X that is the projection of the previous system on the link X is the expected result.

17.6.1.2 Properties

Kahn's paper proves that the result is an infinite stream containing alternatively 0 and 1. For that he proves: **result** $==$ **cons** 0 (**cons** 1 **result**).

This is done in two steps, first he proves that **result** satisfies the following fixpoint equation:

$$\mathtt{result} == \mathtt{cons}\,0\,(\mathtt{cons}\,1\,(f\,(g_1\,\mathtt{result})\,(g_2\,\mathtt{result})))$$

then proves that $f\,(g_1\,s)\,(g_2\,s) == s$.

The first equation is a consequence of two general properties of fixpoints.

(i) A fixpoint on a continuous function is stable by composition: $\mathtt{FIXP}\,f == \mathtt{FIXP}\,(f @\_f) == \mathtt{FIXP}\,f^{n+1}$.

This is a consequence of a general lemma about fixpoint of composition of continuous functions:

$$\forall (f\,g : D \overset{C}{\to} D),$$
$$g @\_f \le f @\_g \to f\,(\mathtt{FIXP}\,g) \le \mathtt{FIXP}\,g \to \mathtt{FIXP}(f @\_g) == \mathtt{FIXP}\,g$$

(ii) Fixpoint on products can be simplified when the output on an index i depends only on the input on the same index i:

$$\forall (I : \mathsf{Type})(D : I \to \mathsf{cpo})(F : \prod D \overset{C}{\to} \prod D)(i : I)(F_i : D\,i \overset{C}{\to} D\,i),$$
$$(\forall p : \prod D, F\,p\,i == F_i\,(p\,i)) \to \mathtt{FIXP}\,F\,i == \mathtt{FIXP}\,F_i.$$

We take the equation `EQN_sys` of type $\prod SA \xrightarrow{C} \prod SA$ associated with the system `sys` together with the empty input stream and we compose it three times. We obtain the equation:

$$\texttt{EQN\_sys}^3 \, p \, (r \, X) = f \, (h \, 0 \, (g_1 \, (p \, (r \, X)))) \, (h \, 1 \, (g_2 \, (p \, (r \, X)))).$$

Consequently the stream `result` which is the fixpoint of `EQN_sys` on the output X is also the fixpoint of `EQN_sys`^{3} on the output X and is also the fixpoint of F_X with $F_X \, s = f \, (h \, 0 \, (g_1 \, s)) \, (h \, 1 \, (g_2 \, s))$. Using the definition of f and h, it is easy to see that: $F_X \, s == \mathsf{cons} \, 0 \, (\mathsf{cons} \, 1 \, (f \, (g_1 \, s) \, (g_2 \, s)))$.

What remains to be proved is that $\forall s, f \, (g_1 \, s) \, (g_2 \, s) == s$. Kahn's paper uses a structural induction which is not appropriate because the stream s is possibly infinite. Instead we use a bisimulation technique.

We use a variation of the bisimulation principle given in Section 17.4.2.4 which is:

$$\forall D \, (R : \mathsf{Str} \, A \to \mathsf{Str} \, A \to \mathsf{Prop}),$$
$$(\forall x_1 \, x_2 \, y_1 \, y_2, R \, x_1 \, y_1 \to x_1 == x_2 \to y_1 == y_2 \to R \, x_2 \, y_2)$$
$$\to (\forall x \, y, (\mathsf{is\_cons} \, x \vee \mathsf{is\_cons} \, y) \to R \, x \, y \to \mathsf{first} \, x == \mathsf{first} \, y)$$
$$\to (\forall x \, y, (\mathsf{is\_cons} \, (\mathsf{rem} \, x) \vee \mathsf{is\_cons} \, (\mathsf{rem} \, y)) \to$$
$$\qquad R \, x \, y \to \mathsf{first} \, (\mathsf{rem} \, x) == \mathsf{first} \, (\mathsf{rem} \, y))$$
$$\to (\forall x \, y, (\mathsf{is\_cons} \, (\mathsf{rem} \, x) \vee \mathsf{is\_cons} \, (\mathsf{rem} \, y)) \to$$
$$\qquad R \, x \, y \to R \, (\mathsf{rem} \, (\mathsf{rem} \, x)) \, (\mathsf{rem} \, (\mathsf{rem} \, y)))$$
$$\to \forall x \, y, R \, x \, y \to x == y.$$

We instantiate this principle by the relation $R \, s \, t \stackrel{\mathrm{def}}{=} t == f \, (g_1 \, s) \, (g_2 \, s)$. The proof is based on algebraic properties of f, g_1, g_2, `rem`, and `first`.

We end up with the expected property $\texttt{result} = \mathsf{cons} \, 0 \, (\mathsf{cons} \, 1 \, \texttt{result})$ from which we deduce that `result` is an infinite stream because its length is infinite.

17.6.2 Sieve of Eratosthenes

The scheme corresponding to the sieve of Eratosthenes is given in Figure 17.2 in Section 17.2. What is interesting is that it is a recursive scheme. The scheme defines a node `sift` which is used as an internal node in the scheme itself. This is done using a fixpoint construction which is possible because the interpretation of a scheme is a continuous function of the nodes themselves.

The node `fdiv` is easily built using `case` and `filter` such that:

$$\texttt{fdiv} \, (\mathsf{cons} \, a \, s) = \texttt{filter} \, (\mathrm{div} \, a) \, s$$

We introduce the input index type I which is just a type with one element i and the output index type J which contains three elements X, Y and o. All the links have type nat, so using the same notation as before we introduce $A : I + J \rightarrow \mathsf{Type}$, $SA : I + J \rightarrow \mathsf{cpo}$, $SA_I : I \rightarrow \mathsf{cpo}$ such that $A\,k = \mathsf{nat}$, $SA\,k = \mathtt{Str\,nat}$ and $SA_I\,i = \mathtt{Str\,nat}$.

We define the functional $\mathtt{Fsift}$ associated with the recursive system which has type $(\mathtt{Str\,nat} \xrightarrow{C} \mathtt{Str\,nat}) \xrightarrow{C} \mathsf{system}\,A$ and is defined by case on the output link with p of type $\prod SA$:

$$\mathtt{Fsift}\,f\,X\,p = \mathtt{fdiv}\,(p\,(l\,i))$$
$$\mathtt{Fsift}\,f\,Y\,p = f\,(p\,(r\,X))$$
$$\mathtt{Fsift}\,f\,o\,p = \mathtt{app}\,(p\,(l\,i))\,(p\,(r\,Y))$$

The construction $\mathtt{SOL\_of\_system}$ introduced in Section 17.5.2 gives us a continuous function from systems to functions of type $\prod SA_I \xrightarrow{C} \prod SA$ from the streams corresponding to input edges to the streams corresponding to all edges.

The composition of $\mathtt{SOL\_of\_system}$ with $\mathtt{Fsift}$ gives us a continuous function from $(\mathtt{Str\,nat} \xrightarrow{C} \mathtt{Str\,nat})$ to $\prod SA_I \xrightarrow{C} \prod SA$.

Now the recursive graphical construction of the system says that $\mathtt{sift}$ is the functional corresponding to the input i and the output o.

Using $\mathtt{pair_1}$ (the continuous trivial function from D to $\prod_{i \in I} D$ when I has only one element), it is easy to build a continuous function $\mathtt{focus}$ of type $(\prod SA_I \xrightarrow{C} \prod SA) \xrightarrow{C} \mathtt{Str\,nat} \xrightarrow{C} \mathtt{Str\,nat}$ such that $\mathtt{focus}\,h\,s = h\,(\mathtt{pair_1}\,s)\,o$.

The composition of $\mathtt{focus}$, $\mathtt{SOL\_of\_system}$ and $\mathtt{Fsift}$ is now a continuous function from $(\mathtt{Str\,nat} \xrightarrow{C} \mathtt{Str\,nat})$ to $(\mathtt{Str\,nat} \xrightarrow{C} \mathtt{Str\,nat})$. We introduce $\mathtt{sift}$ as the fixpoint of this operator.

We can prove, using the fixpoint equation for $\mathtt{sift}$, the following equality:

$$\mathtt{sift} == \mathtt{focus}\,(\mathtt{SOL\_of\_system}\,A\,(\mathtt{Fsift}\,\mathtt{sift})).$$

Using the fixpoint equation for: $\mathtt{SOL\_of\_system}\,A\,(\mathtt{Fsift}\,\mathtt{sift})$, it is easy to derive successively the following equalities for all stream s:

- $\mathtt{SOL\_of\_system}\,A\,(\mathtt{Fsift}\,\mathtt{sift})\,(\mathtt{pair_1}\,s)\,(l\,i) == s$.
- $\mathtt{SOL\_of\_system}\,A\,(\mathtt{Fsift}\,\mathtt{sift})\,(\mathtt{pair_1}\,s)\,(r\,X) == \mathtt{fdiv}\,s$.
- $\mathtt{SOL\_of\_system}\,A\,(\mathtt{Fsift}\,\mathtt{sift})\,(\mathtt{pair_1}\,s)\,(r\,Y) == \mathtt{sift}\,(\mathtt{fdiv}\,s)$.
- $\mathtt{SOL\_of\_system}\,A\,(\mathtt{Fsift}\,\mathtt{sift})\,(\mathtt{pair_1}\,s)\,(r\,o) == \mathtt{app}\,s\,(\mathtt{sift}\,(\mathtt{fdiv}\,s))$.

From these equalities, the property of `fdiv`, and the fixpoint equality for `sift` we easily deduce the expected property of `sift`:

$$\mathtt{sift}\,(\mathtt{cons}\,a\,s) == \mathtt{cons}\,a\,(\mathtt{sift}\,(\mathtt{filter}\,(\mathtt{div}\,a)\,s)) \quad \mathtt{sift}\,\bot == \bot$$

17.7 Conclusion

17.7.1 Contributions

This paper describes three contributions.

The first one is a general Coq library for ω-cpos. This is a constructive version of cpos where there is an explicit function to build the least-upper bound of any monotonic sequence. It contains useful constructions such as generalized products, cpos of monotonic and continuous functions and combinators to manipulate them. It also introduces a fixpoint combinator. This library has also been used in a Coq library for modeling randomized programs as distributions [1, 2].

The second contribution is the definition of the cpo of streams of elements in a type A. This type, defined co-inductively, covers both the case of finite and infinite streams but without any explicit way to decide if the stream is finite or not. The type itself is not very original, it corresponds to an infinite stream with values which can be present or absent. What is interesting is the order defined on that data structure and the derived equality. Modulo this equality, we are able to reason on this data structure by only considering the interesting cases where the streams are equal to (`cons a s`). The most difficult construction on the type of streams was the least-upper bound. The fixpoint given by the cpo structure makes it possible to define in a natural way a function like `filter` that selects the elements of a stream satisfying a predicate P. This function is problematic with most representations of streams in Coq because the output can be finite or infinite depending on the number of elements in the input which satisfies P.

The last contribution is the modeling of Kahn networks as they are described in the paper [11]. We chose a shallow embedding where a system is represented using a set of links and for each noninput link a continuous function corresponding to the node. Each node can possibly take as input all the links of the system. This leads to a very simple and uniform definition of systems which itself can be seen as a cpo.

A system together with streams for inputs defines a continuous function on the streams associated with the links of the system (the history of the system). The fixpoint of this function defines the behavior of the system as a continuous function both from the inputs and the system.

Using this interpretation, we were able to formalize both the main example given by Kahn [11] and the sieve of Eratosthenes, an example of a recursive scheme which was presented by Kahn and MacQueen [12].

17.7.2 Remarks

Coq development The Coq development runs with Coq version 8.1 [15]. It makes an intensive use of the new setoid rewriting tactic. It is available from the author's web page. It contains approximately 1700 lines of definitions and statements and 3000 lines of proofs. The Coq notation mechanism as well as implicit arguments makes it possible to keep notations in Coq quite similar to the ones used in this paper.

What is mainly missing is a syntactic facility in order to automatically build complex continuous functions by composition of simpler functions and functionals.

Synchronous case As we mentioned before, one important application of Kahn networks is their restriction to synchronous languages where no buffer is needed to store the values on the links. The nodes receive the inputs at a regular time given by a clock and instantaneously produce an output. A denotational semantics of this calculus in Coq was given by Boulmé and Hamon [5]. Their approach is to make the type of the stream dependent on the clock (which is an infinite stream of boolean values), so there is a control on which data is available or not. They do that by considering ordinary infinite streams (only the **cons** constructor) with values which can either be an ordinary value in the type A of elements, or an absent value (when the clock is off) or a failure (no value when the clock is on).

We could adapt our development to this particular case by extending the definition of streams to make them dependent on the clock.

```
CoInductive Str A :clock → Type :=
  Eps : ∀ c, Str A c → Str A (false::c)
| cons : ∀ c, A → Str A c → Str A (true::c)
```

Then in order to define the bottom element of a stream on a clock c, it is convenient to have a bottom element in the type A. So the natural framework is to consider a cpo structure on A. Then the order on the streams can be defined in the following way (the clock argument of constructors Eps and cons can be derived from the type of the stream so it is left implicit in the Coq notation).

$$\frac{x \leq y}{\text{Eps } x \leq \text{Eps } y} \qquad \frac{a \leq b \qquad x \leq y}{\text{cons } a\, x \leq \text{cons } b\, y}$$

It is simpler than in our case because we know exactly where the cons constructors are. The construction of lubs is also simplified, when the clock is true, there is a cons constructor in each element of the sequence of streams, we produce a cons constructor in the output with a value corresponding to the lub of the heads. However, some extra properties have to be proved on the sequence if we want to ensure that there is no cons $\perp$ left in the result.

Equations Kahn's paper refers to the paper of Courcelle, Kahn and Vuillemin [9] which proves the decidability of equivalence in a language of fixpoints.[2] We started to write a Coq version of this paper and in particular we defined the notion of terms and built the cpo corresponding to the *canonical interpretation* of equations built on sequences of terms. But the full formalization of this part still remains to be done.

Bibliography

[1]   P. Audebaud and C. Paulin-Mohring. Proofs of randomized algorithms in Coq. In T. Uustalu (ed.) *Mathematics of Program Construction, MPC 2006*, volume 4014, Lecture Notes in Computer Science, Kuressaare, Estonia, July 2006. Springer-Verlag, 2006.

[2]   P. Audebaud and C. Paulin-Mohring. Proofs of randomized algorithms in Coq. To appear in *Science of Computer Programming*. Extended version of [1].

[3]   Y. Bertot. Filters on coinductive streams, an application to Eratosthenes'sieve. In P. Urzyczyn (ed.) *International Conference of Typed Lambda Calculi and Applications*, volume 3461, Lecture Notes in Computer Science, pp. 102–115. Springer-Verlag, 2005.

[4]   Y. Bertot and P. Castéran. *Interactive Theorem Proving and Program Development*. Springer-Verlag, 2004.

[5]   S. Boulmé and G. Hamon. Certifying synchrony for free. In *International Conference on Logic for Programming, Artificial Intelligence and Reasoning (LPAR)*, volume 2250, Lecture Notes in Artificial Intelligence, La Havana, Cuba, December 2001. Springer-Verlag, 2001. Short version of *A clocked denotational semantics for Lucid-Synchrone in Coq*, available as a Technical Report (LIP6), at www.lri.fr/~pouzet.

---

[2]   Editor's note: this article is reproduced in this book.

[6]   V. Capretta. General recursion via coinductive types. *Logical Methods in Computer Science*, 1(2:1):1–28, 2005.

[7]   P. Caspi and M. Pouzet. Synchronous Kahn Networks. In *ACM SIGPLAN International Conference on Functional Programming*, Philadelphia, Pensylvania, May 1996.

[8]   A. Cohen, M. Duranton, C. Eisenbeis, C. Pagetti, F. Plateau and M. Pouzet. *N*-Synchronous Kahn networks: a relaxed model of synchrony for real-time systems. In *ACM International Conference on Principles of Programming Languages (POPL'06)*, Charleston, South Carolina, USA, January 2006.

[9]   B. Courcelle, G. Kahn and J. Vuillemin. Algorithmes d'équivalence et de réduction à des expressions minimales dans une classe d'équations récursives simples. In J. Loeckx (ed.) *Automata, Languages and Programming*, volume 14, Lecture Notes in Computer Science, pp. 200–213. Springer-Verlag, 1974. Translation from French by T. Veldhuizen with original text, a few comments and additional references.

[10]   N. Halbwachs, P. Caspi, P. Raymond and D. Pilaud. The synchronous dataflow programming language lustre. *Proceedings of the IEEE*, 79(9):1305–1320, 1991.

[11]   G. Kahn. The semantics of a simple language for parallel programming. In *Information Processing 74*. North-Holland, 1974.

[12]   G. Kahn and D. MacQueen. Coroutines and networks of parallel processes. In B. Gilchrist (ed.) *Information Processing 77*. North-Holland, 1977.

[13]   G. Kahn and G. D. Plotkin. Concrete domains. *Theoretical Computer Science*, **121**(1& 2):187–277, 1993.

[14]   D. Pilaud, P. Caspi, N. Halbwachs and J. Plaice. Lustre: a declarative language for programming synchronous systems. In *14th ACM Conference on Principles of Programming Languages*, pp. 178–188, Munich, January 1987.

[15]   The Coq Development Team. *The Coq Proof Assistant Reference Manual – Version V8.1*, July 2006. `http://coq.inria.fr`.

18

Asclepios: a research project team at INRIA for the analysis and simulation of biomedical images

N. Ayache, O. Clatz, H. Delingette, G. Malandain,

X. Pennec, and M. Sermesant

INRIA Sophia Antipolis Méditerranée

Abstract

Asclepios[1] is the name of a research project team officially launched on November 1st, 2005 at INRIA Sophia-Antipolis, to study the Analysis and Simulation of Biological and Medical Images. This research project team follows a previous one, called Epidaure, initially dedicated to Medical Imaging and Robotics research. These two project teams were strongly supported by Gilles Kahn, who used to have regular scientific interactions with their members. More generally, Gilles Kahn had a unique vision of the growing importance of the interaction of the Information Technologies and Sciences with the Biological and Medical world. He was one of the originators of the creation of a specific *BIO* theme among the main INRIA research directions, which now regroups 16 different research teams including Asclepios, whose research objectives are described and illustrated in this article.

18.1 Introduction

18.1.1 The revolution of biomedical images and quantitative medicine

There is an irreversible evolution of medical practice toward more quantitative and personalized decision processes for prevention, diagnosis and therapy. This evolution is supported by a continually increasing number of biomedical devices providing *in vivo* measurements of structures and processes inside the human body, at scales varying from the organ to

---

[1] Asclepios was a Greek hero who later became the Greek god of medicine and healing. His most famous sanctuary was located in Epidaurus which is situated in the northeastern Peloponnese (from Ron Leadbetter).

From Semantics to Computer Science Essays in Honour of Gilles Kahn, eds Yves Bertot, Gérard Huet, Jean-Jacques Lévy and Gordon Plotkin. Published by Cambridge University Press. © Cambridge University Press 2009.

the cellular and even molecular level. Among all these measurements, *biomedical images* of various forms increasingly play a central role.

Facing the need for more quantitative and personalized medicine based on larger and more complex sets of measurements, there is a crucial need for developing: (1) advanced image analysis tools capable of extracting the pertinent information from biomedical images and signals; (2) advanced models of the human body to correctly interpret this information; (3) large distributed databases to calibrate and validate these models.

18.1.2 Advanced biomedical image analysis

Tremendous progress has been made in the automated analysis of biomedical images during the past decades. [16, 3].[2] For instance, for rigid parts of the body such as the head, it is now possible to fuse, in a completely automated manner, images of the same patient taken from different imaging modalities (e.g. anatomical and functional), or to track the evolution of a pathology through the automated registration and comparison of a series of images taken at widely spaced time instants [20, 42] (see Fig. 18.1). It is also possible to obtain from a magnetic resonance image of the head an adequate segmentation into skull tissues, white matter, grey matter, and cerebro-spinal fluid [43], or to measure certain functional properties of the heart from dynamic sequences of magnetic resonance [2], ultrasound or nuclear medicine images [22].

Despite these advances one may note that statistical models of anatomy are still very crude, resulting in poor registration results in deformable regions of the body, or between different subjects. If some algorithms exploit the physical modeling of the image acquisition process, only a few actually model the physical or even physiological properties of the human body itself. Coupling biomedical image analysis with anatomical and physiological models of the human body would not only provide a better comprehension of the observed images and signals, but would in addition provide efficient tools to detect anomalies, to predict the evolution of diseases and to simulate and assess the effect of therapies.

---

[2] One can gain a good understanding of the state of the art from the proceedings of the most recent conferences MICCAI (Medical Image Computing and Computer Assisted Intervention) or ISBI (Int. Symp. on Biomedical Imaging) as well as from the most recent issues of journals like *IEEE Trans. on Medical Imaging* or *Medical Image Analysis*.

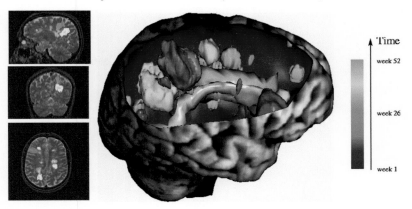

Fig. 18.1. Automatic detection of the evolution of multiple sclerosis lesions from a time sequence of 3D magnetic resonance images of the head of a patient (from D. Rey *et al.* [34]).

18.1.3 Computational models of anatomy and physiology

Computational models of the human body constitute an emerging and rapidly progressing area of research whose objective is to provide a better understanding of anatomical variability (computational anatomy) and of the major functions of the human body (computational physiology), as well as to provide effective algorithmic tools for their realistic numerical simulations [4, 14, 5].

Quite advanced models have already been proposed to study at the molecular, cellular and organic level a number of physiological systems (e.g. cardiac, respiratory, digestive, nervous (central and peripheric), reproductive, etc. [24]). For instance, computational models of the heart have been proposed to interpret the cardiac electromechanical activity from medical images and electrophysiological measurements [6, 9], or to study the properties of physiological flows in blood vessels [33], in order to predict the appearance of cardiovascular diseases. Computational models have also been proposed to explore the structures and the activity of the brain from anatomical and functional images and signals, for instance to better understand a number of brain diseases (e.g. Alzheimer's disease, multiple sclerosis, Creutzfeldt–Jakob disease, epilepsy or schizophrenia) [13]. Advanced models of abdominal organs including the liver [14] and the intestine [21] have been developed in the context of image-guided surgery (cf. Fig. 18.2) and surgery

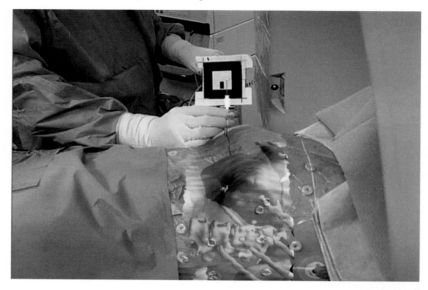

Fig. 18.2. Augmented reality for image-guided radio-frequency ablation of a liver tumor (from S. Nicolau, L. Soler *et al.* [28]).

simulation (cf. Fig. 18.3). Other models have been developed to predict the evolution of cancerous lesions in various organs [39, 38, 25].

It is necessary but not sufficient to develop, refine and validate such models. In addition, new methods must be designed to automatically fit the model parameters to a given person from the available biomedical signals (in particular medical images) and also from prior genetic information. Building such patient-specific models is a challenging goal which requires in particular the development of new data assimilation methods which can cope with massive numbers of measurements and unknowns.

18.1.4 Large distributed databases

Another important milestone towards progress in these directions is the development of large databases of subjects and patients, including biomedical signals and images as well as genetic information, and the development of specific tools to correlate, for instance, the shape and evolution of anatomical structures (phenotype) with the genetic information (genotype) and/or with a certain number of pathologies.

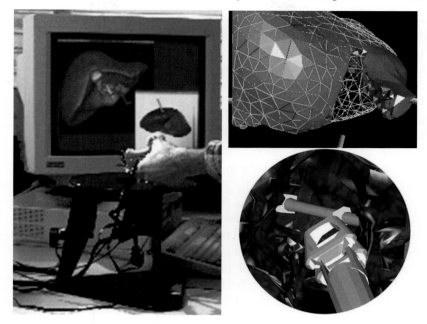

Fig. 18.3. Surgery simulation with visual and force feedback (cf. S. Cotin, G. Picinbono, C. Forest *et al.* [12, 32, 18]).

The construction and exploitation of such databases require the development of specific measurement platforms which can regroup cutting edge imaging facilities with easy access provided to internal and external research teams (e.g. the Neurospin[3] platform of CEA).

Huge computing power is already required to run advanced computational models in their direct mode (for prediction) or inverse mode (to adapt to a specific patient from biomedical measurements). The amount of required computing power to process large databases will require the development of grid-enabled algorithms capable of exploiting distributed computing power and data in large international networks [23].

18.2 From Epidaure to Asclepios

To address the above issues, the Asclepios research project team was launched on November 1st, 2005 at INRIA Sophia Antipolis after

---

[3] URL of Neurospin: http://www.meteoreservice.com/neurospin/.

final approval by the INRIA CEO Gilles Kahn. It built on the results
of the previous research project team Epidaure, initially launched at
INRIA Rocquencourt in 1989 and later installed in Sophia-Antipolis in
October 1992 thanks to the strong support of Gilles Kahn and Pierre
Bernhard (at the time respectively VP for Science and Director of
INRIA Sophia-Antipolis). The original scientific objectives were the
quantitative analysis of medical images and the coupling of medical
imaging with medical robotics and surgery simulation.

Some of the major contributions of the Epidaure project were
published in an invited article in the IEEE Transactions on Medical
Imaging in November 2003 [3]. The Epidaure team has contributed,
in association with a number of other teams, to the establishment of
medical image analysis and simulation as a very distinct discipline in the
field of computer science, with its own scientific community, its scientific
peer-reviewed journals and conferences. In particular we contributed
to the founding of the Medical Image Analysis journal (MedIA) and
the MICCAI conference (Medical Image Computing and Computer
Assisted Intervention), again with the encouragement of Gilles Kahn
who attended the precursor conference CVRMed'95 (Computer Vision,
Virtual Reality and Robotics in Medicine) organized by INRIA in Nice
in April 1995, and the MICCAI'04 conference organized by INRIA in
Saint-Malo in September 2004.

18.2.1 Personalized models for diagnosis and therapy

If several of the problems listed in the original 1989 Epidaure research
proposal have been solved, some important ones remain and new
challenging problems have appeared. The research objectives of the
Asclepios proposal take into account this situation and are organized
around five research directions, namely: (1) medical image analysis;
(2) biological image analysis; (3) computational anatomy; (4) computational physiology; (5) clinical and biological validation. Only directions 1
and (part of) 5 correspond to a continuation of the research objectives
of the former Epidaure project, whereas directions 2, 3 and 4 correspond
to novel objectives related to emerging problems.

Figure 18.4 attempts to summarize the overall objectives of the
Asclepios project. The computational models of the human body that
we consider often have four different primary components which we
characterize as geometry, statistics, physics and physiology. In order to
personalize a generic model, it is necessary to identify its parameters

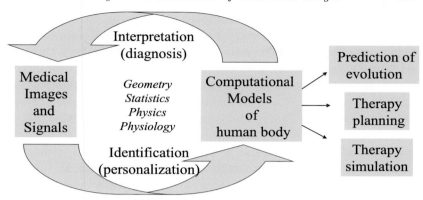

Fig. 18.4. Objectives of the Asclepios project team.

by confronting it to a set of patient-specific biomedical images and other biomedical signals. The personalized model can then, in turn, be projected back onto the images and signals to better interpret them, and to provide support for the diagnosis of disease. The personalized model can also be used to predict the evolution of disease, or to plan and simulate an intervention. This provides support for the prevention and therapy of diseases.

In the remainder of this article we provide four illustrations of several aspects of current research in Asclepios respectively on: (a) the automatic measurement of the variability of the geometry of some brain structures; (b) the simulation of the growth of personalized brain tumors; (c) the simulation of personalized electromechanical activity of cardiac ventricles; (d) the construction of large mosaics of microscopic molecular images acquired *in vivo* and *in situ*. We conclude with a summary section.

18.3 Measuring brain variability from sulcal lines

The objective of computational anatomy is the modeling and analysis of biological variability of the human anatomy.[4] Typical applications cover the simulation of average anatomies and normal variations, the discovery of structural differences between healthy and diseased populations, and the detection and classification of pathologies from structural anomalies.

---

[4] See the summer school organized at UCLA in 2004 and 2008 by P. Thompson (UCLA) and M. Miller (Johns Hopkins) www.ipam.ucla.edu/programs/mbi2008/.

Studying the variability of biological shapes is an old problem (cf. the remarkable book *On Growth and Form* by D'Arcy Thompson [40]). Significant efforts have been made since that time to develop a theory of statistical shape analysis, refer to [15] for a good synthesis, to a specific special issue of *Neuroimage* [41] or more recently to the first international workshop on the *Mathematical Foundations of Computational Anatomy* organized by Xavier Pennec and Sarang Joshi at MICCAI'2006 [30].

Computational anatomy lies at the intersection of geometry, statistics and medical image analysis. A three-stage approach to computing statistics on anatomical shapes was proposed by Miller in [27]: (1) construction from medical images of anatomically representative manifolds based on feature points, curves, surfaces and volumes); (2) assignment of a point-to-point correspondence between these manifolds (possibly through a restricted class of geometric transformations, e.g. rigid, affine, diffeomorphism); (3) generation of probability laws of anatomical variation from these correspondences.

We provide below an illustration of a similar approach applied to the study of the variability of certain brain cortical structures. Through a longstanding collaboration[5] with the LONI research group of UCLA (Professor Paul Thompson), we developed a method to study the variability of the so-called sulcal lines, which are defined by neuroanatomists as the bottoms of brain cortical foldings. These lines can be extracted and labeled manually by experts (in our case on a database of 700 subjects), or automatically by expert systems such as the one developed at CEA by the group led by J.F. Mangin [35].

Figure 18.5 shows a typical set of sulcal lines extracted on the cortical surface of a brain of the LONI database. Together with Arsigny[6] and Fillard, we developed an original approach to register all the images of the database to a common reference frame after an affine normalization, followed by an individual alignment of all homologous sulcal lines. This enabled us to compute for each sulcal line an average sulcal line, and along each of these lines a local measure of variability under the form of covariance matrix computed at regularly sampled points.

As a result of new metrics defined in the space of symmetric positive definite matrices (also called "tensors" in our community), we were able to propose a method to extrapolate this local measure of variability to

---

[5] See Associated Teams BRAIN-ATLAS http://www.inria.fr/sophia/asclepios/ projects/UCLA/.

[6] Vincent Arsigny received in the 2007 runner-up Gilles Kahn PhD prize for his research.

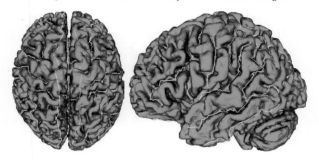

Fig. 18.5. Example of sulcal lines drawn on the cortical surface of one of the brains of the UCLA database (courtesy of P. Thompson).

the whole cortex in a plausible manner [29, 1]. We see in Figure 18.6 a color representation of the variability measured in various regions of the brain which quantitatively confirms previous observations made on a more qualitative basis by neuroanatomists. These results are published in [17].

Statistical information about variability can be used to help guide the superposition of a brain atlas to the brain images of a specific patient. This was shown with a different statistical database and in an image-guided radiotherapy context by Commowick *et al.* in [11].

Another study, conducted during the PhD work of Boisvert [8], concerned the statistical analysis of the variability of the scoliotic spine. By using an articulated model based on the relative position and orientation of successive vertebrae (through rigid body transformations), we were able to estimate the variability of the spine shape over a database of more than 300 patients. This was used to assess the evolution of the deformation during orthopedic treatments; moreover, the first four modes of variation appeared to be closely correlated to the usual clinical classification of scolioses, which reinforces the clinical interest of the chosen approach. Figure 18.7 illustrates a typical result.

18.4 Simulation of tumor growth

Combining anatomical, physical and physiological models of the human body is part of the computational physiology research field, to which the next two examples belong. The first concerns the simulation of diffusive tumor growth based on medical images. The objective is to identify the parameters of a generic dynamic model from a sufficient

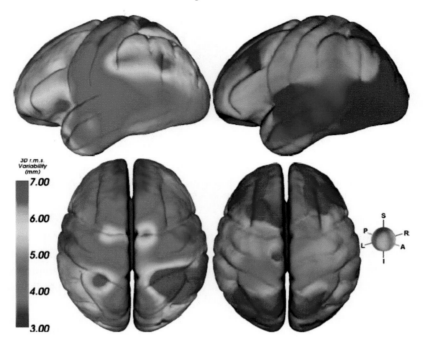

Fig. 18.6. Color maps showing the geometrical variability of the cortical structures extrapolated from the sulcal variability and a mathematical Riemannian framework. Left column shows the amplitude of the variability (hot colors mean high variations among subjects). Right column shows the main direction of variability. (color code: Red: left-right oriented tensor, Green: posterior–anterior oriented, Blue: inferior-superior oriented). Cf. Fillard, Arsigny, et al. [17].

number of observations on a specific patient, in order to better characterize the nature of the observed tumor. This image-based characterization of the tumor aims at better predicting its plausible evolution, and anticipating the effects of possible therapies (e.g. radiotherapy, surgery, chemotherapy).

The work described in [10] includes three main levels of modeling: the first is geometrical and includes the extraction of the main structures of the head from a set of multisequence magnetic resonance images (MRIs). Among these structures are: (1) the skull, (2) the gray and (3) the white matter of the brain, (4) the cerebrospinal fluid and (5) the falx cerebri. Figure 18.8 shows a typical representation of these structures. The accurate geometric description of these structures is

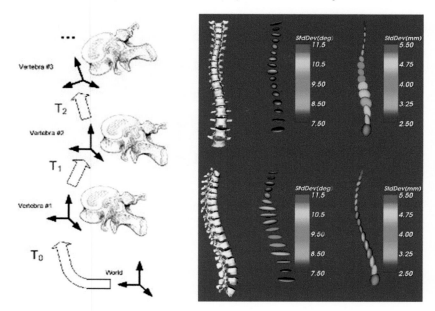

Fig. 18.7. Statistical spine model. From left to right: mean spine model reconstructed from a database of 300 patients with scoliosis, rotation and translation covariance measuring the local variability of each vertebra (color encodes the determinant of the covariance matrices). Top: Postero–anterior view. Bottom: lateral view. (cf. Boisvert [8])

important because the proliferation and migration of glial tumor cells strongly depend on the nature of the tissues and also on the orientation of the white matter fibers.

The second level of modeling refers to biomechanics. The aim is to simulate the deformation of the brain induced by the tumor growth, also called the "mass effect". We built a finite element model of the previously extracted head structures under the hypothesis of inhomogeneous isotropic linear elastic behavior of the biological tissues. Linearity is a reasonable assumption to impose since the amplitude of the deformations is small. Inhomogeneity takes into account the mechanical variability of the tissues.

The third level of modeling concerns the physiopathology of the tumor itself. We consider a macroscopic description of the tumor cell density through a Fisher–Kolmogorov reaction diffusion equation. The reaction component is a second order polynomial which corresponds to a

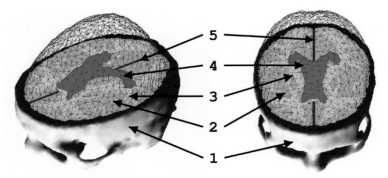

Fig. 18.8. The different tissues included in the biomechanical model of the head. 1 Skull. 2 gray matter. 3 white matter. 4 ventricles. 5 falx cerebri.

logistic proliferation law: exponential increase of number of cells followed by a reduced proliferation rate until an asymptotic value is reached. The diffusion component models the migration of tumor cells in their neighborhood. Because glioma cell migration is preferentially along the white matter fibers, the main bundles of white matter fibers are included in the model, through diffusion tensor MRI. The biomechanical coupling with the reaction–diffusion equation is introduced in the constitutive equation through a local pressure proportional to the tumor cell density.

Figure 18.9 shows a simulation of the progression of a glioblastoma during a 6-month period, with a good correspondence between observations and simulations. The identification of the parameters of the model followed an interactive and semi-automatic procedure. Currently the PhD work of Konukoglu [26] is seeking to identify automatically these parameters from the observations at two time points, and to measure the predictive power of the model against a third time point.

Once validated, we believe that such models could be used to better delineate, for instance, the dosimetry planning in radiotherapy, by proposing a margin outside of the visible contours of the tumor which would take into account the actual proliferation and diffusion parameters of the model, as well as the privileged directions of the main white matter fibers (Fig. 18.10).

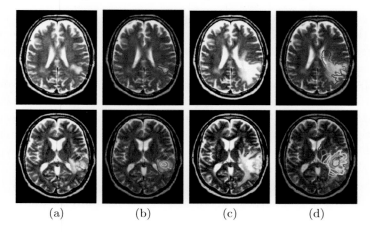

(a)   (b)   (c)   (d)

Fig. 18.9. Six months simulation of a glioblastoma growth. (a) T2 MRI of the patient, March 2002. (b) Previous MRI with superimposed tumor cell isodensity contours used for initialization. (c) T2 MRI of the same patient in September 2002 (6 months later). (d) Previous MRI with superimposed tumor cell isodensity contours simulated with the model.

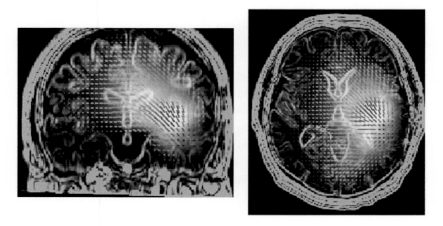

Fig. 18.10. The simulated displacement of the brain parenchyma due to the development of the previous tumor model in (left) coronal and (right) transverse views.

18.5 Personalized electro-mechanical model of the heart

Building a personalized electro-mechanical model of the heart ventricles is an important precursor to the simulation and analysis of the electrical or mechanical activity of the heart of a specific patient.

We began research on this topic at INRIA about seven years ago through a collaborative action ICEMA[7] funded by the scientific management of INRIA. This collaborative action was followed closely and supported by Gilles Kahn. It involved several project teams at INRIA including Sosso, Caiman, Epidaure, Opale and Macs, as well as external research groups at NIH (Mc Veigh), Guy's Hospital (Razavi), and Philips (Gérard). This collaboration was reinforced more recently through a specific INRIA consortium called CardioSense3D,[8] currently involving the INRIA project teams Asclepios, Macs, Reo and Sisyphe, as well as the NIH, Guy's Hospital and Philips research groups.

The current models again include three levels of description [36]. The first is a geometrical description of the anatomy of the cardiac ventricles, which is adapted to the specific geometry of a given patient through image processing methods. The direction of the cardiac fibers is projected onto this geometric model by automatically mapping an average description which comes from a previous statistical analysis [31].

The second level of modeling is a macroscopic description of the evolution of the action potential of cardiac cells, which measures the difference between the extra-cellular and the intra-cellular electrical potentials. This evolution is modeled through a set of reaction diffusion equations (initially proposed by FitzHugh and Nagumo, and later refined by Aliev and Panfilov). These equations take into account the higher conductivity in the direction of the fibers at each point of the previous geometrical description, and enable the realistic simulation of the depolarization and repolarization waves within the cardiac tissues.

The third level of modeling is the electro-mechanical coupling which describes how the action potential variations actually control the contraction and the relaxation of the cardiac fibers. We chose a macroscopic model due to Bestel, Clément and Sorine [7]: a set of partial differential equations combines locally the behavior of an active elastic contractile element controlled by the previous action potential, with in addition two passive elastic elements respectively in parallel and in series. This model, initially inspired by the model of Hill-Maxwell is based on a multiscale analysis from the nanoscopic to the macroscopic scale. We see in Figure 18.11 an illustration of the realistic simulation of the contraction of a generic instance of this model.

---

[7] www-rocq.inria.fr/sosso/icema2/icema2.html.
[8] http://www-sop.inria.fr/CardioSense3D.

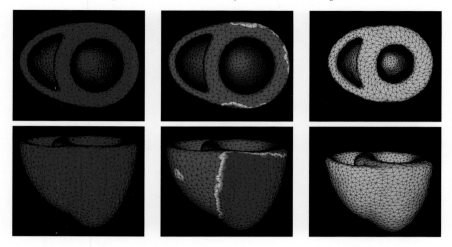

Fig. 18.11. Short axis (top row) and long axis (bottom row) views of an electromechanical heart model during end diastole (left column), ventricular depolarization (middle column) and end systole (right column).

The personalization of such a generic model must then be done through a set of specific measurements obtained through cardiac imaging (e.g. ultrasound, magnetic resonance, computed tomography or nuclear medicine imaging) as well as electrophysiology (typically the electrocardiogram or ECG). This is a difficult inverse problem which can be attacked through several strategies (cf. for instance [37]). Figure 18.12 shows the personalization of the model obtained through tagged magnetic resonance imaging and specific electrophysiological measurements obtained with an endovascular procedure.

The future objectives of this research include the simulation of various therapies, like for instance cardiac resynchronization therapy (CRT), or radiofrequency ablation procedures, or the effect of stem cells therapy.

18.6 Building large mosaics of microscopic images

The last example concerns microscopic imagery. During the past few years, we have initiated a research on the digital processing of microscopic images acquired *in vivo* and *in situ*. This was made possible through the development of new imaging devices enabling the acquisition of confocal microscopic images at the end of a very thin optical probe. The probe can be introduced in the operator canal of an endoscope in

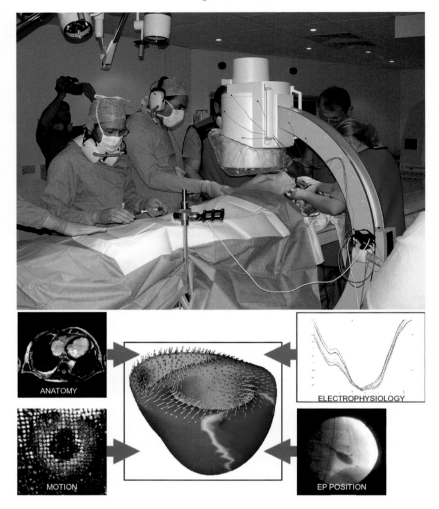

Fig. 18.12. (a) Intervention in the XMR room at Guy's Hospital (Professor Reza Razavi) that allows the combination of MRI and X-ray acquisition. (b) Integration of XMR data providing anatomy, motion and electrophysiology measurements of a specific patient into the previous generic electromechanical model to get a personalized electro-mechanical cardiac model (cf. [37]).

order to provide images of the cellular architecture of suspicious tissues on line. This operation can also be seen as an "optical biopsy".

One of the issues with this type of imaging is the limited field of view of the microscopic images: because such images have a resolution of the order of a micron, the field of view is usually limited to a few hundreds of microns. This poses a problem when the analysis of the cellular architecture requires a larger field of view (this can be the case, for instance, when observing human colonic crypts), or when certain statistical measurements require a larger number of cells or vessels, or simply when it is necessary to reposition the probe exactly in a given location (when doing a temporal series of images at distant time points to study a slow dynamic phenomenon for instance). Through a collaboration with the Mauna Kea Technology company, Vercauteren [44] proposed, during his PhD research, a method to build a larger scene from the video sequence of microscopic images acquired during a smooth motion of the acquisition probe. The mosaic of images is obtained by replacing all of them in a common reference frame. This is a difficult problem because of the possible deformations induced by the motion of the probe and the non-rigid nature of the observed tissues. Figure 18.13 shows a typical example of the reconstruction of such a mosaic. Other work on the construction of large mosaics of 3-D confocal images acquired from *in vitro* samples can be found in [19].

18.7 Conclusion

We have outlined and illustrated in this article the current research objectives of the Asclepios project at INRIA, whose main application areas are in medicine and biology. The pharmaceutical domain is also an application area, as computational models of the human body can be exploited to better predict and quantify the effects of new drugs.

We believe strongly that the development of advanced biomedical image analysis methods combined with specific computational models of living systems will lead to a more profound understanding of the anatomy and physiology of the human body, and of the correlation between anatomical or physiological anomalies with the development of certain pathologies. We also believe that this research effort will be helpful to better exploit the huge amount of available biomedical signals (from *in vivo* molecular and cellular imaging to macroscopic organ imaging) as well as the genetic information potentially available on each patient.

An important clinical objective will be to increase significantly the potential for pre-symptomatic diagnosis and early treatment for a maximum medical efficiency. This research could also help the simulation and evaluation of various therapies, in particular traditional

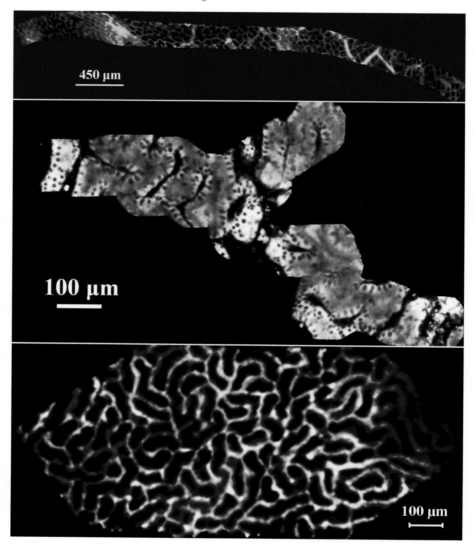

Fig. 18.13. Top: *in vivo* mouse colon vascularization after injection of FITC-Dextran high MW (300 input frames, Courtesy of M. Booth, MGH, Boston, MA); Middle: Ex vivo reflectance imaging of the human colon (mosaic includes 1500 input frames); Bottom: Microcirculation of the peritubular capillaries of a live mouse kidney with FITC-Dextran high MW (31 input frames) (cf. T. Vercauteren *et al.* [44]).

or minimally invasive surgery, radiotherapy, chimiotherapy, and also some currently experimental therapies like genetic or cellular therapy. It should also contribute to the promotion of image guided therapies.

Gilles Kahn strongly encouraged this research while he was the scientific director of INRIA Sophia-Antipolis, later the Vice-President for Science, and finally the CEO of INRIA. Through his numerous scientific interactions with the researchers involved, through his exceptional vision of the future, he stimulated this activity and gave those scientists the necessary confidence to explore new directions sometimes far away from their traditional background. For all these reasons we are proud to dedicate this article to the memory of Gilles Kahn.

18.8 Acknowledgements

The authors wish to thank all the past and current members of the Epidaure and Asclepios research project teams, as well as their collaborators (both academic, clinical and industrial).

Bibliography

[1]   V. Arsigny, P. Fillard, X. Pennec and N. Ayache. Log-euclidean metrics for fast and simple calculus on diffusion tensors. *Magnetic Resonance in Medicine*, **56**(2):411–421, 2006. PMID: 16788917.

[2]   L. Axel, A. Montillo and D. Kim. Tagged magnetic resonance imaging of the heart: a survey. *Medical Image Analysis*, **9**(4):376–393, 2005.

[3]   N. Ayache. Epidaure: a research project in medical image analysis, simulation and robotics at *INRIA*. *IEEE Trans. on Medical Imaging*, **22**(10):1185–1201, 2003.

[4]   N. Ayache (ed.) *Computational Models for the Human Body*. Handbook of Numerical Analysis (Ph. Ciarlet series editor). Elsevier, 2004. 670 pages.

[5]   N. Ayache, J.-P. Boissel, S. Brunak, *et al.* Towards virtual physiological human: Multilevel modelling and simulation of the human anatomy and physiology. Virtual Physiological Human: White paper, EC - DG INFSO and DG JRC, 2006.

[6]   M. E. Belik, T. P. Usyk and A. D. McCulloch. Computational methods for cardiac electrophysiology. In N. Ayache (ed.) *Computational Models for the Human Body*, pp. 129–187. Elsevier, 2004.

[7]   J. Bestel, F. Clément and M. Sorine. A biomechanical model of muscle contraction. In W.J. Niessen and M.A. Viergever (eds) *Proc. of International Conference on Medical Image Computing and Computer Assisted Intervention (MICCAI'01)*, volume 2208, Lecture Notes in Computer Science, pp. 1159–1161. Springer-Verlag, 2001.

[8]   J. Boisvert, X. Pennec, H. Labelle, F. Cheriet and N. Ayache. Principal spine shape deformation modes using Riemannian geometry and articulated

models. In *Proc. of the IV Conference on Articulated Motion and Deformable Objects*, Andratx, Mallorca, Spain, 11–14 July, volume 4069, Lecture Notes in Computer Science, pp. 346–355. Springer-Verlag, 2006. AMDO best paper award 2006.

[9] D. Chapelle, F. Clément, F. Génot, P. Le Tallec, M. Sorine and J. Urquiza. A physiologically-based model for the active cardiac muscle contraction. In T. Katila, I. E. Magnin, P. Clarysse, J. Montagnat and J. Nenonen (eds) *Functional Imaging and Modeling of the Heart (FIMH'01)*, Helsinki, Finland, volume 2230, Lecture Notes in Computer Science. Springer-Verlag, 2001.

[10] O. Clatz, M. Sermesant, P.-Y. Bondiau, *et al.* Realistic simulation of the 3D growth of brain tumors in MR images coupling diffusion with mass effect. *IEEE Transactions on Medical Imaging*, **24**(10):1334–1346, 2005.

[11] O. Commowick, R. Stefanescu, P. Fillard, *et al.* Incorporating statistical measures of anatomical variability in atlas-to-subject registration for conformal brain radiotherapy. In J. Duncan and G. Gerig (eds) *Proceedings of the 8th International Conference on Medical Image Computing and Computer Assisted Intervention - MICCAI 2005, Part II*, Palm Springs, CA, USA, October 26–29, 2005. volume 3750, Lecture Notes in Computer Science, pp. 927–934, Springer-Verlag, 2005.

[12] S. Cotin, H. Delingette and N. Ayache. A hybrid elastic model allowing real-time cutting, deformations and force-feedback for surgery training and simulation. *The Visual Computer*, **16**(8):437–452, 2000.

[13] J. G. Csernansky, L. Wang, S. C. Joshi, J. T. Ratnanather and M. I. Miller. Computational anatomy and neuropsychiatric disease: probabilistic assessment of variation and statistical inference of group difference, hemispheric asymmetry and time-dependent change. *NeuroImage*, **23**(Supplement 1):S56–S68, 2004. Special Issue: Mathematics in Brain Imaging.

[14] H. Delingette, X. Pennec, L. Soler, J. Marescaux and N. Ayache. Computational models for image guided, robot-assisted and simulated medical interventions. *Proceedings of the IEEE*, **94**(9):1678– 1688, 2006.

[15] I. L. Dryden and K. V. Mardia. *Statistical Shape Analysis*. John Wiley and Sons, 1998.

[16] J. Duncan and N. Ayache. Medical image analysis: Progress over two decades and the challenges ahead. *IEEE Transactions on Pattern Analysis and Machine Intelligence*, **22**(1):85–106, 2000.

[17] P. Fillard, V. Arsigny, X. Pennec, K. M. Hayashi, P. M. Thompson and N. Ayache. Measuring brain variability by extrapolating sparse tensor fields measured on sulcal lines. *Neuroimage*, **34**(2):639–650, 2007. Also as INRIA Research Report 5887, April 2006.

[18] C. Forest, H. Delingette and N. Ayache. Removing tetrahedra from manifold tetrahedralisation: application to real-time surgical simulation. *Medical Image Analysis*, **9**(2):113–122, 2005.

[19] C. Fouard, G. Malandain, S. Prohaska and M. Westerhoff. Blockwise processing applied to brain microvascular network study. *IEEE Transactions on Medical Imaging*, **25**(10):1319–1328, 2006.

[20]   N. C. Fox and J. M. Schott. Imaging cerebral atrophy: normal ageing to Alzheimer's disease. *Lancet*, **363**(9406), 2004.

[21]   L. France, A. Angelidis, P. Meseure, *et al.* Implicit representations of the human intestines for surgery simulation. In M. Thiriet (ed.) *Conference on Modelling and Simulation for Computer-aided Medicine and Surgery (MS4CMS'02)*, volume 12, European Series in Applied and Industrial Mathematics, pp. 1–7, 2002.

[22]   A. F. Frangi, W. J. Niessen and M. A. Viergever. Three-dimensional modeling for functional analysis of cardiac images: a review. *IEEE Transactions on Medical Imaging*, **20**(1):2–25, 2001.

[23]   C. Germain, V. Breton, P. Clarysse, *et al.* Grid-enabling medical image analysis. *Journal of Clinical Monitoring and Computing*, **19**(4-5):339–349, 2005. PMID: 16328948.

[24]   P. Hunter. Computational physiology and the physiome project, 2004. "http://nbcr.sdsc.edu/mcmregistration/pdf/Peter_Hunter.pdf".

[25]   S. Jbabdi, E. Mandonnet, H. Duffau, *et al.* Simulation of anisotropic growth of low-grade gliomas using diffusion tensor imaging. *Magnetic Resonance Medicine*, **54**(3):616–624, 2005.

[26]   E. Konukoglu, O. Clatz, P.-Y. Bondiau, H. Delingette and N. Ayache. Extrapolating tumor invasion margins for physiologically determined radiotherapy regions. In *Proc. of the 9th International Conference on Medical Image Computing and Computer Assisted Intervention (MICCAI'06), Part I*, 2–4 October 2006, volume 4190, Lecture Notes in Computer Science, pp. 338–346, Springer-Verlag, 2006.

[27]   M. I. Miller. Computational anatomy: shape, growth and atrophy comparison via diffeomorphisms. *NeuroImage*, **23**(Supplement 1):S19–S33, 2004. Special Issue: Mathematics in Brain Imaging.

[28]   S. Nicolau, A. Garcia, X. Pennec, L. Soler and N. Ayache. An augmented reality system to guide radio-frequency tumor ablation. *Computer Animation and Virtual World (previously the Journal of Visualization & Computer Animation)*, **16**(1):1–10, 2005.

[29]   X. Pennec, P. Fillard and N. Ayache. A Riemannian framework for tensor computing. *International Journal of Computer Vision*, **66**(1):41–66, 2006. A preliminary version appeared as INRIA Research Report 5255, July 2004.

[30]   X. Pennec and S. Joshi (eds). *Proceedings of the First International Workshop on Mathematical Foundations of Computational Anatomy–Geometrical and Statistical Methods for Modelling Biological Shape Variability*, Copenhagen, Denmark, October 2006.

[31]   J.-M. Peyrat, M. Sermesant, H. Delingette, *et al.* Towards a statistical atlas of cardiac fiber structure. In *Proc. of the 9th International Conference on Medical Image Computing and Computer Assisted Intervention (MICCAI'06), Part I*, 2–4 October 2006, volume 4190, Lecture Notes in Computer Science, pp. 297–304. Springer-Verlag, 2006.

[32]   G. Picinbono, H. Delingette and N. Ayache. Non-linear anisotropic elasticity for real-time surgery simulation. *Graphical Models*, **65**(5):305–321, 2003.

[33]   A. Quarteroni and L. Formaggia. Mathematical modeling and numerical simulation of the cardiovascular system. In N. Ayache (ed.) *Computational Models for the Human Body*, pp. 3–128. Elsevier, 2004.

[34]   D. Rey, G. Subsol, H. Delingette and N. Ayache. Automatic detection and segmentation of evolving processes in 3D medical images: Application to multiple sclerosis. *Medical Image Analysis*, **6**(2):163–179, 2002.

[35]   D. Rivière, J.-F. Mangin, D. Papadopoulos-Orfanos, *et al.* Automatic recognition of cortical sulci of the human brain using a congregation of neural networks. *Medical Image Analysis*, 6(2):77–92, 2002.

[36]   M. Sermesant, H. Delingette and N. Ayache. An electromechanical model of the heart for image analysis and simulation. *IEEE Transactions in Medical Imaging*, **25**(5):612–625, 2006.

[37]   M. Sermesant, P. Moireau, O. Camara, *et al.* Cardiac function estimation from MRI using a heart model and data assimilation: Advances and difficulties. *Medical Image Analysis*, **10**(4):642–656, 2006.

[38]   R. Sierra, M. Bajka and G. Székely. Pathology design for surgical training simulators. In *International Symposium on Surgery Simulation and Soft Tissue Modeling*, volume 2673, Lecture Notes in Computer Science, pp. 375–384. Springer-Verlag, 2003.

[39]   K. R. Swanson, E. C. Alvord and J. D. Murray. Virtual brain tumours (gliomas) enhance the reality of medical imaging and highlight inadequacies of current therapy. *British Journal of Cancer*, **86**(1):14–18, 2002.

[40]   D. W. Thompson. *On Growth and Form*. Cambridge University Press, 1917.

[41]   P. M. Thompson, M. I. Miller, J. T. Ratnanather, R. A. Poldrack and T. E. Nichols. Guest editorial. *NeuroImage*, **23**(Supplement 1):S1–S1, 2004. Special Issue: Mathematics in Brain Imaging.

[42]   P. M. Thompson, K. M. Hayashi, E. R. Sowell, *et al.* Mapping cortical change in Alzheimer's disease, brain development, and schizophrenia. *NeuroImage*, **23**(Supplement 1):S2–S18, 2004. Special Issue: Mathematics in Brain Imaging.

[43]   K. V. Leemput, F. Maes, D. Vandermeulen and P. Suetens. A unifying framework for partial volume segmentation of brain MR images. *IEEE Transactions in Medical Imaging*, **22**(1):105–19, 2003.

[44]   T. Vercauteren, A. Perchant, G. Malandain, X. Pennec and N. Ayache. Robust mosaicing with correction of motion distortions and tissue deformation for in vivo fibered microscopy. *Medical Image Analysis*, **10**(5):673–692, 2006. Annual Medical Image Analysis (MedIA) Best Paper Award 2006.

19

Proxy caching in split TCP: dynamics, stability and tail asymptotics

François Baccelli

Ecole Normale Supérieure

Giovanna Carofiglio

Ecole Normale Supérieure and Politecnico di Torino

Serguei Foss

Heriot-Watt University

Abstract

The split of a multihop, point-to-point TCP connection consists in replacing a plain, end-to-end TCP connection by a cascade of TCP connections. In such a cascade, connection n feeds connection $n + 1$ through some proxy node n. This technique is used in a variety of contexts. In overlay networks, proxies are often peers of the underlying peer-to-peer network. split TCP is also already proposed and largely adopted in wireless networks at the wired/wireless interface to separate links with vastly different characteristics. In order to avoid losses in the proxies, a backpressure mechanism is often used in this context.

In this paper we develop a model for such a split TCP connection aimed at the analysis of throughput dynamics on both links as well as of buffer occupancy in the proxy. The two main variants of split TCP are considered: that with backpressure and that without. The study consists of two parts: the first part is purely experimental and is based on *ns2* simulations. It allows us to identify complex interaction phenomena between TCP flow rates and proxy buffer occupancy, which seem to have been ignored by previous work on split TCP. The second part of the paper is of a mathematical nature. We establish the basic equations that govern the evolution of such a cascade and prove some of the experimental observations made in the first part. In particular, we give the conditions for system stability and we show the possibility of heavy tail asymptotics for proxy buffer occupancy and delays in the stationary regime.

From *Semantics to Computer Science Essays in Honour of Gilles Kahn*, eds Yves Bertot, Gérard Huet, Jean-Jacques Lévy and Gordon Plotkin. Published by Cambridge University Press. © Cambridge University Press 2009.

19.1 Introduction

The panorama of access network technologies has been changing at an incredibly fast rate over the past few years, whilst almost any substantial change intervened at transport layer, where TCP has become a "standard de facto".

However, the increasing user demand for high quality services spurs development of performance-enhancing techniques to implement on top of the pre-existing IP infrastructure.

Particularly powerful for content delivery and media streaming in peer-to-peer systems, *overlay networks* have emerged as an attractive solution for throughput improvement without any change of the underlying network architecture.

One of the key features of overlay networks is the *split-connection* mechanism, that yields a considerable throughput improvement for a TCP connection when split in shorter segments on the route between the sender and the receiver host. Intermediate nodes act as proxies: incoming packets are locally acknowledged on each segment (LACKs), then stored and forwarded on the next TCP connection.

In the context of overlay networks, split TCP is addressed in [5] and [19], where, in addition, a backpressure mechanism is proposed to limit the sending rate to the forwarding rate in presence of saturated proxy buffer, thus preventing buffer overflows. In other contexts, split TCP has been shown to be particularly effective when the sender-to-receiver route includes network segments with very different characteristics, like wired and wireless links, that usually cause problems to TCP. In fact, the "split connection" approach was initially proposed in the context of wireless networks where a significant throughput degradation has been observed for TCP. The poor TCP performance in wireless networks is to ascribe to the congestion control that wrongly attributes to congestion losses due to link failures (consequence of mobility or channel errors), or is related to high propagation delays that slacken the growth of the congestion window. In the seminal work of [9] and [10] a new implementation of TCP was proposed, Indirect TCP (I-TCP), which handles the problem of wired-wireless link interaction and introduces the concept of split TCP. Two TCP connections in tandem replace the single TCP connection: the first running on the wired side, the second one running over the wireless link and characterized by different parameters to cope better with larger delays and channel losses. The same approach has been drawn on in [18] where the split TCP scheme is adapted to mobile ad hoc networks to cope with the additional issue of a dynamic placement of the proxy. The aim of the "split-connection" approach is to operate a clear separation between flow control and congestion control functionalities over two different network environments. Similar issues have been studied in *satellite networks* ([20], [16]) where long propagation delays cause TCP throughput degradation by lengthening the slow start duration and slowing the linear growth of the congestion window in the congestion avoidance phase. Such throughput limitations are aggravated by frequent losses related to channel errors or temporary link disconnections. In this context, proxies with specific capabilities, called performance enhancing proxies (PEP), have been introduced to perform a transport layer connection split oblivious to end systems (cf. [25]). Among all the approaches that attempt to isolate issues pertaining to different media, the split connection approach is the only one that does not require any modification of standard TCP implementations, and for that reason it has been the subject of an in-depth study in the literature. The diffusion and implementation of split-connection techniques is documented by a recent measurement study ([28]) where the authors detect, through the use of inference/detection methods, the deployment of split TCP in all commercial networks they consider. They also investigate the throughput improvement provided by split TCP with respect to standard TCP implementation, that can be up to 65%

The majority of related work on split TCP are either measurement or simulation studies targeted to the throughput evaluation along a chain of TCP connections. (e.g.[11]). There are only a few *analytical attempts* in the literature which study split TCP's dynamics.

In [29] the authors study a particular class of split-connection approaches in wired/wireless networks, that adopts a standard version of TCP on wired segment and an "ad hoc" lightweight transport protocol for the wireless hop. In [27] an estimate of the expected throughput is provided for a cascade of standard TCP connections based on the well known square root formula, thus neglecting the dependencies between the two connections. Similar models based on the square root formula for TCP throughput estimation are presented in [15], [19] and [26], where the authors make the assumption that the buffer in the proxy never empties nor fills.

In this work, we make the following analytical contributions: we establish the equations for throughput dynamics jointly with that of buffer occupancy in the proxy. We then determine the stability conditions by exploiting some intrinsic monotonicity and continuity properties of the system. Finally, we focus on the study of buffer occupancy in the proxy and end-to-end delays to derive tail asymptotics. The framework allows us to consider both the case with an infinite buffer at the proxy and that of a limited buffer size, where a backpressure algorithm is needed to limit the sender rate and avoid losses in the proxy.

The paper consist of two parts: the first part (Sections 19.2 and 19.3) exploits some simulation results to make some basic observations on the system dynamics in different scenarios. We identify there the complex interaction that exists between TCP flow rates and proxy buffer occupancy. To the best of our knowledge, this problem is addressed here for the first time and finds an analytical explanation in the second mathematical part of the paper, where we emphasize the role of the buffer size on the total throughput gain for the split. The second part (Section 19.4) contains further mathematical results such as the equations governing the overall dynamics, the stability condition for the case without backpressure. We also compute the tail asymptotics for proxy buffer occupancy and delays in the stationary regime and show that they are surprisingly heavy-tailed under certain natural statistical assumptions of the literature. Finally, Section 19.5 is devoted to discussions on future studies and concludes the paper.

19.2 Simulation scenarios

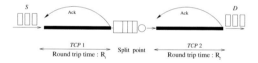

Fig. 19.1. split TCP network scheme.

19.2.1 Network scheme

We consider a saturated traffic source S that sends packets to the destination D through two long-lived TCP-Reno connections $TCP1$, $TCP2$ in cascade as in Figure 19.1. Due to the fact that S is saturated, $TCP1$ always has packets to send.

A layer-4 proxy is placed in the middle and forwards packets from the first link to the second one, sending local acknowledgments to S (LACKs). It prevents the loss of packets that cannot be immediately forwarded on the second link by storing them temporarily in a buffer. When the buffer approaches its maximal capacity, a backpressure mechanism limits the sender rate. The flow control is accomplished through the advertised window indication present on the acknowledgements sent back to the sender S. The transmission window of S is then regulated according to the minimum between the current congestion window and the advertised receiver window. Therefore, as the buffer occupancy approaches the buffer capacity, the backpressure algorithm timely starts working and prevents buffer overflows. In the *ns2* simulator, the backpressure algorithm is implemented by means of ack notifications to the sender of the instantaneous available space in the proxy buffer (RFC compliant).

19.2.2 Assumptions and notation

In the following we introduce the notation that will be used throughout the paper and the assumptions shared by the simulation setting and, thereinafter, by the model.

- The TCP connections are assumed to be in congestion avoidance phase, thus neglecting the initial slow start.
- $X(t)$, $Y(t)$ respectively denote $TCP1$, $TCP2$ rates at time t.
- The proxy buffer has size B. We will generally assume a limited buffer size, though the mathematical part also considers the ideal case of $B = \infty$.
- The local round trip times, R_1, R_2 (of $TCP1$, $TCP2$, respectively) are assumed to be constant, equal to twice the local propagation delay.
- Losses are modelled by two kinds of Poisson processes:
  - homogeneous Poisson processes with constant intensities λ_0, μ_0, which will be referred to as the **rate independent** (RI) case.
  - inhomogeneous Poisson processes with (stochastic) intensities $\lambda_1 X(t)$, $\mu_1 Y(t)$, proportional to the rates $X(t)$ and $Y(t)$, a case that will be referred to as the **rate dependent** (RD) case;

Concerning the loss process assumptions, the RI case corresponds to the physical layer loss pattern of wireless links (fast/slow fading) or some DSL links (multi-users interference), whereas the RD case fits well with the cases where there is a PER (packet error rate) due to congestion (cf. [7]). For example, the self congestion that arises in slow access links. In addition, these models allow one to consider at the same time both transmission error losses and congestion losses. Some interesting models are hybridations of the above simple cases. Here is a typical example to be used in what follows: $TCP1$ is a fast-wired link with a RD loss process and $TCP2$ is a slow DSL or wireless link with RI losses.

19.2.3 Scenarios

The following three scenarios focus on a cascade of two TCP connections. They correspond to different network settings, and contexts of application of split TCP.

- *The slow sender fast forwarder case (SF).*
  When the first TCP connection is "slower" than the second one, i.e. it has a smaller capacity and/or longer RTT and/or higher loss rate, we are in what we call the "SF" scenario. It can be the case in overlay networks, where the traffic of the first TCP connection is forwarded on a faster TCP connection.
- *The fast sender slow forwarder case (FS).*
  We call the "FS" case, the scenario where $TCP1$ is "faster" than $TCP2$. It is the case in hybrid wired/wireless scenarios where the faster reliable wired connection forwards its traffic to a slower lossy wireless connection. In the case of a wired/satellite configurations, in addition, the wireless part is characterized by higher propagation delays. The example where $TCP1$ is a fast link with a RD loss process and $TCP2$ is a slow one with RI losses will be referred to as the FS-RD/RI example.
- *The symmetric case.*
  In the wired/wireless cascade, the two TCP connections are strongly asymmetric, as the two media are notably different. In overlay networks, instead, it can happen for a long TCP connection to be split in smaller symmetric segments. In this setting, the two links have about the same characteristics.

19.2.4 Performance metrics

The majority of related work on split TCP are experimental evaluations of the throughput improvement achieved by splitting connection techniques. In addition to the throughput metric, our work is focused on the analysis of buffer occupancy in the proxy and on packet delays.

19.3 Simulation results

In this section we present a set of *ns2* simulations to illustrate the temporal evolution of congestion windows of $TCP1$ and $TCP2$ as well as the proxy buffer occupancy in the three cases mentioned above.

19.3.1 Rates

Let us start with a rather "symmetric" case, where the links have the same rate, $C_1 = C_2 = 100$ Mbps, similar propagation delays, $R_1 = 100$ ms, $R_2 = 90$ ms, and where losses are generated according to homogeneous (RI) Poisson processes with intensity $\lambda = \mu = 0.3$ losses/s. The proxy buffer can store $B = 15$ pkts and we assume a constant packet size equal to 1500 bytes. Figure 19.2 shows the *ns2* simulation of the congestion window patterns in Congestion Avoidance phase, together with the buffer occupancy $Q(t)$ in the proxy.

Looking at the buffer dynamics in Figure 19.2, we remark that:

Observation 19.1 The rate of $TCP1$ and $TCP2$ interact through the buffer occupancy. One can distinguish three operational phases:

(PH1) as long as the buffer is neither empty nor full, TCP rates X, Y follow the $AIMD$ rule, i.e. they linearly increase until a jump occurs and halves the rate;

(PH2) the rate of $TCP2$, Y exhibits a nonlinear growth when the buffer is empty;

(PH3) the rate of $TCP1$, X exhibits a nonlinear growth when the buffer approaches saturation.

In Figures 19.3 and 19.4, we plot the congestion windows and the proxy buffer occupancy in the SF and FS cases, respectively. In the SF case we maintain the same links capacities ($C_1 = C_2 = 100$ Mbps), the round trip times are $R_1 = 90$ ms, $R_2 = 30$ ms, and loss intensities are $\lambda = \mu = 0.4$ losses/s (still under the assumption of RI losses). The FS case is characterized by $R_1 = 40$ ms, $R_2 = 80$ ms, and $\lambda_0 = 0.4$ losses/s, $\mu_0 = 0.2$ losses/s. In both cases, the proxy buffer size is $B = 20$ pkts. We observe that in both cases, the dynamics of one of the three possible phases can be neglected w.r.t. the others. In the FS scenario the buffer

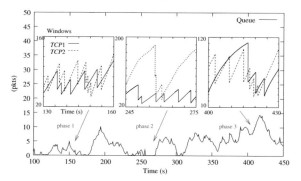

Fig. 19.2. Congestion windows and buffer occupancy in the symmetric case.

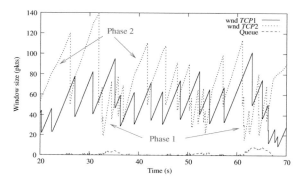

Fig. 19.3. Congestion windows and buffer occupancy in the SF case.

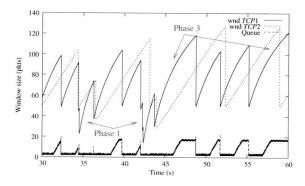

Fig. 19.4. Congestion windows and buffer occupancy in the FS case.

Table 19.1. *Impact of buffer size on stationary throughput averages.*

B (pkt)	Mean throughput (pkt/s)	Throughput improvement
1	780	—
5	1415	81%
10	1840	136%
20	2285	193%
50	2954	278%
100	3340	328 %
1000	3340	328 %

hardly ever empties, therefore the duration of phase 2 is negligible when compared to the other phases, whereas in the SF it is the opposite scenario: the buffer is rarely close to saturation, hence phase 3 is almost never visible. Therefore, we will consider later SF/FS cases with large buffers where only phases 1–2 and 1–3 are taken into account, respectively.

The nonlinear behavior of X or Y bears evidence of the fact that the two TCP connections interact. In particular, the window of $TCP2$ (and therefore its rate) evolves not only according to the windows dynamics of TCP, but also according to the availability of packets in the proxy. Similarly, the window of $TCP1$ (and therefore its rate) evolves not only according to the AIMD rule, but also according to the availability of space in the receiver buffer, advertised by the proxy to the source S via the backpressure mechanism.

In observation 19.1, we have already remarked the role of the buffer content on the interaction between $TCP1$ and $TCP2$. In Table 19.1 we report the mean values of total throughput in steady state for different values of the buffer size in a SF case. Here $C_1 = C_2 = 100$ Mbps, $R_1 = 40$ ms, $R_2 = 20$ ms, $\lambda_0 = \mu_0 = 0.4$ losses/s. Compared to the extreme case of $B = 1$ pkt, we remark a large improvement of total throughput as buffer size increases. At the other extreme, when B is large enough to never saturate, the total thoughput reaches its maximum value, which corresponds to the throughput of $TCP1$ in isolation (the last is computed via the mean throughput formula in Section 19.4.2). An important consideration follows:

Observation 19.2 In the RI case, the end-to-end throughput of split TCP increases with the proxy buffer size.

A large buffer size is beneficial to the total throughput, in that it makes it less common to use the flow control of the backpressure mechanism and it reduces the probability for the buffer to empty, which limits the forwarding rate.

On the TCP rates we observe that:

Observation 19.3 In the finite buffer backpressure case, the long-term average of $TCP1$ coincides with that of $TCP2$ and is strictly smaller than that of each connection in isolation.

This is in contrast with the throughput estimation provided in [15], [26] and [27], through the application of the square root formula. These works rely on the assumption that the two connections are independent and evaluate the overall throughput as the minimum of the throughputs of each connection taken in isolation. As shown in the last table, such a minimum rule is in fact the best case and a significant throughput degradation can be observed w.r.t. this rule in the presence of small buffer size.

The simulation results presented so far share the assumption of RI losses, though all considerations still hold for the RD case. We report in Figure 19.5 a symmetric RD scenario with the following parameters: $C_1 = C_2 = 100\,\mathrm{Mbps}$, $R_1 = R_2 = 60\,\mathrm{ms}$, $\lambda_1 = \mu_1 = 0.03$, where all three phases can be observed.

19.3.2 Buffer occupancy

We present here the statistical analysis of the buffer occupancy in steady state and when $B = \infty$. In order to guarantee the existence of a steady

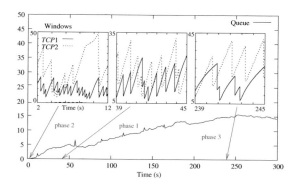

Fig. 19.5. Congestion windows and buffer occupancy in the RD loss case.

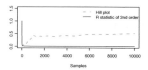

Fig. 19.6. Hill plot and R statistic for the queue tail.

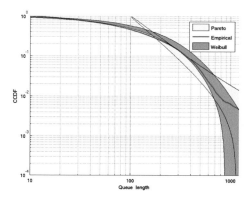

Fig. 19.7. α-Confidence intervals with $\alpha = 0.95$.

state, we consider the SF case (we will give in due time the exact conditions for such a steady state to exist). To infer some preliminary information on the queue distribution, we made a fit with the R software (free clone of S-plus) of the stationary queue distribution from the samples extracted via *ns2* simulation.

19.3.2.1 RI case

In the RI case, the R software suggests a Weibull distribution with shape parameter 0.5; the last parameter was obtained through a maximum likelihood estimator. We can then conjecture that:

Observation 19.4 In the RI case with $B = \infty$, when there is a stationary regime, the stationary buffer occupancy exhibits a heavy tail.

The presence of possible heaviness in the queue tail motivated a further inspection of the moments of Q by means of statistical methods suitable for heavy-tailed distributions.

For this purpose, two statistics were employed: the Hill plot and the R statistic (see definitions an further details of the analysis in [6]).

In Figure 19.6 we plot the parameter γ of the Hill estimator in the above *SF* scenario. It rapidly converges to a value between 0 and 1, which indicates a Pareto-like distribution with infinite second moment. In contrast with this result, the same figure also shows the R statistic for the second moment of the tail distribution, computed on the same set of samples; the fact that it becomes zero supports the thesis of the finiteness of the second moment. The discrepancy between these two results can be explained by looking at α-confidence intervals for the Pareto distribution or for the above-mentioned Weibull distribution in this example. We observe in Figure 19.7 that the 0.95-confidence intervals of a Pareto distribution with $\alpha = 0.5$ and a Weibull distribution with shape parameter 0.5 largely overlap in a way which compromises the inference of the tail distribution. In conclusion, we showed that these statistical methods aimed at the identification of the shape of these heavy tails provide discordant answers.

19.3.2.2 RD case

In the RD case both the Hill plot and the R statistic agree that the distribution of the buffer occupancy has all finite moments. We report in Figure 19.8, the Hill plot and the R statistic for the second moment of the distribution in a SF scenario with such RD losses. The results of statistical test in the RD case allows us to observe that:

Observation 19.5 In the RD case, the buffer occupancy exhibits a light tail decay.

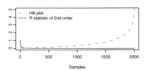

Fig. 19.8. Hill plot for the RD case.

19.4 Mathematical analysis

In this part, we first establish the differential equations which govern the joint evolution of the windows and the rates of the connections and of the buffer content. We then give formal proofs for some of the experimental observations made in the previous sections and add further results. More precisely:

- We address the stability issue, in case of infinite buffers and no backpressure (which is the only case where the stability question is of interest).

- We analyze the tail asymptotics for the buffer occupancy as well as for end-to-end delays.

- We prove that in the finite buffer, backpressured case, the stationary throughput is strictly less than the minimum of the stationary throughput of each connection in isolation.

19.4.1 The single connection model

Let us now briefly revisit the models of [8] and [7] for a single TCP connection. In the congestion avoidance phase, the evolution of the TCP congestion window is described through the following "hybrid" differential equation:

$$dW(t) = \frac{dt}{R} - \frac{W(t)}{2}N(dt) \qquad (19.1)$$

which states that the window increase between two loss events is linear with slope $1/R$, where R denotes the round trip time and that loss events produce jumps of the congestion windows which is cut by half. In this stochastic differential equation, $N(t)$ represents the loss point process. We assume here that this point process has a stochastic intensity (w.r.t. the natural history of $W(t)$ – see [4] for the definition of stochastic intensity), which is either constant or proportional to $W(t)$ depending on the case we consider (RI/RD).

Linked to the congestion window we define the instantaneous rate or throughput (here the two words are interchangeable), as $X(t) = W(t)/R$, a generally accepted assumption in the literature, which can be seen as an avatar of Little's law. The rationale for the linear increase is as follows: TCP stipulates that in the congestion avoidance phase, the window is increased of 1 unit every W ack. In an infinitesimal interval of length dt, the number of acks that arrive is $X(t)dt$. Hence the window increases of $X(t)dt/W(t) = dt/R$. The rationale for the halving of the window in case of a loss is just the multiplicative decrease rule. Systems evolving according to eq. (19.1) were also studied in [22] and [1].

19.4.2 Mean throughput in steady state

The stationary distribution of the rate of each TCP connection *in isolation* has an analytical expression. In particular, the mean throughput of $TCP1$ (resp. $TCP2$), in isolation is given by $\bar{X} = 2\alpha/\lambda$ [resp. $\bar{Y} = 2\beta/\mu$], where $\alpha = 1/R_1^2$, $\beta = 1/R_2^2$. This result follows from the fact that $X(t) - \alpha t + \frac{\lambda}{2}\int_0^t X(u)du$ is a martingale (cfr.[6]). Thanks to the PASTA property, the mean value $E_N^0[X(0-)]$ of the stationary rate just before a loss is equal to stationary rate in continuous time $\bar{X}$. Using this and the fact that the packet loss probability is $p = \lambda/\bar{X}$, we obtain the square root formula

$$\bar{X} = \sqrt{\frac{2\alpha}{p}}, \quad \left(\text{resp. } \bar{Y} = \sqrt{\frac{2\beta}{q}}\right). \tag{19.2}$$

In [8], the following square root formula is derived for the RD case:

$$\bar{X} = \Phi\sqrt{\frac{\alpha}{\lambda}}, \quad \left(\text{resp. } \bar{Y} = \Phi\sqrt{\frac{\beta}{\mu}}\right), \tag{19.3}$$

where $\Phi = \sqrt{\frac{2}{\pi}\frac{\sum_{i=0}^{\infty}(\prod_{j=1}^{i}(1-4^j))^{-1}}{\sum_{i=0}^{\infty}(\prod_{j=1}^{i}(1-4^j))^{-1}2^i}} \approx 1.309$. The mean throughput formulas in the RI and RD case have also appeared respectively in [2] and [24].

19.4.3 The split connection model

Let now introduce the stochastic equations for the split connection model.

With respect to the case of a single TCP connection, as observed in observation 19.1 there are three operational phases.

- Phase 1 or the *free phase*, where the buffer is neither empty nor full, and $X(t)$ and $Y(t)$ evolve independently;
- Phase 2 or the *starvation phase*, when the buffer is empty and Y is limited by the input rate X.
- Phase 3 or the *backpressure phase*, when the buffer has reached its storage capacity B and X is forced by the backpressure algorithm to slow down to the rate Y at which the buffer is drained off.

In the free phase, the AIMD rule gives:

$$\text{on } \{0 < Q(t) < B\} \quad \begin{cases} \mathrm{d}X(t) = \alpha\mathrm{d}t - \frac{X(t)}{2}M(\mathrm{d}t) \\ \mathrm{d}Y(t) = \beta\mathrm{d}t - \frac{Y(t)}{2}N(\mathrm{d}t). \end{cases} \tag{19.4}$$

In the starvation phase, as long as the buffer is empty (which requires that $X(t) \leq Y(t)$), we have:

$$\text{on} \quad \{Q(t) = 0\} \quad \begin{cases} \mathrm{d}X(t) = \alpha\mathrm{d}t - \frac{X(t)}{2}M(\mathrm{d}t) \\ \mathrm{d}Y(t) = \beta\frac{X(t)}{Y(t)}\mathrm{d}t - \frac{Y(t)}{2}N(\mathrm{d}t). \end{cases} \tag{19.5}$$

where $M(t)$, $N(t)$ represent the loss processes on X and Y. The rationale for a linear increase of $Y(t)$ proportional to $\frac{X(t)}{Y(t)} < 1$ is that when the buffer is empty, since $X(t) < Y(t)$, the rate at which packets are injected in $TCP2$ and hence the rate at which $TCP2$ acks arrive is $X(t)$. Hence the window of $TCP2$, W_2, increases of $X(t)\mathrm{d}t/W_2(t) = \mathrm{d}t\frac{X(t)}{R_2Y(t)}$ in the interval $(t, t+\mathrm{d}t)$ and the rate of $TCP2$ thus increases of $\beta\mathrm{d}t\frac{X(t)}{Y(t)}$ during this interval. The ratio $X(t)/Y(t)$ can be interpreted as the *utilization factor* of the congestion window $W_2(t)$: in contrast with what happens in the free phase, where $TCP2$ is "independent" of $TCP1$ and where the window W_2 is fully utilized (draining packets from the buffer), in the starvation phase, the number of packets transmitted by $TCP2$ depends on $X(t)$, which brings the utilization factor below 1 and leads to a nonlinear evolution as observed in observation 19.1.

In the backpressure phase, which lasts until the buffer is saturated (this requires that $X(t) \geq Y(t)$), we have

$$\text{on} \ \{Q(t) = B\} \quad \begin{cases} \mathrm{d}X(t) = \alpha\frac{Y(t)}{X(t)}\mathrm{d}t - \frac{X(t)}{2}M(\mathrm{d}t) \\ \mathrm{d}Y(t) = \beta\mathrm{d}t - \frac{Y(t)}{2}N(\mathrm{d}t). \end{cases} \tag{19.6}$$

The rationale for this should be clear: acks of $TCP1$ now come back at a rate of $Y(t)$. Hence the congestion window, $W_1(t)$ of $TCP1$ grows at the rate $Y(t)/W_1(t)$.

The evolution of the buffer occupancy in the proxy within phase 1 ($Q(t) > 0$) is given by

$$Q(t) = Q(0) + \int_0^t (X(u) - Y(u))\mathrm{d}u. \tag{19.7}$$

Note that the queue at the proxy can be seen as a fluid queue with a fluid input rate $X(t)$ and a fluid output rate $Y(t)$ at time t. Hence we can also write:

$$Q(t) = \max\left(\sup_{0 \leq u \leq t}\int_u^t (X(v) - Y(v))\mathrm{d}v, \right.$$
$$\left. Q(0) + \int_0^t (X(u) - Y(u))\mathrm{d}u\right). \tag{19.8}$$

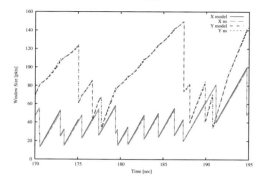

Fig. 19.9. Congestion windows: comparison between the model and *ns2*.

Figure 19.9 shows the perfect agreement between the evolution of congestion windows as predicted by equations (19.4)–(19.7) or provided by *ns2* simulations.

19.4.4 Stability in the infinite buffer, RI case

This subsection is focused on the case $B = \infty$, where only phase 1 and 2 exist. A natural question within this infinite buffer context is that of *system stability*, which is understood here as the finiteness of the stationary buffer occupancy at the proxy. In the stable case, this infinite buffer model is a good approximation of the SF case, whenever B is not too small (we have seen in Section 19.3 that in this case, phase 3 is almost never visited and that we can focus on phase 1/phase 2 dynamics). In the RI case, the stability proofs rely on some monotonicity properties which we introduce in the following paragraph.

19.4.4.1 Monotonicity properties in the RI case

Let us first consider sample paths of $X(t)$ and $Y(t)$ in case $B = \infty$, where the dynamics is governed by (19.4) or (19.5) depending on $Q(t)$.

We denote by Y^f ("free Y") some fictitious process which evolves according to the dynamics of phase 1 only. In the RI case, we can actually choose to make a *coupling* of Y^f and Y by building these two processes from the *same realization* of the Poisson point process N.

We can then state three main properties.

- If we consider two processes, $Y^f(t), \widehat{Y}^f(t)$ based on the same realization of N, but departing from different initial conditions, $Y^f(0) \leq \widehat{Y}^f(0)$, then, $Y^f(t) \leq \widehat{Y}^f(t), \forall t \geq 0$.

- If we consider the process $Y_v^f(t), t \geq v$ which starts from 0 at time v, then $Y_{v_1}^f(t) \geq Y_{v_2}^f(t)$, for all $v_1 < v_2 \leq t$.
- If $Y^f(0) = Y(0)$, then $Y(t) \leq Y^f(t)$, for all $t \geq 0$.

The proofs of the first two properties should be clear. The last one follows from the fact that in phase 2, $X(t) \leq Y(t)$, so that at any continuity point, the slope of $Y(t)$ is always less than or equal to the slope of $Y^f(t)$. Since both processes have the same discontinuity points (thanks to the coupling), the result immediately follows.

Consider now the case B finite with backpressure. The triple $(X(t), Y(t), Q(t))$ forms a continuous time Markov process. Thanks to the fact that Q is bounded from below by 0 and from above by B, one can show that this Markov process admits a unique stationary distribution, and that, starting from any initial value, this Markov process converges to the stationary one in the total variation norm.

We again compare the processes $(X(t), Y(t))$ in the split TCP system and the free processes $(X^f(t), Y^f(t))$. We build these processes on the same realizations of the point processes M and N. Assume the initial conditions to be the same: $(X(0), Y(0)) = (X^f(0), Y^f(0))$. When we are in phase 1, the two processes have exactly the same dynamics, so that if at the beginning of the phase, $(X(.), Y(.)) \leq (X^f(.), Y^f(.))$ coordinatewise, then this holds true at the end of the phase too. In phase 2 (resp. 3), the slope of Y (resp. X) is strictly less than that of Y^f (resp. X^f) and both are halved at the same epochs, whereas X and X^f (resp. Y and Y^f) have exactly the same dynamics. Hence, if $(X(.), Y(.)) \leq (X^f(.), Y^f(.))$ at the beginning of the phase, then $(X(.), Y(.)) < (X^f(.), Y^f(.))$ at the end. This leads to the following confirmation of observation 19.3:

Lemma 19.6 *In the RI case with $B < \infty$, when backpressure is used, the stationary rate of split TCP is* strictly *less than the minimum of that of TCP1 and TCP2 in isolation.*

19.4.4.2 Queue bounds

The triple $(X(t), Y(t), Q(t))$ forms a Markov process. Interestingly enough, the direct stability analysis of this Markov via Liapunov functions is not an easy task. In particular, we were unable to make use of the classical fluid limit techniques for Markov chains here, primarily because of the multiple phases. This is the reason why we use

backward construction techniques to prove stability. This will be done
by introducing two simple bounds on the queue size.

The proposed backward construction (see e.g. [4] Chapter 1 for
classical instances of such constructions) consists in building the queue
size $Q_t(0)$ at time 0 when departing from an appropriate initial condition
at time $t < 0$. The initial condition that we select consists of a queue size
$Q(t) = 0$, a rate for $TCP1$ which is the stationary rate $\widetilde{X}(t)$ of $TCP1$
at time t in isolation, and a rate for $TCP2$ which is the stationary rate
$\widetilde{Y}^f(t)$ of $TCP2$ at time t in isolation. From (19.8), we have

$$Q_t(s) = \sup_{t \leq u \leq s} \int_u^s (\widetilde{X}(v) - Y_t(v)) \mathrm{d}v, \qquad (19.9)$$

for all $s \geq t$, where $Y_t(v)$ denotes the rate of $TCP2$ in the split TCP
system and at time v under the above assumptions.

The stability issue can then be stated in the following terms: does
$Q_t(0)$ have an almost surely (a.s.) finite limsup when t tends to $-\infty$?
This is enough to ensure that the Markov chain $(X(t), Y(t), Q(t))$ is
neither transient nor null recurrent.

We are now in a position to define the lower bound queue. From
monotonicity property 3 and from (19.9), we get

$$Q_t(0) \geq L_t = \sup_{t \leq u \leq 0} \int_u^0 (\widetilde{X}(v) - \widetilde{Y}^f(v)) \mathrm{d}v, \qquad (19.10)$$

where $\widetilde{Y}^f(.)$ is the stationary free process for $TCP2$. In [6], we prove
that the stochastic process $(\widetilde{X}(t), \widetilde{Y}^f(t))$, which describes the fluid input
and the fluid drain in this queue, forms a stationary and geometrically
ergodic Harris chain. In particular we show there that we can apply the
splitting technique of Athreya and Ney (cfr.[3]) for such chains and that
there exist renewal cycles for this process related to its return times to
the compact set $C = [0, x] \times [0, \frac{2\beta}{\alpha}x]$, where x is an arbitrary positive
real number. In what follows, we will denote by T the length of such a
renewal cycle. We now define the upper bound queue. Let $\tau(t)$ denote the
beginning of the last busy period of $Q_t(s)$ before time 0 (0 if $Q_t(0) = 0$
and t if $Q_t(s) > 0$ for all $t < s \leq 0$). We have

$$Q_t(0) = \int_{\tau(t)}^0 (\widetilde{X}(v) - Y_t(v)) \mathrm{d}v \leq \int_{\tau(t)}^0 (\widetilde{X}(v) - Y^f_{\tau(t)}(v)) \mathrm{d}v$$

$$\leq U_t = \sup_{t \leq u \leq 0} \int_u^0 (\widetilde{X}(v) - Y^f_t(v)) \mathrm{d}v, \qquad (19.11)$$

where the first inequality follows from the fact that the dynamics on $(\tau(t), 0)$ is that of the free phase and from the fact that $Y^f_{\tau(t)}(.)$ is the minimal value for the free $TCP2$ process (monotonicity property 1).

19.4.4.3 Stability

Lemma 19.7 *If $\rho < 1$, where $\rho = \alpha\mu_0/\beta\lambda_0$, then the RI system is stable. If $\rho > 1$, then it is unstable.*

Proof We prove first that if $\rho > 1$, then the system is not stable. The equation for L_t is that of a classical fluid queue with *stationary and jointly ergodic* arrival and service processes. The joint ergodicity follows from the fact that the couple $(\widetilde{X}, \widetilde{Y}^f)$ forms a Harris recurrent and geometrically ergodic Markov process (see [6]). We can hence apply classical results on fluid queues stating that under the above stationarity and ergodicity properties, if $\mathrm{E}[\widetilde{X}(0)] > \mathrm{E}[\widetilde{Y}^f(0)]$, then L_t tends a.s. to ∞, which in turn implies that we cannot have $\limsup_{t\to\infty} Q_t(0)$ a.s. finite. Hence $\rho > 1$ implies instability.

We now prove that if $\rho < 1$, then the system is stable. Assume that $\limsup Q_t(0) = \infty$ with a positive probability. Then $\limsup U_t = \infty$ with a positive probability too. As $\widetilde{X}$ and Y^f_t are locally integrable for all t, this together with the second monotonicity property of the last subsection imply that there exists a sequence t_n tending to $-\infty$ and such that a.s.

$$\int_{t_n}^0 (\widetilde{X}(v) - Y^f_{t_n}(v))\mathrm{d}v \to_{n\to\infty} \infty. \tag{19.12}$$

Let us show that this is not possible under the assumption $\rho < 1$. Let θ_t denote the product shift of the point processes M and N (this shift is ergodic). The pointwise ergodic theorem implies that

$$\frac{1}{t}\int_{-t}^0 \widetilde{X}(v)\mathrm{d}v = \frac{1}{t}\int_{-t}^0 \widetilde{X}(0)\circ\theta_v\mathrm{d}v \to_{t\to\infty} \mathrm{E}[\widetilde{X}(0)], \tag{19.13}$$

where the last limit is in the a.s. sense. We show now that the following a.s. limit also holds:

$$\frac{1}{t}\int_{-t}^0 Y^f_{-t}(v)\mathrm{d}v \to_{t\to\infty} \mathrm{E}[\widetilde{Y}^f(0)]. \tag{19.14}$$

This will conclude the proof since equations (19.13)–(19.14) and the assumption

$$E[\widetilde{X}(0)] < E[\widetilde{Y}^f(0)]$$

imply that a.s. $\lim_{t\to\infty} \int_{-t}^0 (\widetilde{X}(v) - Y_{-t}^f(v))dv = -\infty$, which contradicts (19.12).

Let us now prove (19.14). From the monotonicity properties, the function $\varphi_t = \int_{-t}^0 Y_{-t}^f(v)dv$ is super-additive: $\varphi_{t+s} \geq \varphi_t \circ \theta_{-s} + \varphi_s$. Thanks to the sub-additive ergodic theorem, this together with the fact that φ_t is integrable imply that a.s. $\exists \lim_{t\to\infty} \frac{1}{t} \int_{-t}^0 Y_{-t}^f(v)dv = K$, for some constant K which may be finite or infinite. The fact that K is finite follows from the bound $0 < Y_{-t}^f(v) \leq \widetilde{Y}^f(v)$ and from the pointwise ergodic theorem applied to the stationary and ergodic process $\{\widetilde{Y}^f(v)\}$. Since K is finite, the last limit holds both a.s. and in L^1 [21]. Using again super-additivity of the forward process, we get by the same arguments:

$$K = \lim_t \frac{1}{t} \int_{-t}^0 Y_{-t}^f(v)dv = \lim_t E\left(\frac{1}{t} \int_0^t Y_0^f(v)dv\right).$$

But from the fact that $Y_0^f(v)$, $v \geq 0$ is a geometrically ergodic Markov chain,

$$\exists \lim_{t\to\infty} \frac{1}{t} \int_0^t Y_0^f(v)dv = E[\widetilde{Y}^f(0)] \quad \text{a.s.}$$

Hence $K = E[Y^{\tilde{f}}(0)]$, which concludes the proof of (19.14). $\qquad\square$

19.4.5 Stability in the infinite buffer, RD case

In the RD case, we use the same backward construction as above to prove the exact analogue of Lemma 19.7 (in the RD case, ρ is equal to $\alpha\mu_1/\beta\lambda_1$). We only sketch the main ideas of the proof. To get an upper bound on $Q_t(0)$, we consider the following optimization problem: what is the infimum over all $y > 0$ of the integral $\int_u^0 Y_{u,y}^f(v)dv$ where $Y_{u,y}^f(v)$ denotes the value of the free process of $TCP2$ at time $v \geq u$ when starting from an initial value of y at time u? Let us first show that the last optimization problem admits an a.s. unique solution $y^*(u)$, and that this solution is a.s. finite.

For defining such an infimum, we need the following construction which builds the stochastic processes $Y_{u,y}(v)$, $v \geq u$ from a two dimensional homogeneous Poisson point process $\mathcal{N}$ of intensity μ on

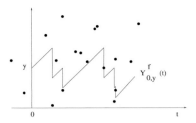

Fig. 19.10. Coupling of the RD processes.

the positive half plane ($t \in \mathrm{R}, y \in \mathrm{R}_+$). We start with $Y_{u,y}^f(u) = y$ and then have a linear growth of slope β until we find a point of $\mathcal{N}$ below the curve $Y_{u,y}^f(.)$. There we halve the value of $Y_{u,y}^f$ at that time and we proceed again using the same rule of a linear growth until the next point below the curve (see Fig. 19.10). It is easy to see that the stochastic intensity of the losses is exactly $\mu Y_{u,y}^f(t)$ at time t, which is precisely what we want. With this construction, all $Y_{u,y}^f(t)$ are defined as deterministic functions of $\mathcal{N}$ and the infimum over all y of $\int_u^{u+t} Y_{u,y}^f(v)\mathrm{d}v$ for fixed $t > 0$ and u is well defined in view of the fact that the function $y \to \int_u^{u+t} Y_{u,y}^f(v)\mathrm{d}v$ is piecewise continuous, with a finite number of discontinuities in any compact, is increasing between discontinuities and tends to ∞ when y tends to ∞. Denote by $Y_u^*(v)$ the function $Y_{u,y^*(u)}^f(v)$. Hence

$$Q_t(0) \leq U_t = \sup_{t \leq u \leq 0} \int_u^0 (\widetilde{X}(v) - Y_u^*(v))\mathrm{d}v. \qquad (19.15)$$

The arguments to prove stability when $\rho < 1$ are then similar to those in the RI case: when t tends to ∞, $\frac{1}{t}\int_{-t}^0 \widetilde{X}(v)\mathrm{d}v$ tends to $\mathrm{E}[\widetilde{X}(0)]$ a.s. from the pointwise ergodic theorem. The function $\varphi_t = \int_{-t}^0 Y_{-t}^*(v))\mathrm{d}v$ is super-additive. We then use the sub-additive ergodic theorem to prove that $\frac{1}{t}\varphi_t$ tends to a constant K a.s. and the pointwise ergodic theorem again to show that this constant is necessarily $\mathrm{E}[\widetilde{Y}^f(0)]$.

The proof of the last property relies on the following two ingredients: (a) for all y, with probability 1, there exists a positive random variable $\epsilon(y) > 0$ such that the functions

$$y \to g_t(y) = \frac{1}{t}\int_0^t Y_{0,y}^f(v)\mathrm{d}v$$

are t-uniformly continuous; (b) let $y^o(t)$ be the initial condition that minimizes $\int_0^t Y_{0,y}^f(v)\mathrm{d}v$; the liminf of the function $y^o(t)$ as t tends to ∞

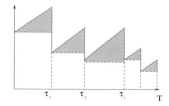

Fig. 19.11. Decomposition of the integral of X in a sum of trapezes.

is 0. From (b), we deduce that there exists a subsequence t_n such that $y^o(t_n)$ converges to 0 a.s. It is easy to see that $g_{t_n}(y^o(t_n))$ converges to K as n tends to infinity. But $g_{t_n}(0)$ converges to $\mathrm{E}\widetilde{Y}^f(0)$ due to the ergodicity of the Harris chain $\widetilde{Y}^f(.)$. This together with the continuity property (a) allow one to conclude that

$$K = \lim_{n\to\infty} g_{t_n}(y^o(t_n)) = \lim_{n\to\infty} g_{t_n}(0) = \mathrm{E}\widetilde{Y}^f(0) \quad \text{a.s.}$$

19.4.6 Tail asymptotics in the RI case

Here, we take up the observation 19.4 and confirm it with the following theoretical result.

Lemma 19.8 *In the RI case, the queue distribution is heavier than a Weibull distribution of shape parameter $k = 0.5$.*

This unexpected result suggests that the buffer occupancy in split TCP is not negligible. It also explains the quite important fluctuations observed on end-to-end delays within this context (Fig. 19.11).

We give the proof of this result in [6]. Let us summarize here the main steps of the proof. It relies on the lower bound of equation (19.10), and it is based on the fact that the fluid input process and the fluid draining process of this lower bound queue are jointly stationary and ergodic and have renewal cycles (see [6]). We denote by T the length of such a renewal cycle and we define

$$\Delta = \int_0^T \widetilde{X}(t) - \widetilde{Y}^f(t)\mathrm{d}t = I_x - I_y.$$

We first study the asymptotics for $\mathbf{P}(\Delta > x)$ as $x \to \infty$. We show that this is lower-bounded by random variables with a Weibull distribution with shape parameter $1/2$. Hence Veraverbeke's theorem ([13]) can be used to show that Q is heavier than a Weibull distribution with shape parameter 1/2. We now provide an intuitive explanation of the result on the tail of Δ. By looking at I_x, we observe that each trapeze area has a triangular lower bound, so that

$$\mathbf{P}\left(\sum_0^{N_T} Trap_i > q\right) \geq \mathbf{P}\left(\sum_0^{N_T} \alpha\frac{\tau_i^2}{2} > q\right),$$

where N_T denotes the number of losses in the cycle. All triangular areas are i.i.d and heavy tailed: as τ_i are i.i.d exponentially distributed, each summand has a tail distribution

$$\mathbf{P}\left(\alpha\frac{\tau^2}{2} > x\right) = \mathbf{P}\left(\tau > \sqrt{\frac{2x}{\alpha}}\right) = e^{-\mu\sqrt{\frac{2x}{\alpha}}},$$

which is Weibull with shape parameter $k = 0.5$. Thanks to the properties of subexponential distributions, the result applies to the integral of $\widetilde{X}$, and then propagates to Q. It is worth noting that such a result is not affected in practice by a limited congestion window (max congestion window). Indeed, if we decompose the integral of $\widetilde{X}$ as above, it is easy to see that the heavy tailness yet arises due to the presence in the sum of some terms like $\tau_i^2/2$ linked to the periods when the window is not clipped to the maximum value.

The communication literature contains many instances of heavy-tailed queues. The most famous example is probably that of a FIFO queue subject to a self-similar input process; it is proved in [23] that the stationary buffer content is then heavy tailed; it is also well known (see e.g. [12]) that such self-similar input processes arise in connection with HTTP traffic, when represented as the superposition of a large number of ON/OFF sources with Pareto on and/or off periods. In this example, heavy-tailed queues arise as a corollary of long-range dependence, which in turn is a consequence of the heavy tailedness of file sizes and off periods. In contrast, the heavy tailedness of the proxy contents in our split TCP model arises as a direct consequence of the AIMD dynamics under the assumption of a RI loss process. Such rate independent loss processes are quite natural in wireless or DSL lines, for example. Note however that the heaviness of the tail is linked to the loss model considered. In the RD case, arguments similar to those used in the RI case let us conjecture that the queue distribution is light, as suggested by observation 19.5.

19.4.7 Phases duality and End delays

The structure of equations (19.5), (19.6) points out the *duality* between phase 2 and 3: we can obtain one equation from the other by exchanging the roles of $X(t)$ and $Y(t)$ (and their parameters). In phase 3, the analogue of $Q(t)$ in phase 2 is what we can call the *antibuffer*: $A(t) = B - Q(t)$, the amount of the proxy buffer space available at time t. Based on this duality between the SF and FS scenarios, we can use the analysis of the tail asymptotics of Q in the SF case to evaluate $A(t) = B - Q(t)$ in the dual FS case.

Let us now look at end-to-end delays. This is the sum of three terms: the two local propagations delays and the proxy buffer waiting and forwarding time. In the FS case and when B is large enough, the processing delay of a packet arriving at time t at the proxy is well approximated by the queue length at time t divided by the mean value of the stationary service rate of $TCP2$, i.e.

$$D(t) \approx \frac{R_1}{2} + \frac{R_2}{2} + \frac{Q(t)}{\mathrm{E}[\tilde{Y}]} = \frac{R_1}{2} + \frac{R_2}{2} + \frac{B}{\mathrm{E}[\tilde{Y}]} - \frac{A(t)}{\mathrm{E}[\tilde{Y}]}. \tag{19.16}$$

The fluctuations of $D(t)$ are then determined by those of $A(t)$. Duality shows that the fluctuations of $A(t)$ in this FS scenario are similar to those of $Q(t)$ in the SF case, namely are heavy tailed.

19.5 Conclusions

The first contribution of the paper is the set of equations (19.4)–(19.7) which, to the best of our knowledge, provides the first mathematical attempt for describing the dynamics of the split TCP system. Previous models neglect the dependence between the two connections, by assuming that the buffer at the intermediate node never empties nor saturates ([15]), whilst we have shown that there exist two phases, (ph. 2, 3) where the interaction between the TCP rates X and Y and buffer occupancy Q cannot be ignored. These equations also allowed us to show that the prediction of the expected throughput in steady state as provided by the square-root formula for the slowest TCP connection in isolation ([19], [27], [15], [26]) is *not* valid unless buffers are very large. Finally, these equations allowed us to identify situations in which the proxy buffer content has either heavy tails or important fluctuations which imply in turn important fluctuations for end-to-end delays. We also expect these equations to open a new analytical track for answering the following list of questions which remain open up to the writing of the present paper.

(i) In the finite buffer backpressured case,

    (a) Is the split TCP stationary rate increasing in B as suggested by observation 19.2.

    (b) What is the value of the stationary rate of the connection?

(ii) In the infinite buffer stable case,

    (a) Is the stationary proxy buffer contents light tailed in the RD case?

    (b) What is the distribution, or the mean value of the stationary buffer content?

Acknowledgments

This work was funded in part by the Euro NF Network of Excellence.

Bibliography

[1] E. Altman, K. Avrachenkov, C. Barakat and R. Nunez-Queija. State-dependent M/G/1 type queueing analysis for congestion control in data networks. *Computer Networks*, **39**(6), 789–808, 2002.

[2] E. Altman, K. Avrachenkov and C. Barakat. A stochastic model of TCP/IP with stationary random losses. *IEEE/ACM Transactions on Networking*, **13**; 356–369, 2005.

[3] K. B. Athreya and P. Ney. A new approach to the limit theory of recurrent Markov chains. *Transactions of the American Mathematical Society*, 1978.

[4] F. Baccelli and P. Bremaud. *Elements of Queueing Theory*, 2nd ed. Wiley, 2003.

[5] F. Baccelli, A. Chaintreau, Z. Liu, A. Riabov and S. Sahu. Scalability of reliable group communication using overlays. *Proceedings of the IEEE Infocom*, February 2004.

[6] F. Baccelli, G. Carofiglio and S. Foss. Proxy Caching in split TCP: Dynamics, Stability and Tail Asymptotics, *INRIA Report*, July 2007.

[7] F. Baccelli, K. B. Kim and D. De Vleeschauwer. Analysis of the competition between wired, DSL and wireless users in an access network. In *Proceedings of IEEE Infocom*, Miami, FL, USA, March 2005.

[8] F. Baccelli, D. McDonald and J. Reynier. A mean-field model for multiple TCP connections through a buffer implementing RED. *Performance Evaluation*, No. 11, 77–97, 2002.

[9] A. Bakre and B. R. Badrinath. I-TCP: Indirect TCP for Mobile Hosts. *Proceedings of the 15th ICDCS*, May 1995.

[10] A.V. Bakre and B.R. Badrinath, Implementation and performance evaluation of Indirect TCP. *IEEE Transactions on Computers*, **46**(3):260–278, 1997.

[11] H. Balakrishnan, V. Padmanabhan, S. Seshan and R. Katz. A comparison of mechanisms for improving TCP performance over wireless links. *IEEE/ACM Transactions on Networking*, **5**(6), 1997.

[12] F. Brichet, J. Roberts, A. Simonian and D. Veitch. Heavy traffic analysis of a storage model with long range dependent on/off sources. *Queueing Systems*, **23**, 1996.

[13] P. Embrechts, C. Kluppelberg and T. Mikosch *Modelling Extremal Events*. Springer, 1997.

[14] S. Foss and S. Zachary, The maximum on a random time interval of a random walk with long-tailed increments and negative drift. *Annals of Applied Probability*, **13**(1):37–53, 2003.

[15] R.B. Jain and T. Ott. Design and Implementation of split TCP in the Linux Kernel. *Proceedings of the Globecom*, San Francisco, November 2006.

[16] M. Karaliopoulos, R. Tafazolli and B. Evans. Modeling split-TCP latency and buffering requirements in GEO satellite networks. *Proceeding of the IEEE Wireless Communications and Networking Conference*, vol. 3, pp. 1509–1514, March 2005.

[17] U. Keller and G. Biersack. A congestion control model for multicast overlay networks and its performance. *Proceedings of the Networked Group Communication*, Boston, MA, 2002.

[18] S. Kopparty, S.V. Krishnamurthy, M. Faloutsos and S. Tripathi. split TCP for mobile ad hoc networks. *Proceedings of IEEE Globecom '02*, Taipei, November 2002.

[19] G. Kwon and J. Byers. ROMA: reliable overlay multicast with loosely coupled TCP connections. *Proceedings of the IEEE Infocom*, February 2004.

[20] M. Luglio, M.Y. Sanadidi, M. Gerla and J. Stepanek. On-board satellite "split TCP" proxy. *IEEE JSAC*, **22**(2), 2004.

[21] T. Liggett, An improved subadditive ergodic theorem. *Annals of Probability*, **13**:1279–1285, 1985.

[22] V. Misra, W.-B. Gong and D. Towsley, Stochastic differential equation modeling and analysis of TCP-windowsize behavior. In *Performance'99*, Istanbul (Turkey), October 1999

[23] I. Norros, A storage model with self-similar input, *Queueing Systems*, **16**:387–396, 1994.

[24] T. Ott, J. Kemperman and M. Mathis, The stationary behavior of ideal TCP congestion avoidance. *Research Report*, 1996, available from T. Ott web page.

[25] http://www.ietf.org/rfc/rfc3135.txt.

[26] P. Rizk, C. Kiddle and R. Simmonds. Improving gridFTP performance with split TCP connections. *Proceeding of IEEE First International Conference on e-Science and Grid-Computing*, 2005.

[27] A. Sundararaj and D. Duchamp. Analytical characterization of the throughput of a split TCP connection. *Technical Report*, Stevens Institute of Technology, 2003.

[28]   W. Wei, C. Zhang, H. Zang, J. Kurose and D. Towsley. Inference and evaluation of Split-Connection Approaches in Cellular Data Networks. *Proceedins of the ACM PAM*, 2006.

[29]   F. Xie, J. Hammond and D. L. Noneaker. Steady state analysis of a split-connection scheme for internet access through a wireless terminal. *IEEE/ACM Transactions on Networking*, **12**(3), 2004.

20

Two-by-two static, evolutionary, and dynamic games

Pierre Bernhard and Frédéric Hamelin

I3S, University of Nice-Sophia Antipolis and CNRS, France

Foreword

Gilles Kahn and I were classmates at École Polytechnique where, in the academic year 1965–1966, he taught me programming (this was in MAGE 2, a translation in French of Fortran 2 I believe, on a punched tape computer SETI PALAS 250), then we met again and became good friends at Stanford University, where he was a computer science student while I was in aeronautics and astronautics. Our paths were to get closer starting in the spring of 1980 when we started planning and, from 1983 on, heading INRIA Sophia-Antipolis together.

Gilles has always believed that game theory was worth pursuing. He was adament that our laboratory should take advantage of my being conversant with that topic. He was instrumental in maintaining it alive in the lab.

He was to be later the president of INRIA who presided over the introduction of "biological systems" as a full-fledged scientific theme of INRIA. Although this was after I had left INRIA, this again met with my personal scientific taste. I had by then embraced behavioural ecology as my main domain of interest and of application of dynamic games, much thanks to Eric Wajnberg, from INRA, but also out of an old desire of looking into the ecological applications of these techniques.

It is why I think fit to write here a few words about games and behavioural ecology, and also population dynamics and evolution, which are closely related topics.

From Semantics to Computer Science Essays in Honour of Gilles Kahn, eds Yves Bertot, Gérard Huet, Jean-Jacques Lévy and Gordon Plotkin. Published by Cambridge University Press. © Cambridge University Press 2009.

Abstract

We discuss related aspects of the simplest possible games, i.e. games where two players have two pure strategies each, and consider static games, population games – a generalization of evolutionary games – and dynamic games.

20.1 Introduction

What follows begins as a form of entertainment with two by two (2×2) games, the very simple structure of such static games shaping the dynamic aspects of evolutionary games, – a topic invented by the biologists – population games and bilinear differential games, of which we show here an example in behavioural ecology where it arises naturally.

We begin with a short taxonomy of 2×2 static games, which will be useful in the sequel. Then we investigate how concepts of evolutionary game theory translate in that simple case. The material up to Section 20.3.3, is reminiscent of [13], may be with more emphasis on the role of our parameter σ. A natural generalization of classical evolutionary games are population games.[1] We develop some very simple, yet probably original, results for such games still in the 2×2 case, and look at their relationship to evolutionary games.

Then we venture into differential games. The literature on differential games bears a striking difference with that on classical game theory in that, while the latter is mainly concerned with mixed strategies – up to the point that ordinary decisions have to be called *pure* strategies to recall that they are not mixed – mixed strategies have had little impact on differential games research. On the one hand, differential games have been mainly concerned with state feedback or non-anticipative strategies, and the concept of mixed state feedback, or, for that matter mixed nonanticipative strategy, is surely not simple. On the other hand, most of that literature has considered continous decision sets, as opposed to finite, thus allowing for enough convexity or concavity without relying on mixed strategies.

However, we recently showed [7] that in the case of a two-player (non-zero-sum) game where each player has only two possible controls – the framework of this article – not only do mixed strategies come up as a natural concept, but moreover they lead to a concept of bi-singular

---

[1] As far as we know, this phrase has been introduced by W. Sandholm [14]

trajectory fields which seems to have no counterpart in control theory. Looking into older literature, this concept should have been uncovered in the late 1960s or early 1970s. We are surprised – and a bit suspicious – that we did not find any mention of it.

We use this theory to investigate a problem of conflict over parental care which has been investigated in the literature on behavioural ecology ([8, 11, 9, 4]) in various forms (static, discrete dynamic, symmetric...). Here we adopt a continuous time model, asymmetric, that fits with the current paper, and is solved in part via our theory of bi-singular trajectory fields. We find that the solution of the more realistic finite horizon version investigated here, shares, to our surprise, some features of the infinite horizon version investigated in [7], but also displays new features.

20.2 Static games

There is a wealth of classical 2×2 static games, starting with the famous Prisoner's Dilemma – a story due to Tucker – including Stag and Hare, Hawk and Doves, Sex War, – four related games that attempt to capture the benefit of cooperation over agression (See [3]). We propose here a taxonomy of all 2×2 games adapted to our use in the sequel.

20.2.1 Notations

Let a two-person game be described by the following 2×2 bi-matrix:

$u_1 \backslash u_2$	1	2
1	a_2 a_1	c_2 b_1
2	b_2 c_1	d_2 d_1

Player 1 chooses the row through his control u_1, his payments – or rewards – are indexed by the subscript 1, while player 2 chooses the column through her control u_2, her payments being indexed by the subscript 2.

We shall all along adopt the convention that when a property holds for indices $i = 1$ and $i = 2$, we shall simply write it with the index i without every time writing $i \in \{1, 2\}$, which shall be implicit. Also, the index j in an expression involving i will mean $j = 3 - i$.

We let

$$A_i = \begin{pmatrix} a_i & b_i \\ c_i & d_i \end{pmatrix}$$

Because of the way we have arranged the bi-matrix of payments, each player chooses the row of his or her own matrix, the opponent chooses the column. Let

$$\delta_i = a_i d_i - b_i c_i \,, \qquad \sigma_i = a_i - b_i - c_i + d_i \,,$$

and when $\sigma_i \neq 0$,

$$p_j^\star = \frac{d_i - b_i}{\sigma_i} \,, \qquad 1 - p_j^\star = \frac{a_i - c_i}{\sigma_i} \,. \qquad (20.1)$$

20.2.2 Interpretation

We notice that if $\sigma_i = 0$, player i has a dominating pure strategy since $a_i - c_i = b_i - d_i$, so that the first strategy dominates the second one if both are positive, and the second dominates if both are negative. (And his choice is void if both are zero.)

Moreover, we also stress that σ_i is the second derivative of the restriction of the quadratic form of $\mathbb{R}^2$

$$x \mapsto \langle x, \frac{1}{2}(A_i + A_i^t)x \rangle$$

to the subspace orthogonal to the vector (1 1). This will have an impact in view of classical theorems on evolutionary stable strategies (ESS).

If we let p_i and $1 - p_i$ be the probabilities that player i chooses his or her first and second pure strategy respectively, $p_i^\star$ is a candidate strategy of player i equalizing for player j, i.e. such that both decisions of j provide the same payment:

$$(\, p_i^\star \quad 1 - p_i^\star \,)A_j = \frac{\delta_j}{\sigma_j}(1 \quad 1)\,.$$

However, $p_i^\star$ can be a mixed strategy only if it belongs to $[0,1]$. If so, any mixed strategy of player j is a best response to that strategy.

The property that $p_i^\star \in (0,1)$ means that player j has a dilemma: the best decision for that player depends on the decision of the other one. Conversely, if either $p_i^\star \leq 0$ or $p_i^\star \geq 1$, one line of A_j dominates the other one (weakly if $p_i^\star$ is at one of the bounds), so that player j can play that decision regardless of the opponent's choice. The dominating line is the first one if $\sigma_j p_i^\star < 0$, and the second one if $\sigma_j p_i^\star > 0$.

Invariance We stress the following invariances and symetries.

- Under addition of the same constant to all four entries of A_i, σ_i and p_j are invariant.
- Interchanging the order of the pure strategies of player i, but not j, changes both σ_i and σ_j to their opposite, leaves $p_j^\star$ invariant, and, obviously, changes $p_i^\star$ to $1 - p_i^\star$.
- In evolutionary games, the sign of σ_i will have a strong meaning. But this is a symmetric game with $A_1 = A_2$, so that one can only interchange the order of the pure strategies of both players simultaneously, thus preserving this sign.

20.2.3 Taxonomy

To avoid unnecessary particular cases, we make the following hypothesis.

Hypothesis 20.1 $a_i \neq c_i \quad \text{and} \quad b_i \neq d_i \,.$

As a consequence both $p_i^\star$ are different from 0 and 1.

Let us list the possibilities that arise.

Theorem 20.2 *Under hypothesis 20.1, occurences of Nash equilibria in* 2×2 *games are as follows:*

(i) *Either of the $\sigma_i = 0$. Then, Player i has a dominating pure strategy, the game has a single Nash equilibrium, which is pure.*

(ii) *Both $\sigma_i \neq 0$, but one at least of the $p_i^\star \notin (0, 1)$. The corresponding player(s) j has a dominating pure strategy. There is a unique Nash equilibrium, which is in pure strategies.*

(iii) *Both $\sigma_i \neq 0$, and both $p_i^\star \in (0, 1)$. Then $(p_1^\star, p_2^\star)$ is a mixed Nash equilibrium. Two subcases arise.*

    (a) *$\sigma_1 \sigma_2 < 0$. There is no Nash equilibrium in pure strategies. The mixed Nash equilibrium is the only one.*

    (b) *$\sigma_1 \sigma_2 > 0$. There are two pure Nash equilibria in addition to the mixed one. They are,*

        1. *if $\sigma_i < 0$, $(0, 1)$ and $(1, 0)$ (in terms of p_1 and p_2).*

        2. *if $\sigma_i > 0$, $(1, 1)$ and $(0, 0)$. (A coordination game, e.g. Sex War.)*

Proof

(i) The case where one $\sigma_i = 0$ has been covered in the Section 20.2.2., entitled "Interpretation" above.

(ii) Assume that both $\sigma_i \neq 0$, but that $p_i^\star \notin (0,1)$. (Remember that our Hypothesis 20.1 rules out the case $p_i^\star \in \{0,1\}$.) Then $p_i^\star$ and $1 - p_i^\star$ have opposite signs. Therefore, according to (20.1) $b_j - d_j$ and $a_j - c_j$ have the same sign. Thus the first line of A_j dominates the second if that common sign is positive, and conversely if it is negative. The domination is strict because of our Hypothesis 20.1. Therefore, a Nash equilibrium has to be pure for player j. But then player i must play his or her best response against that pure strategy, which is pure and unique again due to Hypothesis 20.1. (If both $p_i^\star$ are outside $(0,1)$, both players have a dominating strategy. A typical example is Prisoner's Dilemma.)

(iii) If both $p_i^\star$ belong to $(0,1)$, they constitute a pair of mutually equalizing strategies, hence a mixed Nash equilibrium.

    (a) The only two possibilities for there being no pure Nash equilibrium, is that, for a choice of i and j, $a_i > c_i$ and $d_i > b_i$ while $a_j < c_j$ and $d_j < b_j$. Then, trivially $\sigma_i > 0$ and $\sigma_j < 0$.

    (b) Otherwise, one of the two pairs of diagonally opposite payments are Nash. The cases *i.* or *ii.* of the theorem can be checked by inspection.

$\square$

Remark If the context allows one to number the pure strategies of both players independently, then cases (i) and (ii) of (iii)(b) in Theorem 20.2 above are not different, since, according to the facts pointed out in the paragraph "Invariance", one is converted into the other one by interchanging the numbering of the pure strategies of any one (but one only) of the players.

20.3 Evolutionary and population games

20.3.1 Mixed strategies and dynamics

In this section, we investigate in the particular case of our simple 2×2 games the implications of a simple idea: replace players by populations, and probabilities in mixed strategies by proportions of the population that use a given (pure) strategy. One can still recover a probabilistic interpretation, in that, if an individual is chosen "at random" (with a uniform law among the population), the probabilities that it plays one or the other strategy (that it be of one or the other phenotype) agree with population proportions. Yet, each individual uses a unique strategy (is of a given phenotype).

On the one hand, this gives a much more concrete and convincing interpretation of mixed strategies. On the other hand, this allows naturally for an evolution of the mixed strategies as individuals in the population switch from one pure strategy to another one.

In that respect, Sandholm [14] shows that at least two very natural strategy revision schemes lead to the same strategy dynamics, which are those considered in behavioural ecology if the fitness of a phenotype (the payment associated to a pure strategy) is taken to be the growth rate of the sub-population using it.

We use this last explanation to justify the so-called "replicator equation". We imply that a Nash equilibrium is the credible outcome of a game if it is stable under that dynamics. For the sake of completeness, we shall compare it with the Cournot – or pseudo-gradient – dynamics.

20.3.2 Evolutionary games

20.3.2.1 Taxonomy

Evolutionary games consider a competition between several (here, two) behaviours within a single population. In our wording, this means that, on the one hand $A_1 = A_2 = :A$, and on the other hand, $p_1 = p_2 = :p$.

In that context, two remarks are in order concerning the application of Theorem 20.2. On the one hand, the case (iii)(a) cannot appear. On the other hand, interchanging the numbering of the pure strategies of one player alone is not possible, hence the two sub-cases of case (iii)(b) of Theorem 20.2 are indeed different. And the two pure Nash equilibrium of the sub-case (i) being non-symmetric, they are not Nash equilibria in this context.

The basic concept is that of an *evolutionarily stable strategy* (*ESS*). This is defined by two conditions: on the one hand it is a Nash equilibrium in this symmetric context. On the other hand, in the case of a mixed Nash point, strategies as good as p against p must be less efficient than p against themselves. We state both conditons in the simple form it takes for a 2×2 game.

Definition 20.3 *A symmetric strategy (p, p) of a symmetric game is called an ESS if*

(i) *It is a Nash equilibrium,*

(ii) If $p \notin \{0, 1\}$ (then it has to be $p^\star$ of the previous section), for any $q \in [0, 1]$ different from p, the strategy $(p, 1 - p)$ is a better response to $(q, 1 - q)$ than $(q, 1 - q)$ itself, i.e.

$$(p - q \quad q - p)A \begin{pmatrix} q \\ 1 - q \end{pmatrix} > 0 .$$

The ESS that may arise are now described by this corollary.

Corollary 20.4 *Occurrences of ESS in 2×2 symmetric games are as follows:*

(i) $\sigma = 0$. There is a unique ESS, which is pure. (Typically, Prisoner's Dilemma according to [3].)

(ii) $\sigma \neq 0$ but $p^\star \notin (0, 1)$. There is a unique ESS, which is pure. (Typically, Prisoner's Dilemma, with $c < a < d < b$.)

(iii) $\sigma \neq 0$, $p^\star \in (0, 1)$.

    i If $\sigma < 0$, the only ESS is $p^\star$, (typically, Hawk and Dove),

    ii if $\sigma > 0$, there are two pure ESS : $(0, 0)$ and $(1, 1)$, and no mixed ESS. (Typically, Stag and Hare.)

Proof This is just applying Theorem 20.2 to Definition 20.3, except for the case $p^\star \in (0, 1)$ which requires distinguishing ESS among Nash points. But only symmetric Nash points may be ESS, and a simple calculation shows that

$$(p^\star - p \quad p - p^\star)A \begin{pmatrix} p \\ 1 - p \end{pmatrix} = -\sigma(p - p^\star)^2 .$$

This is positive if and only if $\sigma < 0$. □

Several remarks are in order. The only mixed ESS is therefore obtained when $\sigma < 0$, $p^\star \in (0, 1)$. Embedded into a population with that particular mix, individuals using strategy 1 and 2 fare as well. This characterization of an equilibrium population was first discovered by Wardrop in the context of road traffic [15].

20.3.2.2 Dynamics

Assume payments to pure strategies are to be understood as sub-population growth rates. Let therefore n_i be the number of individuals of type i in the population, and $p = n_1/(n_1 + n_2)$. Assume furthermore that the growth rate of each sub-population is

$$\begin{aligned}
\frac{\dot{n}_1}{n_1} &= ap + b(1-p), \\
\frac{\dot{n}_2}{n_2} &= cp + d(1-p).
\end{aligned} \tag{20.2}$$

A straightforward calculation yields the *replicator dynamics*:

$$\begin{aligned}
\dot{p} &= \sigma p(1-p)(p-p^\star) \quad \text{if } \sigma \neq 0, &(20.3)\\
\dot{p} &= (b-d)p(1-p) \quad\quad \text{if } \sigma = 0. &(20.4)
\end{aligned}$$

It is straightforward to check, concerning (20.3), that if $\sigma < 0$, its only stable equilibrium is $p^\star$, while both 0 and 1 are stable, and not $p^\star$, if $\sigma > 0$. This is an instance of the general theorem that states that ESS are (at least locally) stable points of the replicator dynamics. The same holds for (20.4) which converges to 0 or 1 according to whether $b - d$ is negative or positive.

Stag and Hare's paradox Stag and Hare (after J-J. Rousseau [12]) is a symmetric game with

$$A = \begin{pmatrix} S & 0 \\ 1 & 1 \end{pmatrix}$$

with $S > 1$. This an instance of the case $\sigma = S > 0$, $p^\star = 1/S \in (0,1)$, the last case $(3.b, ii)$ of Theorem 20.2, where there are three symmetric Nash equilibria, but only two pure ESS. Indeed, if the mixed strategy $p^\star$ is considered as a possible outcome of the game, we run into a paradox: the probability of choosing strategy 1 would *decrease* with the payment S of coordinated choices in favor of 1. The solution is in the replicator dynamics : the interval $(p^\star, 1)$ is the attraction basin of the ESS $(1,1)$. And it is *increasing* with S.

20.3.3 Population games

20.3.3.1 Equilibria and stability

We turn now to games between two different populations, each composed of individuals of two different types. This is exactly the framework of (non-symmetric) games, but with players interpreted as populations. The status of Nash equilibria are therefore described by Theorem 20.2. We do not attempt to define the equivalent of an ESS, but rely on the stability of the replicator dynamics to select realistic outcomes of a game.

As mentioned earlier, several natural considerations lead to this same dynamics, either in a learning paradigm (see [14]) or, as we assume here, in an evolutionary context.

We now have two sets (n_{i1}, n_{i2}) of subpopulation numbers, and we extend equations (20.2) to both populations, as well as the definition $p_i = n_{i1}/(n_{i1} + n_{i2})$. Differentiating that last expression, we get, in case both $\sigma_i \neq 0$,

$$\dot{p}_i = \sigma_i p_i (1 - p_i)(p_j - p_j^\star). \tag{20.5}$$

These equations have $(1,1)$, $(1,0)$, $(0,1)$, and $(0,0)$ as equilibria, and $(p_1^\star, p_2^\star)$ if both $p_i^\star \in (0,1)$. The stability of these equilibria are readily seen from the Jacobian

$$J(p_1, p_2) = \begin{pmatrix} -\sigma_1(1 - 2p_1) & \sigma_1 p_1(1 - p_1) \\ \sigma_2 p_2(1 - p_2) & -\sigma_2(1 - 2p_2) \end{pmatrix}.$$

We skip the discussion of the four "pure" cases. The conclusion is that the pure Nash equilibria are stable. Let us concentrate on the phase portrait in case 3 of the theorem. The Jacobian at $(p_1^\star, p_2^\star)$ is

$$J(p_1^\star, p_2^\star) = \begin{pmatrix} 0 & \sigma_1 p_1^\star(1 - p_1^\star) \\ \sigma_2 p_2^\star(1 - p_2^\star) & 0 \end{pmatrix}.$$

Therefore two cases arise

a $\sigma_1 \sigma_2 < 0$. The equilibrium $(p_1^\star, p_2^\star)$ is a center,

b $\sigma_1 \sigma_2 > 0$. The equilibrium $(p_1^\star, p_2^\star)$ is a saddle.

Let us furthermore emphasize the following fact. Consider the functions

$$U_i(p_i) = p_i^\star \ln \frac{p_i^\star}{p_i} + (1 - p_i^\star) \ln \frac{1 - p_i^\star}{1 - p_i}$$

and

$$V(p_1, p_2) = \sigma_2 U_1(p_1) - \sigma_1 U_2(p_2).$$

Lemma 20.5 *The function $V(p_1, p_2)$ is a first integral of the replicator dynamics (20.5).*

Proof The lemma is proved by direct differentiation, checking that the lagrangian derivatives of the U_i's are $\dot{U}_i(p_i) = \sigma_i(p_1 - p_1^\star)(p_2 - p_2^\star)$. $\square$

20.3.3.2 Phase portraits

We can now give a fairly complete description of case 3.

Theorem 20.6 In case both $\sigma_i \neq 0$ and both $p_i^\star \in (0, 1)$,

  (a) If $\sigma_1 \sigma_2 < 0$, the trajectories of the replicator dynamics are all periodic, the center being $(p_1^\star, p_2^\star)$,
  (b) If $\sigma_1 \sigma_2 > 0$, $(p_1^\star, p_2^\star)$ is a saddle. The two pure Nash equilibria are the stable points of the dynamics. Their attraction basins are separated by the curve $V(p_1, p_2) = 0$.

Proof It is a classical fact that, as long as the $p_i^\star \in (0, 1)$, the U_i are positive, null in $p_i^\star$ and strictly convex. Hence, if σ_1 and σ_2 are of opposite signs, V is strictly convex or concave, with its extremum 0 in $(p_1^\star, p_2^\star)$, and the trajectories, lying on level curves of V, are periodic. Otherwise, the curve $V(p_1, p_2) = 0$ has to be a trajectory, and as it passes through $(p_1^\star, p_2^\star)$, the result follows. $\square$

Take $A_1 = A_2 = A$, with $\sigma < 0$. Remark that the stable mixed ESS of the previous section has now turned into a saddle. The ESS dynamics was the diagonal dynamics of the current two-dimensional (2D) game, and indeed, in the saddle, the diagonal is the trajectory heading towards the saddle point. But in this 2D game, it is highly unstable. Whether the stable case can be taken as such depends on the context. Two identical populations are not the same as a single population.

20.3.3.3 Wolves and lynxes

We give here an example of population dynamics taken from a model of intraguild predation. (This is a somewhat formal model.[2] See [1] for a recent review.) In the classical Hawk and Doves game, one investigates the equilibrium between two behaviors in a population of predators competing for prey. Here, we have two different species of predators, say wolves and lynxes hunting deer. "Dog does not eat dog". In our model, the competition is extra-specific, but we still have two possible behaviours, agressive or pacific, in each population.

In that model, Lynxes are at a trophic level above that of wolves. In particular, if two aggressive individuals meet, the lynx is hurt, but the wolf is killed. We also assume that against a pacific (coward) wolf, an

---

[2] The authors thank Frédéric Grognard, of INRIA, and Ludovic Mailleret, of INRA, for a discussion that helped improve this model.

agressive lynx gets less than 1 (the full benefit of the prey), because it has spent unnecessary time and effort chasing a competitor who would have left anyhow.

The result is the following bi-matrix of rewards:

$L\backslash W$	p		a
		$1 - \lambda$	1
p	λ		0
		0	$-\theta$
a	$1 - \mu$		$1 - \nu$

with $\lambda + \mu > 1 > \nu$. In that game, we have $\sigma_1 = \lambda + \mu - \nu$ and $\sigma_2 = -\lambda - \theta$, $p_1^\star = \theta/(\lambda + \theta)$, $p_2^\star = (1 - \nu)/(\lambda + \mu - \nu)$.

A typical example of the resulting phase portrait is depicted in Figure 20.1, where we have taken $\lambda = \nu = 1/2$, $\theta = 2\mu = 1.5$, initial state at $(0.2, 0.2)$. We have integrated with an order 4 Runge Kutta scheme, with a step of 2.5×10^{-2} from $t = 0$ up to $t = 40$.

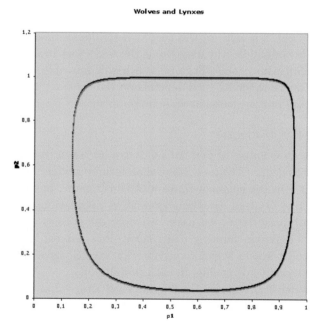

Fig. 20.1. Population dynamics for wolves and lynxes, $\lambda = \nu = 1/2$, $\theta = 2\mu = 1.5$, time span : 40 units.

20.3.3.4 Cournot dynamics

It may be worthwhile to compare the replicator dynamics to the "natural" dynamics whereby the p_i's would evolve according to the gradient of the rewards. (This could be considered the natural extension of Cournot iterations, and is Rosen's pseudo-gradient algorithm.) This leads to

$$\dot{p}_i = \sigma_i(p_j - p_j^\star).$$

This is either an harmonic oscillator or a diverging exponential according to the sign of $\sigma_1\sigma_2$. It does not take into consideration the restriction $p \in [0, 1]$ and does not seem to be a good basis for Nash selection.

20.4 Conflict over parental care, a differential game

We turn now to an application of the theory described in [6, 7] where we show how a mixed Nash equilibrium of a two-player non-zero-sum game where each player has, as here, two pure strategies (two possible phenotypes), can be found via the solution of a pair of uncoupled partial different equations (PDEs), derived from Isaacs' PDE.

20.4.1 The parental care game

Rather than an exhaustive taxonomy, which does not seem feasible, we investigate here a variation of a famous problem in behavioural ecology, the *conflict over parental care*. [2, 9]. We significanty improve, we believe, our own treatment of that question in [6, 7] by allowing for a fixed duration breeding season.

Two animals, 1 and 2, have jointly given birth to an offspring. Each of the two parents may take care of the young, but this time is taken from the time it could spend caring for itself and thus increasing the likelihood of disseminating its genes by other means. Or it may defect, but then the effort put into nesting and giving birth to the young is wasted. We allow each parent a mixed strategy, in the form of a partial rather than full effort.

Let therefore $x \in \mathbb{R}$ be the weight increase of the young. At initial time, $x = 0$. The offspring is adult and viable when $x = 1$. But this must happen during the year it was born, say at or before time T. Let $u_i = 1$

if parent i takes care full time of the young, $u_i = 0$ if it defects. In the "pure" dynamics $\dot{x}$ is given as follows:

$u_1 \backslash u_2$	0	1
0	$-\delta$	α_2
1	α_1	γ

The coefficients α_i, γ and δ are all assumed positive, with $\gamma > \alpha_1 > \alpha_2$. We let $\beta = \gamma - \alpha_1 - \alpha_2$ be the *synergy* coefficient.

Allowing for "mixed strategies" or partial efforts $u_i \in [0, 1]$ leads to

$$\dot{x} = a_1 u_1 + a_2 u_2 + c u_1 u_2 - \delta \qquad (20.6)$$

$$a_i = \alpha_i + \delta, \quad c = \gamma - \alpha_1 - \alpha_2 - \delta.$$

We allow both parents to behave in closed loop, i.e. use controls of the form $u_i = \phi_i(t, x)$. We shall encounter only constant controls, so that the existence of solutions to our dynamic equations is not an issue.

The game ends at $\tau = \min\{t \mid x(t) = 1, T\}$. The reward of the parents are $M(x(\tau)) = 1$ or 0 according to whether the young has achieved viability or not, —i.e. $M(1) = 1$, $M(x) = 0 \ \forall x < 1$—, decreased by the cost of caring, say

$$J_i(u_1(\cdot), u_2(\cdot)) = M(x(\tau)) - \varepsilon_i \int_0^\tau u_i(t) \, dt.$$

20.4.2 Pure equilibria

20.4.2.1 Constant controls

We notice the following simple facts.

Lemma 20.7

(1) Any effort that does not lead to $x(\tau) = 1$ is dominated by 0.
(2) A parent who cares alone should use the pure strategy $u_i = 1$.
(3) The best response to $u_i = 1$ is never $u_j = 1$ unless $\gamma T = 1$.

Proof

(1) If $M(x(\tau)) = 0$, the payoff to each parent is negative, or 0 for whichever has used $u_i = 0$.
(2) If a parent cares alone, to reach $x(\tau) = 1$, it needs to achieve

$$\int_0^\tau (a_i u(t) - \delta) \, dt = 1, \quad \implies \quad a_i \int_0^\tau u_i(t) \, dt = 1 + \delta\tau.$$

Hence its reward is $J_i = 1 - (\varepsilon_i/a_i)(1 + \delta\tau)$ which is decreasing with τ. Hence it should strive to minimize τ.

(3) Against $u_j = 1$, a constant response u_i yields $\tau = 1/[(\gamma - \alpha_j)u_i + \alpha_j]$ which is decreasing with u_i, as is $J_i = 1 - \varepsilon_i\tau u_i$. Hence if $\tau < T$, a $u_i < 1$ still leads to termination before T and a higher reward.

$\square$

This simple fact suffices to allow us to investigate pure Nash equilibria. Consider the game space in the (t, x) plane. Draw the lines $x = 1 - \alpha_i(T-t)$, called $\mathcal{L}_i$, and $x = 1 - \gamma(T-t)$ called $\mathcal{L}_\gamma$, as in Figure 20.1. (We carry the discussion below for $x(0) = 0$, and with respect to the position of 0 on the time axis. This could easily be extended to an arbitary initial pair (t_0, x_0).)

We claim the following (Fig. 20.2)

Theorem 20.8 *The following discussion provides all pure Nash equilibria with constant controls*

Discussion To the right of line $\mathcal{L}_\gamma$, the child cannot be brought to adulthood within the remaining time. Therefore, the only Nash equilibrium is $(0,0)$.

Assume $\alpha_1 > \alpha_2$. To the right of line $\mathcal{L}_1$, no parent can bring the child to adulthood alone. Therefore, if the other parent plays $u_j = 0$, the optimum is $u_i = 0$, and $(0,0)$ is Nash. A joint effort may drive x to 1 before time T, but, according to the lemma, except on the line $\mathcal{L}_\gamma$,

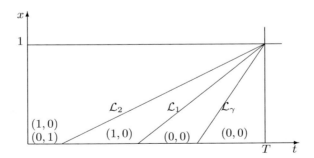

Fig. 20.2. The pure Nash equilibria if the ε_i are small.

$(1, 1)$ cannot be a Nash equilibrium. We shall see mixed equilibria in that region.

Between lines $\mathcal{L}_1$ and $\mathcal{L}_2$, the parent 1 can succeed alone. If its reward in so doing is positive, it is its best response against $u_2 = 0$. And of course $u_2 = 0$ is the best response to $u_1 = 1$ since it yields a reward of 1 to parent 2. Therefore, $(1, 0)$ is the only Nash equilibrium if $\varepsilon_1 < \alpha_1$. Otherwise, the same situation as to the right of $\mathcal{L}_1$ prevails.

To the left of line $\mathcal{L}_2$, both parents are able to succeed alone. Therefore, if both $\varepsilon_i < \alpha_i$, there are two asymmetric Nash equilibria, $(1, 0)$ and $(0, 1)$. If any of the $\varepsilon_i > \alpha_i$, that parent has no incentive to breed the child alone. Therefore, its best response to 0 is 0. Therefore if one only, say 1, is in that situation, the only Nash equilibrium is $(0, 1)$. If both are, again $(0, 0)$ is a Nash equilibrium, and also $(1, 1)$ provided that $\varepsilon_i < \gamma$.

20.4.2.2 Synchronous on-off equilibria

If $c > 0$, Nash equilibria appear, where both parents care or rest simultanesouly. The following sufficient condition has no claim of optimality. Note that we have used $\alpha_1 \geq \alpha_2$ to keep the most stringent of symmetric conditions.

Theorem 20.9 *Assume $c > 0$. Let $\mathcal{T}_0$ be a subset of $[0, T]$ with measure $\tau_0 \leq 1/\varepsilon_i$, $i = 1, 2$. Assume that the controls $\bar{u}_1(t) = \bar{u}_2(t) = \mathbf{1}_{\mathcal{T}_0}(t)$ generate a trajectory $\bar{x}(t)$ ending at $\bar{x}(\tau) = 1$ before time T, and that $(1, \bar{u}_2)$ generate a trajectory ending at τ_1. Assume further that over $[\tau_1, \tau]$, the trajectory $\bar{x}(t)$ lies below the line of slope $\gamma - \alpha_2$ passing through its end-point. Then the pair $(\bar{u}_1, \bar{u}_2)$ is a Nash equilibrum.*

Proof Fix $u_2 = \bar{u}_2$, and pick an arbitrary $u_1(\cdot)$. If the pair $(u_1(\cdot), \bar{u}_2)$ does not lead to termination before time T, parent 1 incurs a negative reward, while the condition $\tau_0 \leq 1/\varepsilon_1$ ensures a positive reward for the pair $(\bar{u}_1, \bar{u}_2)$. Let therefore τ' be the termination time on this new trajectory. Note that, necessarily, $\tau' \geq \tau_1$. Two cases arise depending on whether τ' is less or more than τ.

If $\tau' < \tau$, the support of $\bar{u}_2$ may have been curtailed by the early termination. Let $\mathcal{T}_2$ be that curtailed support, and τ_2 its measure. Let $\mathcal{T}_1 = [0, \tau'] - \mathcal{T}_2$, and let v_1 and w_1 be the integrals of $u_1(\cdot)$, respectively over $\mathcal{T}_1$ and $\mathcal{T}_2$. We have

$$x(\tau') = 1 = a_1(v_1 + w_1) + a_2\tau_2 + cw_1 - \delta\tau' = \bar{x}(\tau) = (a_1 + a_2 + c)\tau_0 - \delta\tau .$$

This can be rearranged in

$$(a_1 + c)(v_1 + w_1 - \tau_0) = cv_1 + a_2(\tau_0 - \tau_2) - \delta(\tau - \tau'). \qquad (20.7)$$

The hypothesis in the theorem can be written, using $\gamma - \alpha_2 = a_1 + c$,

$$\bar{x}(\tau') = (a_1 + a_2 + c)\tau_2 - \delta\tau' \leq (a_1 + a_2 + c)\tau_0 - \delta\tau - (a_1 + c)(\tau - \tau'),$$

which can be rearranged into

$$a_2(\tau_0 - \tau_2) - \delta(\tau - \tau') \geq (a_1 + c)[\tau - \tau' - (\tau_0 - \tau_2)].$$

Combining this with (20.7), and noting that necessarily, $\tau_0 - \tau_2 \leq \tau - \tau'$, we get

$$(a_1 + c)(v_1 + w_1 - \tau_0) \geq cv_1 \geq 0.$$

Since $J_1(u_1(\cdot), \bar{u}_2) - J_1(\bar{u}_1, \bar{u}_2) = -\varepsilon_1(v_1 + w_1 - \tau_0)$, we conclude that J_1 has creased in the change.

Otherwise, if $\tau' \geq \tau$, then $\tau_2 = \tau_0$, and (20.7) directly yields the desired result. $\qquad\qquad\square$

20.4.3 Time-sharing equilibria

If $\beta < 0$, that is $\gamma < \alpha_1 + \alpha_2$, i.e. if no synergy exists between the parents, but to the contrary a law of diminishing return prevails, another family of Nash equilibria shows up, in which the parents agree to take their turn in caring for the child. Assume that $\alpha_1 T > 1$. Pick a time $\tau < T$ such that $\alpha_2\tau < 1 < \alpha_1\tau$. Let

$$\tau_1 = \frac{1 - \alpha_2\tau}{\alpha_1 - \alpha_2} \quad \text{and} \quad \tau_2 = \frac{\alpha_1\tau - 1}{\alpha_1 - \alpha_2}.$$

This way, $\tau_1 + \tau_2 = \tau < T$ and $\alpha_1\tau_1 + \alpha_2\tau_2 = 1$. Choose a partition of $[0, \tau]$ into two (measurable) sets $\mathcal{T}_1$ and $\mathcal{T}_2$ of respective Lebesgue measures τ_1 and τ_2. Choose $\bar{u}_i(t) = \mathbf{1}_{\mathcal{T}_i}(t)$, i.e. 1 if $t \in \mathcal{T}_i$, 0 elsewhere.

We claim the following theorem.

Theorem 20.10 *If $\beta < 0$, and if both $\varepsilon_i\tau_i < 1$, the pair $(\bar{u}_1, \bar{u}_2)$ is a Nash equilibrium.*

Proof Fix $\bar{u}_2$, and choose an arbitrary $u_1(\cdot)$. Let τ' be the time when the game ends, $\mathcal{T}_2'$ of measure $\tau_2' \leq \tau_2$ the support of $\bar{u}_2$ in $[0, \tau']$ – it might be less than τ_2 if the game ends earlier – and $\mathcal{T}_1'$ of measure τ_1' its complement. Let also v_1 and w_1 be the integrals of $u_1(\cdot)$ over $c\mathcal{T}_1'$ and $\mathcal{T}_2'$, respectively. Notice that $v_1 \leq \tau_1'$.

If $(u_1(\cdot), \bar{u}_2)$ do not bring the state to 1 before time T, J_1 is negative. Otherwise, using $v_1 + w_1 = \int u_1 \mathrm{d}t$,

$$J_1(u_1(\cdot), \bar{u}_2) - J_1(\bar{u}_1, \bar{u}_2) = -\varepsilon_1(v_1 + w_1 - \tau_1).$$

Also, writing the dynamics in terms of the Greek parameters, we have that

$$x(\tau') = (\alpha_1 + \delta)v_1 + \alpha_2 \tau_2' + (\gamma - \alpha_2)w_1 - \delta\tau_1' = 1 = \alpha_1\tau_1 + \alpha_2\tau_2.$$

Using the second and the fourth terms of this equality, we easily get that

$$\alpha_1(v_1 + w_1 - \tau_1) = \delta(\tau_1' - v_1) - \beta w_1 + \alpha_2(\tau_2 - \tau_2').$$

If $\beta < 0$, the right-hand side is positive, hence the variation in J_1 is negative. $\qquad\square$

Notice that, contrary to the mixed equilibrium of the next paragraph, this is a strict Nash equilibrium, as the right hand side above can be zero only if $u_1 = \bar{u}_1$.

20.4.4 Mixed equilibria

20.4.4.1 Time-unconstrained trajectories

We now turn to mixed equilibria, using the theory of [7], whereby each player renders the opponent's Hamiltonian singular. This is therefore an pair of "dynamically equalizing strategies". The Isaacs equation is as follows. We let $V_i(t, x)$ be the two Value functions of the players. We write $\lambda_i(t, x)$ for their derivative in x. If they are of class C^1, they satisfy

$$\frac{\partial V_i(t, x)}{\partial t} + \mathcal{H}_i(\lambda_i, \phi_1^\star, \phi_2^\star) = 0, \qquad V_i(\tau, x) = M(x), \qquad (20.8)$$

with

$$\mathcal{H}_i(\lambda_i, u_1, u_2) = \lambda_i(a_1 u_1 + a_2 u_2 + c u_1 u_2 - \delta) - \varepsilon_i u_i.$$

In these equations, $(\phi_1^\star, \phi_2^\star)$ stands for a Nash equilibrium of the 2×2 game whose payoffs are the $\mathcal{H}_i$.

It is useful to rewrite this as

$$
\begin{aligned}
\mathcal{H}_i(\lambda_i, u_1, u_2) &= (\,u_i \quad 1 - u_i\,)\lambda_i A \begin{pmatrix} u_j \\ 1 - u_j \end{pmatrix} - \varepsilon_i u_i \\
&= (\,u_i \quad 1 - u_i\,)H_i \begin{pmatrix} u_j \\ 1 - u_j \end{pmatrix}
\end{aligned}
$$

with

$$A = \begin{pmatrix} \gamma & \alpha_1 \\ \alpha_2 & -\delta \end{pmatrix}, \qquad H_i = \lambda_i A - \varepsilon_i \begin{pmatrix} 1 & 1 \\ 0 & 0 \end{pmatrix}.$$

As a result, the Nash point sought is that of the bi-matrix game

$u_1 \backslash u_2$	1		0
		$\lambda_2 \gamma - \varepsilon_2$	$\lambda_2 \alpha_1$
1	$\lambda_1 \gamma - \varepsilon_1$	$\lambda_1 \alpha_1 - \varepsilon_1$	
		$\lambda_2 \alpha_2 - \varepsilon_2$	$-\lambda_2 \delta$
0	$\lambda_1 \alpha_2$	$-\lambda_1 \delta$	

Notice that in this game, with reference to the notations of the previous sections,

$$\sigma_i = \lambda_i c, \qquad \Delta_i := \det H_i = -\lambda_i^2 (a_1 a_2 + c\delta) + \lambda_i a_j \varepsilon_i. \qquad (20.9)$$

The Nash equilibria of the above bi-matrix game are singular controls in the sense of control theory. They are

$$\phi_i^\star = \frac{\varepsilon_j - \lambda_j a_j}{\lambda_j c} \qquad (20.10)$$

We investigate a field of trajectories reaching the boundary $x = 1$. On such trajectories, locally, the final time is unconstrained. As the rest of the formulation is time invariant, the associated Value is stationary, and $\partial V_i / \partial t = 0$. Placing this and (20.10) in (20.8) yields

$$\phi_i^\star = \frac{\delta}{a_i}, \qquad (20.11)$$

and therefore

$$\dot{x} = \delta \frac{a_1 a_2 + c\delta}{a_1 a_2} = \delta \frac{\alpha_1 \alpha_2 + \gamma \delta}{(\alpha_1 + \delta)(\alpha_2 + \delta)}. \qquad (20.12)$$

This slope is necessarily positive and less than γ. However, depending on c, it may be more or less than α_i.

Theorem 20.11 *If*

$$T > \frac{a_1 a_2}{\delta(a_1 a_2 + c\delta)}, \qquad and \quad \varepsilon_i < \frac{a_1 a_2 + c\delta}{a_j},$$

the mixed strategies (20.11) are a Nash equilibrium over feedback strategies.

Proof Using (20.12), the first condition in the theorem insures that $\tau < T$, hence $M(x(\tau)) = 1$, and using this, the second one insures that both parents get a positive reward. (Otherwise, $u_i = 0$ is better.) If so, the functions

$$V_i(x) = 1 - \frac{\varepsilon_i a_j}{a_1 a_2 + c\delta}(1 - x)$$

satisfy equations (20.8) in the region of the game space covered by the trajectories (20.12), which includes the initial sate of interest, $x(0) = 0$.

□

20.4.4.2 *Time-constrained trajectories*

We investigate now trajectories that end up exactly at time T with $x(T) = 1$, such that both parents get a positive reward. Let $u_i \in [0, 1]$ be such that

$$T[a_1 u_1 + a_2 u_2 + c u_1 u_2 - \delta] = 1, \qquad T\varepsilon_i u_i < 1. \qquad (20.13)$$

Theorem 20.12 *Under conditions (20.13) the pair of constant controls (u_1, u_2) is a Nash equilibrium over feedback strategies if and only if for $i = 1, 2$, either $u_i = 1$ and $1 - T\alpha_i \in [0, (\gamma - \alpha_i)/\varepsilon_j]$, or $u_j \geq \phi_j^\star$ as given by (20.11).*

Proof We compare the constant control u_i to any $u_i + v_i(t)$, assuming that the other parent keeps its control u_j constant. Let τ be the final time on the trajectory generated by these new controls. If $\tau = T$ and $x(T) < 1$, both parents have a negative payoff. Parent i loses in so doing. Therefore, the new control can be better only if $\tau \leq T$, which is impossible to achieve by player i alone if $u_i = 1$.

Assume thus that $u_i = 1$. Since we also assume $x(T) = 1$, this implies $u_j = (\frac{1}{T} - \alpha_i)/(\gamma - \alpha_i)$. This must be non-negative, and yield $1 - \varepsilon_j T u_j > 0$, which is what our condition ensures.

Assume now that $u_i < 1$, and let $w_i = \int_0^\tau v_i(t)\, dt$. We have

$$\tau[a_1 u_1 + a_2 u_2 + c u_1 u_2 - \delta] + (a_i + c u_j)w_i = 1, \qquad (20.14)$$

We assume that indeed $\tau \leq T$, thus that $w_i > 0$. (Recall that $a_i + c u_j \geq 0$, even though c may be negative.) We have also $J_i(u_i + v_i, u_j) = 1 - \varepsilon_i \tau u_i - \varepsilon_i w_i$, Using (20.13) and (20.14) we find that

$$J_i(u_i + v_i, u_j) - J_i(u_i, u_j) = -\varepsilon_i w_i T(a_j u_j - \delta).$$

Therefore, if $a_j u_j - \delta < 0$, the open loop control $u_i + v_i(\cdot)$ improves the reward of player i, and (u_1, u_2) was not Nash. Conversely, if $a_j u_j - \delta \geq 0$, no open loop control can improve J_i, and then no feedback strategy can either. (Just apply the above calculation with $u_i + v_i(t)$ equal to the control of player i generated by a test closed loop strategy and u_j.) Notice also that if $u_j = \phi_j^\star$, the variation in J_i is identically 0. This is the classical equalization property of mixed Nash equilibria. $\square$

The trajectories generated by these new Nash strategies are straight lines through the point $t = T$, $x = 1$. They fill the void between the last bi-singular trajectory and the curve $\mathcal{L}_\gamma$ of Figure 20.2, and cut into the bi-singular field if a $u_i = 1$ is Nash.

20.4.5 Biological implications

Let us mention a few biological considerations drawn from this analysis.

First, let us comment on the parameters of the game. As opposed to previous literature, we have both a fixed level of welfare to reach and a maximum end time. Moreover, we let welfare go down if the child is left without care. Also, we allow male and female to be asymmetric in terms of "cost" of breeding their offspring. One of the two, for instance, might be more prone to predation, either because it is more visible, or less apt to defend its life. Also, we let them differ in their efficiency at gathering food or otherwise breeding the child.

In that respect, intuitively, if $\gamma > \alpha_1 + \alpha_2$, we may consider this as a synergetic effect, since both parents acting together do better than the sum of their lone efforts. But if we consider that the *efficiency* of a parent is in replacing a decrease rate of δ by an increase of α_i, i.e. $a_i = \alpha_i + \delta$, and similarly for the pair $\gamma + \delta$, then the measure of synergy is rather c. Both play a role in the above results.

We do not claim to have described all Nash equilibria. But they are clearly highly non-unique. More analysis in terms of biological interpretations is needed to sort them out. We give here a few hints.

We notice that some regions of the game space have the mixed stratey as their natural outcome. It is particularly so if T is large and the ε_i small enough, so that the pure Nash equilibria are $(1, 0)$ and $(0, 1)$. Then, the mixed equilibrium appears as the "fair" outcome. The link with an ESS in a population comprising both males and females remains to be investigated further.

The peculiarity of the mixed Nash is that each parent does exactly the effort which, if made alone, keeps $\dot{x} = 0$. The interpretation is that this is true on locally time-unconstrained trajectories. Therefore the same reasoning as in [7] holds. The fact that the available time be, globally, constrained by T is reflected, on the one hand, through the possible overlap of the bi-singular field of trajectories with the field $(0,0)$, and on the other hand, by the existence of a new field of mixed equilibria trajectories, filling the gap between the bi-singular field and the fastest trajectory to just-in-time completion of the breeding process.

A last point we want to raise is that of the incentive to defect. It follows from the threshold $\varepsilon_i < a_i + c\delta/a_j$ that, if $c > 0$, increasing the efficiency of the partner j will eventually lead to a choice for i to desert. An apparent paradox. The explanation we propose is that $c > 0$ means a large synergetic effect. In that case, a less efficient mate, having a lower a_j, has a larger $\phi_j^\star = \delta/a_j$. (The threshold is precisely $a_i + c\phi_j^\star$.) Thus, under the mixed strategy, it will be more often present in the nest, and through the synergetic effect, this will compensate and over for its lower efficiency.

Is this a plausible explanation for the paradox of the handicap [5, 17, 16, 10] in sexual selection whereby a morphological trait which is a clear handicap to the individual enhances its sex-appeal ? We doubt, since it has been noticed that, as a rule, accross species, the male takes the less care of the young that the morphological difference is larger.

Bibliography

[1]   C. J. Bampfylde and M. A. Lewis. Biological control through intraguild predation: case studies in pest control, invasive species and range expansion. *Bulletin of Mathematical Biology* **69**:1031–1066, 2007.

[2]   T. H. Clutton-Brock. *The Evolution of Parental Care*, University Press, Oxford, 1991.

[3]   M. Doebeli and C. Hauert. Models of cooperation based on Prisoner's dilemma and Snowdrift games. In *Ecology Letters*, **8**:748–756, 2005.

[4]   C.-O. Ewald, J. M. McNamara and A. Houston. Parental care as a differential game: a dynamic extension of the Houston–Davis game. *Applied Mathematics and Computations*, **190**:1450–1465, 2007.

[5]   R. A. Fisher. *The Genetical Theory of Natural Selection*, University Press, Oxford, 1930.

[6]   F. Hamelin. Jeux dynamiques en écologie du comportement. thèse de doctorat, Université de Nice, soutenue le 4 juillet 2007.

[7]   F. Hamelin and P. Bernhard. Uncoupling Isaacs'equations in two-player nonzero-sum differential games. Parental conflict over care as an example. *Automatica*, **44**:882–885, 2008.

[8]   A. I. Houston and N. B. Davies. The evolution of cooperation and life history in the dunnock Prunella modularis. In *Behavioural Ecology*, R. M. Silby and R. H. Smith (eds) pp. 471–487. Blackwell Scientific Publications, 1985.

[9]   A. I. Houston, T. Szekely and J. M. McNamara. Conflict between parents over care. *Trends in Ecology and Evolution*, **20**:33–38, 2005.

[10]   H. Kokko, M. D. Jennions and R. Brooks. Unifying and testing models of sexual selection. *Annual Reviews of Ecology, Evolution and Systematics*, **37**:43–66, 2006.

[11]   J. M. McNamara, *et al.* A dynamic game-theoretic model of parental care. *Journal of Theoretical Biology* **205**:605–623, 2000.

[12]   J.-J. Rousseau. *Discours sur l'origine et les fondemens de l'inégalité parmi les hommes (Deuxième partie)*, Dijon, 1755.
(See `http://hypo.ge.ch/athena/rousseau/jjr_ineg.html`)

[13]   L. Samuelson. *Evolutionary Games and Equilibrium Selection*. MIT Press, 1998.

[14]   W. H. Sandholm. Population Games and Evolutionary Dynamics. Preprint, `http://www.ssc.edu/~whs/book/index.html`, 2007.

[15]   J. G. Wardrop. Some theoretical aspects of road trafic. *Proceedings of the Institution of Civil Engineers, Part II*, **1**:325–378, 1952.

[16]   T. Winquist and R. E. Lemon. Sexual selection and exaggerated male tail length in birds. *The American Naturalist*, **143**:95–116, 1994.

[17]   A. Zahavi. Mate selection – a selection for the handicap. *Journal of Theoretical Biology*, **53**:205–214, 1975.

21

Reversal strategies for adjoint algorithms

Laurent Hascoët

INRIA Sophia-Antipolis Méditerranée

Abstract

Adjoint algorithms are a powerful way to obtain the gradients that are needed in scientific computing. Automatic differentiation can build adjoint algorithms automatically by source transformation of the direct algorithm. The specific structure of adjoint algorithms strongly relies on reversal of the sequence of computations made by the direct algorithm. This reversal problem is at the same time difficult and interesting. This paper makes a survey of the reversal strategies employed in recent tools and describes some of the more abstract formalizations used to justify these strategies.

21.1 Why build adjoint algorithms?

Gradients are a powerful tool for mathematical optimization. The Newton method for example uses the gradient to find a zero of a function, iteratively, with an excellent accuracy that grows quadratically with the number of iterations. In the context of optimization, the optimum is a zero of the gradient itself, and therefore the Newton method needs second derivatives in addition to the gradient. In scientific computing the most popular optimization methods, such as BFGS [16], all give best performances when provided gradients too.

In real-life engineering, the systems that must be simulated are complex: even when they are modeled by classical mathematical equations, analytic resolution is totally out of reach. Thus, the equations must be discretized on the simulation domain, and then solved, for example, iteratively by a computer algorithm.

From Semantics to Computer Science Essays in Honour of Gilles Kahn, eds Yves Bertot, Gérard Huet, Jean-Jacques Lévy and Gordon Plotkin. Published by Cambridge University Press. © Cambridge University Press 2009.

Optimization comes into play when, after simulating the system for a given set of input parameters, one wants to modify these parameters in order to minimize some cost function defined on the simulation's result. The mathematical local optimization approach requires a gradient of the cost with respect to the input parameters. Notice furthermore that the gradient of the simulated function has several other applications. To quote just one, the gradient characterizes the sensitivity of the system simulation to small variations or inaccuracies of the input parameters.

How can we get this gradient? One can write a system of mathematical equations whose solution is the gradient, and here again analytic resolution is out of reach. Therefore, one must discretize and solve these equations, i.e. do what was done for the original equations. There is however an alternative approach that takes the algorithm that was built to solve the original system, and transforms it into a new *adjoint algorithm* that computes the gradient. This can be done at a relatively low development cost by *algorithmic differentiation*, also known as *automatic differentiation* (*AD*) of algorithms [8, 3, 1].

The fundamental observation of AD is that the original program P, whatever its size and run time, computes a function $F, X \in \mathbb{R}^m \mapsto Y \in \mathbb{R}^n$ which is the composition of the elementary functions computed by each run-time instruction. In other words if P executes a sequence of elementary statements $I_k, k \in [1..p]$, then P actually evaluates

$$F = f_p \circ f_{p-1} \circ \cdots \circ f_1 \ ,$$

where each f_k is the function implemented by I_k. Therefore one can apply the chain rule of calculus to get the *Jacobian* matrix F', i.e. the partial derivatives of each component of Y with respect to each component of X. Calling $X_0 = X$ and $X_k = f_k(X_{k-1})$ the successive values of each intermediate variable, i.e. the successive *states* of the memory, throughout execution of P, we get

$$F'(X) = f'_p(X_{p-1}) \times f'_{p-1}(X_{p-2}) \times \cdots \times f'_1(X_0) \ . \tag{21.1}$$

Recalling now that we are looking for a gradient, which implies strictly speaking that $X_p = Y$ is scalar, we see that equation (21.1) is more efficiently computed from left to right because vector×matrix products are so much cheaper than matrix×matrix. We end up with an iterative *adjoint* algorithm which, for each statement I_k for $k = p$ down to 1, i.e.

in *reverse order*, executes an adjoint code $\overleftarrow{I_k}$ that computes $\overline{X}_{k-1} = \overline{X}_k \times f'_k(X_{k-1})$. In other words, $\overline{X}_k$ is indeed the gradient of the final scalar cost with respect to the variables X_k just before I_k, and finally $\overline{X}_0$ is the required gradient $\overline{X}$. For every variable x in every X_k, we thus define $\overline{x}$ which is the gradient of the final scalar cost with respect to this x, and we will call it the *"gradient on x"* for short.

Before looking further into the problems posed by the AD adjoint algorithm, let's underline its decisive advantage. Observing that the cost of $\overleftarrow{I_k}$ is only a small multiple of the cost of the original statement I_k, with a factor generally between 2 and 4, we see that we get the gradient at a cost which is a small multiple of the cost of P. This cost is independent from the dimension m of the input parameter space. If on the other hand one computes the gradient by evaluating equation (21.1) from right to left, one repeatedly multiplies a matrix $f'_k(X_{k-1})$ by another matrix with m columns. This is called the AD *tangent* algorithm, and its cost is proportional to m. In real applications the number m of optimization parameters can range from several hundred up to several million, and the tangent algorithm is no longer an option.

However, the adjoint algorithm needs and uses the $f'_k(X_{k-1})$ in the reverse order, from $k = p$ down to 1. We call this the program *reversal* problem. For instance the adjoint algorithm first needs X_{p-1}, which in turn requires execution of nearly all the original program P. Then the adjoint algorithm needs X_{p-2}, but going from X_{p-1} back to X_{p-2} is by no means easy. One needs reversal strategies based either on a new run of (a slice of) P, or on undoing statement I_{p-1} possibly using some clever preliminary storage of values before I_{p-1}.

This paper makes a survey of the reversal strategies employed in the most recent AD tools, with some emphasis on the strategies that we implemented and sometimes designed for our AD tool Tapenade. In the sequel, we will organize the reversal problems into reversal of individual statements in Section 21.2, reversal of the data-flow in Section 21.3, and reversal of the control-flow in Section 21.4.

21.2 Reversal of individual statements

Consider a statement I_k from the original simulation program P. We can focus without loss of generality on the case where I_k is an assignment.

Control statements will be dealt with in Section 21.4, procedure calls are out of the scope of this paper and can be considered inlined as a subsequence of statements, and other statements such as I–O statements are of limited effect on gradient computations.

The derivative adjoint code $\overleftarrow{I_k}$ that computes $\overline{X}_{k-1} = \overline{X}_k \times f'_k(X_{k-1})$ is somewhat different from the usual derivatives from textbooks, because the gradients are propagated backwards. Specifically, naming y the variable overwritten by I_k, and considering each variable x used in the right-hand side

$$I_k : \quad \texttt{y=}f_k(\dots\texttt{x}\dots)$$

considering, for the sake of clarity only, that x and y are distinct program variables, the adjoint $\overleftarrow{I_k}$ performs for each x

$$\overline{\texttt{x}} = \overline{\texttt{x}} + \frac{\partial f_k}{\partial \texttt{x}} * \overline{\texttt{y}}$$

and terminates resetting $\overline{\texttt{y}}$=0.0. For example if I_k is:

```
y = x*(a(j)+1.0)
```

its adjoint code is:

```
x̄ = x̄ + (a(j)+1.0)*ȳ
ā(j) = ā(j) + x*ȳ
ȳ = 0.0
```

Let us now focus on the problem of common sub-expressions in the derivative code. Consider an example assignment:

```
res = (tau-w(i,j))*g(i,j)*(z(j)-2.0)/v(j)
```

Its adjoint code is

```
z̄(j) = z̄(j) + g(i, j)*(tau-w(j))*r̄es/v(j)
v̄(j) = v̄(j) - g(i, j)*(tau-w(j))*(z(j)+2.0)*r̄es/v(j)**2
ḡ(i, j) = ḡ(i, j) + (z(j)+2.0)*(tau-w(j))*r̄es/v(j)
t̄au = t̄au + (z(j)+2.0)*g(i, j)*r̄es/v(j)
w̄(j) = w̄(j) - (z(j)+2.0)*g(i, j)*r̄es/v(j)
r̄es = 0.0
```

We see that differentiation has introduced many common subexpressions that slow down the derivative code. This is because the $\frac{\partial f_k}{\partial \dots}$ often share sub-expressions from f_k. This problem differs from the optimal accumulation of partial derivatives addressed by Naumann in [13], which he recently proved to be NP-complete [14]. Instead of looking for the optimal combination of partial derivatives across several successive statements, we are here looking for an optimal common sub-expressions elimination among the expressions that return these partial derivatives for one statement. Instead of leaving this problem to some post-processor, we are going to use the known structure of adjoint codes to eliminate common sub-expressions right from differentiation time. This elimination is governed by cost/benefit considerations and therefore we analyze the cost of the adjoint code of I, looking at the abstract syntax tree of I.

Gradients are computed backward: for any arbitrary sub-tree S of the right-hand side, we can define $\overline{S}$ the gradient on the result of S, which is the product of the gradient on the right-hand side $\overline{\mathtt{res}}$ with the partial derivative of $\mathtt{res}$ with respect to S. Thus, $\overline{S}$ is computed independently of the inside of S, and it is used to compute the gradient on each variable that occurs in S. For example if we take S to be $\mathtt{(z(j)-2.0)/v(j)}$, $\overline{S}$ is $\mathtt{g(i,j)*(tau-w(i,j))*\overline{res}}$, and it occurs twice in the adjoint code, to compute $\overline{\mathtt{z}}\mathtt{(j)}$ and $\overline{\mathtt{v}}\mathtt{(j)}$. Let us evaluate, for each sub-tree S (resp. for its corresponding $\overline{S}$), its evaluation cost c (resp. $\overline{c}$) and the number of times t (resp. $\overline{t}$) it occurs in the adjoint code.

- c is obviously a simple synthesized (bottom-up) attribute.
- $\overline{t}$ is in fact the number of variables inside S, because the gradient on each of these variables uses $\overline{S}$, and no one else does. It is therefore a very simple synthesized attribute.
- $\overline{c}$ is an inherited (top-down) attribute: if S is a child of an expression $P = op(\ldots, S, \ldots)$, then the cost of $\overline{S}$ is the cost of $\overline{P}$, plus one product, plus the cost of $\frac{\partial op}{\partial S}$ which in general depends on the costs of each children of P. According to the operator op, the partial derivative may in fact depend only on some children, and this has a strong impact on the total cost.
- t is also inherited: if S is a child of an expression $P = op(\ldots, S, \ldots)$, then S occurs once inside every occurrence of P, plus each time S is used in the partial derivative $\frac{\partial op}{\partial \ldots}$ of P with respect to any of its children. Here also, this depends on the actual operator op.

The total cost attached to a sub-tree S is tc. It is worth replacing each occurrence of S by a precomputed temporary when tc is larger than the cost of assigning S to the temporary and using it t times, i.e.

$c + 1 + t$, assuming that each access to the temporary costs 1. Similarly, it is worth introducing a temporary for $\overline{S}$ when $\overline{tc} > \overline{c} + 1 + \overline{t}$. Therefore we propose the following adjoint sub-expression elimination algorithm:

```
compute c and t̄ bottom-up on the syntax tree
compute c̄ and t top-down on the syntax tree
while (some sub-tree S has a positive tc − t−c−1 or t̄c̄ − t̄−c̄−1)
   find the S that maximizes max(tc − t−c−1, t̄c̄ − t̄−c̄−1)
   create a temporary variable for S or S̄, whichever is better
   update c and t̄ bottom-up above S
   update c̄ and t top-down on the syntax tree
```

This greedy algorithm is not guaranteed to create a minimal number of temporary variables. On the other hand it is efficient on large expressions and gives good enough results on real codes. Going back to the example assignment, this algorithm produces the following adjoint code

```
tmp1 = (z(j)+2.0)/v(j)
tmp1 = g(i, j)*(tau-w(j))*res/v(j)
tmp2 = tmp1*g(i, j)*res
z(j) = z(j) + tmp1
v(j) = v(j) - tmp1*tmp1
g(i, j) = g(i, j) + tmp1*(tau-w(j))*res
tau = tau + tmp2
w(j) = w(j) - tmp2
res = 0.0
```

Notice that common expression `tau-w(j)` was not eliminated because of the cost/benefit tradeoff. In real engineering codes, long expressions spanning several lines are commonplace. On these codes, we observed speedups up to 20% coming from adjoint sub-expression elimination.

21.3 Reversal of the data-flow

Scientific programs frequently overwrite variables, and there's really no way around that. Programs cannot be turned into single-assignment form because they use iterative solvers and the number of iterations is dynamic. This is the heart of the problem for the adjoint algorithm, since it uses intermediate variables in the reverse order. If the adjoint $\overleftarrow{I_k}$ really uses variable $x \in X_{k-1}$, and if some statement I_{k+l} downstream overwrites x, then the previous value of x must be recovered. We call this the data-flow reversal problem.

To our knowledge, data-flow reversal strategies always apply one of the two approaches (or a combination), sketched in Figure 21.1.

- *Forward recomputation* of the required subset of state X_{k-1}, starting from a stored previous state between X_0 and X_{k-1}. This is done before running $\overleftarrow{I_k}$, and must be repeated similarly before $\overleftarrow{I_{k-1}}$, $\overleftarrow{I_{k-2}}$, and so on.
- *Backward restoration* of the required subset of state X_k, progressively, interleaved with $\overleftarrow{I_p}$ back to $\overleftarrow{I_k}$. In a few cases, this restoration can be done at no cost (think of x = 2.0*x), but in general it requires storage of intermediate values on a stack, known as the *tape*, during a preliminary forward execution of I_1 to I_{p-1} .

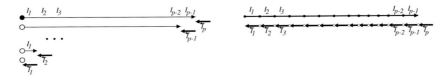

Fig. 21.1. Structure of the adjoint algorithm using Forward recomputation (left) vs. Backward restoration (right).

In Figure 21.1, we represent the actual computation of the derivatives as arrows pointing to the left, and the computation of the original statements I_k that build the required intermediate variables, as arrows pointing to the right. Vertically, we represent time, as what is represented on one line can be done only when all lines above are done. Dots indicate whenever values must be stored (black dots) in order to be retrieved later (white dots).

Figure 21.1 shows the respective merits of the two approaches: recomputation uses little memory but a lot of CPU, opposite for restoration. However, it is clear that neither method can run efficiently on a large program. AD tools, whether they are based on forward recomputation (like TAMC [6], TAF) or on backward restoration (like Adifor [2], Tapenade [12], OpenAD [18]), all use a time/memory trade-off known as checkpointing [8, Chapter 12]. Figure 21.2 illustrates checkpointing of the first half S of a program P. In forward recomputation, a snapshot of the memory is taken so that forward recomputations can restart from it, saving CPU time. In backward restoration, the first half of P is run without storing the intermediate values. It will be run again,

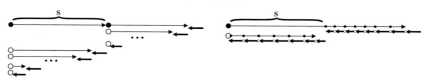

Fig. 21.2. Checkpointing in the context of forward recomputation (left) vs. backward restoration (right).

with storage, when these values are really needed. The maximum size of the stack is roughly divided by two. Checkpoints can be recursively nested. In this case the multiplicative cost factor of the adjoint program compared to the cost of P, both time-wise and memory-wise, grows only like the logarithm of the size of P, which is very good. In this case also, the overall shapes of the adjoint program become quite similar, whether one starts from the forward recomputation extreme or from the backward restoration extreme. These shapes differ only inside the lower-level checkpoints i.e. program fragments that contain no checkpoint.

Checkpointing is certainly a crucial issue for adjoint algorithms, but it is not strictly speaking a reversal problem. In the sequel we will concentrate on the program fragments that contain no checkpoint, i.e. for which the reversal scheme is one from Figure 21.1.

The first class of improvements to the reversal strategies of Figure 21.1 are basically applications of slicing. In the forward recomputation context, it was called the "ERA" improvement [7] for TAMC. Basically, the goal of a recomputation from I_1 to I_{k-1} is to restore state X_{k-1} used by $\overleftarrow{I_{k-1}}$. But in reality I_k uses only some of the available variables, and its adjoint code $\overleftarrow{I_k}$ uses only a subset of these. Therefore recomputation needs to run only a slice, i.e. the statements between I_1 and I_{k-1} that are really involved to compute the desired values.

In the backward restoration context, the similar trick is called "adjoint-liveness" [10] and was devised for Tapenade. Basically, we observe that some of the original I_k in the unique forward sweep, although involved in computing the result of P, are not involved in computing the gradients. Therefore we can take them out of the adjoint algorithm. In addition, this saves extra storage, because some values are not overwritten any more. The recursive equation that computes the set $\overline{\textbf{Live}}(I_k; \ldots; I_p)$ of adjoint-live variables just before I_k is straightforward:

$$\overline{\textbf{Live}}(I_k; D) = \textbf{Use}(\overleftarrow{I_k}) \cup (\overline{\textbf{Live}}(D) \otimes \textbf{Dep}(I_k))$$

which states that a variable is adjoint-live either if it is used in the adjoint code $\overleftarrow{I_k}$ of I_k, or if I_k depends on it to compute some result that is adjoint-live for the tail D of the program. This recursive rule stops when the code tail is empty, for which $\overline{\textbf{Live}}([]) = \emptyset$. When the $\overline{\textbf{Live}}$ sets are computed and we find a statement whose results are out of the following $\overline{\textbf{Live}}$ set, the statement can be taken away.

In the same backward restoration context, there is another slicing-based improvement: it was called the "TBR" improvement [4, 11] for Tapenade and OpenAD. As we said in the "ERA" description, the adjoint code for I_k may not use all the variables that I_k uses. Therefore, it often happens that some value of a variable x is never needed for the derivatives computation. If this happens, then even if x is overwritten we can neglect to restore its value, saving memory space. The "TBR" analysis finds the set of variables from the original program that are indeed used in the partial derivatives. The recursive equation that computes the set $\textbf{TBR}(I_1; \ldots; I_k)$ of variables whose value just after I_k is necessary for the adjoint code of I_1 till I_k is:

$$\textbf{TBR}(U; I_k) = (\textbf{TBR}(U) \setminus \textbf{Kill}(I_k)) \cup \textbf{Use}(\overleftarrow{I_k})$$

This equation states that a variable value is necessary immediately after I_k either if it is used in the adjoint code $\overleftarrow{I_k}$ of I_k, or if it was already necessary before I_k and it was not overwritten by I_k, in which case it is still the same value which is needed. This recursive rule stops when reaching the beginning of P, for which $\textbf{TBR}([]) = \emptyset$. When the $\textbf{TBR}$ sets are computed and we reach a statement that overwrites some variables, only the intersection of these variables with the $\textbf{TBR}$ set just before the statement need to be stored.

Let us now take a closer look at the backward restoration strategies. Storing and retrieving is not the only option: sometimes, inversion is possible. The simplest example is statement x = 2.0*x. If restoration of the upstream x is needed, it can very well be done by x = x/2.0, provided that the downstream x has been restored too. Such statements are not very frequent; however, this can be generalized: statement x =

a-b can also be inverted to restore say, b, provided a and the downstream x have been restored too. In fact the main problem is blending this tactic with memory storage, as there is a combinatorial explosion when looking for the best strategy. This is now becoming a hot topic in the community of AD tool builders.

To gain more insight in the data-flow reversal requires that we consider the data-dependence graph. Figure 21.3 is an magnified view of the right of Figure 21.1, showing a possible data-dependence graph. For clarity, only the necessary anti (read-to-overwrite) dependencies are

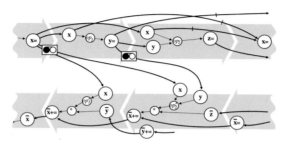

Fig. 21.3. The data-dependence graph of the adjoint algorithm.

shown, and output dependencies (write-to-overwrite) are omitted. The true dependencies are shown, and the computation dependencies inside each instruction are shown with thinner arrows.

The first thing to notice is that the dependencies between the gradient values are symmetric of the dependencies between the original variables in the original code. In [9], we proposed a demonstration of this particularly useful symmetry: this isomorphism between the backward sweep and the forward sweep of the adjoint algorithm tells us that many data-dependence-based properties are preserved, such as parallelizability. The three dependencies labeled with a small tape-recorder symbol are very special: these are indeed true dependencies that *cannot* be satisfied by the algorithm as it is, because the variable gets overwritten before the read operation is made. Therefore, to satisfy these dependencies requires storage of the value during the forward sweep and retrieval during the backward sweep, using the tape. In Figure 21.3, two values are stored, x and y. However, this might not be optimal in terms of memory consumption. Consider the bipartite graph going from the *read* nodes of the forward sweep to the operations nodes of the backward sweep that combine gradient values with partial derivatives depending on the forward sweep (here the two multiplication nodes labeled with *). To minimize memory consumption, one must look for a minimal cut of this bipartite graph. In the example, one could store x op_2' y. In other words, the question is what to store, the intermediate values or the partial derivatives that use them? The answer depends on the actual code. On the example, there is actually a tie since there are two intermediate values x and y, as well as two partial derivatives. The OpenAD tool implements heuristics that sometimes decide to store the partial derivatives. On the other hand, Tapenade and Adifor always store the intermediate values.

If the choice is to store the intermediate values, another question is *when* to push them on the stack. To preserve the convenient stack structure of the tape, the popping order must conform with the order of first uses during the backward sweep. Reversal comes into play here, as the answer is to push x on the stack during the forward sweep, between the *last* use of x and the next overwrite of x. The simplest way to do that is the *save on kill* strategy, which stores x just before it is overwritten.

21.4 Reversal of the control-flow

The topmost level at which reversal is needed is the control-flow. A good introduction to the question can be found e.g. in [15, 17]. Let's start with the representative example of a conditional statement shown by Figure 21.4. If at some time during the original run the control-flow goes to one branch of the conditional, then the adjoint algorithm must go to the adjoint of the same branch. Therefore the direction chosen by the conditional must somehow be retrieved later. The danger that appears on Figure 21.4 is that this must be done by the adjoint algorithm just after $\overleftarrow{I_{16}}$, and not just before $\overleftarrow{I_{10}}$, which would be more consistent with the reversal order.

There are basically two ways to retrieve the chosen direction in the adjoint algorithm.

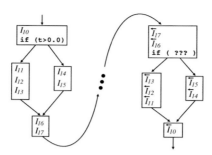

Fig. 21.4. Control-flow reversal of a conditional.

- Either we duplicate the test in the adjoint conditional. This is analogous to the *forward recomputation* strategy of Section 21.3. But because the adjoint test occurs too early, we can employ this strategy only if the variables used in the test (e.g. t) are not modified in the conditional itself.
- Or one stores the direction taken when the conditional actually terminates, so that this direction is available at the beginning of the adjoint conditional. This is analogous to the *backward restoration* of Section 21.3. This amounts to simply storing a boolean on the stack just before the flow merges reaching I_{16}.

Structured loops can be treated in a similar fashion. When the variables that occur in the loop bounds are not modified by the loop body, then the adjoint loop control can be built easily. For example the adjoint loop bounds of a "DO" loop control DO i=2,n,1 is simply DO i=n,2,-1. There are minor technical details, e.g. when the loop length is not a multiple of the loop stride. Again, problems occur when the variables in the loop bounds are modified by the loop. The loop bounds must be stored in temporaries at loop beginning, but these temporaries are stored on the tape only at loop exit, so that they are available at the beginning of the adjoint loop.

Generally speaking, the adjoint of a well-structured code is another well-structured code whose control statements are directly derived from the original control. When the variables in a control statement are modified by the controlled structured statement, a temporary may be necessary. This is usually cheap. The amount of tape memory required to reverse the control-flow is in general very small in comparison with the tape required to reverse the data flow. When, on the other hand, the original program is not well structured, then we must resort to a slightly more brutal strategy, that we call *save control on join*. Specifically, each time control-flow arrows join at the entrance of a basic block, we save on the tape the arrow effectively taken. In the adjoint code, the tape is read to find the adjoint arrow that must be taken. This is indeed the data-flow *save on kill* strategy applied to control-flow. This may increase the total size of the tape significantly, especially on systems where a boolean is actually encoded as an integer.

There are two other classes of reversal questions that we view as extensions of the control-flow reversal problem. AD tools are beginning to consider these questions only now, and we don't know of a tool that treats them fully. The first class is the use of pointers, that effectively control the addresses that are referred to by an expression. Figure 21.5 shows just one representative example, using the C syntax. Pointer p is

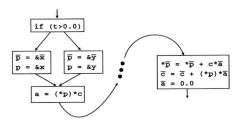

Fig. 21.5. Control-flow reversal with pointer usage.

used to select which variable is read by statement a=2*(*p). To select which gradient variable will be incremented by its adjoint code, we may define a *gradient pointer* $\bar{p}$. This is somewhat surprising as derivatives are usually defined on real numbers only, but this is actually an address memorization strategy. The moment when $\bar{p}$ can be set is exactly when p itself is set, and if ever p is overwritten during the sequel of the original program, then p and $\bar{p}$ must be stored on the tape.

Storing a pointer on the tape works fine as long as the memory it points to is not freed. This is granted for static memory, but we lack a convenient solution for dynamic memory. Suppose the forward sweep of the adjoint program, following the original program, allocates some memory, makes pointer p point into this memory, and then frees this memory. During the backward sweep, some memory will be allocated again when needed, but we cannot guarantee that it is the same memory chunk. The tape mechanism ensures that p recovers its value, but it is an address in the previous memory chunk, not in the new one! There may be a convenient solution if we can request a memory allocation at a specified memory location: we are confident we can prove that the memory freed on the forward sweep is still free when the backward sweep reaches the same location. It would then suffice to allocate exactly the same memory chunk on the way back.

The second class of control reversal questions is related to message-passing parallelism, which is routinely used in the scientific programs we are targeting. As long as communications are one-to-one, control-flow reversal is easy: when process P1 sends a variable x to process P2, the adjoint algorithm must send the gradient variable $\bar{x}$ from P2 back to P1. Communications one-to-all and all-to-one require in addition that the sender of a message be identified in the message itself, so that the adjoint algorithm can send the gradient back. Synchronization may also require care, but so far we saw no application for which synchronization has an effect on differentiable values.

21.5 Automatic differentiation at INRIA

Automatic differentiation has been around for many years: a Russian paper from L.M. Beda mentions the name and concept in 1959, and libraries that execute operations together with propagation of analytical derivatives date from the 1970s (WCOMP, UCOMP). Adjoint algorithms primarily existed as hand-written programs that solve the so-called adjoint state equations from the theory of control. Only in the 1980s did some automatic differentiation tools appear that could generate good enough adjoint algorithms (JAKE, JAKEF), and true awareness of these tools in industrial scientific computing dates from the 1990s.

At INRIA, research on automatic differentiation (AD) was initiated by Jacques Morgenstern and André Galligo in the research team SAFIR. One of the outcomes of this work was the AD tool O∂yssée [5], which very soon featured a successful adjoint mode. Already at that time, this work was warmly supported by Gilles Kahn, who saw the interest of a scientific collaboration between the algorithmic developments of SAFIR and the interactive programming environment Centaur developed by the CROAP team.

In 1999, Valérie Pascual and myself proposed the creation of a new research team TROPICS, to further develop AD for adjoint algorithms. Gilles was again our strongest support. He liked to say facetiously that the difficulties we sometimes experienced in front of skilled hand programmers of adjoint algorithms, sounded like the first compiler programs trying to compete with hand-writing of assembly code.

21.6 Current status and perspectives

Adjoint algorithms produced by AD have made impressive progress in the last few years. Large industrial codes that were simply out of reach are now routinely "adjointed" by AD tools. This is partly due to the development of the reversal strategies described in this paper, as well as to the progress made a few years before in nested checkpointing strategies. AD now produces adjoint algorithms whose quality competes with that of hand-written adjoints, which took months or years of development and debugging. Since the adjoint code must evolve together with its original code, the ability to rebuild it in a matter of minutes is much appreciated.

Problems remain, though, and we discussed some of them. These problems essentially connect to the weaknesses of our static analyses. Undecidability of static analysis of course sets a limit to the power of AD tools. But very far before that, AD tools are already limited by their simplifying assumptions: no AD tool uses the very clever (and expensive) algorithms from parallellization, such as array region analysis or reaching definition analysis.

Maybe the path to overcome these limitations is to develop interaction with the end-user, for example, through directives. An end-user always knows more about the code than any static analysis will find out. Most AD tools are now going in this direction, and TAF is probably ahead in this respect. For the general application domain of adjoint algorithms, i.e. scientific computing, knowledge from the user is even more invaluable than elsewhere. Large parts of the programs correspond to well-known mathematical operations whose properties have been studied for centuries. For example, no static analysis will be able to detect that a code fragment actually solves a symmetric linear system using the latest champion iterative algorithm. Yet if the user provides a clever AD tool with this knowledge, the tool should be able to find that the adjoint is indeed the original solver itself.

Reversal strategies are also explored in other domains. Some debuggers try to keep track of execution before a program crashed, allowing the user to go back in time to discover the true origin of the problem. This is a challenge, even more so when debugging a distributed parallel execution. We hope this paper could spark cross discussions, resulting in improved reversal strategies for adjoint algorithms. I'm sure Gilles would like that.

Bibliography

[1] M. Bücker, G. Corliss, P. Hovland, U. Naumann and B. Norris (eds). *Automatic Differentiation: Applications, Theory, and Implementations.* LNCSE. Springer, 2006. Selected papers from AD2004, Chicago, July 2004.

[2] A. Carle and M. Fagan. *ADIFOR 3.0 overview.* Technical Report CAAM-TR-00-02, Rice University, 2000.

[3] G. Corliss, C. Faure, A. Griewank, L. Hascoët and U. Naumann (eds). *Automatic Differentiation of Algorithms, from Simulation to Optimization.* LNCSE. Springer, 2002. Selected papers from AD2000, Nice, June 2000.

[4] C. Faure and U. Naumann. Minimizing the tape size. In [3], chapter VIII, pp. 293–298. 2002.

[5] C. Faure and Y. Papegay. *Odyssée User's Guide.* Version 1.7. Technical report 224, INRIA, 1998.

[6] R. Giering. *Tangent linear and Adjoint Model Compiler, Users manual.* Technical report, 1997. http://www.autodiff.com/tamc.

[7] R. Giering and T. Kaminski. Generating recomputations in reverse mode AD. In [3], chapter VIII, pp. 283–291. 2002.

[8] A. Griewank. *Evaluating Derivatives: Principles and Techniques of Algorithmic Differentiation.* SIAM, Frontiers in Applied Mathematics, 2000.

[9] L. Hascoët. *The Data-dependence Graph of Adjoint Programs.* Research Report 4167, INRIA, 2001.

[10] L. Hascoët and M. Araya-Polo. The adjoint data-flow analyses: Formalization, properties, and applications. In [1], pp. 135–146. 2006.

[11] L. Hascoët, U. Naumann and V. Pascual. To-be-recorded analysis in reverse mode Automatic Differentiation. *Future Generation Computer System,* **21**(8):1401–1417, 2005.

[12] L. Hascoët and V Pascual. *Tapenade 2.1 user's guide.* Technical report 300, INRIA, 2004.

[13] U. Naumann. Optimal accumulation of Jacobian matrices by elimination methods on the dual computational graph. *Mathematical Programming, Series A,* **99**(3):399–421, 2004.

[14]   U. Naumann. Optimal Jacobian accumulation is NP-complete. *Mathematical Programing*, 2006. in press. Appeared online first.

[15]   U. Naumann, J. Utke, A. Lyons and M. Fagan. Control flow reversal for adjoint code generation. In *Proceedings of the Fourth IEEE International Workshop on Source Code Analysis and Manipulation (SCAM 2004)*, pp. 55–64. IEEE Computer Society, 2004.

[16]   J. Nocedal and S.-J. Wright. *Numerical Optimization.* Springer, Series in Operations Research, 1999.

[17]   J. Utke, A. Lyons and U. Naumann. Efficient reversal of the intra-procedural flow of control in adjoint computations. *J. Syst. Softw.*, 79(9):1280–1294, 2006.

[18]   J. Utke, U. Naumann, M. Fagan, *et al.OpenAD/F: A Modular, Open-source Tool for Automatic Differentiation of Fortran codes.* Technical report ANL/MCS-P1230-0205, Argonne National Laboratory, 2006. Submitted to ACM TOMS.

22

Reflections on INRIA
and the role of Gilles Kahn

Alain Bensoussan

Former president of INRIA, 1984–1996

22.1 Introduction

I have spent 29 years of my life with INRIA. I had seen the beginning of
the institute in 1967. I was appointed president of the institute in 1984
and I left it in 1996, after 12 years as president.

Gilles Kahn joined IRIA in the late 1960s and made his entire career in
the institute. He passed away while he was president, after a courageous
fight against a dreadful illness, which unfortunately did not leave him any
chance. I knew him for more than 35 years and I have an accurate vision
on the role he played in the development of the institute. More globally,
I have seen his influence in the computer science community in France
and in Europe. This article gives me the opportunity to understand what
was behind such a leadership and to recall some of the challenges that
INRIA has faced during more than three decades. What we can learn
from the past and from the action of former great leaders is extremely
helpful for the future.

This is probably the best way to be faithful to Gilles and to remain
close to his thoughts.

22.2 Historical IRIA

22.2.1 Why IRIA?

INRIA was born as an evolution of IRIA.

IRIA was created in 1967 as a part of a set of decisions taken under the
leadership of General de Gaulle. It was a time of bold decisions towards
research at large, based on clear political goals.

General Charles de Gaulle wanted to strengthen France and wanted
a country inspiring respect and influence worldwide. Such a role could

From Semantics to Computer Science Essays in Honour of Gilles Kahn, eds Yves
Bertot, Gérard Huet, Jean-Jacques Lévy and Gordon Plotkin. Published by Cambridge
University Press. © Cambridge University Press 2009.

not become a reality without France being an advanced technological country, and research was the indispensable step towards this objective. IRIA was a part of the "Plan Calcul" whose objective was to provide the country with the capability of being autonomous in producing computers.

IRIA was the research component of the package. Certainly the main element was the industrial decisions concerning the Bull Company. It is interesting to see that while this plan has been globally a failure, the research decisions concerning the creation of IRIA have remained as a significant step forward.

It is fair to say that Bull has survived in a niche activity. Obviously the goal to provide France with an autonomous capability in computer manufacturing was a dream which today looks incredibly unrealistic.

However, in the late 1960s the role of software was not so overwhelming. Computer science was concentrated in building computing machines. The government of General de Gaulle had suffered from a setback in acquiring a CDC computer from the US intended for the CEA, the French Atomic Energy Agency, to be used for developing the French nuclear program. This decision had been vetoed by the US government, accelerating the will of the French government to look for autonomy. The politicians must be commended not to have forgotten research and science in the plan, in spite of the urgency of short-term decisions. However, the role of IRIA has been debated. Was it just the research and development center of the manufacturer, or a long-term government research organization?

Fortunately, the latter format prevailed, thanks to the tenacity of great scientists, J. L. Lions being certainly one of the main leaders defending this orientation. Although Gilles Kahn was a junior scientist in those days, he represented the voice of the young generation and J. L. Lions could be sure to represent them.

22.2.2 Gilles at the beginning?

Interestingly Gilles was an employee of CEA, so he was sensitive to the debate on computing means. In those days the computer science community in France was very limited, with the exception of the talented M. P. Schutzenberger, although a very different personality in comparison to the modern computer scientists. Since also computer science was strongly motivated by performing scientific computations, it is not surprising that the applied mathematicians, the numerical analysts and the combinatorists held the leadership. The fact that a charismatic leader like J. L. Lions was in full activity in those days accelerated this state of affairs.

IRIA played a significant role in preparing a new generation of French computer scientists, providing scholarships to study in the US.

To be trained in Stanford was the most prestigious path for these motivated young and talented students (unfortunately no women among them). Gilles Kahn was one of them. The Stanford connection played an important role in building the base of the present French school of computer scientists. Most of them made at least part of their career at INRIA, and certainly contributed a lot to the orientation of the institute, in particular towards long-term research and science.

Although composed of strong personalities, this community always accepted Gilles Kahn as their leader and their spokesperson. Of course, this pre-eminence did not have any official status, but it was clear that the influence of Gilles Kahn was prevalent.

To a large extent, this was also obvious for the other participants to the IRIA and INRIA adventure, starting with J. L. Lions, who always relied on Gilles Kahn to be aware of the opinion of computer scientists within IRIA and INRIA, to give suggestions on specific aspects of the field or to discuss strategy at large. The same was true with the representatives of the other INRIA communities, those representing control like Pierre Faurre or me, and those representing scientific computing like Roland Glowinski. If I can speak for myself, I have always been impressed by the fact that Gilles was capable of understanding what I was doing, and I know this was true for my colleagues. He was clearly interested by the applications of computer science and he always had the vision that they were the driving force of the importance of computer science at large.

This might look obvious, especially now. However, in those days, the key objective of computer scientists was to develop their science and the tools necessary to build good computing machines. Basic software was one of the main preoccupations. Applications were not so much the concern. The need of good machines and operating systems was prevalent. There was no reason to consider applications directly, that was left to specialists. Probably the fact that Gilles started his career at the CEA helped him to have consciousness of the need of understanding the user's point of view. But, certainly his aptitude to strategic considerations played an essential role. It was always one of Gilles' strong points.

22.3 Creation of INRIA

22.3.1 Why INRIA?

INRIA was created in 1980. The transformation of IRIA into INRIA was not the consequence of the considerable evolution of research after the election of President Mitterrand in 1981. It was rather for reasons linked to urgent political considerations, just as at the creation of IRIA in 1967.

The concern of the government was that the country was lagging behind major industrialized nations in terms of using computer facilities. Consequently, the competitiveness of industry was at stake. The government decided to push demand and its major decision was to create an agency to promote the use of computer means in all activities of society. This was ADI, the Informatics Development Agency. Research was left outside and was supposed to be an activity in regions, leaving a strict minimum at Rocquencourt, the location of IRIA.

Fortunately, J. L. Lions, backed by all IRIA researchers, was influential enough to obtain the creation of a national institute for research in computer science and control called INRIA, with strength in Rocquencourt as well as in regions. The region chosen was Sophia-Antipolis, and the existing IRIA personnel in Rennes, within IRISA, could also constitute an INRIA center. I remember very well the great momentum behind the creation of ADI, obviously the government idea, whereas INRIA was more the result of a compromise between the will of the government and that of the researchers headed by J. L. Lions, who was appointed President of INRIA. It is interesting to see that once again science and research prevailed. In 1987, ADI disappeared while INRIA was reinforced. Research remains a stable and essential need for all nations. Other preoccupations, driven by political considerations rarely survive their political backers.

22.3.2 Gilles Kahn, a scientific leader

Gilles was in charge of software engineering at INRIA. To a large extent, software engineering represented the natural extension of the major domain of operating systems in the previous years. But it is certainly much more than a continuation. It was the evidence that software was becoming the key element of computers, and more importantly of computer systems and networks. Of course, many other great computer scientists at INRIA were also contributing to software engineering, through artificial intelligence, formal methods, complexity, algorithms, parallelism.

I can give only my impression, which is not that of a computer scientist, but that of someone observing the evolution of the field with a direct interest, since I became President in 1984.

I had the impression that the ambitious vision of Gilles was really overwhelming. He certainly was the best to foresee the fantastic evolution of computer science towards what we call now information technology or information science.

Being fully user driven, he anticipated the future needs arising from applications and consequently the types of tools that software developers would require. He was motivated by the fact that software production should be automatized and governed by quality control, as any other production. However software is much more subtle and remains very specific. The quality of software cannot be considered in an intrinsic way. It is system dependent. It is not just the fact that there are no flaws.

That is why Gilles Kahn was perfectly aware of the more focused contributions of his colleagues and he was capable of directing them towards his ambitious objectives. This explains probably his scientific leadership with respect to scientists who were also stars in their domain. When INRIA was invited to cooperate in the Japanese program of fifth generation computers, President J. L. Lions asked Gilles Kahn to coordinate the actions of INRIA. Again, nothing could appear more natural.

Pierre Haren is also a good example. He was motivated by the application of artificial intelligence in specific areas like transport, shipping, and building, more generally in activities requiring fast access to various expertises. He settled in Sophia-Antipolis, to be close to Gilles Kahn, to learn from him, to benefit from his tools and maybe more importantly to benefit from his advices.

22.3.3 Gilles Kahn, a global leader

Pierre Bernhard became the first director of the INRIA centre at Sophia-Antipolis. He had met Gilles Kahn at Stanford, while himself getting a PhD in automatic control. He convinced Gilles to come to Sophia, and there started really a team directorship. Pierre Bernhard was the director, running the center on all matters but relying fully on the scientific leadership of Gilles concerning the research orientations, the new projects and the scientific discussion with the project leaders.

That is where Gilles was so excellent. He was marginally interested by administrative duties, although certainly capable of handling them. He was excellent in his dialogue with researchers and project leaders. His knowledge exceeded his own field and his own research. He liked to learn, to understand and to guide scientists.

His scientific leadership was accepted without any reservation, even by strong personalities who could have a longer list of publications.

This explains why Gilles Kahn became the first computer scientist elected at the French Academy of Sciences, without the slightest reservation from the community of computer scientists or the scientific community at large. Since then, he showed a strong influence in the Academy. He was at the origin of the election of all computer scientists and was listened with authority by all academicians.

I really would like to insist on Gilles Kahn's exceptional charisma. It is not easy to explain such a power, certainly a successful combination of many human qualities: deep intelligence, deep vision, broad interests, large open-mindedness, natural leadership. Probably also important is the fact that Gilles had a goal, I could even say a mission: to obtain for Computer Science the status of a major science, to which the French scientific community would bring the brightest discoveries.

22.4 My personal interaction with Gilles Kahn

22.4.1 Before I became president of INRIA

I was recruited at IRIA at the very beginning in 1967. I made my doctorate, and then became a project leader. At INRIA, under the presidency of J. L. Lions, I became chairman of the project committee, in charge of evaluating current projects and deciding new ones.

I was constantly in contact with Gilles Kahn, first as a colleague then as an essential element of decisions concerning projects. Candidates to new project leadership knew that the position of Gilles Kahn was indispensable. It may look strange, but to create a project without the approval of Gilles Kahn was unthinkable. At the same time everybody was confident that he was fair, positive and helpful. So this situation was completely natural and never challenged.

22.4.2 After I became president of INRIA

I had been appointed President of INRIA in 1984, after J. L. Lions left to become President of CNES. I left INRIA in 1996. In these 12 years

I had so many opportunities to appreciate the intelligence, the strategic vision and the dedication of Gilles Kahn to collective interest.

Gilles himself was not so much interested in becoming president. A President has many solicitations and has to accept many constraints. Gilles Kahn wanted to remain free. It does not mean that Gilles Kahn disliked having power, but he was much more interested by his power of influence than by what is attached to the status of president.

In addition we were on excellent terms, and he knew my admiration for his personality.

I appointed him as scientific director, a position which was fully coherent with his aspirations and interests.

He was a remarkable scientific director, but beyond that he was instrumental in helping me to confront, debate and implement important strategic decisions, in which I was always impressed by the depth of his thoughts and the sharpness of his analysis.

Let me give an example which remains for me striking. In 1993 we suffered what was called the "crisis of informatics", the first one, since later there was the famous Internet Bubble.

All of a sudden, nothing was working well in the informatics sector. A great confusion prevailed, resulting in a serious drop in the economic activity and unfortunately many layoffs. For the first time, this constantly growing sector suffered from lack of jobs, compared to the supply. One year before we had just celebrated our 25th anniversary and the mood was euphoric.

Of course a government research organization is not responsible for economic problems, and is protected from the loss of jobs by its statute.

Nevertheless I was feeling that an essential asset of the country like INRIA could not just continue business as usual and at the very least should give its vision on the best way to contribute to the information society and its economic repercussions. I decided to launch the first strategic plan of the institute. This may seem common now, but was much less so 13 years ago. I thought it essential to refer to some model and to discuss the one most suitable for INRIA to have a significant impact on the economy.

I proposed to center the debate between what I called the Stanford model versus the Fraunhofer model. I clearly expressed my preference for the Stanford model. The point is not to enter into the discussion. I must admit it appeared a little bit abstract to the personel of INRIA, and did not raise much passion. Probably my objectives had not been well understood but my position did not upset anybody.

If I mention this story, it is because the debate appeared important to Gilles Kahn, and I was surprised to see the interest he expressed in considering the implementation of these two models.

Fortunately we were in complete agreement (he was himself trained at Stanford, which was not true in my case), but I was impressed to see his deep interest in the discussions on strategy. When he became President, he recalled to me this discussion that was more than a decade old. In retrospect, to have raised the interest of Gilles Kahn and fortunately of some more at INRIA compensates the feeling of approval with indifference. I guess the interest in strategic discussions has risen as INRIA evolved in size, in importance and in the choice of domains. Gilles Kahn played a key role in this evolution.

We had many more interesting initiatives, in which the support and help of Gilles Kahn was instrumental. I can list the creation in 1987 of ILOG, and later the development of spin-off companies, in coherence with the Stanford model, the creation of ERCIM a little bit later, after the single European Act. At that time Europe was progressing fast on common institutions. An important question for research entities like INRIA was to contribute to the construction of the Europe of innovation. A significant initiative occurred in 1994, when we agreed to form the European branch of the W3C. INRIA has always been at the forefront of the Internet, even at a time when many strong players were opposed to it. Gilles Kahn was a visionary of the role of the Internet, and was himself making the greatest use of it, from the very beginning when the search engines did not exist.

When I left INRIA to become President of CNES, I had unfortunately to face, in June 1996, the failure of the inaugural flight of the new launcher Ariane V. The failure was related to software. I asked the help of INRIA and Gilles Kahn not only participated to the inquiry committee, but also organized a team to work on the validation of software, in similar contexts. A new spin-off was created as a consequence of the successful work of INRIA experts. Gilles Kahn immediately understood what was at stake for the country. He naturally agreed to help. He also understood the importance for INRIA to be involved in the solution of such essential problems. He agreed also to be a member of the technical committee I put in place in CNES.

22.5 Concluding comments

After I left INRIA in 1996, and after P. Bernhard decided not to compete to become my successor, Gilles Kahn was the natural person to become President. Again he preferred not to run and Bernard Larrouturou became President. He naturally confirmed Gilles Kahn as scientific director. Gilles continued in this role until Bernard Larrouturou left.

At some point Gilles could no longer refuse to become president. He was deeply attached to INRIA and he could not remain scientific director after so many years in this position.

Unfortunately, he did not have a long time as president as illness came soon without recovery. Nevertheless Gilles Kahn showed a courage which was beyond belief. I know what the workload of the President of INRIA is, and this can only increase with time. To assume it, while being ill and having intensive care is something which is hard for me to imagine. Once again Gilles Kahn had surprised me. He remains for me an exceptional personality, to whom very few can compare.

23

Can a systems biologist fix a Tamagotchi?

Luca Cardelli

Microsoft Research

Abstract

Gilles Kahn was a serious scientist, but part of his style and effectiveness was in the great sense of curiosity and fun that he injected in the most technical topics. Some of his later projects involved connecting computing and the traditional sciences. I offer a perspective on the culture shock between biology and computing, in the style in which I would have explained it to him.

23.1 The nature of nature

In a now classic peer-reviewed commentary, *"Can a Biologist Fix a Radio?"* [2], Yuri Lazebnik describes the serious difficulties that scientists have in understanding biological systems. As an analogy, he describes the approach biologists would take if they had to study radios, instead of biological organisms, without having prior knowledge of electronics.

We would eventually find how to open the radios and will find objects of various shape, color, and size [. . .]. We would describe and classify them into families according to their appearance. We would describe a family of square metal objects, a family of round brightly colored objects with two legs, round-shaped objects with three legs and so on. Because the objects would vary in color, we will investigate whether changing the colors affects the radio's performance. Although changing the colors would have only attenuating effects (the music is still playing but a trained ear of some people can discern some distortion), this approach will produce many publications and result in a lively debate.

In such a generally humorous style, Lazebnik makes several deep points about the nature of complex systems, and about the concepts and languages that one must develop to even begin to describe them appropriately. One of his main points is that it is not enough to classify

From Semantics to Computer Science Essays in Honour of Gilles Kahn, eds Yves Bertot, Gérard Huet, Jean-Jacques Lévy and Gordon Plotkin. Published by Cambridge University Press. © Cambridge University Press 2009.

or even understand individual components, but one must understand the circuits that arise from them. That point of view has become one of the founding principles of systems biology [3], and is inspiring huge experimental efforts aimed at mapping biological "circuits" in order to eventually learn how to "fix" them rationally rather than empirically. (This is related to earlier rational approaches that include, for example, "fixing radios by thinking" [4].)

Lazebnik's analogy between biological and hardware circuits is illuminating, especially coming from a professional biologist who (unlike me) has full moral authority on such a subject. But the analogy is not particularly accurate when considering whole biological systems. Biologists cannot understand radios without any knowledge of electrical engineering but, similarly, electrical engineers cannot understand mp3 players without any knowledge of software engineering, even though mp3 players play music just like radios. As it turns out, even the simplest biological organisms have a minimum of hundreds of kilobytes of software, in the form of digitally stored genetic information, and can have as much as several megabytes of it (considerably more than mp3 players). There is no life form that is just hardware circuits; not even viruses, which on the contrary are almost purely software. The role of such genetic software is commonly understood as that of "running the organism". All forms of reproduction consist in the software making a copy of itself, by a process that is pretty much standardized across all organisms, and in orchestrating the replication of the required hardware.

Therefore, biologists need to do more than learn how to fix radios. There may come a time when all the "circuits" of a cell will be completely understood, but we will still have little insight on how to go about fixing one. That is because software is not circuits: a full knowledge of microprocessors and radio transmitters is completely irrelevant when trying to understand, for example, why a mobile phone is not fetching email; it has nothing to do with the circuits, usually. Lazebnik's basic analogy might be considered as extending to "software circuits" as well, but it is just too naive to think of software in term of circuits. Software is much more plastic: it could perhaps be defined as dynamically reconfigurable circuits. As such, it is not easily captured by static diagrams, witness the fact that almost no software is written in any notation resembling circuits. Such a fundamental plasticity implies also variability. All radios of a given brand and model have the same circuit, and behave in exactly the same way, assuming the hardware is intact. Instead, genetically identical cells of the same organism behave differently within a population; just like my phone may fetch email, and your absolutely identical phone may not. Therefore, biological organisms do not really behave much like radios, but, to carry forward Lazebnik's work, we can perhaps find another technological analogy where software has a more prominent role.

23.2 A technological organism

The goal of biology is to reverse-engineer biological organisms. We pick a somewhat less ambitious task, by focusing on a "naturally occurring" technological organism instead of a biological one. By choosing technology over biology, we are sure that someone has engineered the organism in the first place, and therefore there can be no doubt that in principle it can be reverse-engineered. Still, even with this simplified task, we will find many practical difficulties that are typical of reverse-engineering biological organisms, including several that are not typical of reverse-engineering radios.

Tamagotchi[1] [5] will be our model organism. In the scientific tradition we use a binomial nomenclature: since it was first observed "in the wild" in Japan, it will thereafter be known as *Tamagotchi nipponensis* (several species and subspecies exist).

Tamagotchi nipponensis is a handheld cyberpet. Morphologically, it consists of an egg-shaped case with a strap, a small bitmap screen, three buttons, sound output, and a highly variable skin pattern. Little else can be easily observed (unless one has the clear-plastic model). An antenna-like appendage appeared in a recent evolutionary turn, but its function is poorly understood. The buttons can be used to manipulate a small character on the screen (a *cyberpet*) that evolves along a wide range of possible stages, lineages, and shapes. The mode and frequency of interaction with the buttons influences the development of the cyberpet, in highly non-trivial ways.

Tamagotchi nipponensis makes an interesting case study because it blurs the boundaries between "devices" and "organisms". Like all life forms, it is primarily an information-processing device: it has inputs, outputs, and internal state. It is governed by software, and is certainly not a full computer, but is not a simple automaton either. Most interestingly, it has a fundamentally *stochastic* behavior, as helpfully explained by Bandai [5]:

---

[1] "Tamagotchi" is a registered trademark of Bandai Co., Ltd. of Tokyo, Japan.

Q: How often do I have to exercise my Tamagotchi?

A: Every Tamagotchi is different. However we do recommend exercising at least three times a day.

Hence, *T. nipponensis* is nondeterministic ("every one is different"), and is stochastic because the *rate* of interaction matters ("at least three times a day"). Without proper interaction, the cyberpet soon passes away, after which the device needs to be reset. Unlike a radio, which can keep playing music without any interaction, the only way to understand *T. nipponensis* is to understand its full dynamic behavior. Any of its steady states, either at any particular instant, or after a long period of constant input, is in fact of no interest to anybody.

How can we go about unraveling such a complex dynamic phenomenon, in order, for example, to grow healthy cyberpets consistently? That is what science is really all about; we cannot rely on rumor, superstition, and blogs: we need to apply a reliable, field-tested, scientific methodology.

23.3 The scientific method

Our task is now simply stated: reverse-engineer *T. nipponensis* legally, that is, by using the *scientific method* (no industrial espionage). The scientific method consists of the following steps.

- Running reproducible experiments that elucidate the phenomenon at hand.
- Building models that explain all past experiments and predict the results of new experiments.

If *T. nipponensis* can be reverse-engineered, then very important applications open up, including the following areas.

- Providing scientifically-based cyberpet consulting services.
- Engineering and selling our own species, *Tamagotchi europaea*.
- Fixing broken *T. nipponensis*, to the joy of kids everywhere.

How can the scientific method be applied to such a problem? Many different approaches, both experimental and theoretical, have been devised over the centuries; let's examine them.

23.3.1 Understanding the principles

This approach assumes that the organism underwent some kind of design and optimization process, either by an intelligent designer, or as the result of competition and evolution, or both. The basic assumption is that there are some *principles*, either deliberate (design principles) or emerging (empirical principles), that somehow determine the organization of the organism, and whose discovery can be helpful in modeling it. According to Charles Darwin, we should be *"grouping facts so that general laws or conclusions may be drawn from them"*. The opposite point of view, in the words of Norbert Wiener, is that there are no organization principles whatsoever: *"The best material model of a cat is another, or preferably the same, cat"*, but we can safely ignore this opinion in the present case.

Here are some typical questions that arise from attempts at understanding principles of organization. We begin with a couple of questions that are not normally asked by biologists, but that we need to consider because they would be first in the mind of technologists.

Q1: Who created it? We actually know the answer to this question (Aki Maita), but it does not help: hiring the creator as a consultant is not considered part of the scientific method. Moreover, how could something so unique and sophisticated as a Tamagotchi have suddenly appeared seemingly out of nowhere? It is such an unlikely and unparalleled phenomenon that we have to question whether we could ever actually understand the mind of the creator, and whether the creator herself truly understands her own design (*"Aki's own Tamagotchi seldom lives longer than its baby stage."* – Apple Daily).

Q2: Where is the documentation? Well, there is no documentation, at least no design manual that explains what its principles are or how it works. Even if we could acquire the design manual from the creator (by industrial espionage), it would be written in the language of the creator, i.e., Japanese, and would be of little use to us. Now, turning to more scientific questions:

Q3: What is its function? What does a Tamagotchi compute? We have here a relatively primitive information processing device, but there is no easy way to explain what its processing function actually is. In fact, its function is not quantifiable; it does not appear to compute anything in particular. And how can we hope to understand its design principles if we cannot say what it *does?*

Q4: Why does it have three buttons? There surely must be
a deep reason for this: three-button devices are comparatively rare in
technology. Did it evolve from archaic two-button devices of which we
have no record? Is three just the closest integer to e? Is there some
general scaling law that relates the size of a device to the number of its
buttons? It seems that none of these questions can be answered from
abstract principles.

Conclusion: Principle-driven understanding fails.

23.3.2 Understanding the mechanism

The mechanistic approach assumes that the organism is a *mechanism*,
and hence can be understood by understanding its parts, and how they
are joined together. And never mind who designed it or why. Laplace
wanted us to understand *"all of the forces that animate nature and the
mutual positions of the beings that compose it"*. Here are some typical
questions for mechanistic understanding.

Q1: What are the parts? As Lazebnik points out, we need to make
a list of parts. Favorite are *moving* parts, because they can be readily
seen to be doing something mechanistic. Unfortunately, *T. nipponensis*
has no moving parts, except for some minor button displacement. It has
parts that never move, and it has a cyberpet moving on the screen, but
it cannot really be called a part because it cannot be separated from the
rest.

Q2: How are the parts connected? If we open it up we can see how
some parts are connected. But what about the cyberpet on the screen;
how is that connected to the rest? It certainly seems to be connected to
the buttons, and to the battery, somehow, and obviously to the screen.
But unfortunately we cannot find any physical connection between it
and the rest. As we said, it is probably not a part, but if it is not a
part, then there can be no mechanistic understanding of it. And if we
cannot understand how the cyberpet is connected, can we ever claim to
understand *T. nipponensis*?

Q3: How does it react to perturbations? This means removing or
changing parts to discover their contribution to the system, or interfering
with their connections (the classic wrench in the clockwork experiment).
Since there are very few discrete parts, removing almost any part just
makes it stop working. And since there are almost no moving parts, and

it is very small, there are very few places where we can usefully stick a wrench, with current technology.

Q4: How is it put together? One way to understand a mechanism is to understand how it is fabricated and assembled. We can call this the *Tamagotchi folding problem*: how do you fold the parts into the whole? Unfortunately, this turns out to be a much harder problem than the original problem. *Tamagotchi nipponensis* is assembled in top-secret factories in Japan, Taiwan, or China, by robots. We do not have access to those assembly lines, and we do not even know where they are. And even if we did, those robots would surely be more difficult to understand than *T. nipponensis* itself, either mechanistically or otherwise.

Conclusion: Mechanistic understanding fails.

23.3.3 Understanding the behavior

The behavioral approach assumes that it is too difficult or premature to try to understand something in mechanistic detail, but we can still try to understand how it behaves. If we can characterize and predict its behavior in future experiments, which is all that the scientific method really requires, then any mechanism that implements it is accidental, and practically irrelevant. However, we first need to identify some suitable behavioral quantities to measure. As Galileo put it, *"measure what is measurable, and make measurable what is not so"*, which is easier said than done: what is there to measure about a Tamagotchi?

Q1: How does it react to stimuli? Well, it has no consistent reaction to stimuli: it is nondeterministic and stochastic, remember? It turns out that its behavior is unpredictable *by design*. We have now discovered a design principle, but not a very useful one. Each individual has a huge range of possible behaviors, and it would take the age of the universe to supply all possible sequences of stimuli. Hence, experiments on individual *T. nipponensis* are not reproducible. Oh, yes, that was a requirement of the scientific method.

Q2: How does it behave in a population? Still, we can get statistics. For example, we can put 1024 *T. nipponensis* in a basket (such baskets are incidentally readily available in Japanese stores), and shake them violently for 3 hours. This will cause buttons to be pressed in a random but very large number of different combinations. Every 10 minutes, we scan the screen of each unit (this requires very expensive equipment or a large number of postdocs), and we plot the number of configurations and how they change over time. The result of such an experiment is publishable; it is after all an indisputable and fairly reproducible fact of nature, but it does not really help us make wide-ranging behavioral predictions.

Q3: How does it communicate? *Tamagotchi nipponensis* is known to communicate with other *T. nipponensis* and with mobile phones through its antenna. (This can be argued, mechanistically, by clipping off the antenna, although strictly speaking one could say only that the antenna is implicated in communication.) Unfortunately, the communication protocol it uses is not an open standard. The question of whether it has a symbolic language, or whether it simply has innate reactions to specific data packets, is still subject to considerable debate.

Q4: How does it react to shock? This is the behavioral version of removing random parts: failures under extreme conditions can provide valuable insights on the structure of a system. Unfortunately, most extreme conditions here result simply in a blank or broken screen, and may void your warranty. Certain temperatures and pressures produce interesting effects on the screen, but again these are completely unrelated to what the cyberpet on the screen is doing.

Conclusion: Behavioral understanding fails.

23.3.4 Understanding the environment

Sometimes it is just not possible to understand an organism in isolation or even as a population. Its properties can only really be explained in the context of its environment and how the organism interacts with it, both cooperatively and competitively. *Tamagotchi nipponensis* could not exist without the Japanese culture and its electronics industry, and hence we must ask how it arose from that marketing environment. To paraphrase Theodosius Dobzhansky: *nothing in consumer electronics makes sense except in the light of competition.*

Q1: How did it evolve? *Tamagotchi nipponensis* evolved and prospered within a modern economic system; unfortunately such systems are just as poorly understood as biological systems. Furthermore, it evolved within the Japanese economic / technological / cultural environment, for which we have no consensus model. It is not entirely known, at present, which other technological organism it evolved from, which it adapted against, and which it displaced from the market: much of that information is proprietary. The archeological record will eventually offer insights through the excavation of Japanese landfills. Provided that adequate funding can be obtained, overcoming those critics who believe that the entire electronics industry was created last Thursday.

Q2: How does it behave in its natural environment? The natural environment of *T. nipponensis* is kids' hands and backpacks, both of which are practically impossible to reproduce in a laboratory. *Tamagotchi nipponensis* has been painstakingly observed in its natural environment by sociology postdocs, but those studies were focused mostly on kid behavior. In any case, it is very difficult to reliably observe a Tamagotchi screen under natural kid–Tamagotchi conditions, and attempts to attach bulky tracking and telemetry devices result in atypical behavior.

Conclusion: Environmental/evolutionary understanding fails.

23.3.5 Understanding the maths

Since Pythagoras, who famously proclaimed that *"Number Rules the Universe"*, scientists have wondered at the inexplicable effectiveness of mathematics at explicating nature. We now seem to have a counterexample:

Q1: What differential equations does *T. nipponensis* **obey?** Hmm. . .

Conclusion: Mathematical understanding fails.

23.4 Standing aghast on the shoulders of giants

Of course, we know very well why the scientific method seems to fail, or at least to be unusually difficult to apply, in such a case. That is because we are trying to reverse-engineer what is a fundamentally a complicated piece of *software* (with some cheap hardware) instead of some kind of circuit, and that turns out to be quite a special kind of activity. Not much progress can be made until we start dumping and disassembling the software itself, provided of course we have some idea of what kind of hardware it is running on.

We also know very well how to reverse-engineer software [6]; it can be quite difficult, but historically it has never been impossible, even when extraordinary steps have been taken to prevent it. Software reverse-engineering techniques include: *tracing* (selectively following the flow of control and the value of variables over time), *breakpointing* (stopping program execution when a certain program point is crossed, or when a certain data structure is modified), *core-dumping* (taking a raw snapshot of the active memory content), *stack-dumping* (taking a snapshot of the active execution context), *packet-sniffing* (examining the traffic on a network wire), *reverse compilation* (partially reconstructing the structured source code from the unstructured binary code, provided that knowledge is available about the source language and the compilation process), *power analysis* (gathering information about a running program from the instantaneous power consumption of the processor), and so on.

Corresponding techniques are often not available in biology (particularly, reverse compilation!), but some are. Tracing is achieved by setting a biological system in a known initial state and then measuring some quantity at timed intervals; the problem is that it is often difficult to measure the quantities of interest. Breakpointing, by various forms of genetic perturbation, is used in biology to stop a pathway at a certain stage, so that one can determine the sequence of events in the pathway. Packet sniffing is commonly used to inspect the nervous system, but it has led so far to limited knowledge of what the packets mean, and what information is actually being transmitted. It is also used to analyze intracellular chemical communication.

In practice, biologists measure all they *can* measure, and sometimes what they do measure would be of extremely little help in reverse-engineering a software system. Core-dumping is partially feasible in biology (e.g. by detecting the phosphorylation state of a large number of proteins), but because of technical difficulties this is usually applied to whole populations of cells. Certainly, averaging millions of software core dumps would produce very low-quality information about the behavior of a program. Stack-dumping is currently extremely popular in biology: microarray technology can determine what parts of the genetic program are currently running by detecting mRNA molecules. But again, this has to be done on whole populations of cells, and only by detecting the difference between the altered and the standard behavior of the genetic network (which is normally not understood). By comparison, averaging the execution stacks of many program runs could lead to some knowledge about the subroutines that are most used, and about their average parameters, but little else. Even when considering a single concurrent program, summing the stack frames from different threads of control would lead to very little insight. Another common inspection tool in biology is gene perturbation experiments. As already mentioned, this technique can provide useful information, but it is also used more blindly, e.g. by deleting in turn *every* single gene in an organism to see what happens. In software engineering, no one has ever seriously proposed to remove each instruction in a program in turn to see what breaks. One might have a slightly better chance of acquiring useful knowledge by removing all pairs or triplets of instructions, but this immediately becomes unfeasible.

In summary, the most popular high-throughput experimental techniques in biology do not provide the right conceptual or technical tools needed to reverse-engineer software, be it digital or biological. In one case, part of the regulatory region of a single gene has been decoded in great detail, but that has required a heroic effort [8]. More promising techniques are just becoming available that can inspect the state of individual cells, and these will certainly lead to significant progress. But even that is not sufficient in itself: Andreas Wagner has given an example of a situation in which no set of classical experiments can recover the structure of a simple biological network, even from single-cell observations [9]. In general, to succeed one must be able to probe the system in sufficient depth, because just measuring a large quantity of superficial properties may not be enough.

What are the chances, eventually, of reverse-engineering the software of life, assuming that the experimental difficulties can be resolved? We have to believe, with Einstein, that nature is subtle but not malicious: it does not encrypt its software just to make it harder for us to copy it or modify it. Still, if the complexity of ordinary software systems is any hint, the task is going to be much more difficult than people generally realize, even after systematically recovering the raw code (*genomics*), taking stack traces (*transcriptomics*), taking core dumps (*proteomics*), monitoring the power supply and the heap size (*metabolomics*), and intercepting the network traffic (*systems biology*). Any additional amount of understanding is going to require extensive measurements and experiments, just like the ones that are being carried out today, but the focus must be on the peculiarities of software systems, not only of hardware systems.

The reverse-engineering task confronting biologists surely looks hopelessly complex, but we should not despair: progress so far has been incredible. Standing on the shoulders of giants is not particularly helpful when confronted with much taller mountains, but we can rely on a steady tradition of fundamental discoveries. Sydney Brenner captured

L. Cardelli

both the scope and the spirit of the endeavor when he said that: *"The problem of biology is not to stand aghast at the complexity but to conquer it"* [7]. And so we must, because we have got things to fix.

Bibliography

[1] Debugging advice can be found at `http://www.wikihow.com/Debug-a-Tamagotchi`.

[2] Y. Lazebnik. Can a biologist fix a radio? Or, what I learned while studying apoptosis. *Cancer Cell* **2**:179–182, 2002.

[3] E. Klipp, R. Herwig, A. Kowald, C. Wierling and H. Lehrach. *Systems Biology in Practice*. Wiley, 2005.

[4] R. Feynman, R. Leighton and E. Hutchings. He fixes radios by thinking. In *Surely You're Joking, Mr. Feynman!: Adventures of a Curious Character*. W.W. Norton, 1985.

[5] Bandai. Tamagotchi Connection. `http://www.tamagotchi.com`

[6] P. Tonella and A. Potrich. *Reverse Engineering of Object-Oriented Code*. Springer, 2005.

[7] S. Brenner. Interview, *Discover Magazine* **25**(4), 2004.

[8] C.-H. Yuh, H. Bolouri and E. H. Davidson. Genomic cis-regulatory logic: experimental and computational analysis of a sea urchin. *Gene. Science*, **279**:1896–1902, 1998.

[9] A. Wagner. How to reconstruct a large genetic network from n gene perturbations in fewer than n^2 easy steps. *Bioinformatics*, **17**(12):1183–1197, 2001.

24

Computational science: a new frontier for computing

Andrew Herbert

Microsoft Research, Cambridge, United Kingdom

Abstract

In 2005 Gilles Kahn discussed with Rick Rashid, Stephen Emmott and myself a proposal for Microsoft Research, Cambridge and INRIA to establish a joint research laboratory in France, building on the long-term informal collaboration between the two institutions. The research focus of the joint laboratory was an important point of discussion. In addition to building on our mutual strengths in areas such as software specification an important topic was a shared desire to create a programme of researching the area of computational science – using the concepts and methods of computer science to accelerate the pace of scientific development and explore the potential for new approaches to science exploiting computer science concepts and methods. This paper explores what computational science is and the contribution it can make to scientific progress. It is in large part abridged from a report "Towards 2020 Science" [1] published by a group of experts assembled by Microsoft Research who met over three intense days to debate and consider the role and future of science, looking towards 2020 and, in particular, the importance and impact of computing and computer science in that vision.

24.1 Introduction

Computers have played an increasingly important role in science for 50 years. At the end of the twentieth century there was a transition from computers supporting scientists to do conventional science to computer science itself becoming part of the fabric of science and how science is done. From the traditional view of science comprising both a theoretical

---

From Semantics to Computer Science Essays in Honour of Gilles Kahn, eds Yves Bertot, Gérard Huet, Jean-Jacques Lévy and Gordon Plotkin. Published by Cambridge University Press. © Cambridge University Press 2009.

and an experimental basis, increasing there is a third leg of "computational" science using computer science tools for modeling, experiment sensing and control, data mining, information interaction and collaboration in addition to pure numerical computation and data processing.

The history of science gives many examples of conceptual and technological tools that have transformed scientific development creating new approaches to science and indeed sometimes new sciences themselves. For example, Fibonacci introduced algebra as a new branch of mathematics when he publish *Liver Abaci* in 1202; in 1604 Galileo invented the telescope creating the science of astronomy, transforming our understanding of our world and the universe.

The developments in science being made possible now by computers have the potential to be at least as transforming as these earlier tools.

24.2 Computational science

Science continually pushes the limits of what is possible in computing, and in some areas is leading to computing advances, making possible experiments that would have been impossible only 10 years ago, and changing the way scientists do science.

There are experiments generating vast volumes of data: the Sanger Centre in Cambridge, UK currently hosts 150 terabytes of genomic data and clusters of computers totaling 2.5 Teraflops. Particle physics is set to generate petabytes of data when the CERN Large Hadron Collider (LHC) comes on-line in 2008. CERN's solution is to use a computing "Grid," one of many being developed world-wide and an example of a vision of e-Infrastructure (EU)/Cyber-infrastructure (USA).

Even with the relatively simple data collected by particle physics experiments, data management is a major issue. The capabilities of a file system to store and transmit bulk data from experiments has to be extended to include indexing and structure to enable efficient query operations. Extensive metadata needs to be kept to describe each experiment and the data it produces. The full power of relational databases is needed to allow effective interactions with the data and a programmatic interface that can be used by tools for visualization and analysis.

Other disciplines bring different challenges. Astronomy has far more emphasis on the collation of federated datasets held at disparate sites and less demand for massive computation – modelling can be done on departmental high-performance computing facilities. Chemistry is different again – teams are often small and there is little computational infrastructure in use today. In the life sciences problems are mostly (but not universally) related to heterogeneous, dispersed, and rich collections of data rather than problems of scale and computation.

24.3 Systems architectures

For most of the twentieth century computing power was driven by Moore's law – as the number of transistors on a chip doubled more-or-less every 18 months this was translated into a doubling of computational throughput. Early in the twenty-first century this is less clear and many predict computers will no longer be exponentially growing in computing power: memories and network bandwidth may be able to continue on an exponential path; latency remains fixed by the speed of light. Thus individual computers may not get much faster, but we will see the development of parallel computers, from multi-core to many-core. From a programming point of view this will require a paradigm shift away from the current sequential approaches to software design to architectures that permit a mix of parallel and distributed processing and are explicitly designed to cope with high latency when a task have to be handed off to a remote machine. This is likely to bring two forms of systems architecture to the fore: "peer-to-peer" and "service-orientated".

Peer-to-peer architectures enable the construction of distributed systems without any centralized control or hierarchical organization [2], and can be designed to scale up to large systems and to use redundancy to provide resilience and performance. Many peer-to-peer architectures are able to automatically balance locality to overcome latency against load-balancing to maximize utilization.

While peer-to-peer systems enable the re-use of memory and computational resources on a massive scale the paradigm of service-oriented architectures [3] assist in the reuse of functionality. The fundamental primitive of service-oriented architectures is the ability to locate and access a computational service across machine and organizational boundaries in both a synchronous (request–response) and asynchronous fashion. The implementation of a service can be a wrapper for legacy scientific applications and resource schedulers providing a migration path. Computational scientists will be able to "orchestrate" these services into scientific workflows to automate many currently manual tasks.

24.4 Semantics of data

A revolution is taking place in the scientific method: "hypothesize, design and run experiment, analyze results" is being replaced by "hypothesize, look up answer in database" [4]. Databases are an essential part of the infrastructure of science: they may contain raw data, results of analyses or simulations or the results of the annotation and organization of data. The current trend is towards the worldwide publication of data.

A major issue is the distributions of data. It has long been known that it is expensive or impossible to move large amounts of data – it is better to take the program code (query) to the data and this is the core of distributed query optimization. Traditionally queries have been optimized for small numbers of databases, but how do we optimize queries for say a network of several million sensors? How do we extend query models developed for tabular business data (records) to spatial queries, text-mining, stream of real-time data and other needs of scientific processing?

These are questions of the base technology that has to be developed. It must be supported by a programming environment that is easy for scientists to use. First and foremost is the semantics of data. This involves understanding the metadata (information about the organization of the data), the quality of the data, where and how it was produced, who owns it and so forth. This data about data is not just for human consumption it will primarily be used by tools that perform data integration and use web services to share, transform or analyze the data.

Attempting to solve the problems of scientific management by building large centralized archival repositories is both dangerous and unworkable. The danger comes from the dependence of ongoing administrative and financial support; unworkable because of scale and the natural desire of scientists to be autonomous and keep control over their information. But by moving to highly distributed and derived data there is the unsolved problem of preserving the scientific record. How do we record the process by which a dataset was derived? How do we record the history of a dataset that is in continual flux? How do we trace the origins of data that has been replicated many times? These are as much social as technical questions and require community standards for publishing metadata, citations and provenance.

24.5 Intelligent interaction and information discovery

The demand for computational resources to perform scientific data analysis is driven by three factors: more sophisticated algorithms consume more instructions per byte of data processed; many algorithms are polynomial in complexity, needing N^2 or N^3 steps to process N data; I/O bandwidth has fallen behind storage capacity. Scientists need better approximate algorithms with near-linear execution time, parallel algorithms that apply many processors (and disks) and they need the ability to steer long-running computations in order to prioritize the production of data that is more likely to be of interest.

Many scientists use packages such as MATLAB to aid in data analysis and hypothesis testing. To bring these symbolic computation tools closer to the data and accessible from mainstream scientific programming languages scientists need programming languages that can capture mathematical models and compilers that turn them into deployable executable software. By the same token, scientists need to extract valid, authentic and actionable patterns, trends and knowledge from large databases using algorithms such as automatic decision tree classifiers, Bayesian prediction, sequence clustering, time series, linear regression directly integrated into database engines.

It is increasingly compelling to integrate precision and accuracy into type systems and to develop first-class data types that perform scientific error propagation and for these to be included in database query, search and data mining tools.

Large observational datasets, the results of numerical computations and high-dimensional analysis all require data visualization to aid intuition and communication of results. Simulations depend on visualization for the interpretation of results and hypothesis formation. Many scientists need to create multi-dimensional aggregations to experiment with correlations between measured and derived quantities. Today much of this processing is done using home-brew software or simple spread-sheets. There is a tremendous opportunity to exploit online analytical processing (OLAP) add-ons to modern database engines. These allow for the construction of "data cubes" serving as caches or replicas of pre-computed, multi-dimensional aggregations that facilitate data analysis from multiple perspectives. Second the support the visualization of data over data partitions. Database technology will aid science first through the transformation of large-scale scientific data sets into schematized small scale formats and then the transformation of small-scale formats into graphical data structures such as meshes, textures and voxels. The first is what OLAP can offer; the second is a challenge for research and development.

To bring together advances in data management, analysis, knowledge discovery and visualization and empower the individual scientist another important component is a truly smart (electronic) lab notebook. Such a device would unlock access to data and make it extremely easy to analyze, discover, visualize and publish new phenomena [5].

24.6 Transforming scientific communication

The web is reshaping scientific publishing and communication. Given that science is a global endeavour and the web is perhaps the most effective global communications medium yet devised this is not a surprise, yet the potential for the web to reshape scientific communication is underestimated. The challenge is not merely to adjust the economics of publishing but to define the very nature of scientific publication.

Online scientific publications will become interactive allowing readers to explore visualizations and data, to search and navigate across all of an author's works, citations of that work and the author's own use of others work. Online pages will be generated at the moment they are requested allowing customization according to a particular time and place, and the reader's access device – which could be a smart phone, a personal computer or richly equipped collaboration environment. Responses will be personalized to the reader: for example when looking outside their main area of research, readers may prefer summaries or tutorials to full articles. Researchers in the field may want to read just the abstract then directly access figures and data. Students may want to read the whole paper including supplementary materials and full explanation of experimental protocols, etc.

Modern scientific communication is dominated by databases and journals, yet these are poorly integrated today. In the future many scientific journals will become databases – the data will be peer reviewed and the author credited for making the data available, even if no immediate conclusions have been drawn from it. The technical challenges are three-fold – managing the volume of data, tracking versions and the provenance of data, and creating open structured machine readable formats.

The web has evolved from a publishing medium to one which enables discussion and dialogue using tools such as *blogs* and *wikis*. These allow users to contribute content and for others to comment on their postings, and automated services to feed notification and summaries of new content to a community of interest. These will become important ways for scientists to organize, share and discover information building and extending on-line collaborative social networks.

24.7 Exploiting computer science concepts

Concepts, theorems and tools developed with computer science are finding wide-ranging application in sciences involving complex systems, notably chemistry and biology. Computer science deals with dynamics in a discrete and reactive sense. In most areas of science the discrete is often not only more central but often harder to deal with – indeed biological systems are the most exciting dynamic systems we know: they are reactive, and they not only respond but also prescribe, cause and indeed program other behavior.

One of the first glimpses of the potential of computer science techniques has been demonstrated in the Human Genome project and the success in structural biology to routinely decipher the three-dimensional structure of proteins. Biologists abstract genes as *strings* and proteins as *labelled graphs* to code their knowledge in a form that is amenable to computer processing and storing in computer databases. The coding of knowledge empowers scientists by allowing them to share, compare, criticize and correct scientific knowledge. It also changes the way science is done: coded scientific knowledge can be analyzed computationally before any experimentation is done. Coded knowledge can be checked for consistency between code theories and for consistency with collected experimental data. Inconsistencies may be resolved by computer-designed experiments, analogous to automated testing for computer hardware and software and computational analysis of theory versus experimental data may suggest additional experiments to be performed manually or even perhaps automatically.

Some computer science concepts are already familiar in other sciences. *Abstraction* is a fundamental tool for looking at a system consistently across different levels of detail. It is a fundamental tool for managing complexity. The concepts of *concurrency theory*, such as processes, non-determinism, communication and synchronization may prove essential for understanding inter- and intra-cellular biological processes. The interchangeability of *program* and *data*, universal computers, compilers, interpreters, partial evaluation and compositional semantics may prove essential to understanding the full role of DNA. *Modularity* and well-defined *interfaces* are key concepts in computer systems design – they ensure that error in one component have a limited effect on other components and therefore can be tracked and fixed. They also ensure designs can be modified and evolved as requirements change. Modularity and evolution appear to be key principles of biology – indeed we can speculate that non-modular systems if they ever existed were not able to evolve and withstand changes in external conditions and accordingly have not survived.

24.8 Integrating theory, experiments and models

By bringing together modelling as a scientific tool and data as a scientific resource we are able to tie together theories, models and experiments. In simplistic terms a model is constructed as a "theory"; a set of inputs are given to the model and behaviours observed. These behaviours are compared to experimental data gathered under similar conditions and if the correspondence between model and experiment holds over a range of inputs, the theory is accepted. Once sufficient confidence is established in the model it can be used in place of experiment or as the input to other models.

This is of course simplistic. In a real setting there are no clean sets of data – experimental data are subject to noise, experiments may be contested and models may be tainted with false assumptions. The model may be congruent with a limited range of inputs but not all. There may be other mechanisms that equally validly predict the experimental outcome. We therefore need a framework in which data, models and the dynamic relationships between them can be managed – this is what a computer scientist would call configuration control and introduces the need for sophisticated version tracking and support for fine-grained scientific workflows alongside static data archiving and computational modelling.

24.9 Complexity and coherence

One of the greatest challenges to science is to understand complexity be it intra-cellular networks, organ systems, ecosystems, social systems and indeed commerce. Paradoxically highly complex systems often produce coherent behaviour and the question has to be how can we understand and predict this? If approaches enabling coherence can be made to emerge from complexity, all areas of applied science will benefit. Systematic approaches, enabled by an ability to predict always trump heuristic ones, not least because they are less costly.

Complexity is grist to the mill of biology, computer science and mathematics. There are opportunities to better reconcile the approaches taken in these different disciplines. In computer science space and time complexity of algorithms is studied – complexity is represented as a function of the size of a problem. Another computer science measure of complexity is Kolmogorov or "descriptive" complexity – given a string, what is the shortest program that can output that string? This metric can perhaps help study biological descriptions such as lineage trees.

A natural representation of complex systems is as a matrix of interconnected elements in which the interactions appear as the pattern of connections in the matrix. In models of this kind the function or failure of individual elements becomes less important than the statistical dynamics or combinations of elements as in "system" or "network" failures and the failure modes of such systems are often invisible. As the number of elements and connections increase the behaviour of the system may become less intuitive and indeed for very-large-scale systems strikingly counter-intuitive. Computational tools can render these counter-intuitive features visible and provide the basis for predictive capability and provide the key for understanding complex systems more successfully. The major problem is determining the structure and topology of networks in complex systems. Studies have shown that most important complex biological networks share elements of topology. Connectivity is generally described by a power law distribution, which gives these systems the robust property that network integrity is only slowly degraded by random failure or deletion of notes, but is very vulnerable to an intelligently targeted attack. Computer science models for network complexity have focused largely on "scale free" topologies and the identification of "hubs" as key nodes on which the integrity of a network depends. Further progress requires improved abilities to measure complex systems; to model the effect of perturbations or designed changes upon them and to change complex systems in desired directions.

24.10 New tools

The invention of new tools, for example the telescope and the electron microscope, typically form the building blocks of scientific revolutions that historically have changed the course of history and society. New conceptual tools are emerging from the intersection of computer science, mathematics, biology, chemistry and engineering which could be equally profound in their impact.

Codification of scientific knowledge – representing scientific knowledge in a code representation in terms of programs and data that are executable and accessible to automatic analysis is a major activity in many areas of science today. Codification has an important property – once obtained it can be right or wrong but importantly it is exactly reproducible and analyzable.

Computer science can be viewed as the codification of information processing knowledge – algorithms and data structures are coded as software or hardware realizations. In mathematics considerable progress has been made in attempts to completely mechanize the production of major mathematical proofs. Moreover many key numerical and symbolic mathematical techniques are already encoded as libraries and tools.

Biology is an area where codification is essential to progress. At the lowest level we have the codification of the genome as strings in a four letter alphabet; at the next level we have proteomics which requires representations of amino acids and three-dimensional structures. These representations are now relatively standardized and tools exist to exploit them. Further efforts involve the coding of metabolic and signalling pathways, where networks of biochemical interactions have to be represented. This is still an open question, although many pathway databases are being created. The hardest problem will be to store, search, compare and analyze biological processes such as cell division. This last example brings into focus that it is not in general sufficient to represent facts as data, but rather as dynamic processes.

Codification is therefore largely an engineering enterprise: there are numerous issues about the best way of representing any particular piece of information. The contribution of computer science is through generally applicable principles to effective codification: abstraction, composition, re-use and scalability.

The value of a scientific theory is its ability to make predictions. In many areas of science the underlying equations are well understood and in principle, predictions simply involve solving these using appropriate numerical or symbolic techniques. Performance improvements in computers enable predictions to be made for larger and more complex systems and in turn these predictions are used by scientists as simulations to explore phenomena where the cost of doing so experimentally would be prohibitive or indeed impossible. In this respect we can look at computers as "prediction machines".

However in most areas of science the complexity of the domain, or the absence of sufficiently precise models prohibit direct simulation. In such cases statistical approaches, in particular machine learning, have proved to be very powerful. The goal of machine learning is to use statistical methods to make predictions: for example, in a supervised learning scenario a large number of input–output response pairs are used to construct a probabilistic model of a system, capturing the underlying trends and extracting them from the noise. The model is then used to predict the responses to new inputs. Machine learning techniques are also used for data visualization, data mining, data filtering and a host of other applications relevant to science.

In biology, *Inductive Logic Programming* – a form of machine learning which represents hypotheses using logic – has been demonstrated on tasks including the discovery of structural principles for major families of protein folds [6], predictions of structure–activity relations in drugs [7] and predictions of toxicity of small molecules [8]. Bayesian networks, whose structure is inferred from observed data, have been used to model the effect of toxins on networks of metabolic reactions within cells.

Research into algorithms and methods for machine learning provide insights into biological information processing systems, including the human brain. For example in low-level visual processing by the brain's cortex there are marked similarities to wavelet feature bases, a technique used in computer vision "object recognition". More speculatively, current research in hybrids of generative and discriminative models of machine learning may shed light on the human brain's remarkable ability to accurately generalize training data which is almost entirely unlabelled.

Machine learning is not limited to batch computation – with *active learning* techniques the adaptation to the data and the prediction process are intimately linked with the model pointing to new regions in the space of variables in which to collect or label data so as to be maximally informative.

Machine learning systems that produce human-comprehensible hypotheses from data will increasingly be used for knowledge discovery with science. Today such systems are open loop with no connection between the machine learning system and the collection of data. A more direct closed loop approach was investigated in the 1990s in work on automating chemistry experiments [9] through the estimation of chemical parameters. Recent advances are at the threshold of "autonomous experimentation" in which artificial intelligence techniques are used to carry out the whole cycle of scientific experimentation including the origination of hypotheses to explain observations, the devising of experiments to test the hypotheses and physical implementation of the experiments using robots to falsify hypotheses. Such a system has already been demonstrated in the "Robot Scientist" project [10], where laboratory robots conducted experiments selected by "active learning".

One exciting development we might expect to see in this area in the next 10 years is the construction of a micro-fluidic robot scientist. The key effects of miniaturizing the technology would be the reduction of the experimental cycle time from hours to milliseconds, with a corresponding increase in the robustness of experimental outcomes. With the confluence of wireless networking of "lab on a chip" sensor technology we can anticipate large-scale applications to environmental monitoring – each sensor node is likely be endowed with a limited supply of wet chemistry and accordingly can only perform a limited number of experiments – the network of such sensors must collectively decide how these resources are spent.

Another key area for robot scientists is where experiments necessarily occur in a place inaccessible to humans and where there is limited bandwidth for remote control – for example, on the seabed, in outer space or other hostile environments. An autonomous robot scientist would decide for itself the next experimental step and data reduction.

These advances will increasingly blur the distinction between the "artificial" and the "living": living cells are the most sophisticated non-systems known. Recent progress in micro-fluidics and nanotechnology has opened this environment to practical engineering experience. Simple laboratory workflows such as sequences of reactions followed by product analysis can be implemented on a single chip for mass production. Specific macromolecules or cells can be specifically separated enabling new types of experiments to be studied, and since small volumes of supplies are consumed more extensive studies can be conducted.

Although lab-on-chip technology allows for control of molecular interactions it pales in comparison to the production capabilities of the living cell. For the past two decades efforts have been underway to modify cells for factory production of chemicals that are either too complex for classical synthesis or can be produced much more efficiently by micro-organisms. So far examples have been relatively simple, but as genome-wide computational models become more complex, these models will enable the construction of cell factories that could change the nature of production in the chemical and pharmaceutical industries. The self-replication capability of cells lends itself to mass production and a shift from static metabolic engineering towards interfacing with the control structure of cells [11] opens the possibility to engineer novel, living biomaterials. Cells tuned for a particular process can be grown in bio-films of communication elements extending on the idea of DNA computers [12] and this is leading the field of *Synthetic Biology*.

An alternative engineering approach would be to design a self-replicating von Neumann computer – in essence a chemical universal Turing machine. Such a device would, in simplistic terms, be an automaton with a reaction flask and a conveyor belt with an arrangement of chemicals (the program). The automaton would have instructions to add and remove chemicals from the flask and control the temperature of the reaction. As a theoretical concept the chemical universal Turing machine unifies lab-on-a-chip and artificial cell concepts: research is required to establish its viability. But, if successful, it could have a dramatic effect on combining theoretical, experimental and modelling approaches to understanding and engineering biology.

24.11 Solving global challenges

The twenty-first century presents some of the most important questions, challenges and opportunities in human history. Some have solutions in scientific advance (e.g. health). Others require political or economic solutions (e.g. poverty). Some require significant scientific advance in order to provide the evidence necessary to make economic and political decisions (e.g. our environment).

There is an urgent need to understand the Earth's life support systems – the biosphere (biodiversity, ecosystems and atmosphere) to the extent we are able to model and predict the effects of human activity on them, and the consequent effect on the ability of life, including human life, to be sustained on the planet. Several areas of science are beginning to tackle this through integrating theory, remote sensing experiments, traditional studies and computational models. It is not just a matter of studying climate – we need to understand biological systems at the geographical scale and how they inter-relate with climate and natural phenomena such as volcanoes and earthquakes. The key trends in this area of computational science are autonomous experimentation, particular remote sensing, distributed data management to mine heterogeneous databases from wide range of ecological and environmental sciences and new algorithms for the analysis, modelling and simulation of large, complex systems.

A recurrent theme in this paper is the role of computational science in understanding biology – particular the emerging discipline of systems biology looking at cell level and higher interactions using models taken from theoretical computer science. It is reasonable to hope that within a decade we will have models of a person's immune system and computational approaches to the design of preventative and therapeutic vaccines. Some go as far as to posit a new approach to personal health care – *theranostics*, in which diagnostic testing is used to diagnose a disease, choose a treatment and monitor the patient response to the therapy. This requires the ability not just to understand the structure of biological systems at the cell level but also to be able to fully understand the dynamics by simulation and analysis.

Computational approaches to systems biology may also help address the challenge of finding sustainable forms of energy, for example from bio-energy crops with near carbon neutrality of grown, harvested and converted efficiently with predictable performance.

At a higher level, understanding the human brain remains a major challenge. Neuroscience has made dramatic strides in recent years – computational circuits are expressed in terms of connectivity between neurons and synapses; complex large-scale connectional systems have been associated with individual brain functions and correlated with physiological properties. It is increasingly understood how neuron function relates to human perception and in turn how this relates to models of regularities and other statistical properties of the world. A complete model of the brain remains intractable, but experimental work has shown that all central sensory systems are somewhat discrete, with each being hierarchical and this opens the opportunity to use computational models for elaborating how complex brain processes interact. The key computer science technology in developing such understanding is likely to be machine learning and inference. It is intriguing that almost all theories of brain function suppose there is no meaningful concept of "software" that applies, so there may also be the potential for neuroscience to propose new computational artefacts and in turn enable greater capabilities for future computational science.

Computational science has several roles to play in confronting global epidemics of infectious disease such as "severe acute respiratory syndrome" (SARS) and avian influenza ("bird 'flu"). First, collection and analysis of genomic and proteomic data for pathogen identification and diagnostic screening. Second, real-time epidemic surveillance at local and regional scale. Third, predictive modelling of disease spread and control measures, both in civil preparedness and medical response to an unfolding outbreak. Fourth, facilitating effective communication and management in ad-hoc global inter-disciplinary teams responding to a new outbreak. Computational models of disease transmission will integrate epidemiological and biological data to give insights into patterns of spread and the effects of interventions. These models will necessarily be at a range of scales from local to global, and a key question will be to discover which controls are the most effect at each scale. Techniques such as agent-based simulation driven by data collected from the field, and integration of location information from transport and mobile telephones to track population behaviour would represent a truly global resource for planning for and responding to future epidemics.

Understanding the origin, workings and ultimate fate of the Universe is one of the great questions. With modern computational tools and methods being used on an unprecedented scale we may be able to answer these questions within a generation. Satellite data has moved cosmology into the realm of precision science. The data are in agreement with the consensus "hot Big Bang" model, however they indicate only 4% of the Universe consists of ordinary matters, and the rest comprises dark matter (23%) and dark energy (73%). It is therefore necessary to investigate the nature of dark energy and dark matter and to understand the properties of the very high gravitational field which would have occurred during the Bang. The data to do this will come from particle physics and experiments in this field are totally reliant on advanced computation, indeed particle physics experiments already reject 99.999% of all collisions before writing them to mass storage, using real-time pattern recognition algorithms running on the detectors themselves. The next generation will require computational tools on an unprecedented scale. For example, the CERN Large Hadron Collider which started operation in 2008 will generate several petabytes of data each year, feed out to a worldwide federation of national "computing grids" linking 100 000 CPUs. More challenging again will be the tools to enable thousands of end users to analyse the physics objects. Usability will be a key since all aspects of data cataloguing and code handling will necessarily have to be automated. A user cannot be expected to know the location of the data required, or the resources required to process it. A completely transparent interface between the scientist's desktop and the computational resources will be needed to allow the user to focus on the science rather than the infrastructure. It will require a move away from batch processing to a more interactive, distributed method of working. This will require data storage solutions combining the features of relational databases and conventional file systems with advanced caching features across wide area network links to avoid intolerable latency issues.

Understanding the large-scale structure of the Universe requires that data from surveys are compared to models which predict the distribution of galaxies. Ideally such comparisons would range over many model parameters and indeed competing models, providing an opportunity for adopting Bayesian machine learning methods to search the parameter spaces efficiently and make robust statistical inferences. There is great potential for tools that steer computation, fit models and automate data analysis.

24.12 Conclusion

From this overview of the state-of-the-art and future prospects for computational science it is evident that cutting edge computer science will play a pivotal role. Across the sciences there are common themes of handling federations of heterogeneous data, modelling complex systems at multiple scales, simulation and visualization and automation of scientific workflows in experimental science, in scientific analysis and in scientific publishing. Seeing this challenge was one of the motivations that led Gilles Kahn to propose a joint laboratory with Microsoft with working on these topics as a key focus.

Bibliography

[1] S. Emmott (ed.). Towards 2020 Science, available from `http://www.research.microsoft.com/towards2020science`.
[2] A. Rowstron and P. Druschel. Pastry: scalable, distributed object location and routing for large scale peer-to-peer systems. *IFIP/ACM International*

Conference on Distributed System Platforms (Middleware), Heidelberg, Germany pp. 329–350, November 2001.

[3]   C. Ferris and J. Farrell. What are web services? *CACM* **46**(6):31, 2003.

[4]   M. Lesk. Online Data and Scientific Progress: Content in Cyberinfrastructure. http://archiv.twoday.net/stories/337419/, 2004 [Accessed 6 December 2005].

[5]   J. Gray, D. T. Liu, M. Nieto-Santisteban, A. S. Szalay, D. De Wiit and G. Heber. Scientific Data Management in the Coming Decade. Technical Report MSR-TR-2005-10, Microsoft Research, 2005.

[6]   A. P. Cootes, S. H. Muggleton and M. J. Sternberg. The automatic discovery of structural principles describing protein fold space. *J. Mol. Biol.* **330**(4):839–850, 2003.

[7]   M. J. E. Stermberg and S. H. Muggleton. Structure Activity Relationships (SAR) and pharmacophore discovery using inductive logic programming (ILP). *QSAR Comb. Sci.* **22**:527–532, 2003.

[8]   S. H. Muggleton, H. Lodhi, A. Amini and M. J. E. Sternberg. Support vector inductive logic programming. In *Proc. 8th International Conference on Discovery Science*, volume 3735, Lecture Notes in Artificial Intelligence, pp. 163–175. Springer Verlag, 2005.

[9]   J. M. Zytkow, J. Zhu and A. Hussam. Automated discovery in a chemistry laboratory. In *Proc. 8th National Conference on Artificial Intelligence, Boston, MA, USA*, pp. 889–894, AAAI Press, MIT Press, 1990.

[10]   R. D. King, K. E. Whelan, F. M. Jones, *et al.* Functional genomic hypothesis generation and experimentation by a robot scientist. *Nature* **427**:247–252, 2004.

[11]   H. Kobayashi, M. Kaern, M. Araki, *et al.* Programmable cells: interfacing natural and engineered gene networks. *Proc. Nat. Acad. Sci., USA,* **101**(22):8414–8419, 2004.

[12]   S. Basu, R. Mehreja, S. Thiberge, M.-T. Chen and R. Weiss. Spatiotemporal control of gene expression with pulse generating networks. *Proc. Nat. Acad. Sci., USA* **101**(17):6355–6360, 2004.

25

The descendants of Centaur:
a personal view on Gilles Kahn's work

Emmanuel Ledinot

Dassault Aviation

Abstract

This paper is an overview of 15 years of collaboration between R&D teams at Dassault Aviation and several research projects at INRIA. This collaboration was related to Gilles Kahn's work on generic programming environments, program transformation, and user interfaces for proof assistants.

It is also an evocation of personal memories about Gilles, my perception of the impact of the research he carried out and supervised, and his dedication to INRIA.

25.1 Introduction

Since 1990, Dassault Aviation has been working on some formal methods and programming tools developed at INRIA by Gilles' research group (CROAP) or by other groups led by scientists close to him such as Gérard Berry and Gérard Huet.

Formal methods, more specifically the synchronous languages Esterel and Lustre or the proof assistant Coq, have been evaluated and introduced in our engineering processes to enhance our development tools for safety critical software, especially software embedded in flight control systems.

As for the programming tools developed by CROAP with the generative environment Centaur [3], it happened that in 1995 some of its language-specific instantiations were targeting scientific computation. More precisely, they were designed to assist some classical transformations of large Fortran codes (ports, parallelization, differentiation). Since Dassault Aviation has always developed its computational fluid

From Semantics to Computer Science Essays in Honour of Gilles Kahn, eds Yves Bertot, Gérard Huet, Jean-Jacques Lévy and Gordon Plotkin. Published by Cambridge University Press. © Cambridge University Press 2009.

dynamics (CFD) codes in-house, there was some motivation in our company to experiment tools that claim to partially automate some time consuming tasks done manually at that time.

I first met Gilles Kahn at INRIA Sophia-Antipolis in 1991, a year or two after I had started a collaboration with Gérard Berry on the Esterel programming language and related verification tools. Georges Gonthier was completing his PhD thesis on the semantics of Esterel V3, which was then implemented into a compiler by Frederic Boussinot and a few colleagues of his. In the meantime Yves Bertot was instantiating the generative programming environment Centaur on the Esterel language.

Two years later, in 1994, I met Gilles again while building-up a 3-year research program between INRIA, Dassault Aviation and Aerospatiale (which later became EADS), that was initiated and funded by the French Ministry of Research.

Gilles shaped this research program, named GENIE,[1] with Pierre Bohn who was then my director and had been in the late 1970s and early 1980s the originator of the first versions of the 3D CAD software CATIA, now the world leader in the field.

He took the opportunity of this research contract to have Dassault Aviation evaluate Foresys, Partita and Odyssée. Although our CFD experts had been collaborating for years with researchers at INRIA, especially with Alain Dervieux's group, these tools were unknown to them at that time. Gilles was eager to know what we would think of his promising youngsters.

He also promoted to me CtCoq, as I was leader of the work package named "design of safety critical software". Puzzled by the "correct by construction" programming paradigm, implemented as extraction of Caml programs from correctness proofs in the Calculus of Inductive Constructions [10], I had started 3 years before an evaluation of the Coq proof assistant [9, 1] developed by Gérard Huet's project at INRIA Rocquencourt. Gilles was still leading CROAP and supervising the development of a Centaur-generated graphical user interface to the Coq system.

As an early industrial user of the Coq system since 1992, I was for Gilles a good candidate to assess the added-value of the CtCoq front-end.

---

[1] In French it stands for GEnération Nouvelle d'IngénieriE, which means New Generation Engineering

I then met him again on several occasions as he was INRIA's Chief Scientist Officer and I had been appointed as a member of INRIA's Evaluation Board.

When Gilles became INRIA's President after Bernard Larrouturou's assignment to French National Scientific Research Center (CNRS), he invited me to join INRIA and become a member of his directorship. It didn't happen, but he explained to me on this occasion how he envisioned the role of INRIA to foster innovation and enterprise creation in France.

As a tribute to him I would like to review these contacts, discussions and memories, and give my perception of Gilles' contribution to research and INRIA. I will focus on industrial relevance and technology transfer.

25.2 Centaur: a generative programming environment

While we visited Gérard Berry at INRIA Sophia in 1990, I remember Gilles having organized a demo of Centaur and commenting with some tempered excitement the TYPOL machinery executing the rules of Esterel's small step semantics. A Prolog engine executed the semantic rules, especially that of Georges Gonthier's potential calculus, and the backtracking mechanism elegantly performed the backward stepping of the generated graphical debugger. Gilles then whispered, as some sort of satisfaction and weariness sigh: "all that time to do that!".

During the same demo, switching to a mini-ML instantiation of Centaur, I was also favourably impressed by Centaur's interactive highlighting feature wired to the structural translation rules. After a click on a mini-ML source level instruction the generated Categorical Abstract Machine (CAM) instructions were highlighted in the target code window. Conversely, when clicking on a CAM object instruction, the originating ML instruction was highlighted in the source code window.

I found it truly impressive that all these functionalities were defined once and for all at a meta level, for any programming language whose syntax was definable in METAL and whose semantics could be axiomatized in TYPOL.

That was the up side. The down side seemed to me two-fold : some lack of reliability, probably due to the complexity of the meta-machinery, and an excessive learning curve to use it, that could be summed-up by the sarcasm I heard once in a conference from a fellow to whom I explained that I was using a Centaur-generated environment: "Hum... Centaur!"

he said, "the tool you have five languages to learn first before doing anything with it..."

To my knowledge, Centaur as a meta-programming environment had no industrial impact. All the features it exemplified turned out to be available in commercial or open source programming environments. But can we state that research on language-independent programming environments preceded and influenced publishers of CASE tools such as Borland, Microsoft, etc.? For parsing and other syntax-related functionalities the meta-level generative approach was adopted, but for semantic related functionalities such as type checking, interpreting, translating and debugging, I'm dubious about a meta-level factoring in CASE product lines...

In real life, compilation has to be optimized and the translation rules can't be purely structural, or syntax driven, as TYPOL rules. Graph-based algorithms are needed.

But as advocated in the following sections, in spite of its lack of industrial outcome, Centaur happened to have successful descendants. By descendants I mean software engineering tools that reused algorithms, principles, or components of Centaur.

Centaur was a sort of chimera with a Prolog head and a Le_Lisp body, that was successful in federating the CROAP team led by Gilles for about 15 years. By the time Gilles handed over the project to Yves Bertot, in 1993, Ilog decided to no longer support Le_Lisp. Centaur's decline started looming then. It was progressively abandoned by its former developers although it still helped support some research activities until 2000–2001.

25.3 Foresys and Partita : re-engineering of Fortran code

Foresys and Partita are two re-engineering tools, which were designed to assist the transformation of large Fortran codes, like those developed in CFD, meteorology or nuclear physics.

They were distributed by two INRIA start-up companies, Connexité and Simulog, that no longer exist. A total of 150 Foresys licences were sold from 1995 to 2003, mainly to big French companies and research centers.

The core of Foresys was generated by Centaur after instantiation on two versions of Fortran: Fortran 77 and Fortran 90. Complemented with static analysis algorithms (data-flow analysis) and rewriting rules,

Foresys was a tool designed to help the port of large codes from Fortran 77 to Fortran 90.

Partita was an additional module of Foresys to help parallelize sequential codes for vector and SPMD-parallel machines.

Partita analysed the data-flow dependencies of the code to be parallelized, and proposed transformation rules consistent with the computed dependencies and the targeted machine.

About 50 licences of Partita were sold, which is a reasonable success considering the niche market addressed by such a tool.

What did Foresys and Partita reuse from Centaur? What was the added-value of the generative approach compared to developing the tools from scratch?

Foresys' and Partita's front-end and back-end modules were generated respectively by the METAL and PPML machineries of Centaur. The representation of programs resorted to the Virtual Tree Processor (VTP) but tree-based only analysis and transformation of programs turned out to be insufficient. Classical graph-based algorithms [4] had to be implemented as "external" Le_Lisp functions. The GUIs of both software were also derived from Centaur's.

In the end, the generative approach truly sped up the development, and the first versions of the two products were developed very quickly, but seemingly to the expense of robustness, as acknowledged by one of their main developers.

25.4 CtCoq: Proof by pointing

This next example of a tool derived from an instantiation of Centaur had no industrial impact, since unlike Foresys and Partita, CtCoq was never industrialized nor commercially distributed.

Although one may say that CtCoq never gained a significant acceptance in the theorem-proving community, even among 'Coqers' [1], it seems to me that Gilles and his colleagues at INRIA were the first to exemplify how sophisticated theorem provers could benefit from sophisticated graphical user-interfaces [7].

Relying on the VTP generic machinery of Centaur, which provided the means to maintain active relations between annotated trees, a sophisticated click-triggered mechanism was designed to synthesize Coq proof script commands from selection of formulas or sub-formulas in the active context (i.e the current goal and the displayed hypotheses).

When the mouse-click selected a deep sub-formula in the context, tens of lines of tedious commands might be generated at once so that the selected sub-formula or the goal appeared in the appropriate way to carry out the next user-significant step of the proof. It was especially useful when the formula to be proven contained many nested logical connectors and quantifiers. It spared the user boring sequences of elimination commands. Elimination of existential quantifiers needed a non-trivial meta-variable mechanism, handled by Coq, but that had to be mirrored in CtCoq's variable binding mechanism.

CtCoq's innovative "proof by pointing" feature [8] was all but sugar-coating of Coq's vernacular editing windows. It provided real productivity leverage on proof-script editing by comparison with the first generation of Coq graphical user interfaces, such as the one developed by Amy Felty in 1991 for instance.

CtCoq also supported useful mathematical notations. Provided you get trained to programming in Centaur's PPML language, you could define your own mathematical notations to pretty-print Coq terms. Display of formulas was far from LaTeX formatting and was limited to read mode, but it provided a first significant comfort increase.

Limited but interesting "rewrite by pointing" functionalities were also prototyped by Yves Bertot in CtCoq during GENIE.

I remember a discussion with Gilles about some issue regarding CtCoq's ergonomics. He was constantly looking for even higher unifying concepts that could underpin the design of CtCoq mouse-clicks or keystrokes. He explained to me, for instance, that I could see any term displayed by CtCoq as a generalized menu, and that it was a powerful way of viewing some key aspect of CtCoq's user-friendliness.

I must confess this higher order unifying concept of asymptotic ergonomics left me a bit sceptical, especially considering some irritating differences[2] between a few basic CtCoq keystroke bindings and their equivalent in Emacs, or the time it took CROAP to add to CtCoq the capability of editing comments in vernacular files. I felt how different is the perception of "value" and development priorities in academia and in industry.

In the end, in spite of the fact that CtCoq gained few aficionados, proof by pointing was implemented in a significant number of theorem provers' GUIs. I regard it as a landmark idea originating from CROAP.

---

[2] but justified by deep and compelling technical reasons stemming from Centaur's very principles.

Why so few CtCoq adopters? My personal feeling is that among many possible reasons lies the fact that to get started with CtCoq one needed to overcome a rather disturbing first contact with the GUI, and to devote a significant amount of time to get comfortable with it. Moreover, benefiting from CtCoq's full potential required too heavy an investment. For instance, I never felt motivated to learn PPML during GENIE (nor did I have time to do so), I lazily subcontracted the programming of my notations to Yves Bertot who kindly accepted to do it for me. Centaur's extension and instantiation capabilities were probably accessible only to its designers and developers. Its complexity was dissuasive for anybody else.

To end these few memories and comments about my use of CtCoq and the related interactions with Gilles and Yves, I would like to mention Gilles' interest in translating proofs encoded as lambda-terms into hopefully readable texts in natural language [5, 6].

On the one hand Centaur provided a framework to handle in a uniform way texts, programs, formulas, proofs and relations between them. On the other hand, Coq had the distinctive feature of storing and type-checking an explicit representation of proofs as CIC lambda-terms.

From an academic point view it was attractive to tackle the challenge of translating into French or English the very detailed "argument" contained in these lambda-terms.

But who would read these automatically generated French or English proof-texts? Gilles wondered whether in the field of aeronautics certification authorities might be interested in reading such texts. He probed my feeling about a possible future introduction of proof assistants such as Coq to perform verification tasks, for instance in DO-178-compliant software development processes.

Meanwhile, he had already started working with Yves Bertot, Laurent Théry and Yann Coscoy on this topic, and certainly intended to continue regardless of my answer. But I felt that he was genuinely open to the industrial point of view I could express, and that he would take it into consideration for his future research priorities.

At that time, in 1994, I had been using Coq for 2 years and like Gilles I was fond of formalization in higher-order logic. I encouraged him to proceed in his research on natural language rewriting of proof-terms, and justified this stance with certification issues.

Thirteen years later I observe Airbus successfully introduced theorem proving (Caveat by CEA) in A380 on-board software development process, and obtained Caveat's qualification by Airworthiness Authorities.

Moreover, DO-178 is being revised (revision C), especially to take greater advantage of formal specification and verification methods.

But airworthiness authorities tend to delegate part of the reviewing processes to the aircraft manufacturers. The industrial relevance of research on how to automatically produce human-readable documents from computer-checked correctness proofs may be questioned.

Reviews of software verification activities might be in the scope of delegations so that such generated documents were more likely to be read by the proof developers or maintainers themselves rather than by external FAA or EASA reviewers.

But at Trusted Logic, a start-up from INRIA in the field of security on smart cards which makes extensive use of Coq, reviews of natural language presentations of the formalizations and proofs are mandatory and crucial to their customers and the certification authorities.

So translation of proof terms and proof scripts into natural language documents may really be an industrially relevant research theme.

25.5 Tapenade: code differentiation

Let us now move back to scientific computation, computational fluid dynamics and numerical solution of Euler and Navier–Stokes equations.

We mentioned previously Foresys and Partita as two program transformation assistants that were successful examples of tools derived from Centaur.

We now deal with automatic code differentiation (AD). It is a topic more loosely connected to Centaur, but to me it was a mark of Gilles' influence as INRIA's Chief Scientific Officer.

First let us introduce briefly what code differentiation is and why it is useful to industry. A code differentiator takes as input a Fortran program and outputs another Fortran program that computes some partial derivatives of the mathematical functions implemented in the input source code.

Just as computer algebra systems like Maple can compute the formal derivatives of polynomials or any explicit analytic formulation of a function, code differentiators compute first-order or, more recently, second-order derivatives of functions whose definition is only accessible through arrays, loops, procedure calls, commons, if then else statements, pointers, etc.

Code differentiation is on the critical path of optimum design, and optimum design is of paramount importance in many design offices.

Considering optimal design of shapes in aerodynamics for instance, CFD codes were limited to performance evaluation of shapes until the mid-1990s. They could not automatically[3] find, after iterative transformations of an initial shape, the shape that would deliver optimal performance under given constraints.[4]

Let us suppose that the performance of a wing may be assessed through pressure, velocity and temperature fields around it, all these fields being computed by some CFD codes. One needs the gradients of these fields with respect to the wing's geometrical parameters (chord, curve, aspect ratio etc.) to compute the suitable directions along which the shape has to be modified to improve its performance. Building the Fortran code that will compute the fields' gradients from the Fortran code that computes the aerodynamic fields is what is at stake with automatic differentiation. It is relevant in any other industrial domain where physics comes into play in product design.

Research on automatic differentiation was initiated at INRIA by Jacques Morgenstern, through a joint project with Nice university called SAFIR, which he led until his early death in 1998. By 1995 when we started the first phase of GENIE, Odyssée, a first prototype differentiator written in Caml by SAFIR, had reached what was considered a level of maturity suitable for first industrial experiments.

Odyssée earned our CFD experts' attention and respect, but by 1997, at the end of GENIE phase 1, it delivered only limited help to differentiate codes. The memory footprint of the pieces of software generated by Odyssée was too large to scale-up. However, the generated programs were useful to help test the software pieces produced by manual differentiation.

The heart of the matter was also to understand how to combine differentiation and parallelization: for a given code was it better to differentiate its parallel version or to parallelize after differentiation?

Morgenstern's demise occurred by the time GENIE phase 2 was to start. As I had been appointed coordinator of GENIE phase 2, I met Gilles more often at that time. He was profoundly affected by the death of SAFIR's scientific leader. The project was closed, but Gilles was deeply convinced that research on automatic differentiation had to go on at INRIA, that the institute was well positioned in the worldwide

---

[3] Derivatives by finite difference could be used in theory but are not tractable in practice.

[4] let us say locally optimal...

academic competition on this subject. He thought it was a good topic for INRIA's commitment to scientific excellence and technology transfer.

Though I have no evidence of that, I guess he used all of his charisma and power of persuasion to convince a few researchers at INRIA Sophia to build a new project on automatic differentiation.

Project TROPICS was created in 2000 with Alain Dervieux and Laurent Hascoët as scientific leaders. Alain Dervieux is a senior researcher in computational fluid dynamics, and Laurent Hascoët is a former member of CROAP. He was the designer and implementer of Partita...

They decided to write a new code differentiator from scratch in Java. Like Odyssee, they chose to put the emphasis on the reverse mode of AD, which computes gradients very efficently, at the cost of a complex program transformation.

Laurent Hascoët explained to me that his experience on Centaur and Partita, as well as his close collaboration with Alain Dervieux, were instrumental in the development of what is presently regarded as the world-best reverse mode differentiator of Fortran code. I feel all the more comfortable to write this chauvinistic statement as I read it in a recommendation letter by one of the top US researcher in AD.

Thanks to Tapenade, our parallel Euler and Navier–Stokes codes (200+ Kloc) have been differentiated with a reasonable amount of manual post-processing on the generated code. Optimum design loops, iterating CFD evaluations and shape transformations, have been operational at Dassault Aviation for viscous and non viscous flows respectively since 2004 and 2001.

Tapenade is also used by Rolls Royce, Cargill, by leading European scientists in oceanography or agronomy, and by a famous English bank.

I consider Tapenade as a major achievement of INRIA, and Gilles played some role in this success.

25.6 Kahn's networks

Surprisingly enough, Gilles and I had no discussion about models of concurrency and Kahn's networks, although I had some activities on Lustre and data-flow synchronous programming at Dassault.

Beside parallel design of sequential control programs using Esterel and Lustre, I was interested in coarse-grain parallelism, multi-tasking and pre-emptive real-time scheduling. Kahn's networks handle concurrency in a way that didn't fit our applications in avionics.

I hope Gilles knew, before he left us in February 2006, that Albert Cohen and Marc Pouzet's paper titled "N-Synchronous Kahn networks" was accepted at ACM POPL'06 [2].

In collaboration with Marc Duranton at Philips Research, now NXP, extensions of Gilles' model of stream concurrency are investigated to support a new design method of stream processing circuits dedicated to HD TV, 3D gaming, medical imaging, etc. Kahn's networks and a specific type system are used to provide a "correct by construction" synthesis method of the size of the bit buffers and of the synchronizing mechanisms that are inserted between the operators of the circuits.

25.7 In memoriam

I would like to end this recollection note with a few more personal memories.

Though I never obtained any evidence to back this assumption, I think I owe my appointment as member of INRIA's evaluation board in 2002 to Gilles.

If my guess is right, I'm very grateful to him for that, as well as to my company which agreed to allow me to be available for this part-time assignment. Since then, I have been participating in INRIA's recruitment competitive examinations and research projects' evaluations. I have participated in many very interesting discussions and presentations in the course of my duties as a member of this board.

It gave me the opportunity to meet Gilles as INRIA's CEO, when he briefed the evaluation board on INRIA's selection and evaluation criteria, or made comments on its strategic plan. Gilles loved INRIA. He was committed to its scientific international posture and to technology transfer to French companies. He sincerely cared for its researchers.

It seemed to me that he was a bit disappointed by the relations between INRIA and companies in France. "I wonder whether we are not working more for US companies than for French ones" he told me once while we were talking together about transfers and INRIA's role regarding innovation and enterprise creation, as expected by the ministry of industry.

I would like also to mention two of his qualities I appreciated most: he knew how to coin a nice synthesizing phrase or a thoughtful question to put back on track a messy discussion. And he had a very concrete way of speaking, full of imagery and humour.

I remember his manner of depicting the situation at Aerospatiale when he visited Dassault's management just after he had been appointed chairman of Ariane 501's inquiry board. As an aside, he told me: "You know, as far as embedded software is concerned there, you have two different cultures, two different people. You have those who build birds, and you have those who build firecrackers... And of course they ignore each other!"

Incidentally about this anecdote, I would like to mention that spurred on by Gilles, Alain Deutsch and a group of researchers at INRIA designed a static analyser to process Ariane 501's on-board software, a huge work that led to the creation of the spin-off company Polyspace Technologies,[5] a few years after Ariane 5 catastrophic maiden flight.

I only met Gilles occasionally over the last 15 years, but it was always with genuine pleasure. I miss his enthusiasm, humour, research news and acute statements.

You accomplished a nice mission among us Gilles. Rest in peace.

25.8 Acknowledgements

Many thanks to Yves Bertot, Laurent Hascoët and Laurence Rideau for their help and comments on early versions of this note.

Bibliography

[1] Y. Bertot and P. Casteran. *Interactive Theorem Proving and Program Development. Coq'Art: The Calculus of Inductive Constructions.* Texts in Theoretical Computer Science. An EATCS Series 2004, XXV, 469 pp.

[2] A. Cohen, M. Duranton, C. Eisenbeis, C. Pagetti, F. Plateau and M. Pouzet. N-sychronous Kahn networks. *In 33th ACM Symp. on Principles of Programming Languages (PoPL'06)*, pp. 180–193, Charleston, South Carolina, January 2006.

[3] P. Borras, D. Clément, T. Despeyroux, *et al.* Centaur: the system. In *Software Engineering Notes*, volume 13(5). Third Symposium on Software Development Environments, 1988.

[4] Aho, Sethi, Ullman. *Compiler Writing: Principles Programming and Tools*, Addison Wesley, 1986.

[5] Y. Coscoy, G. Kahn and L. Théry. Extracting text from proofs. In *Typed Lambda Calculi and Applications TLCA'95*, Edinburgh.

[6] Y. Coscoy. A natural language explanation for formal proofs. In *Logical Aspects of Computational Linguistics*, LACL'96, Nancy France.

---

[5] Now part of the MathsWorks

[7] L. Théry, Y. Bertot and G. Kahn. Real theorem provers deserve real user-interfaces. *ACM SIGSOFT Symposium on Software Development Environments*. 1992.

[8] Y. Bertot, G. Kahn and L. Théry. Proof by pointing. In M. Hagiya and J. C. Mitchell (eds), *Proceedings of the International Symposium on Theoretical Aspects of Computer Software*. volume 789, Lecture Notes in Computer Science, Sendai, Japan, p 141-160, Springer-Verlag, 1994.

[9] *The Calculus of Constructions. Documentation and User's Guide*, Version 4.10. Technical Report 110, INRIA, 1989.

[10] C. Paulin-Mohring and B. Werner. Synthesis of ML programs in the system Coq. *Journal of Symbolic Computation* **15**:607–640, 1993.

Glossary

AD	Automatic Differentiation
CAD	Computer Assisted Design
CEA	Commissariat à l'Energie Atomique. French Nuclear Agency research center.
CIC	Calculus of Inductive Constructions
CFD	Computational Fluid Dynamics
CROAP	Conception et Réalisation d'Outils d'Aide à la Programmation
DO-178	Referential of Software development processes defined by airworthiness authorities
DSP	Digital Signal Processing
EASA	European Aviation Safety Agency
FAA	Federal Airworthiness Authority
GUI	Graphical User Interface
METAL	description language for concrete and abstract syntax
NDA	Non Disclosure Agreement
PPML	Pretty Printer Meta Language
POPL	ACM Symposium on Principles of Programming Languages
TYPOL	Rule language to define static and dynamic semantics
VTP	Virtual Tree Processor

26

The tower of informatic models

Robin Milner

University of Cambridge

Foreword

This essay is dedicated in admiration to the memory of Gilles Kahn, a friend and guide for 35 years. I have been struck by the confidence and warmth expressed towards him by the many French colleagues whom he guided. As a non-Frenchman I can also testify that colleagues in other countries have felt the same.

I begin by recalling two events separated by 30 years; one private to him and me, one public in the UK. I met Gilles in Stanford University in 1972, when he was studying for the PhD degree – which, I came to believe, he found unnecessary to acquire. His study was, I think, thwarted by the misunderstanding of others. I was working on two different things: on computer-assisted reasoning in a logic of Dana Scott based upon domain theory, which inspired me, and on models of interaction – which I believed would grow steadily in importance (as indeed they have). There was hope to unite the two. Yet it was hard to relate domain theory to the non-determinism inherent in interactive processes. I remember, but not in detail, a discussion of this connection with Gilles. The main thing I remember is that he ignited. He had got the idea of the domain of streams which, developed jointly with David MacQueen, became one of the most famous papers in informatics; a model of deterministic processes linked by streams of data.

The public event, in 2002, was the launching workshop of the UK Exercise in Grand Challenges for Computing Research. It identified eight or so Grand Challenge topics that now act as a focus for collaborative research; part of their effect is to unite researchers who would otherwise never have communicated. Before the workshop we had no doubt that Gilles Kahn was the one to invite as keynote speaker. We knew his

From Semantics to Computer Science Essays in Honour of Gilles Kahn, eds Yves Bertot, Gérard Huet, Jean-Jacques Lévy and Gordon Plotkin. Published by Cambridge University Press. © Cambridge University Press 2009.

unique combination of encouragement and probing criticism; just what we needed for the event. And so it turned out. His view of the future of computing, and his cautionary remarks about artificially created goals, are well-remembered. Equally important were his enthusiasm, and his encouragement to aim high.

Abstract

Software science has always dealt with models of computation that associate meaning with syntactical construction. The link between software science and software engineering has for many years been tenuous. A recent initiative, *model-driven engineering* (MDE), has begun to emphasize the role of models in software construction. Hitherto, the notions of 'model' entertained by software scientists and engineers have differed, the former emphasizing meaning and the latter emphasizing tool-based engineering practice. This essay finds the two approaches consistent, and proposes to integrate them in a framework that allows one model to *explain* another, in a sense that includes both implementation and validation.

26.1 Purpose

The purpose of this essay is to suggest, in simple terms, how to harmonize the scientific content of informatics with its engineering practice. Such an exposition should help informaticians[1] both to coordinate their work and to present it to other scientists and to the wider public. It should also clarify the nature of informatics alongside, but in contrast with, the natural sciences.

In attempting this general exposition, let us avoid terminology that is either new or technical. Of course, each instance of modelling – such as engineering a distributed system, or modelling by intelligent agents, or optimizing target code, or verifying a program – has its own technical terms; but the terms used for each are unlikely to cover all instances. And we should minimise the extra term-baggage used to fit these instances together into a whole, even if we use terms that are imprecise.

---

[1] Loosely speaking, informatics is a synonym for computer science, and hence informatician (or informaticist) is a synonym for computer scientist. The 'info' words have an advantage: they express the insight that informatic behavior is wider than what computers do, or what computing is.

26.2 Models

All scientists and engineers will agree that they work with models and modelling. The word 'model' is both verb and noun. Used as a verb, 'M models R' usually means that M that represents (some aspects of) R, a reality. Used as a noun, 'M is a model' means that M may represent one or more unspecified realities; for example, differential equations model many realities. R and M may be singular: R a specific ship, e.g. the Queen Mary, and M a specific plastic replica of R. Or they may be plural; R a family of realities, such as national economies, and M a pack of concepts and equations that represent these economies. We shall avoid the singular kind of model, and say that a model comprises

> A family of *entities*; and
> What these entities *mean*.

This is not a formal definition; it is rather a challenge to seek a notion of model that unites the engineering and scientific aspects of informatics. The purpose of the 'definition' is to insist that a model should not merely enumerate its entities, as in a syntactic definition, but should describe how they work, i.e. their meaning. On this basis we shall propose how models should relate to each other.

The imprecise term 'meaning', synonymous with 'semantics' or 'interpretation', is meant to be inclusive. If the entities are automata or programs or processes, it includes their activity or behavior; if the entities are the sentences of a logic it includes the truth-valuation of those sentences via an interpretation of the function and predicate symbols;[2] if the entities are differential equations, it includes the interdependence of the variables and their derivatives. But the term 'meaning' also includes an informal description of how the entities work.

We avoid a sharp distinction between 'model' and 'reality'.[3] We may wish to say that a reality, say 'clouds and their movement', is an *extremal* model: it doesn't represent anything else. But some realities – e.g. a plastic replica of a ship – are models of other realities, so it is a mistake to say that *all* realities – considered as models – are extremal.

---

[2] Logics are models in the sense of this essay, so we should compare the way we use the term 'model' with the logicians' usage. The striking difference is that a logician speaks of models *of a logic*, and that we (so far) take a logic to be a model *of something else*. The logicians' usage is close to what we call 'meaning'. Thus the two usages differ but can be reconciled.

[3] In this paper, we use 'reality' to mean 'physical reality'. This is for brevity, rather than from a conviction that all reality is physical.

Our informal definition admits artificial realities as well as natural ones; thus it includes all engineered artifacts. In particular, it includes 'computers and what their screens display'; a model of it can then be 'assembly programs and their semantics'. Part of what contrasts engineering with natural science is that the realities are artificial in the first case and natural in the second.

26.3 Explanation

The phrase 'model *of* ...' needs discussion. The '*of*' relationship, between a model and the reality it explains, is central to the whole of science; the same relationship holds in any engineering discipline between a model and the reality it explains. Just as we say that Newton's laws *explain* the movement of bodies with mass, so we can say in informatics that a model consisting of programs and their meaning *explains* the reality of computers and what their screens display.

The artifacts of informatics are not always (physical) realities; they can also be (and are more often) syntactic or symbolic. In fact, they are models. What distinguishes the science of informatics is that its artifacts demand explanation at many levels. Consider Fortran, one of the most influential models in computing history. The model 'Fortran and its behavior' (even though this behavior was informally described) explains the model 'assembly programs and their behavior'; at least, it explains those assembly programs that are the translations of Fortran programs. By transitivity, Fortran also explains the real behavior of the computers on which these assembly programs run. As we shall see later, Fortran – and other symbolic constructions – demand explanation at still higher levels; we begin to see why the term 'tower of models' is appropriate. We shall also argue that the towers have breadth as well as height.

One may feel uneasy about this use of the term 'explanation', because realities normally precede the models that explain them. But informatics deals with artifacts, whether real or symbolic, so the explanation often precedes what its explains. One may then be happier to use 'specify' rather than 'explain'. But there are cases where the artifact precedes the explanation; if a reverse-engineer succeeds in reconstructing the lost Cobol source-code of a legacy assembly-code program, then she would find it natural to call the former an explanation of the latter.[4]

---

[4] We tend to use 'A explains B' as an abbreviation for 'A-entities explain B-entities'. This allows us to dodge the question of how many A-entities are involved in

We shall therefore assume that *explanation* is the principal relationship – with many manifestations – that cements the tower of models that we call informatics. Using near-synonyms we can express 'model A explains model B' in many ways; for example

> model A *represents*, or *specifies*, or *abstracts from*, model B; or
> model B *realizes*, or *implements*, or *refines*, model A.

As a simple illustration, suppose that B is a programming language, whose behavior is defined in one of the usual ways. One way is by structured operational semantics (SOS), which is formal; another way is informal – a description in natural language of how the runtime state changes. An example of the latter is the original description of Algol60, an outstanding example of lucid prose.

Now let A be a specification logic, such as **Z**; its entities are sentences, and its meaning defines the interpretation of each sentence. Then an explanation of the language B by the logic A comprises – for each program P of B – a set S of A-sentences concerning the operations, types, variables, inputs and outputs of P. The explanation provides a way to prove that each sentence of S is satisfied by the behavior of P as described in B. If S pre-exists P then it may be called a specification of P. It is unlikely to determine P uniquely; the larger the set S, the more accurately is P determined.

26.4 Combination

The entities in a model need not be all of the same kind. Consider a model of the flight of informatically controlled aircraft. This heterogeneous model combines at least three parts: a model of the real world (locality, temperature, wind speed, ...) in which the planes fly; an electro-mechanical model of the systems to be controlled; and a specification (or explanation) of the controlling software. Consider also a model of humans interacting with a computer; the model of the human components may involve human attributes such as belief or sensation, as distinct from the way the computer is described. These two examples show the need not only to combine informatic models, but to combine them with others that are not informatic.

Such *combination* is best seen as a construction, not a relationship; it combines the entities of different models, with extra behavioral

---

explaining each B-entity. This surely varies from case to case, but for this essay we shall use the abbreviated form 'A explains B' for all cases.

description of how they interact. Combinations abound in informatics. Further examples: hybrid systems mix differential equations with automata; coordination systems combine different programming languages via shared data structures; and a distributed programming language may be combined with a networking model to create a model of a pervasive system.

26.5 Towers

Let us declare a *tower of models* to be a collection of models built by combination and related by explanation. A tower may be tall and thin, or short and broad. Breadth can arise partly via combination, and partly because explanation is a many-many relation: different aspects of a model B may be explained by different models A_1, A_2,...; equally, a model A may explain different models B_1, B_2,.... However, a tower with no explanations – one that is very short – is of little use.

What role does such a tower play in informatics? Natural sciences pertain to realities that are given. These sciences are anchored in the real world; much of what a natural scientist does is to validate or refute models of this reality by experiment. In contrast, except at the lowest level of silicon or optical fibres, informatics builds its own realities; also, crucially, it builds symbolic models to explain these realities at many levels, shading from reality to abstraction with no sharp distinction between the two. Such levels are – roughly in order from less to more abstract – computers themselves, memories, networks, low-level programming, high-level programming, algorithms, programming frameworks (object-oriented, neural, intelligent agents), program transformation, specification languages, graphical representations, logics, mathematical theories, ... There are many models at each of these levels.

Correspondingly, every model addresses a certain class of *clients*: those for whom its explanations are intended.[5] In the natural sciences many models are designed for the scientist, but models designed for the general public are also essential for public understanding. Clients for informatic models span a huge range of concerns and ability, ranging from the many millions of private end-users, through executives in client companies, through the technical staff in such companies,

---

[5] More generally, every model has a distinct purpose. For example, a single client may use different models of flight-control software for different forms of analysis.

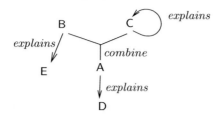

Fig. 26.1. A possible tower of models.

through suppliers of custom-assembled products, through programmers of support software, through software architects, down to academic engineers and theorists.

No-one could attempt to describe the *whole* tower of informatic models. Although the science of informatics has advanced enormously in its sixty years, new technologies continually increase the possible realities, and therefore increase the challenge to build models that explain them. But the notion of a tower, ever incomplete and ever growing, provides a path that the growth of our science can follow; we may build *partial* model-towers, each representing a particular field, with models designed for different clients and cohered by explanation.

Figure 26.1 shows a possible structure for a small model-tower. A is a combination of B with C; A explains D; B explains E; C explains itself. To see that self-explanation makes sense, recall that 'M explains N' is a short way of saying that the entities of model N – say programs – may be explained (e.g. specified) by entities of model M – say a logic. A good example of 'C explains itself' is provided by the refinement ordering invented at Oxford; to refine a specification is to constrain its non-determinism. Thus a coarser specification explains each of its refinements. Such a notion of refinement is also built into Eiffel, an object-oriented language for specification and programming.

For M to explain N, there is no need to require that *every* entity of N is explained by entities of M. For example flowcharts explain some programs, but not those with recursion. When we want more precision we can talk about *full* or *partial* explanations; and the latter should allow that only some entities of N are explained, or that only some aspects of each entity are explained.

Now recall that different models are designed for different clients. For example, if M is designed for senior executives then we may expand 'M

explains N' into the statement 'M explains N *for* senior executives'. In
the example pictured above, suppose B consists of certain differential
equations, and C is a process calculus; then the combination A explains
hybrid systems. However, B is designed to explain only E, the electronic
component of A, to control engineers who need not be familiar with
process calculus. An important function for a model tower is to cohere
the models designed for different clients.

26.6 Examples

The variety of explanations may create unease; can we not formally
define what 'explanation' means? Not yet: this paper aims to arouse
discussion of that very question. To feed the discussion, here are some
examples that illustrate the variety of explanations. In each case we
outline the structure of a small model-tower. To establish firm ground
our first example, though elementary. will be defined precisely; it
indicates that model-towers can be rigorous. The other examples are
treated more informally; indeed, a main purpose of models and their
relationship is to allow informal insight into how software science may
be integrated with software engineering.

Programs We consider both specification and implementation for a
fragmentary programming language; this yields the small tower shown
in Figure 26.2. Research over the past four decades ensures that the
same can be done for realistic languages; but as far as I know these two
activities – specification and implementation – have not previously been
presented as instances of the same general notion, which we are calling
'explanation'.

Let $X = \{x_1, \ldots, x_n\}$ be a fixed set, the program variables. Let V
be a set of values, say the real numbers. A map $m{:}X \to V$ is called a
memory; let M denote the set of memories. Consider three models:

> Programming language P.   An *entity* p is a sequence of assignment
> statements like $x_1{:} = 3x_1 + 2x_2 - 4$. The *meaning* of p is a function
> $\mathcal{P}[\![p]\!]{:}M \to M$, and is defined in the standard way.
>
> Assembly code C.   An *entity* c is a sequence of instructions of the
> form add, mult,..., load$_v$, fetch$_x$, store$_x$ where $v \in V$ and $x \in X$.
> These instructions manipulate a memory $m \in M$ and a stack $s \in V^*$
> in the familiar way, defining the *meaning* of a code c as a function
> $\mathcal{C}[\![c]\!]{:}M \times V^* \to M \times V^*$.

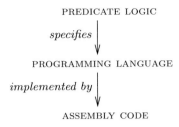

PREDICATE LOGIC

specifies

PROGRAMMING LANGUAGE

implemented by

ASSEMBLY CODE

Fig. 26.2. A small tower of models for programming.

Predicate logic L.   An *entity* ϕ is a logical formula with free variables in X and bound variables distinct from X. The *meaning* of ϕ is a map $\mathcal{L}[\![\phi]\!]:M \to \{\mathsf{true}, \mathsf{false}\}$; this is a standard notion, called by logicians a *valuation* of ϕ in M.

To implement P we define a compiler Comp that translates each assignment $x: = e$ into a sequence of stack operations, in the standard way. The implementation is validated by a theorem stating that if $\mathcal{P}[\![p]\!]m = m'$ then $\mathcal{C}[\![\mathsf{Comp}(p)]\!](m, s) = (m', s)$ for any stack s. Thus the implementation has a formal part – the compiler – relating entities, and a semantic part relating their meanings.

To explain P by L also involves a formal part and a semantic part. The formal part is a relation which may be called 'satisfaction', denoted by $\models$, between programs p and pairs ϕ, ϕ' of logical formulae. If we write $p \models \phi, \phi'$ as $\models \{\phi\}p\{\phi'\}$, we recognise it a 'Hoare triple'; a sentence of Hoare's well-known logic. In that logic such a triple may be proved as a theorem, written $\vdash \{\phi\}p\{\phi'\}$. The explanation is validated by relating these formal triples to their meaning; it asserts that

Whenever $\vdash \{\phi\}p\{\phi'\}$ and $\mathcal{P}[\![p]\!]m = m'$, then $\mathcal{L}[\![\phi]\!]m \Rightarrow \mathcal{L}[\![\phi']\!]m'$.

Thus we have seen how explanation may consist of a formal part, in this case a compiler or a logical proof, that may be executed by a tool, and a semantic part that gives meaning to the work done by the formal part. Both parts are essential to modelling.

Electrical installations The left-hand diagram of Figure 26.3 shows a small tower that coheres two models of an electrical installation; one for the architect and home-owner, the other for the scientist. Architects understand a model of requirements for an electrical installation in a

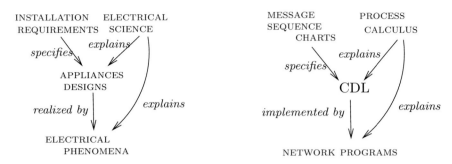

Fig. 26.3. Model towers for electrical installations and for network programs.

house in terms of performance – heating, lighting, refrigeration etc. – also taking account of locality, maintenance, cost and other factors. In these terms they specify the appliances, and home-owners also understand this specification. On the other hand the appliance designs are explained by electrical science, which more generally explains the full range of electrical phenomena. The left-hand diagram shows these model relationships. An important aspect of the example is that a single model – the appliance designs – is explained differently for two different kinds of client: in one case the architect or home-owner, in the other case the electrical engineer or scientist.

Business protocols An analogous tower is shown in the right-hand diagram of Figure 26.3; it concerns a software platform for the computer-assisted enaction of business processes. Such a platform is being designed by a working group of the Worldwide Web consortium (W3C). The workhorse of this platform is the Choreography Description Language (CDL), which has been designed and intensively analysed by the working group. This collaboration allowed a rigorous explanation of CDL in terms of process calculus, which also explains network programs; the implementation of CDL in a low-level language can thus be validated.

The clients of CDL are application programmers, and their concerns are different from those of the scientists, who are clients of the process calculus. They differ again from the concerns of executives in the client companies; these executives in turn understand message-sequence charts, a simple graphical model that represents at least some of the communicational behavior defined in CDL.

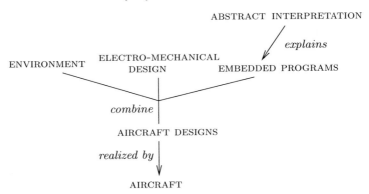

Fig. 26.4. A simplified model tower for aircraft construction.

Before leaving this example, it is worth mentioning that the right-hand tower extends naturally both 'upwards' (more abstract) and 'downwards' (more concrete). Downwards, the low-level network programs are realised by a combination of physical computers and physical networks; upwards, a process calculus can be explained by a special kind of logic.

The airbus Our final example applies rigorous modelling to a safety-critical system. After the failed launch of the Ariane 5 spacecraft, the Institut National de Recherche en Informatique et en Automatique (INRIA) in France – of which Gilles Kahn was then Scientific Director – undertook to analyse the failure. The analysis was informative. As a consequence, Kahn proposed that INRIA should conduct rigorous analysis for the informatic aspects of the design of the forthcoming Airbus.

Such an analysis can often be based upon a specification in logical model, perhaps a temporal logic; the logical sentences are chosen to characterize the desired behavior of the embedded software (the program model). This software model has to be combined – as remarked earlier – with an electro-mechanical model of the plane, as well as a model of the plane's environment. Thus we arrive at a tower like that shown in Figure 26.4; of course this is only a simplification. The method chosen for analysis, based upon *abstract interpretation*, can be seen as a refinement of the logic-based approach. An abstract interpretation of a program is a simplification of the program, omitting certain details and making certain approximations, with the aim of rendering detailed analysis feasible. Such abstraction is essential in situations where the state-space is very large; but, to be sound, it must not conceal any undesirable behavior. Thus, instead of choosing a fixed specification, one may choose an abstraction specifically to match those aspects of behavior that are essential. In the case of the Airbus, by a careful choice of different abstractions, the analysis required to validate the embedded programs was reduced to the extent that, with the assistance of programmed tools, it could be completed.

The Airbus example illustrates that explanations and their validation can be customised within the framework of a tower of models. It also illustrates the importance of programmed analytical tools.

This concludes our examples. It is a good moment to answer a possible criticism of our notions of model and explanation. The criticism is that whenever a model is defined, the meaning of its entities – which are often symbolic – has to be expressed in some formalism; thus a model does no more than translate between formalisms, and our search for real meaning leads to an infinite regress.

Our answer is in two parts. First, every model-designer clearly has *some* meaning in mind. A programming language, or a logic, or a process calculus, or a graphical representation is never just a class of symbolic entities; its intended behavior is always described, even if informally. Thus it is clearly inadequate to call such a class a model in itself. Second, as we move from entities to meaning within a model, or indeed as we move from the entities of model B to those of model A which explains B, we typically move from a specialised entity-class to a class belonging to a more general model. This can be seen clearly in all our examples; e.g. CDL is more specific than a process calculus, so in explaining it we move to a model for which there is already a body of knowledge.

Our examples show that scientific work in informatics consists not only in designing models, but even more in relating them to each other. The former is essential, but only the latter can provide the coherence that will enable both other scientists and the general public to grasp the quality of informatics.

26.7 Divergent approaches

Increasingly, over 60 years, informatic theory and applications have diverged from each other. At present, their relationship is almost tangential; few people understand or practice both. On the one hand an impressive range of theoretical concepts, inspired by applications, have emerged and been developed. Here is an incomplete list, roughly in order of discovery: universal machines; automata theory; formal language theory; automation of logics; program semantics; specification and verification disciplines; abstract interpretation; object-orientation; type theories; process calculi; neural nets; temporal and modal logics; calculi for mobile systems; intelligent agents; semi-structured data; game-theoretic models; quantum computing; separation logic; ... . On the other hand the industrial production of software has developed sophisticated processes for implementation and management, stimulated by a huge and growing market demand. These two developments, theoretical and industrial, are largely independent of one another. It is hard to see how this could have been avoided. No scientific and technological discipline in human history has been so rapid or so global. Responding to hungry demand has preoccupied the industrial wing of informatics; competition in the market has made it virtually impossible to win contracts while maintaining a rigorous standard of validation, or even documentation, of software. On the other hand, building models for rigorous analysis is a daunting intellectual challenge, especially as technological advance continually creates startling new realities – such as pervasive or ubiquitous systems – to be modelled.

Despite the frequent delay and technical failure of software systems, and despite the fact that future software systems – especially pervasive systems – will be larger and more complex than ever, there is a danger that this disconnection between software engineering and analysis becomes accepted as a norm. There is evidence for this acceptance. For example, in a report entitled *The Challenge of Complex IT Systems* produced jointly by the UK's Royal Academy of Engineering and the British Computer Society, the phenomenon of defective IT systems was examined in detail. Many cases were studied, and valuable recommendations were made from the point of view of management and the software production process. But virtually no mention was made of the need for, and possibility of, rigorous analysis based upon fully developed theories.

26.8 Rapprochement?

Paradoxically, while the need for scientific system analysis has been neglected by some, there is currently a strong drive in other quarters to base software development and production on models. This trend has been called 'model-driven engineering' (MDE). The academic research carried out under this heading is very varied, and the author is not equipped to summarise it. An optimistic view is that, while the MDE approach may appear superficially incompatible with the framework proposed here, the approaches differ only in terminology and emphasis. One purpose of the present essay is to induce a rapprochement between the approaches; such a rapprochement is not only possible, but absolutely necessary, for informatics to gain its proper position as an integration of scientific understanding with industrial construction.

An extreme form of MDE has, as its prime concern, that software production be based upon automatic tools which transform one class of syntactic entities into another. Sometimes such an entity-class, e.g. the syntax of a programming language, is called a model. This conflicts with the notion of model proposed here; and while terminology is conceptually unimportant, such a conflict may inhibit rapprochement. In this particular case, it may inhibit the union that I am advocating between science and engineering, since the scientific sense of 'model' lays emphasis on the notion of meaning, which is absent from syntactic entities in themselves.

The MDE research community also – in varying degrees – seeks this union. This essay has proposed that the union can be found via a notion of model which associates meaning with every syntactic entity, and via a notion of explanation between models that includes not only a transformation between syntax-classes, but also a representation between their corresponding meaning-classes. Both the transformation and the representation can be highly engineered as tools; thus the union itself can be engineered! This essay will have achieved its goal if it promotes a constructive debate, involving both engineers and scientists, upon the notion of 'model'.

Acknowledgements

I am grateful to all those, including Gilles Kahn himself, with whom I have discussed these questions, and to the anonymous referees for their helpful comments. They have made my suggestions (which are hardly original) seem plausible to me, even though there are many difficulties to be overcome before convergence between the engineering and science of informatics becomes real. Next steps on the path must include reports of detailed case studies, with detailed bibliography, that appear to contribute to the convergence.